This Terrible War
The Civil War and Its Aftermath

Second Edition

Michael Fellman
Simon Fraser University

Lesley J. Gordon
University of Akron

Daniel E. Sutherland
University of Arkansas

PEARSON
Longman

New York San Francisco Boston
London Toronto Sydney Tokyo Singapore Madrid
Mexico City Munich Paris Cape Town Hong Kong Montreal

Executive Editor: Michael Boezi
Executive Marketing Manager: Sue Westmoreland
Production Manager: Denise Phillip
Editorial Assistant: Vanessa Gennarelli
Project Coordination, Text Design, and Electronic Page Makeup: Electronic Publishing
  Services Inc., NYC
Cover Design Manager: Wendy Ann Fredericks
Cover Designer: Nancy Saks
Cover Art: Bridgeman Art Library, London/SuperStock
Photo Researcher: Photosearch, Inc.
Manufacturing Buyer: Lucy Hebard
Printer and Binder: Courier Corporation
Cover Printer: Courier Corporation

Library of Congress Cataloging-in-Publication Data

Fellman, Michael.
  This terrible war : the Civil War and Its aftermath / Michael Fellman, Lesley J. Gordon, Daniel
E. Sutherland.
        p. cm.
  Includes bibliographical references and index.
  ISBN 978-0-321-38960-2
  1. United States--History--Civil War, 1861-1865. 2. United States--History--Civil War, 1861-
1865--Social aspects. 3. United States--History--Civil War, 1861-1865--Influence. 4. United
States--Politics and government--1849-1877. I. Gordon, Lesley J. (Lesley Jill) II. Sutherland,
Daniel E. III. Title.
  E468.F45 2008
  973.7'1--dc22

                                                  2007010004

Please visit us at www.ablongman.com

ISBN 13: 978-0-321-38960-2
ISBN 10:   0-321-38960-3

3 4 5 6 7 8 9 10—CRS—10 09

For Mei Ning, Liz, Rebecca, Sara, and Samuel
Michael Fellman

For John
Lesley J. Gordon

For Gordie, Joe, and Harvey, with gratitude
Daniel E. Sutherland

Contents

Part I   Before the War

1   *Commonalties and Conflict:*
Slavery and the American Republic   **11**

2   *War and Political Collapse: 1846–1860*   **43**

Part II   Civil War

3 Southerners Secede and Amateurs Go to War: December 1860–December 1861   79

4 Discovering the Scope of War: 1861–1862   113

5 Reckoning with Slavery, Reckoning with Freedom   146

9   A War of Exhaustion: 1864–1865   264

Part III   Aftermath of War

10   Northern Politics and Southern Reconstruction: 1863–1870   298

11   White and Black Reconstruction in the South: 1865–1872   323

12   Destroying Reconstruction   353

Epilogue: Remembering and Forgetting the Civil War: 1865–Present   383

Documents

Preface

We wrote this book because our students told us to write it. They reinforced our concerns over limitations and shortcomings we found in available textbooks about the Civil War. The organization of the existing books did not suit us, or their illustrations did not complement the narrative. Common soldiers and everyday people were left out, and the focus was primarily on famous leaders and famous battles. Most textbooks failed to address issues we thought important, or they interpreted events differently than did we. Many seemed still to be fighting the war for one side or the other. Or they separated the Civil War as a historical experience from long-term American issues, especially those of race relations and the development of governmental solutions to social problems.

Picking up on our frustration, students voiced their own grievances. They found the maps in these books confusing. They wanted more concise explanations of certain events, and sharper, more detached analysis of controversial questions. They thought the books were too dense with detail and lacking in narrative appeal. They complained, we complained, and then came their challenge: "Well, why don't you write your own textbook?" So we did.

Recalling those shared concerns, we have created a book that addresses the needs of students and teachers who, like us, seek an alternative to traditional approaches to the war. We think, too, that our approach will appeal to many general readers. Rather than burdening readers with an encyclopedic compilation of detail, we have sought to engage them with an analytic and admittedly argumentative narrative. Most chapters, while maintaining a distinctive chronological thrust, are equally concerned with topical development and analysis, and we have clearly identified those themes that we believe are crucial for understanding the war and its aftermath.

We have made *This Terrible War* as unlike a textbook as possible, but we have also organized it—with a prologue, twelve chapters, and an epilogue—to correspond with a standard college semester. In order to maintain the narrative flow of the story, we use marginal glosses—rather than obtrusive subheadings—to help readers identify main themes and topics. Appendices provide a collection of pivotal documents. The narrative itself offers a generous sampling of excerpts from contemporary letters, diaries, newspapers, songs, and poems. We have designed the maps, charts, and illustrations to serve as integral parts of the narrative. A topically organized bibliography directs readers to the most useful recent writings on the Civil War era.

Our prologue is set in 1859, the year of John Brown's raid on Harpers Ferry. This violent act, and Brown's subsequent public execution, capped a decade of growing political tension between North and South, but it was also an unpredictable event that made a huge and violent impact, one that divided Americans as never before. Even northerners who had previously rejected violence as a means of settling sectional differences over slavery could not bring themselves to disavow Brown's act and aim entirely. Their hesitation as much as the raid itself confirmed the worst fears of southerners. The North would never rest, slaveholders believed, until slavery had been abolished. When northern voters gave the Republican Party control of the national government one year later, a majority of the South saw no alternative but to leave the Union.

In Part I we backtrack to explain how the nation reached this desperate impasse and why an impassioned debate over slavery caused the South to secede. An important theme here concerns the similarities and differences between northern and southern society on the eve of the war. We find that the two sections had much in common: shared language, religious values, politics, and economic energy. They certainly did not form two separate and distinct cultures, a neofeudal South and an industrialized or "modernizing" North. Yet the South, unlike the North, did depend on slave labor, and the two sections could not agree on the future of this increasingly outdated system. The imposing shadow of slavery increasingly cast a dark cloud over the Republic, obscuring commonalties and magnifying differences.

The debate over slavery also took place at a time of social stress and discord, which further complicated matters. By 1848, when the real trouble over slavery began, antebellum America was in the midst of rapid, chaotic, and unpredictable social, economic, and technological change. Although most Americans rejoiced in much of the resulting growth and progress, they also harbored anxiety about the pace and implications of change, and some changes they did not like at all.

These subtle threats to older social and economic orders were exacerbated further by a still immature government and political system that broke under the strain of the slavery debate in the 1850s. Many other issues, related directly to the bewildering pace of social change, contributed to this collapse, but slavery and the diverging economic interests of North and South were the central problems. The seemingly solid alliances that had allowed political leaders to skillfully negotiate and resolve these issues in the past now splintered, and an accompanying exaggeration of political rhetoric reduced the chances for compromise. National institutions were too weak to deal with such fundamental fissures.

We conclude in Part I, then, that the war was not inevitable, although it did carry with it an unanticipated note of urgency. The original sectional conflict had been over the expansion, not the existence, of slavery. Southerners believed they were entitled to take slaves—their property—into new western territories. Northerners disputed that right. Things got out of hand when both sides turned the political question of property rights into an issue of moral justice, of right versus wrong. The reaction to John Brown's raid demonstrated that while most white northerners still spoke in terms of containing slavery, a small but influential group had its eye on the eventual destruction of the slave system.

Part II begins by describing the South's reaction to the election of Abraham Lincoln as president, but most of the seven chapters in this portion of the book focus on the war itself. A major theme here is the disorganized, amateurish, improvised way in which the United States and Confederate States mobilized their armies and governments for war. Both sides managed war in more efficient ways as the fighting progressed, and the conflict evolved into what we would recognize as a "modern" war in its massive casualties and the rampant destruction it carried in its wake.

In discussing the major military campaigns, we devote less space to the tactical details of battles than do some other accounts of the war. We include the stories and words of common soldiers mixed with discussions of campaign strategies and military leadership. We also challenge the traditional view that the most important battles were fought in the East. Rather, we believe that the western campaigns determined the outcome of the war. There are extended sections describing the naval war and the importance of combined operations. We fully portray the confused and unglamorous nature of combat, and we explore the intriguing question of why men fight.

Another important theme in Part II concerns the home front, which is where most Americans experienced the war. We show why the localized and dispersed nature of the fighting meant that much of the war's violence and suffering came not on the battlefield but behind Confederate lines. Guerrilla warfare, clashes between warring neighbors, and the invasion and occupation of rebel territory by Union armies entangled noncombatants in a degree of violence and destruction that no one had anticipated. Northern communities experienced relatively little violence, but they were racked by grief, uncertainty, and political turmoil. The war drew women as much as men into the conflict as participants and as victims. Families were broken and personal relationships deeply scarred. This was a brutal, horrifying, and cruel civil war.

Never losing track of the cause of the war—slavery—we also trace the complex role of African Americans—in and out of the military—during the conflict and explain the gradual turn of the U.S. government toward the abolition of slavery. Finally, we conclude that northern victory came primarily as a result of superior numbers and resources. Other factors, including strong northern political leadership, a balanced economy, and deep national loyalties, played important roles, but large, well-equipped Union armies were the primary reasons for it. Moreover the Confederate States did as much to lose the war as the North did to win it. Whatever sense of national unity or identity Confederates had—and we believe it was never as strong as in the North—could not prevent public morale from disintegrating as Union armies occupied an ever expanding area of the South, as the southern economy crumbled, and as the South continued to lose irreplaceable numbers of men. Confederate communities gradually lost hope that their national government and armies could protect them from the horrors of war.

Part III, consisting of three chapters, describes the aftermath of the war. We stress "aftermath," rather than the more familiar term "reconstruction," because the full story of the war does not end with the failed northern attempt to restructure the South politically and socially. Our principal theme for the postwar years is the northern retreat from its disjointed efforts toward racial justice. After some significant early strides in this direction—mainly the Thirteenth, Fourteenth, and Fifteenth Amendments—the national government failed to enforce its will. The fate of black Americans proved to be a far lower priority for white Americans, north and south, than did the pursuit of wealth and political power. Southern white leaders destroyed Reconstruction, seized back power in their states, and imposed segregation—a racial caste system. Because white Americans in general preferred national peace to social revolution, the initial promise of a racially integrated society stalled. The U.S. Supreme Court sanctified this segregated society in 1896, and so we conclude our narrative in that year, with the vanquished ex-Confederates and their sons nationally sanctioned as lords of their vast domain.

Our epilogue deals with how Americans came to remember their Civil War in later years. Almost inevitably, the war became less horrible in memory than it had been in fact. Forgotten was the war's complicated origins and bitter divisiveness. As southerners fashioned their myth of the Lost Cause, and northerners congratulated themselves on the triumph of racial justice, the golden stain of time obscured the bitter feelings that caused the conflict. For many Americans, the Civil War became the nation's great morality tale, demonstrating the importance of believing in a cause and fighting for "what is right." In memory, the war became a romantic, glorified pageant that bore little resemblance to those terrible times.

Changes to this Edition

In the four years since our first edition, we have received a great deal of input from students and professors who have read or studied *This Terrible War* in the classroom. Many instructors were generous with their time and insight, giving the book a close, critical read.

Our new edition responds to their suggestions, to the best of fresh scholarship and to our own evolving thoughts. We have enhanced and energized the narrative to make it more concise, clear and contextualized, while preserving its flow. We have reorganized and rewritten the opening chapter, including richer analyses of slavery's beginning, the Quakers and antislavery, the Second Great Awakening and reform movements, planters and the economy of slavery. To subsequent chapters we have added more discussion about women's political roles, westward expansion, African-American army regiments, naval warfare, and the daily life of sailors. We have intensified analysis of many battles, including Antietam, Chancellorsville, Chickamauga and Chattanooga, Gettysburg, The Seven Says, the Red River, and Chambersburg. We have clarified and enriched the chapter on Guerrilla Warfare, and have deepened the discussion of the political views of a variety of leading Union generals. For the postwar chapters we have elucidated Andrew Johnson's plans for Reconstruction and those of the Joint Congressional Committee on Reconstruction. We have added an in-depth analysis of the election of 1868. In addition, as a reflection of the creative explosion of writing on war and memory, we have tripled the length of the epilogue on Civil War in historical memory. We have also improved several maps and updated the bibliography.

We would like to thank especially: Paul Anderson, Clemson University; Jonathan Atkins, Berry College; Scott Barton, East Central University; Frederick

Beatty, Troy University-Montgomery; Thomas Best, Monmouth College; Jamie Bronstein, New Mexico State University; Vernon Burton, University of Illinois at Urbana-Champaign; Frank Byrne, State University of New York-Oswego; Peter Carmichael, University of North Carolina-Greensboro; Joan Cashin, Ohio State University; Michael B. Chesson, University of Massachusetts-Boston; Edward Crowther, Adams State College; Douglas Cupples, University of Memphis; John Daley, Pittsburgh State University; Joseph Dawson, Texas A&M University-College Station; Donald O. Dewey, California State University-Los Angeles; Carol Faulkner, State University of New York-Geneseo; John Fowler, Kennesaw State University; William Furdell, University of Great Falls; Richard Frucht, Northwest Missouri State University; Matt Gallman, University of Florida; Mark Grimsley, Ohio State University; James Hedtke, Cabrini College; Matthew Hiner, Northampton Community College; W. Sherman Jackson, Miami University of Ohio; Lawrence Kohl, University of Alabama; Bryan Lamkin, Azusa Pacific University; Virginia Laas, Missouri Southern State College; Elizabeth Leonard, Colby College; Bruce Mactavish, Washburn University; Carl H. Moneyhon, University of Arkansas-Little Rock; Kenneth Noe, Auburn University; Christopher Phillips, University of Cincinnati; Sarah Purcell, Grinnell College; Robert Reinhardt, Linn-Benton Community College; Ann Sarah Rubin, University of Maryland-Baltimore County; Robert Sawrey, Marshall University; Andrew Slap, East Tennessee State University; Scott Stephan, Ball State University; Robert Taylor, Florida Institute of Technology; Thomas Turner, Bridgewater State College; Steve Trip, Grand Valley State University; Robert S. Weise, Eastern Kentucky University; Stephen Weisner, Springfield Technical Community College; and Nancy Zens, Central Oregon Community College.

Today, as the United States remains engaged in war abroad, it is all the more urgent to understand the manifold historical relationships of war and society. We are not of a romantic persuasion about war, nor do we think it is the preferred means to solve basic social problems. While it is true that nothing but civil war ended the institution of slavery, the war did not solve underlying issues of racial injustice. And the costs of war were terribly high. This does not mean that we are pacifists; rather, we believe it is of utmost importance for all citizens—students included—to gain a realistic understanding of the costs of the Civil War as well as its benefits. As we point out in our epilogue, legends about this war have great historical importance taken in themselves. But such stories painted far more glorious pictures than a more detached and historical approach would indicate had been the case. Whatever we might deduce to be the long-term gains for freedom in America, the Civil War and its aftermath were filled with ambiguities and negation as well as sacrifice and fellow feeling. Caught up in this long, tumultuous struggle, our forebears often paid terrible prices.

Michael Fellman
Lesley J. Gordon
Daniel E. Sutherland

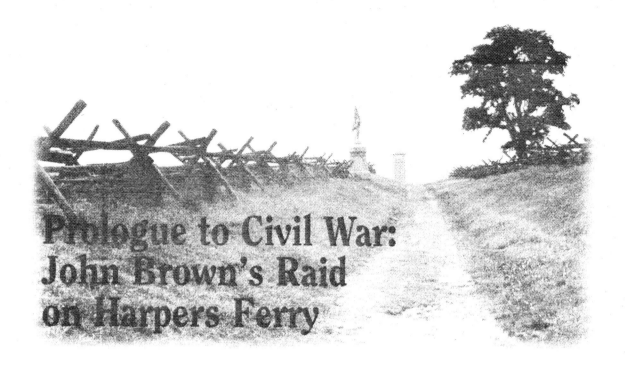

Prologue to Civil War: John Brown's Raid on Harpers Ferry

A s he stood before the judge who would sentence him to hang, John Brown spoke to the nation: "Now, if it is deemed necessary that I should forfeit my life for the furtherance of the ends of justice and mingle my blood further with the blood of my children and with the blood of millions in this slave country whose rights are disregarded by wicked, cruel, and unjust enactments,—I submit; so let it be done!"

It was November 2, 1859. Six months earlier, Brown had stood to interrupt a drowsy meeting of the New England Antislavery Society: "Talk! Talk! Talk! That will never free the slaves. . . . What is needed is action!—action!"

By leading his terrorist band into Harpers Ferry on Sunday night, October 16, 1859, and seizing the federal arsenal there in an attempt to ignite a vast slave insurrection, Brown took the fatal leap from angry talk to revolutionary action. Although his raid failed, his actions inflamed the long-simmering sectional antagonisms between the nonslave North and the slaveholding South. From that time forward, public apprehension ran high until mounting sectional hatreds burst into civil war eighteen months later. Contradictions had placed the nation in this trajectory. But the war was not the automatic outcome of its structural preconditions. Before John Brown, the economic, social, and political system had proved sufficiently coherent to hold the nation together. After his revolutionary act, the United States moved toward war with an almost unabated rush.

The Raid on Harpers Ferry

HARPERS FERRY: Here, on October 16, 1859, John Brown and his band of twenty-one men raided the government arsenal, hoping to set off a massive slave revolt. Brown was quickly captured, and hanged on December 2, but his act and his fearless comportment polarized the nation, speeding the onset of civil war.

Military Defeat; Political Victory

John Brown lost, but his military defeat and death were only prologue to his ultimate victory. Brown had long believed that slaves were not only capable but eager for violent insurrection and that his mission was to make that happen. Preparing for battle, he commissioned the forging of a thousand pikes, which he would supplement with the stands of rifles he would seize at the arsenal. He assumed that when slaves heard of his daring initiative, they would rush to him at the arsenal and then, protected in the mountains, travel south where slaves ex-

ON OCTOBER 16, 1859, John Brown and twenty-one men, six of them black, seized the federal arsenal in Harpers Ferry, Virginia. Driven out of the arsenal by local militias the next day, several of Brown's men were killed, and seven escaped, while Brown and four of his men took hostages and barricaded themselves in the thick-walled fire-engine house, seen in the left foreground of this photograph. That night, Col. Robert E. Lee and a company of Marines stormed the engine house, killing two of Brown's men while wounding and capturing him.

isted in greater numbers, creating a spontaneous, chain-reaction revolution. To begin this uprising, Brown and his band of twenty-one men, including three of his sons and six black men, seized the arsenal and took thirty hostages, among whom were ten quite bewildered slaves. Yet not a single slave came to join Brown and his men at Harpers Ferry. His assumption unfulfilled, as if transfixed, Brown and his men barricaded themselves inside a brick-walled fire-engine house, only to be surrounded first by local citizens and then by a company of U.S. Marines commanded by Col. Robert E. Lee. The federal soldiers stormed in the next day, killing several of Brown's band and severely wounding Brown.

Militarily, the raid was a disaster, which Brown would soon concede. He was imprisoned, tried, and hanged within six weeks. Before his death, however, his eloquence, embedded in the language and the traditions of biblical prophecy, made his trial and execution a powerful national drama.

Brown had remained in the engine house rather than taking off for the surrounding hills, in part because of a deep ambivalence about actually committing the slaughter he prophesied and planned. Three days after the raid, Brown told his captors, "I should have gone away, but I had thirty odd prisoners, whose wives and daughters were in tears for their safety, and I felt for them. Besides I wanted to allay the fears of those who believed we came here to burn and kill." Right before his stirring conclusion at his sentencing about mingling his blood with that of millions of slaves, Brown asserted that he had come to free slaves and take them northward and that "I never did intend murder or treason or to excite or incite slaves to rebellion or to make insurrection." This was a lie but also a defense that demonstrated Brown's deep sympathy for the underdog, which was applied even to his hostages and his potential slaveholder victims. Not that Brown was incapable of cold-blooded killing: in Kansas, at Pottawatomie Creek, on May 24, 1856, he had led a small company of men who hacked five proslavery settlers to death and mangled their bodies. But once the Harpers Ferry insurrection failed, Brown disavowed his murderous intent in the name of his larger humanitarian goals.

Brown Welcomes Martyrdom

This defense, which retrospectively elevated his motives, was part of Brown's wider, intuitive strategy to turn himself into a Christ-like martyr, welcoming death as the climax of a vivid morality pageant about the evils of slavery. Brown did not seek martyrdom, but he understood what remained available to him after his capture. He told his wife that although he was "disappointed in not keeping up to my own [military] plan," he now felt "entirely reconciled to God's plan," which was even better. Repeating a biblical image just written by the great African American abolitionist Frederick Douglass, who had known of Brown's plan and had refused to join him, Brown wrote, "Had Samson kept to his determination of not telling Delilah wherein his great strength lay, he probably would never have overturned the house." His folly had snared him, but God's wisdom had shown him his life's true and final moral meaning.

Others tried to mount a defense of insanity—something that ran in Brown's family—but Brown rejected the strategy, and any plans to rescue him were rendered absurd by the military guard around him, which swelled to 1,500 on execution day. Under these circumstances, Brown wrote to a northern clergyman, "it is a great comfort to feel assured that I am permitted to die (for a cause) not merely to pay the debt of nature (as all must)." He anticipated with great clarity the meaning his death would achieve, writing to his wife and children: "I have not lived altogether in vain. I can trust God with both the time and manner of my death, believing, as I now do that for me at this time to seal my testimony for God and humanity will do vastly more toward advancing the cause I have earnestly endeavored to promote than all I have done in my life before." Brown also asserted that his very failure had cleansed his motivations—the violent means had collapsed and were as nothing, but the ends had soared into

AFTER A SWIFT TRIAL, during which his eloquent abolitionist testimony electrified the North and horrified the South, John Brown was hanged on December 2, 1859. Just before he peacefully and confidently mounted the gallows steps, Brown handed one of the Virginia authorities a prophetic message: "I John Brown, am now *quite certain* that the crimes of this *guilty land;* will never be purged away; but with Blood."

purity. "I pity the poor in bondage that have none to help them: that is why I am here, not any personal animosity, revenge or vindictive spirit," he told his slaveholder prosecutors. "It is my sympathy with the oppressed and the wronged that are as good as you and as precious in the eyes of God."

As he walked toward the cart that would take him to the scaffold, the calm and cheerful Brown handed a note to one of his captors. It insisted that his form of insurrection would be insufficient; indeed, only a vast civil war could end the violent slave system: "I John Brown," he wrote, "am now *quite certain* that the crimes of this *guilty land*; will never be purged away; but with Blood."

Brown's deed and words sped across the nation by telegraph and newspaper, producing in the North a wave of surprise and revulsion for the deed, but also a surge of awe and admiration for the eloquent captive, often within the same persons. Brown had expressed, with perfect timing and uncanny insight, a conclusive reckoning with slavery as had no one before him—his actions and words were an elemental purification ritual for many who attended to them. Even the normally reserved Ralph Waldo Emerson thrilled to the act: Brown, he told audiences in Boston and Concord, was "that new saint, than whom none

Purification Ritual

was purer or more brave. . .the new saint awaiting his martyrdom. . .who. . .will make the gallows as glorious as the cross." On the day of Brown's hanging, to hisses and applause at a Philadelphia meeting, the Reverend Theodore Tilton agreed that "this scaffold in Virginia. . .will abide forever, as the monument of a Christian man who lived a hero and died a martyr." The dedicated pacifist abolitionist, William Lloyd Garrison abandoned his nonresistant position of thirty years standing and subscribed to Brown's violence, applauding him for having taken "weapons out of the scale of despotism and thrown them into the scale of freedom."

Another pacifist abolitionist, Henry David Thoreau, recognized in Brown the noblest Transcendentalist of them all, a man who "did not value his bodily life in comparison with ideal things." Here was a fellow anarchist who, Thoreau seemed to concede, had gone beyond his own pacifism into a cleansing and ennobling violence, placing himself, by his willingness to sacrifice his life, squarely against the corrupt state and false laws. "No man in America has ever stood up so persistently and effectively for the dignity of human nature, knowing himself for a man, and the equal of any and all governments." The Virginian preacher Moncure Conway, who had fled the South and joined the northern abolitionist ranks, clarified the obvious political implication of Brown's sacrificial act and death: "Out of the ashes of our martyr a Revolution must come."

Brown's raid also electrified the black population of the North. In New York, the powerfully outspoken Reverend Henry Highland Garnet decreed to a meeting in his African Methodist Episcopal Church that henceforth December 2, the date of Brown's execution, be known as Martyr's Day, and other black congregations joined this appeal. At Garnet's meeting, the Reverend Sampson White insisted that Brown had followed in the tradition of American revolutionaries who had taken as their motto that "Resistance to tyrants is obedience to God." White then argued for black identification with Brown's militant act: "I have an arm—God has given me power, and whenever and wherever my God given rights are invaded, I shall feel it my duty to use it."

In sum, John Brown had converted the entire radical wing of northern opinion, small though it might have been, to the necessity of national redemption through war. Indeed, six young abolitionists had funded and supported Brown as he prepared his blow. And Brown had gained the friendship and support of several leading political abolitionists, including the wealthy Gerrit Smith of New York, and Frederick Douglass, the leading black abolitionist, who later expressed regret that he had not had the nerve to join Brown at Harpers Ferry, although he knew at the time that Brown was leading his men into what Douglass called a "steel trap." On December 2, 1859, nonviolent, moral arguments against slavery died, as Brown insisted they must, and the obvious necessity of "manly" purification through war became an increasingly urgent antislavery theme, uttered with a sudden release of power that must have horrified even such figures as Garrison, Emerson, Thoreau, and Gerrit Smith, all of whom Brown had radicalized.

Although they were far more conservative than the radical abolitionists, many Republicans found themselves awestruck by John Brown's attempted insurrection and martyrdom. If they hoped ever to be elected, they had, of course, to deny and denounce support for such subversive destructiveness, and most condemned Brown as a madman. Salmon P. Chase, a veteran political antislavery leader from Ohio who was running for the Republican presidential nomination, interpreted Brown's actions: "Poor old man! How sadly misled by his own imagination! How rash—how mad—how criminal thus to stir up insurrection which if successful would deluge the land with blood and make void the fairest hopes of mankind!" However, if Chase denounced the sinful actions, he could not help praising their perpetrator, almost despite himself, for Brown's "unselfish desire to set free the oppressed—the bravery—the humanity toward the prisoners which defeated his purposes!. . .Men will condemn his act and pity his fate forever." Then Chase further projected a future in which the South would justly suffer the fate Brown enunciated: "How stern will be the reprobation which must fall" on proslavery politicians and upon "slavery itself, which underlies it all." Divine retribution might be inevitable, Chase asserted, but sometimes, he implied, it was speeded along by human agency, even if by a madman.

Political Reckoning

Even the cautious and moderate Illinois Republican Abraham Lincoln could not exclude Brown from his political calculations. Lincoln frequently discussed Brown, always calling him wrong, sometimes calling him insane, noting that "an enthusiast broods over the oppression of a people till he feels commissioned by Heaven to liberate them. . .which ends in little else than his own execution." In the face of attacks from Democrats, Lincoln repeatedly denied that a single Republican had supported Brown. On December 5, 1859, he told a Kansas audience, "Old John Brown has just been executed for treason against a state. We cannot object, even though he agreed with us in thinking slavery wrong. That cannot excuse violence, bloodshed and treason. It could avail [Brown] nothing that he might think himself right." Lincoln frequently used John Brown as a kind of warning, as he did in his famous Cooper Union address on February 27, 1860, when he predicted that if the Democrats succeeded in using the specter of John Brown to break up the Republican party, many antislavery proponents would turn away from "the peaceful channel of the ballot box" and instead embrace the very same violent means advocated by Brown and his cohorts.

In these subtle but telling ways, Lincoln did not utterly disavow someone who was willing to go to the gallows due to his hatred of slavery, which, deep in his soul, Lincoln shared. He found a use for Brown as a bogeyman with whom to warn voters about the consequences should they not follow Republican moderation, and yet in so doing, with whatever criticisms he made, he ascribed great force to Brown's legacy: in the final analysis Lincoln could not disconnect Brown from his own distaste for slavery nor his larger antislavery political goals. Brown indeed had heightened the contradictions of the wider political landscape of his era. It would not be long before northern soldiers of many backgrounds would march together into the South singing "John Brown's body lies amouldering in the grave, but his truth goes marching on."

Southern Reaction to Brown

Not merely John Brown's words and deeds but also the northern reaction to them terrified and infuriated southerners. White southerners believed that, behind a smoke screen of abolitionist anger and Republican moderation, they saw the true enemy in the body of John Brown, the first of an undoubted wave of slave insurrectionists who, not content to parry the advance of slavery in the West or to denounce slaveholder morality in the abstract, would march right into the heart of the South and help black insurrectionists destroy slavery, social hierarchy, and the southern white race.

Because the threat now seemed so much more fundamental, southern responses to Harpers Ferry and its aftermath were visceral and apoplectic. J. D. B. De Bow, a renowned Louisiana periodical editor, proclaimed that the North "has sanctioned and applauded theft, murder, treason. . . . There is—there can be no peace." John Brown was obviously "the first act in the grand tragedy of emancipation, and the subjugation of the South in bloody treason. . . . The vanguard of the great army intended for our subjugation has crossed our borders on Southern soil and shed Southern blood." To "save our wives and daughters," an independent southern nation was the only remaining solution.

What was a purification ritual for northerners was a ritual of horrific pollution for white southerners. However much his raid had failed in itself, John Brown had addressed the deepest fears of southerners, to which the most direct response would be destruction in return for destruction. Amanda Virginia Edmonds, the twenty-year-old daughter of a large plantation owner in Fauquier County, Virginia, for example, wrote in her diary after reading of Brown's execution, "I would see the fire kindled and those who did it singed and burned until the last drop of blood was dried within them and every bone smouldered to ashes. Ah! but couldn't I! I don't think my heart would harbour feelings of sympathy for heartless ungrateful wretches." The actual hanging was "an awfully sublime, glorious, charmed scene." In the heart of this young belle, though she was a bit shocked by the vengefulness of her own reaction, only fire fighting fire could repurify the contaminated southern soil.

With uncanny insight, the captive John Brown had played directly both into these fears and with them. When asked by the southern prosecutors who had sent him on his mission, Brown refused to name any names, which only amplified his frightfulness, as the conspiracy they knew existed might be as immense as their most fevered imaginings. Furthermore, Brown replied, "No man sent me here; it was my own prompting and that of my Maker, or that of the Devil,—whichever you please to ascribe it to." If in his own eyes he was a messenger of an avenging God, Brown here also accepted the southern notion that he was the Antichrist, the conscious missionary of the devils of their innermost fears. The southern reaction was to accept Brown's idealism and his sincerity and to make of him the sum of all northern aggression against their way of life, the prophet of a future racial catastrophe.

AN 1885 ENGRAVING of what one artist invented as the last moments of John Brown's life, depicting Brown as humbly kissing a black baby, while haughty but somewhat awestruck Virginia civil authorities and Federal soldiers look on. Soon enough, some of those soldiers would be fighting for the Confederacy, while others would be marching for the Union to the cadences of the song, "John Brown's body lies amouldering in his grave, but his truth goes marching on."

Under these circumstances, white southerners assumed all northerners to be evil unless they proved themselves otherwise. Six days after Brown's hanging, Julia Gardiner Tyler, a genteel Virginia teenager, wrote to her mother: "If there is not an important demonstration on the part of the North towards the South, I think disunion will be the consequence." But if Brown had been sincere, and if he was being heralded in the North, what demonstration could possibly suffice? Therefore the most common reaction was to call for armed southern unity in

South versus North

the face of the aggressor. Future Confederate commander James L. Kemper told the Virginia General Assembly that "all Virginia should stand forth as one man to say to fanaticism, in her own language, whenever you advance a hostile foot upon our soil, we will welcome you with bloody hands," and Assemblyman O. G. Memminger added, more simply, "The North and South are standing in battle array."

It was not just John Brown nor his shadowy circle of unnamed co-conspirators whom southerners knew they had to fight, but the whole "North," embodied in what they called the Black Republican Party, for whom they believed John Brown had served as a vanguard and a stalking horse. Despite Abraham Lincoln and his party's efforts to distance themselves from Brown, southerners angrily tied Brown and his raid directly to the Republicans during the ensuing months.

As Governor John W. Ellis of North Carolina put it early in 1860, "How can the South expect protection to property from those who aid and abet the assassin and murderer as this party did in the case of John Brown?" A Mississippi politician editorialized that the Republicans "are our enemies and we are theirs. [They] have declared war upon us and I am for fighting it out until the bitter end."

John Brown soon would have his prophetic way. The Union would crumble within a year of his execution, and civil war would follow. Whether the ensuing mass sacrifice could purge the nation remained to be seen, but the spectacle would be terrible to behold.

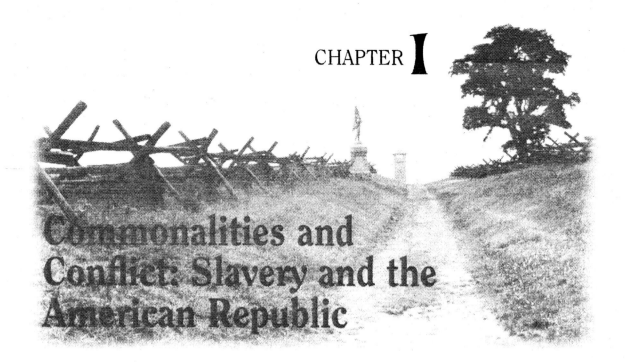

CHAPTER I

Commonalities and Conflict: Slavery and the American Republic

In the aftermath of John Brown's raid, the United States seemed deeply and permanently divided. The North and the South appeared to have very little in common except fear and anxiety about the future of the Republic. So divisive was the reaction to Brown's raid that the idea of disunion and even civil war, notions largely inconceivable just months before, became increasingly prevalent. Yet, beneath the angry talk of sectionalism, Americans still shared a great deal, even as late as 1859. It was slavery, an institution older than the Republic itself, that ultimately cast a dark cloud over the nation, overshadowing commonalties, polarizing sections, and oversimplifying complex questions and issues. Slavery severed the nation and would eventually lead to secession and bloody civil war.

Americans at midcentury partook of a lively and evolving nationality, including a shared history, language, religion, and a booming market economy. They took pride in their revolutionary heritage, republican ideals, and Christian—overwhelmingly Protestant—beliefs. Americans in both the North and the South believed in progress and wanted their republic to move forward. Hard work and self-denial were valued by most, and most sought to control themselves with abstemious morals, although, of course, they often fell far short of that goal. At one and the same time, Americans were enormous imbibers of alcohol as well as of evangelical revivalism. Families were large and

Commonalities

11

patriarchal, where male identity subsumed that of the female. Americans dressed similarly and enjoyed much of the same sentimental music, art, and poetry, raucous politics, and long-winded oratory. The majority of Americans were farmers, tilling the soil, raising livestock, and living by the sweat of their brows.

The Market Revolution

During the first half of the nineteenth century, a series of economic revolutions swept this agricultural nation, bringing more industry to the country, bonding Americans closer together, and helping to create a unique American identity. By 1815 an *industrial revolution* was well under way in the Northeast. By the 1850s it embraced the manufacture of textiles, hats, shoes, and machinery and had spread to the Midwest and, to a lesser extent, the South. The nation was still a long way from becoming an industrial giant, and even most northern laborers would have preferred farm and village life to toiling in factories and cities. But with 1.3 million Americans employed in manufacturing by 1860, albeit the overwhelming majority of them in small workshops of ten or fewer employees, the face of the workforce and its economic future had begun to tilt.

A *technological revolution* facilitated many of the industrial changes, even as it altered other dimensions of American life. The telegraph collapsed time and distance, speeding commerce and nationalizing the news. Machines to plant and harvest grains reduced the need for agricultural laborers. Newfangled "refrigerators" (iceboxes lined with zinc and tin) and increasing numbers of processed foods changed people's diets. Charles Goodyear found a way to make rubber more elastic and durable. And, again, the pace of change was astounding. Between 1820 and 1830, the U.S. Patent Office issued an average of 535 patents per year; in the 1850s, the yearly average grew to 2,525.

Technology also contributed mightily to the *transportation revolution*. It began modestly enough, with crude roads pushing westward and connecting settled regions along the Atlantic seaboard, but soon the main roads were graded and paved with crushed stone. Canals connected rivers and lakes to offer water transportation on a wider, more reliable, and much cheaper scale. The steam engine powered grand boats up and down the nation's rivers, along its coasts, and across oceans. The steam engine also made possible the railroad, the most important technological and transportation innovation of the century. In 1815 there were 23 miles of railroad in the United States. By 1860 there were more than 30,000 miles, further tying the nation together and reorienting trade in an east–west manner, to the advantage of Chicago and New York City at the expense of St. Louis and New Orleans.

Industrialization and the new technology were tied to a *managerial revolution*. Banks expanded in size and geographical reach, sending out lines of commerce into the developing countryside. They drew farmers into commercial webs that strengthened the growing business centers, which banks also boosted by amassing (partly from Europe) unprecedented levels of funding that they passed into the hands of merchants and manufacturers. Improvements in bookkeeping, sales, and advertising pushed both production and consumerism. At the same time, many merchants streamlined and cheapened production by dividing crafts into segments that could be completed by unskilled laborers, often poor people who worked out of their houses or tenements, thus cutting overhead costs for manufacturers.

An *urban revolution* also materialized from this whirlwind of change. In 1820 only 6 percent of the population resided in urban areas—urban was defined by the Census Bureau as a place with 2,500 or more inhabitants. By 1860 that proportion rose to 20 percent. After 1845 a fresh wave of immigrants—mostly Irish and Germans—swelled the urban masses.

New technologies supported a *literary revolution,* helping to tie the nation further together and making Americans the best-informed people in the world. As early as 1840, 78 percent of the free population could read and write—91 percent if one counted only whites. The number of American newspapers more than doubled between 1830 and 1860 to 3,000. The nearly 700 magazines published by 1850 offered specialized coverage of virtually every topic, from national politics to women's fashions. The telegraph and the introduction of a national wire service made "news" fresher, while updated paper-making processes and the steam-powered printing press dramatically lowered publication costs; the railroad permitted wider and more rapid distribution for the printed word.

The nation and the world were shrinking. People were becoming more mobile and better informed. And as manufacturing, communication, farming, and transportation became more efficient, they produced a commercial or *market revolution* that gradually but relentlessly transformed the economic basis of daily life. Small farmers who had seldom bought or sold goods outside their communities gained access to other parts of the nation, entire regions exchanged goods, and eastern seaports by extension could trade more easily and more profitably with Europe. Transportation links stitched northern cities to midwestern and even southern farms, and the nation was becoming increasingly unified. Americans journeyed east to west, seeking fresh land and fresh opportunities in new lands, opened up by the enormous territorial gains made by the United States during the first half of the nineteenth century. The drive for profit seemed universal.

Foreign travelers found Americans infused with a fearless, "hurry-up" attitude that characterized all that they did, thought, and said. When Hungarian visitor Theresa Pulsky asked how Americans could drink the muddy Mississippi River water, a southerner responded: "We are such a *go-a-head* people that we have no time to filter our water." English actress Fanny Kemble believed Americans to be "impetuous" in their concern for internal improvements, having "all the impatience of children about the trying of a new thing, often greatly retarding their own progress by hurrying unduly the completion of their works, or using them in a perilous state of incompleteness."

With all these revolutionary changes, a strong sense of nationalism emerged, but so did feelings of sectionalism and a stubborn belief that the "North" and the "South" were fundamentally different civilizations that held opposing interests. As industrialism, immigration, and urbanization grew, southerners increasingly and strongly claimed that they were untouched by these volatile and

Perceptions of Sectionalism

MANY EUROPEANS disdained what they believed to be antebellum Americans' "hurry-up" attitude. This English drawing depicts uncouth Americans in an eating frenzy.

unnerving forces of change. By 1861, Georgia planter Charles Colcock Jones Jr. pronounced: "In this country have arisen two races which, although claiming a common parentage, have been so entirely separated by climate, by morals, by religion, and by estimates so totally opposite to all that constitutes honor, truth, and manliness, that they can no longer exist under the same government."

To be sure, certain factors did distinguish the regions from each other. The northeastern and midwestern parts of the country experienced more of the revolutionary economic transformations sweeping the country than did the South, including greater industrial change, greater population growth, and more immigration. The South had fewer and smaller cities. In 1860 New York (including Brooklyn) had 1.1 million people and Philadelphia over 565,000, while New Orleans and Baltimore exceeded 100,000 people, and only Richmond, Charleston, and Louisville had 35,000 to 100,000 people. The extensive system of roads, canals, and railroads stopped, essentially, at the Mississippi River. By 1860 only 30 percent of the nation's railroad track ran South of the Ohio River.

Other factors divided the regions and segmented Americans. Settled areas had post offices and a smattering of customhouses, but the vast new western territories lacked even these small federal institutional anchors. The dramatic technological changes had not been coupled with a stable national monetary system, and the shared written language, having been defined by Noah Webster's *American Dictionary* in 1828, disguised numerous regional and local dialects. The nation's history, though celebrated by most Americans as glorious, was ridiculously short and not above regional interpretations. Customs and traditions were likewise as much regional and local as national, even for such holidays as Independence Day and Christmas, and while Protestants ruled the religious roost, dissenters against the norm, especially Catholics, were a numerous and growing minority.

The North as a whole was wealthier than the South, having a particularly dynamic and thriving market economy that absorbed much of the increase in population. Although the vast majority of northerners remained small farmers, they were becoming more connected to the market economy by the rapidly expanding transportation system and improvements in banking and large-scale marketing. Northerners invested their capital in internal improvements, factories, and schools as well as in vast new regions of farmland. Public education was available and widespread, especially in New England, where literacy rates were the highest in the nation. Increased wealth, population, industrialization, and education also produced both a distinctive class structure and widening gaps between rich and poor. The North's middle class self-consciously set itself apart from the working class in its occupations, dress, homes, and conspicuous consumption. The North's bourgeoisie began to celebrate their residences and their women as "havens in a heartless world."

The Antebellum North

Although working-class men, women, and children, especially immigrants, toiled in poorly ventilated, filthy workshops and factories, with boys and girls working alongside their parents and with paltry pay and excessively long hours, northerners of all classes self-consciously believed that their society was far more progressive than the—to them—slovenly South. They shared a free labor ideology that promised that today's laborers would one day, through hard work, saving, and clean living, become tomorrow's owners or masters in a workshop, employing workers of their own. Immigrants tended to write home less about their struggles than their increasing prosperity in the new land, urging others to join them.

While northerners took pride in their accomplishments and frequently considered themselves superior to the South, they did so by overlooking their own problems. Many rural areas remained isolated, impoverished and resistant to change. Bigotry and intolerance ran rampant in the North, and most northern whites were just as hostile to notions of racial equality as their southern counterparts. Northern workers were often violently antiblack. Fearing competition from black workers, and angry that anyone would relate hard physical labor to slavish labor, many sought brotherhood with all white men. Even poor immigrants quickly discovered the power of racism to raise themselves above the most lowly members of American society in conjunction with other white men.

And yet, foreign laborers themselves were more commonly shunned than welcomed. The nativist movement, based on fear and hatred of foreigners, and aiming to curtail immigration (and, for some nativists, to drive foreigners back to Europe), enjoyed great support in the northern states, especially in urban areas where the immigrant population was highest. Northern communities were segregated, not just by race, but by class, ethnicity, and religion. Catholics in particular, including vast numbers of impoverished Irish immigrants, suffered terrible discrimination and harassment, viewed as they were by many native-born, white Protestants as unchristian traitors who had come to undercut fair wages. An 1831 poster in a Massachusetts's city street proclaimed: "All Catholics and all persons in favor of the Catholic Church, are a set of vile imposters, liars, villains and cowardly cut-throats." Apartment and job listings frequently read: "No Irish need apply." Such sentiments led to numerous incidences of anti-Catholic violence, including church burnings, riots, and beatings. Northern factory workers (most of them immigrants) clustered in the region's overcrowded, sordid, and crime-infested urban centers, living hand to mouth. Some struggled to unionize and protect themselves from greedy employers and the harsh reality of the nation's boom-and-bust market economy. Before 1860 there was a handful of unions, but most of them were weak, poorly organized, and incapable of protecting workers' jobs and rights, let alone bringing lasting change to the workplace. Many seasonal workers wandered the countryside as tramps or squatted on marginal land to eke out meager livelihoods.

The Antebellum South

Nor was "the South" a monolithic entity. Geography and weather might seem common characteristics to the entire region, but land conditions and climate varied widely, from the gently rolling Blue Ridge Mountains of Virginia to the swampy bayous of Louisiana. The Smoky Mountains of Tennessee often had snow; the Florida coast often had tropical hurricanes. In fact, the antebellum South was really a number of "Souths," including the deep southern states of Georgia, Alabama, Mississippi, Louisiana, Texas, and Florida; the upper southern states of Tennessee, North Carolina, Virginia, and Arkansas; and the border states of Kentucky, Missouri, Maryland, and Delaware.

The people who inhabited this vast southern land were also diverse. Native Americans, though dwindling in number, continued to live in the South. The majority of whites came from Celtic roots, but there were also pockets of Germans, and Spanish and French influences carried forward from colonial times in such states as Louisiana, North Carolina, Alabama, and Florida. A good many southerners were Evangelical Protestants, affected deeply by the religious revivalism that swept across the region in the late eighteenth and early nineteenth centuries, but there were also Jews and Catholics, especially in such port cities as Savannah and Charleston. And, of course, there were African Americans, mostly enslaved.

Yet, the South as a region did have some unique distinctions. It was predominately agricultural, its people tied closely by kin, community, and religion. By 1860, fewer than 10 percent of all southerners lived in urban centers of 2,500 or more people, compared to 36 percent of northeasterners and 16 percent of midwesterners. Population was sparser than that of the Northeast. During a visit to Virginia, northern journalist Frederick Law Olmsted noted: "For hours and hours one has to ride through the unlimited and continual, all-shadowing, all embracing forest, following roads in the making of which not more labor has been given than was necessary to remove timber which would obstruct the passage of wagons and even for days and days he may sometimes travel and see never two dwellings of mankind within sight of each other." Accents and regional dialects also set southerners apart from most other Americans (although the same could be said of New Englanders). Southerners preferred spoken expressions to the written word, and they valued formal education less than did northerners. Modest farmers, who made up the majority of the white population, seemed to enjoy leisure time more than northerners and appeared to indulge more in carnal pleasures, such as drinking, smoking, fighting, and hunting. These plain folk were fiercely independent: success for them meant owning their own land and living as they pleased. These distinctions struck Olmsted: "The Southerner has no pleasure in labor. He enjoys life itself. He is content with being. Here is the grand distinction between him and the Northerner; for the Northerner enjoys progress in itself. He finds happiness in doing. Rest, in itself, is irksome and offensive to him."

Such differences, in and of themselves, do not inalterably divide nations or cause wars. Rather, for the United States, it was the institution of slavery, particularly its expansion westward, that forced disunion. Slavery profoundly influenced the social, racial, economic and political structures of the South, and by disrupting the nation's political system, it became the determining factor that pitted North against South.

Slavery Divides the Nation

The beginnings of slavery are difficult to pinpoint. Early evidence records the arrival in 1619 of a Dutch warship bringing twenty Africans to Jamestown colony from the Caribbean. But these new arrivals were not, it seems, immediately treated as slaves bound for life to their owners. Instead, these first Africans initially coexisted with white indentured servants—mainly poor, unmarried males who sold seven years of their labor for passage to the New World. Once their time of servitude expired, whether black or white, these laborers would be free and ideally could obtain their own plot of land. (Few of either race actually made it to freedom, but in theory they could.) Before the codification of racial slavery, lines were blurred between the social and economic status of slaves and indentured servants. Africans, both free and enslaved, participated directly in the burgeoning market economy—buying, selling, owning, and trading with white and black alike.

Tobacco was the impetus that brought large-scale racial slavery to the Chesapeake colonies. The "noxious weed," as King James I called it, stirred a frenzy of planting in the Virginia colony that later spread to North Carolina and Maryland. Tobacco was a huge, expensive fad in England, and like tea from the Orient and spices from India, the product created seemingly insatiable demand. Tobacco farming was backbreaking and labor-intensive work but, at least initially, an extremely profitable endeavor. Colonists tried to enslave North American Indians, but these efforts failed. Native Americans proved a difficult population to control and coerce. During the late seventeenth century, colonial elites felt anxious over the growing number of newly freed indentured servants. Nathaniel Bacon's unsuccessful rebellion in Virginia in 1676, when he attempted to overturn colonial rulers by leading an army of restless, landless white males, added to the elite's conviction that enslaving

Africans was less dangerous than continuing indentured servitude. By the 1680s, the number of indentured servants imported to the colonies was dropping anyway. The African slave trade was already well established by other Europeans, and English colonists perceived owning slaves to be a better long-term investment. Whites also reasoned that Africans were more easily discernable by the color of their skin, and because these slaves were brought to an entirely new continent, owners believed that black slaves would be easier to subdue. The fact that they were Africans, considered by most Europeans to be primitive, savage, and inferior heathens, also helped to justify their exploitation through brutal domination. By the late seventeenth century, African slaves increasingly replaced white indentured servants working tobacco and other cash crops.

Slavery in the North
During the middle decades of the eighteenth century, labor shortages in the North made African slaves a viable commodity. By the 1740s, 15 percent of Philadelphia's workingmen were slaves; by the 1770s, nearly 14 percent of New York's population was black. In Boston, Philadelphia, Newport (Rhode Island), and New York, as much as in Charleston and Williamsburg, owning slaves became a recognizable badge of status for the urban elite. Slaves could be found toiling as servants, in artisan workshops, on ships and docks, and on northern farms, working alongside whites—sometimes resented and other times appreciated.

Southern Staple Agriculture
Two factors dramatically changed the nature of slavery in the American colonies: the profitability of southern staple crops—first tobacco, rice, and indigo; later sugar, and cotton—and the ongoing demand for labor. Slavery became more codified and rigid, more exclusive to the southern regions, and more racially based. In 1640, Maryland statutes detailed treatment of slaves; in 1641, Virginia laws distinguished between the status of black slaves and white indentured servants; and in 1664, Maryland declared that slaves were slaves for life. New laws were passed banning intermarriage between whites and blacks and prohibiting miscegenation. By 1705 the codification of slavery was complete. Relationships between masters and slaves changed too, becoming more distant and formal. By this time, being a slave in America meant being of African ancestry. The line separating free blacks from slaves blurred as racial slavery became increasingly entrenched in colonial society.

The African Slave Trade
Long before this dramatic shift from indentured servitude to chattel slavery occurred in the English colonies, the African slave trade was well established by other European powers. The Dutch, the Portuguese, and the Spanish brought slavery to their colonies, seeing it thrive in the Caribbean and Latin America. England's dominance of the seas meshed well with the demand for African slaves, and England joined these other European colonial powers in the exchange of human chattel. Slaves became part of the profitable triangular trade that involved New Englanders as well as African and Arab traders.

African men, women, and children captured in the interior, in most cases by fellow Africans, were marched to Africa's west coast and then forcefully crammed onto ships bound for the New World. White Europeans paid little regard to the regional distinctions by which Africans defined themselves; all slaves were profitable property and valued workers, and all were labeled "Africans."

But, as one historian has remarked, "If Africa provided few common experiences, enslavement did." Tens of thousands of these Africans, especially young men, found themselves transported across the ocean in horrific conditions, crowded onto disease-infested ships. Most were sent to the Caribbean and Latin America, while relatively few went to North America. Those that did not die en route to the New World arrived to discover lives of toil and oppression.

The Middle Passage

Olaudah Equiano was only ten years old when he and his sister were forcibly taken from their home in present-day Nigeria. Equiano was familiar with slavery; his father owned slaves. Still, the version spread by European colonizers through the Americas, with its emphasis on perceived racial difference and gang labor, was different from slavery in Africa and many other locales, although there were commonalities as well. In other times and places, slavery was not solely a system of forced labor; nor was race always the essential characteristic that distinguished owner from chattel, although it was in many places, particularly in the Middle East. Slaves in ancient Rome, the Ottoman Empire, Africa, the Near East, and Asia, for example, served as warriors, concubines, government officials, and eunuchs. But, similarly to the American South, in vast stretches of the Roman Empire, huge land owners used gang labor to produce cash crops, especially wheat. Muslims and Christians held "heathens" in bondage, and warring tribes in Africa enslaved captured foes. However, Euro-American slavery was primarily a system of coerced toil to produce cash crops and to fuel the industrial and market revolutions. Although a handful of blacks owned slaves and a relatively small number of American Indians were enslaved as experiments, the racial makeup of American slavery was largely singular: people of African descent owned by people of white European descent. Young males like Equiano were highly prized.

Equiano later recalled his terror when he first realized that he was bound for a slave ship that would take him far from his homeland: "When I looked round the ship too, and saw a large furnace of copper boiling, and a multitude of black people of every description chained together, every one of their countenances expressing dejection and sorrow, I no longer doubted my fate, and quite overpowered with horror and anguish, I fell motionless on the deck and fainted." Equiano survived the awful Middle Passage to the Americas and was bought and sold several times before he finally purchased his own freedom in 1776.

The same year that Equiano gained his freedom, the thirteen English colonies formally declared their independence from Great Britain. Thomas Jefferson's phrase that "all men are created equal" seemed to contradict the very notion of owning human beings, although Jefferson and other prominent leaders of the American Revolution were slave owners. Until this revolution, slavery was an accepted and growing institution among the elite and the poor, the educated and the illiterate. It proved adaptable in a variety of environments, in both the North and the South. Yet, the American Revolution and revolutions in

Slavery and the American Revolution

France and Haiti proved to be crucial turning points in both the history of slavery and the beginnings of sectionalism. These political rebellions unleashed new ideas that opened new avenues for freedom. Echoing Enlightenment philosophy that emphasized individualism and self-autonomy, America's Declaration of Independence and France's Declaration of the Rights of Man stipulated specific "inalienable rights" for "all men," including freedom of speech, press, and religion, and the equality of all persons before the law.

Such powerful revolutionary rhetoric made many slave owners uncomfortable; they realized that owning human beings as property did not fit with the ideals of a republican government—a voluntary compact formed by free and equal men. Jefferson had originally included in his list of grievances expressed in the Declaration of Independence the accusation that King George had "waged cruel war against human nature itself, violating its most sacred rights of life and liberty in the persons of a distant people who never offended him, captivating and carrying them into slavery in another hemisphere, or to incur miserable death in their transportation hither." Fellow southerners persuaded Jefferson to strike this passage from the document.

Even with Jefferson's words condemning slavery excised from the Declaration, just the intense and divisive nature of the American War of Independence helped slaves begin to challenge the political power of the ruling elite over their lives. Slaves closer to the battlefront found it easier to gain their freedom, and when the British-appointed governor of Virginia, Lord Dunmore, offered freedom to slaves who fought against the patriots in 1775, slave owners faced a serious challenge to their institution. American rebels countered by granting freedom to slaves who fought against the British. It is estimated that 5,000 enslaved and free blacks fought in the American army, while some 30,000 served in the British forces.

In the aftermath of the War for Independence, slave states, especially in the border South, changed manumission laws, making it easier for masters to free their slaves. Many now wondered how a libertarian republic could stay virtuous with slavery. Abolitionism, a relatively new and radical notion in the history of the Western world, began to gain ground.

Debates at the Constitutional Convention

At the Constitutional Convention in 1787, delegates openly debated the institution, but the lines were quickly drawn between North and South. Founding Fathers such as George Washington and Thomas Jefferson, both large slave owners, had already voiced concerns about the future of slavery and pondered its eventual demise. (It also should be emphasized that while Washington freed all his slaves in his will, Jefferson manumitted only a few, and Jefferson was enmeshed in the slave system in many ways, such as keeping a slave mistress, Sally Hemmings, and writing one of the first arguments for "scientific racism" in his *Notes on Virginia*.) One delegate to the Constitutional Convention attacked the international slave trade as discouraging white emigrants "who really enrich & strengthen a Country." Most southerners, especially from the deep South, disagreed and sought instead greater national protection of their property and labor system in the new government. Some southerners con-

AT THE CONSTITUTIONAL CONVENTION in 1787, delegates laid the groundwork for the new republic, but sectional division over slavery was apparent.

ceded the problematic human implications of the system but saw it as socially and economically necessary and refused to support talk of general emancipation. The result was one of the first sectional compromises that leaders of the new nation would implement.

The word *slave* does not appear anywhere in the Constitution, but southerners gained several important concessions to protect the institution. Article IV, section 2, addresses the extradition of fugitive slaves by stating that anyone "held to Service or Labour" who escapes "shall be delivered up on Claim of the Party to whom such Service or Labour may be due." The Constitution also allowed for, but did not require, the end of the Atlantic slave trade in 1808. Southerners gained only a partial victory with the "three-fifths" clause: Article I, section 2, stipulated that "all other persons" than free persons, Indians excluded, would count as three-fifths of a person in determining direct taxes and representatives to the House of Representatives. This was a significant compromise for southerners, who wanted slaves counted as whole persons so they could gain greater representation in Congress. Some of the writers of the Constitution, including many slaveholders, considered slavery a "necessary evil," as they could not imagine how to deal with blacks should they be freed. This might have been one reason for the 1808 clause—by cutting off the slave trade, the increasingly enlightened nation would witness the natural decline of slavery, many hoped (naively, as it transpired).

The most concerted efforts to make the Constitution an antislavery document, however, came from many among the Quakers. The Society of Friends had been petitioning individual states and Congress to prohibit the owning of human chattel since hostilities with England ended. Their antislavery beliefs dating to the seventeenth century, Quakers were among the earliest white abolitionists to

Quakers and Abolition

emerge in America. By 1775, they had formed the world's first antislavery society in Philadelphia. As devout activists, eager entrepreneurs, and egalitarians, Quakers believed in an individual's inner light, in universal love, and in the evil of physical coercion. They condemned what one believer in 1688 had called "the traffic of men's body" and "the handling of men as cattle." Quakers, following the Enlightenment view that Western society was gradually progressing for the better, sought to end slavery but also wanted to remove the slaves themselves and colonize them in Africa. Entrusting Ben Franklin, delegate to the convention and president of the Pennsylvania Abolition Society, as their advocate, Quakers believed their time had finally come. At the last minute, however, Franklin withheld their petition, fearing the angry reaction of southern delegates. Quakers failed in Philadelphia, but the antislavery crusade had just begun.

The Second Great Awakening

It is not surprising that a religious group such as the Quakers would play a prominent role in affecting American attitudes toward slavery and sectionalism. Religion was an integral part of everyday life in the new republic. From the late eighteenth century through the 1830s, an evangelical Christian movement, called by historians the *Second Great Awakening,* swept the nation, welcoming anyone and everyone into the fold. Stirring messages of personal and collective salvation were preached to young and old, male and female, poor and rich, white and black. Sinfulness might be but a temporary moral lapse, with each heart carrying the inward capacity to free itself in choosing salvation. All were equal in the eyes of God, and every man was his brother's keeper, affirmed the circuit riders and revival sermonizers, reinforcing conceptions of egalitarianism and social activism spread by the Revolution. All had the moral tools to bring about social conditions that would lead to an era of public redemption fit for Christ's return to earth. This *premillennialism,* which dominated the Second Great Awakening, carried a radical, activist vigor, unlike the more passive and negative *postmillennialism* of later decades (and our own day) that would stress humans' innate depravity and the necessity of preparing for a Second Coming as Christ willed it. Postmillennialism would focus not on social reform but on the apocalypse—a universal social catastrophe rather than human progress. But in the 1830s, calls for social reform and progress characterized evangelical preaching.

Reform Movements

The Second Great Awakening had roused the nation's moral zeal, and a romantic spirit of individualism inspired many Americans to seek perfection in themselves and society. But the consequences of the Awakening varied from North to South. In the North, an emerging northern middle class embraced evangelicalism and its message of redemption and, by 1815, began to apply it, not only to themselves but to changing the world around them. Seeking individual and societal perfection, these reformers turned their energies toward a variety of causes and movements, including temperance, prison and school reform, utopian communitarianism, and abolition. Politicians seemed corrupt; the immigrants and poor appeared to be ignorant and easily misled. To many reformers, slavery was an outdated, barbaric practice that did not fit with the general spirit of their Christian faith. Most worked for change within the existing society, but other "utopian" reformers believed that progress must be born of model communities, such as New Harmony, in Indiana; Oneida, in western New York; and Brook Farm, near Boston.

Southern Protestants, however, seeing their primary life task as preserving and improving their deeply rooted way of life, tended to read the message of the Second Great Awakening in more personal terms: each person should free himself or herself from sin; each person should be kind and encouraging to others. This might lead to prescriptions for better treatment of slaves, but it would never lead to emancipation. Indeed the whole emphasis on slavery as a sin and slaveholders as special sinners struck them as outrageously self-righteous on the part of the abolitionists. Far from sinners, they were God's stewards to the pitiful slaves; far from evil, their system was a "positive good," not only for themselves but for the slaves, whom they regarded not as mere workers (in contrast to the degraded wage slaves of the North), but as their "people." Improvement might be possible, but mere mortals should not try to change the underpinnings of God's perfect design or upset the delicate balance of the universe. Thus evangelical Christianity mixed with the agricultural slaveholding society and strengthened a tendency toward traditional conservatism. To many southerners, this was a virtue rather than a shortcoming. By midcentury it would seem to some slaveholders that slavery was acting as a safeguard in keeping out what they saw as dangerous social activism. Congressmen E. Carrington Cabell in 1850 warned northerners that the "*conservatism of slavery* may be necessary to save you from the thousand destructive *isms* infecting the social organization of your section." The southern reform that did occur centered on improving slavery, making it more "humane" to confront abolitionist challenges.

The Decline of Slavery in the North

Economic changes after the Revolution also divided the nation and made slavery a more divisive issue. Slavery was in its essence an economic system, but in the North this form of labor became less and less viable as capital and labor became more mobile as means of production changed. Concepts of property shifted: white southerners accepted slaves as measurable property, but many northerners were troubled by the idea. In a society built on the accumulation of property, only free and self-actualizing workers could join in the growth of both a free-market economy and democratic society. In the North, owning humans had never been very practical: most northern farms were small, family-oriented concerns, and northern crops and climate worked against extensive use of slaves. By 1800 fewer northerners owned slaves, and by the second decade of the century the northeastern economy was a vigorous mix of farming, commerce, and industry. Having before them undeniable proof that a society could grow and succeed without slavery, northern whites adjusted their attitudes and values to the world around them and deemed that the economic future of the nation rested on free labor.

Vermont in 1777, Massachusetts in 1780, and New Hampshire in 1783 incorporated gradual emancipation provisions into their state constitutions. Gradual abolition legislation passed in Pennsylvania in 1780, in Rhode Island and

Connecticut in 1784, in New York in 1799, and in New Jersey in 1804. The Northwest Ordinance of 1787 banned slavery in what became the new states of Ohio, Illinois, Indiana, Michigan, Wisconsin, and part of Minnesota. New York followed up its prior move toward eventual emancipation by declaring in 1817 that all slavery would be entirely abolished on July 4, 1827. Step by step, as the century progressed, the northern states halted the spread of slavery.

Southern Society

While it withered and died in the North, slavery expanded in the South. A small but self-confident and increasingly wealthy planter class stood at the apex of southern society. In 1860 the white population of the South was about 8 million. Of this number, only 25 percent owned slaves, and most slaveholders owned fewer than five slaves. Only 12 percent of all slave owners qualified as planters—usually defined as people who owned twenty or more slaves. As a class, planters lived in the best homes, ate the best food, wore the best clothes, had the best education. Some lived in comfortable farmhouses, others in opulent mansions, and many also owned elegant town houses in places such as Charleston and New Orleans. They thought of themselves as custodians of society who must care for the less powerful, including not only their own slaves but the plain white folk in their locale. They believed that they were not oppressors but benevolently paternalistic guardians of black and white alike. But they were also proud of being shrewd and up-to-date businesspeople. A planter could display unmistakable traits of a savvy capitalist one day, carefully calculating investments, and the next day show the traits of traditional precapitalists by bartering with neighbors and swapping labor and services with little apparent concern for cash. In truth, most planters were a bit of both. Tied directly to the booming market economy, they self-consciously saw themselves and their "South" as removed from the negative social byproducts of industrialism that they believed afflicted the North.

Plantation mistresses enjoyed the benefits of race and class, but their husbands, fathers, and brothers reigned supreme. These women managed the household, supervised care of the children, and often attended to sick slaves, but all of their domestic duties depended heavily on slave labor. It was difficult also to ignore the sexual liaisons that went on regularly between many white men and female slaves. Mary Chesnut, wife of prominent South Carolinian James Chesnut, angrily wrote: "Like the patriarchs of old our men live all in one house with their wives and their concubines, and the mulattoes one sees in every family exactly resemble the white children—and every lady tells you who is the father of all the mulatto children in everybody's household, but those in her own she seems to think drop from the clouds, or pretends so to think." A former slave recalled an exchange among children on the plantation, one set claiming to share the "same daddy" as the master's children. "He is our daddy," these light-skinned youngsters announced, "and we call him daddy when he comes to our house to see our mama."

Small farmers and herders made up the majority of the South's white population. Southern farmers, sometimes called yeomen, crackers, or simply plain

MOST WHITE SOUTHERNERS lived modestly on small farms with few or no slaves. Although proud of their independence and self-reliance, many aspired to be wealthy planters.

folk, possessed few, if any, slaves and farmed between 80 and 160 acres of land. Like their northern counterparts, many owned their own land and were essentially self-sufficient. Southern farmers prided themselves on their independence and self-reliance, and yet it was their willingness and desire to own slaves that set them apart from northern farmers. Many of these plain folk were already related to planters through ties of blood and marriage. Farmers often relied on nearby plantations to gin their cotton and as places to sell surplus corn, hogs, or other products. Some of them served as overseers on large plantations, and they rode in slave patrols to police black slaves. Should they amass sufficient wealth, many were eager to buy some slaves to grow more crops and increase their holdings, just as they saw planters do. Profoundly affected by the Second Great Awakening, southern small farmers embraced their egalitarian message of universal depravity and redemption, but they replicated the planters' social hierarchy in their own homes. Men exuded paternalistic control over their wives, their children, and a scattering of slaves.

Like planters, yeomen mixed capitalism and noncapitalism. Some lived on the frontier, far removed from market society, eking out just enough food to exist; others followed cotton prices and anxiously sought to make a profit from their crops. John Flintoff, a North Carolinian yeoman who was "impatient to get along in the world," traveled to Louisiana and Mississippi to try to make his fortune. Employed as an overseer, he eventually returned to North Carolina, where he acquired enough slaves and land to get himself out of debt, and he planned to send his sons to college. But he never became the wealthy cotton planter of his aspirations. Ferdinand L. Steele also left North Carolina and went west to make his fortune. He worked hard as a hatter and a riverboatman, then took up farming in Mississippi, hoping to turn a profit on the cotton crop he planted and picked himself. Unable to raise his family above its subsistence existence, the intensely religious Steele reflected in a resigned fashion: "My life is one of toil, but blessed be to God it is well with me as it is."

The South too had what might be considered a "middle class" comparable to that of the North. These included manufacturers, merchants, bankers, doctors, clergy, lawyers, and teachers. Many of these people also owned or rented slaves, often because they needed the labor, but sometimes because slaves were symbols of prosperity.

Landless whites made up a small percentage of the southern population. Their number differed from state to state, but most regions in the South counted 10–15 percent landless whites. Some were overseers on plantations, others were tenant farmers, and still others were day laborers who were paid to do specific tasks. Many were young, and some were immigrant Irish, clustered in the South's few urban centers. Olmsted was struck by their presence and was told that these poor whites were "worse off in almost all respects than the slaves." He observed: "That their condition is not as unfortunate by any means as that of the negroes, however, is most obvious, since from among them, men *sometimes* elevate themselves to positions and habits of usefulness, and respectability." Upper-class whites had little positive to say of these poor, accusing them of "corrupting" blacks with liquor and having licentious relationships with them. "They seem, nevertheless," Olmsted concluded, "more than any other portion of the community, to hate and despise the negroes."

The South often seemed a contradictory mix of hierarchy and egalitarianism. Southern whites shared interests in agriculture, ties of kinship, feelings of localism, and a stubborn sense of independence. Race bonded all whites, giving even the poorest farmer social and political benefits merely because of skin color. As the black population grew, whites also shared fears of slave rebellion. Thus, even for whites not tied economically to the slave system, the institution remained the vital and apparently indispensable means of controlling a potentially dangerous population. Still, honor, name, and place mattered, and personal relationships defined the most mundane interactions. Planters expected a certain deference, given their affluence and status, and wealthier slave owners frequently spoke disparagingly of lower classes.

Free Blacks in the South

At the bottom of the southern hierarchy were free blacks and slaves. Since the mid-seventeenth century, there had been a small but steady population of free blacks living in the South. Some had arrived in the New World free; others gained their freedom after indentured service. Still others were freed upon their master's death. The Revolution and the Great Awakenings ushered in new waves of manumission, increasing the number of free blacks, especially in the upper South. From 1790 to 1810 their number increased more than threefold, from about 32,000 to more than 108,000. In 1860 there were 261,918 free blacks living in the South. The majority of these people lived as tenant farmers, hiring out their labor to nearby whites. About a third lived in urban areas, employed as skilled craftsworkers or in the region's limited industry. Their rights were still limited by the color of their skin, although they could own property and make contracts. A small number of free blacks owned their own land or business, and a few of them owned slaves. Some blacks became "masters" by purchasing their wives or children, a means either of freeing them or of preventing them from being sold to whites.

Free blacks still suffered from discrimination and lacked most of the legal rights enjoyed by even the poorest whites. They were favorite targets whenever slaveholders feared uprisings. In 1859 a free black woman named Lucy Andrews petitioned the state of South Carolina to become a slave. Her petition stated that she was "dissatisfied with her present condition being compelled to go about from place to place, to seek employment for her support, and not permitted to stay at any place, more than a week or two at a time, no one caring about employing her." She preferred enslavement to her "isolated condition of freedom."

Slaves were, as South Carolinian planter and senator James Henry Hammond once described, the "mudsill class." There were significant variations among slaves, depending on time, region, and place. Slavery in the deep South was unlike that in the upper South or the middle South, and slave life in such urban centers as New Orleans or Mobile differed from slavery experienced on the vast rice plantations of the South Carolina low country.

Despite the variety of slave life experiences, some generalizations can be made. By the eve of the Civil War, the majority of slaves resided in the lower South, laboring in large gangs to plant and harvest cotton, rice, sugar, and tobacco. Some learned skilled trades; others worked as house servants, cooking, cleaning, and supervising children for their white owners. First and foremost, slaves were workers, and thus their daily existence revolved around constant toil, often from sunup to sundown. In the South Carolina rice regions, slaves worked under a task system: once they completed a specific task, they were free to use the rest of the day as they wished, most often on their own garden plots. This unusual arrangement was due to rice planters' absenting themselves during the hot summer months when malaria ran rampant. Most slaves, however, did not follow the task system and instead worked from sunup to sundown under the watchful eyes of whites, who rode among them, whip in hand. Although planting and harvesting crops was seasonal, there were other chores to keep slaves busy. Slaves mainly lived in rough conditions, usually in one-room cabins with minimal light, warmth, and comfort. Many strove to create a world away from their master's control. Every aspect of their existence, from their family relations to their religious beliefs, was deeply imprinted with the reality of their bondage. Slaves lived in constant fear of being physically and mentally abused or being sold far from their loved ones. As one historian has commented: "It was the random potential for horror, not just its prevalence, that made slavery so wrong."

Slave Life

Ethan Allen Andrew, a Latin teacher and northerner who visited the South during the 1830s, likened the situation to sleeping "on the verge of a volcano." Slave owners often spoke affectionately and earnestly of their family "white and black," expressing real affection for their slaves, but distrust and fear hovered over all relations between master and slave. As Andrew noted: "The real sentiments and feelings of the negroes, in respect to their situation, it is very difficult for any white person to ascertain, and for a stranger, it is nearly impossible." He found that whenever a white man asked slaves about their condition, "they are at once put upon their guard, and either make indefinite and vague replies, or directly contradict their real sentiments." This distrust makes a slave see "all white men, and especially strangers, as the friends of his master, and does not dare trust his sacred wishes to those who may immediately betray him."

The Cotton Kingdom

Meanwhile, complex interests helped to regionalize slavery, increase its profitability, and create the Cotton Kingdom. Before the 1770s, cotton was grown in small amounts on the Sea Islands of South Carolina and Georgia; often slaves planted it in their gardens to make their own homespun cloth. The Revolutionary War's interruption of trade made imported cloth, especially English wool, fall into short supply; domestic production of cotton increased, but cultivation was laborious and profits were limited. Long-staple cotton grew only in limited coastal regions of the South, and the threads of the short-staple variety, which flourished all over the region, were harder to separate from the seeds. Enter Eli Whitney and his famed cotton gin (gin was short for engine). Northern-born, Yale-educated, and savvy, Whitney claimed all the credit (and great profits) for his invention, although varying methods used to separate lint from cotton seeds dated back centuries. In 1794 Whitney, along with his business partner Phineas Miller, patented their gadget—a cylinder with wire teeth that turned against drums of cotton. Even though Whitney's gin tangled and tore the fiber and was nearly unusable, his boast of producing 2,500 pounds of cotton per day with only two laborers inspired improvements. Quantity over quality became the goal, and by the early 1790s, production of short-staple cotton sky-rocketed.

The change was phenomenal. By the 1820s, highly mechanized British and New England textile mills were demanding great quantities of southern cotton, and the gin, along with improved baling methods, enabled planters to keep pace. By the 1850s, feeding the worldwide boom in cheap cotton cloth, the South was producing 70 percent of all the world's cotton. The crop had been transformed from a favorite in slaves' gardens to staple produce. Cotton plantations stretched through the deep South states of Louisiana, Mississippi, Alabama, Georgia, and South Carolina. They also extended into Texas, Tennessee, Arkansas, Kentucky, Virginia, and North Carolina.

"Cotton is King," proclaimed many southerners, and so it seemed. Much of the deep South's climate and geography was perfectly suited for cotton planting, and cotton traveled well; once ginned, the bolls kept for months without spoiling. Rice, in comparison, thrived in very limited areas, most notably South

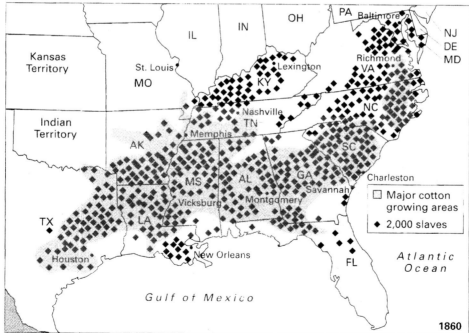

BETWEEN 1820 AND 1860, large-scale slavery spread south and west into regions where cotton growing was most prevalent and most profitable.

Carolina and Georgia's Sea Islands. And unlike rice, cotton did not require elaborate dykes, floodgates, and canals. Cotton came to dominate everything else that southern farmers produced. To be sure, southern farmers planted more than just one crop: They grew vegetables, raised poultry, and exchanged some products in the local community. Owning livestock was more widespread than owning slaves or planting cotton. But even a modest small farmer could plant a patch of cotton and turn a profit, and cotton made the big planters the wealthiest group of men in the United States, enabling them to pursue an opulent lifestyle. As one historian puts it, for rich and poor, cotton was the "main chance in the ante-bellum South, and southerners pursued it furiously." By the 1850s, even more than during the prior fifty years, the expanding world market in textiles, woven mainly in England but increasingly in New England and France, had turned the American South into a boom economy.

To fill this seemingly ever-growing market for cotton, and because cotton cultivation rapidly depleted the soil, slavery, well suited for cotton cultivation, had to expand. During the late 1850s, for example, vast new acreage was opened in southeast Arkansas and east Texas, quite often by plantation owners from older portions of the deep South. In addition, cotton growing reintensified in such places as the black belt of Mississippi and Alabama, where an earlier "Alabama fever" for the soft white fiber had occurred years earlier. Cotton growing also expanded toward the hill country in such states as Alabama, Georgia, and South Carolina. With the spread of the railroad, the South experienced a rapid expansion of cotton growing and exportation, and the movers and the shakers—the younger and more aggressive men, including the most ambitious poor whites—experienced sudden prosperity. And they became more deeply committed to cotton and to slavery. Because of the great profitability of cotton, most planters invested their money in more land and more slaves. They created veritable factories in the field with large gangs of slaves using simple tools in a concerted and well-organized fashion. There were other ways to generate wealth in the South, but whites of all classes recognized landowning and slaveholding as the best routes to prosperity.

Slavery Expands Westward

Far from awaiting the natural death of slavery, as the 1808 clause in the Constitution had suggested, masters, abetted by efficient slave traders, found little problem in vigorously expanding their peculiar institution. The slave South expanded dynamically as slaveholders drove their labor force westward when they migrated onto fresh lands acquired by the United States. In such older eastern-seaboard states as Virginia and North Carolina, where soil depletion and a falling tobacco market made slavery less profitable, farmers concentrated on corn, wheat, hemp, and livestock. These products were very much needed by the cotton South and in port cities such as Charleston, Savannah, Mobile, and New Orleans. The surplus slaves left over from these less labor-intensive endeavors, an estimated 2 million between 1820 and 1840, were sold farther south, creating a booming domestic slave trade—and dividing black families forever.

This expansion alarmed many northerners who saw the West as free land to be taken up by free labor and free men, uncontaminated by what they consid-

SLAVES ENDURED COUNTLESS CRUELTIES and humiliations at the hands of whites. Perhaps one of the most demeaning aspects of their lowly status was the dreaded inspection and sale, where they were prodded and pricked like farm animals at an auction.

ered the degrading use of black slaves, indeed by any physical presence of the alien black race. This was to them a fundamental culture clash, not just another form of competition for land; it concerned the whole future of the United States.

Indian Removal

One element of southern expansion did not seem to be of much concern to northern whites—the concerted action of state and federal governments to push the Indians off the land they believed was destined for their use. Following the Indian Removal Act of 1830, in 1838–1839 the army banished the Cherokee tribe, who had become Christian farmers, from Georgia. Of the 16,000 exiles forced to Oklahoma along the "Trail of Tears," approximately 4,000 died of starvation and disease. In more protracted, if episodic wars, such as the Seminole Wars of 1817–1818, 1835–1842, and 1855–1858, state militias and federal forces either drove Indians from their land or penned them up on reservations. When they envisioned the virgin prairies ready for their plows, northerners wanted them clear of both African Americans and Indians.

The Missouri Compromise

In 1819 the first real political crisis over slavery's expansion westward erupted. Missouri, part of the 1803 Louisiana Purchase, was ready to apply for statehood. Slavery had existed in this region during Spanish, French, and

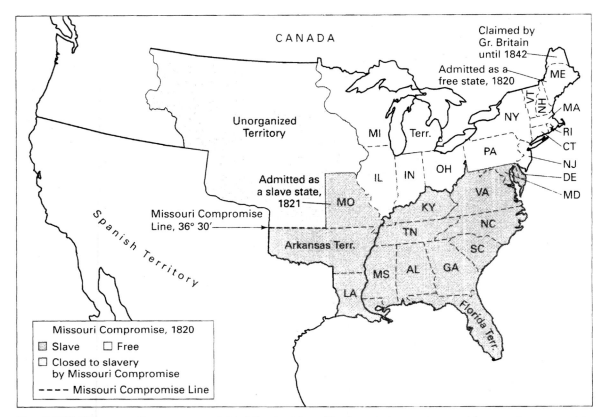

THE 1820 MISSOURI COMPROMISE divided the Louisiana Purchase between slave and free. and was meant to quiet political debate over the institution.

American rule, and it seemed the territory would enter the Union as a slave state. But when Congressman James Tallmadge Jr. of New York unexpectedly added an amendment to the bill for Missouri statehood that would bar any more slaves from entering the region and would include a plan for gradual manumission, what many thought would be a smooth process turned abruptly rocky.

Before 1819 new states, free and slave, had entered the Union with relatively little controversy. In fact, by 1819 a balance of eleven slave states and eleven free states had been achieved, all east of what seemed to be the natural boundary of the Mississippi River. However, some northerners, irritated by what they perceived as increasing southern domination of the House of Representatives due to the Constitution's "three-fifths" clause, believed that slave owners' political power needed to be checked. Tallmadge's amendment ignited a political firestorm that raged for more than a year.

Heated congressional debates over political power, sectional interests, and the future of slavery shook the very foundation of the Republic. Proslavery advocates began to push their "positive-good" theory of slavery, convinced that the institution had to spread to stay alive. The two sides divided over how much power Congress could have over a state entering the Union. Thomas Jefferson, aging but still politically alert, likened the Missouri crisis to a "fire-bell in the night," warning that serious division could lead to civil war. Tallmadge himself declared: "If a dissolution of the Union must take place, *let it be so!* If civil war, which gentlemen so much threaten, must come, I can say, *let it come!*" Instead, thanks largely to the efforts of Speaker of the House Henry Clay, Congress achieved a compromise. Missouri entered the Union as a slave state, but Maine, originally part of Massachusetts, entered as a free state, keeping the balance of free to slave states equal. *The Missouri Compromise* of 1820 also forbade any more slave states above 36°30′, banning the institution "forever" from a sizable area of the West. The "fire-bell" Jefferson heard had been muffled, and the nation resumed its stunning growth and expansion.

Within a decade, sectionalism reared its ugly head again, and fears of disunion resurfaced. In 1828 the South Carolina legislature published *The South Carolina Exposition and Protest*, attacking the Tariff of 1828, and proposing that a state could veto a federal law that it deemed unconstitutional. The *tariff*, a protective tax on imports, was in effect a subsidy for American manufacturers, almost all of whom were in the North. It was widely unpopular among southern slave states, which were more dependent on imports than were the northern industrial states, and which bought finished goods from the North at a higher price due to the tariff, while they sold their cotton onto an unprotected world market. Slaveholders called the 1828 tax, the highest in U.S. history, an "abomination" and clamored for its reduction. South Carolina in particular, the only southern state with more slaves than whites, was especially sensitive to the tariff and issued its protest.

The Nullification Crisis

The author of the *South Carolina Exposition* was Vice President John C. Calhoun, a native South Carolinian with considerable political experience, influence, and intellect. Once described by English author Harriet Martineau as "the cast-iron man, who looks like he had never been born and never could be extinguished," Calhoun had a formidable reputation as a devout protector of states' rights. His *Exposition*, initially published anonymously to safeguard Calhoun's electoral prospects as Andrew Jackson's running mate in the upcoming 1828 presidential election, was his first public statement of what came to be known as his *Theory of Nullification*. Calhoun, drawing on arguments presented by Jefferson and Madison in their Kentucky and Virginia resolutions, reasoned that the Union was a voluntary compact among the states and that the Constitution granted the federal government very specific and limited powers. Congress could tax to raise revenue but not to shelter domestic industries from foreign competition. Such laws made southerners the "serfs of the system—out of whose labor is raised, not only the money paid into the Treasury, but the funds out of which are drawn the rich rewards of the manufacturer and his associates in interest." Calhoun proposed that if a state deemed a federal law, such as the tariff, outside the bounds of the federal government's constitutional

SOUTH CAROLINIAN JOHN C. CAL-HOUN emerged during the 1830s as the most strident voice favoring states' rights and defending the institution of slavery. His "Theory of Nullification" laid the groundwork for southern secession.

domain, that state could veto or nullify it. Calhoun would later elaborate that the federal government would then be left with two choices: either to accept the decision of the state to refuse to follow the law, or to pass an amendment to make the law constitutional. Calhoun maintained that if the federal government refused to recognize the state's power to nullify, the state could secede, or leave the Union.

In 1828 South Carolina approved Calhoun's *Exposition*, but believing that the new president, Andrew Jackson, would side with their position on the tariff, the state stopped short of nullifying the law. However, Jackson, himself a native of the state and a resident of Tennessee, was not supportive of South Carolina's position. The whole idea of nullification appalled him. In a famous confrontation in 1830, Jackson arose at a banquet to toast the nation. Glaring at his vice president, he proclaimed: "Our Federal Union—it must and shall be preserved." Calhoun stood to respond, his glass shaking in his hand: "The Union—next to our liberty most dear." Calhoun soon resigned as vice president but returned to Washington as a South Carolina senator. The confrontation over the tariff and states' rights was far from over.

The tariff was the stated reason for the dispute, but slavery lay at the heart of the debate. It was slavery that made southern states more dependent on imports of finished goods than the industrializing North, and more dependent on the export of raw materials. Calhoun himself admitted as much in a letter to a friend. On September 11, 1830, he wrote Virgil Maxey: "I consider the Tariff, but as the occasion, rather than the real cause of the present unhappy state of things." He confessed: "The truth can no longer be disguised, that the present domestick institutions of the Southern States, and the constant direction which that and her soil and climate have given to her industry, has placed them in regard to taxation and appropriation in opposite relation to the majority of the Union." The slave South, the minority in Calhoun's mind, had to have some way to counter the majority position of manufacture-minded northerners.

On November 24, 1832, just weeks after Jackson's reelection to the presidency, a South Carolina state convention passed an ordinance of nullification, rejecting the Tariff of 1828 as well as a lower tariff passed in 1832. If the federal government opposed the convention's action, South Carolina would secede from the Union. In December the state legislature moved to implement the ordinance, to allocate money to buy arms and to raise troops.

Jackson moved quickly to silence South Carolina's dissenters. He persuaded Congress to pass the *Force Act*, authorizing him to use federal troops to enforce federal law in South Carolina. He dispatched soldiers into forts in Charleston harbor and appointed Winfield Scott to prepare for a military confrontation. A civil war almost began. Armed confrontation was avoided, thanks largely to the efforts of Henry Clay and other political leaders, who believed that lowering the tariff would end the crisis. Despite the widespread unpopularity of the tariff among southern slaveholders, no other southern state joined South Carolina in its open defiance of the federal government. South Carolina stood alone.

In the end, with the passage of the Tariff Act of 1833, the hated tax was gradually reduced, and the nullifiers backed down. South Carolina assembled another convention to repeal its nullification ordinance, but in a final act of bravado, the South Carolina convention also vetoed the Force Act. The crisis was over, but the sectional strife that the tariff issue exposed was hard to ignore.

Slave Rebellion

At the same time that South Carolina shook the national tree, forces outside the political and economic realms added a note of urgency to the slavery debate. Most slaves never escaped slavery, nor did they violently oppose it. The few examples of large uprisings were all failed ones with deadly consequences—enough to discourage rebellious slaves. The largest and most successful attempt at organized rebellion occurred in Southampton County, Virginia, in August 1831. Nat Turner was a charismatic and eloquent slave preacher whose religious convictions and biblically oriented mysticism led him to believe that he heard voices and perceived signs instructing him to lead an uprising of slaves against their white owners. He and his followers killed about sixty white men, women, and children in the county and were able to wreak havoc throughout the region before suffering capture and execution. More than 400 blacks were killed in retaliation. A local doctor, Thomas Gray, obtained a confession from Turner, who said that a "loud voice from the heavens" told him that the "time was fast approaching when the first should be last and the last should be first." Turner's cool composure and honest confession shocked Gray. "I looked on him," Gray wrote, "and my blood curdled in my veins."

Nat Turner's rebellion deeply frightened many whites throughout the South. The uprising led directly to a series of debates on emancipation in Virginia's state legislature. Compared to its widespread growth and success in such cotton states as Georgia and Alabama, slavery in Virginia was on the decline, although the Old Dominion state, like other upper southern states, participated actively in the domestic slave trade, selling slaves to new lands to the south and west. But ridding Virginia of the institution was another matter, and for several weeks, delegates seriously debated the pros and cons of slavery. Most supporters of emancipation also supported colonization in Africa; few whites could envision freed blacks becoming fellow citizens in their own state. In the end, the seeming impracticality of emancipation and its high monetary cost silenced discussion. The Virginia debates marked the end of open antislavery discussion in the South just as a revived abolitionist movement was gaining momentum in the North.

The Abolitionist Movement

Although abolitionists were always a minority of the American population, southerners increasingly believed that abolition defined the North and threatened their political, social, and economic autonomy. After 1831 a more militant, more political, more influential abolitionist movement *was* growing in the North, assailing the slave South and calling for an immediate end to slavery.

Before 1831, most abolitionists were *gradualists,* antislavery proponents who sought a slow end to slavery with compensation to slave owners for their economic loss. Many gradualists further believed that slaves should be deported to Africa, slowly obliterating slavery as well as the freed blacks themselves from American society. The American Colonization Society, founded in 1817, had little success in freeing slaves and relocating them to Africa. Nonetheless, colonization was popular among some slaveholders and both northern and southern whites. There were those who sincerely despised slavery but believed that whites and blacks could not live peacefully side by side as equal citizens. There were also those who merely wanted to be rid of blacks, whether free or slave. And there were those—southern slaveholders in particular—who believed as Jefferson did that slavery was a troublesome and inherently problematic institution that increasingly hurt the Republic the longer it lasted.

In the early 1830s, however, the gradualist position gave way to a more militant, more emotional form of abolitionism: *immediatists* demanded an immediate end to slavery. They refused to temporize with what they believed was the mortal sin of slavery. How could Americans claim to live in a true democracy, how could they claim to be Christians, if they did not destroy slavery? To usher in the American millennium that they believed was at hand, they had to root out and destroy the cancer of the slave power that was spreading corruption wherever it went—and they had to begin immediately rather than waiting on some indefinite future. Thus would these abolitionists witness their faith through action.

The best-known and most radical member of this combative wing of the antislavery movement was William Lloyd Garrison, a young, impassioned printer from Boston. Deserted by his alcoholic father and raised by his pious mother, stirred by the millennialist impulses of the Second Great Awakening, Garrison became intent on both moral perfection and social recognition. Denouncing the pragmatic gradualists in 1831, Garrison angrily declared: "Tell a man whose house is on fire to give a moderate alarm; tell him to moderately rescue his wife from the hands of the ravisher; tell the mother to gradually extricate her babe from the fire into which it has fallen;—but urge me not to use moderation in a cause like the present." Insisting "I am in earnest," Garrison proclaimed: "I will not retreat a single inch—and *I will be heard.*" Heard he was, mainly through his newspaper the *Liberator*, with its masthead reading "No Union with slaveholders." In 1833 he authored the American Anti-Slavery Society's "Declaration of Sentiments" that stated: "No man has a right to enslave or imbrute his brother—to hold or acknowledge him, for one moment, as a piece of merchandise—to keep back his hire by fraud—or to brutalize his mind by denying him the means of intellectual, social and moral improvement." Garrison once publicly burned a copy of the Constitution, proclaiming it "a covenant with death and an agreement with Hell."

Immediatists also included blacks themselves. In the expanding institutions of black newspapers and black churches, African American leaders created an increasingly militant stance toward striking off the chains that bound their slave brothers and sisters. David Walker, a free black from Wilmington, North Carolina, who relocated to Boston, mocked the language of the Declaration of Independence in his 1829 *Appeals in Four Articles*. "See your Declaration Americans!!!! Do you understand your own language?" After citing the famed document and pointing to the "cruelties and murders" slavery inflicted on innocent blacks, Walker proclaimed: "Now Americans! I ask you candidly, was your sufferings under Great Britain, one hundredth part as cruel and tyrannical as you have rendered ours under you?" He denounced notions of white superiority and black submissiveness and urged whites to treat African Americans as human beings, not brutes. "Remember Americans," Walker pronounced, "that we must and shall be free and enlightened as you are, will you wait until we shall under God, obtain our liberty by the crushing arm of power?" Predicting the horrific casualties and destruction of civil war, Walker declared: "And wo, wo, will be to you if we have to obtain our freedom by fighting."

Such militant abolitionism, although growing, attracted only a small minority of the northern population. And yet, so threatening was their message that southerners conflated them with all antislavery people, thereby amplifying the abolitionists' impact. Literature produced by such immediatists as Walker and Garrison so incensed southerners that many of these writings were banned in the South. Post offices suspected of carrying antislavery publications were looted and vandalized. President Andrew Jackson, himself a large slave owner, endorsed a government prohibition on sending antislavery literature south. When abolitionists flooded Congress with antislavery petitions, the federal government passed a *gag rule* that lasted from 1836 to 1844, tabling all such petitions from discussion. In turn, in the House of Representatives, former President John

Quincy Adams, now a congressman from Massachusetts, turned this proscription into a freedom of speech campaign, thereby broadening the appeal of northern antislavery efforts and dealing with slaveholders as tyrants who not only lorded over their enslaved workers but destroyed freedom for all Americans in the name of security for the defense of their brutal institution.

Resistance to Abolitionism

Even with abolitionism growing and slavery fading in the North, however, few white northerners wanted to ban slavery in the South. In the 1830s and 1840s, there was a good deal of resistance to talk of abolition, and there were efforts to silence it, including the gag rule in Congress. In the North, violent antiabolition mobs attacked prominent antislavery advocates, destroying property and in some cases killing abolitionist activists. The abolition message of emancipation struck a raw nerve for many whites by seeming to imply the threat of competition for work from freed slaves and a rearrangement of the nation's racial and social order. Ties to British abolitionists further heightened fears of foreign agitators in the North. It seemed that abolitionists threatened the very Union itself. Community leaders had little trouble whipping crowds into a frenzy with references to "amalgamation" and racial intermarriage.

Antiabolition violence exploded throughout the North, including New England. In 1833 a Quaker teacher, Prudence Crandall, sought to open a boarding school for black girls in the small town of Canterbury, Connecticut. With the help of Garrison, Crandall recruited fifteen or twenty children to attend. The local community reacted with fury, instantly seeking to shut down the school. Store owners refused to sell anything to Crandall; townspeople terrorized students, smeared filth on the school doors and steps, and poisoned the well. In May 1833 the Connecticut legislature outlawed schools for black children, and about a month later Crandall was arrested for operating the school. A trial ensued without any conclusive results, but the school eventually closed for good, and Crandall left the state.

In October 1835 mob violence erupted in the heart of the abolitionist movement, Boston, Massachusetts. A combination of factors caused the outbreak, including increased resentment toward Garrison's outspoken views, the promised appearance of a prominent British abolitionist, and anger at the scheduled meeting of the Boston Female Anti-Slavery Society—an unwelcome intrusion of women into the public sphere. A crowd that formed outside the meeting place refused to disperse, even when appealed to by the mayor. Rioters attempted to break down the door, chanting: "Garrison! Garrison! We must have Garrison! Out with him! Lynch him!" Slipping out the back door into a nearby carpenter's shop, Garrison could not escape the angry mob. They soon found him, put a rope around his body, and marched him through the streets. Garrison managed to get free of the rope, and the sheriff and his deputies tried to escort him to safety. He recalled: "They led me along bareheaded, (for I had lost my hat), through a mighty crowd, ever and anon shouting, 'He shan't be hurt! You shan't hurt him! Don't hurt him! He is an American, etc, etc.' This seemed to excite sympathy among many of the crowd and they reiterated the cry, 'He shan't be hurt!' " Turned over to the mayor's office, Garrison was then transferred to the city jail, the only place where town officials thought they could keep him protected. Charged as a disturber of the peace, Garrison was locked in his cell, "safe from my persecutors, accompanied by two delightful associates, a good conscience and a cheerful mind." The next morning, he scribbled on the jail walls: "Wm. Lloyd Garrison was put into this cell on Wednesday afternoon Oct. 21, 1835, to save him from the violence of a 'respectable and influential' mob, who sought to destroy him for preaching the abominable and dangerous doctrine that 'all men are created equal,' and that all oppression is odious in the sight of God." Later that day, he was released and left the city for a few days. But he soon returned and continued his abolition activities.

Two years later, Reverend Elijah P. Lovejoy became the most prominent victim of antiabolition violence. In 1836 Lovejoy started an abolitionist newspaper, the *Alton Observer,* and preached his views in churches in and around his home in Alton, Illinois. His words stirred anger and threats. In a letter to a friend in October 1837, he described keeping a loaded musket at his bedside to protect his pregnant wife and sick child. One mob member angrily accused Lovejoy of inciting a black man to rape his wife. "I feel that I do not walk the streets in safety, and every night when I lie down, it is with the deep settled conviction, that there are those near and around me, who seek my life." Less than a month later, a mob murdered Lovejoy as he fled the burning building that housed his newspaper.

Just as the antiabolition violence escalated, the movement showed signs of division. Shocked by the fury of northern antiabolitionists, antislavery leaders began to reconsider their methods and goals. Some believed that they should establish political parties and attack slavery through the legal system; others, like Garrison, wanted nothing to do with government institutions and organized churches, particularly ones that supported slavery. Garrison also promoted pacifism—believing that coercion of all sorts, not just slavery, was evil—while others were more militant. Gradualists continued to believe that slave owners should be compensated and that slavery could not and should not be abolished quickly. In central New York, supporters of using politics to attack the institution rallied around the wealthy Gerrit Smith. In New York City, Lewis Tappan led a wing of church-oriented activists who remained committed to their belief that a Christian nation had no place for slavery. A scattering of abolitionists, including Smith, founded their own party, the Liberty Party, which ran presidential candidates in the elections of 1840 and 1844. One contemporary noted that the key interest of this new party was not solely the welfare of the slave: "The negro's pick of corn a week, his stripes and the sundering [of] his family are legitimate subjects for the discussion of the Liberty Party man, only in so far as they may be prejudicial to the interests of the white man."

Abolitionists also argued over the role of women in their ranks and the active involvement and leadership of blacks. For many it seemed obvious that degradation by race and degradation by gender were parts of a general abuse of power, and that freedom and equality had to be extended to women as well as blacks. Indeed, the first woman's movement derived from the ranks of abolitionist

Abolitionists Divided

women. For other abolitionists it was important to remain focused on slavery, lest the movement dissipate its energies in other issues, causes that would narrow the base of their appeal in the North, frightening off many potential converts.

Two sisters, Angelina and Sarah Grimké, fled their slave-owning family in Charleston to become outspoken immediatists and devout Quakers. In 1837 the Grimkés found themselves attacked by conservative clergy who were shocked by the idea of women speaking in public. They were opposed as well by another prominent woman, Catharine Beecher, the older sister of Harriet Beecher Stowe and the daughter of outspoken gradualist Lyman Beecher. Angelina responded to Catharine Beecher by publishing a letter that blasted the entire gradualist position: "I have seen too much of slavery to be a gradualist. I dare not, in view of such a system, tell the slaveholder that 'he is physically unable to emancipate his slaves.' I say *he is able* to let the oppressed go free, and that such heaven-daring atrocities ought to *cease now*, henceforth and forever. Oh my very soul is grieved to find a northern woman thus 'sewing pillows under all armholes' framing and fitting soft excuses for the slaveholder's conscience, whilst with the same pen she is professing to regard slavery as a sin. An open enemy is better than such a secret friend."

Proslavery Defense

As the abolitionists argued over members and methods, proslavery advocates united, pushed in part by the horrors of Nat Turner's rebellion that led slaveholders to an increasing militancy. Slavery certainly was not showing any signs of dying in the South. On the contrary, it was growing. Nor was racism abating; in fact, almost all white Americans viewed blacks as inferior and insisted that theirs was a white republic. As an English traveler noted in 1855: "There seems, in short, to be a fixed notion throughout the whole of the states, whether slave or free, that the colored is by nature a subordinate race; and that, in no circumstances can it be considered equal to the white." Proslavery proponents constructed an elaborate defense that drew not only on these well-accepted racial attitudes, but also on popular notions of history, religion, and nature. Slavery was immensely profitable, even for the most modest slave owner, but proslavery apologists rarely emphasized the monetary value of slavery. Instead, they stressed the religious and historical precedents that supported the institution. They drew on passages from the Old and New Testament that dealt with the curse of Cain (that curse being black skin), the descendents of Ham, and Paul imploring slaves to be faithful and dutiful in this life and await for the hereafter to be free. They noted that nowhere in the Bible was slavery condemned, even by Jesus Christ, and they criticized abolitionists for failing to follow the Bible's literal text. "The South is to be damned," remarked South Carolinian Lawrence Keitt, "into a change of its institutions by virtue of pseudo-scriptures, edited with notes and exegesis tacked to them by Yankee exponents of bogus Gospel law." Historically, they cited the examples of Greece and Rome, both ancient republican civilizations that held slaves, and argued that no wealthy civilization succeeded without relying on the labor of others.

By the third decade of the nineteenth century, some slaveholders used political and social theory to justify slavery. Some pointed to their plantations as model communities, condemning the industrializing North and the concepts of free labor. Depicting themselves as considerate masters, and portraying slaves as helpless children, slave owners such as South Carolina congressman and governor James Henry Hammond maintained: "I have no hesitation in saying that our slaveholders are kind masters, as men usually are kind husbands, parents and friends—as a general rule, kinder. A bad master—he who overworks his slaves, provides ill for them, or treats them with undue severity—loses the esteem and respect of his fellow-citizens to as great an extent he would for the violation of any of his social and most of his moral obligations." Southern publisher H. Manly agreed, arguing in 1836 that a slave "never suffers from inordinate labour—he never sickens from unwholesome food. No fear of want disturbs his slumbers. Hunger and cold are strangers to him; and in sickness or age he knows that he has a protector and a friend able and willing to shield him from suffering." Manly asserted that slavery offered "complete equality among whites." "Colour alone," he declared, "is here the badge of distinction, the true mark of aristocracy, and all who are white are equal in spite of variety of occupation."

In 1854 George Fitzhugh compared the slave South to the North and Europe and concluded: "At the slaveholding South all is peace, quiet, plenty and contentment. We have no mobs, no trade unions, no strikes for higher wages, no armed resistance to the law, but little jealousy of the rich by the poor." According to this view, the northern labor system degraded and exploited its workers, casting them out into the cold during bad times or when they could no longer work due to illness of injury, making "wage-slaves" of supposedly free workers, while southern slavery protected its workers with paternalistic care from cradle to grave.

Others studied the seeming physical differences between black and white, concluding that blacks were not only inferior to whites but were of a different and lesser species. Exploring the new field of ethnology, these proslavery proponents went so far as to argue that black people's brains were smaller and less developed than whites and that the inner organs and bodily fluids of slaves were somehow darker than that of whites. Although these ideas of "scientific racism" clashed with the views of religious literalists—who were doubtless a majority among southern whites, and who believed that it was clear in the Book of Genesis that God created one human species, not two or more—the result was the same. All proslavery theorists concluded that Africans were fated to play a submissive role in the world and to remain under the protective control of the superior white man. The proslavery argument had evolved from accepting slavery as a necessary evil to proclaiming it to be a natural, historical, moral, positive good as well as a scientifically and politically justified system of labor. The abolition and proslavery sides could not have been more polarized.

As the slavery debate became more heated, the nation continued to expand westward at dizzying speed. Since the turn of the century, the United States had begun to acquire vast amounts of land, first in 1803 with the Louisiana Purchase, followed by the acquisition of Florida, and in 1845 the annexation of Texas. Americans sought these new lands to farm, to spread political and religious

Slavery in the Territories

ideals, to mine gold and silver, and to wrest the territory from "savage" Indians. A journalist labeled the belief that Americans were destined to stretch their boundaries from coast to coast *Manifest Destiny*. "We are the nation of human progress," John O'Sullivan professed in 1845, "and who will, what can, set limits to our onward march?"

But slavery did set limits to this march westward, not by preventing Americans from feverishly acquiring more and more land, but by preventing it from being an easy, uncontested process. Most everyone agreed that slavery must spread to survive. Southerners wanted slavery to expand westward, and not just for economic reasons; it was also politically and racially important to them. Their plantation economy was flourishing, and fresh western land would ensure more opportunities and potential profits. Keeping the balance between slave states and nonslave states in Congress remained vital in the minds of southerners, who were wary and suspicious of northern interests. Nor did many white southerners feel comfortable with a large and concentrated population of black slaves. Expanding the Cotton Kingdom westward was key to keeping a racial balance as much as a political one. At the same time, white northerners wanted the new territories to be free of slavery and free of blacks. Northern workers and members of the middle class feared a "slaveocracy"—an increasingly united and powerful "slave power" secretly conspiring to dominate all of American society—an un-American elite that would destroy wage labor, stifle economic mobility, redefine conceptions of property, and force slaveless but independent whites into poverty. They were hardly abolitionists; instead, they wanted western territories for white laborers, not wealthy planters and their slaves.

The Annexation of Texas

The crisis over Missouri first revealed the politically combustible combination of western expansion and slavery. The annexation of the slave state of Texas was another flash point. Texas had initially gained independence from Mexico in 1836 through its own armed revolution. But soon the Lone Star Republic's many slaveholders, mostly Americans themselves, reasoned that annexation to the United States would bring considerable advantages, including protection from Mexico, which continued to challenge their independence. Texans also sought safeguards for their slaves. Texas became a slave state in 1845, but the heated clash over its annexation, which dominated the election of 1844, centered on slavery's expansion westward. The debate remained on the boil.

By the mid-1840s bitter sectionalism was growing, leading no one yet knew where. Slavery, an institution initially accepted by most white Americans and practiced throughout the new republic, was increasingly regionalized and was proving troublesome to national unity. Few could predict what the nation was about to endure as the winds of war began to gather just south of the Texas border in Mexico.

CHAPTER 2

War and Political Collapse: 1846–1860

As U.S. soldiers returned from Mexico in the summer of 1848, enthusiastic crowds celebrated their resounding victory. Americans called it the Mexican War and it had been a wondrous thing. The young republic, with its popularly elected government and citizen soldiers, had whipped the conscripts of a despotic neighbor and done it on Mexico's own soil. That was something to crow about. "Woe to the crowned head that interferes with rising, onward, onward America!" exalted one soldier. In just seventeen months, the nation had acquired nearly a half-million square miles of territory reaching from the western border of Texas to the Pacific Ocean. Add to that the Oregon Territory, acquired through a treaty with Great Britain two years earlier, and the United States had grown by nearly 25 percent.

However, during the next twelve years, this vast new tract of real estate would throw the United States into turmoil. Even before the war ended, people wanted to know if slavery would be permitted there. It seemed natural to southerners that slavery should expand, but increasing portions of northern society, whose opposition to slavery had been voiced ever more strongly in the 1830s and 1840s, thought otherwise. The inability of Congress and the courts to answer that question to everyone's satisfaction contributed significantly to a metamorphosis of the political party system, pushed sectional passions and paranoia to dangerous levels, and caused most of the slave states to leave the

Union. The so-called territorial question, which began as a dispute about property rights and the balance of political power, became a moral issue, just the sort of thing that the American political system, based on a willingness to compromise and make deals, found difficult to resolve.

President Polk and Manifest Destiny

James K. Polk, eleventh president of the United States, could not have foreseen all that when he initiated the war against Mexico. The lean, determined, and rather colorless former congressman and governor from Tennessee leaped into the national political scene when a deadlocked Democratic convention made him the first "dark horse" presidential candidate in American politics. Henry Clay, his far more famous Whig opponent from Kentucky, scornfully asked, "Who is James K. Polk?" but Polk squeaked out a victory. Most of the country liked his confident, expansionist language and his pledge to push American claims in Oregon, reduce the tariff, reestablish the independent treasury, and, most especially, annex Texas. Polk achieved all that in a single term as president, although he eventually settled for just half of the American claim to Oregon. The Mexican territory would become a rather spectacular bonus.

Polk milked the symbolic value of the Mexican victory by signing the Treaty of Guadalupe Hidalgo on July 4, 1848. He had already helped to dedicate the huge marble cornerstone of what would become the Washington Monument that morning. The two events occurring on the same festive day suggested that this American nation occupied a special place in history. To have attained such size and potential power barely two generations after the American Revolution was breathtaking. One could imagine the ghosts of the founders hovering as guardian angels. Indeed, a grandson of George Washington had joined Polk in dedicating the monument, as had Dolley Madison—a living icon—and the widow of Alexander Hamilton. No wonder Americans had spoken in recent years of their *manifest destiny,* an unflinching belief that they had a divine mission to spread democracy and Christianity across the continent.

Other signs of impending greatness appeared in 1848. Gold had been discovered in California in January, an event that no one could have predicted when the war with Mexico began. Much of Europe had been convulsed by political revolutions that year, another indication that as the Old World crumbled it must inevitably acknowledge the leadership of this brash, vital republic. The United States had entered "a new epoch in its history," declared one American magazine. "From this year we take a new start in national development; one that must, more than ever before, draw the world's history into the stream of ours." President Polk decreed at year's end that Americans were the "most favored people on the face of the earth."

Slavery and Expansion

Favored, perhaps, but the Almighty has a long history of testing even a chosen people. "I can't help feeling a little anxiety for the future and a little of that sadness for the past that the dying out of a new year always awakens," confessed a New Yorker in his final diary entry for 1848. Not least of his concerns was "the possible rupture between North and South on the slavery question." He had good reason to worry. In August 1846, shortly after the fighting with Mexico commenced, a portly young freshman Democratic congressman from

Pennsylvania named David Wilmot had proposed that "neither slavery nor involuntary servitude" be permitted in any new territory acquired in the war. Congress eventually rejected his proviso, but Wilmot had resurrected a volatile issue that most Americans—and certainly most politicians—had sought to avoid since the tense days of the Missouri Compromise.

Few citizens, outside of abolitionist protesters and a handful of southern planters, seem to have appreciated the impact that the war would have on slavery. Manifest Destiny had been the national cry; chastisement of chaotic, polyglot, Catholic Mexico had been the justification. The goal had been to acquire California, where the people—at least the American minority—hungered for stable government and democratic rule. One young army lieutenant had predicted in 1845 that the conflict would "be an infinite benefit" to the army and the country. "Our national divisions and sections and strifes would be healed," he asserted, "and a common interest would bring us together." Those few nonabolitionists who disapproved of the war—mostly Whig politicians—railed more against the naked aggression of the act than against slavery. Not even many southerners thought it likely that slavery would spread beyond Texas. California, Americans agreed, would be a prize for merchants and whalers, the golden coast from which the Columbian dream of trade with the Far East would be realized. The Wilmot Proviso—and the opposition to it—had been inspired as much by disagreements over tariff policy, sectional jealousies within the Democratic Party, and the recent acquisition of Oregon as by discord over slavery.

But with the Mexican War over, what had not been apparent in 1846 became obvious to both the opponents and defenders of slavery. The sudden geographical expansion required a political and economic maturity and a solid institutional base that the nation lacked. Judicious decisions involving extraordinarily complex issues would be needed, and the country was ill prepared to make them. The nation's capital was a mere village, its Capitol building still under construction. The Washington obelisk was to have been the nation's first national monument, but political bickering in the mid-1850s would halt construction for twenty-five years. Symbolic of the national divide to come, it would remain uncompleted until 1884.

Stress of Expansion

What was more, the times and the nation were in flux. The dominant force in American life since at least 1815 had been *expansion,* and although expansion implies growth, and growth is deemed by most people to be a good thing, expansion and growth also bring change, and change—especially rapid change that threatens old ways, old values, and familiar patterns of life—makes people anxious. This point is worth emphasizing. The country in 1848 was already reeling from the recent "revolutions" that had overtaken—and continued to alter—American industry, technology, transportation, cities, and markets. So, too, the enthusiasm for social reform both excited and alarmed people. The suddenly accelerated rate of physical expansion seemed no less a revolution. It was all tremendously exciting, to be sure, and had produced a prosperous, vigorous, *potentially* powerful nation, but when stacked against

THE U.S. CAPITOL seen from Pennsylvania Avenue in 1860. Like the unfinished Washington Monument a mile and a half to its front, the building's dome represented the still unfulfilled potential of a young nation.

the country's undeveloped sense of national identity and its even weaker institutional center, the cumulative effect of these growing pains—physical and otherwise—would be to divide its people.

Political Party System

Central to all this was the nation's still raw and immature political party system. It had been born just a half-century earlier, and the two principal parties—the Democrats and the Whigs—were less than half that old. Both parties swore devotion to *democracy*—a government operated by "the people"—and to *republicanism*—a societal commitment to liberty and equality for "the people"—but they frequently disagreed over the best means of achieving those admirable ends. Democrats, who claimed lineage as the heirs of Thomas Jefferson's Democratic-Republican Party, placed a premium on the power of *state* governments, favored a strict interpretation of constitutional powers, opposed financial monopolies of any sort (be they private corporations or a government-directed national bank), and detested restrictions on individual freedom. The Whig Party, led from its inception by Henry Clay of Kentucky, advocated a relatively stronger role for the *national* government as a facilitator of social change, as the protector of republican liberties, and as an agent of economic growth (including a national bank, a nationally funded transportation system, and a high tariff to protect both the development of American manufacturing and the wages of American workers).

Had Americans still huddled east of the Mississippi River or been content to limit their physical expansion to the Louisiana Purchase, perhaps even to Oregon and Texas, this political system might have proved equal to the task. Party lines remained just fuzzy enough to permit cooperation and compromise on most issues, even slavery. But pressure for the immediate settlement and organization of the Mexican territory put an enormous strain on the parties. It exposed them for what they were *not*: genuinely national organizations. They were, instead, sectional—even local—coalitions in which national party loyalties remained fragile and dependent on compromise. In a very real sense they only became national parties every four years, when they chose a presidential candidate. When the victor chose his cabinet and dealt with Congress, everything dissolved once again. Those fragile partisan loyalties had not been seriously challenged in the 1830s and 1840s, so it remained to be seen if they could stand up to a desperate, bare-knuckles brawl.

These weak party coalitions had also been shaped by a complex and constantly shifting *political culture*—expressed in commonly held beliefs, values, and assumptions—that must be taken into account. Secular ideals such as democracy, republicanism, and liberty formed an important part of that culture, but so did religion. The emotional intensity of *evangelical religion* helped to politicize the most important reform issues of the 1840s and 1850s: temperance, nativism, and slavery. Evangelicals voted for candidates who were "right" on these issues and supported the party that spoke most directly to their moral and ethical, as well as material, concerns. The Whigs, with their greater reliance on government activism to improve society, benefited more often than Democrats from this enthusiasm, but both parties ignored the opinions of local clergy and reformers at their peril. Religion even affected the style of American politics. Torchlight parades, stump speaking, monster rallies, songs and slogans, and the cult of personality had turned political campaigns into secular revival meetings since the 1820s.

At the same time, the churches provided a dangerous precedent for the politicians. In 1845 the nation's two largest Protestant denominations, Methodists and Baptists, split along North–South lines over the slavery issue. Presbyterians would not officially divide until 1861, but a theological schism within the church had recognized different sectional loyalties since the mid-1830s. In each case, these divisions expressed disagreement over the extent to which the churches should promote social change and whether the Bible defended or condemned slavery and slaveholders. Such contortions among the mainstream religious faiths showed how involved Protestantism had become in the nation's political debate, but they also fostered a new confrontational climate in politics that offered a dire—though universally ignored—warning of the party upheaval to come.

The churches also gave women an opportunity to help shape the political culture. American women, idealized as bastions of moral virtue, had served for many years within their families and churches as civilizing influences on men and moral instructors to children. In the early nineteenth century, benevolent organizations recruited thousands of middle-class women to serve those same functions on a wider scale. It shocked many people to see women invade even this semipublic realm, but reformers believed that female crusaders enhanced

Political Culture and Religion

Political Roles of Women

the nobility of their causes. What was more, women contributed in very practical ways by circulating petitions, raising funds, speaking publicly to support their favorite charities and reforms, and writing for the many newspapers and magazines that were devoted to reform.

That was only the beginning. Having expended so much energy on behalf of others, some of these women sought wider freedoms for themselves, including equality with men in employment opportunities, wages, legal protection, and political rights. Like the antislavery movements in which these early feminists played such visible roles, their own program also exploited the nation's Revolutionary rhetoric by insisting that men and women were created equal. The symbolic beginning of their fledgling movement, which gained the support of relatively few male reformers, came in July 1848 when the first national women's rights meeting convened at Seneca Falls, New York. Like the churches, activist women would also be a force in the sectional contest to come.

Sectional Tensions

In the face of such dislocation and fervor, the new territorial question might appear to be but a slight additional burden, but it held deadly potential. Politicians believed that a balanced, two-party political system reduced the risks of sectional bickering, and certainly past divisions over national issues, even the existence of slavery, had been resolved amicably. But many Americans sensed a dangerously shifting situation in the summer of 1848. Traditional differences between Democrats and Whigs over the tariff, the national bank, and internal improvements were already disappearing, thus loosening the cement of *national* party loyalties and placing more importance on *sectional* and *local* alliances. An issue such as slavery expansion, which tended to split national opinion geographically, could, in this new atmosphere, destroy the old political loyalties. "The Southern men will sustain no one for the Presidency who does not pledge himself against the Wilmot proviso," observed wealthy Philadelphian Sidney George Fisher in June. "When the question comes fairly to be raised—which shall govern, South or North—then the Union will be in imminent danger." Even more ominously, he continued, "Party leaders cannot much longer control public opinion, new combinations will be formed, are forming, and there is great reason to fear that ere long there will be a Northern party and a Southern party, and that the former. . .will attempt the entire abolition of slavery. This would be the signal for civil war."

Issue of Property

The crux of this new territorial problem was that slavery formed the core of a southern economic-social-legal system at odds with the northern definition of *property*. Southerners claimed that if they did not have the right to carry slave property wherever they chose, they would be second-class citizens in their own nation. "We have no wish to propagate slavery, but every man at the South does wish to insist to enter the territories upon terms of perfect equality with the North," a Virginian declared. "He may not exercise the right, but he will not give it up [because] by surrendering it, [he] should be acknowledging an inequality." Southerners would never relinquish their republican rights to govern themselves and to control their own slaves. John C. Calhoun cut to the heart of the issue, just as he had in clarifying the South's theory of nullification.

He stated the case for expanding slavery this way in 1848: "Our right to go there with our property is unquestionable, and guarantied and supported by the Constitution. The Territory belongs to us—to the United States."

The most hopeful sign in 1848, as the presidential election drew near, was that neither Democrats nor Whigs wanted to appear to be guided by sectional interests; both wished to appeal to both northern and southern voters. The Whigs selected Zachary Taylor as their standard bearer. As *General* Taylor, "Old Rough and Ready" had been one of the military heroes of the Mexican War. More than that, he was a slave-owning Louisiana planter (though born in Virginia). That the Whig Party, which had raised the loudest objections to the war, should nominate Taylor shows their desire to avoid the slavery issue during the campaign. Taylor—short and stocky in appearance, honest and plainspoken by reputation—had never held political office and espoused no firm political views; rather, he presented himself as a bipartisan man of the people, a *democrat* who, quite frankly, the Whig power brokers hoped would appeal to the rank and file of the *Democratic* Party. Taylor would be the Whig version of Andrew Jackson, the first U.S. president to have identified himself with the "common man."

Election of 1848

Meanwhile, when President Polk stood by an earlier promise to serve but a single term as president, *real* Democrats turned to Lewis Cass. Both Taylor and Cass had served in the War of 1812, but while Taylor remained in the army, Cass embarked on a political career. He subsequently served in the Ohio legislature, as territorial governor of Michigan, in Andrew Jackson's cabinet, as minister to France, and as U.S. senator from Michigan. A brilliant man and formidable speaker, Cass had impeccable credentials as a nationalist and expansionist, and he now proposed a bold and pragmatic new solution to the territorial problem. In contrast to Taylor, who implied that Congress should determine the policy for expansion, Cass wanted people living in the territories to decide the fate of slavery there; let *popular sovereignty* settle the issue, Cass said, rather than some arbitrary geographical division established by Congress.

Further complicating matters, a third "Democrat," a wild card, entered the race. Former president Martin Van Buren, who as Andrew Jackson's vice president and successor had labored in the shadow of "Old Hickory" for two decades, now boldly opposed the extension of slavery. He became the candidate of the Free-Soil Party, an odd assortment of antislavery Democrats, New England Whigs (known as "Conscience" Whigs), and remnants of the defunct Liberty Party, which had run the nation's first antislavery political campaign in 1844. The slogan of this new antislavery party—"Free soil, free speech, free labor, and free men"—summed up its opposition to the expansion of slavery, its support of a homestead act (to provide cheap western land to settlers), and its abhorrence of the "slave power." It was a telling if somewhat misleading credo, for most Free-Soilers envisioned new lands settled by white people, unthreatened by black labor of any kind. However, the Free-Soilers did speak to settlers who feared the *competition* of black labor, and as the slavery debate continued through the decade, this would be a preeminent concern for all laborers in an age of expanding markets and economic growth.

The stark sectionalism of the Free-Soilers was not yet in step with the times, but they influenced events far beyond their numbers. Taylor won the election with the support of eight slave states and seven nonslave states, while Cass earned the same number of states in reverse geographical proportion. That left no electoral votes for Van Buren, even though this wily politician, known as the Little Magician, captured a very respectable 10 percent of the popular vote. However, Van Buren cut deeply enough into the Democratic vote of New York to give the state and the election to Taylor. Equally important, by winning 13 seats in the House of Representatives, the upstart Free-Soilers held the balance of power between 112 Democrats and 109 Whigs. The mischievous Van Buren must have been tickled, for Lewis Cass had been instrumental in denying him his party's presidential nomination in 1844.

Taylor's Compromise Plan

Northerners feared that the election of Taylor meant a "southern" victory on the territorial question, but the subsequent, hard-fought Compromise of 1850 proved to be reasonably balanced despite the deep divisiveness its consideration engendered. Congress heatedly discussed the fate of the Mexican territory between January and September 1850 in one of the greatest series of debates in its history. The Senate's imposing, if aged, triumvirate of Calhoun, Clay, and Daniel Webster stole the oratorical show, but President Taylor, to nearly everyone's surprise, became the pivotal player. Taylor had proposed in December 1849 that California be admitted to the Union immediately, with New Mexico to follow "at no very distinct period." So confident was he that Congress would accept his plan that the president had urged Californians the previous summer to elect a government and to write a constitution for congressional approval. By December, New Mexico, too, had established a territorial government. As for slavery, Taylor recommended that the inhabitants of all new states, rather than Congress, be allowed to decide the issue for themselves. He had cleverly appropriated, without actually using the phrase, Cass's doctrine of popular sovereignty.

Southern Concerns

Southerners felt betrayed by Taylor. Despite northern charges and apprehension, few southerners expected plantation slavery to be profitable beyond Texas. Although a few people noted the potential value of slave labor in California's gold mines, the soil and climate of the Far West did not suit their cash crops. Still, there remained the firm conviction that slavery had to expand to survive. And southerners were determined, as new territory was acquired and new states carved from it, that the congressional balance between slave and nonslave states be maintained. It was a concern as old as the nation. It had produced the three-fifths clause of the Constitution, the Missouri Compromise, and the ordered admission of new states to the Union since 1816. In 1850, there were fifteen slave states and fifteen nonslave states. California, which had already voted to prohibit slavery, and New Mexico, which gave every sign of following suit, would throw that balance seriously out of kilter. Given the more rapid population and economic expansion in the North, and with the Oregon Territory and the remaining unorganized portion of the Louisiana Purchase unlikely to embrace slavery, the South might soon be un-

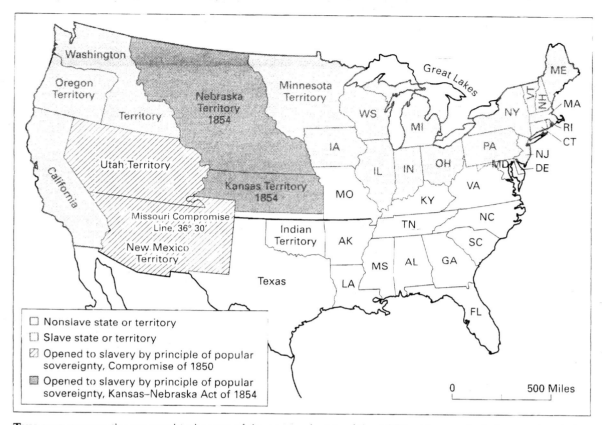

THIS MAP SHOWS the geographical scope of the sectional crisis of the 1850s. Unprecedented expansion during the preceding two decades forced the United States to address the controversial issue of slavery expansion. Each new addition of territory seemed to incite new political battles.

able to muster enough congressional votes on issues it deemed crucial to its interests, especially those connected to property rights. As if that were not bad enough, some northerners still insisted that the Wilmot Proviso be made part of any territorial settlement.

So the great debate raged until, on July 9, the nation was stunned by the death of its president. Following an Independence Day ceremony at the unfinished Washington Monument, the sixty-five-year-old Taylor had returned to the White House with an intense thirst. After downing quantities of iced milk and raw fruit and vegetables, he suffered an attack of acute gastroenteritis. Four days later, Millard Fillmore, a former New York congressman of no great distinction who had been installed as Taylor's vice president to heal a party riff in the Empire State, became president. Suddenly, the apparent congressional deadlock, which Taylor had threatened to resolve by ramming through his own plan, was thrown open to a genuine compromise.

Fillmore Becomes President

Fillmore's ascension proved a blessing because the new president favored a series of compromise bills cobbled together during the previous months as an alternative to the Taylor plan. The new president's dignified bearing and suave manners disguised his humble origins as a virtually illiterate tailor's apprentice. People had always underestimated him, and now he surprised everyone again. Unlike his southern predecessor, the antislavery Fillmore did not insist on statehood for New Mexico, and with that obstacle removed, everything else fell into place. Henry Clay had earlier proposed an "omnibus" bill in which the various compromise measures—some favored by the North, others by the South—would be voted on as a package. The bill had failed, and the effort had so exhausted the seventy-three-year-old Kentuckian that he left the capital in August to recuperate. Stephen A. Douglas, a first-term Democratic senator from Illinois, stepped in to gain passage of essentially the same bills by presenting them separately for consideration.

Compromise of 1850

Douglas, with Fillmore's backing, managed this maneuver by exploiting the sectional patterns that had stymied Clay. Rather than encourage harmony, he played off the strength of one section against that of the other. The most important parts of the final compromises, passed in September 1850, stated: (1) California would be admitted to the Union as a nonslave state. (2) New Mexico would remain a territory with no restrictions on slavery until such time as it applied for statehood. Then the people would vote to determine the fate of the institution. In addition, the boundary between New Mexico and Texas, which had been hotly contested in the West, was set. (3) Utah would be recognized as a territory under the same guidelines as New Mexico. (4) A federally enforced fugitive slave law would ensure that runaway slaves were returned to their masters. (5) The public sale of slaves (but not slavery) would be abolished in the District of Columbia.

A degree of caution dampened the national rejoicing that accompanied this compromise. "All look upon the question as settled and no fears are felt in relation to the movements in either North or South," declared one observer. Yet by most definitions of *compromise,* the acts of 1850 left much to be desired. A sectional truce had been reached, perhaps even an armistice, but North and South had really only agreed to continue disagreeing on the subject of slavery in the territories. As Salmon P. Chase, a first-term Free-Soil senator from Ohio, insisted, "The question of slavery in the territories has been avoided. It has not been settled."

Still, given the bitter feeling that had prevailed just a few weeks earlier, people breathed easier. Sectional feeling still ran high in Congress, but the political process had worked, as it had in 1819–1820 and 1832–1833. If someone had suggested that the nation would be torn apart by war just ten years on, most Americans would have scoffed. The mood of the country did not warrant such a dire prediction.

Nashville Convention

A little noticed yet symbolically telling event in Nashville, Tennessee, that June gave further proof that the potential for secession, let alone a destructive war, did not exist. Uncertain of what action Congress would take in its debates, nine of the fifteen slave states sent representatives to a convention in Nashville to discuss the merits of the proposed compromise. Radical southern nationalists, or *fire-eaters*, such as Robert Barnwell Rhett of South Carolina and Edmund Ruffin of Virginia, hoped that southern Whigs and Democrats would raise a single voice in defense of southern rights and against compromise, but they failed to rally much support among the mostly moderate delegates. Like most southerners, the Nashville delegates agreed on the importance of protecting their interests, but they divided badly over the means of doing it, and they overwhelmingly disapproved the solution being urged by the fire-eaters: secession from the Union.

The Nashville delegates did no more than endorse a proposal to extend the Missouri Compromise line to the Pacific Ocean and agree to meet again after Congress had taken action on the territories. Only seven states participated in the second meeting, held in November. The fire-eaters dominated that convention, and they passed a resolution that condemned the compromise and asserted the right of secession, but it was a hollow victory. With most southerners content to live by the congressional compromise, unionist sentiment prevailed in the South. For the moment, at least, the fire-eaters remained marginal and largely discredited political actors.

The next presidential election, in 1852, seemed to strengthen the fragile sense of national rejuvenation and unity. The Democrats reclaimed the executive mansion with Franklin Pierce, a relatively obscure forty-eight-year-old New Hampshire lawyer. The charming, handsome, and loquacious Pierce had retired from the Senate a decade earlier, partly because of intemperate habits, but he wrested the nomination from party stalwarts Cass, Douglas, and James Buchanan of Pennsylvania in an exhausting battle of attrition. Even with Cass and Douglas tainted by their ties to popular sovereignty, Pierce could not claim victory at the party's convention until the forty-ninth ballot.

Election of 1852

The election against Whig candidate Winfield Scott, principal hero of the war with Mexico, proved much easier. The pompous and politically naive Scott was no match for Pierce, whose popular-vote margin of nearly 7 percent was the biggest for any president since Andrew Jackson in 1832. Equally important as hopeful portents of sectional peace, the Free-Soil Party all but disappeared in the election, and Martin Van Buren returned to the Democratic fold. Voter turnout was the lowest since 1836 (just 70 percent), but that may have reflected the absence of crucial issues; the nation faced no crisis.

However, the Whigs had suffered more than an electoral defeat, and therein lies the more troubling legacy of 1852. Scott, like Pierce, had won his party's nomination in a sharp convention fight, not defeating Millard Fillmore until the fifty-third ballot. The overwhelming majority of his support came from northern Whigs, and during the following year, many southern Whigs, disappointed with the party's growing opposition to the expansion of slavery, went over to the Democrats. The Whigs never recovered from this sectional division, and the entire nation would soon reap the whirlwind. The sectional balance of the two-party system, so necessary for maintaining consensus and avoiding chaos, had been seriously compromised. If the Democrats should stumble in similar fashion, the future would be difficult to predict.

Young America

For the moment, however, the Democrats waxed strong. Pierce, committed to keeping the slavery issue out of politics, embodied the spirit of a largely Democratic movement known as *Young America*. Devoted to Manifest Destiny, free trade, and the revolutionary liberal upheavals that had convulsed Europe in 1848, Young America had grown out of the vigorous expansionism of the mid-1840s. Its adherents dismissed the Whig resurgence of 1848–1852 as an unaccountable but temporary setback. They intended to resume the course of prosperity and harmony that the United States had set for itself before the war with Mexico, a war that Pierce, in contrast to the Whigs, proudly proclaimed as "just and necessary." Let "decadent monarchies" abroad and "Old Fogies" at home beware, crowed Young America at midcentury. Join our bold march into the future or be left behind. We are ready to lead the world.

The muscular assertiveness of Young America also embraced a form of cultural nationalism, a phase of the broader "romantic" influence witnessed in the arts and literature for several decades past. Literature especially had been animated by the "spirit of democracy," by American themes and virtues fitted to "the New Man in the New Age." That spirit shaped the early careers of many of the nation's chief male literary figures, including Ralph Waldo Emerson, Nathaniel Hawthorne, Herman Melville, and most especially Walt Whitman. The chief organ for the movement, at once literary and political, became the *Democratic Review*, edited in New York by John L. O'Sullivan, the man who in 1845 had coined the expression *Manifest Destiny*, and who Pierce named as U.S. minister to Portugal. With something approaching missionary zeal, Pierce also tagged South Carolinian Edwin DeLeon, creator of the expression *Young America*, to carry the movement's spirit abroad as consul general to Egypt.

Opposition to the Fugitive Slave Law

Not everyone succumbed to the nationalist enthusiasm of Young America. Antislavery people, like southern fire-eaters, refused to accept the congressional compromise on slavery, especially the fugitive slave law. This law not only made the federal government responsible for returning runaway slaves to the South, but it also forced northern residents, on pain of fine and imprisonment, to assist in this work. What was more, the law was retroactive: slaves who had escaped northward before 1850 and who may have been living as free people for years were to be apprehended and returned. It even threatened the liberty of free-born African Americans who could not *prove* their nativity. Thousands of free blacks, fearful of being kidnapped, eventually fled to Canada. William Lloyd Garrison, Theodore Parker, and other notable abolitionists attacked the law unsparingly and, in Parker's case, incited northerners to thwart it by physical force. Daring rescues of recaptured runaways, sometimes resulting in mob violence, occurred in New York, Massachusetts, Pennsylvania, Michigan, Ohio, and elsewhere.

One widely publicized episode occurred in 1854 when Parker called a mass meeting to protest the arrest in Boston of Anthony Burns, a fugitive slave from Virginia. "There *was* a Boston once," he told the assembly. "Now there is a North suburb to the city of Alexandria." His audience muttered bitterly in agreement, but Parker wanted more than that; he demanded action. "I have

CAUTION!!
COLORED PEOPLE
OF BOSTON, ONE & ALL,

You are hereby respectfully CAUTIONED and advised, to avoid conversing with the

Watchmen and Police Officers of Boston,

For since the recent ORDER OF THE MAYOR & ALDERMEN, they are empowered to act as

KIDNAPPERS
AND
Slave Catchers,

And they have already been actually employed in KIDNAPPING, CATCHING, AND KEEPING SLAVES. Therefore, if you value your LIBERTY, and the *Welfare of the Fugitives* among you, Shun them in every possible manner, as so many *HOUNDS* on the track of the most unfortunate of your race.

Keep a Sharp Look Out for
KIDNAPPERS, and have
TOP EYE open.

APRIL 24, 1851.

THIS ANTISLAVERY HANDBILL of 1851 shows that the Compromise of 1850 had not satisfied everyone. The fugitive slave law—an important part of the compromise—angered antislavery northerners, who protested the legal obligation of returning runaway slaves to their masters.

heard hurrahs and cheers for liberty many times," he continued; "I have not seen a great many deeds done for liberty. I ask you are we to have deeds as well as words?. . .I am a clergyman and a man of peace; I love peace. But there is a means and an end: Liberty is the end, and sometimes peace is not the means toward it." He so aroused the crowd that it attacked the courthouse where Burns was being held, killing a policeman in the process. Angry abolitionists such as Parker, who openly admitted to hating not only the sin of slavery but also the "slave-hunters, slave-breeders, [and] slave-holders," had abandoned nonviolent protest, and they would add significantly to the fevered atmosphere of the 1850s.

Uncle Tom's Cabin

Yet the most far-reaching response to the fugitive slave law came from the soft-spoken wife of a New England college professor. On June 15, 1851, the *National Era,* an abolitionist journal, published the first installment of a serial novel entitled *Uncle Tom's Cabin.* By the time Franklin Pierce took office, Harriet Beecher Stowe's completed work had appeared in book form (in two volumes), had sold more than 300,000 copies in the United States, and had been published in separate editions in England, Scotland, France, and Germany. By August 1852 it had been adapted for the stage and was being performed in both the United States and England. It inspired a cottage industry that churned out a string of

HARRIET BEECHER STOWE, whose Christian-based antislavery novel *Uncle Tom's Cabin* became an international best seller. While demonstrating a degree of sympathy for the dilemma of southern slaveholders, her book, published serially in 1851–1852, was the first of a number of dramatic northern challenges during the 1850s to the moral certitude and honor of the South.

derivative novels, songs, pamphlets, and poetry. Stowe said that she wrote the book "to illustrate the cruelties of slavery," and she certainly succeeded. Her relentless attack on the brutality and injustice of the institution rallied the flagging abolitionist cause. "Never, since books were first printed," proclaimed one northern magazine, "has the success of *Uncle Tom's Cabin* been equalled; the history of literature contains nothing parallel to it, or approaching it."

Stowe's success unnerved Young America and the South. Even some northerners considered her book "a tool of abolition. . .and a political instrument for undermining the influence of republican institutions." It left white southerners seething. Southern book reviewers pilloried Stowe, not only for her attack on southern society but because she seemed to be the worst sort of northern feminist, a woman who sought "a footing of political equality with man. . .in the administration of public affairs." What most offended them, though they did not say as much, was the human face she put on slavery and the way she used Christianity—through biblical quotes and allusions—to undermine, rather than to defend, the institution. Some thirty "anti-*Uncle Tom*" novels appeared, nearly half of them published within two years of Stowe's book. One of the earliest of these proslavery rebuttals was Virginian Mary Eastman's novel *Aunt Phillis's Cabin; Or Southern Life as It Is.*

Altered Political Role of Women   There is some irony in this female dimension of the slavery debate, one, too, that illustrates a subtle shift in the roles of white women in public life at this time. When reformers, including thousands of middle-class women, lost faith in the ability of "moral suasion" to transform society in the 1840s, they turned from their benevolent societies toward political activism. The Whig Party, which had been in the forefront of many social reform movements, profited most from this influx. The women could not vote or hold public office, but they raised funds, circulated petitions, spoke at public meetings, joined marches and processions, attended rallies, and, as they had done in the reform movements, sanctified the party and its goals. Crafty political managers also exploited the power of persuasion that women were reputed to have over their men. Thus, in the presidential campaign of 1852, Whigs sang joyously:

> The Ladies fair, with grateful art,
> Will lead their beaux to take a part;
> They'll pledge them first in whispers tender,
> Vote for SCOTT and I'll surrender!

The Democrats belatedly and reluctantly welcomed women into the political process, but after the election of 1852, female activists faced restrictions in both parties. Southern women, especially, almost disappeared for a time as political speakers. In the case of the Whigs, this was simply a matter of the party disintegrating after the beating it took in 1852. For Democrats, the rise of a more militant form of feminism in the North and the high visibility of female abolitionists caused a backlash. They quietly persuaded their female activists to be less visible in politics. Women continued to publish literary defenses of the South and slavery, but they were encouraged to be less strident, less "partisan," when speaking publicly. Instead, they should promote sectional harmony, a more natural feminine role in any case, thought many Americans. As things turned out, even southern women were only restrained temporarily. Political anarchy ruled after John Brown's raid, and partisanship became a virtue. However, the parties' concerns over their image in the mid-1850s suggest the power of reawakened sectional tensions.

Pierce's Miscalculations

The boyish and intellectually superficial Pierce set the sectional pot roiling again, too, through a series of political miscalculations. At the heart of the problem was his naïveté about northern sensitivities on the territorial question. First, in late 1853, he found himself in a tussle to win congressional approval of the Gadsden Purchase. The president wanted to buy this strip of land—which forms the lower portions of modern-day Arizona and New Mexico—to facilitate construction of a railroad across the southern United States. Northern senators resisted both the hefty price tag of $15 million and the acquisition of any more land that might be opened to slavery. Pierce won that battle, but he encountered more serious resistance when he next tried to organize what remained of the Louisiana Purchase. This modest goal also started with railroads, but it sparked a chain reaction that shattered the fragile armistice of 1850, toppling the American party system and provoking bloodshed.

Origins of the Kansas-Nebraska Bill

While most Americans living in the Midwest and Southwest recognized the benefits of a railroad to connect the eastern half of the country with California, they angrily disputed the best route. Quite simply, northerners wanted a northern route, and southerners wanted a southern one. While the territory necessary to build a southern railroad had been properly organized by 1853, that portion of the Louisiana Purchase over which a northern route might be constructed—either from Chicago or St. Louis—remained unorganized. Thus a sense of urgency led some midwestern politicians to champion the creation of a new territory they called Nebraska. Stephen Douglas, who owned lands in Illinois and Michigan that would soar in value if a railroad ran through Nebraska, happened to chair the Senate Committee on Territories, and he promised to shepherd the legislation through Congress. But just here, things became complicated, and to this day the motives and actions of many key players in the drama are hard to untangle.

The diminutive (5 feet, 4 inches) but pugnacious "Little Giant," as Douglas was known, may have stood to profit personally from a settled, stable territory, but as a hero of Young America, and being attuned to the wishes of his Illinois constituents, he also had advocated the measured economic development of the West (including a transcontinental railroad, telegraph lines, overland mail service, and free land for homesteaders) since the mid-1840s. Similar interests—specifically, construction of a railroad linking Chicago to the Mississippi River—had influenced his support for the Compromise of 1850. Faced with southern opposition to a northern railroad route through the West and a local political fight in Missouri that threatened the new Nebraska plan, Douglas negotiated another armistice. He recommended that Congress abandon the old Missouri Compromise, which had guaranteed the exclusion of slavery north of Missouri's southern border (36°30′), and apply popular sovereignty to the unorganized portion of the Louisiana Purchase. In addition, he proposed that the Nebraska Territory be divided in half, with the southern portion called Kansas.

Opposition to the Kansas-Nebraska Bill

Antislavery forces of all stripes exploded over this Kansas-Nebraska Bill. Northern Whigs and Democrats, Free-Soilers, and Know-Nothings (a rapidly rising new party) all denounced the plan as a slave-state conspiracy. The ambitious Douglas, they charged, posed as a front man for slaveholders to secure their support for a future run at the presidency. The maneuvering, posturing, bitter debate, and threatened violence that followed, both behind closed doors and on the floor of Congress, lasted three months. When the vote came, twenty-three slave-state and fourteen nonslave-state senators supported the bill; two slave-state and twelve nonslave-state senators opposed it. In the House, sixty-nine slave-state and forty-four nonslave-state representatives approved it; nine slave-state and ninety-one nonslave-state representatives voted nay.

It is impossible to overstate the turmoil created by these results. The tenuous handshakes and half-smiles of 1850 disappeared altogether. The antislavery forces vowed to thwart Kansas-Nebraska, the fugitive slave law, and every other symbol of slavery expansion. The doctrine of popular sovereignty, initially seen as a plausible solution to the slavery issue, was now condemned as part of an insidious slave-power conspiracy.

Antislavery advocates misconstrued the situation, just as southerners had always exaggerated the influence of the abolitionists. Douglas had railroads on his mind, and southerners had paid little attention to the Kansas issue until he was attacked as their dupe. But none of that mattered in the combustible atmosphere of 1854. Douglas's hopes that his proposal would "destroy all sectional parties and sectional agitations" were dashed. Paranoia ran rampant in both North and South, and the suspicions would only deepen.

The Kansas-Nebraska Act also added to an already existing popular distrust of politicians. The bargaining and deal-making of American politicians repulsed many citizens, and reports of widespread corruption in Congress and statehouses convinced them that officeholders sought only to plunder the public trough. With their finely honed eye for conspiratorial forces, American voters could easily believe that politicians put their own best interests above those of the Republic. A New York newspaper stated the case most bluntly in December 1855: "Their machinery of intrigue, their shuffling evasions, the dodges, the chicanery and the deception of their leaders have excited universal disgust, and have created a general readiness in the public mind for any new organization that shall promise to shun their vices."

Distrust of Politicians

Bribery, fraud, rigged elections—there seemed no end to the depravity. Lobbyists swarmed over Washington, D.C., and state capitals from Maine to Texas. Congressional investigating committees had full agendas, and the country's growing number of newspapers kept the public informed and inflamed about every new dodge and scam. In ordinary times, the consequences might have been slight, but in the poisoned atmosphere of suspicion that engulfed the nation in the 1850s, they had tragic overtones. How could politicians who accepted bribes and winked at corruption be trusted to tell the truth and keep their word? How could parties and sections trust one another to compromise on such sensitive issues as slavery and territorial expansion when honor had no champion? "The time to compromise with a system of rank corruption has now gone by forever," responded one northerner who opposed the Kansas-Nebraska Act. "As a body," countered a Virginian, "the majority of northern members of congress are as corrupt & destitute of private integrity, as the majority of southern members are the reverse."

The situation seemed particularly grave because both Democrats and Whigs suffered from a leadership void. The past four presidents—Polk, Taylor, Fillmore, and Pierce—had been a weak lot, all of them bland compromise candidates. Forcible, dynamic leaders such as Clay and Webster, even Van Buren and Douglas, having accumulated too much political baggage, were viewed with suspicion. Calhoun, Clay, and Webster were all dead by late 1852, and most of their political heirs—except for the unfortunate Douglas—had yet to prove their mettle. More than that, too many Americans believed that neither party effectively addressed the issues that most concerned them. Old solutions and patchwork compromises no longer answered national needs.

The people demonstrated their dissatisfaction in the state and congressional elections of 1854 and 1855, further weakening the two major parties and forcing several telling political realignments. Northern Democrats, more than ever out of place in a party that had tended to support the expansion of slavery, were slaughtered at the polls. At the national level, they lost two-thirds of their congressional seats in 1854 alone. The Whig Party, having already lost most of its southern wing in 1852–1853, was in even worse shape as its northern wing

Democratic and Whig Losses

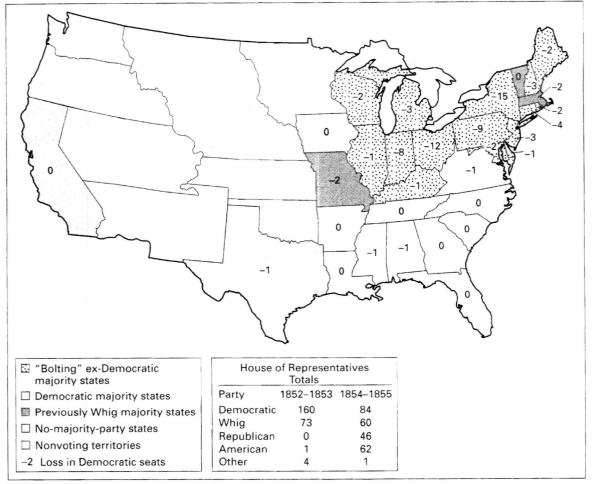

	House of Representatives Totals		
Party	1852–1853	1854–1855	
Democratic	160	84	
Whig	73	60	
Republican	0	46	
American	1	62	
Other	4	1	

Legend:
- ⊡ "Bolting" ex-Democratic majority states
- ☐ Democratic majority states
- ▦ Previously Whig majority states
- ☐ No-majority-party states
- ☐ Nonvoting territories
- –2 Loss in Democratic seats

THE CONGRESSIONAL ELECTIONS OF 1854 signaled both the rise of new political parties and the end of the sectional balance that had characterized the old two-party system. The American and Republican parties reflected not only northern displeasure with the Kansas-Nebraska Act but also deep concern about the moral decay of American society, as nativism and temperance joined with abolitionism to reshape the political landscape.

crumbled internally in 1854–1855 over such cultural and ethnic issues as temperance and nativism. "We are utterly wrecked," eulogized one lost soul. "It is altogether idle to think of a reconstruction of the Whig Party. It is past all surgery, past all medicines."

The decline of the old parties would not have been so steep or immediate had not the winners in these northern elections, two hungry new political coalitions, already begun wooing disenchanted Whigs and Democrats. During the next six years, the Know-Nothings and the Republicans would set the nation on a very different course from that of 1848–1854, even though the direction of that course was not readily apparent in 1855 and was certainly not inevitable. As one northerner judged in late 1854, "Parties are now in a state of disorganization—rather of utter anarchy. What is to come out of it, none can foresee." Indeed, the whys and wherefores of that tragic journey, which would end in secession, are complex and controversial.

Students of the war have not always appreciated the complexity of this process because the so-called *Civil War synthesis* has emphasized national issues—especially those directly connected with slavery—as harbingers of an inevitable war, while ignoring or discounting the importance of local concerns. This half-vision of the past has seriously handicapped our understanding of the realignment of political parties in the 1850s—a crucial episode in the drift toward secession—because some of the most important reasons for that realignment originated and grew in localized battles scattered in communities across the country. In this same vein, it is important to remember that the splintering, weakening, and collapse of the existing party system occurred not everywhere at once, but rather quite gradually and haphazardly, state by state.

Civil War Synthesis

The outcome of elections often hinged on local issues such as tariffs, railroads, and land reform, but cultural and ethnic issues, especially temperance and nativism, played the most conspicuous roles. Many people had long predicted that the moral corruption of American society would destroy the Republic more quickly and more surely than the expansion of slavery. The national addiction to alcohol, measured by an annual per capita consumption of seven gallons by the 1830s, was one of the earliest signs of this apparent decline. The temperance crusade that became the most popular of the many moral reform movements to sweep the nation had begun long before the abolitionist movement took root. Even the Free-Soil Party, despite its name, image, and most touted issue, had drawn strong temperance people away from the Whigs by cleverly endorsing prohibition.

Cultural and Ethnic Issues

Temperance, in turn, was absorbed by the nativist movement, and it was on the crucial coupling of these two issues that much of the impending reshuffling of parties would hinge after 1854. The tide of foreign immigrants into the United States had risen sharply since the mid-1840s, thanks to European wars, famines, and revolutions. More than 2.6 million foreigners entered the country between 1848 and 1855, and although their numbers gradually declined in the last half of the decade, the consequences had already been felt. Native-born white Americans feared these immigrants, many of whom were impoverished Irish Catholics, as drunkards, religious agents of the pope, and a cheap labor force that would drive down wages and steal jobs. They had expressed their displeasure in the 1830s and early 1840s with violent and destructive riots against Catholics and foreigners. By the mid-1840s, they turned more often to political protest.

At this time, the American Party—better known by its popular name of the Know-Nothings—stepped in to shape party realignment in the wake of Kansas-Nebraska. The party evolved in the late 1840s and early 1850s from a collection of scattered, semisecret, anti-immigrant fraternal orders—the Order

Know-Nothing Party

of United Americans, United Sons of America, the Order of the Star-Spangled Banner—in New York, Pennsylvania, and Massachusetts. Even so, it acted more as a political pressure group, like the old temperance societies, until 1854. Only when it began to exploit local ethnic and cultural anxieties in elections, thus culminating a decade of evangelical agitation on the temperance and nativist questions, did it gain political prominence.

Tradition has it that the Know-Nothings acquired their nickname because early members consistently pleaded ignorance when questioned about the secret lodges that had spawned the movement. This explanation has never been proven, but we do know that by 1854 many disenchanted Whigs rushed to join the party, whose first national platform called for the exclusion of Catholics and immigrants from public office and demanded a twenty-one-year waiting period for naturalized citizenship. The strength of its appeal startled everyone. "The Whigs are desperate—ready to ally themselves with any faction," commented an observer in June 1854; "This new order, so far, is secret and intangible—they talk of their *principles,* but they avow none—and the clandestine manner in which they proceed, fills timid people with alarm—and even *old politicians* are led away, *by fear,* or *desire of favour."* The party held less appeal for southerners, who did not embrace temperance so fervently and whose region had attracted few Catholic immigrants, but even a Mississippi Democrat could moan, "*Know Nothingism* like the *measles* is catching."

The Republican Party

The Republicans, second of the new renegade parties, took a different path to power. In direct response to Kansas-Nebraska, this party formed during the summer of 1854 from an assortment of old Free-Soilers, antislavery Democrats, Conscience Whigs, and other political dissidents outraged more by the territorial issue than by a few too many Irish. A series of rallies in the Midwest had shown impressive support for the Republican platform, which demanded repeal of the fugitive slave law and abolition of slavery in Washington, D.C. Unlike the nativists, the Republicans attracted no southern supporters, and for that reason they seemed less likely than the Know-Nothings to succeed. While Kansas-Nebraska had clearly angered many citizens, it seemed an issue unlikely to attract national support. As one member acknowledged glumly in November 1855, "Nobody believes that this Republican movement can prove the basis of a permanent party."

The chief obstacle to Republican success was its murky stance on slavery. Most Republicans shared the same racist assumptions that had denied black suffrage in the North and maintained segregation in schools, public transportation, restaurants, and hotels in most northern communities. They were antislavery, but as an organization they neither directly attacked northern caste arrangements nor pressed for equal citizenship or equal rights. They even tolerated slavery as long as it did not spread into the western territories. In fact, their electoral strategy was based to a considerable extent on an appeal to voter fears of competition with black labor, free or slave. Many Republicans found slavery morally repulsive and believed that halting its spread into the territories must lead to its eventual demise. Yet at the same time, the party supported the curious double standard of opposing both slavery and any significant black presence in the North and West. This seemingly benign confusion did not fool white southerners. For them, the Republicans remained an exclusively northern party devoted to destroying their right to property in slaves, and they believed that stopping the expansion of slavery was the stealthy first step to abolition. In this context, the new party posed a radical political problem for the Union, however softly it peddled its opposition to slavery.

Because the nonsectional agenda of the Know-Nothings held much popular appeal, that party seized a slew of local and state offices in head-to-head competition with the Republicans. By 1855 they controlled most of the state legislatures in New England and had replaced the Whigs as the nation's second-largest party. More than sixty Know-Nothings sat in Congress.

Party Realignment

Yet the possibility of cooperation between the Know-Nothings and the Republicans soon became evident. Both parties drew support from the same rural Protestant constituency so that most nativists were also antislavery, and most antislavery advocates tended to be nativists. The Republicans, coming belatedly to this realization, quickly embraced nativism too. Furthermore, both parties pledged themselves to the destruction of sinister conspiracies. Know-Nothings claimed that Catholics and immigrants, as tools in a popish plot to rule America, posed a grave threat to American political and moral values. Republicans warned that to permit slavery to spread through the territories would be equally disastrous for white farmers and laborers who had to compete with slave labor. That so many people eagerly accepted these images of an imperialistic pope and a united, expansionist slave power—just as southerners raged against an abolitionist conspiracy to usurp their sovereignty—points to the volatility of the times.

Then, in 1855, the Know-Nothings made a fatal error. Under pressure from ex-president Millard Fillmore—one of their most influential members—they tried to escape the sectional quagmire by billing themselves as a sectionally neutral "Union" party. Seeing an opportunity to pull away from the one-dimensional Republicans and attract both Democrats and Whigs, the American Party tried to live up to its name and bridge the "chasm between the slave and free states." Nativism remained its principal article of faith, but the party also endorsed the "existing laws" regarding slavery, including the fugitive slave law and the Kansas-Nebraska Act, and declared the slavery issue resolved. However, the new direction disgusted the party's antislavery advocates, many of whom went over to the Republicans. The Know-Nothings never recovered.

These realignments weakened still further the national constituencies of the Whigs and the Democrats and made the loyalties of both politicians and voters "very foggy." Even more dangerously, the old parties, having been fragmented by a divisive sectional issue, and the untested new parties, born largely of local and regional concerns, immediately faced a series of national crises that required the sort of national consensus and compromise they could not provide.

First, a miniwar broke out in Kansas. Tension had built steadily in the territory during 1854–1855. When Congress told Kansans to determine the fate of slavery in their own land, both slavery and antislavery partisans jockeyed for

Bleeding Kansas

Voting on the future of Kansas. Many Americans believed popular sovereignty was a reasonable solution to the territorial issue, but hardly any foresaw the violence and bitter feelings it would inspire. Although relatively few people died in "Bleeding Kansas," much property was destroyed, and western residents showed their willingness to use intimidation and violence as a means to political ends. Kansas did not join the Union until 1861.

power. There would have been commotion enough had the decision been left to the people who already resided there, but from the beginning of the contest, outsiders escalated passions and incited violence. Several northern states, especially Massachusetts, promoted emigration to Kansas to bolster the antislavery forces there. The actual number of settlers resulting from this movement proved negligible, no more than a few thousand, but the intrusion angered proslavery advocates, especially in neighboring Missouri, who then sent their own people—so-called Border Ruffians—into the territory. Both sides armed themselves; neither side would back down.

The outsiders intended to influence elections for a territorial governor and legislature, and they did a first-rate job. By the end of 1855, following a series of bitter elections, two separate governments operating under two different constitutions—one proslavery, entrenched at Lecompton; one antislavery, at Topeka—claimed to speak for "the people." The Topeka government called for more settlers and weapons. New Englanders responded by sending hundreds of rifles, known popularly as Beecher's Bibles in honor of Reverend Henry Ward Beecher, a noted abolitionist and brother of Harriet Beecher Stowe.

Venomous words encouraged people to use their rifles. Northern journalists derided the Missouri settlers—most of them poor whites who owned no slaves—as "pukes," mere minions of southern planters, brutish and savage. Even Charles B. Stearns, one of the few peaceful "Garrisonian" abolitionists in the territory, abandoned his lifelong pacifism to demean Missourians as "wild beasts" and "drunken ourang-outans" and declare his intention "to aid in killing them off." Stearns elaborated, "When I deal with men made in God's image, I will never shoot them; but these pro-slavery Missourians are demons from the bottomless pit and may be shot with impunity." Southern propagandists returned insult for insult and threat for threat. "Oh! those long-faced, sanctimonious Yankees!" fumed one proslavery Kansas newspaper. "Who else would call Sharpes rifles moral weapons to be used in place of the Bible. . . . Surely none but the Yankee abolitionists would go to such heights and depths of duplicity, falsehood and hypocrisy."

The first murder came in November 1855, and periodic spurts of violence followed over the next several years. The press soon called the territory *Bleeding Kansas*, although more looting and intimidation occurred than actual bloodshed (approximately 52 deaths and 200 injured between 1855 and 1858). Even when a proslavery gang of several hundred men "sacked" the town of Lawrence in May 1856, only one person—a proslavery attacker—died, and that from an accident. The raiders wrecked a couple of newspaper offices, burned a hotel, and partially destroyed the mansion of the proslavery "governor," but they spent most of their energy getting drunk and vandalizing shops and homes. Yet, these scattered reports of violence aroused people, North and South. Both sides bristled at the arrogance and conspiratorial tactics used by the other. Most alarmingly, Kansas showed that Americans were willing to spill blood as well as spew hate over the expansion of slavery.

No one exploited Bleeding Kansas better than Charles Sumner, an intelligent, cultivated, but often arrogant and intolerant antislavery crusader from Massachusetts. The day before the "sack of Lawrence," Sumner, a founder of the Republican Party, concluded an impassioned, two-day speech, laden with insulting and often sexual imagery, on the Senate floor. He denounced proslavery bullies and their "Crime Against Kansas"; he raged against the South and slavery. He verbally attacked Democratic senators Stephen Douglas, James M. Mason of Virginia, and, most notably, sixty-year-old Andrew P. Butler, a kindly and conscientious legislator from South Carolina. Sumner scoffed at Butler's reputation as a "chivalrous knight" when, in fact, the Carolinian had debased himself by embracing "the harlot slavery," a mistress who, "though ugly to others. . .[and] polluted in the sight of the world," remained "always lovely. . .[and] chaste in his sight." The embarrassing allusion to interracial sex was the meanest insult he could have hurled at a southern gentleman, but Sumner had not finished with Butler, who was not present to hear the diatribe. He went on to mock a speech impediment that caused the elderly senator to drool. "With incoherent phrase," the New Englander sneered, Butler "discharges the loose expectoration of his speech. . . . He cannot open his mouth, but out flies a blunder. . . . [He] touches nothing which he does not disfigure."

Even members of Sumner's own party found the speech offensive, but no one took more umbrage than a young South Carolina congressman named Preston S. Brooks, a kinsman of Butler. Two days after the speech, on May 22, 1856, Brooks confronted Sumner as he sat at his desk in the Senate chamber. Denouncing the

Sumner-Brooks Affair

SOUTHERN CHIVALRY — ARGUMENT versus CLUB'S.

THE CANING OF CHARLES SUMNER of Massachusetts by Preston S. Brooks of South Carolina in 1856. Sumner's passionate but intemperate denunciation of the defenders of slavery exemplified the uncompromising nature of political debate in the 1850s. Brooks's violent reaction to Summer's "Bleeding Kansas" speech demonstrated the hypersensitivity of southerners to attacks on their personal and sectional honor.

senator's crude remarks as a libel on both South Carolina and Butler, Brooks began to beat Sumner with a cane. Intending at first only to flog him, Brooks became so frenzied that he pounded Sumner into an insensible, bloody pulp.

Both North and South claimed victory in the Sumner-Brooks affair. "Bully" Brooks, as northerners quickly dubbed him, paid for his defense of southern and family honor by resigning from Congress, although the South lionized him and his admiring constituents soon reelected him. Sumner, for his part, became a martyr to free speech and the antislavery cause. "Violence reigns in the streets of Washington," declared the outraged poet and editor William Cullen Bryant in his newspaper, the *New York Evening Post;* "violence has now found its way into the Senate Chamber. . . . In short, violence is the order of the day; the North is to be pushed to the wall by it, and this plot will succeed if the people of the free states are as apathetic as the slaveholders are insolent." The forty-five-year-old Sumner was so physically incapacitated and emotionally traumatized by the attack that he did not return to the Senate for two and a half years.

Pottawatomie Massacre

But whatever high ground the antislavery cause might have taken disappeared two days after the caning of Sumner. Back in Kansas, a recently arrived Connecticut emigrant named John Brown, outraged by the sack of Lawrence, wreaked his own vengeance. The fifty-six-year-old abolitionist, who regarded himself as God's avenging prophet, led a band of seven men, mostly his sons, in a grisly rampage against several proslavery families living along the Pottawatomie Creek. They left five proslavery men dead, their skulls split open, their bodies hacked to pieces.

As though all this was not enough to provoke sectional mistrust, the Pierce administration added to tensions with a series of foreign-policy blunders in 1853–1855. Unlike Presidents Taylor and Fillmore, who had discouraged further expansion, Franklin Pierce looked upon the western hemisphere as the new frontier for Manifest Destiny. He was encouraged in his vision by the misplaced idealism of Young America and the desire of some southerners to expand slavery abroad. The Knights of the Golden Circle, for example, a largely southern organization formed in 1854, advocated a great slave empire, which, with Cuba at its hub, would embrace in a sweeping "golden circle" the American South, Mexico, Central America, and the Caribbean. Pierce, too, considered Cuba the key acquisition, and his plans gained a degree of urgency when the Cuban government—with the approval of Spain, which owned Cuba—announced in September 1853 that it would soon end the African slave trade to the island and liberate a large part of its slave population.

Foreign Policy and Cuba

The announcement of this policy of "Africanization" accelerated plans already in place to seize Cuba with a *filibustering* expedition. American filibusters—taken from the Spanish word *filibustero*, or "freebooter"—were soldiers of fortune who had advocated the takeover of several Latin American countries since the 1840s. Pierce had encouraged one of most notorious of these men, John A. Quitman, to support revolutionaries in Cuba with a military expedition to the island, much as the United States had done in California prior to the Mexican War. Paradoxically, it appears that the Cubans decided to emancipate their slaves largely to create a black army that would discourage American adventurers like Quitman. A former governor of Mississippi who had already faced federal prosecution for an earlier filibuster scheme, Quitman was poised to make his move when, after much stalling and hesitation, Pierce withdrew his support for the expedition in the spring of 1854.

The president's change of heart came in response to an altered and exceedingly complex situation. Following up on its defiant emancipation policy, the Cubans, in February 1854, had seized a U.S. merchant ship at Havana. The Spanish government eventually apologized and paid reparations to the United States, but the incident occurred just as Congress began its heated debate of the Kansas-Nebraska Bill. Under these circumstances, Pierce decided that it might be easier and safer to purchase the Spanish-owned island, but the Spanish refused to consider U.S. overtures. Faced with a mounting diplomatic crisis, the Pierce administration directed the U.S. foreign ministers (ambassadors) to England, France, and Spain to meet at Ostend, Belgium, in October 1854 and decide on a course of action.

Ostend Manifesto

The resulting Ostend Manifesto caused a political uproar in the United States. The document declared that Cuba was "as necessary to the North

American republic as any of its present members" and denounced recent Cuban actions as a danger to the "internal peace" of the United States. Under such circumstances, concluded the foreign ministers, the United States would be justified "by every law, human and Divine" in seizing Cuba. When the semi-secret Ostend agreement became known to the public in March 1855, the timing could not have been worse for Pierce. The New York *Tribune* condemned this "Manifesto of the Brigands" as a thinly veiled pretext "to grasp, to rob, to murder, to grow rich on the spoils of provinces and toils of slaves." The national consensus that popularized Manifest Destiny and Young America in the 1840s had faded by the mid-1850s. Far more northerners than in 1848 had grown hostile to expansion, which always seemed to open new territory to slavery. Appeals to Manifest Destiny had lost much of their patriotic allure.

The foreign connection also worried people. Although most citizens, regardless of section, had supported the march to the Pacific, they regarded the manifesto, filibuster expeditions, and Knights of the Golden Circle as but tentacles of a slave-power conspiracy. It was not a completely accurate picture, for many American merchants and investors, not just floundering fire-eaters and slaveholders, welcomed the commercial opportunities promised by expansion into Latin America and the Caribbean. Still, you could not convince the average northerner of that, and antislavery people would not buy it at all. Their suspicions seemed confirmed when, in May 1856, President Pierce recognized a new filibuster government in Nicaragua. Established by William Walker, the regime soon collapsed, although it would take a Honduran firing squad in 1860 to end the Central American scheming of this Tennessee adventurer.

Election of 1856   Pierce's foreign policy blunders, along with the controversy over Kansas, ruined his hopes for reelection in 1856. The Democrats, refusing even to renominate him, turned instead to previous presidential contender and veteran Pennsylvania politico James Buchanan. With forty years of experience as a congressman, senator, cabinet member, and diplomat, this "northern man with southern principles," as he was called, seemed the perfect choice to maintain party unity. Few Democrats cared that Buchanan, as Pierce's ambassador to England, had been intimately involved in writing the Ostend Manifesto. They seemed more pleased that, despite four decades in public life, Buchanan had escaped serious controversy and remained an appeaser at heart. "Even among close friends," revealed one senator, "he very rarely expressed his opinions at all upon disputed questions, except in language especially marked with a cautious circumspection almost amounting to timidity."

The Republicans hammered away at the manifesto and Kansas that election year, but Buchanan escaped with a narrow victory. Even in a lackluster field, he had been unusually vulnerable. He won only 45 percent of the popular vote—the lowest winning margin since 1824. The Know-Nothings, running Millard Fillmore (who was also endorsed by the Whigs), captured 22 percent of the voters. The Republicans pinned their hopes on the bold soldier-explorer John C. Frémont. Although the famous "Pathfinder" had never held public office, possessed no particularly strong beliefs, and lacked political savvy, he shocked the

Party Upheaval

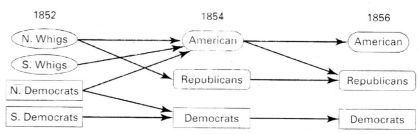

THIS DIAGRAM SHOWS how the regionally integrated two-party political system of 1852 became a regionally segregated three-party system by 1856. By 1860 only the Republicans and Democrats would represent viable national parties, and the Democrats wasted their majority status at their national convention that summer by dividing along sectional lines.

nation by carrying all but five northern states with a whopping 33 percent of the vote. Equally impressive was the fact that Frémont had endured false campaign rumors that he was a Catholic.

New Republican Strategy

The Republicans learned a valuable lesson from the election. By muting their strong antislavery message and appealing to voters on a wider variety of issues, they could become the strongest *northern* party, and during the next four years, they did just that. They reached out to both nativists and Free-Soilers by shaping an anti-immigrant message that distinguished between sober, hard-working Protestant immigrants (such as Germans and Scandinavians) and the supposedly ignorant, lazy Catholic Irish. Opposition to the expansion of slavery remained the core of their message, but they tailored their rhetoric to attract outright abolitionists (which most Republicans were not), "antislavery" people who only wished to exclude slavery from the territories, and potential western settlers who wished to keep all black labor—slave and free—away from "free" soil. As heirs of the northern Whigs, the Republicans also welcomed women activists to the party. Unlike their Democratic counterparts, Republican women played highly visible roles in the campaign of 1856, including public speaking. Many northern women were drawn to the Republicans because they equated the slavery issue with their own demands for political rights. They were also attracted by the feisty Jessie Frémont—"Our Jessie"—wife of the presidential candidate and an influential figure in his campaign.

Attack on Slavocracy

All of these groups, the Republicans realized, shared one thing: an abiding fear, distrust, and growing hatred of southern slave owners. Consequently, the party stressed that they opposed not the entire South but the *slavocracy*, the arrogant, ignorant, and depraved slave owners and politicians who insisted on spreading the cancer of slavery westward. The Republicans convinced an increasing number of northerners that once established in Kansas, slavery could just as easily be declared legal in Ohio or Pennsylvania. A line must be drawn, they declared. The slavocracy had blustered and bullied for too long. It could not be allowed to threaten free men and free labor as well as free soil. It was a brilliant strategy.

Dred Scott   The idea of a slave-power conspiracy was not new, but no previous antislavery party had hammered at it so relentlessly as the Republicans, and they soon claimed to have more proof of that conspiracy. Two days after Buchanan delivered his inaugural address, which condemned the agitation over slavery and endorsed popular sovereignty in the territories, the Supreme Court ruled on the Dred Scott case. Scott, a "small pleasant-looking" Missouri slave, had sued for his freedom in the federal courts more than a decade earlier, following the death of his master. Scott insisted that by residing with his master in Illinois and Wisconsin, he had become a free man. Years of complex litigation that involved the widow of Scott's deceased master, the family of a former master, Scott's wife (who had also sued for her freedom), and antislavery attorneys who championed Scott finally landed his case in the high court in 1856. The nine justices, including seven Democrats, six of whom had decidedly prosouthern leanings, decided that African Americans were not citizens and that Scott had no right even to sue in federal court. In the words of Chief Justice Roger Taney, himself a former slave owner from Maryland, blacks possessed "no rights which the white man was bound to respect." In any event, went the majority decision, a temporary residence in nonslave territory did not bestow freedom or abrogate the rights of property.

All of that might have passed with little public comment had not some members of the Court also maintained, in an aside to the principal decision,

DRED SCOTT'S LEGAL SUIT to obtain his freedom brought the Supreme Court into the territorial controversy in 1857. The southern-leaning justices not only denied Scott his freedom but also complicated the sectional debate by declaring the old Missouri Compromise line unconstitutional.

that the Missouri Compromise and all such congressional efforts to restrict slavery geographically were unconstitutional. No citizen, went this line of reasoning, could be prohibited from carrying *property*, be it a slave or a mule, into the territories. Republicans shouted "conspiracy" and charged collusion between the Court and the president, who in his inaugural address had cryptically promised that the slavery issue would be "speedily and finally settled" quite soon. In all probability no such collusion had occurred, but appearances counted more than established facts in the tumultuous 1850s.

To northerners, it appeared as though the tide of political corruption, which seemed everywhere so apparent, had now tainted even the Supreme Court. Certainly the Court had emasculated Congress, charged Republicans, and the oft repeated warning of conspiracy seemed a step closer to fulfillment. With their ability to halt the march of slavery by legal/constitutional means seemingly endangered, Republicans turned to moral outrage. The nation's flag, suggested William Cullen Bryant, "should be dyed black, and its device should be the whip and the fetter," all symbols of shame, bondage, and disgrace. "If slaves are recognized as property by the Constitution," pointed out a northern newspaper, "no local or State law can either prevent property being . . . held as such wherever its owner may choose to hold it." The nation should be prepared to witness slave auctions in Boston, warned another northerner, and slave ships, "protected by the guns of United States frigates," landing their cargo on Plymouth Rock.

Before worrying about Boston, the nation had first to settle the slavery issue in Kansas, where the Missouri Compromise line was already a moot point. In November 1857 a proslavery constitutional convention in Lecompton—which antislavery citizens refused to recognize—completed a state constitution for congressional approval. Unhappily, it became a tainted document, for Kansans were not given an opportunity to disapprove it. In a December referendum, they were given a choice only of accepting the constitution with unlimited slavery or accepting the constitution with limited slavery, meaning that slaves already in the territory (and their progeny) would remain enslaved. Neither side seemed to care that only about one hundred slaves resided in the territory at the time.

Kansas Politics and the Lecompton Controversy

The resulting political battle over this Lecompton constitution carried over into the next summer and destroyed the tottering sectional balance of the Democratic Party in Congress. Buchanan, who unwisely supported the document in hopes of settling the Kansas dispute and restoring national harmony, quarreled with the leaders of Congress, chiefly Stephen Douglas. Douglas, sincerely distressed by the obvious fraud that had produced the constitution, charged that it mocked the spirit of popular sovereignty and violated a "fundamental principle of free government." At the same time, he saw an opportunity to regain his standing with northern Democrats and challenge Buchanan for leadership of the party. After much debate in Congress and no little maneuvering behind the scenes, the people of Kansas were given another chance. Voting on the constitution as a whole, the territory's substantial antislavery majority rejected it 11,300 to 1,788. Rather than accept slavery, they had decided not to enter the Union for the present and would not do so until 1861.

The Lecompton fiasco cost Buchanan the support of many northerners in his party and presented Republicans with another emotional campaign issue in 1858. Local matters continued to reign supreme in some places, and not a few contests hinged on the tariff and land reform, but no single controversy affected so many contests as the ill-fated Kansas constitution. The Republicans cashed in immediately. Northern Democrats lost twenty-one seats in the House of Representatives in 1858, and with twelve "anti-Lecompton" Democrats elected to oppose the president's policies, the administration lost effective control of the House. The party remained strong in the South, with sixty-nine members elected to the House and a majority in the Senate, but that only made the party appear more sectional, thus weakening its national appeal.

Panic of 1857   Economic woes made the campaign even tenser. The problems began with the *Panic of 1857*, sparked that August by the failure of the New York branch of the Ohio Life Insurance and Trust Company. Heated speculation in land and railroads, the most frequent cause of nineteenth-century financial panics, was the culprit. As a consequence, the stock market tumbled, banks and businesses failed, prices rose, and people lost jobs. A fledgling national labor movement also suffered as several newly formed trade unions folded. "A nightmare broods over society," observed a Philadelphian. "Scores of thousands are out of work. Bread riots are dreaded. . . . God alone foresees the history of the next six months."

Like so many other events in this season of sectional distrust and political animosity, some Americans attributed even the economic depression to a sectional conspiracy. Specifically, southerners blamed the collapse on northern avarice and the hated tariff. As long as the South remained tied to northern bankers, northern merchants, and a tariff policy that protected northern manufacturers, they cried, it would remain "the very slave of the North." In fact, the depression hit the Northeast and the Midwest hardest, inspiring a bout of religious revivals, mostly in the cities, and causing some Republicans to soften their stand on the tariff. When southern agriculture recovered more quickly than did the northern economy, southerners pointed triumphantly to the superiority of their economic system and way of life. Proslavery advocates mocked the North for championing the free labor system where workers suffered hunger and want, more so, they insisted, than did slaves.

Sectional   Still, not even the depression could detract from the unresolved territorial
Tensions   question. Public debate grew ever more shrill, inflamed, and exaggerated, with
Increase   words as violent as the acts perpetrated against Sumner and the mutilated farmers of Pottawatomie Creek. Both sections feared domination; both remained convinced that the other side would stop at nothing to achieve domination. "The South is not satisfied with what she is fairly entitled to under the Constitution," declared an Illinois newspaper. "She wants more. She aspires to nothing short of absolute supremacy. . . . On behalf of the interests of freedom, the Republicans in self-defense have been compelled to resist; and thus the contest will go on, until one or the other shall have achieved an undisputed supremacy." Southerners, for

their part, feared "the filthy, fanatical abolitionist, who, regardless of all right and justice, [was] seeking to *usurp* the control of the government, destroy the equality of the States, and trample in the dust the sacred guarantees of the Constitution."

This sort of talk had been tossed around for years by abolitionists and fire-eaters, but it had rarely invaded legislative halls nor been part of the mainstream political culture. When William H. Seward, as a Whig senator from New York, declared during the congressional debates of 1850 "all legislative compromises radically wrong and essentially vicious," he had received no more support than did the secessionists at the Nashville Convention. When he appealed in that same speech to "a higher law than the Constitution," politicians shrank from the prospect of investing political issues with moral authority, and with placing moral conviction ahead of constitutional law. Yet, as the sectionally balanced Whigs and Democrats lost ground to new, strongly sectional political coalitions—the Republicans and a southern-dominated Democratic Party—that all changed. The confrontational style of the evangelicals held sway. The territorial debate became a question of "right" versus "wrong," and the chances for compromise and consensus faded accordingly.

Seward and Irrepressible Conflict

By 1858 Seward was a Republican, and his denunciations of slavery seemed perfectly acceptable to much of his party. Recognizing that the unparalleled expansion of the nation and its economic system had placed northern and southern values at odds, Seward warned in October 1858 that a "collision" was inevitable. "It is an irrepressible conflict between opposing and enduring forces," the New Yorker declared, "and it means that the United States must and will, sooner or later, become either entirely a slaveholding nation or entirely a free-labor nation." That frightening phrase, *irrepressible conflict,* entered into the lexicon of American history.

Abraham Lincoln, another former Whig turned Republican, catapulted onto the national political scene during the snarling sectional exchanges of 1858–1859. Lincoln had served in the Illinois legislature (1834–1841) and in Congress (1847–1849) before retiring from politics to establish a lucrative law practice. With a number of corporate clients, including the Illinois Central Railroad, Lincoln became a respected member of his community, but he remained politically ambitious and increasingly concerned about the expansion of slavery. The Kansas-Nebraska Act and the upstart Republican Party soon lured him back into the political arena. Campaigning for Frémont in 1856, Lincoln impressed party leaders with his dogged style. By June 1858, speaking at an Illinois Republican convention, he was insisting that "a house divided against itself cannot stand." The government could not endure permanently "half slave and half free," reasoned Lincoln: "I do not expect the Union to be dissolved; I do not expect the house to fall; but I do expect it will cease to be divided. It will become all one thing or all the other." Lincoln spoke even more forcibly later that summer when he challenged Stephen Douglas for his Senate seat. Tangling with the formidable "Little Giant" in a famous series of debates, Lincoln called slavery "a moral, a social, and a political wrong." Douglas won the election, but Lincoln made his mark as a rising star in the Republican Party.

Emergence of Lincoln

Still, no matter how heated the passions or heightened the rhetoric, politicians had managed since 1854 to disagree about slavery within the strictures of political convention and the laws of the land. By 1859, as the economic crisis passed and the Kansas question sputtered to a momentary impasse, the public seemed almost grateful for the respite. People of action despaired. "Times are so dull that we seem just creeping along on the cold surface of the world," complained Lincoln's law partner, William Herndon, in early 1859. "There is nothing to animate—elate—fire us up to the blazing point." Sectional and party tensions may have grown, but few reasonable people believed the nation's political turmoil must necessarily lead to dissolution of the nation, let alone war.

Democratic Convention of 1860

That all changed when John Brown and his band rode into Harpers Ferry, not only for antislavery people, but even more significantly for the fire-eaters. Talk of secession immediately gained new currency in the South. Even southerners who had held fast to the Union through the political upheaval of the 1850s could foresee circumstances where separation might be the only guarantee for southern security and prosperity. It was all the Democrats could talk about when they met at Charleston, South Carolina, in April 1860 to select their presidential candidate. Southern delegates demanded that the party support a federal law to guarantee slavery in the territories, even though they knew northern Democrats would reject it. Stephen Douglas, fearing just such a move and anticipating that he would be the party's presidential nominee, had warned southerners several months earlier that a proslavery platform would cost precious northern votes. At the convention, George A. Pugh of Ohio issued a similar caution to the southern delegates: "Gentlemen of the South, you mistake us—you mistake us—we will not do it."

Pugh was right. The convention voted down the proslavery platform along stark sectional lines, upon which the delegates from eight slave states, led by Alabama, marched out of the hall. Without enough voting delegates to conduct their business, the Democrats agreed to reconvene six weeks later at Baltimore. There, following a nasty fight over which southern delegates to permit in the hall, six more slave states, plus California and Oregon, joined the original bolters in a separate convention. They approved their proslavery platform and nominated Kentuckian John C. Breckinridge, then serving as Buchanan's vice president, to head their ticket. The stunned northern Democrats plowed ahead and nominated Douglas. The two conventions had completed the work of the Whigs, the Know-Nothings, and the Republicans: they had destroyed the only remaining party that could lay a reasonable claim to being "national."

Southern disunionists rejoiced. William L. Yancey of Alabama, the loudest fire-eater of them all, proclaimed that his goal was not to win the national election but to deny it to Douglas. A Republican victory, he reasoned, would lead to secession and an independent southern nation. As a South Carolina editor put it, "We do not care a fig about the Convention or election of another President, as we are convinced that the safety of the South lies only outside the present Union—and this we believe to be the judgment of a large majority of our people." In point of fact, the majority of southerners did *not* share this view, but the fire-eaters, seemingly dead and buried after the Compromise of 1850, had been resurrected.

Meanwhile, the Republicans had held a jubilant convention in Chicago. They met under awkward circumstances, having convened after the *first* Democratic meeting had adjourned but before the *second* dual conventions had complicated the race to such an uncommon degree. Still, they handled it all masterfully. Fully appreciating the damage the Democrats had already done themselves, and anticipating that Douglas would be the eventual candidate, the Republicans continued to soften their antislavery message to attract disenchanted northern Democrats and other swing voters. Their platform still opposed the extension of slavery, but it also condemned John Brown's raid as a grave crime and affirmed the right of existing states to "control their own domestic institutions." It further advocated a protective tariff, cheap western lands for homesteaders, construction of a transcontinental railroad, and citizenship for foreign immigrants.

Republican Convention

The party took a similarly moderate approach in selecting a presidential candidate. Bypassing the two principal contenders—Seward, whose blunt outspokenness threatened to alienate voters outside the party, and Salmon P. Chase, who was widely known as an antislavery radical—the Republicans nominated everyone's next choice: Abraham Lincoln. Lincoln was helped tremendously by the fact that the convention was held in his own state of Illinois and that his supporters, who packed the Chicago convention hall to cheer their man, lobbied relentlessly for his nomination. However, his reputation as an antislavery moderate and his status as a "western" man who could defeat Douglas in crucial midwestern states were Lincoln's most important strengths. His image as a folksy, self-made common man also appealed to many delegates, although, in truth, this particular rail splitter was a corporate lawyer and skilled, ambitious politician who possessed a keen analytical mind.

Republicans also waxed confident because, fragmenting the electorate still further, another party had entered the contest. The Constitutional Union Party had been founded earlier that year by a disparate group of Know-Nothings and moderate Democrats and Whigs, mostly from the border states. They denounced the extremists of both major parties and appealed for national harmony. Only they, of all the contending players, the Constitutional Unionists maintained, were still committed to compromise. Their ranks included some illustrious though quite aged figures, such as Winfield Scott, John J. Crittenden of Kentucky, Edward Bates of Missouri, and Sam Houston of Texas, but they selected as their presidential candidate ex-Whig John Bell, a lackluster Tennessean who had no chance of being elected.

Constitutional Union Party

It was a curious campaign. It had the festive air that Americans had come to expect of their elections since the 1820s, complete with mass rallies, parades, stump speeches, campaign buttons, and barbecues. Yet, mirroring the composition of the new political parties, it was a bizarrely fragmented, largely sectional affair. Republicans and Douglas Democrats battled in the North, while Breckinridge Democrats and Constitutional Unionists had the South largely to themselves. Only Douglas, who made several forays deep into Breckinridge territory, tried to wage a national campaign. He was also the only presidential candidate to make frequent public appearances. Lincoln, by contrast, gave not a single public speech.

Sectional Campaign

Campaign messages were similarly fragmented. Only Bell and Douglas found it advantageous to stress that the election might well determine the fate of the Union. Lincoln, as he had done throughout the 1850s, made light of that possibility: southern threats of secession were all a bluff—"humbug," he had called it—"nothing but folly." Breckinridge, too, downplayed the possibility of secession, preferring to emphasize the devotion of the South to the Union. All sides made clear their positions on slavery, but that did not necessarily help matters. Southern Democrats insisted on congressional protection of slavery in the territories; Douglas clung to popular sovereignty; the Republicans pledged themselves to keeping the territories "free soil."

Mood of the South

A combustible combination of paranoia, fear, and anger simmered in the South during the unusually hot summer of 1860. Still raw memories of John Brown made white southerners shudder at the very thought of a Lincoln victory. Most of them did not wish to disrupt the Union, and few desired an independent southern republic, but they had become convinced that the region's dwindling political influence threatened to make them second-class citizens in the existing Union and that a Republican victory would threaten their economy, way of life, and physical safety. They read reports that Lincoln's "black Republicans" meant to surround them with a "cordon of Free States. . .hem them in. . .by free and happy communities, rejoicing in perfect liberty" and growing prosperity. Once they controlled the national government, crowed some Republicans, "slavery must gradually die out."

In southern minds, danger lurked everywhere. A long summer drought in the deep South produced food shortages and fires from Alabama to Texas. Although the fires likely resulted from the spontaneous combustion of phosphorus matches, a new invention that lacked a safety retardant, white southerners at the time discerned a well-organized conspiracy by northern abolitionists who had come south to stir up slave revolts. Southerners beefed up slave patrols and formed militia and "Minute Men" units to protect communities. Suspicious characters, mainly Yankee peddlers and teachers and free blacks, endured daily threats if not outright physical attacks. "Now the time has come for wiping these creatures out," insisted a Montgomery, Alabama, newspaper. "Let a strict search everywhere reveal them—it will bring them to light—and let the ROPE do the rest."

White southerners closed ranks across class lines as the perception grew that a remorseless and implacable alien foe lay to the north. Those who did not own slaves would not lose property and profits in the impending abolitionist onslaught, whatever its eventual form. However, all white people living in regions populated by slaves feared insurrections, in which, it was assumed, white women would be raped and small children butchered. Even more importantly, slaveholders and nonslaveholders alike dreaded the collapse of a racial order that gave even the poorest white person some degree of social status. They feared the debasement of white society, the galling spectacle of black "citizens" claiming republican equality with them. Some men even believed this northern challenge somehow threatened their freedom to control other parts of their world, including families and hired hands.

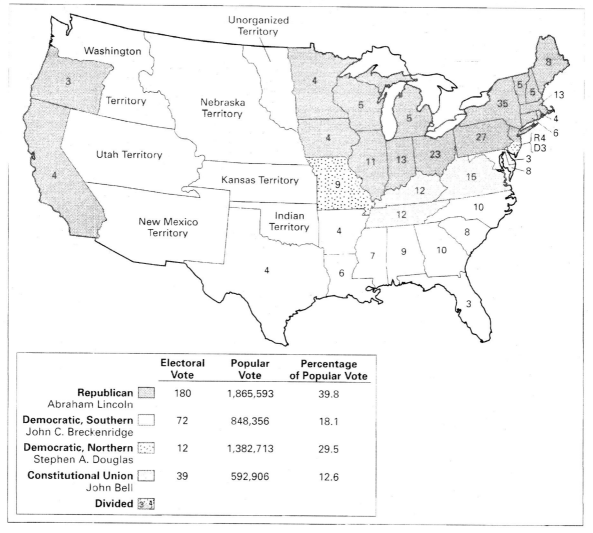

	Electoral Vote	Popular Vote	Percentage of Popular Vote
Republican Abraham Lincoln	180	1,865,593	39.8
Democratic, Southern John C. Breckenridge	72	848,356	18.1
Democratic, Northern Stephen A. Douglas	12	1,382,713	29.5
Constitutional Union John Bell	39	592,906	12.6
Divided			

REPUBLICAN VICTORY in the presidential election of 1860 did not necessarily mean war, but it did convince many southerners that secession was the only way to protect slavery and regional self-determination. The Democrats had little hope of winning the election when they failed to compromise on a candidate and a platform that both the northern and southern wings of their party could endorse.

Election Results

North and South, voters realized that the stakes in this election were enormously high, that the future of the nation—politically, economically, socially, and racially—hung in the balance. More than 80 percent of the American electorate—the second-highest percentage in history—went to the polls in November 1860. Lincoln garnered less than 40 percent of the votes, but he and his party swept the North and won the election. Their strongest showing came in the upper tier of northern states where the Republican antislavery message held its broadest appeal. More remarkably, Lincoln won 50 percent of the vote in the lower portions of the North, where Democrats had traditionally made strong showings. Douglas carried only Missouri, although he finished second everywhere in the North and had the second-highest popular vote. Virginia, Kentucky, and Tennessee went to Bell, while Breckinridge won the rest of the South. Even had one candidate carried every slave state, the balance of population would have made it impossible for him to win a strictly sectional election. Lincoln racked up 180 electoral votes to a combined 123 for his opponents.

During the next three months, the slave states of the deep South reacted to Lincoln's victory by seceding from the Union. The fire-eaters, seemingly ignored ten years earlier, finally triumphed. Secession, which had seemed unthinkable to most Americans—North and South—gained favor because southerners had lost faith in the political system. The new western territories, which had at first seemed like a blessing, had caused nothing but trouble. The root of that trouble was the issue of slavery expansion. Beginning in 1848 as a question of political balance in Congress and conflicting definitions of property, the political debate had evolved by 1860 to become an issue of right versus wrong, a question of fundamental morality. It was too passionate an issue for an immature citizenry and a distended and shallow national political system to resolve amicably. Still, even at that, the triumph of the Republicans did not necessarily mean war, and the final steps toward that terrible event require explanation.

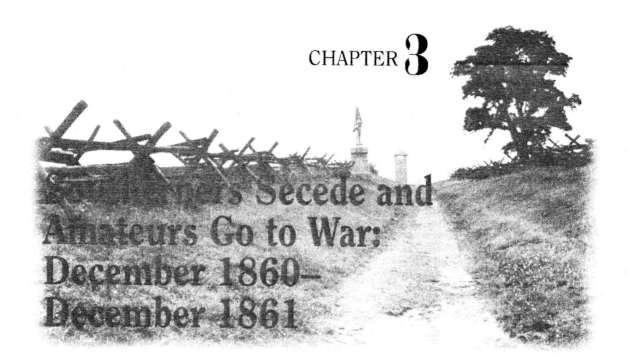

CHAPTER 3

Southerners Secede and Amateurs Go to War: December 1860– December 1861

The twelve months that followed Lincoln's election as president produced some of the most tumultuous times in American history. Within a single year, the nation was transformed from a unified if troubled union of states to two separate warring nations. Amateur armies and navies rushed to fight, the first shots were fired, and the first blood spilled. Civil war had come to America, and it gradually dawned on both northerners and southerners that it had come for an extended stay. By year's end, hopes that this would be a short, almost bloodless affair faded: the slaughter was just beginning.

The presidential election of 1860 was a shock to the South. Many white southerners responded with fear and loathing: fear of the Republicans and loathing for what the Union had seemingly become. In western Alabama, Andrew Henry, a young Irish immigrant, trumpeted: "submit to be governed by a sectional party whose grand aim is not to raise the negro . . . but to sink the southern white men to an equality with the negro! Submit to have our wives and daughters choose between death and satisfying the hellish lust of the negro! Submit to have our children murdered, our dwellings burnt and our country desolated!! Far better ten thousand deaths than submission to Black Republicanism."

Repeatedly, disunionists used this profound aversion to blacks to rally non-slaveholders to the banner of southern independence. If Republicans prevailed, they would destroy slavery, many such arguments went, and the resulting

Southern Response to Lincoln's Election

cataclysm would engulf all whites. The noted Georgia politician Joseph E. Brown articulated this position quite clearly on December 7, 1860, when he argued that blacks would drive poor whites downward were they free to compete with them economically. "It is sickening to contemplate the [ensuing] miseries of our poor white people[s.] They are in no sense placed down upon a level with the negro. They are a superior race, and they feel and know it. Abolish slavery," Brown argued, "and you make the negroes their equals."

While examples varied, the horror story was always the same: succumb to the black Republican plan to limit slavery, and all whites would be impoverished, legally degraded, and—worst of all—racially poisoned. Whites' anxieties about emancipation had a decidedly gendered dimension: the black male slave, a docile and happy fellow, would become in freedom the "buck negro," a savage rapist who would destroy the virtue of all white women and children.

Calmer southern voices attested to the sweeping social impact of such angry, racist rhetoric. One Tuscaloosa editor wrote, "it is considered heretical and unsafe to utter a sentiment in favor of reconciling our differences with the North, even were such a thing possible," while Sereno Watson, a northerner managing his brother's plantation in the black belt of Alabama, wrote that ever since Lincoln's election, the people had "gone crazy"; everyone, of all prior political sentiments, now united in denouncing submission to Lincoln's administration.

The Deep South Secedes

In such an environment, with most dissenting voices muffled, South Carolina seceded from the Union on December 20, 1860, followed during the next six weeks by Mississippi, Florida, Alabama, Georgia, Louisiana, and Texas—the entire cotton South. Even while deliberating secession, these states sent commissioners to the other slaveholding states, urging secession as the only means to preserve slavery. These politicians also frequently employed virulently racist rhetoric. For example, Stephen F. Hale, the Alabama commissioner, argued to the Kentucky legislature on December 27, 1860, that Lincoln's election was an "open declaration of war" and that Republican doctrine "destroys the property of the South, lays waste her fields . . . and inaugurates . . . servile insurrection, consigning . . . her wives and daughters to pollution and violation to gratify the lust of half-civilized Africans."

On February 4, 1861, striking while the iron sizzled, delegates from these states gathered in Montgomery, Alabama, drafted a constitution for the Confederate States of America, and elected as president the experienced, non-fire-eating, Mississippi politician Jefferson Davis. Believing, in conjunction with many in the North, that Abraham Lincoln's election constituted an incipient revolution, the Confederates joined in a sectional coup d'état.

President Buchanan's Reaction to Secession

Abraham Lincoln would not be inaugurated until March 4, 1861, nearly four months after his election. In the interim, President James Buchanan, a "dough-face" Democrat—that is, a northern man of southern principles—and an especially weak lame duck, would be the one to face southern secession. In his clearest statement concerning the Confederate gauntlet, Buchanan argued that secession was illegal but that the national government had no right to coerce seceded states back into the Union. His stance nullified him and his administration as potential actors. In this vacuum, many politicians, especially older and more conservative ones from the border and upper South states, scrambled to create a compromise that would lead the Confederate states to return to the Union and prevent the other slave states—Arkansas, Delaware, Kentucky, Maryland, Missouri, North Carolina, Tennessee, and Virginia—from leaving and vastly increasing the power of the rebel nation.

All the various compromise proposals floated in those desperate months would have conceded a great deal to the South. The most fully developed of them was the *Crittenden Compromise*, named after its chief sponsor, Senator John J. Crittenden, from the badly divided border state of Kentucky. Crittenden's compromise was an "unamendable" amendment that reaffirmed the 36°30' line established by the Missouri Compromise of 1820, banning slavery above the line and allowing it below. Other proposals for reconciliation also resolved to protect constitutional slavery in the southern parts of the West, encourage American proslavery adventures in the Caribbean and Latin America, and safeguard the rights of slaveholders in the free states. These defenses of the slave system were not necessarily new to northerners, but it remained unclear whether the Confederates would consider them sufficient to end their rebellion.

Attempts at Compromise

On the other side of the political ledger, most Republicans were at best wary of any such concessions, and the more radical among them were hostile. On this issue, the president-elect, while explicitly refusing to make public statements before his inauguration, stood firm against accepting any proposals to extend slavery into even one inch of the territories. As early as December 11, 1860, Lincoln wrote to a Republican congressman who was joining a select House committee to discuss possible remedies for secessionists, "Entertain no proposition for a compromise in regard to the *extension* of slavery. The instant you do that, they have us under again, all our labor is lost, and sooner or later must be done over. . . . Have none of it. The tug has to come & better now than later."

Lincoln believed that if the Republicans abandoned their steadfast conviction—that slavery not spread into new lands—they would lose the reason for their existence and become just another political party, one incapable of halting the slave power. Lincoln, in many ways a practical and conservative politician, did in this way insist on a bottom line that he would not compromise. The secessionists were trying to win by threats and political extremism what they had lost at the ballot box. They had radically altered the normal political game, and so had Lincoln by refusing to back down as had generations of northern politicians before him. All efforts to find a new sectional compromise failed—the middle ground had collapsed—and American politics permanently changed. Abraham Lincoln had been all too prescient in his earlier argument that "a house divided against itself cannot stand." Or, as the Mississippi declaration of secession put it: "Utter subjugation awaits us in the Union. . . . We must either submit to degradation . . . or we must secede."

Not all southerners in the seceded states had been secessionists, and in those slave states that were still in the Union, there remained many who were hesitant to rush to secession. Such men argued that the upper South's key economic

The Upper South Delays Secession

interests lay more with the Union than with the Confederate states, that southern disunionists had conspired to induce a panic among southern voters, that secession was a mass delusion, that the South misunderstood northern intentions both deliberately and out of unreasonable fear, and that the Republican Party might be able to stop the drift to war. Calming voices did retard the secession process, but most of them were also convinced that the national government had to guarantee independence of action concerning slavery within the slave states, rather than coerce them back into line.

Lincoln's First Inaugural Address

On March 4, 1861, in his carefully crafted inaugural address, Abraham Lincoln addressed southern moderates more than anyone else. He pledged that his government would not interfere with slavery where it existed, including an offer to sponsor a constitutional amendment to that effect, and he promised to enforce the fugitive slave law. He also sought to assuage southern fears by rhetorically narrowing the issues at stake. Discussing the fugitive slave law, which had led to so much passionate mutual recrimination and bloodshed, Lincoln said blandly, "there is some difference of opinion whether this clause should be enforced by national or by state authority; but surely that difference is not a very material one." Lincoln described the division simply: "One section of our country believes slavery is *right*, and ought to be extended, while the other believes it is *wrong*, and ought not to be extended," adding, "this is the only substantial dispute." In the past, Lincoln had often said that the wrong side ought to submit to the right one, and he certainly believed that the Republican Party, opposed to the expansion of slavery and hopeful of its ultimate extinction, was the right one, but here, in his first speech as president over a shattered nation, he downplayed the enormity of the sectional divide. Lincoln appeared to be acting on his understanding of the obligations of his office, and struggling personally with the implications of secession.

Lincoln further argued that secession was the "essence of anarchy," that the Union was a "perpetual" contract that could not be broken by the states, and that he would execute federal laws within all the states. He aimed this portion of his speech at his Republican listeners, who responded with gratitude for his nationalist firmness. At the same time, Lincoln promised not to instigate bloodshed, although he did not indicate how he would enforce a law in a Confederate state by other means. Instead, he shifted the burden of future actions onto the South. "In *your* hands, my dissatisfied fellow countrymen, and not in *mine*, is the momentous issue of civil war. The government will not assail *you*. You can have no conflict without being yourselves the aggressors." In effect, Lincoln abnegated his executive power to the aggrieved portion of the citizenry. Should the tidal wave sweep over the nation, they and not he would be the final cause.

Lincoln's contradictory address was a kind of lawyer's attempt to calm the nation, but at the close, the new president appealed emotionally to a certain set of southerners who, he believed, shared his love of the Union but were temporarily silenced by the better organized revolutionary secessionist minority. "We are not enemies but friends. We must not be enemies," Lincoln concluded. "Though passion may have strained, it must not break our bonds of affection.

The mystic chords of memory, stretching from every battle-field and patriot grave, to every living heart and hearthstone, all over this broad land, will yet swell the chorus of the Union, when again touched, as surely they will be, by the better angels of our nature."

Facing the threatening unknown—the incomprehensible notion of actual civil war—Lincoln along with many other northern politicians expressed wishful thinking. He simply could not predict which way the remainder of the South would turn should some form of bloodshed occur to which he would have to react. Nor did he know which way the antisecessionists would turn should war begin. There are many indications, however, that out of almost wistful optimism, Lincoln fundamentally misread such people as committed unionists when they were in fact conditional in their allegiance to the national state, that condition being Lincoln's refraining from protecting the Union by force against the South.

Upon taking office, Lincoln faced a major problem left over from the Buchanan administration that went to the heart of the issue of potential war— whether to resupply two forts off the southern coast, the more important of which was Fort Sumter in Charleston harbor, at the very mouth of the hottest secessionist state. The Confederacy had ringed the harbor with cannons and had cut supplies off from the small Union garrison. If Lincoln were to give meaning to that portion of his inaugural address that insisted on executing federal law in all federal areas, he would have to do something about this situation, but he did not want to be drawn into firing the first shot in a war.

Fort Sumter Crisis

Soon after his inauguration, Lincoln discussed with Virginia unionists the possibility of giving up Fort Sumter in exchange for their pledge to stay in the Union. His old political competitor and new secretary of state, William H. Seward, who suggested to Lincoln that a war with Europe would unite the nation and solve the entire crisis, was secretly assuring Confederate emissaries that the United States would evacuate the fort. Later in March, impatient with indecision and inaction, Republican newspapers and northern public opinion swung behind a firmer line. When military and bureaucratic incompetence wrecked plans to reinforce Fort Pickens—the second and more easily approached of the two forts—at Pensacola, Florida, Lincoln moved to resolve the situation in South Carolina. He decided on the expedient of resupplying the fort but only with nonmilitary goods, primarily food. The Union fleet would sail into Charleston harbor but with an unwarlike intent.

Fort Sumter also weighed heavily on the mind of Confederate president Jefferson Davis. The Federals' continued presence in Charleston harbor challenged the fledgling nation's very legitimacy. In February the Confederate provisional Congress had recommended that all such forts, including Sumter, be attained "either by negotiation or force." Some Confederate leaders believed that a show of force in Charleston would convince the hesitant upper South to join them. The longer, too, that the crisis lasted without a resolution, the more chance southerners, even in the seceded deep South, might have second thoughts. Davis knew he had to act.

SKETCH OF THE INTERIOR of Fort Sumter. South Carolina. soon after the federal garrison endured a thirty-four-hour bombardment and surrendered to Confederates.

On April 9, with the near unanimous support of his cabinet (Secretary of State Robert Toombs was the only holdout), Davis ordered Confederate commander Gen. Pierre Gustave Toutant Beauregard to deliver an ultimatum to the fort's commander, Maj. Robert Anderson, that he evacuate immediately. Anderson, a Kentucky slaveholder who wished to avoid war, agreed to surrender by noon on April 15, "should I not receive prior to that time controlling instructions from my Government or additional supplies." Those additional supplies, Beauregard knew, were in fact en route. In the early morning hours of April 12, the Confederates began their bombardment of Fort Sumter. After thirty-four hours, his garrison crumbling, his ammunition running out, his honor maintained, and miraculously none of his men killed, Anderson surrendered.

Lincoln Responds to the Firing on Fort Sumter

If Lincoln had gained a bit of moral leverage from the southern initiation of battle, he still had the fundamental problem of how to respond. Without hesitating, he called on the governors of all the states still in the Union to supply 75,000 militia troops for ninety days service, "to favor, facilitate and aid this effort to maintain the honor, the integrity, and the existence of our National Union and the perpetuity of popular government" and more specifically "to repossess the forts, places and property which have been seized from the Union." Lincoln also issued a "command" that "the persons composing the combinations" of disloyalty disperse and return to their homes. A few days later, Lincoln proclaimed a naval blockade of southern ports. The assumption that such measures and such a relatively small body of men (that was, nevertheless, more than five times larger than the regular army), operating for such a short period of time, could suppress the rebellion soon appeared extremely shortsighted. Also, if Lincoln believed that peace-loving unionist southerners would either sit on the sidelines or fight for the old flag, he was immediately proven wrong in four of the eight remaining slave states.

What Lincoln had thought to be southern unionism had in fact been many citizens in the upper South taking a wait-and-see attitude with a southern bias. When Lincoln responded to the Confederate cannons, his call to arms liberated them from any remaining ambivalence concerning their essentially southern loyalties. On April 17, Virginia's convention, already in session, voted for secession; Arkansas, North Carolina, and Tennessee followed in short order. The significance of the secession of these four states cannot be overstated. More than half of the meager industrial resources of the new nation were located in Virginia and Tennessee, not to mention the production of livestock and foodstuffs. These four states also doubled the white population of the Confederacy. The Confederacy would still be outnumbered 20 million to 8 million (plus 4 million slaves), but a war of any duration without these additional people and resources would have been highly unlikely.

The Upper South Secedes

As had been true in 1776, Virginia was still the essential state in terms of geography, population, wealth, and leadership traditions. Acknowledging the Old Dominion's symbolic importance, Confederates quickly moved their capital from sleepy and remote Montgomery, Alabama, to the urban, more populated, and more accessible—by both rail and sea—Richmond, Virginia. President Jefferson Davis settled with his wife Varina and their three young children into a gray stucco mansion just a few blocks from the capitol building, where a statue of Revolutionary war hero and native Virginian George Washington stood guard.

Although many Virginians, Tennesseans, and others from the upper South left the Union in great heat and even joy, others went with their states more reluctantly as a matter of following a more local loyalty than their continuing American nationalism. The zealots had taken the lead, and now reluctant southerners (most of them at any rate, and at least for a certain period of time) joined in the cause.

However, the divisions between unionist and secessionist sentiments were more nearly equal in southern regions where slavery was less entrenched and of diminishing importance. Delaware, Kentucky, Maryland, and Missouri, all slaveholding states, remained in the Union. Indeed, at the start of the war, Maryland, Missouri, and Kentucky were linchpin states strategically, and so, to keep them in the Union, Lincoln moved slowly on any measure that would abolish slavery. The hidden unionism so untrue of other slave states did have a greater meaning in these border states.

The Border South Stays in the Union

Southern Unionism

Unionism remained powerful in regions with few slaves or free blacks, including the western portions of Virginia, the eastern portions of Tennessee, and the hill country of deep southern states such as Georgia and Alabama. In all these places, especially after the first enthusiasm for sticking with an abstraction called "the South" wore off, unionism would reemerge, and this would lead to guerrilla warfare against both Confederate neighbors and the Confederate army. Contrarily, Confederate sentiments would cause many Missourians and Kentuckians to fight their unionist neighbors and Union soldiers holding their state. Such guerrilla fighting would become the most brutal and dehumanizing aspect of the larger civil war.

Americans Unprepared for War

In the spring of 1861, however, few Americans had any idea how awful and gruesome this war would be, and they were ill prepared to fight it. Putting great faith in their innate martial readiness, Americans had always been loath to fund a large peacetime army. The military, with its inherent system of hierarchy and conformity, seemed contradictory to the ideals of the free and virtuous republic. Even the United States Military Academy at West Point, New York, had come under periodic attack as elitist.

The South's Perceived Martialism

Wrapped up in northern and southern perceptions of sectionalism was a conviction that the South was somehow more martial and violent than the North. It seemed to many that the existence of slavery and the region's sparse frontier environment meant that southern white males learned early to defend their homes, their honor, and their property. Living far from what they saw as the corrosive effects of urbanization and manufacturing, southerners maintained that their rural-bred, hearty masculinity made them better soldiers. They also believed that northern men, particularly those from the industrializing northeast, were cowardly and lacking in the values of patriotism, independence, and courage so vital to a warrior.

Regional Martialism Compared

But like so much of the sectional rhetoric, the differences between northerners and southerners were greatly exaggerated, and perception mattered more than reality. There were military academies in the North as well as in the South; the nation's militia periodicals were published in the North; the majority of West Point graduates between 1820 and 1860 were from the North; and southern officers did not stay in the army any longer than northern men. The image of the violent southerner was as much a product of northern distaste for slavery as anything else. The North was certainly not free of violence or brutality: angry antiabolition mobs, increasing urban crime, and the dirty and dangerous sweatshops where so many immigrants toiled did not point to a more compassionate, more tolerant society. Northern farmers worked as hard, if not harder, than southern farmers, placed their well-worn muskets over their mantels at night, and learned early to shoot and fight.

These distorted perceptions helped to convince Americans that war was the only option. Northern newspapers printed cartoons that depicted savage-looking southerners, thirsting for combat. Southern illustrators pictured pasty-faced northerners in awkward-fitting uniforms, not knowing from which side to shoot their rifles. A Virginia newspaper predicted that one "Southerner could lick five Northern mudsills." A New York lawyer reflected in his diary soon after Fort Sumter that northerners were "mostly men of peace, unlike the Southern sepoy . . . who habitually carries his knife or revolver." What would happen when the allegedly more martial South met on the battlefield the allegedly more peaceful North? Both sides waited in nervous anticipation to see if these popular perceptions held true.

Lincoln's call for troops on April 15, 1861, managed to unify both North and South. The entire country teemed with excited young recruits rushing to join in the biggest adventure of their lives. Males of all ages felt the urge to go to war; females of all ages felt the urge to send their husbands, fathers, and sons to war. Men made bombastic speeches and dressed in colorful uniforms. Women stitched flags and lined small-town streets to cheer on their local troops.

The North and the South Prepare for War

In the North, states competed to fill Lincoln's request for 75,000 volunteers, easily surpassing that number in a matter of weeks. Harvard professor George Ticknor recalled: "I never knew before what popular excitement can be. Holiday enthusiasm I have seen often enough, and anxious crowds I remember during the war of 1812–15, but never anything like this."

In the South too, Lincoln's call for troops unified the new nation. Southern regiments formed rapidly and eagerly. With names like "Grayson's Daredevils" and "Montgomery Fencibles," they donned an eclectic array of uniforms and bore weapons of all types. Some units wore British havelocks to protect their necks from the sun; others wore brightly colored Zouave uniforms. A steady stream of visitors poured into the hastily founded camps where volunteers learned the fundamentals of drill. Women congregated in public halls, lecture rooms, and churches to sew uniforms and flags. Mothers, daughters, wives, and sisters, anxious to keep their new warriors well fed and well protected, handed out pies and cakes, slippers, even umbrellas. A Virginia woman remembered these as the "gala days of war," when smiling ladies presented flags and waved handkerchiefs, and fresh-faced soldiers cheered and posed for ambrotype or tintype photographs. This fervid martialism struck English journalist Edward Dicey while traveling in the North. "I recollect," he wrote in his journal, "a Northern lady telling me that till within a year before, she could not recall the name of a single person whom she had ever known in the army, and that now she had sixty friends and relatives who were serving in the war; and her case was by no means an uncommon one."

Despite the passionate martial spirit spreading through North and South, the transition from civilian to soldier was not easy. Few men on either side were prepared for military discipline and instruction, and most early volunteers clung tenaciously to their democratic individualism. Virginian Randolph Shotwell observed: "In the earlier stages of the war when our men were well dressed and cleanly—every company having its wagon for extra baggage—enabling the private soldier to have a change of clothing and necessary toilet articles—the men retained much of their individuality as citizen—soldiers, volunteering to undergo for a time, the privations and perils of army life, but never forgetting that they were *citizens* and gentlemen." Warren Goss, an eager enlistee in the Second

Civilians Become Soldiers

VOLUNTEERS LIKE GEORGIAN Pvt. William S. Askew rushed to enlist with little idea of how long and bloody the war would become.

Massachusetts Artillery, recalled his first day of drill. Tired and bored, he innocently announced to his drill sergeant, "Let's stop this fooling and go over to the grocery." The drill sergeant turned to the corporal and angrily ordered him to "take this man out and drill him like hell." Goss and Shotwell, like so many other green recruits, learned quickly that actual soldiering little resembled their naive expectations, and efforts to maintain their proud individuality and egalitarianism would become harder and harder the longer the war lasted.

The Volunteers   Most 1861 volunteers were young, single, white males with no military experience. The majority were native born and farmers, although the federal army had a larger number of foreign-born soldiers (25 percent of the whole) and men from a variety of occupations. Eventually, both armies counted some Native American soldiers, and even a few women who disguised themselves as men to serve. After the issuance of the Emancipation Proclamation in 1863, the Union army mustered nearly 180,000 African Americans in its ranks. By the war's end, some 3 million people from all walks of life had served in the Civil War armies.

Three Branches of the Army   Both armies had three branches of service: the infantry, the artillery, and the cavalry. Ideally, each branch would work in tandem to exploit the enemy's position. The tactics of Napoleon Bonaparte—the French emperor and general whom all nineteenth-century soldiers sought to emulate—utilized artillery first to weaken the opponent, infantry second, to secure the main position, and cavalry last to make the final, decisive blow. Most Civil War soldiers served in the infantry. Infantry volunteer *regiments*, designated by number and state, consisted of approximately ten *companies* of one hundred men, although these numbers diminished with time and the effects of attrition. The men elected their company commanders (captains and lieutenants), who in turn elected regimental officers (colonels, lieutenant colonels, and majors). State governors issued commissions to these regimental officers, although political appointments irrespective of military qualifications were common.

Unit Identity

Unit identity, pride, and feelings of solidarity were especially strong within companies and regiments. Companies often included men from the same locale, lifelong friends, and acquaintances. The everyday experience of soldiering, let alone actual battle, bonded men even more closely together, especially among messmates who shared the same tent or daily meals. A Union corporal referred to the individuals he tented with as "our family." "I am very proud of this company," a South Carolinian stated in explaining why he did not want a transfer, "& I am too attached to my intimate friends to seek an opportunity of parting with them." A Connecticut soldier affirmed: "Every true soldier believes in his own regiment. He holds himself in perpetual readiness to demonstrate that no other battalion, brigade, divisions or corps ever passed in review so handsomely, marched so far, fought so bravely, or suffered so much, as his own."

Army Organization

Beyond the company and the regiment, military units became more cumbersome and less personal. Three to five regiments formed a *brigade*, led by a brigadier general. Two to five brigades made a *division*, commanded by a major general. The largest partition of the Civil War armies was the *corps*, consisting of two or more divisions and led on the Union side by a major general and on the Confederate side by a lieutenant general. Two or more corps made an *army*. With a few exceptions, the Confederacy named its armies after regions of land, the Union after bodies of water. For example, the Federals had the Army of the Potomac, the Army of the Ohio, and the Army of the Cumberland; the Confederates had the Army of Northern Virginia and the Army of Tennessee. The two sides would frequently assign different names to their battles, following this same pattern. It is not clear why this occurred, although after the war former Confederate D. H. Hill suggested that because "troops from the North came mainly from cities, towns and villages," they were more impressed by "some natural object near the scene of the conflict and named the battle from it. Soldiers from the South were chiefly from the country and were therefore impressed by some artificial object near the field of battle."

The Artillery

Only about 5 percent of Civil War soldiers served in the artillery. When the war began, artillery *batteries* usually consisted of four to six guns with 80–156 officers and men. Most individual batteries were eventually grouped into *battalions* under one commander and assigned to a specific infantry brigade, regiment, or battalion. Until later in the war, when armies designated separate chiefs of artillery to act independently from infantry corps commanders, artillery officers often found themselves outranked by infantry officers. Manning

CAVALRYMEN SUCH AS THE FEDERALS pictured here had only limited tactical use during the Civil War, serving essentially as the army's "eyes and ears," gathering information and screening the infantry's movements.

cannons was hard and difficult work, but artillerymen generally suffered lower casualties in battles than did infantrymen. Also, although the ideal of massed cannon fire rarely occurred, the presence of artillery was critical in many large-scale engagements, if mainly for the shock value of large guns in helping to demoralize the enemy. Artillery barrages were common before frontal infantry assaults, and their use in defending fortifications remained significant.

The Cavalry   Cavalry, like field artillery, never reached its full tactical potential during the Civil War. In most cases, the cavalry served primarily as the "eyes and ears" of the army, doing reconnaissance and gathering information on the enemy's position, size, and strategy. Fourteen percent of all Union soldiers served in the cavalry; 20 percent of all Confederates were horsemen. Occasionally, cavalry functioned as a striking force in its own right, and some units performed as mounted infantry, riding into battle, dismounting, and fighting like foot soldiers. But it was extremely expensive to maintain and supply cavalrymen; just the horse itself was costly, let alone the necessary saddle, horseshoes, pistols, sabers, and riding boots. Confederate cavalrymen provided their own horses, but even this led to problems when wealthy horsemen felt free to forage, seek fresh remounts, or simply go home on their own accord. Thus, most Civil War cavalry units were small, scattered, and of limited use. Pure cavalry engagements were rare, and by the last year of the war, cavalry raids occurred more frequently against the enemy homefront rather than on the battlefront. Nonetheless, there was a certain romance associated with cavalrymen, and individual commanders such as J. E. B. Stuart, Nathan Bedford Forrest, Phillip Sheridan, George A. Custer, and John Buford earned lasting reputations as dashing and formidable fighters. Sheridan in particular saw the powerful role that well-armed and well-trained cavalry could perform in battle, but he was an exception.

Yet, what made men want to join any of these branches of the army? This question has perplexed historians for decades. Most scholars agree that there were both ideological and practical reasons to go to war and that these reasons sometimes shifted and changed. The motivations that caused a man to join the military were not necessarily the same ones that kept him at the front, fighting and enduring; this was especially true for the first wave of volunteers in 1861. These early volunteers enlisted because they felt a sense of duty and an obligation to serve; others had a strong love of Union or, in the case of the South, their state or the region. In 1861, not yet aware of the hardships they would face, men were caught up in the emotion of the time and eagerly volunteered, worried only that the war would end before they made it to the front.

Motivations to Enlist

America's revolutionary heritage inspired men on both sides to fight. Southerners believed they were following the example of the Founding Fathers in breaking free of a seeming tyranny; northerners believed they were protecting the union of states that those same founders sacrificed so much to create. Defense of home was a strong motivation for Confederates, especially since Union armies were "invading" their new nation. Proving one's manhood, too, was a powerful influence that combined with many other factors, such as duty, patriotism, and defense of home, to inspire enlistment. Others joined because there was communal or peer pressure to do so, and staying behind would have been far too embarrassing. Money also played a role in luring men to enlist, especially in the North, where bounties were higher. Monthly pay for Union privates in the infantry and artillery was $11; cavalrymen received a dollar more. This amount was later raised to $13 for all arms in August 1861 and increased again in May 1864 to $16. Confederate artillery and infantrymen were paid $11 at the start of the war, and cavalrymen were paid $12. In 1864 the monthly pay was raised by $7 for all branches of the southern army.

Curiously, slavery, which was the underlying cause of the war, was not the cause for which most Civil War soldiers volunteered to serve. To be sure, Confederate soldiers believed firmly that they had to protect their "way of life" and beat back hated Yankee aggression, but they seldom enlisted to defend slavery per se. Similarly, Union white soldiers, especially in 1861, although convinced that they faced a "slaveocracy" that threatened their free-labor economy, were none too keen on the notion of emancipation, let alone racial equality. There were true abolitionists in the ranks of the Union from the war's start, but their number was always a minority, even when the war became one to end slavery.

Whatever the motivator in the spring of 1861, men on both sides were eager to "see the elephant." This was a nineteenth-century expression used to describe any dramatic or perilous undertaking. For Civil War recruits, it meant facing the danger of combat. Young Tennessean James Cooper remembered his enthusiasm and apprehension upon joining: "I was tormented by feverish anxiety before I joined my regiment for fear the fighting would be over before I got into it."

Anticipating Battle

Soldiers were not the only ones eager for battle. "On to Richmond," shrieked northern newspaper headlines, and northern politicians urged that some military action be taken before the Confederate Congress convened in the city on July 20. Lincoln was anxious to do something about the growing number of southern troops massing just across the Potomac River. Ending the rebellion was crucial, but he also faced more immediate problems: Maryland threatened to secede, and Lincoln needed an army to protect the northern capital. He consulted with his chief military advisor Winfield Scott, the failed Whig presidential candidate of 1852. Born in 1786 in Virginia, Scott had spent his entire adult life in uniform. He served in the War of 1812 and led the victorious Army of Occupation into Mexico City in 1847. Tall, fat, and quick tempered, he was nicknamed "Old Fuss and Feathers." Despite his southern roots, Scott's allegiance to the Union was undeniable. "I have served my country, under the flag of the Union, for more than fifty years," he declared. "I will defend the flag with my sword even if my native state assails it."

The Anaconda Plan

Scott, who was not eager to shed blood on southern soil, proposed subjecting the rebellious states to a massive siege that would eventually strangle the Confederacy to death. Hesitant to initiate a major land campaign until Union troops could be properly trained and armed, and worried about protecting Washington, D.C., Scott recommended a naval blockade of the coastal South combined with a show of force on major rivers, most notably the Mississippi. Seeking to capitalize on northern industrial might, Scott envisioned dispatching some 60,000 men on gunboats down the Mississippi in order to diminish severely the Confederacy's ability to transport goods and wage war. Like a city under siege, the Confederacy, Scott predicted, would eventually surrender, and the war would be over with relatively little loss of human life. But the northern public and press had rejected Scott's plan by the summer of 1861. They clamored for real fighting and a decisive battle. Newspapers derisively labeled Scott's proposal the "Anaconda Plan," likening it to a snake slowly strangling its victim. Union strategic thinking quickly swung toward winning a dramatic and decisive land battle in a Napoleonic *strategy of annihilation*.

Theaters of War

The principal obstacle to delivering a single, knockout blow was the gigantic size of the Confederacy. In fact, the wartime map may be divided into three large theaters of war: the Eastern Theater consisted mainly of Virginia, West Virginia, Pennsylvania, and Maryland; the Western Theater essentially covered the area between the Appalachian Mountains and the Mississippi River, including Kentucky, Tennessee, Georgia, Alabama, and Mississippi; the Trans-Mississippi Theater consisted of Arkansas, Missouri, Texas, the Indian Territory, and Louisiana west of the Mississippi. Still, these geographical categories faltered sometimes. Where, for example, does one place North Carolina, South Carolina, and Florida, or expeditions that involved a combination of sea and land forces and seemed as much naval battles as land campaigns? Historians, too, have hotly debated the importance of these different theaters to the war's outcome; some argue that the war was won and lost in the East; others insist that it was in the West. Each of these theaters had its own distinctive history, and in some ways even the armies were different. Midwesterners and southerners from the Gulf states did most of the fighting in the West; men from the Northeast and the upper South did most of the fighting in the East.

The man chosen to lead the North's eastern army to speedy victory was Irvin McDowell. McDowell was forty-two years old in the spring of 1861, an Ohio native and a U.S. Military Academy graduate. Although he had served as a staff officer in Mexico and had taught tactics at West Point, he had never led so much as a company of men into battle. Blue-eyed, bearded, and robust, McDowell refused liquor and tobacco and seemed to lack a sense of humor. He was brusque, testy, and aloof, but he had friends in high places, including Secretary of the Treasury Salmon P. Chase and Secretary of War Simon Cameron. By late May 1861, McDowell was a brigadier general in command of the Department of Northeastern Virginia, responsible for protecting Washington, D.C., and destroying the rebel army just south of the capital.

Irvin McDowell

The Confederacy was also searching for leaders and a strategy. With the secession of Virginia, North Carolina, Arkansas, and Tennessee, a fresh wave of West Point–trained officers offered their services to the new southern nation. Virginians Robert E. Lee, Thomas Jonathan Jackson, and Joseph E. Johnston each applied for commissions in the Confederate army. Lee, whom Scott believed was the most talented officer in the regular U.S. Army (and to whom he had offered command of the Union army, which Lee declined), was made major general and given command of all Virginia state forces. Thirty-seven-year-old Jackson had left his position as an instructor at the Virginia Military Institute in Lexington to join the Confederacy; his first assignment placed him at Harpers Ferry to train volunteers. Jackson's students at VMI, who had always thought him strange and eccentric, had nicknamed him "Tom Fool" and "Old Blue Light." As he drilled his green and undisciplined troops unmercifully, Jackson was viewed by these recruits as an intensely religious and overly strict commander. He inspired a mixture of both dislike and awe. Eventually, the awe would almost entirely displace the dislike.

Confederate Military Leaders

Virginian Joseph E. Johnston was also a West Pointer. He, like Lee, had made the army his career and moved through the ranks, but with the outbreak of hostilities in 1861, Johnston, as brigadier general and quartermaster general, was the second highest ranking officer in the U.S. Army after Samuel Cooper. Assured that his rank would transfer into the new Confederate army, the small and slight Johnston was sensitive to this issue from the start.

The Union had the more challenging strategic role in seeking to seize control of the South and its armies, while the Confederacy had comparatively more modest offensive goals. Although the North had the advantage of more men,

Strategy

supplies, and industry, with military and government infrastructures already in place, rebel commanders benefited from familiarity with the region, interior lines of communication, and a mostly friendly civilian population. In 1861 the U.S. War Department did not even have an accurate map of the South.

President Davis gave a speech on April 29, 1861, two weeks after the fall of Fort Sumter, in which he reiterated his original inaugural pronouncement that the Confederacy wanted peace. Davis proclaimed: "We protest solemnly in the face of mankind that we desire peace at any sacrifice save that of honor and independence; we seek no conquest, no aggrandizement, no concession of any kind from the States with which we were lately confederate." He stated plainly: "All we ask is to be let alone." Davis, however, was being somewhat disingenuous, as he had every hope of bringing the slave states of Missouri, Kentucky, and Maryland and the southwestern territories into the Confederacy. The rebels considered these places natural extensions of their nation, and just as Lincoln believed in the latent unionist sympathies of much of the South, so Davis trusted in the prosecessionist sentiments of the border states. Davis, himself a West Point graduate and Mexican War veteran, looked to George Washington as his model strategist. Convinced that the Confederacy just needed to hold out until a *strategy of attrition* wore down Union armies, he believed he had time, geography, and history on his side. But Davis confronted a political obstacle not faced by Washington: in a nation founded upon states' rights, Davis had to balance the needs of the varying eleven states in his Confederacy more carefully than Washington had had to do with the thirteen colonies. In fact, Washington had given up a good deal of land and significant positions, including New York and the capital at Philadelphia, to the British. Davis could not consider such concessions. He wanted to hold everything, although it became clear early on that he lacked the men and the material to protect every part of his vast Confederacy.

The Battle of Bull Run

By mid-June 1861, North and South had collected thousands of men for battle in and around northern Virginia. The Confederacy had 22,000 soldiers under command of the hero of Fort Sumter, Pierre G. T. Beauregard, at Manassas Junction, a major railroad center just 25 miles southwest of Washington, D.C. Joe Johnston was in the Shenandoah Valley with 10,000 Confederates near the town of Winchester. Rail lines linked these two armies by a few hours, and Davis proposed combining them by train to push back a federal advance against Manassas. The Union meanwhile had assembled 35,000 men under McDowell at Centreville, Virginia, and another 18,000 under veteran General Robert Patterson at Harpers Ferry. Patterson was another career army officer, just six years younger than Scott, and a veteran of the War of 1812.

The Confederates expected McDowell's advance, thanks to the intelligence gathered by two spies, Bettie Duval and Rose Greenhow, and broadcast openly by northern newspapers. His intentions became clear on July 18, when Confederate troops under James Longstreet and Jubal Early encountered and pushed back McDowell's advance brigade at Blackburn's Ford. In response, Johnston received orders to transfer his men eastward "if practicable." On July 19, 1861,

THE BATTLE OF MANASSAS, July 21, 1861. To counter Union Gen. Irvin McDowell's advance toward Manassas Junction, Confederates rushed reinforcements from various parts of Virginia, including Theophilus Holmes's brigade at Aquia Creek, Wade Hampton's legion in Richmond, and Joseph E. Johnston's troops in the Shenandoah Valley. The timely arrival of Johnston's forces via train resulted in a northern rout.

Joe Johnston's men slipped away from the unwatchful eyes of Robert Patterson and boarded trains for Manassas Junction, some 34 miles to the east. The trains were sluggish, and only a portion of the troops could travel at a time. Some soldiers were on the cars for forty-eight hours, but their arrival would turn the tide of battle and provide an early example of the strategic, even tactical role of railroads in this railroad war.

On the morning of Sunday, July 21, 1861, fighting commenced in and around the gently rolling farmland at Manassas Junction. Men in the ranks, wearing a variety of colors and styles of uniform, could not always distinguish friend from foe. The Second Wisconsin and the Eighth New York Infantry regiments both donned gray, and several senior Confederate officers still wore their blue U.S. Army uniforms. Northerners and southerners fumbled with their rifles, strained to hear unfamiliar orders, and tried to remain calm. Shot and shell tore through trees and bodies without prejudice. The smoke grew thick, the noise became deafening, and the very ground shook. The air was hot and heavy with the acrid smell of carbon and death. Soldiers felt intense fear, excitement, and overwhelming thirst, often at the same time. For most men, actual combat was like nothing they had anticipated and like nothing they had ever experienced in their lives.

Not merely were men in the ranks caught off guard by the thunderous chaos of battle; neither army had provided them with adequate food or water, and medical facilities and personnel were nearly nonexistent. It was as if no one had foreseen that there would be wounded, let alone dead, after the two armies engaged in large-scale conflict. Command structures were as yet haphazard and unwieldy, staff work often sloppy. To make matters worse, inaccurate maps caused the Union commander to miscalculate distances and the nature of the terrain.

Among the masses of men caught in the battle's whirlwind of turmoil, violence, and death was Colonel Jackson, who by day's end would earn a famous nickname. There are various accounts of how this happened, but most agree that as Confederate Gen. Bernard Bee tried desperately to restore confidence in his broken command on the back slope of Henry Hill, he spotted Colonel Jackson's brigade of Virginians. "Look Men! There stands Jackson like a stone wall!" Bee exclaimed. "Rally behind the Virginians!" Bee died, but the legend of "Stonewall" Jackson was born.

Civilians were also swept into the melee, including a group of U.S. congressmen and senators and their wives who had come down from Washington to watch the Sunday battle. Arriving in fancy carriages and carrying picnic baskets and binoculars, they joined hundreds of other spectators assembled on a hill a few miles from the scene of slaughter. William Howard Russell, an English journalist, stood nearby and overheard a woman as she peered through her opera glasses: "That is splendid. Oh, my! Is not this first rate? I guess we will be in Richmond this time tomorrow." Some ventured closer to the fighting, including a Massachusetts congressman who was captured by Confederate soldiers. Local Confederate civilians were also there, not to watch but to inquire about loved ones and try to protect their homes and property. The very idea that civilians for any reason would hover near a battle underscores how unprepared Americans were for the brutal and vicious war unfolding before them.

Jefferson Davis arrived on the field from Richmond soon after hearing word of the fight, anxious to resume his former role as a military commander. Ignoring the concerned pleas of several staff officers, Davis rushed into the fray astride a horse. Encountering some shaken troops who were retreating, he excitedly declared: "I am President Davis! Follow me back to the field."

Until about 3 p.m. on July 21, it did seem that the battle of Bull Run would prove a decisive Union victory. McDowell's men managed to push back the rebels and take essential positions on high ground, but after Jackson's bold stand and a lull in the fighting, fresh Confederate reinforcements arrived to reverse the entire momentum of battle. The Union troops were soon in full retreat. Some northern soldiers withdrew in good order, but many others, inexperienced, exhausted, and scared, panicked. Fearing the pursuit of rebel cavalry, they fled blindly toward Washington, D.C. Newspaper correspondent William Russell witnessed the frenzy: "Infantry soldiers on mules and draft horses with the harness clinging to their heels as much frightened as their riders; Negro servants on their masters' chargers; ambulances crowded with unwounded soldiers; wagons swarming with men who threw out the contents in the road to make room, grinding through a shouting screaming mass of men on foot who were literally yelling with rage at every halt and shrieking out: 'Here are the cavalry! Will you get on?' " The fleeing soldiers quickly mixed with the equally horrified spectators, only adding to the chaos.

The battle of Bull Run, called the battle of Manassas by the Confederates, shocked the North. It was the bloodiest battle yet recorded in the western hemisphere. Its close proximity to both capitals made it even more significant. The Federals lost just fewer than 3,000 dead, wounded, and captured, but the battle took a psychological toll far beyond the blood and pain: it refueled old stereotypes of a soft, impotent North and a robust, manly South. Soon after the battle, rumors spread of alleged rebel barbarity. Newspapers printed descriptions of southern soldiers slashing the throats of northern prisoners and using wounded Yankees for target practice. On August 17, 1861, a disturbing illustration appeared in *Harper's Weekly* that depicted rebels plunging bayonets into the bodies of helpless wounded Federals. The *New York Times* angrily declared: "The Southern character is infinitely boastful, vainglorious, full of dash, without endurance, treacherous, cunning, timid and revengeful."

Aftermath of Bull Run

For the Confederates, Bull Run affirmed their belief in their martial superiority over northerners. Confederate losses numbered some 1,000 less than those suffered by the North, and although a bitter controversy erupted among Davis, Beauregard, and Johnston over the feasibility of pursuing the fleeing Federals—something highly unlikely, given the shaken and disorganized condition of the rebel troops—the victory seemed to verify that the South had superior leaders and better soldiers.

The Union loss curbed war euphoria in the North as many people realized that this was not going to be a romantic lark. The day after the battle, Congress increased the call for Union volunteers to 500,000 to serve for no more than three years but no less than six months. Three-month volunteers were no longer adequate. Col. William T. Sherman called Bull Run "but the beginning of a long war." Sherman hoped he was wrong and that the people of the South would "yet see the folly of the unjust rebellion against the most mild and paternal government ever designed for men," but for some northerners, the feeling of defeat was overwhelming. "Never in my life," wrote New York diarist Maria Daly on July 22, "did I feel as badly as when I saw this fearful, disgraceful news in the paper yesterday. It will prolong the war another year, if not three, and give European powers cause to consider the matter of recognizing the Confederacy as very probably their very best policy." After the federal debacle, Edwin M. Stanton, soon to be Lincoln's secretary of war, wrote to ex-President Buchanan referring to the battle as "the dreadful disaster." He predicted that

SOON AFTER THE BATTLE at Bull Run, or Manassas, rumors spread throughout the North that the Confederates were guilty of atrocities. This illustration from the August 17, 1861, issue of *Harper's Weekly* depicts Confederates brutally killing defenseless, wounded federal soldiers after the fighting stopped.

Washington would fall to the enemy: "The rout, overthrow, and utter demoralization of the whole army is complete. Even now I doubt whether any serious opposition to the entrance of the Confederate forces [into Washington, D.C.] could be offered."

George McClellan Takes Command

Lincoln wanted a new commander. As both armies rested not far from the battlefield at Manassas, Winfield Scott urged him to replace McDowell with George Brinton McClellan, and on July 27 the president followed his advice. McClellan seemed one of the few bright spots on the North's bleak military horizon in the summer of 1861. McClellan, a native of Pennsylvania, was a West Pointer and decorated Mexican War veteran who had left the military in 1857 to pursue a successful career in civil engineering. Short and handsome, intelligent and avowedly anti-Republican, the thirty-four-year-old McClellan seemed in 1861 a very promising military commander. When the war began, he resided in Cincinnati and readily accepted when Governor William Dennison appointed him major general of Ohio volunteers.

Soon becoming a major general in the regular army, McClellan was placed in command of the Department of the Ohio, which included western Virginia, an area traditionally nonslaveholding and defiantly independent from the rest of the Dominion State. Northwestern Virginia had significant strategic value be-

UNION GEN. GEORGE B. MCCLELLAN, pictured here with his wife. Ellen. held great promise when he became commander of the Army of the Potomac in the summer of 1861.

cause of the Ohio River and the Baltimore and Ohio Railroad—two crucial transportation arteries. Control of northwestern Virginia also ensured a buffer zone, protecting not only eastern Ohio and western Pennsylvania, but also the Shenandoah Valley and even eastern Kentucky. In June 1861, 20,000 soldiers under McClellan's departmental command entered western Virginia and in just over a month appeared to have secured the region for the pro-Union residents. This campaign, including engagements at Philippi on June 3, Laurel Hill on July 10, Rich Mountain on July 11, and Carrick's Ford on July 12, was not overly large or costly, and McClellan's actual involvement in all but the small action at Phillipi was minimal. However, he took the credit for the campaign's overall success, and that was enough to gain him national attention. On July 16, McClellan issued a congratulatory address to his men that was full of bombast and pride: "Soldiers! I have confidence in you, and I trust you have learned to confide in me. Remember that discipline and subordination are qualities of equal value with courage."

McClellan's first tasks were to strengthen the defenses in and around Washington, D.C., and to provide better organization and training for the demoralized troops. A man who knew how to build and maintain an army, he proved adept as an administrator and quickly won the affection of the soldiers, but he bickered openly with Winfield Scott, Secretary of War Edwin Stanton, and Secretary of the Treasury Salmon Chase. He agreed with Lincoln's conciliatory war policy—seeking to avoid the destruction of civilian property and the displacement of noncombatants—although for somewhat different reasons. A Democrat in politics, McClellan was no enemy of slavery, and he did not wish to see the South unduly punished. Lincoln hoped that "the Young Napoleon" would push the northern war effort forward, and on November 1, 1861, after the more or less forced retirement of Winfield Scott, which McClellan himself connived to bring about, the president appointed McClellan general-in-chief of the U.S. Army.

Western Virginia Campaign

Although McClellan left the region to assume greater responsibilities in Washington, sporadic fighting continued in western Virginia during the late summer and fall of 1861 as federal forces pushed farther into the region. Unionists in these mountainous counties, seeking complete political separation from the rest of seceded Virginia and the Confederacy, began to assemble a reorganized government at Wheeling with plans to create a new state.

Jefferson Davis, troubled by the worsening situation in northwest Virginia, dispatched Robert E. Lee in late July as "coordinator" to tour and inspect the region and, it would seem, to bring a better sense of military order to operations there. But Lee's portfolio was unclear, and he hesitated to involve himself in a bitter feud raging between political generals Henry Wise and John B. Floyd. Lee discovered the enlisted men sick, cold, and hungry and the weather soggy, hardly ideal conditions upon which to launch an offensive and to regain lost territory. Lee tried nonetheless in his first real campaign of the Civil War. He began his advance on September 10 through treacherous terrain and chilly, wet weather. For the next five days, Lee attempted to push forward, but his men soon grew demoralized and tired, and his command floundered. Lee finally withdrew on September 15, and the battle of Cheat Mountain, a minor action, was a major disappointment. "I cannot tell you my regret & mortification at the untoward events that caused the failure of the plan," Lee wrote his wife on September 17. After botching another attempt to engage the enemy at Sewell Mountain, Lee returned to Richmond in late October, his future as a field commander somewhat in doubt. West Virginia formally joined the Union in 1863, and the Confederates waged a bitter guerrilla campaign there for the remainder of the war.

The Battle of Ball's Bluff

Except for these limited engagements in western Virginia, military operations in the eastern theater appeared to grind to a standstill. The battle of Ball's Bluff on October 21, 1861, was a notable exception to the quiet. This "melancholy disaster" in which Confederate troops literally drove a Federal force into the Potomac River, resulted in more than 900 Union casualties. Among the dead was Col. Edward Baker, a friend of Lincoln and a senator from Oregon. The U.S. Congress created the Committee on the Conduct of War to investigate the causes of this rout. The committee, which enjoyed broad investigative powers, played a controversial role in northern politics for the remainder of the war.

All Quiet along the Potomac

Six weeks after Ball's Bluff, Ethel Lynn Beers published a poem in *Harper's Weekly* entitled "The Pickett Guard" that spoke to soldiers' sense of loneliness and anonymity in this vast war. When the poem was set to music and retitled "All Quiet along the Potomac," an oft-repeated newspaper headline describing the state of affairs in northern Virginia, it quickly became a favorite among the troops on both sides of the river:

> All quiet along the Potomac,
> Except now and then a stray picket
> Is shot, as he walks on his beat to and fro,
> By a rifleman hid in the thicket.
> 'Tis nothing—a private or two now and then
> Will not count in the news of the battle;
> Not an officer lost—only one of the men,
> Moaning out, all alone, the death rattle.

Meantime, the Confederates believed that their amazingly lopsided victories at Manassas and Ball's Bluff presented a marvelous opportunity to gain foreign aid. If a major power such as England or France would recognize them as a legitimate, independent nation, the North might be compelled to end its efforts to restore the Union. Unfortunately, the South had already made a series of miscalculations in foreign affairs that hurt their ability to wage an extended war. The mistakes started with Davis. Even before hostilities commenced, Davis had entrusted the issue of foreign recognition to men poorly suited for such an important task. In February 1861 he dispatched a three-man commission to Europe consisting of the Alabama fire-eater William Yancey, the overly verbose Ambrose Dudley Mann, and a Louisiana judge, Pierre Rost, chosen only because he spoke French. For his secretary of state, Davis selected Georgian lawyer and former U.S. senator Robert Toombs, who had years of experience in state and federal government but no experience in foreign affairs. The special European commission was to request the governments of England, France, Russia, and Belgium to admit the Confederacy "into the family of independent nations, and "ask for that acknowledgement and friendly recognition which are due every people capable of self government and possessed of the power to maintain independence."

The Confederacy and Foreign Diplomacy

But Europe was wary of rushing into the American crisis, and by the summer of 1861, Toombs and Yancey, bored and discouraged by their tasks, tendered their resignations. Toombs's successor, Robert M. T. Hunter of Virginia, was no more qualified than the others, and his tenure lasted only until March 1862, when he resigned to seek office in the Confederate Congress. Judah P. Benjamin of Louisiana became the third and final secretary of state, and although he had more foreign experience than the others did, he was no diplomat and proved no more successful than the others in gaining recognition.

Yet, even if the Confederates had had a skilled diplomat at the helm of their state department, their diplomatic strategy was naive and wrongheaded. Cotton had been king in the prewar South, and many Confederate leaders hoped to use the threat of a cotton embargo to force the dominant world powers, England in particular, to support their war effort. Surely, those English textile factories, reasoned Confederate politicians, could not function without southern cotton, which everyone acknowledged to be the finest and most plentiful in the world.

The Confederate government never officially sanctioned the cotton embargo, and not everyone believed that a boycott would force the Europeans' hand. Benjamin, in fact, urged the government to sell as much cotton as possible early in the war to establish credit with Europe and to obtain necessary war materials. Most Confederate leaders, believing that the war would be over in a few months, ignored his argument, and from the summer of 1861 to the spring of 1862, rebel farmers and merchants participated in a voluntary effort to stop overseas cotton shipments. Production slowed, while thousands of bales of cotton sat untouched in southern warehouses. By the spring of 1861, Europe had already received most of its annual cotton shipments from the American South; in fact, there was a surplus of cotton in British warehouses. These surpluses would begin to disappear in mid-1862, but as English and French textile production shifted to Indian, Turkish, and Egyptian cotton, the loss of southern cotton mattered less. Confederate leaders realized too late their mistake. Cotton diplomacy ultimately proved a disaster.

Confederates also misjudged the willingness of Europeans, particularly the British, to risk war with the North. Portraying themselves as freedom fighters and northerners as tyrants, southerners downplayed the issue of slavery, convinced that Europeans would be sympathetic to their struggle for independence. Diplomatic envoys were sent not only to France, Russia, Belgium, and England, but also to Spain, the Vatican, and the various dominions of Mexico. Although on the surface it seemed that the British aristocracy would openly support the South, English attitudes were mixed. Some British elites applauded the Confederates, perceiving the conflict as a potential check on the spread of U.S. economic strength and influence; moreover, worried about pressure from their own lower orders, these elites were pleased to see the experiment in democracy faltering from within. The British press, notably the London *Times* and the *Standard,* were stridently pro-Confederate. It was also very common for southern gentry to associate themselves proudly with British aristocracy. But this bond was not as deep as Confederates hoped. Many British artistocrats were quite ambivalent toward the South and hesitant to involve the nation in the war, nervous that a divided United States could lead to further instability across the western hemisphere. And among the populace, workers, merchants, and manufacturers were more pro-Union than pro-Confederate, taking the progressive, democratic North, not the aristocratic South, as the bellwether of where they wanted their own nation to head. It would take some time for the Confederates to realize that neither the government nor the people of Great Britain was their natural ally.

The United States and Foreign Affairs

There were other reasons, however, for the Confederacy to be encouraged in 1861, especially when relations between the United States and Britain appeared to be on a crash course. The British were quite suspicious of the new administration and the ill effects of war. In February, before Lincoln was inaugurated, British foreign minister Lord John Russell sternly warned the United States that if its efforts to suppress the rebellion interfered with British trade, there could be serious consequences, including British recognition of Confederate independence. Lincoln's inauguration did not ease their fears, particularly after the declaration of the blockade and the passage of the Morrill Tariff, an act that doubled duties on imports. A South Carolina planter reasoned: "The United States have lately increased their Tariff so high on many articles of European manufacture, as to amount almost to prohibition; whilst the Confederate States have lessened theirs from the old standard, & have it in contemplation to reduce still more. The case then stands thus: We furnish what is absolutely essential to their commercial & manufacturing prosperity, & we alone—We offer them a market for their goods on better terms than heretofore."

U.S. Secretary of State William Seward further alienated Europeans. Seward, an intelligent, well-traveled, experienced politician, also was woefully tactless. He was sorely disappointed not to have won the Republican nomination for president in 1860, and as a member of Lincoln's cabinet, he was determined to assert his power, even to the extent of starting a foreign war. It was Seward who, during the tense weeks leading up to the firing at Fort Sumter, proposed that a foreign conflict would unify the country and end the crisis. The United States was, in fact, facing direct challenges to the Monroe Doctrine, first in March when Spain invaded Santo Domingo and then when it appeared that the French were considering doing the same in Haiti. On April 1, 1861, Seward urged Lincoln to demand an explanation from Spain and from France about their activities in the Caribbean. If their responses proved unsatisfactory, Seward advised Lincoln, the president should "convene Congress and declare war against them." Lincoln ignored the secretary's advice, but Seward's belligerent reputation intensified.

England, France, even Russia appeared on the verge of acknowledging southern independence. Already, the French and the Russian ministers to the United States had advised their governments to open diplomatic relations with the southern nation. Lord Russell unofficially granted interviews with the Confederate commissioners on May 3 and May 9. Then on May 14, 1861, Queen Victoria issued a proclamation recognizing the state of belligerency in America and declaring British neutrality. Other European countries, including Spain and France, soon followed suit, and this seemed a huge step toward formal recognition of Confederate independence. With their subsequent victory at Bull Run in July and their continued conviction that this would be a short war, Confederates were sanguine through much of 1861 that foreign recognition, even intervention, was just a matter of time.

Lincoln's minister to Great Britain, Charles Francis Adams, was instrumental in helping to soothe British nerves. Adams arrived in London the day of the queen's proclamation with firm instructions from Seward to cut off all interaction with the British as long as they continued to interfere in American affairs. Lincoln could not have chosen a better man to counter Seward's saber rattling than Adams, the son and grandson of two presidents. Thoughtful, judicious, and proficient in reading the British political climate, Adams worked to reaffirm the United States's relationship with Britain and convinced Lord Russell not to have any further interviews, informal or formal, with southern commissioners.

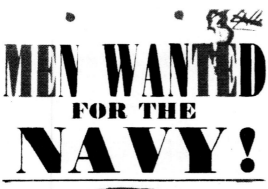

MEN WANTED FOR THE NAVY!

All able-bodied men not in the employment of the Army, will be enlisted into the Navy upon application at the Naval Rendezvous, on Craven Street, next door to the Printing Office.

H. K. DAVENPORT,
. Com'r. & Senior Naval Officer.

New Berne, N. C.,
Nov. 2d, 1863.

BOTH SIDES NEEDED MEN to serve in their navies, but the Confederacy was especially desperate for sailors. Despite intensive efforts at recruitment, conscription, and transfers from the army, the Confederate navy failed to attract enough sailors.

Adams's diplomatic skills would again be tested in November 1861 with the *Trent* Affair, but for the summer and early fall at least, England and the rest of Europe merely watched and waited.

The Confederate Navy

Meanwhile, Confederates busily developed another vital branch of their military: a navy. The Civil War would prove the strong interdependence of military operations on land and water. Waterways were essential to transportation, communication, and control of strategic locations. The Confederacy consisted of more than 3,500 nautical miles of coastline and more than 189 harbors. In addition, the South had miles and miles of inland waterways and extensive rivers. The Mississippi River, more than 1,000 nautical miles long, was the Confederacy's lifeline, flowing north to south from the border states of Kentucky and Missouri to the deep Delta states and the Gulf of Mexico. Changes in transportation, most notably the invention of the steamboat and armorclads, would make waterways crucial to war making.

Despite these facts, Jefferson Davis never was a strong advocate of the navy. Unable to appreciate the importance of sea power, convinced that manning a formidable fleet would be nearly impossible for the agricultural South, and confident, especially at first, that the war would be a short one, Davis reverted to a relic of the past: issuing letters of marque to privateers to prey on northern merchant ships. On April 17, two days after Lincoln's initial call for troops, Davis made his controversial pronouncement, which helped prompt the Union to establish a blockade. Letters of marque were meant to distinguish privateers from pirates and to give privateers legitimacy as agents of the Confederacy. International law had long permitted privateering, including the submission of captured ships and cargo to the judgment of a prize court in a friendly or neutral port, but these rules had not always been observed, and in 1856 the European powers signed a treaty called the Declaration of Paris to ban privateering. The United States refused to sign the treaty, and privateering remained a disputed international issue. On June 1, 1861, after England closed its ports to prizes brought in by either the North or the South, the United States suddenly sought to reopen negotiations to adhere to the Declaration of Paris. Even the threat of Confederate privateers hurt northern commerce, especially during the war's early months. Maritime insurance costs went up, and British freighters offered lower rates than northern ships.

Although Davis had little interest in developing a navy, he did appoint a strong naval advocate to be his secretary of the navy: Stephen Russell Mallory. Mallory, nearly fifty years old, was a moderate Democrat and former senator from Florida who had served as chair of the Senate Committee on Naval Affairs. Resourceful and imaginative, Mallory would prove the essential ingredient in creating a navy from practically nothing. Physically, he was unimpressive: contemporaries described him as red-faced, stumpy, "plethoric," and prone to "the highest living." Nor was he particularly popular with the public, the press, or many naval officers. He ran the department almost entirely on his own, acting as head administrator, chief naval strategist, and overseer of maritime and coastal operations. Yet, due to Mallory's tireless efforts, the Confederacy would have a navy, hardly as formidable as that of the United States, but a navy nonetheless, one that incorporated some of the newest innovations in water transportation and naval warfare available.

Mallory's greatest challenge as Confederate naval secretary was funding. He needed money to purchase and maintain ships, and he realized quickly that he would have to compete with the army for financial support. The army always gained more public and political support than the navy. Only Jefferson Davis's Richmond residence received less funding, and most able-bodied men—even those with some naval experience—preferred to serve on land rather than on water. Efforts to shift men from the army to the navy were unsuccessful: army commanders ignored transfer laws, and soldiers-turned-sailors deserted in high numbers. In 1864 the C.S. Navy reached its highest manpower level, just under 6,000 men and officers in the navy and the marines.

Civil War navies, like Civil War armies, reflected the changes brought on by the Industrial Revolution. During the 1850s, great advances in ship construction and armaments had been made. The steam engine, armored ships, and explorations into underwater warfare were just some of the developments

New Naval Technology

emerging at midcentury. These new inventions also affected naval strategy. Although the Confederacy lagged behind the Union in industrial might and technology, the Confederate navy was creative and resourceful, relying on new technologies to overcome numerical weaknesses. Water mines, torpedo boats, submarines, and ironclads were all tried and tested by the Confederacy. Not all were successful, and some, such as the submarine, proved deadly to their crews. Still, Mallory was convinced that new technologies in armored steamships, rifled guns, and underwater warfare would lessen the Confederacy's numerous disadvantages. England and France had already begun to experiment with ironclads—wooden ships fitted with iron plates and an iron ram. The offensive-minded Mallory, believing that these rams could do more than simply protect the South's coast, wanted to use such ships to cripple the Union's essentially wooden navy. The Confederate Congress agreed and appropriated $2 million for the purchase of ironclads in Europe. Mallory dispatched a special envoy, Lt. James H. North, overseas to buy ironclads. When the unimaginative North came home empty-handed, Mallory changed his strategy: if he could not buy ironclads abroad, he would build them at home. The question was: where?

His answer came soon after the capture of the Gosport Navy Yard near Norfolk, Virginia. The secession of Virginia gave the Confederacy Gosport, one of the largest and most modern shipyards in the country, stocked with arms, munitions, and boats. On the evening of April 20, just before abandoning the yard to Virginia militia, the U.S. commander ordered everything burned and the ships scuttled. The fires that glowed through the night shocked citizens in and around Norfolk. New York newspaper editor Horace Greeley, equally stunned, labeled the abandonment of Gosport "the most shameful, cowardly, disastrous performance that stains the annals of the American Navy." In fact, all was not destroyed, and the Confederates worked quickly to salvage what they could from the ruins.

The CSS *Virginia*   One of the ships retrieved from the ruins of Gosport was the five-year-old steam frigate *Merrimack,* which had been in dry dock awaiting repairs when it was burned and scuttled. Rescued by Virginia soldiers, the ship's hull and engine were found to be in remarkably good shape, so much so that Confederates began in June 1861 to convert the ship to an ironclad. Furnished with an armor-plated casemate that contained ten heavy guns and an iron ram on its bow, the newly named CSS *Virginia* was the first ship of its kind. Its sides were sloped so that projectiles would glance off its surface, and except for the casemate, most of the vessel stayed submerged below the waterline. Time would tell how much damage the ironclad could wreak on the Union navy.

Confederate Naval Troubles   Mallory would have his ironclad, but the Confederacy still lacked many essential ingredients to form an effective navy. In particular, there was a severe lack of skilled workmen—blacksmiths, smelters, and mechanics—who were crucial to building and maintaining a fleet. Although the South was rich in such raw materials as lumber, turpentine, and iron, transporting these items to coastal ports was problematic. The army needed iron too, so again Mallory faced major constraints in creating a legitimate navy and the industry necessary to support it. In addition, the Confederate navy, like the southern armies, was also hampered by states' rights. When the war began, many southern states organized their own navies. The Confederate navy was supposed to absorb each of these state navies, but the problem of state versus central control was never entirely solved. Finding competent commanders was another important problem, and although some officers defected from the U.S. Navy to the South in 1861, more trained personnel were needed. On March 16, 1861, the Confederate Congress authorized the creation of a naval academy in Richmond, although it was not actually established until 1863.

Mallory did not give up on European help. In addition to sending Lieutenant North abroad, he dispatched Lt. James Dunwoody Bullock to England, seeking cruisers. Bullock, a well-organized and able navy officer, quickly realized that building ships was more practical than trying to buy them. Using great secrecy, changing names, and faking documents, Bullock enlisted the help of private investors and British shipbuilders, who were forbidden from arming the ships until they were entirely finished. The South soon had new ships built in Europe but officially commissioned in Confederate service.

Raphael Semmes

One of the men who eventually commanded one of these European vessels was Raphael Semmes, a thirty-five-year veteran of the navy who was anxious to serve as a commissioned officer with a commissioned ship for the Confederacy. By July 1861 Semmes had his ship, the CSS *Sumter,* and had captured eight Union merchant ships carrying valuable cargoes of sugar, but his daring exploits also brought danger. Pursued by six U.S. warships, the *Sumter* reached Gibraltar with its engines overtaxed and its hull leaking. The following summer, Semmes took command of one of the freshly completed vessels built in England for the Confederacy, the CSS *Alabama*.

The U.S. Navy

The United States was also enlarging its navy and investigating new technology, including ironclads. Although the Union had clear advantages in manpower and numbers of ships, it needed enormously more of both, especially when, on April 19, 1861, Lincoln declared a blockade of the rebelling southern states. Initially, Lincoln moved cautiously for two days after Davis issued a call for privateers. He first considered closing southern ports, but when it was clear that the British would view such an act negatively, perhaps even provoking them to intervene on the part of the South, Lincoln opted for the blockade. This, too, was risky. There was first a question of legality: How could the United States, refusing to recognize the legitimacy of the Confederacy, blockade its own coastline? Second, how could the U.S. Navy establish what international law deemed an "effective" blockade on the vast southern coast?

In 1861 the U.S. Navy had ninety ships on paper, including forty steamers and fifty sailing vessels. But most sailing ships were outmoded, and many steamers were unprepared for action. A navy that was barely adequate in peacetime suddenly looked extremely inadequate during war, especially in a war against a foe five times larger than France, with thousands of miles of seacoast, rivers, and tributaries. There was also a need for more sailors. Although

THE UNION NAVY, like the Confederate one. struggled to fill its ranks with able-bodied sailors, despite the fact that life on a ship was relatively safer and healthier than life in the army. This photograph shows sailors relaxing on the deck of the Union's famed ironclad. the USS *Monitor*.

fewer men left the U.S. Navy than the U.S. Army to join the Confederacy, naval recruiters competing with those of the army never attracted as many volunteers. Of those sailors who remained in the service, most were trained for deep-water service and were ill prepared for shore or coastal responsibilities. Further, many high-ranking administrators were too elderly for active duty, and the U.S. Naval Academy, located at Annapolis, Maryland, was vulnerable to attack. To make matters worse, U.S. Navy squadrons were scattered across the globe, some as far away as Japan and the East Indies. It would take weeks, even months, to bring these ships home.

Gideon Welles   The practical and shrewd Gideon Welles served as Lincoln's secretary of the navy. Fifty-eight years old when appointed to Lincoln's cabinet, Welles was a former Democrat who had experience as a Connecticut newspaper editor and postmaster but little expertise in naval affairs, except for a short stint as chief of the Naval Bureau of Provisions and Clothing during the Mexican War. Fortunately, Welles was aided by a navy veteran, Gustavus V. Fox, who proved an excellent and energetic administrator. As assistant secretary of the navy, Fox was instrumental in strengthening the fleet and planning some of its most successful expeditions.

Quickly, Welles and Fox began to initiate significant changes. Talented ship designers such as John Ericsson, Charles Ellet Jr., and Samuel Pook were put to work building and converting hundreds of ships for battle. It is estimated that by 1865 the Union navy had placed in action more than 600 vessels of all kinds.

Although the Confederacy took the first step toward developing ironclads, the North also moved to develop this new technology. In June 1861 the Quartermaster Department, under orders from Winfield Scott, began to build a river squadron of ironclad gunboats, equipped and manned by the navy. By mid-October, the United States had constructed its first vessel, the *St. Louis*. Other ironclads would quickly follow, totaling about sixty-five by war's end. This number included the *Monitor*, designed and built by Ericsson in early 1862, and the Ellet Ram fleet, a group of speedy river steamers converted to rams in the spring of 1862. The western river squadron also consisted of seven newly armored gunboats, under the command of Capt. Andrew Hull Foote, that was used innovatively for joint army–navy operations in the Western Theater.

The U.S. Navy also grew in manpower from an estimated 7,600 sailors in 1861 to about 118,000 men and officers in 1865. Like their counterparts on land, the individuals who served in the Civil War navies were predominately young, white, single males with limited military experience, but unlike army regiments that drew from the same state and community, naval crews were more heterogeneous. Where 75 percent of Union soldiers were native born, only 55 percent of sailors were, and the immigrant contingent included a hefty 20 percent born in Ireland. Sailors from various backgrounds, ethnicities, and races lived in extremely tight quarters for extended periods of time, cut off from larger society. Life on a ship assumed its own separate existence. Racism and bigotry were of course just as common among Civil War sailors as among Civil War soldiers. Many ships were segregated, with blacks excluded from firing guns, and often beaten and discriminated against in other ways by their mates. Nevertheless, due to manpower shortages and because operating ships depended on close communal cooperation, men of different backgrounds were compelled to work together. Black sailors enjoyed greater equity of pay, provisions, and medical care than did black soldiers. In fact, all Union sailors had fresher and more food, better medical care, and generally less chance of death or illness than did Union soldiers serving on land. Many men called joining the navy "coming clean," believing that shipboard life was bound to be less onerous than camp life and marching in the army, and that their risk of death would be reduced.

The Union Navy Grows and Expands

Yet, the U.S. Navy struggled to attract enough new recruits. Attempts were made to raise its bounties, and recruiting officers emphasized the possibilities of sharing "prizes" seized from the Confederates, promises rarely delivered. On the rivers, many sailors developed considerable skill in seizing valuable cotton from southern civilians for resale. Some men joined the navy to avoid the army draft, and other soldiers transferred from the army to the navy, although as Gideon Welles complained in July 1862, "They [the transfers] are generally not of very good character and of little benefit to the service." Late in the war, the Union navy became so desperate for manpower that it resorted to using Confederate prisoners to fill its ranks. There were various reasons why it was so difficult to draw good men into the navy. Although large-scale naval engagements were few, when they did occur, casualty rates were much higher

Problems Recruiting Sailors

than those that occurred on land. When a ship went down, so did its crew. Sailors most feared exploding boilers and enemy mines, which led to terrible deaths with little hope of escape. Civil War naval warfare also offered fewer opportunities to demonstrate individual bravery in battle. There were climactic and heroic duels on the water, to be sure, but the common Civil War sailor rarely shared in the battle laurels; most of the credit went to the ship's commander and the ship itself.

Although food was plentiful and danger relatively less than that faced by the armies, everyday conditions at sea were still difficult. The bowels of wooden and ironclad vessels were hot, cramped, damp, and rat infested. Manning the blockade was particularly monotonous and unglamorous duty: sailors filled their days scrubbing the decks, making repairs, drilling, and taking target practice. In their free time, they sang, drank, wrote letters, gambled, prayed, and complained about the long weeks at sea, growing ever more isolated and depressed with the passing months. Frequently, whole crews broke into fistfights, which the sailors called "skylarking," and the crews of several ships staged full-scale mutinies.

Until August 1862 the harsh sailor life was relieved by two glasses of whiskey each day, which made the navy especially attractive to alcoholics, and when the navy attempted to forbid this practice, an energetic bootleg trade replaced the official rations. "Jack Ratlin's Lament," written by seaman James Eggo, laid out the grievances of many Union sailors:

> But the greatest cause of all my woe, I am just about to mention,
> It's another abolition scheme, of their black heart's invention.
> You know that day by day we drank our Uncle's health in whiskey,
> Which kept us our weary way, contented, gay, and frisky.
> But those d____d abolitionists to gratify their passion,
> Not content with freeing contrabands, they've stopped the spirit ration;
> But if they'll just take my advice, though they may treat it slightly,
> They'll give the sailors back their grog, give the niggers hell or Hayti.

Battle of Hatteras Inlet

One of the Union navy's first offensive expeditions was a *combined operation*—that is, using both army and navy personnel—that targeted the Hatteras Inlet on the North Carolina coast, a gaping hole in the blockade and a haven for Confederate runners and privateers. On August 26, 1861, seven warships commanded by Adm. Silas H. Stringham left Hampton Roads, Virginia. Three days later, outgunned and poorly protected from the intensive naval bombardment, two Confederate forts guarding the inlet yielded 670 prisoners and 35 cannon. This expedition, showcasing the power of naval guns over shore batteries, enabled the U.S. Navy to seal off the sounds of North Carolina to privateers and blockade runners and caused a near panic on the eastern coast of the state.

Battle of Port Royal

Six weeks later, the Union navy gained an even more dramatic victory at Port Royal, South Carolina. In late October 1861 a fleet of 75 vessels, 12,000 infantrymen, and 600 marines under Flag Officer Samuel F. du Pont was dispatched from Hampton Roads, bound for the South Carolina coast. On the morning of November 7, du Pont's steam-powered gunboats attacked two forts guarding Port Royal sound, and by early afternoon the Confederates had surrendered one of the finest natural harbors on the eastern seaboard. The battle of Port Royal resulted in relatively few human casualties—31 Federals and 66 Confederates—but the victory gave the North an important coaling, refitting, and supply station to maintain the blockade and to provide a strategic location from which to launch attacks on other coastal cities.

At about the same time, an international incident revived rebel hopes for British intervention. On November 8, 1861, near Havana, Cuba, the British mail steamer *Trent* was stopped by the Union warship *San Jacinto* commanded by Capt. Charles Wilkes. Wilkes, acting entirely on his own recognizance, was hot on the trail of two Confederate emissaries who were rumored to be aboard the British vessel. After ordering two shots fired across the *Trent*'s bow, he sent an armed boarding party to search the ship for the men. Wilkes found his prize: James Murray Mason and John Slidell (with his wife and four children) were indeed on board. Both men, prominent and powerful southerners with a long history in politics, were bound for London and Paris to replace the Yancey commission and to seek English and French recognition of the Confederacy. The Union boarding party led Mason and Slidell off the *Trent* at bayonet point and allowed the ship to resume its voyage. The *San Jacinto* then turned north and on November 24 arrived in Boston harbor, where Mason and Slidell were imprisoned at Fort Warren.

The *Trent* Affair

Almost overnight, Wilkes became a Union hero, despite the fact that his conduct was wholly unauthorized and that his actions were readily comparable to the hated British practice of impressment. Nonetheless, the arrest of the two Confederate commissioners bolstered Union morale. Even Lincoln, who seemed cheered by the event, made no effort to censure Wilkes. There were eulogies in Congress, and the House of Representatives passed a resolution heralding Wilkes for his "brave, adroit and patriotic conduct." Across the ocean, however, the outraged British demanded immediate release of the prisoners and prepared for war. One British newspaper blamed a "feeble confused" Lincoln and that "firebrand" Seward for deliberately provoking "a quarrel with all of Europe, in that sprit of senseless egotism that induces the Americans, with their dwarf fleet & shapeless mass of incoherent squads they call an army, to fancy themselves the equals of France by land and of Great Britain by sea." The British dispatched some 3,000 troops to Canada and readied a naval fleet. For a few anxious weeks, it appeared that Mason and Slidell, through no direct action of their own, would bring more than Confederate recognition from Europe; their capture might signal war against the Union.

Eventually, cooler heads prevailed on both sides of the Atlantic. In the British government, Prince Albert, who died tragically in the midst of the turmoil, was among those urging caution. The costs of sufficiently reinforcing Canada were prohibitive, and the long-term dangers of the American navy and army were threatening. Even Secretary of State Seward, seemingly so instrumental in stirring tensions with the British, sought a peaceful resolution. Following the suggestion of a British member of Parliament, he proposed releasing the prisoners and, while admitting no wrongdoing, praising the British for upholding the doctrines of international law. The proposal diffused the controversy. Mason and Slidell were released and were soon safely en route for London; Great Britain and the United States breathed collective sighs of relief. For the Confederacy, on the other hand, the *Trent* affair marked the closest any European country came to intervening formally in the American conflict.

As 1861 drew to a close, New York diarist and lawyer George Templeton Strong reflected on the past twelve months: "Poor old 1861 just going. It has been a gloomy year of trouble and disaster. I should be glad of its departure, were it not that 1862 is likely to be no better." Strong was right. The war had just begun; its violence and destruction would continue for three more long years.

CHAPTER 4

Discovering the Scope of War: 1861–1862

Newspapers called it "the hardest fight yet on the American continent." One participant even insisted that it had been "the severest battle since Waterloo." From the perspective of the private soldier, it had been "a might mean-fowt fight," and years later a combatant still recalled it as "one of the stubbornest and bloodiest battles of the war." Americans reading their newspapers in August 1861 looked at each other quizzically: Where on earth was Wilson's Creek? Some 1,300 Union men had been killed, wounded, or listed as missing there, and 1,230 Confederates had met the same fates. That was nearly 25 percent of the combined armies, which made it, for its size, one of the most deadly battles of the century.

Wilson's Creek meandered through southwest Missouri, near the town of Springfield. The battle fought there proved to be just one of many life-and-death struggles in obscure, out-of-the-way places that no one in Washington or Richmond had anticipated in April 1861. The geographical sprawl of the fighting became one of the major surprises of this unplanned war. It stretched eventually far into the western territories, and few states, even those north of the Ohio River, escaped all violence and bloodshed. Equally important, besides the staggering extent and degree of the mayhem, the war turned topsy-turvy the entire structure of American life. It had been a ramshackle structure in any event, uncontrolled by government bureaucracies or organizations, a society that, unlike

THE BATTLE OF WILSON'S CREEK, fought near Springfield, Missouri, in August 1861, gave Americans their first hint of the geographical scope of the war. This contemporary sketch of the battle depicts Gen. Nathaniel Lyon as he led a regiment of Iowa soldiers in a counterattack. Lyon reportedly waved his hat and called out, "Come on, my brave boys, I will lead you forward!" Within seconds, he fell from his horse mortally wounded.

the great European states, was not built for war. So from the daily lives of civilians, to the organization of governments, to economic and diplomatic policies, to assumptions about science and technology, to people's very understanding of why the war was being fought, everything in America changed radically. The lives people had led and the assumptions they had made would never be the same.

Border Strategy in the West Militarily, the war expanded far beyond the anticipated seat of fighting in Maryland and Virginia in 1861–1862. As the North mustered its troops for invasion and the South prepared to defend itself, they did so not only in the vicinity of the national capitals, but across the entire breadth of the divided nation. The bulk of the early fighting would be conducted in the slaveholding border states of Kentucky, Tennessee, and Missouri, crucial states for both sides to control. Two of those states—Missouri and Kentucky—had not seceded, and the divisions between secessionists and unionists ran deep in all three. The results of the fighting there would go a long way toward defining military, political, economic, and diplomatic objectives and options for the remainder of the war.

Early strategy along the border was not complex. Union armies made a show of strength that was intended to convince rebels that secession was foolish and war futile, but they had orders to respect the personal and property rights—including slaves—of all citizens in hopes that such restraint would persuade rebels to return quietly to the fold. Confederate armies, for their part, established a passive *cordon defense* along the border, with troops concentrated at key strategic points in Tennessee, Kentucky, and Missouri.

It all sounds very placid and civilized, but things did not stay that way for long. Even before these strategies were fully implemented, the situation turned nasty in Missouri. Rich in both agriculture and manufacturing, Missouri stuck to the Union during the secession crisis, but the loyalties of many people remained up for grabs. Pro-Confederate sentiment increased in Missouri after Lincoln's call for volunteers, if not to the point of endorsing secession, then at least with a marked determination to remain neutral. Governor Claiborne Jackson and the state legislature shared that view, but both secessionists and antisecessionists recruited and organized troops within the state.

War in Missouri

Hopes for neutrality dimmed when a battalion of U.S. Army regulars, reinforced by four regiments of Union volunteers—about 10,000 men in all—forced an encampment of 700 pro-Confederate militia to surrender in St. Louis on May 10, 1861. A day of rioting and bloodshed followed, not unlike the attack on a Massachusetts regiment marching through Baltimore several weeks earlier, as mobs attacked the Union troops with stones and clods of earth. The soldiers, answering with muskets, killed more than two dozen civilians, and the state exploded. Bands of rebel home guards, operating essentially as guerrillas, attacked unionist neighbors and destroyed railroads and telegraph lines for the remainder of that spring and summer.

German immigrants became a particular target of the rebels, not only because most of them were unionists, but also because many of the Union troops in St. Louis were German. The foreign-born population of Missouri, both German and Irish, outnumbered the state's southern-born residents by 1860, and most of them lived in St. Louis. Nativist animosity ran high, and rumors that German soldiers, "drunk with beer and reeking of sauerkraut," had mowed down citizens during the riots poisoned public attitudes toward the "blood thirsty Dutch" and the Lincoln government. One outraged woman confided to her diary, "Think of it! The German rabble, composed of soldiers of the lower element of the city, recruited from the saloons and dives . . . taking as prisoner the sons and husbands of the leading families of St. Louis!"

Missouri's distress brought neighboring Iowa and Kansas into the fray. As terrified Missouri unionists fled to those two states, men flocked to defend their borders. Guerrilla raids across their southern border alerted Iowans to the dangerous potential for a genuine invasion. Consequently, Iowa militia occasionally entered Missouri to reinforce Union troops. However, that was nothing compared to the reaction in the new state of Kansas, which had finally joined the Union in January 1861. Antislavery Kansans, who had grown accustomed to bloodshed during the previous half-decade, saw the war as a contest between "two systems of civilization for the mastery of the continent," and they rejoiced that the issue would now "be settled by the sword."

Iowa and Kansas Respond

MISSOURI AND ARKANSAS witnessed the most significant early fighting in the trans-Mississippi during 1861–1862. The map shows the principal towns and geographical features mentioned in this chapter's discussion of those conflicts, especially at Wilson's Creek and Pea Ridge. Both states were also ravaged by guerrilla warfare, Missouri from the earliest days of the war, Arkansas by the spring of 1862.

Many *jayhawkers*—a nickname for Kansans that was rapidly becoming synonymous with marauders and robbers—believed that the best way to defend their state was to give Missourians "something to do at home." Men such as James Lane, James Montgomery, and Charles R. Jennison had been staging raids into Missouri to liberate slaves since late 1860. Rebel guerrillas retaliated with occasional forays into Kansas, but most of the ensuing havoc engulfed Missouri. With jayhawkers pouring over the border and Confederate guerrillas still prowling the central and western parts of the state, beatings, robberies, and ambushes became commonplace. By comparison, easterners had no idea of what war meant.

Missouri's pro-Confederate legislature joined the frenzy by authorizing former governor and Mexican War hero Sterling Price to organize a "state guard." At fifty-two years, the imposing (250 pounds) "Pap," as the white-haired Price was affectionately known to his men, stood tall and carried himself with a dignity that inspired respect. He would be one of the central figures in this trans-Mississippi war. Opposing him—a contrast in virtually every way—stood Gen. Nathaniel Lyon, a militant freesoiler and professional soldier who had commanded Union troops during the St. Louis "massacre" and now led all Union forces in Missouri. Lyon shattered any remaining thoughts of Missouri neutrality on June 11 by declaring war on the rebels: "Rather than concede to the State of Missouri for one single instant the right to dictate to my government in any matter however important, I would see . . . every man, woman, and child in the State, dead and buried!"

Divided Missouri

During the next few weeks, Lyon conducted a series of precise, lightning strikes against the rebels that gave him control of the state capital at Jefferson City and forced Price southward to Springfield. Price, still scurrying to assemble an effective force, found himself hamstrung by the refusal of Jefferson Davis to order Confederate troops into Missouri. Davis maintained that he could not legally send Confederate soldiers into a state that had not seceded, but having learned that Price and Governor Jackson had tried to negotiate an armed truce with the Union forces in June, Davis also distrusted Missourians.

Finally relenting, Davis allowed a tough but soft-spoken old Texas Ranger named Ben McCulloch to lead 5,700 troops into the state from Arkansas. With Price as his second in command, McCulloch added the 9,000-man Missouri State Guard to his own force of Texans, Louisianans, and Arkansans and marched toward Springfield. These were the Confederates who clashed with Lyon's men at Wilson's Creek, or Oak Hills as the Confederates called it, on August 10. Lyon attacked the rebels with only 5,400 troops, including Kansas and Iowa volunteers alongside his regulars. In an exhausting, five-hour, see-saw action, the rebels prevailed.

This second major battle of the war may not have been another Waterloo, but it did resemble Bull Run. The men were mostly farmers with meager training as soldiers. McCulloch called Price's home guard "badly organized," "ill-disciplined," and "badly armed." Some Federals donned gray uniforms, and thousands of men, especially among the rebels, wore only their work-a-day farm clothes. The victorious Confederates, like those at Manassas, were too tired and disorganized to pursue the routed enemy. The courageous Lyon, perhaps the most able Union commander in the West at the time, fell mortally wounded, a bullet through his heart, while seeking to rally his men in the thick of the fighting. Price, when less seriously wounded under similar circumstances, complained jokingly to a staff officer before learning of Lyon's fate, "That isn't fair; if I were as slim as Lyon that fellow would have missed me entirely."

The rebels pressed their advantage for several months in Missouri. When the disorganized Federals retreated more than 100 miles northeast to Rolla, Missouri, McCulloch returned to Arkansas, but "Pap" Price remained to defend Confederate claims to the state. Gen. John C. Frémont, the former Republican presidential candidate who commanded the Union's Western Department from St. Louis, responded to the defeat and to the continuing threat of rebel guerrillas by declaring martial law. He also emancipated all rebel-owned slaves, although a cautious Lincoln soon reversed this measure and eventually removed Frémont from command as a consequence. Meanwhile, Price, after capturing and briefly holding Lexington, Missouri, assembled his troops that October in Neosho, where Governor Jackson and a secessionist rump of the state legislature passed an ordinance of secession. With a new unionist legislature and a governor already installed at Jefferson City, this act may have seemed like a bit of bravado, but another rebel battlefield victory on November 7 at Belmont, in the southeastern corner of the state, caused consternation in the North. "Our troops have suffered a bad defeat," acknowledged a Chicago newspaper. "The rebels have been elated and emboldened while our troops have been depressed, if not discouraged."

War in Kentucky   Events in Missouri begot Kentucky. Control of the Bluegrass state, birthplace of both Abraham Lincoln and Jefferson Davis, became a point of personal pride for the two presidents, but both, too, appreciated the state's strategic value. With its northern border formed by the Ohio River, Kentucky provided both sides with a buffer against the invasion of more interior states. Federal occupation of Kentucky would leave Tennessee, arguably the most important manufacturing and food-producing state in the Confederacy, terribly exposed. Rebel control would put Confederate troops within easy striking distance of Cincinnati, Indianapolis, even Chicago. "I think to lose Kentucky is nearly the same as to lose the whole game," declared Lincoln. "Kentucky gone, we cannot hold Missouri, nor, as I think, Maryland." But Kentucky, like Missouri, had not seceded from the Union, and many of its inhabitants, like many Missourians, hoped to maintain their neutrality by warding off "invaders" from both North and South.

President Davis, seeing the necessity of prompt action in Kentucky, had allowed Confederate troops to occupy Columbus, Kentucky, on the Mississippi River since early September. He then permitted Gen. Albert Sidney Johnston, commander of the Western Department, to establish his headquarters at Bowling Green. This move also gave Johnston, a native Kentuckian whom most people considered the South's best general, control of the Louisville and Nashville Railroad. The thirty-five-year army veteran, with only 40,000 men to defend a line that stretched from the Appalachian Mountains to the Mississippi River, would need that railroad.

At the same time that Johnston was establishing his cordon defense in southern Kentucky, the Federals were positioning themselves to capture the state's most valuable assets, its rivers. Union troops at Paducah and Smithland already had a good grip on the lower Ohio River. Of more immediate concern were the Mississippi, the Cumberland, and the Tennessee rivers that could provide Union armies with water highways deep into Confederate territory. The Mississippi, forming Kentucky's western border, ran all the way to the Gulf of Mexico. The Cumberland ran south through the breadth of the state before meandering eastward to Nashville, Tennessee. The Tennessee ran northward through the state from Florence, Alabama, to enter the Ohio River at Paducah. One of the main goals of Union strategy in the West from late 1861 would be to gain control of these and other rivers by capturing the Confederate forts that guarded them and deploying heavily armed naval forces to patrol their waters. Their first targets were Forts Henry and Donelson, which protected the Tennessee and Cumberland rivers, respectively, along Tennessee's northern border. **Importance of Western Rivers**

The task of capturing Forts Henry and Donelson fell to thirty-nine-year-old Gen. Ulysses S. Grant. A West Point graduate and Mexican War veteran, Grant had quit the army in 1854 to be a farmer. He had failed at that, as well as in several subsequent business ventures, before resuming the profession of arms when the war started. It was Grant whom the rebels had defeated at the battle of Belmont, amid rumors of his old fondness for liquor. Seeking redemption, Grant welcomed orders to move against Forts Henry and Donelson. Fifty-six-year-old Flag Officer Andrew H. Foote, a taciturn Connecticut Yankee who abhorred both slavery and whiskey, assisted him. Foote reinforced the movement of Grant's ground troops with seven steam-powered *gunboats*, four of them ironclads. This sort of combined operation, involving cooperation between the army and navy, came to typify military operations in the West, where many of the campaigns were conducted along strategically important rivers. **Forts Henry and Donelson**

Grant achieved an easy victory against his first target, Fort Henry. Both Henry and Donelson were earthen fortifications, constructed from the labor of slaves and soldiers, but the uncompleted Fort Henry was flooded and sorely undermanned when Grant attacked it with 15,000 men on February 6, 1862. His infantry became bogged down in the muddy terrain, but a bombardment by Foote's gunboats soon convinced the 100-man garrison to surrender with what remained of its fifteen heavy guns. The elated Foote sent a portion of his flotilla 150 miles southward into northern Alabama. Along the way, naval gunners destroyed a railroad bridge, disabled some rebel gunboats, and confiscated much war material. Hundreds of civilians fled in terror as the warships approached, although federal reports emphasized the many unionist citizens who crowded the river bank to cheer and hail "their national flag with an enthusiasm there was no mistaking." The Federals had penetrated Confederate territory in dramatic fashion.

THE USS *ST. LOUIS*, launched at Carondelet, Missouri, in October 1861, was the first Union ironclad. It carried 251 officers and men and was armed with 11 cannon. Warships like this one played a crucial role in the Union's ability to advance along western waters and capture important Confederate port towns. The *St. Louis* was sunk in action on the Yazoo River in July 1863.

When the gunboats returned to Fort Henry on February 12, Grant advanced eastward toward Fort Donelson. His command, which had been reinforced to 27,000 men, marched 10 miles directly overland, while Foote's gunboats chugged back north to the Ohio River and thence entered the Cumberland. Donelson presented a more formidable obstacle than Henry. Its heavier guns mauled Foote's flotilla, and 21,000 infantrymen—most of them sent from Bowling Green when Johnston decided to abandon that town—easily repulsed Grant's initial ground assaults. Then the weather turned bitterly cold. A blizzard swept over the region, and nighttime temperatures dropped to 10 degrees. Soldiers on both sides suffered, but especially the more exposed Union troops, most of whom had discarded their blankets and winter coats during fair weather on the march from Henry.

On the third day of the siege, February 15, a surprise attack by the rebels opened a gaping hole in Grant's thin, 5-mile-long line. Gen. John B. Floyd, a lawyer, planter, former governor of Virginia, and senior commander at Donelson, could have evacuated his garrison to Nashville, 70 miles away, by exploiting the breakthrough, but the opportunity passed while he and his two senior officers, generals Gideon Pillow and Simon B. Buckner, argued about it. When the Federals restored their line, the necessity of Confederate surrender seemed imminent. Floyd, who had been one of Lee's bickering subordinates in western

Virginia, and Pillow—another lawyer and politician—feared execution if captured, so they escaped to safety with a few thousand men across the Cumberland on the only available river transports. Col. Nathan Bedford Forrest led the garrison's cavalry regiment to safety.

That left Buckner, a native Kentuckian and West Point graduate, to surrender the fort. If he expected generous terms from Grant, an old army friend, Buckner was disappointed, for Grant demanded "unconditional" and immediate surrender. Foote had insisted on the same terms at Fort Henry, but the newspapers "puffed" the capitulation of Donelson, which netted nearly 15,000 prisoners, 20,000 muskets, 65 cannon, and thousands of horses. Playing on the initials of his name, the press started to call U. S. Grant *Unconditional Surrender* Grant.

Union Gains in the Heartland

The Union victory stunned the Confederate nation, which had been victorious on most other fronts. Not only was all of Kentucky lost (Columbus was evacuated on February 20), but suddenly, too, western and central Tennessee lay exposed, and beyond that the northern portions of Mississippi, Alabama, and Georgia. The Federals had penetrated the Confederate heartland, with its rich agricultural, mining, and industrial resources and valuable railroads. Western railroads would henceforth be as important as rivers to the U.S. advance, which now threatened machine shops, foundries, ordnance works, powder mills, and the manufacture of military accouterments in Memphis and Nashville and possibly, in a very short time, even Montgomery, Atlanta, and Macon.

In Tennessee, many citizens of Nashville fled in panic. Governor Isham Harris and the state legislature scurried to Memphis. Without a shot being fired, the rebels abandoned the second most important city in the Western Theater (after New Orleans) and a state capital. Along with Nashville went a vital railroad junction, an army arsenal, two gunpowder mills, and scores of factories, many of which had produced cannon, muskets, percussion caps, saddles, swords, and uniforms. Equally important, by abandoning the enormously productive farming region of central Tennessee, the Confederacy lost potentially tons of foodstuffs and tens of thousands of livestock. Ironically, only eastern Tennessee, the region of the state most loyal to the Union, remained under Confederate rule.

War in Far West

As widespread as fighting had become across the upper South, the Confederate government was intent, if need be, on spreading it even farther. For one thing, the rebels yearned to control the territory taken from Mexico in 1848. The goldfields of California, Nevada, and Colorado also beckoned, and if the Confederates could claim even a portion of the Pacific Coast, they would create an imposing nation indeed, one that would stretch an already overextended Union naval blockade even thinner. Old filibusters continued to dream about expansion through Central America and the Caribbean. Without the "Puritans and the Devil" to curb them, crowed a South Carolina newspaper, the entire "Gulf country" could be added to the Confederacy. A Georgia newspaper predicted early in 1861, "Then will the proudest nations of the earth come to woo and worship at the shrine of our imperial Confederacy."

But Mexico and Cuba would have to wait. The Confederacy's first "imperial" objective would be the "Golden West," and many people in the territories of New Mexico, Utah, and Colorado were inclined to join the new nation. Colorado had a small number of secessionists, but that minority—about 7,500—mobilized quickly and threatened to seize Union forts in the southern part of the territory. Mormon-controlled Utah, if not keen on joining the rebels, at least would not support the Union. The Mormons, longtime targets of persecution in the United States, had always felt like outcasts, especially after 1857 when the government had sent a military expedition into Utah to put down a reported Mormon rebellion. Ultimately the Latter-Day Saints were content to curse both North and South. Their leader, Brigham Young, spoke for them: "I am no abolitionist, neither am I a pro-slavery man; I hate some of their principles and especially some of their conduct, as I do the gates of hell."

Few people doubted the Confederate sympathies of New Mexico, at least not in the southern part of the territory. This was also the more important half, the one adjacent to southern California, and when the territorial legislature at Santa Fe balked at joining the Confederacy, prosecessionists held a convention in March 1861 to pledge allegiance to the rebel government. By August, emboldened by the arrival of Col. John R. Baylor and 350 Texans, they planned to reorganize the southern half into a separate territory of Arizona.

Still, conquering the Far West was a tall order. The region was enormous, and hostile Native Americans threatened the operations of both Union and Confederate forces. Many Texans had voted to join the Confederacy because the U.S. government had failed to protect them against marauding tribes, and the situation only worsened in 1861 as the United States, underestimating the strategic significance of the territories, surrendered or abandoned most of its western forts. The absence of armed authority encouraged western tribes to escalate their raids on largely defenseless ranches, especially in Confederate Arizona and Texas, to rustle horses, cattle, and sheep. White settlers had been encroaching on their domain and disrupting their way of life for a generation. Now, with the white men squaring off against each other, these Indians struck for revenge. They attacked small detachments of soldiers, supply trains, and mail couriers, too. Indeed, during the first few months of the war, Indians killed more Confederate troops than did the Federals.

New Mexico Campaign

The rebels struck first in this season of uncertainty. Gen. Henry H. Sibley, a hard-drinking Louisianan with a chin that looked like a block of granite, convinced Jefferson Davis that he could secure New Mexico and provide a solid base from which to turn west toward California. The forty-seven-year-old West Point graduate and Mexican War veteran had spent most of the 1850s in frontier service. His experience fighting Plains Indians had even inspired him to design a tent for the army—known thereafter as a *Sibley tent*—modeled after a Sioux wigwam. In early January 1862, he set out with his Army of New Mexico—consisting of nearly 4,000 Texans—to conquer the Southwest.

Only Col. Edward R. S. Canby, whose military experience closely mirrored Sibley's career, stood in the way. Canby commanded Fort Craig, an adobe fortification with about 3,800 U.S. troops on the northern edge of Arizona territory. He had a core of army regulars, but most of his men were volunteer militia from New Mexico. Led by the likes of Col. Christopher "Kit" Carson, the famous mountaineer and scout, many of these men—like most of Sibley's army—had more combat experience than did the green troops then grappling with each other east of the Mississippi. At the very least, these westerners had engaged in sporadic fighting against bands of Apache, Kiowa, Navajo, and Comanche. Yet, like the easterners, they remained undisciplined and poorly armed.

These weaknesses betrayed themselves on February 21, 1862, in the battle of Val Verde (Spanish for "Green Valley"), the largest Civil War battle in the Far West. Fought 6 miles north of Fort Craig in a 5-mile-long, 2-mile-wide oasis of grass and cottonwood trees, the affair began almost haphazardly with early morning skirmishing along the icy Rio Grande. Neither side presented a very uniform appearance, and the rebels in particular bore a motley array of weapons, including old squirrel guns, machetes, and Bowie knives. Much of the fighting was hand to hand, although artillery also ripped large holes in attacking lines. "The field was covered with blood, horses, torn and dismembered limbs, and heads separated from bodies," reported a Union soldier, "a spectacle that was horrible." The turning point came when Col. Tom Green, a middle-aged Virginian who had settled in Texas during the 1830s, drove the Federals back into Fort Craig with his Texas cavalry. All told, the Federals lost 263 killed and wounded, and the Confederates 187, but the Union also destroyed nearly 1,000 Confederate horses and mules, a heavy blow for a mostly cavalry force traversing arid terrain.

Sibley had retired to his tent during the fight, complaining of heat exhaustion, although rumors said that the "Walking Whiskey Wagon," as he was known, had been just plain drunk. Deciding that Canby's whipped garrison posed no further threat, and running far too low on provisions to risk a lengthy siege of Fort Craig, Sibley continued the march into New Mexico. He entered Santa Fe unopposed on March 1 and claimed Albuquerque four days later, but then the campaign turned sour. Sibley's army suffered crippling loses in men, animals, and supplies in late March while fighting against tough Union volunteers from the Colorado goldfields—known as Pike's Peakers—at Apache Pass and Glorieta Pass. The latter engagement was something of a tactical victory for Sibley, yet it all but ended Confederate hopes for a southwestern empire. The depleted army tumbled back through Albuquerque, where, in mid-April, Canby's men joined the Pike's Peakers in pursuit.

With the Federals sniping at its heels, a hungry, thirsty, demoralized, and bone-weary Army of New Mexico, by then reduced to 2,000 men, straggled back to San Antonio. A long line of wrecked or burned wagons, dead horses and mules, and discarded equipment and personal items littered its path through the desert. "Except for geographical position, the Territory of New Mexico is not worth a quarter of the blood and treasure expended in its conquest," a disgusted Sibley reported to Richmond. "As a field for military operations it possesses not a single element, except in the multiplicity of its defensible positions." The Confederates had squandered the initiative in the Far West, and as setbacks east of the territories required ever more men and equipment to defend the rebel states, they never regained it. Occasional skirmishes would follow, but most of them resembled engagements like the one at Picacho Pass, in Arizona territory, where on April 15, 1862, a column of fewer than 300 Union troops from California brushed aside less than two dozen rebels in the westernmost "battle" of the war.

Battle of Pea Ridge   On March 7–8, as a still hopeful Sibley planned his advance beyond Albuquerque, Confederate hopes of holding Missouri died at the battle of Pea Ridge (or Elk Horn Tavern) in northwest Arkansas. A month earlier, Price had been forced to retreat from Missouri, and the Confederate government, finally appreciating the need to strengthen and coordinate its forces in that state and Arkansas, had assigned Gen. Earl Van Dorn, a handsome, forty-one-year-old West Pointer, to head the Trans-Mississippi Department. Determined to reenter Missouri, Van Dorn pieced together his 16,500-man Army of the West by combining Sterling Price's Missouri Guard, Ben McCulloch's command, and nearly 1,000 Cherokee, Chickasaw, Choctaw, and Creek Indians under Gen. Albert Pike, a prominent and gifted Arkansas lawyer, poet, and newspaper publisher who headed the Department of Indian Territory. As Van Dorn advanced from Fayetteville, Arkansas, toward the Missouri border, Gen. Samuel R. Curtis and his 10,250-man Army of the Southwest, coming from the opposite direction, barred the rebel line of march.

Van Dorn maneuvered to attack the Union rear, but his tired men, who had been marching for three days on short rations in bitterly cold weather, moved sluggishly, and Curtis, a quiet West Pointer who had left the army to become a prominent engineer and Iowa politician, detected the ruse. Curtis swung his line around so quickly to meet the Confederate advance that Van Dorn had to divide his command. Price's column reached the army's objective near Elk Horn Tavern, an inn 3 miles north of Curtis on the old Butterfield Stage route between St. Louis and Fayetteville, but McCulloch and Pike lagged several miles behind, and they were separated from Price by a 150-foot-high plateau known as Pea Ridge. When Union artillery forced this rear segment of Van Dorn's men off the road and into line of battle, what should have been a single battle became two separate engagements fought over two days.

The Federals prevailed on both sides of the field, thanks largely to the death of McCulloch on March 7 and a shortage of rebel ammunition on March 8. Curtis counted 1,384 of his men killed, wounded, and missing, but the Confederates, who reunited at the tavern for the second day of fighting, had suffered more than 2,000 casualties and had lost all semblance of discipline and organization. Van Dorn guided what troops he could muster southward to the Arkansas River during the next two weeks. On April 6 he effectively abandoned northern Arkansas and all Missouri to Union control by transferring his men, weapons, equipment, and animals to Mississippi. To fill the void, Arkansas Confederates resorted to guerrilla warfare, a crucial ingredient of the conflict in the state thereafter, even after a new conventional army was assembled to defend it.

Role of Native Americans   The Confederate Cherokees did not follow Van Dorn, but their presence and actions at Pea Ridge further illustrate the expanding scope of war. The Indians fought well in the early stages of the battle before panicking when Union artillery shells exploded in their ranks. However, before fleeing, a few Cherokee were said to have "tomahawked, scalped and shamefully mangled" several wounded Federals. The U.S. government bitterly denounced this episode, and Congress investigated the matter, just as it had some alleged "rebel barbarities" at Bull Run. The Pea Ridge culprits were never identified, but all evidence pointed to the Cherokees, and that was who everyone blamed.

Native Americans endangered Federal soldiers in the Far West throughout the war, although not in the name of the Confederacy. The Apache, led by Cochise and Mangus Coloradas, were a mortal threat in the farthest reaches of Arizona, and Colorado tribes, mostly Arapaho and Cheyenne, gave nearly as much trouble. Indeed, the latter tribes forced the U.S. government to build a new string of forts on the high plains of Nebraska, Kansas, and Colorado. By the summer of 1862, the attacks had spread northward, with an uprising by the Sioux in Minnesota. Only in Utah, where local militia, Union troops, and a series of treaties secured safe travel along the Overland Mail route, would the Indian threat be fully contained.

Looking at the larger picture, the 50,000 Native Americans who inhabited Indian Territory—mostly the Five Civilized Tribes of Cherokee, Choctaw, Chickasaw, Creek, and Seminole—expanded the scope of war by forming, in effect, another border state. Resting on the western edge of Arkansas, Indian Territory (roughly, modern Oklahoma) served as a buffer between Kansas and Texas. Both the United States and Confederate States sought its allegiance, but the Confederates gained an early advantage. Most of the tribes had long-standing grievances against the U.S. government, and many of them had adopted "southern" ways of life, including slavery. The rebels also acted swiftly to secure their friendship by creating a Bureau of Indian Affairs and assigning Albert Pike, who spoke most tribal languages and had defended Indian rights before the U.S. Supreme Court, as commissioner to the Indian Territory. The tribes, like white southerners, divided over secession and war, but by early October 1861, Pike had negotiated treaties that guaranteed their sovereignty and permitted them to send nonvoting delegates to the Confederate Congress. The tribes, in return, provided 3,000 fighting men to the Confederacy.

Still, the rebels never secured a firm grip on Indian Territory. A faction of Cherokee, led by Chief John Ross, refused to acknowledge the Confederacy, as did a large contingent of Creeks, led by Opothleyahola, which took on Texas troops and Confederate Indians in fights at Round Mountain, Chusto-Talasah, and Chustenahlah in November–December 1861. The Creeks lost those battles, which forced some 7,000 of them into Kansas early the next year. The suffering of these Creek unionists, many of them with "not rags enough to hide their bodies," was pitiable, and hundreds died. Another 2,000 refugees from the Ross band followed them later that year, and many in that exodus had fought for the rebels at Pea Ridge. Then Pike resigned as commissioner because he could not acquire sufficient supplies for his Indian troops. By the end of 1862, Confederate control of the territory had become tenuous.

Confederate Setbacks in the Western Theater

The year 1862 would be no kinder to Confederate hopes east of the Mississippi. The euphoria inspired by victories at Wilson's Creek and Val Verde had all but dissipated, and the U.S. drive through Tennessee had barely paused at Forts Henry and Donelson. Still holding to their plan of advancing southward along the rivers and rebel railroads, Union troops under Grant pushed south along the Tennessee River nearly to the Mississippi state border by April 1862. In the Confederacy, a public outcry for Sidney Johnston to resign followed his abandonment of Kentucky and Nashville. The stoic and dutiful general offered to step down, but Jefferson Davis, who idolized him, refused to hear of it. "If Sidney Johnston is not a general," Davis told a congressional delegation seeking Johnston's hide, "we had better give up the war, for we have no general."

New Confederate Strategy

Nonetheless, the Confederates adopted a more aggressive, *offensive-defensive strategy* in the West. Johnston had been spread far too thin in Kentucky, but now the Federals bore that burden. The farther south they moved, the longer and more vulnerable became their supply and communications lines, and the more territory they had to defend. The Confederates could exploit the situation by sending raiders behind Union lines, attacking Union weak points, and reentering lost territory. Sidney Johnston, who had established his new base at the important railroad junction of Corinth, Mississippi, saw a chance to defeat Grant with this strategy and to salvage his public reputation. Drawing troops from as far away as western Florida, Johnston believed that if he moved swiftly and struck before Grant concentrated his then divided force, he would drive the Federals out of Tennessee. Johnston nearly succeeded.

Shiloh Campaign

At daybreak on April 6, 1862, 44,000 rebels rolled over 40,000 surprised Federals encamped around the Shiloh Methodist Church near Pittsburg Landing, some 20 miles northeast of Corinth. "Our men raised a yell," recalled one of the rebel attackers, "and burst out into the wildest yelling it has ever been my lot to hear. It drove all sanity and order from among us." In a few short hours, they pushed the Yankees back, nearly to the banks of the Tennessee River. However, in the process, Johnston lost the initiative. Many of his troops, even a year into the war, were still untested in combat. They remained undisciplined and lacked the training necessary to carry out the complex plan of battle drawn up by Johnston's second in command, Gen. "Gus" Beauregard, who had become a national hero at Fort Sumter and Bull Run. Their lines advanced unevenly across a 4-mile front. The broken terrain, heavily wooded and honeycombed with thickets and ravines, made it difficult to maintain alignment. Entire regiments and brigades became as entangled as the thick undergrowth. The enemy's camps posed yet another physical obstacle, not least of all when men paused to scavenge.

Still, most of the Union troops were fighting in their first major battle, too, and the fearful din, accentuated by a rebel artillery barrage of sixty-two cannon—the largest concentration yet witnessed in North America—unnerved them. A stalwart band of about 2,500 soldiers, mostly midwesterners, saved the day by establishing a makeshift defensive line in an old wagon trace, or *sunken road*, to slow the rebel pursuit. So ferocious was this fighting that the

THE BATTLE OF SHILOH (or Pittsburg Landing). Tennessee. fought on April 6–7. 1862. was one of the decisive military engagements in the Western Theater. It led to the permanent Union occupation of western Tennessee and gave the Federals a springboard into Mississippi. This contemporary drawing shows fighting in a peach orchard on the Union left flank during the first day of the battle.

Union position became known as the Hornet's Nest. "This line was desperately engaged," recalled an Illinois soldier assigned to the perilous spot. "I remember as we . . . began firing, about the first thing that met my gaze was what out West we would call a 'windrow' of dead men in blue; some doubled up face downward, others with their white faces upturned to the sky, brave boys who had been shot to death in 'holding the line.' Here we stayed until our last cartridge was shot away."

The heroic stand gave Grant, who had not been present when the fight started, time to bring up 25,000 reinforcements and a pair of gunboats by nightfall. Then, too, Johnston bled to death early that afternoon when his aides failed to apply a tourniquet to a leg wound. The loss of his leadership took the steam out of the rebel attack and offset whatever early advantage the Confederates had earned. When action resumed on the next day, April 7, the numerically superior Federals finally forced the Confederates to retreat after another exhausting bout of combat.

Waged across a front nearly 2 miles long, the battle of Shiloh (or Pittsburg Landing) was the largest and bloodiest duel of the war to that time. Indeed, *slaughter* is not too strong a word for it. The Confederates absorbed nearly 10,700 casualties, while the victorious Federals lost 12,500. This was double the number of combined dead and wounded at Bull Run, Wilson's Creek, Fort Donelson, and Pea Ridge combined. A northern journalist counted 200 bodies within a single acre of ground; an Iowa soldier was repulsed by "the groans and shrieks of the dying and wounded, the pools of blood, the dead and dying at every few steps." Overcrowded field hospitals presented grisly sights. "Arms, legs, hands, and feet, just amputated lay scattered about," reported a southerner. Wounded men begged piteously for water, and the dead had to be hurriedly dumped into mass graves. "I dread tomorrow," confessed an Indiana soldier detailed to help bury corpses. "They are so swollen and smell so awful and terrible many of them."

Shiloh not only awakened everyone to the realization that this would be a long war, but it also solidified Union dominance in the West. "Though not conclusive," acknowledged Gen. William T. Sherman after the war, the Union victories at Pea Ridge, Fort Donelson, and Shiloh "gave the keynote to all subsequent events of the war. They encouraged us and discouraged our too sanguine opponents, thereby leading to all our Western successes which were conclusive of the final outcome."

Additional Union Gains

Farther to the west, Confederate defenders on Island No. 10, the equivalent of a blockhouse in a bend of the Mississippi River at the Missouri–Kentucky border, surrendered on April 7. Rebel control of the Mississippi valley seemed to be unraveling. Then New Orleans—which, despite being the largest city in the Confederacy, had been left woefully underdefended by the Richmond government—surrendered near the end of April to the naval squadron of Adm. David G. Farragut, a Tennessean by birth. Union gunboats now prowled the mouth of the Father of Waters unimpeded as far north as Baton Rouge. Memphis, the sixth-largest city in the Confederacy and the most important remaining river port, surrendered without a battle on June 6.

Meanwhile, Beauregard returned to Corinth from the bloody fields of Shiloh. When the Federals pursued, he withdrew farther south to Tupelo. When the Federals kept coming and finally laid siege to his command with more than 100,000 men, a weary Beauregard, suffering from a chronic throat ailment, thought it a good time to seek medical attention in Mobile. Without informing Jefferson Davis of his plans, he temporarily turned the army over to Gen. Braxton Bragg in mid-June. That was a mistake. The president, who blamed Beauregard for the defeat at Shiloh and believed that he had unnecessarily abandoned a crucial railroad junction at Corinth, stripped Beauregard of his command. Bragg would now lead the Confederacy's largest western army, soon to be called the Army of Tennessee.

Confederate Conscription

As though all this was not reason enough for alarm in Richmond, rebel armies were shrinking by the spring of 1862. The Confederate Congress responded to the emergency by taking one of the most momentous steps of the war: conscription. The army had been losing men not only to battlefield casual-

THE WESTERN THEATER IN 1861–1862 witnessed several important campaigns. This map, which shows the principal rivers, railroads, towns, and battle sites of those campaigns, will allow readers to locate the fighting at Forts Henry and Donelson, Shiloh, Iuka, Corinth, Perryville, and Murfreesboro. Important campaigns would be conducted in 1863–1864 in the areas around Knoxville, Chattanooga, and Nashville.

ties, sickness, and disease, but also to expired enlistments and desertion. The exhaustion, discomfort, and carnage of war had sobered recruits once inspired by patriotic fervor and romantic visions of martial valor. The brave, confident volunteers of 1861 had enlisted for only six to twelve months of duty, and many of them, having fulfilled their obligation, wanted to go home. Yet, the departure of potentially thousands of men would have depleted the army at a time when the Federals were gaining momentum and gobbling up large chunks of real estate. The only way to save the nation, decided rebel politicians, was to force men to serve. So on April 16, 1862, the first of three Confederate conscription acts became law. All able-bodied white men between eighteen and thirty-five (later extended to seventeen and fifty) would serve under arms for three years. Men already in the army had their enlistments extended by that same length of time.

The action was unprecedented in American history, and large numbers of citizens complained. Men caught in the snares of the draft or soldiers whose enlistments had been extended cried coercion, and unionists were distraught at having to fight for a cause they opposed. Additional protests targeted a lengthy list of occupations exempt from the draft, including government officials, teachers, millers, some artisans, and laborers engaged in industries—mines, railroads, textile mills—necessary to the war effort. Some people also protested conscription on ideological grounds. The law, they pointed out, enabled the central government to usurp the authority of the states. Northerners responded in similar fashion a year later when the Union also resorted to a draft. Desperation led both sides, drawing on European precedents of a nation in arms, to expand national power in a new yet socially incendiary way. Interesting enough, northern conscription would pay more homage to localism than did the southern plan, as northerners were drafted only if enlistment quotas for their congressional districts were not met.

Southerners also complained about two specific exemption clauses in their conscription acts: the overseer clause and substitution. The former provision exempted one white male from each plantation with twenty or more slaves. The logic behind this clause assumed that at least one man was needed to manage large numbers of slaves, but many nonplanters and nonslaveholding farmers claimed that it gave preferential treatment to planters and their sons. In point of fact, overseers were the most likely people to benefit from the provision, which was modified toward the end of the war, in any case, to apply only to plantations owned by minors, women, or the physically disabled, but the overseer clause did arouse considerable class resentment against the government. So did substitution, and perhaps more legitimately. Substitution allowed a draftee to avoid military service by finding someone—usually by hiring the person—to take his place. This clause, too, seemed to favor the wealthy, although the extent to which this was true is difficult to know.

George McClellan
Despite all these Confederate problems and Union military successes in the West, trans-Mississippi, and Far West, the war remained a stalemate in mid-1862, a circumstance many northerners blamed on Gen. George McClellan. This confident, able, and quite promising soldier was proving to be an unsatisfactory general-in-chief. He was overly cautious when it came to committing troops to combat, and he never thought he had enough men for the task at hand. He consistently overestimated the size, strength, and resources of the enemy, which led him to see more formidable obstacles than actually existed. Like most of the war's professional soldiers, he resented politicians who interfered with his military plans, and he was especially irked by President Lincoln's habit of assigning far more men than McClellan thought necessary for the defense of Washington. His resentment of Lincoln, whom he called a fool and worse, would become brazen.

Union War Board
The first sign of serious disagreement between president and general came in March 1862 when Lincoln authorized formation of the *War Board*. Directed by Secretary of War Edwin M. Stanton, this new organization—composed of the heads of the various bureaus of the War Department—emasculated the position

THE EASTERN THEATER IN 1862 provided the Confederates with significant victories that offset their losses in the West. This map, which shows the principal rivers, towns, and battle sites of those campaigns, will allow readers to locate the fighting on the Virginia peninsula and at Cedar Mountain, Second Bull Run, Antietam, and Fredericksburg.

of general-in-chief by giving Stanton and Lincoln more direct control over Union military strategy. In time, the new board would prove to be an important step toward a modern general staff, but Lincoln's immediate goal was to bypass slow-moving professional generals like McClellan and do something to deflect mounting public and political criticism of the slaughter in the West and the lack of military success in the East. The president had come to realize that western victories counted for little so long as a defiant rebel government sat less than 100 miles from Washington. Even significant accomplishments in the East, such as the surrenders of Port Royal and Hilton Head, South Carolina, in November 1861 and of Fort Pulaski, which had protected the important rebel port of Savannah, Georgia, in mid-April 1862, did not pacify the public for long.

Peninsula Campaign

However, the president still wanted the charismatic "Little Mac," as his adoring soldiers called the 5-feet, 8-inch but powerfully built McClellan, to lead the Army of the Potomac, the largest of the Union armies, against Richmond. McClellan had to abandon an earlier plan to attack Richmond from the north—the so-called Urbana plan—because he waited too long to implement it. Now, in the spring of 1862, he developed a new scheme, one that would allow him to strike at the lightly defended southern side of the city by leading his army up the peninsula formed by the York and the James rivers. This bold maneuver was made considerably safer on March 9, 1862, when the USS *Monitor* fought its rebel rival the CSS *Virginia* to a draw at Hampton Roads, the gateway to the Peninsula. When the *Virginia* withdrew to Norfolk for repairs, this first battle in history between ironclad warships cleared the way for McClellan. He could now safely transport his army and supplies by sea to Union-held Fort Monroe at the foot of the Peninsula—just 75 miles from Richmond. More good news came two months later when the rebels abandoned Norfolk and the Gosport Navy Yard, which opened the James River to McClellan. Because Norfolk had been the only port capable of sheltering the *Virginia*, the rebels had to scuttle their fearsome warship.

By early April, nearly 400 Union ships and barges had delivered more than 100,000 men, nearly 15,000 animals, 1,200 wagons and ambulances, and hundreds of cannon to Fort Monroe. McClellan had every manpower and material advantage, including a field telegraph system and reconnaissance balloons (used for the first time in the war). Only 15,000 rebels stood between him and Richmond, but he twice failed to capture the city. McClellan moved far too cautiously at first, wasting one full month laying siege to a mere 10,000 rebels (who eventually retreated) at Yorktown. By then, with roads turned to mud and rivers made impassable by heavy rains, Confederate general Joseph Johnston had mustered 42,000 defenders and defeated a like number of isolated Federal troops in the battle of Seven Pines and Fair Oaks (May 31), just 6 miles from Richmond.

Lee Takes Command

This first round of fighting not only saved the rebel capital but also resulted in Jefferson Davis making one of the most fateful decisions of the war. Joe Johnston was severely wounded at Seven Pines. To replace him, the president ordered Robert E. Lee, who had recently returned to the capital as a military advisor, into the field. Lee's newly designated Army of Northern Virginia—the first army Lee had ever commanded—would, under his leadership, become the most famous of all Confederate armies.

Lee made an important decision of his own soon after assuming field command. To boost the size of his army, he summoned Stonewall Jackson and his 18,000 men from the Shenandoah Valley, where Jackson had been conducting another important military operation that spring. The 165-mile-long valley, which stretched northeast from Lexington to Harpers Ferry, served both as a major supplier of grain, fruit, and livestock for the Confederacy and as a strategic highway for any rebel army intent on invading Maryland or attacking Washington. From March through June, Jackson had directed a dazzling defensive campaign in this valley. He had weaved, dodged, and feinted while pummeling three different Union commanders and four times his number of men. At the same time, the threat Jackson posed to Washington forced an almost desperately apprehensive Lincoln to bolster defenses around the capital and deploy troops against him that could have been used elsewhere. His mission accomplished in the Valley, Jackson joined Lee with his "foot cavalry" to defend the Confederate capital. The partnership between the two men, though lasting less than a year, would become legendary.

Jackson in the Shenandoah Valley

Lee was now ready for McClellan: When the Federals regrouped and advanced on Richmond a second time, he stopped them cold in the Seven Days' battles (June 25–July 1, 1862). Lee pounded the Federals in a series of bloody encounters—Mechanicsville, Gaines's Mill, Savage Station, and White Oak Swamp—that drove McClellan southward, away from Richmond and toward the James River. It was not a flawless performance. The usually swift-moving Jackson was strangely lethargic. His division was consistently out of position, perhaps exhausted after the Valley campaign, perhaps hesitant in the unfamiliar terrain. Lee, in any case, had not been able to map the area properly, a serious handicap in a region covered with swamps, bramble-infested ravines, and wooded hills. Lee also sacrificed men in needless charges on the final day of fighting at Malvern Hill. The rebels, trying to advance uphill, across open fields, and against massed artillery, lost more than 5,000 men at Malvern, a quarter of their total losses for the week. One Confederate general said of the battle, "It was not war—it was murder." Not heeding several generals on his staff who urged a counterattack against their weakened foe, the psychologically whipped McClellan retreated that night, July 1, the rest of the way to the James River, stymied, frustrated, and embarrassed but with most of his still formidable army intact.

Seven Days' Battles

The Seven Days proved that northern and southern generals had learned little after more than a year of fighting except how to kill men more recklessly. The human cost in these battles was staggering. "The dead lay almost thick enough in some places to have walked on," reported a Louisiana soldier of the twisted and grotesque mass of bodies he saw after the fighting on June 27. "The scene was one never to be forgotten. . . . Language would in no way express the true picture as it really was." The Federals lost more than 1,700 killed, 8,000 wounded, and 6,000 captured or missing. The *victorious* Confederates suffered more than 3,000 killed, 16,000 wounded, and almost 1,000 captured or missing. The South could not afford many such victories, and yet this would remain the pattern for most of the war. Even when the rebels had lower *numerical* casualties, they almost always incurred higher *proportional* losses than the Union.

Despite the loss of men, the Seven Days represented a significant political and moral victory for the Confederates. Lee had, as it were, driven the wolf from the door and saved the capital, quite possibly the Confederate nation. His victory balanced the depressing string of western defeats and increased the already intense political pressure on Lincoln to do something more in the East than capture a few coastal forts. From this time forward, the Confederacy would lean heavily on Lee for similarly timely, morale-boosting battlefield heroics.

New Union Strategy The Seven Days also marked a turning point for the North and especially for Abraham Lincoln. The demand by radical politicians in the president's own party for a tougher war policy had grown through the spring and summer. Following the disaster on the Peninsula, Lincoln began to think that the politicians might be right. He decided to abandon the "kid-glove warfare" of the preceding year and wage a no-holds-barred, relentless war against a formidable foe.

Lincoln's change of heart was also rooted in disappointment. He had always believed that the majority of white southerners, especially in the upper South, retained strong attachments to the Union. Given a little time, thought the president, those old patriotic feelings would resurface, and the people would rise up to help overthrow the Confederacy. He had thus ordered advancing Union armies to treat noncombatants with respect, to win the trust of white southerners by showing that the United States had no desire to injure them or despoil their region. Yet, outside of northwest Virginia, no widespread unionist revolt had come. Instead, hundreds had taken up arms as guerrillas and assisted the Confederacy's conventional armies by murdering Union soldiers. Lincoln had to concede that his conciliatory policy had failed.

Lincoln also decided that the new strategy must include some form of black emancipation. In calling for a harsher war policy, the more energetic and radical Republican politicians had insisted on this point. Emancipation, they said, would revitalize the war effort. In this, too, they had been pushing Lincoln in a direction and at a speed he was not prepared to go, but by the summer of 1862, the president had little choice. He had to still the political clamor, and given the need for a tougher military policy, there was no question that emancipation would also undermine the Confederate war machine.

The consequences of the movement toward emancipation will be discussed in the next chapter, but here is how Lincoln pursued his new military policy. Deciding that his three-month experiment in managing the eastern war had been a fiasco, the president picked a new general-in-chief to coordinate the armies and formulate strategy. McClellan would continue to command the Army of the Potomac, but his defeat in the Seven Days as well as his efforts to avoid responsibility for the failure turned Lincoln against him. Moreover, McClellan had written an unwise letter to Lincoln a week after his retreat from Malvern Hill (the so-called Harrison Landing letter) in which he denounced the administration's new military policy. Consequently, the president, mindful of the successes of his western armies, tapped his senior western general, Henry W. Halleck, for the job. Perhaps those westerners, Lincoln thought, knew something about winning battles that eluded eastern commanders.

Lincoln had high hopes for Halleck, a West Point graduate in his mid-forties with a reputation as an intellectual. "Old Brains," as he was known, possessed of "great chunks of wisdom," had written both an army tactical manual and a treatise on international law before the war. He enjoyed a thriving law practice in California, where he had also helped to write the state constitution. As commander first of the Department of the Missouri and then of the Department of the Mississippi, Halleck had directed much of the successful Union military effort in the West, although he was a better administrator than field officer. His reputation as a conquering general had been acquired largely through the victories of subordinates, particularly those of Grant, toward whom Halleck displayed signs of jealousy. Halleck also shirked responsibility when things went wrong, an unbecoming trait that eventually led Lincoln and his cabinet to become disillusioned with him. Even so, Halleck would remain a major player in the Union high command for the remainder of the war, often serving as a mediator between the army and the administration.

Halleck as General-in-Chief

Halleck joined another western general already in the East. Lincoln had summoned John Pope, one of Halleck's most dependable western subordinates, a month earlier to lead the newly created Army of Virginia. Indeed, Pope had recommended Halleck for his new job. He was another of those tough western generals who had shown an ability to handle guerrillas, keep defiant rebel civilians in line, and win battles. Openly scoffing at the Union's seemingly soft eastern armies and generals, Pope took command of his army with the intention of applying western methods in the East. He ordered his men, assigned to sever railroad connections between Richmond and the Shenandoah Valley south of the Rappahannock River, to live off the abundance of rebel farms and to execute without trial civilians suspected of being spies or of bushwhacking Union troops. The new policy unfortunately led to much wanton destruction of private property and the unnecessary intimidation of noncombatants, but it also placed Pope in a position either to move deeper into Virginia or to turn eastward toward Richmond.

John Pope

Pope's campaign so angered and worried Lee that he dispatched Stonewall Jackson in mid-July to dispose of the "miscreant" Union general. Jackson defeated but did not quash Pope at the battle of Cedar Mountain on August 9, 1862, so when McClellan abandoned the Peninsula in mid-August, Lee also withdrew to concentrate his entire army against Pope before he could be reinforced. Pope retreated across the Rappahannock River upon his arrival, but Lee developed a daring plan to corner and destroy him. Dividing his force, Lee sent Jackson and 24,000 men on a rapid march around Pope's right flank to capture the Union army's supply depot at Manassas Junction and block its line of retreat. When Pope fell back to protect his rear, Lee followed with his remaining 30,000 men, intent on crushing the Federals between the halves of his army.

Second Bull Run Campaign

The resulting battle of Second Bull Run (or Second Manassas) was a three-day affair (August 29–31, 1862), grander in every way than the comparatively innocent skirmish fought over much of the same ground the previous summer. Lee's army suffered more than 9,000 casualties (19 percent of his force), but he wrecked the Army of Virginia by inflicting 16,000 casualties (21 percent), although 6,000 of that number were men captured or missing, as opposed to killed or wounded. The victory cleared northern Virginia of virtually all federal troops and added significantly to a growing aura of invincibility surrounding Lee and his men. Seven Days, Cedar Mountain, and Second Bull Run had been the only bright spots in an otherwise dismal year for the Confederacy. That they had been won in the East—seat of the government and center of rebel population, commerce, and industry—lent the victories particular renown. That they displayed a more offensive-minded strategy was also significant.

Antietam Campaign

Lee's early victories now emboldened him to make an even more audacious move. The Virginian had always preferred the *offensive* part of the Confederacy's offensive-defensive strategy, and although he and Jefferson Davis worked well together, the general was clearly more impulsive than the president—and perhaps more contemptuous of the enemy. With the Federals reeling from his blows, he wanted to carry the war into Union territory. Thinking to complement a bold Confederate advance already underway in Kentucky—to be explained momentarily—Lee decided to enter another border slave state controlled by the Federals: Maryland.

Lee saw several advantages to a raid into Maryland. He could, he presumed, attract recruits to Confederate service, move the fighting out of Virginia during the coming harvest season, live off the Maryland countryside, replenish his declining supply of horses and mules, draw Union troops from the West, hurt the Republican Party in that fall's northern congressional elections, and put diplomatic pressure on Europe to recognize the Confederacy as a sovereign nation. A single impressive victory could thus accomplish much, and his mere presence across the Potomac, Lee believed, would spread panic through the North.

Lee entered Maryland during the first week of September 1862, but he had trouble from the start. First, a stubborn Union garrison at Harpers Ferry stood its ground as Lee approached and threatened his communication lines should he bypass it. Jackson's corps had to stay behind to force a surrender while the rest of the army moved forward. Then, one of Lee's staff officers lost a copy of the army's projected movements for the campaign. A Union patrol, investigating the sudden show of rebel force in Maryland, found the orders—wrapped, as improbable as it sounds, around some cigars—and turned them over to General McClellan. When the Union commander, taking advantage of this bit of luck, moved more swiftly than customarily to intercept the rebel army, Lee sensed that something was amiss; this was not the cautious McClellan he had come to know. Lee, with his army divided, considered withdrawing from Maryland until he received word that Jackson had captured Harpers Ferry and would soon rejoin him. The rebel chieftain decided to make a stand at the little town of Sharpsburg.

The battle of Sharpsburg (or Antietam) began with an infantry attack against Lee's left flank at 5:30 a.m. on September 17. The 35,000 Confederates, spread north and south of the town on a line 2 miles long, absorbed charge after charge by McClellan's 87,000 men in some historic clashes. Fighting rolled over expansive cornfields and pastures and swirled through the woods surrounding a small Dunker church. In the center of the rebel line, dead and dying Confederates soon filled a sunken road, known thereafter as the Bloody Lane. Lee had anchored his left flank on the Potomac River, which looped lazily behind rebel lines. It was a dangerous position, for had the Federals turned either flank or penetrated his defenses, Lee's army would have been pushed back into the river, virtually annihilated.

Union failure resulted primarily from the sluggish performance of several corps commanders who failed to attack at the appointed time. The assault unfolded piecemeal, never mustering enough weight for a knockout punch. "There seems to be no doubt that if McClellan's orders had been carried out," a Union officer surmised shortly after the battle, "the attack would have been so complete a success that but little of the rebel army would have escaped." As it was, "Lee was always able to concentrate on the point where the attack was made." The best Union chance came against the thinly manned Confederate right flank, positioned on some bluffs overlooking Antietam Creek. About 500 Georgians held off 12,000 Federals for three hours as the Yankees tried to cross the creek's narrow bridge. The blue-coated soldiers finally broke through, but just as they prepared to turn and attack the exposed and badly weakened center of Lee's line, Gen. Ambrose P. Hill arrived with the last of Stonewall Jackson's men from Harpers Ferry. They crashed into the flank of this final threat and saved the day for Lee.

"No tongue can tell, no mind conceive, no pen portray the horrible sights I witnessed this morning," a Union soldier confided to his diary on September 17. Many soldiers wrote similar lines following every battle of the war, but these words, written on this evening, told a special truth. After twelve hours of hellish combat, 2,100 dead Federals and 1,500 Confederates lay scattered over the fields surrounding Sharpsburg. In addition, the Federals had 9,500 wounded men; the Confederates, 7,700. It proved to be the single bloodiest day of the war. "We were glad to march over the field at night," confessed one soldier in a letter to his parents, "for we could not see the horrible sights so well. Oh what a smell. Some of the men vomit as they went along."

Political Results of Antietam

The battle was a draw, but given their advantages in numbers and terrain as well as their advance intelligence of Confederate intentions, the Federals should have beaten Lee. When the rebels withdrew toward Virginia the night of September 18, McClellan did not pursue. The Confederates, even in retreat, could claim a moral victory, and Lee, as it turned out, had gained at least one of his objectives—the political one. The Republican Party took a drubbing in that fall's elections, a result that must be attributed at least partly to Lee's raid. Democrats won the governorships of New York and New Jersey, gained thirty-five congressional seats, and piled up huge majorities in Lincoln's home state of Illinois. It was not enough to dismiss the outcome as a typical off-year election dip for the majority party, or to say that many of the victories came in Democratic strongholds. All understood that military defeats had spawned political ones. "The people," reported an Ohio newspaper, "are depressed by the interminable nature of this war, as so far conducted, and by the rapid exhaustion of the national resources without progress." Even Lincoln admitted that the "ill-success of the war had much to do" with voter displeasure.

Emancipation Proclamation

Yet, the Antietam campaign produced another, even more profound political consequence, one not at all intended by Lee. Lincoln, as suggested, had been planning since July to introduce the abolition of slavery as a new Union war aim. He had delayed making the announcement only because he wanted to do so on a positive note, namely a military victory. When McClellan marched out to intercept Lee in Maryland, the president told his cabinet that he would regard a Union win as "an indication of Divine will . . . to move forward in the cause of emancipation." Lincoln did not get the glistening triumph for which he had hoped, but it was a good enough omen to satisfy him. When Lincoln is-

THIS PHOTOGRAPH WAS PART of the "Dead of Antietam" exhibition that awakened northerners to the merciless reality of war. The bloated and stiffened corpses seen here provide a stark contrast to the romantic depictions of battle shown earlier in this chapter.

sued his Emancipation Proclamation on September 22, to take effect on the following New Year's Day, he changed the entire nature of the war.

Antietam produced one other nonmilitary result, a chillingly emotional and psychological one for northerners. Within a day of the fighting, while the stiff, bloated carcasses of men and animals and the wreckage of battle still littered the fields, northern photographers working for Mathew Brady, the most famous photographer of the war, rushed to the scene. Brady exhibited the stark images they took the following month in his New York City gallery. A far cry from the romantic paintings and engravings of victorious charges and sanitized fighting that people were accustomed to seeing, the "Dead of Antietam," as the exhibit was called, gave northern civilians their first look at the real consequences of war. Not the long casualty lists printed in newspapers after each battle nor even the thousands of written descriptions of battle sent home by soldiers to their families (which often shied away from graphic details of the carnage) could convey a fraction of the horrors conveyed by those static black-and-white images. They portrayed, as one newspaper reporter wrote, "the terrible reality and earnestness of war."

Dead of Antietam

That autumn's final campaign in the West ended on an earnest note, too. By the summer of 1862, U.S. troops controlled the Cumberland Gap—Daniel Boone's old stomping grounds and the gateway to Tennessee, Kentucky, and Virginia—but the rebels held the key railroad and river towns of Chattanooga and Knoxville. Halleck had sent Gen. Don Carlos Buell to capture Chattanooga while still commanding in the West, and Buell was making progress until July, when Col. John Hunt Morgan and Nathan Bedford Forrest staged a series of raids through Kentucky and central Tennessee that disrupted federal communication and supply lines. Neither Morgan nor Forrest was a professional soldier, but they shared a talent for the hit-and-run tactics of guerrilla warfare. Buell still might have advanced on Chattanooga, but much like McClellan, he was a cautious, deliberate soldier who tended to plod rather than dash. Then, too, he had not reckoned with the new Confederate commander in Mississippi, Braxton Bragg.

Kentucky Campaign

The forty-five-year-old Bragg, another West Point graduate and Mexican War veteran, had retired from the army in 1856 to operate a Louisiana sugar plantation (inherited from his new bride), but his military experience and friendship with Jefferson Davis made him, by April 1862, the fifth-ranking officer in the Confederate army. He was a fierce disciplinarian, not normally loved by his men, but Bragg quickly refitted the Army of Tennessee, restored its morale, and designed a plan to save Chattanooga by exploiting the chaos caused by the Morgan-Forrest raids. He hoped, too, that his plan would force Grant, still sitting at Corinth with 60,000 men, and Buell, then in northern Alabama, to fall back into central Tennessee, perhaps even Kentucky. Leaving 16,000 troops to hold Tupelo and sending another 16,000 to Vicksburg—the obvious target for any new Union advance down the Mississippi River—he rushed his remaining 31,000 men by railroad to eastern Tennessee. The transfer required a circuitous route of 776 miles by way of Mobile, Montgomery, and Atlanta, but Bragg had his army in Chattanooga in less than a week.

Braxton Bragg

The plan worked so well that Bragg found himself taking another bold step. Gen. Edmund Kirby Smith, who commanded Confederate troops in east Tennessee, was eager to lead a new campaign to liberate Kentucky. He apparently convinced Bragg that Kentuckians would cheer the expulsion of the Federals (probably true) and welcome the establishment of a Confederate government (definitely not true). An unenthusiastic Bragg, agreeing to cooperate, led a portion of his army into Kentucky, where on September 14, 1862, he issued this grandiloquent proclamation: "Kentuckians, I have entered your State with the Confederate Army of the West, and offer you an opportunity to free yourselves from the tyranny of a despotic ruler. We come not as conquerors or despoilers, but to restore to you the liberties of which you have been deprived by a cruel and relentless foe." He then proceeded to set up a Confederate state government at Frankfort and announce his intention to enforce the Conscription Act. His actions met with little enthusiasm. Those Kentuckians inclined to support the Confederacy had already gone south to join the army. The fence-sitters who remained showed no more inclination to follow Bragg's banner than they did the U.S. flag. They still hoped to spare themselves and their property—including slaves—the ravages of war. Worst for Bragg's army, however, were those staunch unionists who operated as bushwhackers against the advancing columns. It was the sort of resistance Lincoln had hoped would materialize across the upper South.

By early October, Bragg had a more serious problem than bushwhackers. Buell's army, as he had hoped it would do, followed him into Kentucky. However, Buell also became unexpectedly aggressive. He sent four separate columns against the widely dispersed forces of Bragg and Kirby Smith, some 135,000 Federals against less than 50,000 Confederates. When one column of about 25,000 men moved to block Bragg's line of retreat through central Kentucky, Bragg attacked at Perryville on October 8. Bragg lost 3,100 of his 16,000 men. Buell lost 3,700, but he had another 32,000 troops within a few hours march. Five days later, Bragg returned to Tennessee. His Kentucky campaign—the last Confederate attempt to win the state—was a disaster. Moreover, this failure came hard on the heels of two rebel defeats in Mississippi, where Van Dorn and Sterling Price, the Confederate commanders from Pea Ridge, had botched a well-intended effort to prevent Union troops from reinforcing Buell. The results were losses at Iuka (September 19) and Corinth (October 4).

Military Impact   So stood the military situation in the autumn of 1862—a far cry from the brief, narrowly confined, clearly defined conflict most Americans had expected. Surprisingly, most of the fighting had taken place in the West, where the Union claimed large amounts of Confederate territory. Meantime, a stalemate had developed in the East, the place where most people expected the contest would be decided. Another unexpected turn came with northern talk of emancipation and the adoption of a harsher war policy, to which many rebels responded by "raising the Black Flag," meaning showing no mercy, even though, as a Louisiana woman observed, "such a war" was "too horrible to think of." Worse still, there was no end in sight. "Our war on rebellion languishes," declared a

New Yorker in late October. "We make no forward movements and gain no victories." One heard the same lament within the armies. "The only conversation here is of the probable duration of the war," reported a Massachusetts soldier serving under McClellan. "Everyone wants to know what the people at the North say, and if they think the war is ever going to end." A Virginian was struck by the apparent inability of either army to gain a decisive edge. Battle after battle had produced rivers of blood but "no conclusive victory."

The brooding horror of such a slugfest not only stunned people but also overwhelmed the organizational capacity of both sides to wage war. Finding, feeding, clothing, equipping, and transporting hundreds of thousands of men, caring for the wounded, burying the dead, and paying for it all could not be handled within the traditional, hopelessly decentralized structure of local volunteerism within which the war began. New and vastly expanded bureaucratic procedures would have to be improvised and somehow coordinated to overcome the inertia of older practices and to galvanize citizens into active, earnest commitment.

Problems of Decentralized Government

The material costs of the war were staggering and unprecedented in every way. According to the most recent studies by economic historians, direct money costs were approximately $4.8 billion in 1861 dollars, not including the long-term economic consequences of the loss of human lives, and the total cost ran to perhaps $15 billion. Military procurement became a source of rampant corruption and profiteering in North and South, with bribes, kickbacks, the production of shoddy goods, and illegal trading with the enemy causing problems in the field. In terms of consumer investment, the North would not recover fully from its "victory" until 1879, the South not until 1909.

Material Costs of War

The South began with an enormous economic disadvantage, as 90 percent of the nation's industrial capacity remained in the Union. Only the Tredegar Iron Works in Richmond and another foundry rushed into production at Selma, Alabama, could produce heavy iron products, and both mills had to manufacture artillery rather than rails, while the North had sufficient capacity for both. Worn-out southern railroads could be repaired only by ripping up feeder lines. To maintain its armies in the field, the Confederates had to capture Union war material, trade for it on the Union black market, or purchase supplies in Europe and run them through a tightening Union blockade at ever increasing risk and cost. Although the South produced sufficient gunpowder and bullets for this relatively low technology war, they were often of uneven quality. Even such products as soap grew scarce, and manufactured shoes were nearly nonexistent.

Confederate Economic Weaknesses

Southern finances also rested on a shaky foundation. The government's power to tax remained limited, and bond sales went dry because of a shortage of capital at home and hesitation in Europe to invest in such a desperate gamble. The government resorted to the printing press, which resulted in runaway inflation, spiraling prices, and much civilian suffering. By the end of the war, one dollar in Confederate currency was worth only two cents in gold. Farmers stopped accepting payment in Confederate money by the midpoint of the war, which led to government confiscation of goods and hard feelings by the farmers. Mobs of

THE TREDEGAR IRON WORKS in Richmond. Virginia, was the most important industrial plant in the Confederacy. It manufactured nearly one-half of the 2,200 cannon produced in the Confederate states, and at its peak of production in 1863, 2,500 people worked in the foundry.

angry women led food riots in several towns in early 1863 when merchants raised the prices of staples beyond the means of ordinary people. None of the financial improvisations worked, and the wonder is that Confederate spirits did not crumble more quickly than they did. Despite the increasing bleakness on the home front, Confederate armies remained the repository of rebel pride and morale. Standing off the North in the face of enormous economic dislocation, they continued to spearhead the Confederate rebellion.

Union Economic Response

Union leaders learned to marshal their superior resources, but it was an uneven and inefficient process. They increased revenue by raising tariffs (illegal in the Confederacy) and introducing an unprecedented array of license fees, excise taxes, and manufacturing levies. They also imposed a graduated income tax, although the highest tax bracket was a paltry 5 percent. (The South introduced an income tax in 1864, with a high tax bracket of 15 percent, but it was rarely collected by local officials.) Such taxes increased federal revenues from $56 million in 1860 to $334 million in 1865, but expenditures skyrocketed from $63 million to $1.3 billion during the same years. In addition, the national debt rose from $59 million in 1859 to $2.756 billion in 1866, with interest accumulating at $200 million per year during the war, more than three times the entire national budget of 1860.

Taxation financed only one-third of the Union war effort, the shortfall being taken up by bonds and paper money. The government lacked the banking controls and resources to have the Treasury Department sell bonds, so it jobbed out the task to New York entrepreneur Jay Cooke, who enriched himself with sales at home and abroad. *Greenbacks,* as federal currency became known, were a major innovation in early 1862, but they could not be exchanged for gold, which flowed out of the country at a steady rate for foreign purchases. However, the value of northern currency, unlike its Confederate equivalent, never fell below thirty-three cents in gold on the dollar, and so the dislocation of the northern economy, as severely as it affected the wages of many working people, never became as desperate as in the South.

Paper money and bonds also created pressure for systematic financial reform, although this would not be accomplished until 1864. The National Banking Act chartered local banks that would deposit a portion of their assets—in government bonds—with the federal government. In return, they received 90 percent of the bonds' value in National Bank Notes, exchangeable across the country. Few banks signed up until 1865, when Congress taxed state bank notes—the main form of paper currency before the war—by 10 percent, which made them less valuable than federal greenbacks. Ever since Andrew Jackson had slain the National Bank in the mid-1830s, American investors had preferred state and local banks, and it would take time to convince them that another central banking system, which could provide cash reserves to state and local banks, could protect them from economic recessions. Gold coins, the staple of the antebellum money system, were also in short supply. Many people substituted postage stamps for the hard currency, but these tended to disintegrate quickly.

If the war strained the ramshackle financial "system," the nascent industry **Industrial** and technology of North and South underwent similar stresses. Both sections **Challenges** responded with a series of relatively uncoordinated improvisations rather than centrally controlled, unifying strategies.

Railroads offer a major example. Given the poor quality of most railroads, **Railroads** land transport was slow, cumbersome, expensive, and unsafe. Canals and rivers were utilized wherever they ran, one reason the war along such western rivers as the Mississippi, the Arkansas, the Tennessee, and the Cumberland became so intense, but in the East, water transportation up rivers from the seacoast reached few militarily vital sectors. Horse- or mule-drawn wagons had supplied armies for centuries, and they would continue to provision most Civil War armies, but the nation's railroad network, thrown up mainly in the 1850s, provided the brightest hope for moving masses of men and material.

However, numerous obstacles reduced the usefulness of railroads. The tracks, for example, had no standard gauge, which meant that axles had to be adjusted or contents shifted at many junctions. Rolling stock was fragile and required frequent repair. Engines either were not standardized or were not powerful enough for major hauling. Skilled railroad workers grew scarcer as the war dragged on. Most grievously, most rails were made of iron until near the end of the war, when steel rails were introduced, and iron deteriorates rapidly from use and cold weather. Consequently, wartime maps that show the ostensible location of railroads can be misleading, for the lines were frequently unusable.

Such problems were especially severe in the South, where, in any event, the miles of track numbered half of those in the North. Hampered by insufficiencies of every kind, the Confederates could not count on their roads much of the time. In fact, some historians maintain that the shortages of food and equipment associated with Confederate armies were not caused by the unavailability of supplies so much as by an inability to transport them over an increasingly decrepit rail system. Then, too, the South often resorted to destroying its own railroads to deny Union troops their use. In addition, several states, especially Georgia, held back supplies for the use of state troops. States' rights trumped the Confederacy's rights more often than they trumped the U.S. government's.

Superior productive capacities permitted the North to maintain its routes and to repair southern lines it needed, but traffic bottlenecks plagued the vital northeast corridor between New York and Washington. Even double tracking, slow to come, proved insufficient. Major improvements did not occur until 1862 when the United States Military Railroad (USMRR) system was chartered to operate captured rebel railroads. By the end of the war, the USMRR system oversaw an impressive 2,105 miles of railroad with 419 engines and 6,330 cars. These lines were the most important routes through the border states to places where U.S. troops would campaign, and this primitive step toward wartime socialism demonstrated what could be done if property were considered essentially public rather than private.

Although this attack on the sanctity of private property was politically acceptable where enemy property was the target, the government never considered full federal management, much less ownership, of the roads, which remained relatively independent and profit oriented. Northern railroads avoided similar treatment only because they took to heart Secretary of War Stanton's advice to cooperate voluntarily in standardizing their tracks (something the Confederacy never achieved), giving priority to military traffic, and agreeing to reasonable rates for the government. Not until the twentieth century would American wartime socialism and centralization be implemented fully.

Northern Industry The overall impact of the war on northern industrialization has proven difficult to measure. The current consensus among economic historians is that the war somewhat retarded the rate of industrial development because heightened military expenditures and procurement did not compensate for other losses of markets and dislocations. Pig iron production remained steady, and woolens and watches did better than before, but on the whole, industry experienced relative losses. The major exception to this trend was the agricultural sector, where labor shortages led to an accelerated rate of mechanization. The rate of increase of the production of farm machinery, which had grown by 110 percent from 1849 to 1859, rose 140 percent in 1859–1869 and fell to 95 percent in the next decade. Capital investment in farm machinery rose 300 percent from 1860 to 1870. In the Midwest, labor productivity, which had grown by 8 percent over the 1850s, increased by 13 percent over the 1860s. Despite inflation and the market-driven rather than the regulatory priorities placed on production for the military, the northern standard of living rose during the war, and rationing was never considered.

THE DEPOT OF THE U.S. MILITARY RAILROAD SYSTEM at City Point, Virginia, in 1864. Authorized by Congress in January 1862, the system operated railroads in hostile or occupied territory. This became a crucial agency for the U.S. government in a war that depended on railroads for many tactical, strategic, and logistical movements. By the end of the war, the USMRR operated 2,100 miles of track, 419 locomotives, and 6,330 cars.

Efforts to enhance the efficiency of other parts of the Union and Confederate war machines, such as the medical care of soldiers, will be described in later chapters, but the pattern would remain much the same. Decentralized national governments, searching for untested solutions to unprecedented challenges, would continue to rely on the volunteer enthusiasms of its citizens to offset improvised and disorganized military and political bureaucracies. Whichever side could mobilize and sustain that spirit more efficiently would gain the advantage. Yet both sides quickly learned that Mars is a harsh God, a devourer of youthful idealism. As Americans in a divided nation marched behind their respective flags, both literally and figuratively, they lost the innocent romanticism that had propelled so many of them into the conflict. After more than a year of fighting that promised no end, and in the face of the war's overwhelming human suffering, they developed a ruthless stoicism, so savage and so deep that it would harden them forever.

CHAPTER 5

Reckoning with Slavery, Reckoning with Freedom

Slavery was the underlying cause of the Civil War: when southerners argued for their constitutional states' rights, the right they most often had in mind was the continuance of slavery. Ending the expansion of slavery—the central goal of the Republican Party, an exclusively northern political movement—was understood by secessionists as the first step toward complete destruction of their peculiar institution. The Republicans denied that their strategy implied emancipation, loudly if somewhat insincerely. As the war lengthened, far from going away, reckoning with slavery deepened as a problem. The fundamental implicit meaning of unionism after the Republican-dominated national government went to war against states that had seceded over slavery was how to reunite the nation without capitulating to the South over slavery, thereby entrenching an institution they wished to curtail.

Republican Ambivalence toward Blacks

Nevertheless, even if Republicans considered slavery an evil that they should put on the road to ultimate extinction, it did not follow that they also believed in taking action to promote equality and racial justice for African Americans. On these issues they were ambivalent when not indifferent or hostile. Hatred or fear of blacks was often as virulent in the North, where there were few blacks, as in the South, where there were millions. This was "aversive racism," a desire to avoid all contact with what many whites believed to be a polluting lower race. Even in many of the states where the Republican vote was rapidly climbing, white voters had rejected black suffrage by large margins before the war, and several of the so-called *free states* had forbidden free blacks to enter or settle, though these laws were rarely enforced. Other forms of public discrimination, such as segregation in the schools and on public transport, were not decreasing, and private prejudice undercut black opportunities in many ways. Republicans were not concerned with setting black citizenship on an equal plane with white—they just opposed the spread of slavery and, more vaguely, its moral standing.

Neither did the Republicans have a coherent strategy for ending slavery when they came to power in 1861—in fact, at first they vigorously denied that such was their intent. Rather, the exigencies of war itself—anger at the Confederates, abolitionist pressure from without as well as within Congress, and the actions of blacks in responding to the opportunities that secession and war between the whites offered—had as much to do with the ending of slavery as did anything the Union government initiated. In the fluidity of war in an already weak nation-state, many new actors became involved. Emancipation grew in a complex dialectical political process where Congress and the Lincoln administration reacted to developments with a messy, halting, often ambiguous process; this finally led to the complete abolition of slavery, but only with the ratification of the Thirteenth Amendment in December 1865, after the war had ended.

Whatever racial ambivalence might have characterized Union beliefs, the longer the ever deepening war continued, reckoning with slavery and with black freedom grew as the central issue driving much of Union political, military, and even diplomatic policy, just as maintaining slavery remained the primary right for which Confederates fought. How blacks were to be employed, both as soldiers and on the land, and what the legal and social shapes their postwar lives might assume were inescapable problems for authorities on both sides. Also, far more than had been the case during slavery times, given the division of white authority structures and the opportunities offered by the flux of war, blacks took active roles in determining their futures, profoundly affecting what choices governments would make.

By instinct, Abraham Lincoln believed slavery a "monstrous injustice," as he put it in a speech in 1854, coining a phrase he repeated during the celebrated Lincoln–Douglas debates of 1858. But equally by instinct, he believed that blacks would never reach an equal footing with whites. He also believed that he lacked the authority to end slavery within the Union—which included the four slave states of Missouri, Kentucky, Maryland, and Delaware—believing that constitutional limits prevented the president from acting unilaterally to outlaw the institution. Politically, Lincoln did everything he could to keep those slave states in the Union, because he was certain that their support was crucial to his success. In particular, he was sure that if he alienated and lost Kentucky, he would lose the war. Therefore, whatever his attitude about slavery, he temporized with the slave owners in the border states, who had considerable power to help or hurt the Union. He long sought masters' cooperation in ending slavery through a system of compensation to the slaveholders, and he argued well into

Lincoln's Views of Slavery

1864 that it would be best for blacks as well as whites that African Americans be colonized outside the United States, in Latin America perhaps.

As for white prejudice, Lincoln was on the whole a fatalistic conservative. He never overtly subscribed to white supremacy but accepted as a fact that white Americans had deeply ingrained prejudices against blacks and that he could do nothing to change that. In fact, he was certain that he had to accommodate white beliefs. With such a view of race relations, which he knew to be terrible for blacks, Lincoln doubted the wisdom of any scheme of emancipation that would leave blacks free among whites. He could not imagine blacks as full citizens of the American republic. And he was angry that the race problem existed. At one famous meeting with African American leaders in the White House on August 14, 1862, Lincoln went so far as to blame the slaves for having been the cause of the war: "Our white men [are] cutting one another's throats. . . . But for your race among us there could not be war," he told them. This position led Frederick Douglass to remark in print that Lincoln was blaming the horse for the crime of the horse stealer.

Yet, fatalistic conservatism was not the whole story of Lincoln's conflicted beliefs. He was at war within himself over these issues, and whatever his own racial beliefs, during the complex political evolution that accompanied the long, brutal war, he moved in the direction of emancipation. Never a radical, Lincoln remained engaged with the congressional Radicals in his party, who had an agenda more ambitious and clearer than his own. They saw no point in preserving the Union with slavery maintained; the issue had to be settled. In this, the Radicals understood the deeper logic of the war more quickly than did those who thought reunion could be based on yet another sectional political compromise. Even more important, whatever Lincoln's ambivalence, he prosecuted the war in an increasingly vigorous manner that propelled him and the Union toward the logic of emancipation, if not necessarily to racial justice.

When the war began, Lincoln believed that the national government should strive to restore and preserve the Union rather than to end slavery, the position of almost all Republicans. In the field, most soldiers would have agreed with William Reed, who wrote back to a friend in Iowa, "I am as much in favor for the Union as any one but I am not in favor of shedding my blood for the sake of the black tribe although I think Slavery is a ruination to our government." At the start, in conformity with general sentiments and in particular to placate slaveholding unionists, especially in Kentucky, Lincoln moved cautiously, with the support of his party.

Flight to Freedom   Almost immediately, war and black responses to it changed forever the political configuration of slavery. Despite Lincoln's dallying, and however lukewarm Republican feelings about justice for them, blacks perceived Lincoln's election and the onset of war as biblically symbolic. Slaves reenacted their own version of the Book of Exodus by fleeing their homes and masters for the Promised Land. As many as 500,000 slaves migrated north during the war, thus helping to weaken the Confederacy and strengthen the Union, even if northern authorities did not immediately mobilize them for the war effort.

Other political figures wanted to move on emancipation more quickly than Lincoln, and as some of them were now political generals, they had opportunities to take action. On May 24, 1861, just five weeks after Fort Sumter, when Union forces occupied a corner of Confederate Virginia, at Fort Monroe, hundreds of slaves fled their plantations for the Union encampment. Union general Benjamin F. Butler, in command of this expedition, declared these fugitive slaves to be "contraband of war" and put them to work. Although it was hardly ennobling to blacks to call them a species of property, by responding this way to black initiative, Butler demonstrated his awareness that at the very least the loss of Confederate assets in slaves could be Union gains. At least some of his men agreed with Butler. One Maryland master reported that when he attempted to retrieve his fugitives, soldiers in the white regiment to whom they had fled cried, "shoot him, bayonet him, kill him, pitch him out, the nigger stealer, the nigger driver," stoned the man and drove him from camp without his former slaves.

Other Union generals, however, returned fugitive slaves to their masters. In effect, there was no general policy but only the whims of local commanders, a haphazard situation that would remain unresolved for more than a year. On August 6, 1861, Congress passed the First Confiscation Act, which nullified masters' claims to their fugitive slaves if they had been used for Confederate military purposes, or if the masters had contributed to the Confederate war effort, something hard either to prove or disprove. The bill failed to provide clear direction to Union officers, and it also seemed to reinforce the claims of loyal masters in Union slave states.

Haphazard Union Policy

On August 30, 1861, Gen. John C. Frémont, heroic explorer, 1856 Republican presidential candidate, and a man who took his independent standing very seriously, declared martial law in the Department of the Missouri, which he commanded, and emancipated the slaves of all disloyal masters. After Frémont

Abolitionist Union Officials

THIS PORTRAIT of John C. Frémont appeared in *Harper's Weekly* in November 1861. In May 1861 Lincoln gave Frémont command of the Western Department, where in July the general took it upon himself to issue an emancipation proclamation for his command region. Trying to bolster Union fortunes in border slave states, Lincoln rescinded the proclamation and fired Frémont, although many antislavery Republicans continued to admire him for the stance he had taken.

refused Lincoln's polite request that he mute his declaration to conform to the Confiscation Act, the president ordered him to do so and then fired him on November 2. Nevertheless, Frémont had let the cat out of the bag; by articulating what appeared at the time an extreme measure, he had placed it on the political agenda. Frémont had sharpened the antislavery potential of the war. Abolitionists, particularly black abolitionists, rallied to Frémont's position and grew increasingly vocal in their criticism of the, to them, slow-moving Lincoln.

In his December 1861 annual report, Secretary of War Simon Cameron proposed that blacks be freed and armed. Lincoln recalled the report, excised the proposal, and fired Cameron the next month, presumably for corrupt administration, though many believed Cameron's stance on slavery was the deeper cause. In the spring of 1862, another antislavery Union general, David Hunter, in command of the Sea Islands off the South Carolina shore that had been captured by the Union navy in November 1861, again escalated the emancipationist agenda. After the War Department ignored his request to arm former slaves in his command who had been abandoned by their fleeing masters, Hunter went right ahead and did it on his own on May 9, 1862. He told Abraham Lincoln, in a letter that reached the antislavery press, that his experiment was "a complete and even marvelous success. [The freedmen] are sober, docile, attentive and enthusiastic, displaying great natural capacities for acquiring the duties of the soldier. They are eager beyond all things to take the field and be led into action." The following month, when Hunter proclaimed the freedom of slaves in South Carolina, Georgia, and Florida, Lincoln nullified his order, and the War Department refused to equip or pay his black troops, thus ending Hunter's independent experiment. Once more, however, a local Union commander had broached an antislavery policy—the use of black troops—thus rendering it thinkable. That same summer, commanders in Louisiana and Kansas undertook similar initiatives. To a considerable extent, they were responding to pressures from black freedmen, many of whom were eager to pick up the rifle to liberate their compatriots.

1862: Union War Aims Deepen As the war deepened—the battle at Shiloh in early April 1862 and the bloody and losing Peninsula campaign in late June coming as special shocks because of their magnitude—and as Union forces occupying Confederate territory discovered that white civilians often remained treacherous enemies, whether they stayed at home and resisted Union rule passively or took to the brush as guerrillas—blacks seemed increasingly plausible adjuncts to Union war aims. Awareness that many white young men were reacting to the increasing slaughter by resisting recruitment only sharpened the belief in black potential in many quarters. Desires to punish the South and to use blacks to do so grew in tandem. Not only would black troops fight, but their very appearance would also do much to humiliate their former masters, turning the southern political world upside down. In northern legislatures and in Congress, antislaveholder action intensified, which always had abolitionist meanings, whether or not that was the chief intention of the legislators. Meanwhile, in Virginia, Union soldiers began to attack Confederate civilian property with greatly increased intensity, following harsh new policies issued by McClellan's replacement, John Pope, a Republican close to many congressional Radicals.

On March 13, 1862, Congress prohibited federal soldiers from returning fugitive slaves to their owners, and on April 16 it abolished slavery in the District of Columbia, the first act of actual emancipation. This was followed on June 19 by a congressional act prohibiting slavery in the western territories. Yet, even these actions were limited by reservations, most of which came from President Lincoln. On April 10 Congress accepted Lincoln's plan to compensate masters financially in any state that would undertake gradual emancipation. In the District of Columbia emancipation bill, masters were offered a $300-per-head compensation, and funds were earmarked to pay for the colonization of former slaves out of the United States. British Honduras, Panama, and Liberia were considered as destinations during the war (and there would be one disastrous experiment in Haiti). Clearly, Lincoln sought to craft this bill to serve as a general model for emancipation. **Congressional Emancipation Measures**

This was Lincoln's plan, to which Congress was willing to accede, although with rapidly growing reluctance: gradual emancipation, compensation to masters for their property, black deportation. This unwieldy and improbable attempt at temperate change was scuttled not by abolitionists but by conservative congressmen from slaveholding Union states. On July 12, 1862, Lincoln called a group of these legislators to the White House, asked them to accept his scheme immediately, and warned with great foresight that as an alternative, slavery would be "extinguished by mere friction and abrasion—by the mere incidents of war." On July 14 they rejected the proposal. The war-driven erosion of the peculiar institution would thus continue, and Lincoln's scheme also withered. At this point, given increasing public and congressional pressure to act on slavery, realizing that the very men he had intended to aid had sabotaged his preferred plan, Lincoln had to rethink his political strategy. **Lincoln and Gradual Emancipation**

In the meantime, Congress continued to push forward vigorously. On July 17 it passed the Second Confiscation Act, which permitted the government to seize all rebel property, forbade any member of the armed forces from returning fugitive slaves, and licensed the president to employ blacks in any way he deemed fit to fight the Confederacy. This bill ended ambiguity and varying ad hoc policies among officers of different political persuasions on the fugitive slave issue. On the same day, Congress passed the Militia Act, which opened the way to the use of black troops and granted freedom to slaves who joined the army. These bills came just four months after David Hunter's first failed attempt to enlist freedmen. In late August, several black militia units in New Orleans were sworn into the federal service, and David Hunter was finally authorized to recruit Sea Island blacks. **The Second Confiscation Act**

The politically astute Lincoln consented to these congressional initiatives, although he did cause Congress to moderate the confiscation measure before he would sign it. He realized that he needed to maintain some presidential control over the emancipation process before the Radicals preempted him, and he also understood that confiscation and emancipation could be used to fashion a tougher military policy against the rebels, which he favored.

The Emancipation Proclamation

In this atmosphere of accelerating engagement of blacks in an altogether harsher war effort, Lincoln drafted a proclamation to free Confederate-owned slaves on July 22. When he brought the executive order to his cabinet, William Seward convinced Lincoln to postpone the announcement of the proclamation until after a major Union victory, lest it appear to be an act of desperation during hard military times. It was at this juncture that Lincoln wrote to renowned editor Horace Greeley of the New York *Tribune*, on August 22, 1862, "my paramount object in this struggle *is* to save the Union, and is *not* either to save or destroy slavery. If I could save the Union without freeing *any* slave I would do it; and if I could save it by freeing *all* the slaves I would do it; and if I could save it by freeing some and leaving others alone I would also do that." Lincoln added that this purpose grew from his view of his "*official*" duty" rather than from his "*personal*" wish that all men every where could be free." Addressing a

THOUGH HOPES WERE HIGH that the Emancipation Proclamation of 1863 would ring in a new era of freedom, this cartoon from 1866 illustrates that changes were superficial. Here, Thomas Nast depicts the continuing evils of the slavery system. Before emancipation, blacks could be sold like cattle, as shown on the left. Yet, as seen on the right, even three years later whites were still whipping black freemen as punishment for crimes, proclaiming their "states rights" to control the blacks.

broad range of public opinion, much of which remained hostile to emancipation, Lincoln put a conservative slant on a dramatic forthcoming proposal, while at the same time signaling abolitionists that his heart was with them.

The withdrawal southward of the Confederate army after the bloody and indecisive battle at Antietam on September 17 served well enough as victory for Seward and Lincoln, and so, on September 22, the president issued his Preliminary Emancipation Proclamation. The following New Year's Day would be the day of liberation.

Far from being stirring, as one might have expected from Lincoln's eloquent pen, this historic declaration read like a lawyer's contract, hedged and bland. At the onset of the document, Lincoln repeated his offer of compensated, gradual emancipation followed by colonization. Only after reiterating these conservative proposals, which by this time he probably knew could never be enacted, did he declare that as of January 1, 1863, "all persons held as slaves within any state...the people whereof shall then be in rebellion against the United States shall be then, thenceforward and forever free." The government, Lincoln continued, "will do no act or acts to repress such persons, or any of them, in any efforts they may make for their actual freedom." Committed antislavery people greeted the proclamation with incredulity, as it freed only those slaves not within the Union, leaving slavery alone in Union slave states. For his part, Lincoln clearly believed that as president he had no constitutional authority to free slaves within the United States.

Nevertheless, and this must be emphasized, the proclamation was indeed a monumental shift in policy disguised in lawyer's talk. Even if only on paper at first, it freed the vast majority of slaves and clearly was a step that would be almost impossible to reverse. On January 1, 1863, in the cities of the North and occupied portions of the South, freedmen paraded in triumph. "Thence forward and forever free"—that phrase had a ring that overcame the rest of the document. It announced the "Kingdom Coming" and the "Year of Jubilee." For a celebration at the Boston Music Hall, Ralph Waldo Emerson chanted a hymn that included the lines:

Welcoming the Emancipation Proclamation in the North

> I break your bonds and masterships.
> And I unchain the slave:
> Free be his heart and hand henceforth:
> As wind and wandering wave.

Meanwhile, at Tremont Temple, Boston's blacks held their own joyous festivity. Frederick Douglass proclaimed that the dark yesterdays of enslavement were now to be followed "by the rosy dawning of the new truth of freedom," and the congregation joined him in booming out the words of an old spiritual: "Blow ye the trumpet blow, Sound the loud timbrel o'er Egypt's dark sea, Jehovah hath triumphed, his people are free." Black services greeted the proclamation across the North and the Union-occupied South. Also on that day, Lincoln announced a vigorous program to enlist black troops, and massive recruitment soon began.

**The Effects
of the
Proclamation**

The revolutionary implications of the Emancipation Proclamation also were not lost on northern Democrats, who violently objected to making emancipation and the arming of blacks, rather than reunion, the center of the war effort, and they began work to roll it back. For example, on January 7, 1863, the Democratic-controlled Illinois state legislature resolved that the proclamation was a "gigantic usurpation" and "subversion" of constitutional authority by the president, designed to turn the war into a "crusade for the sudden, unconditional and violent liberation" of the slaves. It was a "revolution in the social organization of the Southern States" and an invitation to slaves to make a "servile insurrection," colored by "inhumanity and diabolism." There remained a powerful *northern* opposition to Lincoln's policy, one that would have long-term implications for the acceptance of the notion of equal justice for black people.

**Black
Enlistment and
the Confederacy**

Emancipation linked to black enlistment profoundly deepened the war in many ways. For the Confederates, it meant that unless a peace-at-any-price party came to power in the North, any likely conclusion to the war would be premised on southern acceptance of abolition. To achieve peace, they would have to give up their slaves as well as their political independence—and that, they resolved, would never happen. So committed were the vast majority of slaveholders to maintaining slavery that they would not submit to compromise on the issue. Thus, both sides dug in for a long and bloody struggle.

**Effects of the
Proclamation
Abroad**

Emancipation also altered the diplomatic dimension of the war. Before then, many in Britain—the superpower of the day—and in France and the other continental powers had considerable sympathy with the Confederate proposition that the Union was fighting a war of imperial conquest over an oppressed people seeking to be free. Many in the British aristocracy had some sense of identification with the southern gentry and antipathy with materialistic northerners who were well on the road to outstripping Britain as an industrial power; it was tempting for them to fish in troubled waters to weaken America. Such sentiments never dominated the government of the day, however, as the British had too much to lose through casual adventure—Canada for starters—and as British middle-class and working-class public opinion, growing in importance at this time, never supported the South, seeing in the Republican's policies support for their own efforts to democratize their nation.

With the Emancipation Proclamation, however, talk of recognizing the South decreased dramatically. After all, Britain had led the way in abolishing the slave trade and, in 1834, ending slavery in her colonies. The moral capital accumulated by this long-term reform policy meant that to the degree that the Union was fighting a war against slavery and not simply against political dissidents, the British would tend to align with the party of freedom. Union military victories perhaps did more to convince the British to stay out of the war, particularly as they watched the Union army and navy become increasingly powerful, presenting the possibility of anti-British American imperialism in the post–Civil War world.

**The Limits of
Emancipation**

Too much should not be made of the independent importance of the Emancipation Proclamation however. Both before and after that event, the incursions of Union troops into the South, much of which they occupied, and the ever in-

WHENEVER UNION TROOPS approached southern plantations, many slaves would bundle up their possessions, seize their masters' livestock and wagon, and flee toward the Union lines. In July or August 1862, Timothy O'Sullivan photographed this group of self-emancipated slaves, as they crossed the Rappahannock River in Virginia on their way north to freedom.

creasing mass flight of slaves to sectors secured by Union troops, provided much of the emancipationist energy of the Civil War. One Virginia refugee exclaimed in 1865 about the significance of his earlier escape: "It used to be five hundred miles to git to Canada from Lexington, but now it's only eighteen miles! *Camp Nelson* is now *our* Canada!" Setting off from Louisiana to Texas to carry the family slaves beyond reach of Union troops, Mary Williams Pugh reported to her mother, "the first night Sylvester left—the next night at Bayou B. about 25 of Pa's best hands left & the next day nearly all the women & children started—but this Pa found out in time to catch them all except one man & one woman. Altogether he had lost about 60 of his best men." Confederate authorities were well aware of the implications of such flight but could do less and less to stop more and more of it.

Once again, the Union had done no planning for this unprecedented population movement, and they greeted the liberated slave families with a confused mixture of empathy, indifference, hostility, and exploitation. All those black hands and bodies were potentially useful to the Union cause, many Union officials soon realized despite their underlying racial attitudes. One Democrat from Ohio wrote, "my doctrine has been anything to weaken the enemy," which meant that blacks ought to be made "serviceable" to the Union, whether with spade or musket. In Washington on March 31, 1863, Henry Halleck wrote to General Grant, "Every slave withdrawn from the enemy, is equivalent to a white man put *hors de combat.*" Black men could be put to immediate use to relieve the

Black Refugees

army of such onerous tasks as digging fortifications and serving as teamsters, while women could be used as cooks and cleaners and in hospitals for the worst jobs. Realizing the simple calculation that their loss in labor could be a direct Union gain, the Confederates tried to ship many slaves deeper into their territory and to conscript others into their service digging entrenchments and performing other hard labor on the war front, which only served to accelerate black flight to the Union whenever opportunity arose. Whole families fled, not just men—this was a permanent population movement.

Union Abuses of Freedmen

Despite this basic federal understanding of the labor potential of fugitive slaves, much of the treatment of blacks was abysmal. When the army employed ever increasing numbers of black men in drudge labor, no national policy prescribed pay or working conditions. The principle of wages was recognized, but more often than not, black men received only inadequate food and clothing and a little cash, irregularly if at all. Black families that depended on such payments often suffered because of the stingy treatment accorded laborers. To take just one example, three white officers—the chaplain and two

INUNDATED WITH SELF-LIBERATED African Americans, the Union army settled many of them in "contraband camps"—contraband being their somewhat dehumanizing name for such former slaves. In this 1863 photograph, dozens of ex-slaves, mainly women and children, are seen in their government quarters at what had been the Baton Rouge, Louisiana, Female Seminary. Most of the missing young male members of these families were soldiers enlisted in the new "colored" regiments of the Union army.

surgeons—in Helena, Arkansas, writing to the commander of the Department of the Missouri on December 29, 1862, charged that some black families who had been paid had been robbed and sometimes killed by Union soldiers who went unpunished. Some of the wives had been "molested by soldiers to gratify their licentious lust, and their husbands murdered" when defending their wives, again without punishment. Many black men received no pay and only their own meals, no provision being made for families who were thus "left in a helpless & starving position."

Some refugees protested this treatment. A group of men on Roanoke Island, North Carolina, even wrote to President Lincoln on March 9, 1865, to complain that for the past three years they had been paid rarely, subjected to corporal punishment, and often ordered around at the point of bayonets. They insisted that they would do any tasks assigned them but that they were "not willing to be pull and haul about by those head men." Large numbers of men conscripted for labor at the front had never returned, and when the Union army had taken them, recorded one black, "they treated us mean as our owners ever did...just like we had been dum beast." Other men from Roanoke Island informed the secretary of war that the man in charge of the local commissary house kicked out hungry women and children who were begging for supplies and then sold food earmarked for freedmen for his own profit, while white soldiers broke into their houses to steal their chickens and garden produce.

Black Protests over Union Abuses

In many areas of Union occupation, having fled their home plantations in search of work, black families had no place to live. As a public health measure, fugitive slaves were driven out of many cities and towns by army authorities unless they were in the direct employ of a white person who would take responsibility for them. All over the South, shantytowns sprang up at the edges of cities and in the countryside—living conditions true for many white war refugees as well. People threw together whatever shacks they could, only skimpy construction materials being available. In these windowless, unventilated, damp, and filthy refugee camps, epidemic disease ran rampant.

The Wandering Life of Refugees

Thousands of blacks became camp followers to Union armies—vagrants really—moving through the South. These desperate people provided menial services in exchange for whatever food and clothing soldiers would toss them, but many Union commanders, who considered such additions to their baggage trains a great nuisance, sought to get rid of them. In a case that became notorious in the northern press, Jefferson C. Davis, one of William T. Sherman's corps commanders during the March to the Sea in 1864, pulled up his pontoon bridge after getting his troops safely across a rain-swollen Georgia river, abandoning the blacks in his train to the pistols and sabers of Gen. Joseph Wheeler's approaching Confederate cavalry, or to the river, where many drowned. When questioned about the affair, it is reported that Davis told Sherman he had forbidden the refugees to follow him, "but that they would come along and he took up his pontoon bridges, not because he wanted to leave them, but because he wanted his bridge." Assured by Davis that Wheeler had not killed any fugitives, Sherman took his unsubstantiated word as that of one honorable white officer to another and dismissed the story of abandonment as "cock-and-bull." There is no record of the number of African American lives destroyed that day.

Experiments on Abandoned Lands

Because excursions into the urban labor pool or camp-following were such dismal choices, Union officials considered two major alternatives for organizing the labor of the newly freed slaves in the countryside, where 95 percent of them had resided before the war. The first plan would somehow reconstitute the plantation system, using wage labor. The second would put the blacks on rental land of their own. The third possibility, something of a mixture of the first two, would be to superintend blacks on abandoned plantations, renamed "government farms," under white overseers. These experiments were tried only in a few places, especially areas that the Union occupied early in the war, notably the Sea Islands off the South Carolina coast and the area around New Orleans and along the lower reaches of the Mississippi River.

In certain instances, northern men came south or left the army to take up the abandoned plantations of departed southern owners, most of whom were in the Confederate army. In many other instances, plantation owners who remained on their land still needed black labor, which the army sought to regulate. Two very different views of the ex-slaves determined which approach was taken. The harsher and more cynical view was that these were "rude, childlike people," as one white superintendent of black farmers argued, and that slavery therefore had to be replaced by another paternalistic, white-dominated system. Other whites took a more favorable view. For example, the abolitionist Francis W. Bird testified on December 24, 1863, to a commission established by the secretary of war that slaves working rented land "regard it as a great boon" that they were allowed a share of their own crops. All that needed to be done to build a "loyal and prosperous" black community, Bird insisted, would be to allow them to own their own soil.

The Carolina Sea Islands Experiment

Union officials tried several different modes of placing freed blacks on ex-Confederate lands, but none resulted in widespread black land ownership. On the Sea Islands of South Carolina, when the Union gunboats drove out the Confederate army early in 1862, the plantation owners fled, leaving behind 10,000 slaves. What followed was confused experimentation. Left on their own, at first the slaves sacked and often burned the great houses and then began to grow food crops for themselves while avoiding planting cotton—the great symbol of their enslavement. Several dozen young male and female white abolitionists—Gideon's Band as they became known—came down from New England to teach the freedmen reading, writing, and arithmetic, as well as to instill free labor values such as punctuality and thrift and to help them acquire land. However, sensing big profits to be made in cotton, treasury agents seized the abandoned lands for nonpayment of taxes and auctioned them off to northern speculators and officials, many of whom colluded with those treasury officials to make inside deals. Few blacks could muster the resources, even if they joined together, to purchase land.

The freedmen did not accept this turn of events passively. They organized local associations in many locales and pushed federal authorities for title to the

IN ADDITION TO WORK, food, shelter, and some security, fugitive slaves desired education. Often with the help of free blacks and white teachers from the North, ex-slaves founded schools at their contraband camps, such as this one on St. Helena Island, South Carolina, part of the Port Royal experiment in wartime reconstruction.

land. These nascent political organizations lasted into the Reconstruction period, where they formed part of the wider agenda of African American Union League political clubs. In a sense, from the start, the freedmen set themselves in a political and economic tension with their northern rulers—they sought a voice, and they knew that the Union needed them, and thus did a people politicize themselves.

One Boston consortium, which purchased eleven plantations, about 8,000 acres in all, sent Edward Philbrick down to manage them. He hired nearly 1,000 laborers, and divided the land into family-size lots that black families farmed for a share of the crop. Philbrick was not devoid of idealism, but the profit he hoped to turn proved disappointing to him, and so, by 1865, he sold off the land and went back to Boston. For their part, if they could not own their own land, blacks wanted to make enough cash for security and to remain independent of white domination, even from the paternalism of the best-intentioned northern philanthropist.

Another model was tried at Davis Bend, Mississippi, on the huge plantations of Jefferson Davis and his brother, Joseph. The Davises always had accorded their slaves a considerable amount of independence in assigning themselves tasks and in forming slave courts to judge bad behavior and impose sanctions. This policy had the unintentional effect of encouraging them to

Another Experiment: Davis Bend

teach themselves self-government without owners. In 1864, in the absence of the Davis brothers, after the Union occupied this region, the ex-slaves leased the plantations from the federal government and continued to plant cotton as well as food, setting up their own local government. They made tidy profits, but this successful model did not spread.

Labor Relations in Louisiana

In Louisiana, some of the rice planters were unionists, and others took loyalty oaths after the Union occupation in 1862. There the army tried to enforce a system of fair wages for ex-slaves, based on contracts freedmen signed with their former owners. Union officials also insisted that, as a condition of their contract, the freedmen had to remain on the land unless granted permission to leave by the owners, in effect creating a form of peonage—a kind of hybrid form between slave and free labor. This system resembled that implemented by Gen. Lorenzo Thomas in leasing the Mississippi Valley plantations of Confederates to loyal men coming down from the north. Seeking quick profits, many unscrupulous entrepreneurs took up the leases. Thomas compelled black men either to serve in the army as laborers or to sign contracts to work on the plantations. Thomas had set low wage levels, and the new plantation bosses frequently exploited their workers even more severely than had the prior owners, so many freedmen remained mired in the squalid shantytowns they had built immediately after their plantations had crumbled. Many black workers resisted their new bosses, and the whole system proved unprofitable, highly discouraging, and often brutalizing.

LORENZO THOMAS, adjutant general of the Union army. After falling out with Secretary of War Edwin M. Stanton, Thomas was assigned to endless inspection tours and to organize black regiments in the Mississippi River Valley, where he also formulated a system to lease out the plantations of departed Confederates to northern white entrepreneurs.

Surprisingly, in 1864, none other than the negrophobe Gen. William T. Sherman promulgated the most radical experimental plan for southern land and black labor. Sherman had done everything in his power to keep black troops out of his army, including disobeying direct orders from Abraham Lincoln to use them. Under the urging of Secretary of War Stanton, who arrived in Savannah on January 11, 1865, to assign black troops to Sherman's command and to urge him to do something about his reputation among blacks, Sherman, on January 16, proposed that coastal lands "abandoned" by their former owners—who in fact had fled—be distributed in 40-acre lots to former slaves, who were to be given a "possessory title in writing." Under this plan, land was distributed to about 40,000 ex-slaves along the Georgia and South Carolina coast. Sherman put abolitionist Gen. Rufus Saxton, a man he despised, in charge of the project. Special Field Orders No. 15 satisfied Sherman by allowing him both to get rid of slaves following his army and to rub salt into wounded southern white pride by showing them their powerlessness.

Land Redistribution Schemes

This was almost certainly the model and impetus for the demand of "forty acres and a mule"—the land redistribution for which freedmen pushed after the war was over. However, in 1866, under the prodding of President Andrew Johnson, who supported the claims of plantation owners, the government called Special Field Orders No. 15 a temporary wartime measure, took back title to the land, and returned it to the former white owners. Blacks were dispossessed in the Sea Islands as well after the war. For those in power in Washington, the sanctity of private property was a fundamental social and economic value that precluded land seizure and redistribution, even as a means to punish one's worst enemies.

To rationalize this terrible mess over land and black labor, although some centralized governmental response had been discussed as early as 1863, only in March 1865 did Congress establish the Bureau of Refugees, Freedmen, and Abandoned Lands, commonly called the Freedmen's Bureau. Americans had never used the government to solve deep social problems with permanent bureaucratic structures, and therefore even this bureau proved short lived. Of all the various forms of black labor attempted during the war, working for wages or for shares of the crop on plantations owned by whites became the predominant modes after the war, and the bureau's main postwar role was in trying to secure fair contracts for blacks within these forms. Both offered a modicum of protection for blacks while supporting white efforts to create an efficient, productive outcome using coercive—and sometimes punitive—controls. Within a few years, sharecropping became the predominant mode of labor relations, mainly because blacks desired to work without direct white supervision. Interestingly enough, sharecropping also spread among poor whites when white land owners came to appreciate the flexibility and relatively easy domination sharecropping afforded them.

The Freedmen's Bureau

While this checkered experience was occurring in the Confederate states to which the Emancipation Proclamation applied, slavery disintegrated in the Union slave states of Maryland, Missouri, Delaware, and Kentucky, where the proclamation did not apply. This not-so-gradual collapse took place despite sometimes strident efforts of slaveholders to maintain the institution. After

Disintegration of Slavery in the Union Slave States

1863 the chief means of change was black enlistment in the army, for with enlistment came freedom. Because the laws governing enlistment were new and murky, blacks learned to manipulate them to their advantage in an unstated collusion with the army, which wanted and needed them, and against the master class, which wished to retain them.

In Maryland, where nearly half of African Americans were already free before the war—the highest proportion of free blacks in any slave state—slaveholders feared that recruiting free blacks would lead to recruiting their slaves, and they were right. After enlistment of free blacks started in earnest in June 1863, Maryland unionist masters convinced Abraham Lincoln to suspend recruitment of slaves. However, given overwhelming manpower needs, Union officials resumed active enlistment of slaves in October. Furthermore, the army sent out black soldiers to guarantee safe passage for slaves wishing to enlist, which created more anger among slaveholders. The same pattern was repeated in Missouri, where 40 percent of slave men joined the army, and in Kentucky, where the figure was 60 percent. In many cases, families went along to army camps with the men, not in the least because owners frequently retaliated against family members left behind. In addition, many of those slaves who remained in their home region often refused to work unless they were paid wages, and employers desperate for workers increasingly overlooked the slave origins of potential employees.

In less than two years, slavery in Union slave states collapsed. The formal abolition of slavery in these places was more an acknowledgment that the institution had decayed than a stirring affirmation of abolitionist sentiments. On November 1, 1864, Maryland became the first Union slave state to abolish slavery in a new state constitution, with Missouri following suit on January 11, 1865. Kentucky and Delaware never formally abolished the institution, although it was rapidly disintegrating in both places. All ambiguities about the dissolution of slavery were not ended until the ratification of the Thirteenth Amendment to the U.S. Constitution on December 18, 1865. Earlier state actions reflected an often begrudging recognition that the slaves had done much to end slavery, with help from an army that desperately needed their manpower, and the strong support of a relatively small cadre of committed abolitionists. Indeed, while many, perhaps most, black men had volunteered for the army—whether as laborers or soldiers—others had been impressed into service, pulled off the streets, sometimes taken from churches on Sunday, often seized from their homes without being allowed to don their shoes or coats or make their good-byes.

African Americans in the Union Army Emancipation and picking up the gun made an enormous impact on blacks and on relationships between whites and blacks. When joining the army, African American men immediately sought the rewards of citizenship that white citizens took for granted, and many of them understood that injury or death in battle would forward the freedom of their people. A significant and often vocal minority of whites agreed with this supposition. For example, on March 23, 1863, Governor John Andrew of Massachusetts rejoiced to his constituent, George A. Downing, a well-known black abolitionist and businessman, that black enlistment "pledges the honor of the Nation in the same degree

IN MAY 1862, at Charleston, South Carolina, the slave Robert Smalls boldly commandeered the *Planter,* a Confederate warship, and sailed it out to the Union fleet blockading the harbor. Immediately lionized by the northern press, Smalls was rewarded with the job of pilot for the Union fleet, and he went on to a political career in his home state during Reconstruction. This engraving appeared in *Harper's Weekly,* June 14, 1862.

and to the same rights with all other troops. They will be soldiers of the Union—nothing less and nothing different [and] will earn for themselves an honorable fame, vindicating their race and redeeming their future from dispersions of the past." Although nearly all blacks agreed with this program, the vast majority of whites did not. They remained convinced that blacks were a debased and worthless race that belonged at the bottom of society. There ensued for black troops one of the most troubling chapters of the Civil War, a military experience not of welcoming and triumph, but of discrimination and struggle for a modicum of justice. By the end of the war, more than 180,000 black soldiers and sailors served the Union, about 20 percent of black men of military age North and South. This included 34,000 free northern blacks, an astonishingly high 15 percent of the entire black population of the North. Much of their military experience replicated the discrimination they had always faced and against which they had always had to contend. In a sense, black men had to fight a war to be allowed to fight the war.

White Officers and Black Men

De facto army policy prohibited black men from serving as officers. In Louisiana, several black militia regiments had formed under free black officers prior to their being called into national service. When that time came, Gen. Nathaniel P. Banks, in charge in Louisiana, insisted that those officers resign. Among all subsequent black regiments, until the spring of 1865, when a few exceptions were made for black junior officers, white officers always were placed in charge.

Some of these white officers were idealistic, but perhaps more of them saw a practical opportunity to advance in pay and in rank by leading new black troops. In other cases, some officers of white regiments, in order to get rid of difficult subordinates, encouraged men they disliked to try their chances with black troops. To screen and train potential officers, the army established a Bureau of Colored Troops in May 1863, which set prescribed examinations for prospective officers. Finding that nearly half of the potential officers failed the exam, the army later established a Free Military School for Applicants for Commands of Colored Troops, which graduated up to thirty candidates per week, achieving a success rate of 96 percent. This was the first American experiment with any sort of officer's candidate training school.

Whatever their training, most of these officers reflected the racial attitudes common to white America. Many of them believed black soldiers were child-like, "simple, docile, and affectionate almost to the point of absurdity," in the words of one officer, who doubtless believed his to be a caring attitude. They were given to "indolence and acting carelessly," wrote other officers, to "stupidity and slow motion, natural or assumed." They lacked independence and self-reliance. These attitudes led to an implicit double jeopardy in the treatment that such officers meted out: harsh discipline might correct childish attitudes, but it would squelch black initiative. In either case, black soldiers were diminished in the eyes of their paternalistic officers.

Grudging Acceptance of Black Troops

Over time, although some officers gained increased sympathy and respect for their troops, other officers' prejudices hardened. One insisted, "it is useless to talk about being lenient with them for if you give them an inch they will take a mile." Another man concluded, after leading black soldiers for nine months, "I no longer wonder slave drivers were cruel. I am. I no longer have any bowels of mercy."

White enlisted men as well as white officers frequently discriminated against black troops. They often complained that they felt "demeaned" to be fighting alongside black troops, doubting the trustworthiness and courage of blacks. A Massachusetts private declared that blacks would be bound to flee the field of battle and that he would gladly shoot them in the back when that happened. "The feeling against the niggers is intensely strong in this army," he generalized, noting that they were seen as the principal cause of the war. The initial response of most white enlisted men to the Emancipation Proclamation had been almost uniformly negative. "We thought we were fighting for the stars and stripes, but we found out it is for the d—d nigger," one private wrote home, and he was certain that all his mates agreed with him.

Many enlisted men came to a grudging acceptance of black troops. "It is nothing but a neger war an so let the negers fight as well as the whites," a Pennsylvania private concluded, and many other men backed into the position that black troops, if despicable, were useful.

It must be noted that much of the historical record about the maltreatment of black troops came from white soldiers who found the abuses offensive. For example, Col. James C. Beecher, from the famous abolitionist family, protested to his superiors on September 13, 1863, about the onerous conditions while digging ditches and building forts that had landed 25 percent of his North Carolina black regiment on the sick list. "They have been slaves and are just learning to be men. It is a drawback that they are regarded as, and called 'd——d Niggers' by so-called gentlemen in uniform of U.S. Officers, but when they send them to do menial work for white regiments [this] simply throws them back where they were before and reduces them to the position of slaves again." Gen. James S. Brisbin, in Kentucky, noted on October 20, 1864, that on the march his black troops were "made the subject of much ridicule and many insulting remarks" and petty annoyances by white troops, such as pulling off their caps and stealing their horses. However, Brisbin was pleased to see that once some black troops had faced a Confederate charge with great bravery and considerable losses, "those who had scoffed...were silent."

These white troops may not have cheered their black comrades at arms, but at least they no longer jeered. Indeed, for a number of white officers, experience heightened their opinions of their black men. One such officer wrote that these were "very remarkable men" and that their behavior as soldiers deepened his "faith in negro character and intellect." Another officer insisted that he was getting to "liking them more & more," and beginning to believe, "as they say sometimes round here, a white man is most as good as a nigger." Although their language frequently remained condescending when not overtly racist, such officers were actually discovering the humanity of their men. Almost certainly, those with positive outlooks got better results.

Prejudice also clouded white attitudes toward black soldiers' families. Many officers assumed that the black women who followed their regiments were just there for sex—part of the barely latent savagery that they believed characterized blacks—though many were wives of the soldiers. Apparently ignorant of this fact, some white officers made sexual advances on these black women, to the deep offense of their men, of a sort that they would not have tried on white women.

Not just officers and men on the line but the entire Union governmental structure often discriminated against the black men they so eagerly enlisted. Black troops were the last to be given good arms, food, and clothing. Most galling to the troops, they were paid less than whites. Where white privates received $13 per month plus clothing or its equivalent of $3.50 in cash, blacks were offered $10 per month, the $3.50 having been deducted for clothing. As a form of protest, many regiments refused their pay, at times joined in this boycott by their white officers. Not until June 15, 1864, did Congress make black pay equal to white, retroactive to the date of first enlistment.

Official Union Discrimination

Discrimination also had the effect of accelerating morbidity rates among black soldiers. The rate of death from disease in black regiments was 18 percent, two-and-one-half times greater than that for whites. Much of this discrepancy was caused by poor camp conditions and food, and medical care was also far worse for blacks. Few white doctors were willing to serve black soldiers, and there were very few black physicians because medical schools turned black applicants away. The dearth of supplies and even basic cleanliness in segregated black hospitals made them veritable death traps.

Widely believed to be unworthy of combat by white officers and men, blacks were almost always assigned to camp duties, often performing heavy manual labor, another reason for the high rates of death by disease. While 6 percent of white Union soldiers died in battle, the figure for blacks was about 1.5 percent, a figure that demonstrates the degree to which they were kept out of combat zones. Their assignment to the rear echelons angered and depressed them. If they had to die, reasoned the men, they wanted it to be in battle, where they could demonstrate their manly courage and feel as though they had contributed to the emancipation of their race. Their frustration led many blacks to desert, although black rates of desertion were about equal to that of whites.

Caught for desertion or arrested for other crimes, black soldiers were far more likely to be executed. Twenty-one percent of all soldiers executed were black, though they comprised about 12 percent of the entire army, and many of these men were hanged or shot for allegedly raping white women, while white soldiers rarely were executed for rape and almost never tried for the rape of black women. In addition, an astounding 80 percent of Union soldiers executed for mutiny were black, which suggests the heavy burdens under which they were placed and also the far greater likelihood that the mutinous actions of white soldiers would be overlooked.

Sherman's Policies Facing discrimination throughout the Union army, blacks encountered special hostility in the Western Theater of William Tecumseh Sherman in 1864–1865. Senator John Sherman of Ohio warned his brother that, in refusing to use black troops, he was isolating himself from a basic Union war aim, but the general ignored this advice and continued to berate the whole idea of arming blacks. He expressed himself most clearly on this issue on July 30, 1864, in what he called his "nigger letter," an utterly intemperate broadside that he circulated so widely among his subordinates that it was soon published. Sherman asked in this letter, "is not a negro as good as a white man to stop a bullet. Yes and a sandbag is better. . . . Can they improvise . . . sorties, flank movements, etc., like a white man? I say no . . . Negroes are not equal to this." He added in another letter, "I like niggers well enough as niggers, but when fools & idiots try & make niggers better than ourselves I have an opinion."

Despite Secretary of War Stanton's visit to Sherman in January 1865, when he steamed down from Washington to meet with the general and assign black troops to Sherman's army, Sherman ignored the directions of Lincoln and Stanton, taking away the black troops' guns and handing them shovels. His men, doubtless understanding and sharing their commander's beliefs, severely hazed these soldiers, beating many and killing two or three while in camp. This regiment did not join the march up through the Carolinas in early 1865. In contrast, in the Army of the Potomac, Gen. Ulysses S. Grant supported the enlistment of blacks, although he usually acceded to the prejudices of his subordinates when they placed black regiments in labor brigades or camps far from the front lines.

Abraham Lincoln evinced greater moral sensitivity on the issue of black troops and took a more affirmative position than most of his generals. To be sure, he was capable of advocating military *realpolitik*, as when he wrote a conservative unionist on September 12, 1864, "Any different policy in regard to the colored man [than black recruitment] deprives us of his help, and this is more than we can bear. . . . This is not a question of sentiment or taste, but one of physical force which can be measured and estimated as [can] horsepower and steampower. . . . Keep it and you can save the Union. Throw it away and the Union goes with it." However, in a more idealistic vein, Lincoln also argued that blacks, "like other people," were motivated by self-interest—in this case the promise of freedom. He also comprehended black honor, for he understood the liberation of the spirit that military action would bring to the freedmen. On August 26, 1863, Lincoln wrote in another letter: "There will be some black men who can remember that with silent tongue, and clenched teeth, and steady eye, and well-poised bayonet, they have helped mankind on to this great consummation" of freedom. Lincoln also insisted that white men who opposed the use of black troops "with malignant heart and deceitful speech" would be ashamed in later years of their spiritual dishonor. This was one of those moments of insight and introspection that kept Lincoln open to the opinions of abolitionists and the Radicals and that placed him toward the more liberal end of the spectrum of white opinion, even if he continued to argue for black deportation.

Lincoln's Policies

Despite systemic discrimination, even during the first months of Union service, undertrained black troops fought valiantly in several major engagements when permitted to do so. On May 27, 1863, the First and Third Louisiana Native Guards bravely launched several assaults on a powerfully entrenched Confederate force at Port Hudson, Louisiana. Ten days later, at Milliken's Bend on the Mississippi River, another black regiment held off a bayonet assault by a larger Confederate contingent, keeping to the field even after white Union soldiers broke and ran. And on July 18, the Fifty-fourth Massachusetts Colored Infantry, under the command of the Boston Brahmin Robert Gould Shaw, attempted heroically, if unsuccessfully, to storm the ramparts of Fort Wagner, South Carolina. As an act of contempt, the Confederates buried the fallen Shaw alongside his black men in a mass grave. However, many in Massachusetts, including Shaw's father, expressed pride in the young officer's death and the biracial manner of his interment.

Blacks in Combat

This well-publicized assault held considerable propaganda value for black troops and their supporters, and yet its impact on the use of black troops should not be overstated. White commanders most often remained unwilling to use blacks in combat, despite their powerful performances at places like Port Hudson and Fort Wagner. Blacks rarely figured prominently in Union offensive tactics.

Perhaps the best-known example of official hesitancy came in the battle of the Crater on July 30, 1864. With both sides stuck in siege warfare, Union sappers tunneled under the powerful Confederate trenches at Petersburg, Virginia, while black troops drilled thoroughly to lead an assault after dynamite would collapse the Confederate defenses. At the last moment, untrained white

ON JULY 18, 1863, Col. Robert Gould Shaw, a young Boston aristocrat, died leading the Fifty-fourth Massachusetts Colored Regiment, as they unsuccessfully but heroically stormed the ramparts of Fort Wagner, South Carolina. This feat impressed many in the Union about the martial value of black soldiers.

troops were substituted, in part because Grant and Meade feared the political backlash should it appear they were using black soldiers as cannon fodder, and in part because they did not fully trust black troops. When untrained white Union soldiers wandered ineffectively into the base of the crater that the explosion had created, they and the black troops who followed them got entangled, thus giving time for the Confederates to surround the crater. What ensued was slaughter, especially of blacks. As Maj. Matthew Love of North Carolina wrote his mother after the battle, "ther men were principally negroes and we shot them down untill we got near enough and then run them through with the Bayonet . . . we was not very particular whether we captured or killed them the only thing we did not like to be pestered berrying the heathens."

Prisoners of War   This massacre was not exceptional. Generally speaking during the Civil War, white prisoners were not shot, except in theaters of guerrilla warfare, although there were summary executions of prisoners by both sides. When it came to Confederates capturing black Union troops and their white officers, shooting prisoners was the norm, at least for a significant portion of the time. In addition to the Crater in the East, there were several major examples in the West.

Massacre at Fort Pillow   On April 12, 1864, Confederate troops under the command of the renowned Gen. Nathan Bedford Forrest (who had acquired great wealth in the slave trade before the war) screamed, "No quarter!" and "Kill the damn niggers, shoot them down!" as they overran Fort Pillow, Tennessee. Following Forrest's orders to shoot the defenders like dogs, Forrest's men massacred more than 100 blacks who had surrendered, and they also shot some whites. The rebels buried some wounded blacks alive, set fire to tents that contained injured African American soldiers, and murdered four little black boys and two black women, whose bodies they threw into the Mississippi River. That same month, at Poison Spring,

ON APRIL 12, 1864, screaming "No Quarter! . . . Kill the damn niggers." Confederate cavalry under the command of Nathan Bedford Forrest stormed into Fort Pillow, Tennessee, and massacred over 100 black Union soldiers who were attempting to surrender. There were many such incidents, demonstrating that the Civil War was also a race war.

Arkansas, other Confederates under Gen. John S. Marmaduke, a well-bred Missourian, executed a perhaps larger number of wounded blacks and others who were attempting to escape. Many of the slain blacks then were scalped, stripped, and mutilated by a Confederate regiment of Choctaw Indians.

Subsequently, according to reliable accounts, black soldiers shouting "Remember Fort Pillow!" sometimes murdered Confederate prisoners in return. Near the end of the war, at Fort Blakely, Alabama, black units threw the rebels into a panic when they charged into their fortifications. Many Confederates jumped into the river and drowned or were shot in the water. Others threw down their arms and ran toward white Union units, "to save themselves being butchered by our niggers," reported a white Union infantryman. The black troops "did not take a prisoner, [but] killed all they took to a man." At those moments when the Civil War became a race war, soldiers viciously lowered the threshold of violence.

On other occasions, Confederates shot white officers of colored regiments and reenslaved black Union troops. One outcome of such actions—and one certainly unintended by the Confederates—was to cause black men and white officers to feel greater camaraderie, as all were at mortal risk if captured. The southern response to black Union troops also contributed to the collapse of the

Reenslavement of Captured Black Soldiers

policy on exchanging prisoners of war that authorities on both sides had arranged, using European precedents. Earlier cartels had placed varying values on men of different ranks and had used arithmetical balance to exchange large numbers of prisoners, sometimes by the thousands. Although exchanged prisoners pledged not to take up arms again, many did so. One immediate response of Jefferson Davis and the Confederate Congress to the Emancipation Proclamation and the enlistment of black troops was to label white officers in black regiments fomenters of slave insurrection. These officers were to be turned over to state governments for the appropriate punishment if taken captive, death by hanging being implied. Captured black soldiers were to be returned to their states of origin, presumably into reenslavement. In part because of fear of retaliation, imprisonment was the outcome for most captured white officers (the ones not executed when captured), while substantial numbers of blacks evidently were returned to slavery, as were black civilians recaptured by Confederate troops. The fog of war closed in on these prisoners, obscuring their fates.

Prisoner Exchanges Collapse

In the fall of 1864, after the massive battles of Grant's Wilderness campaign had produced thousands of prisoners on both sides, Robert E. Lee, "with a view of alleviating the sufferings of our soldiers," proposed a man-for-man exchange of prisoners based on the earlier cartel. Grant immediately inquired whether Lee intended to deliver black prisoners as well as white, to which Lee replied, "Negroes belonging to our citizens are not considered subjects of exchange," although he would return blacks who had been free before the war. Asserting that the Union was "bound to secure to all persons received into her armies the rights due to soldiers," Grant broke off negotiations. At about the same time, Lee assigned black captives to work reinforcing the Petersburg trenches, where they might easily be killed. When Grant retaliated, using white Confederate prisoners to strengthen his works, Lee backed down in practice though never in principle.

Forgoing prisoner exchanges injured the South far more than the North, because captured Union soldiers could be otherwise replaced—often by blacks—while the southern manpower pool was nearing exhaustion. White supremacy, the southern priority, came at a considerable material cost to the Confederate war aims. And Grant was consciously willing to leave Union prisoners to their fates as part of a war of exhaustion that the South could not win. There was an element of cynicism in Grant's appearing to insist that it was the Confederate refusal to swap black prisoners that caused him to shut down exchanges. For public consumption he could make what appeared to be a principled and even idealistic stance, while his deeper aim was to keep those Confederate prisoners from returning to the war effort, even at the expense of Union prisoners, white and black.

Finally, in January 1865, the Confederacy agreed to include all Union prisoners in exchanges, which then were renewed but at a relatively low level. Consequently, prisoners continued to die in considerable numbers until the end of the war. Much of the resulting suffering and 56,000 prison deaths can thus be considered at least in part as the by-product of American race relations. Most of those deaths were of white men, caught in the web of the Confederate understanding that black ex-slaves in the Union army could never be granted equal standing with white prisoners.

Amid the pain of their great dislocation and the treatment accorded them from the North as well as the South, African Americans could feel triumph in their emancipation. For those who had fought, freedom was sealed with action. Wrote one former slave: "This was the biggest thing that ever happened in my life. I felt like a man with a uniform on and a gun in my hand." Elijah Marrs, another black soldier, later recalled that while standing at attention with his comrades during his first roll call, "I felt freedom in my bones." In the later stages of the war, ex-slaves were living on the property of former masters, joining the Union army, forming their own churches, and to a considerable extent controlling their own lives, none of which had been remotely possible during slavery.

Black Triumph

On October 18, 1859, the United States had sent troops under the command of Col. Robert E. Lee into Harpers Ferry to quash John Brown's insurrection, exercising federal support for the institution of slavery. Less than six year later, on February 18, 1865, a regiment of United States Colored Troops, recently freed from slavery, marched into Charleston, South Carolina, to receive the surrender of that city, the inner sanctum of southern secessionism. Surely these were signs of a great social and political revolution.

And yet, there was plenty of evidence that northern soldiers and authorities systemically discriminated against blacks during the war, that despite the change from slavery to freedom there remained a bedrock of race-based prejudice and discrimination. Even when it became an avowedly antislavery war, the Union war effort never became a concerted struggle for racial equality or justice for blacks. Although blacks strove mightily to give full expression to their freedom, and although they had supporters in the North who helped them, the bleak record did not augur well for whatever might come after organized warfare ceased. To say that the Emancipation Proclamation and the enlistment of black troops were steps on the road to eventual racial justice is to take such a long-term and partial view that it fails to deal sufficiently with the great wartime and postwar suffering of blacks, soldiers and civilians alike.

Petitioning the Tennessee legislature in January 1865, several black leaders asserted, concerning the nearly 180,000 black men under arms, "What higher order of citizen is there than the soldier? . . . If we are called on to do military service, why should we be denied the privilege of voting against the rebel citizens at the ballot box?" Black veterans frequently voiced their belief that wartime service gave them claim to equal opportunity. "With the nation we have suffered, and as part of this nation, we must rise with it," wrote a black private stationed in Memphis in September 1865, while Sgt. Henry Maxwell observed, "We want two more boxes besides the cartridge box, the ballot [box] and the jury box." Many progressive northerners would respond to such African American demands for citizenship. Yet, ominously, black efforts and those of their white allies remained set in a social and political environment that were in many respects deeply hostile to them, as wartime experience had demonstrated.

Black Veterans' Claims to Freedom

CHAPTER 6

Attack and Die: November 1862– January 1863

B y the fall of 1862, more than a year of war had ground on, leaving thousands of soldiers dead, maimed, or suffering from debilitating disease. Families were divided, communities wrecked, wealth lost, lives destroyed. The issuance of the Emancipation Proclamation changed the war's moral tenor and political consequences but moved neither side any closer to peace. No end to the killing was yet in sight. If anything, the proclamation deepened the war, as it meant that the South would have to fight on with no hope for a political compromise unless Lincoln were to lose the election of 1864.

Ambrose Burnside Takes Command

After the awful carnage of Antietam, followed by weeks of inactivity, President Lincoln had seen enough of the "Young Napoleon." On November 7, 1862, Lincoln fired Gen. George B. McClellan from command of the Army of the Potomac. Lincoln's act spread consternation in the army, where McClellan remained very popular. Many officers hated what they considered outside political interference, and they identified with their commander, who had spent a great deal of energy fighting the Republican administration. One infantry lieutenant asked, "how can we succeed when mere trickster politicians control the movements of our generals and dictate how and when they must act?" Col. Charles Wainwright concluded in his diary that even those who blamed McClellan for the army's shortcomings felt the "greatest indignation" about Lincoln's intervention. And when McClellan took his formal leave, Wainwright

IN EARLY NOVEMBER 1862, Gen. Ambrose E. Burnside became President Lincoln's third attempt to find a competent and reliable commander for the Army of the Potomac.

noted, "Such a sight I shall never see again. Not a word was spoken, no noisy demonstration of regret at losing him, but there was hardly a dry eye in the ranks. Very many of the men wept like children, while others could be seen gazing after him in mute grief, one may almost say despair." The general himself was quite overwhelmed, as well he might be, to see such affection and devotion testified toward him. Some officers considered resigning in protest but stayed, a junior staff officer believed, only because of "a general order from the boss at the War Dept. threatening dishonorable dismissal to all officers who gave McClellan's removal as the reason of their resignation."

Lincoln replaced McClellan with Gen. Ambrose Everett Burnside, who had performed ably as a corps commander but had twice turned down the opportunity to lead the army. Burnside still did not want the job, but this time he accepted when urged by fellow officers, who preferred him to the bombastic Joseph Hooker. Tall, balding, and burly, his face framed by thick muttonchops that merged into a hefty mustache, the thirty-eight-year-old Burnside was the son of a South Carolina slave owner who had relocated to Indiana after freeing his slaves. Burnside attended West Point with the likes of George McClellan, George Pickett, and James Longstreet but left the army in the mid-1850s to open a gun factory in Rhode Island. He proved a poor businessman, losing the patent to his "Burnside carbine" and declaring bankruptcy. He then worked for McClellan in railroads until the war started, when he helped to organize the First Rhode Island Volunteers. Easygoing and affable, Burnside showed great promise early in the war, and Lincoln liked him. Compared to the boastful and arrogant McClellan, Burnside promised a modest breath of fresh air, although modesty might better have been called insecurity, even well-founded insecurity.

Burnside moved quickly to distract the troops from their displeasure with the loss of their beloved "Little Mac" by reorganizing the army into three "Grand Divisions," replete with new badges, and preparing them for an active campaign. The weather turned colder, and usually when winter came, Civil War armies rested. But Burnside sensed pressure from Lincoln and Halleck, as well as from congressional and public opinion, to do something before spring arrived. He quickly made plans to advance on the Confederate capital by way of Hanover Junction, the shortest overland route from the northeast. First, though, his army of some 120,000 men would have to cross the Rappahannock River.

Lee, meanwhile, after retreating south from Maryland, rested his exhausted army below the Rappahannock. He had failed in his attempt to bring the war north and rally Maryland behind the Confederacy, and his Army of Northern Virginia was badly bloodied. Still desperate for supplies and now with several weeks of inactivity on their hands, Lee's men gave in to common soldier vices: drinking and gambling. Already annoyed with his troops for their straggling and sometimes looting on the way into Virginia, Lee responded by prohibiting gambling and stopping furloughs. The Confederate cause, the devoutly religious Lee proclaimed, demanded the "highest virtue and purest morality."

The Fredericksburg Campaign

By November 19, Burnside moved his army to the east bank of the Rappahannock, just across from the town of Fredericksburg. He was in a position, if he acted swiftly, to cross the river and come between Lee's army and Richmond, but here his plans stalled. Bad weather, bad roads, and bureaucratic bungling in Washington delayed the arrival of the pontoon trains necessary for the army to traverse the river. Not until November 25 did the pontoon trains arrive.

By then, Lee, discovering Burnside's design, moved to stop him. On November 20, he telegraphed Davis somewhat disbelievingly: "I think Burnside is concentrating his whole army opposite Fredericksburg." Amassing his army at the old colonial town, Lee doubted that Burnside would attempt to cross the river. Nor did Lee want to provoke a fight during the winter, but he determined to make a stand nonetheless. He still wanted to strike the Federals hard, and if Fredericksburg was going to be the place, so be it. Jackson's II Corps arrived from the Shenandoah Valley on November 30, and Longstreet's I Corps traveled from Culpeper. All told, the Confederates had 78,000 men and 300 cannon on hand, considerably less than the Federals, but their position, anchored on the left along a high ridge called Marye's Heights and on the right, several miles distance, by Prospect Hill, seemed impregnable.

On the morning of December 11, Union volunteer engineers tried to construct pontoon bridges across the river. Confederates hidden on rooftops and in buildings, and sheltered by a thick fog, showered them with deadly fire. Union artillerists sought to blast out the rebel marksmen but only succeeded in tearing up the town. Citizens who had not already abandoned their homes fled in terror as parts of Fredericksburg burst into flame. It occurred to some sol-

THE BATTLE OF FREDERICKSBURG, December 13, 1862. Throughout the afternoon of December 13, Gen. Ambrose Burnside stubbornly ordered a succession of fourteen futile and costly charges against Confederate commander Robert E. Lee's nearly impregnable position along Mayre's Heights. The battle of Fredericksburg was a stunning Confederate victory.

diers that this was the first time in the war that Union guns had been purposely unleashed on a southern town. "I have just been a looker-on in a new phase of military operations, that of shelling a city," observed a New York artillerist. "Judging from the fires in the city and its general appearance . . . the city must be nearly or quite ruined."

Even so, the engineers could not complete the bridges until, toward midafternoon, three regiments of Union troops paddled across the river in pontoons to secure a foothold and drive the rebel defenders out of Fredericksburg. Meanwhile, bridges were also thrown across the Rappahannock at another site downriver. Before nightfall, U.S. troops came pouring over the bridges onto the rebel side of the river. Many of the men who filed into Fredericksburg disgraced themselves by pillaging the town. "Everything that they could not eat or wear, they destroyed in pure wantonness," reported a disgusted comrade. "Beautiful pictures, books, jewelry, ladies dresses, silverware, and in fact all kinds of household furniture."

Only light skirmishing followed the next day, December 12, as Burnside pondered his options. He wanted to launch simultaneous assaults all along the rebel line, although such frontal attacks uphill against well-positioned artillery and infantry seemed suicidal to most everyone else. When Burnside asked a New York colonel what he thought, the officer exclaimed: "If you make the attack as contemplated it will be the greatest slaughter of the war; there isn't infantry enough in our whole army to carry those heights if they are well defended."

Burnside, still determined to exploit his manpower advantage, ordered an attack on December 13 with a modified plan. He wanted first to capture Prospect Hill—the Confederate right, defended by Stonewall Jackson's corps—and then wheel his men along the ridge that ran back toward Marye's Heights and strike Longstreet's flank. An attack against the heights by troops in Fredericksburg would support this second movement. It was a good plan, but when the fight against Jackson sputtered, Burnside erred by ordering the men in Fredericksburg to assail Longstreet's position on their own. The attack turned into a slaughter, the most uneven Confederate victory of the war. Throughout the day, Burnside ordered repeated frontal assaults on the Confederate left at Marye's Heights. These attacks were piecemeal, usually one regiment at a time. Charging up the slope through the fog and smoke, many soldiers were convinced of their doom, but they followed orders, thrust forward, and fell. Confederate William Owen, a member of the Washington Artillery stationed along the ridge, later recalled the scene as wave after wave of blue marched forward: "On they came in beautiful array and seemingly more determined to hold the plain than before; but our fire was murderous, and no troops on earth could stand the *feu d'enfer* we were giving them." Fire from hell indeed.

The carnage continued all afternoon, with thousands of the dead and wounded, piled three bodies deep in some places, littering the plain between the town and the heights. Men mangled and mutilated by shot and shell crammed the sunken road at the base of the hill, and yet the Federals kept pressing forward "with stubborn determination to obey orders and do their duty." One Union soldier, a Mexican War veteran, commented: "I had never before seen fighting like that, nothing approaching it in terrible uproar and destruction." One of the attackers had a leg ripped from his body by a blast of cannon fire. As he fell, the soldier's neck came to rest grotesquely on the shattered limb. Ignoring his condition and still possessing a wealth of gumption, he raised up on his elbow, "waved his hat and cheered for the old flag" before collapsing dead. The gesture symbolized the Union army's valiant yet futile effort on that day.

Burnside seemed caught in a funk, unwilling to stop the slaughter. Late in the day, after fourteen failed frontal assaults, he announced plans to continue the attacks the next morning at the head of his own IX Corps. Perhaps he was feeling suicidal, but by the next day, after each of his generals expressed their strong disapproval of his plan, he came to his senses and changed his mind. The battle of Fredericksburg was mercifully over.

Meantime, as night fell upon the battlefield, details of men set out to collect the wounded and to identify the dead. Joshua Chamberlain, a professor-turned-warrior from Maine, was part of one of these details on the night of December 13. He described the eerie quiet that engulfed the battleground as darkness approached and the fighting ebbed: "But of that silence from the battle's crash and roar rose new sounds more appalling still: rose or fell, you knew not which, or whether from the earth or from the air; a strange ventriloquism, of which you could not locate the source, a smothered moan that seemed to come from distances beyond the reach of the natural sense, a wail so far and deep and wide, as if a thousand discords were flowing together into a keynote weird, unearthly, terrible to hear and bear, yet startling with its nearness." He heard cries for water, screams for pity, pleas for God's help. Some soldiers called out desperately for loved ones to ease their pain. Chamberlain also perceived "underneath all the time, that deep bass note from closed lips, too hopeless or too heroic to articulate their agony." After two more days of inactivity, the Union army slipped back across the Rappahannock on the night of December 15.

Federal casualties numbered more than 12,000; those of the Confederates totaled much less, about 5,300, with 600 killed. "The battle did no good at all," one northern survivor of Fredericksburg wrote home. "Great many lives were lost and for nothing, but I think they have got about enough of the rebs." He gloomily predicted: "We shall have to give up to them, the sooner the better." Further up the chain of command, Montgomery Meigs, the quartermaster general, wrote, "exhaustion steals across the country. Confidence and hope are dying." Indeed, anger and disillusionment spread across the North as details of the battle became apparent. Lincoln, perhaps feeling guilty at having pressured Burnside to act, despaired, telling one of his aides, "If there is a worse place than Hell, I am in it." When Congress ordered an investigation, the president had to act deftly to ward off the effort by some Radical Republicans to force changes in his cabinet.

Fredericksburg was a much needed victory for the Confederacy, but Lee remained unsatisfied. After battle he was bitterly disappointed that there was no more enemy bloodletting on December 14. "I . . . could not believe they would relinquish their purpose—after all their boasting and preparations," Lee wrote to his wife, Mary. "They went as they came, in the night." He knew his army had inflicted damage on the enemy, but he admitted to Mary that he wanted the chance to do more: "They suffered heavily as far as the battle went, but it did not go far enough to satisfy me." Lee still hoped for one climactic victory that would destroy his enemy forever—and Fredericksburg only whetted his appetite for that martial culmination.

Burnside, equally displeased, was determined to try again despite the onset of winter weather. For more than a month, his army sat quietly across the river as he contemplated his next move. Finally, on January 20, 1863, the Federals began to march upstream to attempt a wide movement around Lee's left. But torrential rains struck, turning roads to quagmires and drenching the troops. By January 23 his "Mud March" was over, and soon, too, was Burnside's tenure in command of the Army of the Potomac. Joe Hooker replaced him. The brash and boastful Hooker received his appointment due to a combination of intrigue within the officer corps and Lincoln's need for a commander known for boldness. Lincoln would later find that Hooker brought his own problems as commander.

William S. Rosecrans In the Western Theater, where the Confederates had also tried to invade Union-occupied territory, the Federals received slightly brighter news. In Kentucky, after the battle of Perryville, Braxton Bragg retreated into eastern Tennessee, while in northern Mississippi, Confederate forces also pulled back after engagements at Iuka and Corinth. Gen. William S. Rosecrans, credited with

GEN. WILLIAM S. ROSECRANS, an Ohio native, had a reputation for personal courage and a tireless work ethic. Although popular with his men, he clashed with his superiors, including Ulysses S. Grant, who resented Rosecrans's blatant ambition and outspokenness.

victory in both Mississippi battles, came to Nashville, Tennessee, to replace Don Carlos Buell, who had lost Lincoln's confidence by failing to anticipate the Confederate's Kentucky campaign and by not pursuing Bragg after the battle of Perryville. Equally damning, Buell had proved to be an overly cautious and politically conservative commander of the McClellan stripe. Still clinging to the discredited conciliatory policy, he had failed to embrace the far bolder new war aims. Consequently, on October 30, 1862, the administration appointed Rosecrans commander of the Army of the Ohio, soon to be renamed the Army of the Cumberland.

A native of Ohio, a West Point graduate, and a talented inventor and engineer, Rosecrans had gained recognition early in the war for his successes in western Virginia. He worked well with volunteer troops and exhibited great personal courage in battle. He was a tireless worker and a devout Catholic who often kept his staff up late at night discussing theological questions, but "Old Rosey," as he was called, had his enemies, including U.S. Grant and Edwin Stanton. Grant in particular resented Rosecrans's public popularity and found him arrogant and annoying. Rosecrans *was* a man of high emotion, with a quick temper. Sometimes in battle he became so excited that he stuttered, making it hard for his aides to understand him. He also was extremely sensitive to rank and openly ambitious. Gen. Jacob Cox recalled: "His impulsiveness was plain to all who approached him; his irritation quickly flashed out in words when he was crossed and his social geniality would show itself in smiles and in almost caressing gestures when he was pleased." Nonetheless, in the fall of 1862, Rosecrans, like Burnside, seemed the man to turn the tide for the Union.

Rosecrans began inauspiciously, postponing an active campaign for two months as he reorganized and prepared his army for battle. The Union War Department was eager for action, and in early December, Henry Halleck urged Rosecrans to move. Halleck warned: "Twice have I been asked to designate someone else to command your army. If you remain one more week at Nashville, I cannot prevent your removal. As I wrote you when you took the command, the Government demands action, and if you cannot respond to that demand someone else will be tried." Rosecrans responded by denying that he had wasted any time and defiantly affirmed: "To threats of removal or the like I may be permitted to say that I am insensible."

Finally, late in December, Rosecrans moved his 41,000 troops out of Nashville. Bragg, who had shifted his army to Murfreesboro, less than 30 miles to the southeast, waited for him. Having lost Kentucky, Bragg was determined to claim at least a share of agriculturally rich middle Tennessee. Murfreesboro, an important market town that sat astride the railroad running from Nashville to Chattanooga, would serve as his base.

On the cold, blustery night of December 30, Rosecrans issued a general order to his troops, proclaiming that the "eyes of the whole nation are upon you; the very fate of the nation may be said to hang on the issue of this day's battle." "Close steadily on the enemy," he urged his men, "and, when you get within charging distance, rush on him with the bayonet. Do this, and the victory will

**Battle of
Stones River**

THE BATTLE OF STONES RIVER, December 31, 1862–January 2, 1863. The three-day battle between Union Gen. William S. Rosecrans's Army of the Cumberland and Confederate Gen. Braxton Bragg's Army of Tennessee was one of the bloodiest engagements of the war. This drawing illustrates action on the first day, when Bragg broke Rosecrans's right flank and pushed him back to the Tennessee River.

certainly be yours." But it was Bragg who attacked first, advancing on Rosecrans's right flank in the predawn darkness of December 31. The resulting three-day battle of Stones River was fierce and gory, with casualties totaling nearly 24,000. Bragg's Army of Tennessee, numbering 34,000, successfully pushed forward on the first day by smashing Rosecrans's right flank and pressing the enemy's back to the river. Capt. Armistead T. M. Cockerill of the Twenty-fourth Ohio likened the Confederate onslaught to "a tornado that would destroy everything in its path." Another Ohioan professed, "Oh such a sight I never want to see again. Just think . . . men running every way and no one knew where to go but to try and get out of the danger."

Little fighting occurred the second day, but on the third, Bragg ordered a desperate advance of John C. Breckinridge's division across treacherous terrain, including the icy Stones River, on the Union left. Braxton Bragg, like many Civil War commanders, clung to the prewar belief that a spirited frontal infantry charge could break any defensive position, but he, like Burnside at Fredericksburg and Lee at Malvern Hill, was dead wrong. After nearly an hour and a half of combat, the rebels fell back in panicked retreat. One Confederate Kentuckian, who witnessed Bragg's ill-advised final attack, watched in shock as murderous enemy fire hurled his comrades in every direction. "Many another gallant Kentuckian, some of the finest line and field officers, were left on the field," in what the rebel bitterly judged "a sacrifice to stupidity and revenge." Tennessee Pvt. Sam Watkins described "Rebels falling like leaves of autumn in a hurricane."

In the end, Stones River was more of a draw than a clear victory for either side, but Bragg evacuated Murfreesboro and abandoned middle Tennessee for good. More than 1,300 of his men were dead, with another 9,000 wounded and missing. After the battle, Bragg, brusque and obstinate, faced mounting criticism from the rebel press, his own soldiers, and his subordinate officers. One of his men recalled: "None of Bragg's soldiers ever loved him. They had no faith in his ability as a general. He was looked on as a merciless tyrant." Bitter squabbles with his subordinates undermined his leadership, but President Davis, maintaining his faith in Bragg, would keep his old friend in command for the near future.

Rosecrans's army, meanwhile, was terribly bruised and bloodied from the fray, having lost 13,000 men. Yet, in light of Fredericksburg, Stones River looked like a spectacular win for the North, and Lincoln proclaimed it as such. Just a few weeks before the fight, midwestern Peace Democrats had boldly called for recognition of the Confederacy and an end to "all constitutional relations with the New England states." Now, with a fresh victory, antiwar rhetoric in the North faded, at least for a time. Lincoln excitedly commended Rosecrans: "God bless you and all with you. Please tend to all, and accept for yourself the nation's gratitude for your and their skill, endurance and dauntless courage."

War's Destruction

At one point during his wildly lopsided win at Fredericksburg, Lee allegedly mused: "It is well that war is so terrible, else we should grow too fond of it." Fond of war? By the end of 1862, few Americans, North or South, had any fondness for it at all. The twin butcheries at Fredericksburg and Stones River were of little lasting strategic purpose, as had been true of the even greater slaughters of Shiloh and Antietam earlier in the year. The concept that one decisive battle could end the fighting completely and bring total victory permanently was proving destructively illusory for both sides. The war just raged on and on. It appeared as if this savage conflict had assumed a mind of its own, uncontrolled by humans. War's almost animate hunger for destruction, pain, and death seemed insatiable.

Soldier Motivation

War, however, is not a natural or even a supernatural occurrence: it is a deliberate human-made process, as much so as peace, and a multitude of individuals at the very heights of power, as well as those at the very bottom, willingly chose to fight the Civil War. Why? Why in particular did ordinary soldiers, the men who faced the worst hardships, dangers, and horrors, voluntarily continue to battle on? For what did Civil War soldiers fight? This question, like the question of why men enlisted in the first place, has long perplexed historians, especially recent generations of skeptical scholars who have been disillusioned by modern warfare. Did ideology play a role? If so, what ideology? If not, what else motivated soldiers? What gave them the "will to combat"?

Leading scholars on this issue have argued that a variety of motives, some ideological, some not, worked together to sustain soldiers through the weeks and months of drill, the filthy, disease-ridden, and boring camp life, the seemingly endless campaigns, and the threat of injury or even death in battle. Just as there were practical and ideological reasons to join the army, so too were there practical and ideological reasons to stay and face the horrors of combat. Soldiers called it "seeing the elephant," which in the nineteenth century meant confronting the most formidable monster. The "Cause" remained a powerful motivator for many. Confederates were determined to defend their homes and maintain their way of life. Most northerners, for their part, intended to save the Union, and a growing number wanted to end slavery. Love of liberty motivated both sides, although it carried two distinctly different meanings. Confederates defined it as freedom from tyranny and "slavery"; for Federals, liberty meant freedom from the tyrannical slavocracy and secessionist efforts to destroy the "sacred" Union.

Inherent and abstract notions of duty and honor also played roles. Northerners, convinced that the Union must be preserved to ensure the longevity of free institutions, individual rights, and what they considered the best government in the world, felt duty bound to protect the Union for themselves and future generations. "It is a duty I owe my country and to my children," a Missouri officer proclaimed, "to do what I can to preserve this government as I shudder to think what it is ahead for them if this government should be overthrown." Abraham Lincoln himself insisted that the Union was the last best hope on earth for the spread of democratic institutions, a sense of international, not just national, moral obligation.

Confederates felt obligated to drive out the Yankee invader: "Now, in the condition in which our country is now plunged," a Virginian urged his cousin, "it is the *duty* of every man, woman and child who can understand the difference between Liberty and Vassalism, to do all in their power no matter what that may be . . . and assist in driving back the foe." Many rebel soldiers believed that it was they who were being true to the ideals of American individual, local, and state independence by standing up to an encroaching and destructive national state.

Young men who came of age during the 1850s and early 1860s also felt a duty of sorts to prove themselves in war. Looking back, especially to the Revolutionary War era, many young American males sought to demonstrate their personal and generational mettle. Sacrificing for a cause larger than themselves seemed to bind them to their heroic forbears. In a sense, theirs was a sort of adventure in ultimate maleness, risking everything on a dare and even a whim.

Honor was important to Confederates and Federals, although here again, the same word often meant different things in the two sections. For white southerners, honor meant a passionate concern with one's public reputation, a respect for social and racial hierarchy, and an adherence to an accepted code of conduct. Honor also kept southern males in the ranks, especially members of the upper class, for fear that deserting would publicly shame not only themselves but also their families. Northern honor was more individual and less communal, calling for greater personal self-restraint and respect for the law. Both forms of honor motivated military enlistment and long-term service, convincing men that to appear dishonorable was worse than suffering injury or death on the battlefield. "Life is sweet," a Mississippi sergeant wrote his sister, "but I would always prefer an honorable death to a disgraceful and shameful life. I much rather be numbered among the slain than those that stay at home for it will be a brand upon their name as long as a southerner lives."

Honor driven and duty bound to serve, Civil War soldiers were anxious to display courage in battle, thus proving their manhood. Green troops in particular agonized about whether they would be able to keep their composure in battle. Many soldiers would have agreed with the Connecticut private who wrote after one battle, "I must confess that the horrid screams of those infernal shells came near lowering my heart into the seat of my pants. But I didn't feel like running away. I felt satisfied of doing my duty, and if it falls to my lot to be in another fight [I] shall not shrink from that duty."

Civil War soldiers also fought because of their most compelling relationships, those with their comrades. Powerful bonds formed among men who shared common dangers and privations, cementing them in place when it came time to face the trials of combat. This "small-group cohesion" sometimes forged relationships more intimate than any other the men would know. Civil War soldiers enlisted with their friends and family members as well as with the boyhood chums from their home towns, and the emotional experience of soldiering, which often involved a good deal of shared suffering, only strengthened those associations. Soldiers cared what the folks back home would think of them. They were anxious to know what their families in general but their wives or sweethearts in particular made of their soldiering. And if one of their "brothers" fell in battle, revenge became an additional potent motivator for staying fiercely at war.

Religion, too, played a role. Patriotic rhetoric on both sides was rich in religious metaphors and references to the Christian warrior. Religious revivals in camp also buoyed soldiers' fortitude and kept them fighting for "God's cause." Soldiers on both sides prayed to the same Christian God, as Lincoln himself noted, but Americans had a concept of death and suffering different from today's, conceiving of death in much more religious terms. There were rituals to death that required last rites, religious prayer, and proper burial. Even in prison, soldiers strove to follow those rituals.

A fatalistic sense of having placed one's life in God's hands also spread through the ranks. One Iowa soldier confessed after battle: "The zip of rifle balls has a peculiar stinging sound, and the shriek of bursting shells causes one to dodge instinctively; but I think that each soldier is impressed with the belief that he will not be struck. . . . It is a remarkable fact that in nearly every instance when a man is struck he impulsively exclaims 'Oh, my God!' or in some similar language addresses his Maker." A Confederate officer put it this way before charging into the battle of Corinth: "I gave myself to God and got ahead of my company." This faith, peace of mind, delusion, or whatever name to give it, when added to the sense of invulnerability characteristic of young men everywhere, could inure men to the notion of being killed or wounded. "I noticed a very unpleasant hum of bullets above my ears," wrote one veteran, "but I had no idea of getting hit."

Any number of other factors might weigh more or less heavily on one soldier or the next in determining his will to combat. As soldiers learned something about the army's code of discipline, and as many witnessed the elaborate ritual killing of recaptured deserters by firing squads, fear of punishment became a coercive force to keep them in the ranks. So, too, would be the drawn swords or pistols of their officers standing behind them in battle, ready at times to cut down deserters on the spot.

In seeming contradiction, loyalty to brave or inspirational officers also could convince men to stand their ground or to charge into the face of almost certain death. "False courage," in the form of alcohol, fortified more than a few men during the course of the war. Then, too, outright hatred of the enemy became a driving force for men who had witnessed the death of friends or heard of enemy depredations. A Union lieutenant explained, "A feeling of intense hatred of the enemy possesses him as the charge is made and he sees his comrades falling about him, and he is carried away with a wild desire to kill and slay in turn. For the moment those opposing him are not human beings, but devils and demons whom it is his duty to slaughter without mercy."

Historians have disagreed over the question of whether motivation, particularly ideological motivation, waned as the war progressed. Some scholars maintain that it did and that a growing gap developed between soldiers disillusioned and embittered by the hardships of war and civilians whose support for the abstract principles of the war remained high. But other scholars have

HISTORIANS OFFER A VARIETY of reasons to explain why men, both North and South, willingly left their homes and families to go to war. This postwar picture depicts a scene common to many households throughout the conflict.

maintained that there was no real deviation from 1861 to 1865, especially among the early volunteers of 1861 and 1862. Civil War soldiers, these historians argue, overcame the horrors of combat and remained unwavering in their duty. Many of them developed what amounted to a cult of toughness—almost a professional hardening in the face of deprivation and danger. They shared an insider's faith that they knew would never be understood by the soft folks back home, the politicians, or even the brass in their own regiments, all of whom became in many ways aliens to the brotherhood of soldiers.

It seems likely that both of these views are accurate. There were soldiers who expressed commitment to the war no matter what and remained remarkably resilient to the ordeal. Yet there were also those, dejected and shaken by battle, disease, and homesickness, who gave up hope. Still others changed their views based on circumstances. One day a soldier might feel inspired, the next day wholly depressed. Of course, the people to whom they revealed these feelings also made a difference. A husband might express more homesickness to his wife than he would to his aging father, or vice versa. A Confederate prison diary might sound more despondent than that of a Union veteran stationed on garrison duty. Occupation, education, age, and class—even military rank, race, and ethnicity—could also affect the tone and content of personal correspondence.

News from home also influenced soldier motivation. Good news and reassurances from loved ones bolstered morale and calmed fears. Bad news left soldiers feeling anxious, worried, and distracted. Reports of illness, death, financial problems, or war weariness made soldiers on both sides feel helpless and disillusioned. How could a man faithfully serve his country when his own family suffered hundreds of miles away? Nineteenth-century conceptions of duty and honor demanded that males protect and provide for their families, but war strained their abilities to be dutiful both to their families and to their nation. When Alabaman John W. Cotton learned that his young daughter had died while he served in faraway Tennessee, he struggled to find words of comfort. "I hant mutch to rite to console you for I am in two mutch trouble myself I shall bee uneasy til I here that all the children has had the measles and well of them I never new what pleasure home afforded to a man before," he wrote. "If it wer not for the love of my country and family and the patriotism that bury in my bosom for them," Cotton confessed, "I would bee glad to come home and stay there but I no I have as much to fite for as any body else but I were there I no I could not stay so I have to take it as easy as possible."

Civilians and War

The conduct and attitudes of civilians who opposed the war and those who seemed only concerned with their own skins or with making a profit discouraged some volunteers. Frederick Pettit wrote his family in western Pennsylvania that critics of the U.S. government would find "but little sympathy among the soldiers. The soldiers are for the government and the prosecution of the war. If enough of us ever get home there will be quite a change in the politics of the country." A few months later, he reiterated how he and his comrades viewed peace advocates at home: "We have endured untold sufferings and risked our lives for our homes and country's rights, while these copperheads have been enjoying all the peace and comforts of home." A Connecticut soldier angrily denounced northern Peace Democrats, wishing that "a portion of one army could be at hom[e] and shoot the traitors there." After the Peninsula campaign in the summer of 1862, Charles Harvey Brewster wondered where all the giddy martialism from his home state of Massachusetts had gone: "Where are all the brave ones who were 'coming after us, when they were actually needed'? there were thousands of them when we came away. Why don't they come on? Don't they think they are needed yet?" He wrote his mother: "It is not half so pleasant to be out here in the woods and swamps as tis to stay at home so I don't wonder at them much only there were so many coming 'when they were really needed' that I almost wonder that if the fifteen thousand from Mass are not on the way already, perhaps they have not heard that they are needed."

Indeed, in some communities, civilians seemed to turn a deaf ear to the war, particularly in northern locales. New Yorker Maria Daly was dismayed at "how people spend despite the present distress. The artists say they have never been so busy . . . and every place of amusement is crowded." Cornelia Jay, the granddaughter of former chief justice John Jay, similarly observed from New York on December 31, 1862: "People seem perfectly callous about the War or indeed everything relating to public affairs." Northern newspapers frequently chided northern businessmen and industrialists who were profiting from the war's economic boon. William Cullen Bryant decried the "extravagance" and "luxury" displayed by some. "What business have Americans at any time with such vain show, with such useless magnificence," he asked. "But especially how can they justify it to themselves in this time of war? Some men have gained great fortunes during the past two or three years, but that does not excuse their extravagance."

There were accusations of civilian insensitivity and selfishness in the Confederacy, too, especially directed toward elite women who late in the war seemed intent on frivolous revelry. Robert E. Lee himself frequently chastised his daughters for going to parties when they ought to be focused on the war. He extended his criticism to his own army, where civilian lassitude seemed to be settling. "Many officers have too many selfish views to . . . induce them to undertake the task of instructing and disciplining their troops," he wrote to Jefferson Davis in 1863. "To succeed it is necessary to set the example, & this necessarily confines them to their duties, their camp & mess, which is disagreeable & deprives them of pleasant visits, dinners, &c."

Southern Home Front

In the South, it was harder to avoid or ignore the war's negative effects, especially in regions invaded by Union troops. In the Confederacy's few urban areas and many rural communities, the war forcefully hit home. Cities became overcrowded with military personnel, bureaucrats, and refugees displaced by war. Inflation sent prices of essential commodities skyrocketing. There were terrible shortages of basic foodstuffs such as meat and salt, and people found themselves eating animals they had considered vermin before the war. In Richmond and Vicksburg, it was not an uncommon sight to find dressed rats sold in butcher shops for high prices and dog meat passed off as lamb. Hungry southerners also devoured cats, crows, frogs, locusts, snails, snakes, and worms. Confederate War Clerk John B. Jones described an exchange between a destitute woman and a Richmond merchant. When the merchant demanded $70 for one barrel of flour, the woman exclaimed, "My God! How can I pay such prices? I have seven children; what shall I do?" The merchant snidely answered: "I don't know, Madam. Unless you eat your children."

Small farmers, who before the war prided themselves on their independence and self-sufficiency, struggled to feed their families. Left at home while their men went to the front, southern white women worked to keep their farms running. Planters faced labor problems, too, as slaves left by the hundreds, seeking the freedom promised by the Union army. Although the Confederate draft exempted one white male on each plantation that owned twenty slaves or more, the lack of white male supervision took its toll.

For southern white women, the absence of their men at the front appeared to expose a troubling contradiction in Confederate rhetoric and ideology. If this crisis was about protecting home, what were women to do if the demands of war left them utterly unprotected? The parties and dances staged by elite white women late in the war seemed a way for them to exhibit their resentment toward the Confederacy's unyielding demand for female self-sacrifice. Frustrated by their own inability to take an active role in the war, many plantation mistresses expressed anger that they could not be men. "O! If I was only a man!" a Louisiana woman scribbled in her diary. "Then I could don the breeches, and slay them with a will! If some few southern women were in the ranks, they could set the men an example they would not blush to follow." As will be shown in the following chapter, many thousands of women would find ways to participate in the war.

War deeply affected family life. Courtships and marriages were rushed, and separations between parents and children, husbands and wives were long and sometimes permanent. The war created an untold number of widows and orphans forever scarred by the death of their loved ones. Losing a father or husband was painful enough, but when a soldier's death meant that a family lacked its sole financial provider, the loss had even deeper repercussions, particularly as a depleted pool of single men cut down opportunities for remarriage.

War also loosened conventional sexual mores on the home front. Left without their menfolk, women took liberties with roaming soldiers that they never would have considered during peacetime. Females anxious and desperate for protection, money, or companionship turned to strangers, sometimes willingly, other times when forced. As soldiers wandered through communities empty of men, sexual dalliances and liaisons were frequent. In Arkansas, Union Cpl. Seth Kelly discovered "Several pretty women, secesh, bewitching. Good circumstances, no men." Federal cavalry Sgt. W. W. Moses recounted the story of a mother and a daughter seduced by two officers while their husband/father served in the army. The sixteen-year-old daughter remained convinced that she would become her lover's wife, "unaware," Moses perceived, "that disgrace and disappointment are in store. She does not know that Henry has a family at home." Moses concluded, "Alas how this war has corrupted the morals, destroyed the health and blighted the fond hopes and joys of our land. Virtue is indeed scarce."

"The life we are leading now is a miserable, frightened one—living in constant dread of great danger," Kate Stone wrote from her Louisiana plantation that was swarming with Union troops, "not knowing what form it may take, and utterly helpless to protect ourselves. It is a painful present and a dark future with the wearing anxiety and suspense about our loved ones."

As the war lengthened and the casualty numbers swelled, a gnawing suspense hung heavy over the home front. When would the fighting end? When would loved ones finally come home? Northern civilians grew reluctant to accept the growing casualties of a seemingly endless war. Southerners, too, became increasingly anxious and terrified by the war's costs. It was not so much that civilians entirely lost faith in their section's cause, but that the conflict's scope and destructiveness intimidated and alarmed civilians. Was any cause worth such frightful human cost?

Political leaders, grappling with these very issues, sought to keep their nations unified and focused on victory. Keeping peace on the home front, despite the sufferings and sacrifices, was just as important—perhaps even more important—than winning battles. Abraham Lincoln told a crowd of volunteer civilian workers in Philadelphia, "War, at the best, is terrible, and this war of ours, in its magnitude and duration, is one of the most terrible." Lincoln assessed the high toll the war had taken on the northern home front, but he easily could

DEATH AND MOURNING were commonplace throughout the long war. This *Harper's Weekly* illustration from January 1864 portrayed a widow grieving at her soldier-husband's grave.

have been describing the South as well: "It [the war] has deranged business, totally in many localities. It has destroyed property and ruined homes; it has produced a national debt and taxation unprecedented, at least in this country; it has carried mourning to almost every home, until it can almost be said that the 'heavens are hung in black.' "

Nearly all soldiers craved reminders of home. Homesickness was rampant among men who had never before left their tightly knit communities, much less ventured hundreds or thousands of miles from their families, nor for such protracted periods of time. With furloughs infrequent, soldiers anxiously awaited mail call, eager for word from home. Occasionally, family members and friends visited the front, but mail was the main link between soldiers and civilians, and there never seemed to be enough letters from home. Often, soldiers chided friends and loved ones for not writing enough and forgetting them. Some counted the letters they received and the ones they sent, keeping careful record in diaries. Michigan soldier George Henry Ewing included a poem in his letter to his parents that contained the following lines:

Soldiers and the Home Front

> Write to me very often
> Letters are links that bind,
> Truthful hearts to each other;
> Fettering mind to mind,
> Giving to kindly spirits
> Lasting and true delight.
> If you would strengthen friendship
> Never forget to write.

Soldiers wrote home with accounts of camp life, news of family and friends in the military, and occasional depictions of battle. But more often than not, soldiers hungered for news from home and details of the everyday life they had left behind. Husbands and fathers filled letters with emotional words of love and affection and with practical questions about their family's financial condition. Husbands-turned-soldiers struggled to justify abandoning their families for military service. Marshall Phillips, a member of the Fifth Maine, tried to keep focused on doing his duty and to "keep up good courage," but as he confessed to his wife, Diana, "when I lay down and think of you and the family, I feel sometimes as if I done wrong by enlisting and leaving you with a family of small children."

Many men tried to maintain their traditional roles from a distance. Edgeworth Bird, stationed in Virginia far from his large farm in Georgia, wrote numerous letters to instruct his wife, Sallie, on how to harvest the corn, feed the hogs, care for the sheep, and shoe the mules. He also advised her on how to get along with their many slaves: "Take pains to gain the affection of the negroes," he told her. "You can attach them to you and govern them through their hearts better than any overseer can through fear." He yearned to be home, convinced that he could do a better job of running the farm than his wife: "Were I only at home, I know we'd have a greater abundance on the plantation, for it has always been a very peculiar business and one that I love and of course, I could conduct more successfully." Husbands also needed to console their wives and to urge them to be strong. "Be a woman," a Mississippi solder urged his lonely and anxious wife. He suggested: "Think of the noble women of ancient and modern times."

Women and War　　Women responded as best they could, but they often shouldered far more responsibility than they had before the war. They had to pay mortgages, sell crops, hire help, and operate businesses, besides looking after households and caring for children. The lucky ones had family and friends close at hand to lend advice or to assist with the work, and many others carried on running conversations via correspondence with their soldier-husbands about how best to manage things. Most shouldered their burdens every bit as nobly as their men at the front. An Illinois farm woman, following several weeks of correspondence with her husband about legal and tax problems that might have forced her to sell their farm, finally took a stand. She would not sell, she decided: "I shall stay here until you come home again and will try to do the best that I can towards paying for the land also the other debts and I think we shall come out all right in the end."

Wives' correspondence to their soldier-husbands included details of family life and financial concerns and words of support and love. Some discussed the newfound autonomy forced upon them by war. Mattie Blanchard, whose husband, Caleb, served in the Eighteenth Connecticut, developed a keen interest in state politics. She asked her husband whether he thought state officials would "let the soldiers wives vote" while their husbands were at the front. Not all women were as enthusiastic as Mattie Blanchard. In fact, some openly resented the demands war made upon them. One North Carolina woman felt so desperate, she asked her husband how he would feel about "going back into the Union" and whether that "would be better than to have all our men killed," adding, "I often think if I could make peace how soon I would have you and all my loved ones with me."

Soldier Life　　It was difficult for men on either side to hear these sorts of sentiments from home. They needed all the positive reinforcement they could get from their friends and families, for a soldier's life was not an easy one. The reality on most days of service was a grinding and rather predictable routine. There were weeks or even months of drill and camp life, relieved abruptly by intensive and exhausting marches, skirmishes, and occasional battles. Wisconsin soldier Rufus R. Dawes remarked: "Military life in camp is the most monotonous in the world. It is the same routine over and over every day." Confederates and Federals might begin a typical day with roll call at six, breakfast at seven, then two hours of squad or company drill. After a noontime meal, there was battalion drill for two hours, dress parade at five, supper at six, roll call at nine, and taps at nine thirty. There might also be some bayonet exercises or target practice. Such drills, so important to maintaining order and discipline in a volunteer army, were unpopular among men accustomed to their individual independence and personal autonomy. They were also tedious. "The first thing in the morning is drill, then drill, then drill again," one Pennsylvanian explained.

CIVIL WAR SOLDIERS found various ways to supplement their diets and fill their free time. Confederate soldier William L. Sheppard's drawing illustrates the fun and mayhem involved in trying to catch a rabbit in camp.

"Then drill, drill, a little more drill. Then drill, and lastly drill. Between drills, we drill and sometimes stop to eat a little and have roll call." Guard detail and picket duty interrupted an otherwise predictable cycle, forcing men to leave the familiar confines of camp for temporary, at times hazardous duty. There were also less-military tasks to do—chopping wood, washing clothes, or cooking— although there were many camp followers who performed these jobs. During winter camp or when on garrison duty, soldiers might resume their prewar occupations, such as blacksmithing, printing, or carpentry.

Soldiers spent their free time doing a variety of activities, including reading, writing letters, and singing. They formed debating societies, Bible study groups, and theatrical companies. Desperate for ways to pass the time, soldiers also turned to more physically rigorous activities like baseball, hunting, fishing, horse racing, cock fights, wrestling, and general tomfoolery. Men capable of such appalling violence in battle demonstrated a playful love of fun and good humor in camp. A Confederate lieutenant marveled at the ability of soldiers to entertain themselves: "Let one cackle like a hen, and the monotony of camp is broken by the encore of 'S-h-o-o!' Then other cacklers take it up, until it sounds like a poultry yard stirred up over a mink or a weasel. Let one bray like an ass, others take it up until the whole regiment will personate the sound, seemingly like a fair ground of asses."

Snowball fights were common during the winter months, and sometimes officers participated, calling forth their units with the same earnestness they would in a real battle. One day in January 1863, near Fredericksburg, two Vermont and New Jersey regiments engaged in a snowball fight that had many of the trappings of actual combat: "Both regiments formed a line of battle, each officered by its line and field officers, the latter mounted. At the signal the battle commenced; charges and counter-charges were made, prisoners were taken on either side, the air was filled with white missiles, and stentorian cheers went up as one or the other party gained an advantage." The Vermonters, perhaps more adept at snowballing than their neighbors farther south, were victorious.

Real rivalries did exist within the ranks, pitting men against officers, lower-class volunteers against upper-class soldiers, native-born soldiers against immigrants, enlisted men against recruits, and state regiments against state regiments. From their lowly existence, privates were convinced that officers fared better in every possible way. Officers were far better paid and usually got more and better food, better housing, more frequent and longer furloughs, and more visitors from home. In general, they enjoyed greater safety in battle and more overall autonomy. These disparities between officers and men are common in any army, but to Civil War volunteers used to individual rights for all, such inequalities were hard to accept. Michigan Pvt. George H. Ewing was convinced that if "som of the big off[ic]ers . . . had to put up with the faire that we do thay would fetch it to a close in a week and so do moste all the men think so." If an officer made a point of sharing the common soldiers' burdens and displaying fearlessness in battle, he gained respect from his men. The war's best-loved commanders, such as Lee, Jackson, Sherman, and Grant, earned their armies' affection because they rejected many of the benefits enjoyed by the elite officer corps and freely exposed themselves to harsh living conditions and to danger.

There were also rivalries between different states and regions. North Carolinians and Virginians were notoriously resentful of one another; so were Federal troops from the Northeast and the Midwest. Native-born Americans resented immigrants in the ranks, too, and once black troops entered Federal service, race divided Union soldiers against one another.

Despite these inner and outer tensions of army life, the military was a markedly masculine world. Cut off from their prewar lives and, it seemed, their prewar selves, soldiers felt removed from the moral and decidedly feminine influence of home. They turned to the less virtuous and distinctively male vices of drinking, swearing, smoking, and gambling. As mentioned above, sexual mores loosened considerably between female civilians and male soldiers on the homefront. Visits to prostitutes were common among Civil War soldiers. Men stationed near cities like Richmond, Memphis, Washington, D.C., and Nashville had easy access to bordellos, but women seeking money for sex made themselves available just about anywhere troops appeared. A South Carolina soldier disclosed to his wife that prostitutes had descended into camp, but he assured her that he resisted temptation: "If you could be here on those occasions you would think that there was not a married man in the regiment but me." Pennsylvania corporal Frederick Pettit declared that war "makes men wicked." "Not because it destroys life and property," he wrote his family; "this is the smallest loss." Pettit feared that war would destroy the nation's morality: "I dread to see the day when this army comes home. Religion will be driven from the country."

Besides tedium, vice, and more harmless pastimes of soldier life, there was the constantly looming presence of illness. Sometimes, more than half the names of a regiment appeared on the sick rolls. Army life mixed hundreds of individuals together, men who had no realization that germs bred disease, the germ theory of illness only being developed in the 1880s. Contaminated water, lack of personal hygiene, exposure, and fatigue all contributed to the armies' poor health. Limited medical attention and supplies only worsened the situation. Diarrhea, often called the soldier's sickness, and dysentery were common (there were 1 million cases of acute diarrhea alone), but there were also frequent occurrences of typhoid, malaria, smallpox, tuberculosis, and rheumatism. Communicable diseases such as measles and mumps, virtually unknown to most of the men who did not live in crowded towns and cities, also ran rampant among the armies. An immunization for smallpox had been developed prior to the Civil War, but men from rural areas had not had access to it. Sexually transmitted diseases such as syphilis and gonorrhea also plagued soldiers, especially men stationed near cities with easy access to prostitutes.

Soldier Illness and Disease

DISEASE KILLED MORE Civil War soldiers than guns did. Sick and wounded men pose in this wartime photograph of the Armory Square Hospital in Washington, D.C.

Ailing from any of these illnesses seemed so much less manly than suffering from a battle wound, and death from disease was so much less heroic than death from the enemy's bullets. Union general and future president James Garfield once remarked: "This fighting with disease is infinitely more horrible than battle. This is the price of saving the Union. My God, what a costly sacrifice!" An estimated 225,000 Federals and 194,000 Confederates died of disease during the war, well over half of the total casualties. It is unclear how many veterans later succumbed to illnesses acquired during their years of service, nor is it known how many wives shared their husband's sexual maladies when they returned from the front.

Soldiers' Diet

Poor diet and improper handling of food played a major role in causing illnesses, particularly the high rates of bowel diseases. Wisconsin volunteer Chauncey Cooke wrote his mother soon after enlisting that the food in training camp was awful. "The boys threaten to riot every day for the bad beef and spoilt bread issued to us," he stated, "and all this in our home state of Wisconsin." Once at the front, obtaining food became a soldier's prime concern. In neither army were provisions particularly plentiful, nutritionally healthy, or fresh. Food preparation was frequently unsanitary, and hungry soldiers often ate raw meat or uncooked corn that played havoc on their digestive systems. The army rations of both Confederates and Federals included varying amounts of meat, bread, and flour, but Union troops almost always had more food and more variety than the rebels. Coffee, sugar, molasses, beans, vinegar, salt, desiccated (or dried) vegetables, dried fruits, pickles, even alcohol sometimes appeared in the standard army ration, but more customarily men obtained these extras from *sutlers* (merchants who traveled with the Union army) or from home. Soldiers also supplemented their diets by hunting and fishing, foraging in the countryside, purchasing from farmers and city dwellers, or simply stealing farmers' produce or livestock. Foraging in particular became a pleasure for the belly and a form of revenge against enemy civilians.

Confederates had a harder time obtaining coffee, a highly valued commodity in both armies. To make up for this deficiency, a good deal of unauthorized trading went on between the lines, the rebels trading tobacco for Yankee coffee. Confederate soldiers and civilians experimented with chicory, acorns, dandelion roots, peanuts, sugarcane seeds, corn, and even beets and potato peelings to find a drinkable substitute, but none was entirely satisfactory.

Confederate Shortages

It was not only coffee that the Confederates lacked: They suffered from serious food shortages throughout the war, not so much because of the South's lack of food, but because of its inability to distribute rations to its armies. Inflation, lack of transportation, and incompetence in the Confederate Subsistence Department combined to diminish the amount of food that actually reached the soldiers. Stacks of rations often sat spoiling at railroad depots far from the hungry troops who so desperately needed them. The Confederate commissary general was Col. Lucius Bellinger Northrop, a loyal and close friend of President Davis. By most accounts, Northrop was prickly, arrogant, stubborn, and woefully ill-suited for this crucial task, but failing to feed the troops was not entirely his fault. The Confederate government severely impaired Northrop's abilities by its unpopular policy of impressing food from farmers and providing only limited funding for procurement.

The Confederacy also struggled to clothe its soldiers. The South's continued problems with transportation and industry meant that soldiers often wanted for adequate military attire. Virginian Randolph Shotwell bitterly remembered Lee's army crossing the Potomac River *"barefooted, blanketless and hatless!* The roads were lined with stragglers limping in swollen and blistered feet, shivering all night, (for despite the heat of the day the nights were chilly), for want of blankets, and utterly devoid of underclothes—if indeed they possessed so much as one shirt!" Within the same unit, there was often a combination of gray and butternut, cotton and wool uniforms, with a mixture of headgear.

Uniforms

In the Union army, clothing was more abundant and consistent. Mass-produced blue wool uniforms became the standard, although there were a few exceptions, such as the colorful Zouave outfits of regiments from Pennsylvania and New York. Most infantrymen donned kepi hats, although one could find occasional variety, as with the tall black hats of the famed "Iron Brigade" of the West.

Uniforms of any type were usually ill fitting, and they quickly became dirty, smelly, and lice infested. Tennessean Sam Watkins recalled that every soldier he encountered "had a brigade of lice on him, and I have seen fellows so busily engaged in cracking them that it reminded me of an old woman knitting." "At first," Watkins explained, "the boys would go off in the woods and hide to louse themselves, but that was unnecessary, the ground fairly crawled with lice." Soap was in short supply, especially among Confederates, so Civil War soldiers marched, fought, slept, and generally lived in the same dingy clothes for weeks. If a soldier wore underwear—and many did not—it too became soiled and foul smelling. "Months and months they were without a change of underclothing, or a chance to wash that they had worn so long," one Virginian remembered; "hence it became actually coated with grease and dust, moistened with daily perspiration under the broiling sun."

Soldiers carried an enormous amount of equipment early in the war, but veterans quickly learned to lighten their loads for long-term campaigning. Yet, even after shedding such nonessential items that they had brought from home as umbrellas, stools, handkerchiefs, and pocket mirrors, the average soldier still hauled a considerable load. Their knapsacks were stuffed with ammunition and select personal effects, such as Bibles, diaries, photographs, pens, ink, and paper. Their haversacks, used to carry rations, smelled strongly of stale bread, uncooked meat, tobacco, and coffee. Some men, particularly hard-marching Confederates, discarded the knapsacks entirely and used their haversacks for both ammunition and food. Additional accouterments included a cartridge box, a canteen (or merely a tin cup for some), a belt, a rubber blanket, a wool blanket, and a tent, but the most important item for any soldier was his weapon.

Soldier Equipment

The standard weapon carried by Civil War infantrymen was the rifle, a relatively recent invention. Eventually, both sides were able to supply sufficient rifles for their soldiers, the Confederacy through a combination of purchases

Weapons

abroad, domestic manufacturing, and capturing weapons from the enemy. In the North, after initial buying in Europe, new and expanded factories kept up with the demand. The greatest technological advantage of such arms over the smooth-bore muskets used in Napoleonic armies was rifling, a spiral groove cut inside the length of the barrel that put a spin on lead bullets and increased the effective killing range from 50 to 400 yards.

There were two standard makes of rifled muskets: the Enfield and the Springfield. The Enfield measured 54 inches long, weighed slightly more than 9 pounds with a bayonet, and had a bore diameter (or caliber) of 0.577 inches. It was manufactured in England and found more commonly in Confederate armies. The Springfield rifle was American made, a bit shorter and lighter than the Enfield, and had a 0.58 diameter. Both weapons fired identical rounds, most commonly a minié "ball," a conical projectile with a hollow base, created by a French army captain, that further improved the rifle's accuracy and range. When these whirling bullets made contact with human flesh, they tore up muscles and nerve endings, smashed bones, slashed through vital organs, and caused gruesome blood loss. And even though rifled muskets remained muzzle loading, which meant that, between each shot, the infantryman had to ram home powder and a bullet from the end of the barrel and fit a percussion cap to the firing plate, the increased range gave a decided advantage to the tactical defense, particularly after troops learned to dig in and put up log or dirt barriers to fend off attackers.

However, many Civil War soldiers, especially early in the war, struggled to master the rifle and take advantage of its improved range and accuracy. Prior to 1863, infantry regiments often carried a variety of weapons, including rifles, smoothbores, and pistols, with differing types of ammunition. Also, early in the war the quality and quantity of rifles was not always consistent. It was common, especially for Confederates, to scour the battlefield after fights to salvage more and better guns. Even when equipped with good quality rifles, Civil War soldiers failed to use them properly. Although a skilled rifleman could load and fire three rounds per minute, many Civil War infantrymen lacked the training and ability to shoot accurately, especially in the heat of battle. Men forgot to extract ramrods, or they stuffed multiple cartridges down the barrel without firing. Such incidents of mishandling, misfiring, and poor aim countered the technological advantage of the rifle.

Rifling improved artillery, too, although here the change also was limited. The standard artillery piece on both sides was the muzzle-loading, smoothbore Napoleon. Confederate Napoleons were iron, those of the Union bronze. These guns fired four types of ammunition: (1) *solid shot,* which had the greatest range (up to a mile) but did the least damage against human targets; (2) *shells,* which detonated in the air and could travel three-quarters of a mile; (3) *spherical case shot,* made up of marble-size iron balls packed in an iron container that, when exploded overhead, dropped balls as far as 800 yards away; and (4) *canister,* a tin container of large lead balls that scattered immediately, like a shotgun blast, on leaving the gun's muzzle. Canister's effective range was 200 yards or less.

Rifled guns, like the 3-inch Ordinance gun and the 10-pound Parrot, had ranges up to 400 yards and greater accuracy than the smoothbores, but they were used only infrequently. Most artillerymen simply preferred the longer range and larger solid shot (12 pounds) of the Napoleon. In any event, production of the new rifled guns was low: the Union produced approximately 700 canons during the war, the Confederacy perhaps 20 percent of that number. The Union also produced 4 million small arms.

If authorities dragged their feet in producing rifled artillery, even more striking was the reluctance of the Union ordnance department to bring vastly improved breech-loading rifles into production. In Europe, the Prussian infantry already was armed with "needle guns"—breech-loading rifles using preassembled copper cartridges—and other European powers were racing to catch up. By 1861 not only single-shot but multishot breech-loading rifles of American design had been tested and were ready for production, but the seven-shot Spencer rifle, which could fire fourteen rounds per minute as opposed to the muzzle-loader's two to three, was not mass produced and placed in the hands of Union cavalry until 1864. Machine-gun technology was ready for speeded testing and production, but almost none of these weapons reached Union troops during the war.

The single greatest impediment to the production and deployment of new weaponry was Gen. James W. Ripley, born in 1794, who directed the Union Ordnance department. Although extremely honest and hard working, Ripley considered inventors to be hare-brained self-promoters, and he used his considerable influence to resist innovation until he left office in 1863. Convinced that repeating rifles would only waste ammunition, he blocked their use by the infantry entirely, although some federal troops bought their own. In a sense, Ripley leveled the technological battlefield for the Confederates, and no countervailing force could budge him in ways that might have helped to overwhelm the Confederates earlier in the war.

Tactics

Civil War field commanders also remained stubbornly conservative on the battlefield, either unwilling or unable to adjust their infantry tactics to the greater range of the improved rifles. Napoleonic tactics rested on the idea that the three branches of service "checked" one another: artillery could blast holes in infantry; cavalry could outmaneuver cannoneers; and infantry, formed in tight squares, could fire at cavalry from all directions and intimidate horses. The bayonet and the saber were also considered highly effective in "shock" attacks. However, the rifle's accuracy and range changed all this by giving infantrymen unique advantages over artillery and cavalry. The rifle's accuracy meant that defenders had the advantage in repelling attacking columns and that attackers faced severe casualties if they remained in close formation. Even West Point professor Dennis Mahan, a devout believer in Swiss military theorist Antoine Henri Jomini's emphasis on maneuver and surprise, taught cadets before the war that frontal assaults needlessly wasted America's citizen-soldiers. He encouraged the use of field fortifications long before the advent of rifled musketry.

Still, the tactical offensive remained well entrenched in the American military psyche. During the Mexican War, frontal charges, bold maneuvers, and flank attacks worked against a numerically superior enemy, even when that enemy was ensconced in seemingly impregnable defensive positions. But Mexican troops had been easily demoralized and poorly led, and the tactical lessons of Mexico gave false confidence to future Civil War generals. Most Civil War attacks came in the form of several long rows of closely packed men moving at a trot, which only improved the efficiency of fields of fire laid down by entrenched defenders. Not until well after the war would the American army formally revise its small-group tactics to deal with the slaughter it had experienced.

Leading officers on both sides failed to come to grips with these simple technological advances. Honor, which demanded unquestioning bravery during even the most suicidal mass attack, impeded a reasonable reform of infantry tactics and increased the death rate exponentially. Southerners seemed particularly enamored with the costly, bloody frontal assault. There were practical reasons, too, why battle tactics did not change more quickly. It was hard to control these large citizen-soldier armies in the field. Technological advances in communication failed to keep pace with those of weaponry, which made it very difficult to coordinate large masses of men in the heat of a fight. Bugle calls, flag waving, drum beats, and men screaming orders were still the time-honored ways of signaling troop movements in battle. As the battlefield expanded, no central command post could observe, much less direct, combat, and sending written orders back and forth by horseback courier often simply confused unit commanders. Improvisation took place in a decentralized manner. The brain of the army was too small for its sprawling body. Is it any wonder that slaughter and confusion defined Civil War combat?

CHAPTER 7

The Other War

The images are stark and frequently terrible. A dozen scruffy, grim-visaged men, each armed with several revolvers and a bowie knife, gallop up to an isolated farmhouse just before dawn. It is the home of an avowed unionist. The ruffians burst into the house, seize the farmer, and shove and kick him into the yard as his wife and children shout hysterically and plead for mercy. Within minutes the men gallop away, but they leave the farmer, a noose secured around his neck, swinging from a tree limb in his own orchard. Elsewhere a sutler's train, bound for a Union encampment, winds its way along a solitary forest trail. Suddenly, a horde of shouting, gray-clad mounted men crash through the underbrush and trees that line the trail. Pistol shots explode. Startled wagon mules bray and veer off the trail. Frightened teamsters leap from their seats and rush for safety as the armed men, now laughing gleefully, dismount to ransack the wagons.

Similar scenes unfolded daily across the South, especially in those areas where neither Union nor Confederate military forces held sway. Many—perhaps most—southern civilians never glimpsed large armies, never heard the boom of artillery, never saw the carnage of large-scale battles. Yet they were frequently victims of other types of warfare and of an escalating cycle of violence and hardship. Soldiers and civilians alike were overwhelmed by unimaginable horrors as the war rapidly deteriorated into something brutish and ignoble. Always there was the *other war,* a war no one had anticipated, a war not waged on battlefields.

Irregular warfare—more popularly known as *guerrilla* warfare—accounted for much of the deterioration, but it was only the most deadly and least restrained source of dislocation on the home front. In addition, the Union army made war on rebel civilians and property. Political dissenters, protesting restrictions on personal freedoms and assumptions of power by the central government, caused turmoil in North and South. Thousands of white southerners, rebels and unionists alike, became refugees, forced from their homes by economic necessity and threats of violence. Northern and southern women joined the war effort, if not in arms, then in roles that relieved the pain and suffering of fellow citizens. These were sides of the war often overshadowed by more dramatic battlefield exploits but just as vital to the progress and outcome of the fighting.

Guerrilla Warfare　　The circumstances under which men—and some women—waged guerrilla warfare varied widely. The guerrilla war had few rules, displayed very little mercy, and was waged by far more people and to a far larger extent than has been credited. In some parts of the South, it was the *real* war, the most frequently encountered and most effective means of protecting friends and van-

"JOHN MORGAN'S HIGHWAYMEN Sacking a Peaceful Village in the West" was the original caption for this illustration in a northern newspaper. While Morgan's men were cavalry raiders rather than genuine guerrillas and not known for committing the atrocities pictured here, the drawing does suggest the range of horrors that became associated with the guerrilla war.

quishing foes. It began in the border states—Missouri, Kentucky, Tennessee, and Virginia—because that is where Union invasion or occupation first threatened. Guerrilla warfare is the ultimate "people's war," the most immediate means by which citizens can respond to invasion. The deeper Union armies penetrated the South, the more widespread became the irregular war. It was easy to be a guerrilla. All it required was a gun and a will to use it. Guns were plentiful in the South, and Confederates had plenty of reasons to use them. Consequently, irregulars "bushwhacked"—that is, *ambushed*—army patrols and supply trains, executed captured soldiers, destroyed railroads, and fired on transports and gunboats that plied southern rivers.

As early as June 1861, Edmund Ruffin, one of Virginia's fiercest fire-eaters, reported: "Guerrilla fighting has begun, and with great effect, near Alexandria & also near Hampton. Some of our people, acting alone, or in small parties, & at their own discretion, have crept upon and shot many of the sentinels & scouts. It is only necessary for the people generally to resort to these means to overcome any invading army, even if greatly inferior to it in regular military force." Of course, Ruffin was not a military man, but many soldiers also saw the necessity of using irregular tactics. In the West and trans-Mississippi, where the Confederate government did not assign sufficient numbers of troops for defense, local commanders depended on irregulars to help combat Union troops.

Fewer northerners—outside of Kansas, anyway, where such men as Charles R. Jennison and James H. Lane soon led raids into Missouri—advocated similar preparations for war. One explanation for this sectional difference is that people seemed to understand that guerrillas operated more effectively on the *defensive* rather than the offensive, and that Union armies would be carrying the war into the rebellious states. Consequently, the northerners who most frequently promoted guerrilla combat lived in midwestern states such as Iowa, Illinois, Indiana, and Ohio that were threatened by rebel guerrilla raids and flooded by unionist refugees from the bushwhacker war. In addition, the U.S. government discouraged the use of guerrillas more forcefully than did the Confederate government, going so far as to tell one hopeful guerrilla chieftain, "It is not the policy of this Government to recognize marauding or guerilla expeditions in the support of its just and equitable laws."

Yet, this use of irregular warfare as a *military tool*, an adjunct to volunteer armies, defined only one brand of guerrilla fighting, and perhaps the most tame. In a second type of guerrilla war, irregular bands of secessionists and unionists waged a bitter struggle to maintain law and order in their communities as well as to harass the enemy. This second type of guerrilla war, waged in the name of *community control*, was not so much a contest between North and South as it was a struggle between neighbors. It was Bleeding Kansas writ large across the South, and it appeared wherever civilians divided most earnestly over secession or were most ambivalent about the wisdom of the war. These struggles began even before the armies arrived, and they persisted after the armies passed, or they raged in places where armies never appeared. Both sides in these local contests considered themselves arbiters of justice whose

Types of Guerrilla Warfare

mission it was to restore order to communities in chaos. Both sides sought to control their neighborhoods by forcing "enemies" to submit or flee. Significantly, given the association so many rebels made between the secession movement and the American Revolution, loyal Confederates referred to their unionist foes as *Tories*, the name that had been used to curse American colonists who had supported England. As a Georgia rebel enthused in 1861:

> We'll teach these shot-gun boys the tricks
> By which a war is won;
> Especially how Seventy-six
> Took Tories on the run.

The stakes were high, and winners wasted little sympathy on the losers. When unionists in east Tennessee tried to disrupt rebel supply lines and troop movements in 1861 by burning the region's railroad bridges, they were captured and hanged. The chilling episode caused hundreds of unionist men to flee north to Kentucky and Ohio, fearful that the "reign of terror" would result in their own arrest. Similar episodes occurred time and again during the war, often with far less provocation than in Tennessee. Rebel militia hanged forty-

GUERRILLAS ON BOTH SIDES often took extralegal actions such as lynching to punish or intimidate their enemies. This particular scene depicts the execution of Tennessee unionists by rebels.

four unionists who were thought to be part of a secret organization that was aligned with Kansas jayhawkers at Gainesville, Texas, in October 1862. Twenty-two unionists, accused of treason after deserting the Confederate army to join the Federals, were hanged at Kinston, North Carolina, in February 1864.

Much of this locally inspired violence was gratuitous and mean spirited, as the crisis atmosphere allowed people with long-standing personal grudges to carry out vendettas that had little to do with the politics of the war. Vengeance became a prime consideration in the minds of many people. The war became an excuse to settle scores and redress wrongs against neighbors who had taken the "wrong" side. To steal the livestock of such people, to drive them from their homes, even to lynch them seemed legitimate actions. Defense of home and family became confused with a desire to throttle old foes. A form of vigilante justice spread through the South, especially in isolated areas where neither rebel nor unionist civilians could depend on the armies to establish legitimate authority.

Worse yet, a third type of guerrilla warfare soon appeared. Most Confederate and Union guerrillas considered themselves loyal to their respective causes. They struck only at those people who they believed endangered their community or nation. However, as ever more people advocated an unrelenting contest waged under the "black flag" of *no quarter,* large numbers of malcontents— army deserters, draft dodgers, thieves, bullies, and genuine outlaws—exploited the irregular war to loot, pillage, murder, and destroy without any regard for the recognized rules of war. These guerrilla bands frequently cloaked their actions in the name of either the Union or the Confederacy, but they sought mainly to take advantage of the chaos and lax standards of morality that accompany every war. They subverted the legitimate use of the irregular war and turned it into a form of *outlawry.* The war became a game for them, a form of *blood sport,* and their outrages not only caused the guerrilla war to career out of control, but it also tainted all guerrillas with an unsavory reputation.

Third Type of Guerrilla Warfare

The upper South bred the largest number of outlaw bands, but they could also be found in such interior southern states as Mississippi, Alabama, and Georgia, particularly in more remote (and more unionist) hill regions. Moreover, both sides joined in this third form of guerrilla action, and even legitimate military units sometimes crossed the line. A Missouri woman described a raid by Jennison's Jayhawkers—organized officially as the Seventh Kansas Cavalry but named for their colonel, the erstwhile Kansas politician—on the home of a neighbor. "One night while the family was asleep," it was reported, "the door . . . was broken open and a squad of noisy [jayhawkers] rushed into the [bedroom]. The alarmed lady entreated them to retire until she could put on her clothes, but they cursed her and told her to get up pretty damn quick. . . . A bright fire was burning in the open hearth; the wretches took blazing brands and carried them about as they ransacked the closets, dresser drawers and trunks. . . . The outlaws then turned their attention to the girls, using insulting terms, searched their persons for valuables, all the while singing ribald songs or telling obscene jokes. . . . Three of the wretches took by force three of the girls into the yard and marched them back and forth in the moonlight, making most vicious threats and insinuations. . . . After several hours of this atrocious conduct the creatures started away."

Jennison's Confederate counterpart on the western border was William C. Quantrill, an Ohio-born drifter in his mid-twenties. Quantrill had earned his living primarily as a schoolteacher before becoming involved in the Kansas-Missouri border war in 1859. A man with no firm political loyalties, he eventually sided with the proslavery faction because it offered the best opportunities for plunder. Educated, a fine horseman, and a dead shot, Quantrill quickly rose to command the largest rebel guerrilla band in the trans-Mississippi.

Quantrill's most notorious action occurred in August 1863 when he led 450 men in the sacking of Lawrence, Kansas, that state's recognized center of anti-slavery agitation. His gang looted and burned the town and murdered some 150 men and boys in just a few hours. When they fled back to Missouri, the raiders left behind a scene of desolation rarely matched in the war. "One saw the dead everywhere, on the sidewalk, in the streets, among the weeds in the gardens," reported one survivor. "The fires were still glowing in the cellars. The brick and stone walls were . . . standing bare and blackened. . . . Here and there among the embers could be seen the bones of those who had perished."

Impact of Guerrilla Warfare

Whichever type of guerrilla warfare engulfed a community—and most often, people experienced a combination of the three—it affected the spirits of southerners every bit as much as news from the battlefields. Depending on which side—unionists or rebels—gained the upper hand, the other side felt that they had lost control of their lives, and thus the war. Losing the war for community control meant that law and order had been extinguished; justice and mercy had been forfeit. News of victory or defeat from the armies could hearten or discourage people, but the immediate contest for survival had even deeper consequences. "I dread guerrilla warfare more than the shock of vast armies in battle array," confessed a despondent Kentucky unionist in 1862. "Guerrillas are never still—life, liberty & property are not safe an hour." Two years later, a Confederate woman in Arkansas insisted, "Things are far worse than they ever have been. The whole country is full of bands of robbers and murderers." Roaming bands of deserters from both armies, she explained, preyed on both sides, regardless of loyalties. Conditions had deteriorated to the point that she even welcomed Union occupation, "anything for Peace and established Laws again." Under these circumstances, the need for security trumped political loyalty.

Official Confederate Attitudes

The Confederate government was of two minds about the guerrilla war. On the one hand, Jefferson Davis and his counselors, while not inclined to encourage bushwhacking, had turned a blind eye to it early in the war when it seemed the only way to resist Union occupation of such states as Missouri, Kentucky, and western Virginia. It would take time, they reasoned, to organize, equip, and train sufficient numbers of conventional soldiers to defend the South. Guerrillas could perform valuable service until that was accomplished. Confederate leaders also knew that federal authorities had retaliated so dramatically against rebel irregulars, not *only* because they deemed them an affront to "civilized warfare," but also because the guerrillas posed real dangers to federal operations. During the course of the war, the Union army had to reassign thousands of men from its combat units to guard communication lines—both railroads and rivers—and to protect loyal territory against possible raids, ambushes, and other deviltry. Rebel guerrillas also caused multiple political problems for Lincoln and the governors of northern and loyal southern border states. These leaders worried until the very last year of the conventional war about how the guerrilla war threatened the lives and loyalties of northern citizens and southern unionists.

On the other hand, Confederate authorities could not help but be embarrassed by their own guerrillas. Enthusiasm for the cause was one thing—patriotic fervor was fine—but the Confederate government sensed a clear danger in becoming too closely aligned with bushwhackers. Unrestricted guerrilla warfare, regardless of its effectiveness, had proven extremely difficult to control, too often shading into outlawry. If it continued as it had begun, it would create a worldwide public relations nightmare. The new government, which wanted desperately to be accepted abroad as a legitimate state and which portrayed itself as a Christian commonwealth governed by gentlemen, would be denounced by the Federals as a barbaric rabble. And they did not want to lend authority to unwashed lowlife types who could then claim a political role.

The Confederate government sought a remedy in the Partisan Ranger Act, passed almost unnoticed in April 1862, just a few days after Congress introduced conscription. The legislation was intended to regulate existing guerrilla bands and to spruce up their image by bringing them under government control. It gave President Davis the exclusive power to authorize bands of *partisans* (the term used for irregular soldiers during the American Revolution, before *guerrillas* was popularized in the Napoleonic era) and required that they operate under the local Confederate commander. The government hoped that by making partisans "subject to the same regulations as other soldiers," it could curb the excesses of unrestrained guerrilla warfare. Unhappily, these attempts failed. The independent nature of irregular service and the proliferation of outlaw bands made them ungovernable. Moreover, the Partisan Ranger Act did not place Confederate commanders and political officers into guerrilla bands, the way other governments have managed to control guerrillas, at least to some extent. By 1864 the degree of violence perpetrated by the guerrillas and conventional soldiers of both armies reached a frightening scale. Confederates repealed the Partisan Ranger Act and disavowed nearly all of its irregular units.

Partisan Ranger Act

To protect its soldiers and loyal civilians from bushwhacker butchery and lawlessness, the Union army responded with harsh retaliatory measures that only made matters worse. As early as 1861, Union commanders in western Virginia and Missouri ordered that captured guerrillas be shot without trial. By 1863 all Union armies had received instructions to treat irregulars in this fashion. Army officers spoke of "hunting" and "exterminating" guerrillas, as though they were tracking wild animals. Guerrilla bands always "infested" an area, rather than occupying it. The members of these bands were not regarded as soldiers but as "villains," "assassins," and "subhuman fiends."

Union Response

What was worse—and here was a crucial element for the deterioration of the war—when the Federals saw that rebel guerrillas could not be intimidated, they included noncombatants in their antiguerrilla edicts. "People of the neighborhood," complained a Union general in Louisiana, "harbor and feed these lawless men, . . . and it [is only] by punishing them that this detestable practice will be stopped." Unfortunately, he was correct. It is a time-honored dictum that guerrillas can only be successful if they have the support of the civilian population. The U.S. government, quickly grasping this fact, made Confederate *civilians* bear the brunt of irregular operations by forcing them to pay for the damage done to local railroads, bridges, or telegraph lines; destroying or confiscating their property; taking them hostage; forcing them out of their homes; even sweeping away whole communities.

For example, Gen. William T. Sherman, long before his destructive "march to the sea" in 1864, torched the village of Randolph, Tennessee, to retaliate against guerrilla attacks on Mississippi River steamers in September 1862. Another Union general did the same to Hopefield, Arkansas, which he proclaimed to be "a mere shelter for guerrillas." The navy, too, pursued this policy. In October 1862, Adm. David Dixon Porter assured his squadron on the Mississippi River, "There is no impropriety in destroying houses supposed to be affording shelter to rebels, and it is the only way to stop guerrilla warfare. Should innocent persons suffer it will be their own fault."

New Union Military Policies

As the dates of these events suggest, mid-1862 marked a turning point in the war, not just in the guerrilla war but also in the larger contest. Chapters 4 and 5 have shown how the political and popular pressure on Lincoln to end slavery and prosecute the war more energetically was building at this time. Lincoln settled the slavery issue in bold fashion by announcing the Emancipation Proclamation and permitting the recruitment of black soldiers. He addressed the military issue by unleashing John Pope's army on central Virginia. The treatment of rebel guerrillas reflected that same toughness. The government and the president had clearly broken with the earlier, if somewhat inconsistent, policy of "conciliation" toward rebels.

A harder, more determined, and somewhat desperate Lincoln emerged in the spring and summer of 1862. "I expect to maintain this contest until successful," he informed William Seward in late June, "or till I die, or am conquered, or my term expires, or Congress or the country forsakes me." A few weeks later, he told Congress, "That those who make a causeless war should be compelled to pay the cost of it, is too obviously just, to be called in question." Lincoln still made occasional references to tempering justice with mercy, but such nuances were easily obscured and often forgotten in the crisis atmosphere. "I am a patient man—always willing to forgive on the Christian terms of repentance," Lincoln told a Louisianan, "and also to give ample *time* for repentance. Still I must save the government if possible. . . . [And] it may as well be understood, once for all, that I shall not surrender this game leaving any available card unplayed."

Confiscation of rebel property (legally justified under the Confiscation Act) increased steadily during the next three years. Military confiscation, especially of livestock and foodstuffs, had long been an accepted practice in war. Both North and South established guidelines to regulate it, such as requiring their armies to give "loyal" citizens written receipts for all property seized. But the rules were not always followed, and freebooting soldiers without any authority at all simply took what they wanted when *foraging*. After all, from the northern perspective, southerners were the "enemy," which fully justified in the soldiers' eyes gratuitous destruction of houses, theft of cash, and "confiscation" of such personal property as clothing and jewelry. "War is awful in the extreme," acknowledged a Union officer in late 1862, "but if *we* can risk *life & limb* do not hesitate over a few paltry *chattels* of the *enemy*." Even popular northern songs such as "Uncle Sam, What Ails You?" encouraged rough treatment:

> Confiscate their stocks and farms,
> Do it with a vigor,
> If it will our Union save,
> Confiscate the——[nigger].
> Confiscate all, everything,
> Even to the whiskey,
> Till they find that to rebel
> Is getting rather risky.

THIS UNION FORAGING PARTY was typical of the way in which both armies sustained themselves during a campaign. These operations were supposed to be conducted in an orderly fashion under the direction of commissioned officers for the benefit of the entire army, but as seen in this episode, soldiers frequently confiscated food and other property for their own personal use.

Prejudices of Union Soldiers

It is important to understand Union soldiers' preconceived attitudes toward the rebels. Generations of political rhetoric had bred a degree of contempt for their southern countrymen even before they invaded Dixie. Southerners, they believed, formed a low, ignorant, and ignoble race. The worst of them were slaveholders, and even nonslaveholders lacked the moral fiber of the most shiftless northerner. One Union officer described the Ozark Mountains of Arkansas as "very thinly settled by a wild semi-civilized race of backwoodsmen." Another man elaborated, "There is a general appearance of slovenliness, as if they had all come to the conclusion that there was no use trying to be decent." The people were "ignorant and lazy," wrote an Iowa soldier, the whole region "decidedly a land of corndodgers and poor fiddlers." Arkansans were "indolent, go-easy, do nothing squatters" who would "make the fairest, sunniest land in the world look dark and gloomy."

Then, too, as Union troops occupied an area, distinctions between combatants and noncombatants became blurred. "These people will conceal their weapons and appear as good Union men," complained an officer of one apparently benign farming community, only to bushwhack men sitting by a campfire or bathing in local creeks. "They are committing murders daily, lying in ambush for that purpose," warned one observer of secessionists in western Virginia. "They steal upon our pickets and murder them. They shoot down their neighbors daytime and at night, and burn their property to ashes." Potential spies, saboteurs, and snipers lurked everywhere, which caused Union troops to trust no one and to treat all rebels as deadly threats. The enemy, as one soldier in Virginia complained, "had friends and spies in every house from Alexandria to Manassas."

Such negative impressions and latent hostility allowed Union soldiers to pillage without conscience or remorse. One man confessed that he and his comrades enjoyed "desolating the country" over which they marched. Another man admitted: "Desolation marks every section of the country through which the army has passed. Houses are deserted and fast going to ruin; fences are pulled down and burned up; orchards are ruined by hitching horses and mules to the trees; fields are left uncultivated and an air of sickening desolation is everywhere visible." And from a third soldier: "Fields are all burned out, houses, barns, . . . and fences burned, and the smoke mingling with the dust darkens the heavens. . . . No white man is found. Women crying but makes little impression on us."

Confederate Excesses

Of course, Confederate troops did their own share of foraging and confiscating. They treated unionists as roughly as Federals handled rebels. Yet, even loyal rebels found reason to complain about excesses. Confederate civilians may have grumbled less when turning over their hogs and corn to gray-clad soldiers—assuming that they were paid—and their private possessions and homes may have been less endangered, but the toll of countless rounds of confiscation by both armies mounted. One rebel watched helplessly as Confederate soldiers felled "a whole hill-side of timber" on her farm. The family suddenly had to worry about how it would stave off the cold of an approaching winter. Another person observed after the Confederate army had "foraged upon the country for some time" that "but little [was] left behind," or as one woman put it, "It is truly a hard case to be spared by neither friend nor foe."

Few people had anticipated the war of retaliation and counter-retaliation, of guerrillas and outlaws, of confiscation and ruin that emerged by the midpoint of the war. The shock of it severely tested the will and spirit of noncombatants caught in its crosshairs. More than that, it contributed to growing public protests over a whole range of other issues, North and South. Both governments discovered that war required unpopular political and legal measures. Dissenters and troublemakers popped up everywhere, sometimes posing significant threats to the stability and unity of the home front.

Dissent on the Home Front

The biggest threat to northern conformity came from the so-called *Copperheads*. Democratic in their politics and located mostly in the Midwest, Copperheads opposed the Lincoln administration on nearly every score. Like most Democrats, traditionally wary of a strong central government, they resisted emancipation, the use of black troops, conscription, and the confiscation of rebel property, but these *Peace Democrats* parted company with *War Democrats* on the morality of the war. War Democrats, while disagreeing with Lincoln about *how* to fight the war, still believed that the war was necessary. Copperheads, on the other hand, insisted that the North had no right to force the South to remain in the Union. It was an unjust war, they said, and it must cease. Interestingly, many people also voiced this conviction because they were themselves southern born, part of a large migration to the lower Midwest from the upper South in the antebellum years. Most Copperheads, devoted to working within the political process, challenged the Republicans in Congress and in elections. However, a few zealots plotted to free rebels from prisoner-of-war camps in Indiana, Illinois, and Ohio, and they encouraged northerners to resist the draft. Most historians believe that the danger posed by these antiwar extremists was exaggerated, but Lincoln and his Republican governors considered the risks to be genuine.

Copperheads

Antiwar protestors threatened more than the stability of the home front, reasoned Republicans; they also undermined the morale of the army. By late 1862, when northern reverses on eastern battlefields gave momentum to the Copperhead cause, Union soldiers wondered aloud about the malignant spirit at home. They cursed the "desperadoes" and "foul miscreants" who had caused so "much dissatisfaction in the army." It angered soldiers to think that they were bearing the hardships and dangers of an unpopular war that the government might be forced to abandon. Whole regiments circulated petitions to denounce the Peace Democrats as traitors. Men vowed to preserve the Union "in spite of the copperheads" and threatened to return home and "give them that *Peace* that Knows no Wakening. By the Bayonet, or U.S. Union Pill [a bullet]." Like so many episodes and issues in the war, this one, too, found its way into popular song. "What's the Matter?" expressed displeasure with Copperhead "traitors," who, in a reversal of rebel vernacular, became the "Tories" of the North:

> Firing on our armies' rear,
> Trying to scatter
> Disaffection far and near;
> That what's the matter.
> "Take your proclamation back;
> Take your armies off the track,"
> Cry aloud this tory pack;
> That's what's the matter!

Lincoln's Response

Lincoln responded to Copperheads and other dissenters by extending the suspension of habeas corpus in Maryland to the nation at large, shutting down disloyal newspapers, and arresting outspoken protestors. The government arrested at least 14,000 civilians during the war on charges of draft evasion, defrauding the government, smuggling, encouraging desertion, treasonable language, and "disloyalty." Some members of Lincoln's cabinet, such as Gideon Welles, and such political allies as Senator Lyman Trumbull of Illinois worried about the legality, necessity, and political wisdom of these actions. Yet, public protests over apparent infringements of civil liberties remained relatively mild, especially outside of the Democratic Party. Most of the people arrested resided in border slave states—Missouri, Maryland, and Kentucky—where both the United States and the Confederate States maneuvered for political control and military supremacy. Even the majority of newspapers that Lincoln shut down—his most frequently protested action—were published in Missouri and Maryland.

Vallandigham Case

Lincoln's most celebrated action against dissent involved the banishment of former Ohio congressman Clement L. Vallandigham. Defeated for reelection in 1862 by political maneuvering within his state, Vallandigham caused a ruckus before leaving Congress by calling for European intervention in the war and "practical recognition" of the Confederacy. When he continued to speak out against the despotism of "King Lincoln," Vallandigham was arrested in May 1863, found guilty by a military tribunal of expressing sympathy for the enemy, and deported to the Confederate States.

The case stands as Lincoln's most serious misreading of public opinion on the issue of dissent. Even conservative Republicans and War Democrats criticized the president. Yet Lincoln, always the patient and skilled political operator, answered his critics with a deft justification for his heavy-handed tactics. Far from being "King Lincoln," protested the president, he had treated the admittedly delicate issue of civil liberties according to the constitutional sanctions permitted during times "of Rebellion or Invasion [when] the public Safety may require it." In the Vallandigham case, Lincoln insisted that this "wiley agitator" had been arrested, tried, and sentenced not for opposing Republican political policies but "because he was damaging the army, upon the existence and vigor of which, the life of the nation depends." More dramatic wartime events eventually overshadowed the incident and Vallandigham soon made his way to Canada, from where he campaigned unsuccessfully for the Ohio governorship in 1863. When he silently reentered the United States a year later, Lincoln ignored him. The president had made his point. By selectively exiling Vallandigham, the most visible and vocal of his critics, he had warned all Copperheads.

Further protests developed over the government's handling of conscription, black emancipation, the use of black troops, and military strategy. So even though the northern home front was relatively prosperous, free from any form of rationing, and largely untouched by the physical destruction of war, the citizenry remained politically divided. The nation's sense of unity and resolve rose and fell with news from the battlefield. Even Lincoln, as will be shown in chapter 9, doubted his own ability to guide the Union to victory as late as the presidential election of 1864.

Additional Northern Protests

Jefferson Davis responded in like fashion to similar protests, but the Confederate president faced an additional challenge. The Confederate States had been formed in the name of *states' rights,* a philosophy that relegated the interests of the *nation* to second place. Yet, as the war progressed, Davis became convinced that his nation could survive only with a marked increase in government *centralization.* He took most of the same actions against dissenters as Lincoln—suspended habeas corpus, limited freedom of speech and press, instituted military conscription, declared martial law—and in some ways went even further. Davis also requisitioned slaves to work for the government, impressed farm products to feed the army, nationalized key war industries, and instituted an internal passport system to regulate movement in and out of major towns and cities. By 1863 these actions caused much public grumbling about how the South was "tending too much to resemble Lincolndom." By 1864 popular discontent with the role of the Confederate government had placed Davis in a difficult position.

Davis's Response to Protest

Davis was no fool, but he lacked many of the political skills that Lincoln wielded so deftly. To his credit, Davis understood that the Confederacy had to pool its resources and centralize its power if it hoped to defeat the more populous, wealthier, and potentially stronger states to the north. But correct as the president's instincts may have been, he seemed incapable of rallying the nation to his vision. Even many friends acknowledged his faults. He could be slow to compromise, undiplomatic, aloof, quarrelsome, prone to favoritism, and unable to delegate authority. Whereas Lincoln trusted his cabinet members to manage the day-to-day operations of their departments, Davis overburdened himself with useless tasks. Where Lincoln was nimble enough to dodge political brickbats, the obstinate Davis was constantly clobbered by them. Where Lincoln used diplomacy, humor, and patient doggedness to disarm potential foes, Davis had a propensity for alienating friends. The loyal and self-effacing James A. Seddon, fourth and best of Davis's five secretaries of war, once complained that "the President was the most difficult man to get along with he had ever seen." This led Seddon's secretary to remark, "If the President cannot get along with a man as smooth and yielding as Mr. Seddon, nobody can please him."

Lincoln and Davis Compared

A useful way to understand the differences between Davis and Lincoln is to recall their pre-political careers. Lincoln was a lawyer, gregarious, and with a passion for language. He knew that every issue had at least two sides, and he believed most people so ornery that he could find someone to disagree with nearly any proposition. He expected conflict more often than harmony. In court, Lincoln had learned to woo, persuade, and cajole when making his case, sometimes by marshaling the facts, sometimes by telling a joke, but always seeking to minimize hard feelings.

Davis, trained as an engineer at West Point, retained something of the rigidity common to that profession. He was precise, almost mathematically so. He approached political problems as he would the construction of a bridge, observing the terrain, calculating the obstacles, measuring his response, and deciding on a course of action. Once he settled on a policy, he rarely swayed from that position. Always certain that his view of things was correct, he had the utmost confidence that everyone else would come to appreciate the sturdiness of his plan and the wisdom of his vision. Years before the war, his future wife, Varina, gave this assessment upon meeting Davis: "He impresses me as a remarkable kind of man, but of uncertain temper, and has a way of taking for granted that everybody agrees with him when he expresses an opinion."

Ill Health of Davis

Davis suffered not only from a rigid temperament but also from physical debility. Plagued by a variety of ailments—primarily neuralgia, bronchitis, and dyspepsia—for most of his adult life, Davis, even his friends noticed, became more impatient and confrontational when feeling unwell. Although only a year older than Lincoln, he was frequently bedridden during his presidency. At such times, his cabinet, and especially Judah P. Benjamin, Davis's most trusted advisor, had to perform his duties. Most annoying to some people, the protective Varina, with her own "lofty if not . . . hasty temper," limited access to the president on many such occasions, presuming to speak for him, and sometimes, when he was ill, forging his signature on official documents. People soon called her "the empress."

Confederate Political Parties

The Confederacy's political party system—or rather, lack of one—exacerbated Davis's woes. After their near religious adherence to states' rights, the next most fervent political belief among Confederates was that the petty factionalism bred by a two-party political system had ruined the old Republic and led to the breakup of the Union. Determined to avoid the errors of the past, they intended to base their new republic on common goals and virtues that would free them from the self-destructive machinations of political parties. Yet, political differences were inevitable, and when disputes arose over such public policies as conscription, impressment, and habeas corpus, people aligned themselves into pro-Davis and anti-Davis factions. Thus broad philosophical differences over policy acquired a personal tone and subjected Davis to even more abuse than northerners heaped on Lincoln.

Personal Opposition to Davis

The attacks became most heated when influential political leaders turned political disagreements into bitter public disputes with Davis. Several governors, who jealously guarded the power bestowed on them by the Confederate system of government, challenged the president head on. Joseph E. Brown, governor of Georgia, berated Davis for assuming the role of "emperor," which would apparently make him an even bigger tyrant than "King Lincoln." Brown was especially incensed by military conscription and shielded all Georgians subject to the draft by enrolling them in his state militia. Zebulon B. Vance, governor of North Carolina, exempted state officials from the draft and fought congressional efforts to control North Carolina industries.

In Congress, Georgian Robert Toombs, whose reputation as a fire-eater and penchant for drink eliminated him from consideration as Confederate president, opposed centralization in no uncertain terms. He called Davis a "false and hypocritical wretch" and announced that he would oppose the suspension of habeas corpus by "advising resistance, resistance to death, to his law." Most notable of all, Vice President Alexander Stephens became so upset by the government's drift toward centralization and the curtailment of civil liberties that he refused to reside in Richmond for much of the war. While not so personally opposed to Davis as some people, Stephens was no less adamant about his own position. "My hostility and wrath is not against him," he said of Davis, "or any man or men, but against the measures and the policy which I see is leading us to despotism."

The Confederacy also remained fragmented by unionists and a variety of Confederates who became unhappy with the war or their government. The so-called *unconditional* unionists, who had been the heart of the antisecessionist movement and who, some historians estimate, formed as much as 10 percent of the South's white population, encouraged opposition to the Confederacy and sought to end the war at all costs. This sort of political warfare found its most effective expression in such places as east Tennessee and west Virginia, but another

Southern Unionists

THIS CLANDESTINE MEETING of Tennessee unionists illustrates the divided loyalties of the South. While the clear majority of white southerners supported the rebellion, a large minority was determined to resist the establishment of an independent South. The men in this picture may have wanted to join the Union army, organize a guerrilla band, or serve as spies and guides for federal troops, but they clearly have resolved to preserve the Union.

strain of unionism emerged when many once loyal Confederates, appalled by the mounting human and material costs of war, called for a peaceful settlement to the conflict. Their unionism, more pragmatic than ideological, was fostered more by war weariness than by political considerations. They did not object to seeing the Union rejoined, but unlike the Tories, they feared any settlement or treaty that failed to protect southern interests.

Historians have long puzzled over the group identity of southern unionists, at least the white ones. It perhaps goes without saying that most blacks, especially slaves, opposed the Confederacy. To that extent, blacks might also be considered unionists, but white unionists remain hard to label. Broadly speaking, most of them appear to have been northern-born emigrants to the South, former Whigs, or small—and generally poor—farmers. Yet, any one of these three groups could be diametrically opposed to another for a variety of social, economic, or political reasons. We also know that some peace advocates were pacifists or religious dissenters. The Quakers of the North Carolina Piedmont and some German communities in Texas offer good examples of people whose loyalties were defined more by cultural than political or economic factors.

Occupations and professions also must be considered, although here, too, the evidence is conflicting. Some historians believe that townspeople—merchants and professionals—were more likely to be unionists, while other historians identify farmers and planters as the best candidates for that label. Age could be a factor, too, with older southerners—say those older than thirty-five or forty—more likely than younger people to oppose secession. Having lived a longer part of their lives under the Stars and Stripes, middle-aged folk had strong emotional attachments to the Union. They may have disagreed with how the old United States had managed its affairs, perhaps even resented the way Congress—from their perspective—always gave southerners the short end of the stick, but they still regretted the disruption of the old union of states.

Antigovernment Confederates

Then there were what may be called *antigovernment* Confederates, the protestors who sided with Joe Brown, Zeb Vance, and Robert Toombs. They believed the Davis government had bungled the war at enormous cost to the citizenry. What was more, they opposed the centralizing policies of the Confederacy, most especially conscription and confiscation. They became bitter, even to the point of occasionally aligning themselves with the unionists, yet they parted company with any group of dissenters who considered reunion an acceptable solution to the war. Antigovernment Confederates welcomed an armistice but not a surrender. They wanted Confederate policies altered but did not want the Confederacy toppled. This was a fine line, to be sure, but then that is what makes distinguishing unionism from Confederate opposition so difficult.

Another indication of the complexity of this issue may be seen in the fact that unionists sometimes expressed conflicting sentiments. Some contradictions were inevitable, inspired as they were by changing military and political fortunes during four years of war. One day, people might be fervent and firm in their desire to see the nation rejoined; a few months later, the shifting tides of war and altered personal circumstances could make the same people more cautious, less certain that the Union should be repaired without political or constitutional guarantees being extended to the South. Ambivalence rather than certainty colored the attitudes of many white southerners.

The protestors, whether hardened unionists or more circumspect antigovernment Confederates, formed only a fraction of most communities, although their ranks sometimes included locally prominent and influential people. Because they often feared being persecuted by neighbors or arrested by Confederate authorities, they maintained a low public profile. Neighbors may have suspected their sympathies, but it would have been foolish to draw community ire needlessly. Unionists were never sure whom to trust, and they often became known to each other only after many conversations and much hemming and hawing on the "delicate subject" of the war. They were "afraid to trust each other," admitted a Virginia unionist. Still, the number of unionists grew as the war dragged on, and they caused plenty of turmoil.

General Confederate Dissent

Unionists and antigovernment Confederates expressed their displeasure in a number of ways. Many people—and this occasionally meant entire communities—declared that they would not support the Confederacy or its laws. Conscription officers, tax collectors, and other government agents confronted such people or entered anti-Confederate neighborhoods at their peril. Jones County, Mississippi, which actually declared itself an independent republic, is the best-known example of an entire community opposing the rebel cause, but places in North Carolina, Tennessee, Florida, and elsewhere did likewise.

Dissenters formed secret peace societies, too, the largest ones being in North Carolina, eastern Tennessee, northern Alabama, and northern Arkansas. All of those regions, it might be noted, were geographically isolated and characterized by formidable hills or rugged mountains. Most of the peace societies organized to resist conscription, although they do not appear to have formed any sort of coordinated national movement. The Confederate army broke up most of these organizations, in some instances dragging the members off to prison in chains, but at least two groups, in North Carolina and Georgia, evolved into political factions that elected several members to the Confederate Congress in 1863 and 1864.

Bolder people contributed directly to the Union military effort. They acted as spies for the Union army, and once Federal troops entered their neighborhoods, they became guides, procured food, and nursed the sick and wounded. Of course, by doing so, they betrayed their loyalties and often had to flee their homes if the Union troops moved on or were forced out. In an ultimate demonstration of discontent, close to 100,000 white southerners—mostly from the border states—enlisted in the Union army. Many of these men came from that large pool of northerners who had settled in the South before the war. Many of them were also recruited to serve in antiguerrilla units in their home states and counties, where they knew the terrain, the favored haunts of rebel guerrillas, and the sympathies of their neighbors.

All of these dissenters were subject to punishment if apprehended. Peace societies' members were imprisoned, while people offering armed resistance might be hanged. The numbers arrested and punished by the Confederacy are difficult to determine, but there must have been thousands. The Davis government, aware of the exaggerated sense of honor and insistence on personal freedom for white men that prevailed in the South, was slower to restrict civil liberties than was Lincoln, but southern arrests appear to have been made for similar reasons—disloyalty and suspicious activities—as those in the North and in the border states. By contrast, the Confederate government shut down few newspapers, but all of its actions, like those in the North, were dictated by pragmatic (if sometimes alarmist) assessments of the dangers posed by internal dissent. The rebel government also forced people to submit to its rule by threatening to arrest and exile them under the Enemy Aliens Act and to confiscate their property through the Sequestration Act, both passed in August 1861.

Confederate Nationalism   Such widespread dissent and disillusionment raises an issue hotly contested among historians: *Confederate nationalism.* How strong were the ties of loyalty between southerners and their government? Clearly, the rebels expressed much national feeling at the start of the war, even as they justified secession in terms of states' rights, and they always spoke of "national" independence. Yet, genuine national sentiment needs time to grow. It is very much a process, an evolution, and sometimes an extremely slow one. Just because rebel leaders declared the Confederate States a nation did not make them so. There was little discernable "national" sentiment in 1776 when the Continental Congress christened the United States. Pennsylvanians still thought of themselves first and foremost as Pennsylvanians, likewise Virginians, and so, too, New Yorkers. It took several years after winning independence just to agree on a form of national government, and many more years were required to forge a national identity.

It is unreasonable to think that Confederate citizens would be immediately imbued with such consciousness or that it was a simple matter of transferring their loyalties from the United States to the Confederate States. Nor could their *regional* identity—and loyalty—as *southerners* be converted automatically into a new national allegiance. White southerners clearly believed that political and economic interests set them apart from northerners. They even felt a degree of pride in being different from their northern brethren. But most southern unionists, to take an obvious example, could not conceive of dividing the nation for the sake of the region. They remained attached to the Union by what Lincoln called "mystic chords of memory." Not even loyal Confederates could entirely escape the echoes of those chords.

The many discordant elements of the other war helped slowly to erode whatever vitality Confederate nationalism may have possessed, and no element better illustrates the problem than the multiple guerrilla conflicts. Not even regional loyalty could withstand this powerfully disruptive force. Recall that much of the peculiar ferocity and intractable nature of the guerrilla war sprang from a desire to maintain law and order within communities. Similarly, when their communities were threatened by outside forces—namely, the Union army—Confederates thought primarily in terms of *local defense.* The rebels, of course, fought to win *national* independence, but many of them defined the "nation" in terms of their own communities. Most guerrilla bands were organized to protect particular neighborhoods, whether against Union troops, southern unionists, or rampaging gangs of deserters. Southerners of all stripes saw the war not so much as a struggle between two sections of the country, or even between states, but as a showdown to decide who would control thousands of individual neighborhoods across the South. In this context, the concept of *states' rights* meant not only the right to defend the interests of the South against the government in Washington, D.C., but also the ability of individual states to ensure the safety of their citizens. It also meant that the principal test of loyalty to any new national government would be the ability of that government to protect individual communities. It may have been an unfair requirement, and it was certainly an impossible task, but whenever the Confederate government failed to meet that obligation, it lost support.

States' rights and attachment to place are bywords of southern culture, but in this context, they dramatically impeded the creation of Confederate nationalism. Some historians believe that strong local attachments are not necessarily at odds with nationalism, that the two can, in fact, coexist and be mutually reinforcing. These scholars are correct up to a point. However, it is equally clear that the concern of so many Confederates for local defense overrode national zeal and loyalty nearly every time. Localism did not prevail everywhere or entirely in the South, but it did so often enough, in enough places, and to a sufficient degree to cast suspicion on the strength of national identity. As Arkansas governor Harris Flanagin told Jefferson Davis in early 1863, "Soldiers do not enter the service to maintain the Southern Confederacy alone but also to protect their property and defend their homes and families."

More selfish considerations could also erode patriotism. Calls from Confederate political and military leaders for devotion to the cause could fall on deaf ears where personal safety or financial gain were in jeopardy. Manufacturers, farmers, planters, anyone who saw an opportunity to turn a profit through speculation, trading on the black market (especially in cotton), or simply charging whatever the open market would bear often put mammon above patriotism. Robert E. Lee, as a member of the gentry class that most often called for self-sacrifice from all Confederates, excoriated profiteers and businesspeople who seemed more interested in the fate of their property than in the survival of the nation. "We have at the South had so easy and comfortable a time, that it is difficult for us to practice the self-denial and labour necessary [in war]," Lee declared. "It will require misfortune & suffering . . . to induce us to do what we ought to do."

Southern Refugees

In any event, the accumulated turmoil of this other war—the guerrillas, the confiscation, the infringements on civil liberties, the cries of dissent—when added to the threat posed by enemy armies, produced a degree of chaos and significant psychic shock in the South. It ultimately forced tens of thousands of people (it is impossible to say exactly how many) to flee homes and communities where they had spent their entire lives. "Many families in this country have left," reported a Virginia rebel in 1861, "some at the approach of our army and some at that of the enemy." Traveling south on one road were "vehicles of

THIS WOEFUL-LOOKING GROUP of unionist refugees in Arkansas could just as easily be Confederate exiles in Virginia. Countless civilians on both sides were forced to leave their homes and live as exiles. Some people had friends with whom to stay or the money to rent or purchase comfortable accommodations. However, the majority of refugees lived a nomadic existence.

all . . . description, filled with women and children, . . . men on horseback and on foot, a continual stream." Just a few miles away, on the same day, an equal number of people heading north left behind "vacant firesides" and villages bereft of "the ploughmans song and the waggons rattle."

Unionists, hoping to remain in their homes and to contest control of their neighborhoods until the Union army appeared, endured as long as possible, but community pressure, threats of personal violence, or the prospect of arrest often sent them on the road north. Highly visible people, such as Tennessee newspaper publisher William G. Brownlow, got away only after being released from prison for verbal or printed attacks on the Confederacy. Others fled even after the arrival of Union troops if federal officers could not ensure adequate protection against guerrillas, harassment by rebel neighbors, or the misbehavior of their own men. An Arkansas unionist in such circumstances observed: "It was like tempting Providence to remain longer, and I decided to seek, if not a home, at least a refuge, in some peaceful land."

Even larger numbers of rebels abandoned their homes, as unfounded rumors of the vengeance to be unleashed by Union soldiers—raping women, hanging old men, burning farms—spread swiftly and went unquestioned. Terrified residents of the border states scattered first, but a more general exodus commenced in 1862 as Union armies advanced. Following the surrender of Fort Donelson, for example, Nashville "became perfectly paralyzed . . . panic stricken." One observer reported: "All who could do so packed up and fled." Confederate soldiers, hearing of the approach of the enemy toward their homes, sometimes sent instructions to their wives and mothers to leave. A few refugees stayed with friends or relatives in Union territory, but most of them sought out secure parts of the Confederacy. Some people retreated only for the moment, perhaps for a few weeks or months. More often, they left for the balance of the war. Some did not go far, perhaps only to a patch of nearby woods or a secluded valley. Others wanted to put as much distance as possible between themselves and the enemy.

Braver, more defiant, and just plain stubborn folk persevered even with the arrival of the enemy, but the resulting privations, the strain of living under martial law, and threats of violence eventually drove them away. In Knoxville, Tennessee, one woman, deciding she could no longer tolerate the federal presence in her city, left in despair. "We were robbed of everything—houses burned, ladies insulted," she explained. "I asked [a Union soldier] how he would like for his mother and sisters to be so treated, he said if they were rebels he would think it all right."

Other people hung on until they were ordered from their homes, as army officers commandeered them for living quarters or military offices. Union generals often required rebels under their jurisdiction either to swear allegiance to the Union or to leave their farms and communities. They also banished people they suspected of being spies or of collaborating with the enemy. Gen. Benjamin Butler ordered a woman out of New Orleans for laughing at the funeral procession of a Union soldier. The provost marshal in Knoxville ordered a young woman named Ellen House to leave that city for allegedly insulting the wife of a Union officer. House was also suspected of spying. "They had a great many charges against me," she confided to her diary, "and they had been thinking of sending me South for some time."

Large-scale banishment also occurred. Gen. William T. Sherman ordered both secessionists and most unionists out of Atlanta in 1864. The most notorious mass exodus of the war came when Sherman's brother-in-law, Gen. Thomas Ewing Jr., in retaliation for Quantrill's raid on Lawrence, Kansas, required rebel civilians living more than 1 mile from a U.S. military post to abandon four western Missouri counties—this in a Union state. As a result, thousands of people, mostly old men, women, and children, trudged into southern Missouri and Arkansas. U.S. troops pursued and robbed many of these refugees, while other soldiers burned their abandoned homes.

Gen. Ambrose Burnside threatened to retaliate against the people of Fredericksburg, Virginia, in November 1862 by bombarding their town. They had been supplying Robert E. Lee's army, encamped in the hills behind them, with provisions and clothing, insisted Burnside, as well as allowing the rebels to fire on federal pickets from snipers' nests in the town. People fled on foot, in wagons, and by rail, crowded into foul cattle cars. They choked all available roads and soon flooded the countryside, for most had no place to go on such short notice. "I was so sorry for the pore little innocent children," reported a Georgia soldier who witnessed the scene, "and the ladies seemed to be scared out of anything like reason."

Rebels also had to confront their old fear of slave rebellion whenever the Union army occupied an area. Having withstood one visit by a band of armed blacks that pillaged its house, a Louisiana family decided to depart when rumors spread that worse was to come. "The next evening, the Negroes from all the inhabited places around commenced flocking to Mr. Hardison's," wrote a family member in her diary, "and they completely sacked the place in broad daylight. That more than anything else frightened Mamma and determined her to leave, though at the sacrifice of everything we owned."

Both unionist and Confederate refugees encountered unforeseen trials and dangers in flight. The fortunate ones had friends or relatives to greet them at the end of their journey; others depended on generous strangers to provide them with food and shelter. Many of the homeless resided in tents supplied by the army or in caves and abandoned buildings. The perils of the road included exposure to foul weather, deadly infectious diseases (such as cholera and typhoid), and attacks by guerrillas and robbers. Some communities turned away large groups, as concern about sharing already slender resources led them to tell refugees to "move on." In towns and cities that were overrun by newcomers, residents blamed the refugees for rising crime rates—especially theft—and they accused not a few women of being prostitutes. In the last half of the war, soaring economic inflation and shortages made food and housing enormously expensive, while the anxiety of life on the road proved to be the heaviest burden for many people.

All Americans, North or South, who felt the least concern about the fate of their nation, or the survival of loved ones, endured some emotional strain: "war is a crushing machine," decided a South Carolina refugee, "whose mainspring is anxiety, whose turnscrew is apprehension. Are my brothers all dead? Are my father and mother still living? These questions put me to the rack when I allow myself to ask them." The longer the war dragged on, the more dreadful became the uncertainty. Never knowing from one day to the next how long the war would last drained people. Would it continue for another week, another month, another year? Even soldiers, engaged in the fighting and able to believe they had some control over events, knew something of this feeling, but noncombatants could only wait and watch. A victory momentarily raised their spirits, but a defeat, or news that a neighbor's son had perished, or rumors of an impending raid drained any reservoir of confidence and hope. There were gradations of hopelessness. Southern noncombatants, subject at any moment to invasion and occupation, had it worse than northerners, but southern refugees

AMERICANS—MOSTLY NORTHERNERS—continued to move to western states and territories during the war. The destination of this family, shown in a photograph taken sometime in the 1860s, is unknown. Similarly, there is no way to know what inspired these particular people to make the trek westward. Yet they represent a widespread desire to escape the confusion and dangers of the conflict.

had it worst of all. "This is a *horrible war*," declared a rebel refugee in mid-1862, "& I have no idea now that it will end for five years."

These people may have avoided the battlefield, may never have felt their flesh ripped open by bullets or shrapnel, but they bore the indelible psychic wounds of the other war. Rare was the refugee who declared, as did one Tennessean, "I am too thankful for my escape to grieve for what I left behind." No historian has attempted to assess the mental scarring or calculate the losses of property and human life of this large refugee population, but although generally unrecorded, they were immense.

Westward Emigration

Another set of white refugees, almost forgotten in the rush to go north and south, headed west. Tens of thousands of people, mostly northerners and a surprising number of southerners, emigrated to Kansas, California, and all stops in between, especially during the last half of the war. They went for many of the same reasons that had propelled Americans westward for decades, with the exception, perhaps, of the severely tarnished notion of Manifest Destiny. Gold and silver mines still beckoned. Utah remained the golden land for Mormons. Inexpensive farming and grazing lands promised security and independence. The wide open spaces, high wages, and plentiful employment lured draft dodgers and rebels who had lost hope in their cause. Samuel L. Clemens, who deserted the Confederate army after two weeks in a Missouri militia company, would become the most famous wartime emigrant. Going first to the silver mines of Nevada,

Clemens eventually landed in California. While in Virginia City, Nevada, he also worked as a journalist and first began to assume the pen name Mark Twain.

Twain later wrote of his decision to abandon the war in a poignant yet perceptive story entitled "The Private History of a Campaign That Failed." His "history" was "a not unfair picture of what went on in many and many a militia camp in the first months of the rebellion," Twain maintained, "when the green recruits were without discipline, without the steadying and heartening influence of trained leaders; when all their circumstances were new and strange, and charged with exaggerated terrors, and before the invaluable experience of collision in the field had turned them from rabbits into soldiers." Twain's personal "collision" came in a sudden and shocking moment when he and several of his comrades fired in panic at a solitary horseman riding down a lonely forest path beneath a veiled moon. The man, who was a stranger to them, fell dead, and they quickly discovered that he wore no uniform and carried no weapon. The episode haunted the then twenty-five-year-old Twain. So this was war, he thought, "the killing of strangers against whom you feel no personal animosity; strangers whom in other circumstances, you would help if you found them in trouble." Deciding he was "not rightly equipped for this awful business," he went home. Five months later, he was in Nevada.

Yet, the war was never far away, not even on the Plains. A Wisconsin farmer was crossing Kansas on his way to California in 1863 when a "tall slim Missourian dressed in a suit of Butternut colored jeans" approached him and asked if he had any news of a rumored battle in Virginia. Yes, replied the farmer, he had chanced to hear some talk of it while passing through Fort Kearny. "There had been a great battle [at Chancellorsville] and our troops have been badly beaten," he reported. The Missourian thanked him for the information and walked away, but he returned a moment later to ask, "Say mister who do you mean by our troops?"

The U.S. government could claim credit for much of this westward migration. Taking advantage of the absence of its southern members, Congress passed the Homestead Act in May 1862. The law provided 160 acres of *free* western land to any adult citizen, man or woman, of the *United States* who settled and lived on the land for at least five years. Republicans had secured a means by which to flood the West with antislavery farmers. A few weeks later, northern congressmen achieved yet another antebellum goal that had been previously stymied by southern congressmen when they approved construction of a railroad between Omaha, Nebraska Territory (Nebraska would not become a state until 1867), and Sacramento, California. This first "transcontinental" railroad would not be completed until 1869, but Congress had ensured a "northern" route that would link the Pacific to Chicago and points east.

Women Combatants and Spies

Many women, whether or not they became refugees, learned that the best way to cope with war was to throw themselves into the winning of it. A few of them took the dangerous course of fighting in the armies. Women could not legally enlist as soldiers or sailors, but several hundred (as best historians can judge) donned uniforms by disguising their gender. Some of these women had already assumed identities as men before the war started. Twenty-year-old Sarah Edmonds, for example, was known as Franklin Thompson when she joined the Second Michigan Infantry in 1861. The authorities discovered most of these subterfuges (although Edmonds, still undetected, deserted in 1863 to work as a female nurse), but several women fought through the war.

A few women also joined guerrilla bands or acted as spies. Unlike their counterparts in the ranks, female guerrillas did not often join in combat, but they proved useful in cutting telegraph wires, delivering messages, smuggling supplies, and serving on scouting parties. Both North and South had some famous female spies, Belle Boyd and Rose Greenhow for the South and Pauline Cushman for the North being perhaps the best known. But many lesser-known women—usually totally *un*known—provided valuable intelligence to local commanders. They appeared in enemy camps as harmless laundresses or vendors, or they entertained officers who occupied their towns, all the while noting information that might aid their side.

What motivated these women to engage in such perilous service is an open question. Doubtless many, like the men, acted from patriotism or a spirit of adventure. Some women enlisted in the army to be near husbands or lovers, while prostitutes occasionally joined the ranks to practice their profession. Some poor women, especially immigrants, signed up for the pay and the assurance of food and shelter. This seems to have been the case with Canadian-born Sarah Edmonds. Others, like Rosetta Wakeman, sought to support their families. Rosetta, a sturdy farm girl from near Afton, New York, had been working on a coal barge when she enlisted in the 153rd New York Infantry as Lyons Wakeman. "I got 100 and 52$ in money," she informed her undoubtedly shocked parents from training camp. "All the money i send you i want you should spend it for the family in clothing or something to eat. Don't save it for me for i can get all the money i want." Wakeman served for eighteen months before dying of chronic diarrhea in Louisiana.

Far more women sustained the armies by serving behind the lines. Just as they had flocked to antebellum reform and charitable activities, so, too, did they join a variety of wartime organizations that provided aid and comfort to soldiers at the front. Northern reformers formed the United States Sanitary Commission (USSC) in 1861, and later its regional offshoot, the Western Sanitary Commission, to assist the government in caring for sick and wounded soldiers. Although organized and led by prominent clergymen, businessmen, and civic leaders, thousands of women from the middle and upper classes propelled these voluntary commissions. They made dressings, collected medical supplies, and organized "Sanitary Fairs" that raised many millions of dollars to purchase blankets, medicine, ambulances, and even hospital boats for the armies. The commissions also served as watchdogs to promote healthy and sanitary conditions in army hospitals, kitchens, and camps, including proper waste disposal, adequate drainage, and clean drinking water.

Charitable Work

Another volunteer agency, the United States Christian Commission, worked in conjunction with the USSC to tend souls rather than bodies. Its agents distributed

THESE U.S. SANITARY COMMISSION volunteers on duty at Fredericksburg, Virginia, in 1864 were among the thousands of northern civilians who labored to relieve physical, emotional, and spiritual suffering of Union soldiers.

1.5 million Bibles, an unknown number of prayer books, 1 million hymnals, and 39 million religious tracts to Union armies. They also encouraged soldiers to write home regularly, led prayer meetings in army camps, and warned against immoral pastimes (mostly drinking and gambling).

One historian has suggested that such civilian agencies permitted conservative, elite northerners to issue powerful calls for self-sacrifice, encourage the subordination of personal gain to the good of the nation, and promote a romantic mood of "hard-bitten stoicism." Indeed, the professed goal of the USSC was not so much kindness to wounded soldiers as a desire to return the men quickly to the firing line. Other expressions of this stern, self-sacrificing nationalism included the formation of patriotic organizations such as the Union League and Loyal Publication Society, which distributed thousands of pro-Union pamphlets to "rebuke . . . all disloyalty" and instill "absolute and unqualified loyalty to the government of the United States" among both soldiers and civilians. Such propaganda assaults on rebellion and revolution also served to undercut Confederate efforts to link their struggle for "independence" to the American Revolution. After the war, northern elites founded a series of social science organizations to foster these same bureaucratic, managerial, and nationalizing sensibilities. This spirit surfaced first in the private sector and in local government, but it spread gradually by the end of the century to the operation of the federal government.

Northern women outside of the principal cities and towns did not often join either wartime commission, and southerners had no such national networks; but virtually every community in both North and South had a charitable society or church group that aided the war effort. In just one month, two-score women in Center Ridge, Alabama, contributed 422 shirts, 551 pairs of drawers, 80 pairs of socks, 3 pairs of gloves, 6 boxes of hospital stores, 128 pounds of tapioca, and $418 cash to the Confederate government. The women of Springfield, Illinois, provided in one year 50 shirts, 522 pairs of drawers, 381 pairs of socks, 213 handkerchiefs, 234 towels, 2,492 bandages, "large quantities of cornstarch, barley, tea, crackers, soap, jars, jellies, pickles, fruits," and much more. Charity balls and fairs raised money by selling homemade pies and jellies, handcrafted quilts and baskets, or chances on lotteries or raffles. Northern schools had "onion days" and "potato days" to collect produce for the armies.

Nurses Thousands of women served as nurses during the war, a more surprising—not to say shocking—development than it sounds. With no professional schools of nursing before the 1870s, Americans were not accustomed to women filling this role outside their homes. Some people worried about the propriety of exposing the fairer sex to the blood, excrement, and bare bodies of a hospital ward, but patriotism, compassion, and a determination to be useful led women to ignore precedent and defy public opinion. Clara Barton, one of the North's most famous nursing volunteers and the first to treat wounded men on the front lines, responded to critics by saying that tending wounded and sick men was no more "rough and unseemly for a *woman*" than fighting was "rough and unseemly for *men*."

North and South began to use women nurses during the first year of the war. Fifty-nine-year-old Dorothea Dix, already famous for her antebellum work in reforming the nation's mental institutions, received a commission as

THIS CLASS FOR VOLUNTEER NURSES in a New York City hospital in 1861 was a rarity. While thousands of northern and southern women worked as nurses for long hours and little compensation, few of them received any formal training.

superintendent of women nurses in Washington. Sally L. Tompkins was Dix's counterpart in Richmond, while many other women on both sides helped to organize these committed volunteers. Dix tried to limit their ranks to "matronly" women between the ages of thirty-five and fifty, fearful that young, attractive women would be more of a distraction than a help for male surgeons and patients, but such were the nation's needs that anyone who wished to serve eventually found a place.

Most nurses received their only training while on the job, although one prominent exception to this was a training program operated by the Women's Central Relief Association, an adjunct of the USSC, in New York. Dr. Elizabeth Blackwell, the first woman to receive a medical degree in the United States, directed the program. Yet many of the demands on these women did not require profound technical skill. They dressed wounds and assisted with operations, but they spent far more time simply comforting patients. They wrote letters to the families of their patients, held their hands as they endured fever or pain, whispered words of faith and hope to dying soldiers. "They call to me . . . like a set of boys after their mother," related a Virginian, "and tell me they should give up and die if I left them."

Women nurses had few material inducements to stay. The Confederate government began to pay limited numbers of nurses—up to six of them per government hospital—between $34 and $40 per month, in addition to their food and lodging, in 1861. The U.S. Congress authorized 40 cents per day plus subsistence for Union nurses in 1862, but not a few women served without financial compensation, insisting that the work was their reward.

Whatever compensation they received, the women earned it. Besides the open contempt and hostility of many doctors, female nurses had to withstand hunger, exhaustion, disease, and the frustration of seldom having adequate supplies. "Everything cut off, nothing but coffee . . . bread and [tough] meat," reported a Union nurse. "One day it was past all bearing. I was positively so hungry I could have eaten cat's meat. I sat over the fire after supper, tired and hungry and wondered if the good I did was balanced by my suffering." Another nurse confessed to the strain of treating so many horribly injured men. "I do not suffer under the sights," she confessed; "but oh! the sounds and screams of men. It is when I think of it afterwards that it is so dreadful."

Assistance for Families   After the soldiers, their dependents became the next most important object of public charity. "Another army besides that in the field must be supported—the army at home," explained a Mississippian. "Their preservation and their comfort are as essential to our success as that of soldiers in the field." Most states and communities offered some form of assistance to the families of soldiers, although many needy people refused the aid because applying for charity bore a stigma of pauperism. Then again, resources became so depleted in the Confederate states that relief there was meager at best. In the last year of the war, one Virginia county—typical of many—authorized a $20,000 loan against its credit to purchase food for the indigent. Widows in the county ranked as the first priority, followed by women "whose husbands are in the Confederate service & then to such others as . . . are most needy." Unfortunately, no family, regardless of size or need, could be permitted more than a single barrel of flour.

Many women—though mostly unmarried ones—sought to cope by taking new employment opportunities in factories and offices. Women had worked in northeastern factories since the earliest days of the Industrial Revolution, but they were in even higher demand with so many men gone to the army. The so-called *government girls*, on the other hand, were something new. Labor shortages in the federal government, most notably in the War, Treasury, and Post Office Departments, opened positions as copyists and clerks to hundreds of young women, and Lincoln appointed several soldiers' widows as local "post-mistresses." Public reaction to these innovations was mixed. Critics predicted a moral crisis by having men and women working together. The Treasury Department, identified as "a house for orgies and bacchanals," actually underwent a congressional investigation. In actual practice, most women served the Union well and escaped with their honor unsullied.

Female Employment

Confederate women, living in the midst of the war, faced even tougher problems. With fewer chances to work in offices, factories, and munitions works, they strove to maintain plantations and family farms in the face of extraordinary adversity. Saddled with the management of slaves, the planting

FEMALE WORKERS LEAVING THE TREASURY BUILDING in Washington, D.C. Many northern and southern women took advantage of employment opportunities created by the war. With so many men serving in the armies, they filled the expanded wartime needs of industry and government.

and marketing of crops, and the raising of children, they had to deal not just with the absence of their men but also with the constant threat of invasion and a markedly more depressed economy. "I can't manage a farm well enough to make a surporte," pleaded a Georgian in seeking to have her husband discharged from the army. "If you dount send him home," pleaded a Virginian in the same situation to the War Department, "I am bound to louse my crop and cum to suffer." A well-to-do Arkansas woman retreated from reality into drugs. "I took a little pill of opium in the morning and all day was in a singular state of being," she recorded in her diary. The next day, a Sunday, she even failed to attend church, it being "too far off, for one under the dying influences of opium, to go."

Changing Status of Women
The extent to which all of these wartime demands permanently changed the roles and status of white women in the North and South is unclear. Some of the jobs that became available to them, especially in clerical work and nursing, would offer continuing postwar employment opportunities; others, including those in factories, would be largely closed when the men returned home. The increased freedom to travel and interact on an equal basis with men helped to break down restrictive social prejudices. More educational options became available, and the roles thought acceptable for women to pursue outside the domestic sphere extended far beyond the antebellum realms of benevolent work and social reform. Indeed, women who lost husbands or fathers during the war frequently had little choice but to become more self-sufficient and worldly. Clara Barton declared toward the end of the 1880s that the war had catapulted women "at least fifty years in advance of the normal position which continued peace . . . would have assigned her." Julia Ward Howe spoke for many women when she declared that wartime experiences had made it impossible for her "to return to her chimney corner life of the fifties."

Yet, solid and substantial change was slow in coming. Society had accepted the new public roles of women as wartime necessities, but more conservative elements expected that women would return to their prewar domestic worlds once those unusual circumstances had passed. Many women also desired a return to the seeming orderliness, stability, and simplicity of that prewar world, even though others had rebellion in mind. The latter group used wartime experiences to reassert antebellum demands for broader social and political rights, especially the vote. White southerners, including women, continued to be more conservative than Americans in other parts of the country. Woman's "business," as one female phrased it, was "to refine and elevate society"; her "mission" was "moral rather than intellectual, domestic rather than political." Still, the restrictions on women's lives, social as well as political, economic as well as cultural, would never be as rigid as they had been before the war. And in the most personal sphere, this war, like all others, loosened sexual decorum, allowing many women to explore territory forbidden to them in peacetime.

Lack of Change
It is also important to remember that, despite the seemingly universal upheaval and carnage, the daily lives of many men and women *during* the war changed very little from what they had been in 1860. People still had to make a living, farms had to be tended, factories had to be operated, business and trade

had to continue. It was somewhat easier for northerners to compartmentalize the war, but neither northerners nor southerners, even those with friends and relatives fighting in the armies, could have functioned without finding distractions and diversions totally divorced from the national crisis. Just as soldiers found time to play games and go fishing, so the nation's noncombatants went to the theater and the circus, attended school, gave birthday parties, held weddings, built homes.

Even in the South, people not plagued by guerrillas or living in the paths of the armies could sometimes forget about the war as they labored to raise families and keep bread on the table. Consider the concerns of a forty-year-old farmer in the South Carolina Piedmont. In October 1864, he wrote in his diary, "I am in a peck of trouble. I have a whole field of corn pulled down and nothing to pull it home." His oxen, which he would normally use for this task, had wandered off. "I am awfully afraid they have broken into someones corn field and killed themselves eating peas," he continued. "They are very mischevous." The health of his family and slaves, the price of calico, and the challenge of getting his crops to market concerned this farmer more than the fate of the Confederacy. In November, cold weather and heavy rain made him wonder how he could sow his wheat and maintain his sanity: "I have been having some corn shucked and shelled to send to mill while the ground is too wet to plow. I am trying hard to make a support. I have not been well today. The children have been confined to the house. Their noise and confusion and the trials that I see in the future have made me a miserable day. I have felt crazy. I could almost feel the wrinkles coming on my face and the hair turn gray on my head."

There were, it would seem, many wars to be fought between 1861 and 1865.

CHAPTER 8

An Inconclusive Year: 1863

Two different stories grabbed the front pages of northern and southern newspapers in early January 1863, two different but familiar stories. The Confederacy's principal western army, the Army of Tennessee, was in retreat once again, this time from Stones River. At the same time, people were only beginning to appreciate the staggering magnitude of Robert E. Lee's victory at Fredericksburg. It was an old refrain: Union triumph in the West, Confederate dominance in the East. The Confederates had achieved some western successes late in 1862. They had destroyed a Union supply depot at Holly Springs, Mississippi, and so turned back Ulysses S. Grant's advance against Vicksburg, but this bold stroke had not regained any of their lost territory or done much damage to the Union war machine. The rebels had also recaptured Galveston, Texas, on New Year's Day, thus liberating the only Federal-occupied portion of Texas, but people were paying less and less attention to the trans-Mississippi.

Still, a perceptive observer could see subtle differences in the old patterns. First of all, Braxton Bragg had not really lost at Stones River. His men knew that. "I can't see for my life why Bragg left Murfreesboro after whipping them so badly," one amazed rebel private wrote to his family. Another man claimed, "There is no doubt but that the Yankees were badly whipped. . . . [M]any think that there was no reason for the retreat from Murfreesboro." It had been a close-run thing, to be sure, and Bragg had managed an orderly withdrawal and suffered fewer casualties than William S. Rosecrans, who, for his part, had no idea that he had "won" anything. His army certainly remained in no condition to pursue Bragg. Much the same could be said of Lee and George McClellan after the battle of Antietam: Lee had withdrawn from Maryland, but no one in the Army of Northern Virginia, the Confederate government, or the rebel populace had considered that a defeat. Bragg, however, had a very different reputation from that of Marse Robert. "No cheer salutes him as he passes," observed one of Bragg's own generals during the retreat. "We obey but do not tremble, and enter action without hope of honor or renown and retreat with sullen indifference and discontent."

This confused pattern typified the year 1863. It began as had the early months of the war, with the Confederacy seeming to hold a military edge; it concluded with the rebels back on their heels and losing ground on every front, from the trans-Mississippi to Virginia. Two of the biggest Union victories of the war—Gettysburg and Vicksburg—came at midyear. The Confederacy lost its last best chance for foreign intervention, and widespread public opposition to the government made a forceful appearance. Yet, none of this made defeat of the Confederate nation inevitable. The Union continued to face equally grave internal divisions, and even as Lincoln issued his most profound statement on the nature of the war—his Gettysburg address—he continued to search for a competent commanding general. As both northern and southern home fronts coped with the physical suffering and emotional anguish of war, there was no end in sight.

Nearly every event, whether political or military, seemed to possess hidden depths, a case in point being Lee's lopsided victory at Fredericksburg. It had been almost *too* easy, the "simplest and easiest won battle of the war," a Confederate officer would later say. If Bragg's men were unnecessarily disheartened, Lee's legions had become dangerously overconfident. "Our army seems somewhat spoilt," admitted James Longstreet, always the realist and conscience of that army. "The troops seem to think they can whip the Yankees with the greatest ease whenever they may choose to come, and wherever they come." A Virginia soldier agreed. "The morale of the army is superb," he declared. "The idea of a defeat never occurs to them so great is their confidence in their own prowess, and the skill of their generals." Another rebel predicted, "When we meet [the Army of the Potomac] in the spring the result will be the same old tale. They have never been accustomed to any thing else [but] defeat and disaster from us and they will hardly look for anything else now." Even Lee was now calling his army "invincible."

It was a dangerous frame of mind. Lee's hold on the Rappahannock River— the Dare Mark, as one Confederate called it, a line the Union army had to cross to threaten Richmond—seemed complete, but the Union army still sat opposite him, on the northern bank of the river, and Lincoln wanted to renew the fight for the Rappahannock come spring. Lincoln also wanted a more aggressive general than Burnside to lead the army, so in late January 1863, he appointed Joseph Hooker, known as Fighting Joe, to command the Army of the Potomac.

Confederate Morale

Joseph Hooker
Hooker was a forty-eight-year-old bachelor, tall, sandy haired, and clean shaven, with blue-gray eyes and a reputation for hard drinking (not entirely deserved), womanizing (thoroughly deserved), and bragging. A West Pointer and a decorated Mexican War veteran, he had informed Lincoln following the Union fiasco at First Bull Run that he could have won that battle and that he was "a damned sight better general than any you, sir, had on that field." Lincoln liked his confident style. He made Hooker a general, and the brash Massachusetts native served bravely, although he earned his bold moniker in curious fashion. During the Peninsula campaign of 1862, a newspaper headline mistakenly omitted punctuation between the words *Fighting* and *Joe Hooker* to create *Fighting Joe Hooker.* The name stuck.

Lincoln believed the cocky and conceited general could instill a spirit of self-assurance in the Army of the Potomac. In a letter informing him of his promotion, Lincoln praised Hooker's bravery, skill, and confidence, even though the president also let it be known that he had heard Hooker's rumored pronouncement "that both the Army and the Government needed a dictator," a dangerous statement for a general to make. "Of course it was not for this," Lincoln observed, "but in spite of it, that I have given you the command." He closed with a blunt warning: "Beware of rashness, but with energy and sleepless vigilance go forward and give us victories."

Chastened by Lincoln's blunt yet fatherly tone, Hooker initially took the president's words to heart. For the next three months, he carefully prepared his men for battle. He reorganized the army into seven infantry corps complete with distinctive badges, and he united all cavalry into a single separate corps. Hooker drilled his men relentlessly but bolstered morale by improving their diet and enacting a furlough system. A Vermont private observed: "Nobody but a soldier who has seen nearly two years of active service, knows what a boon a furlough is." Sick rolls declined because Hooker's surgeons improved sanitary conditions, and the army soon appeared fit and ready to fight, numbering some 134,000 men. Hooker called it the "finest army on the planet."

Hooker's Plan for the Chancellorsville Campaign
By the end of April, Hooker had designed an aggressive plan to destroy the Army of Northern Virginia. He would leave one-third of his troops under Gen. John Sedgwick to face Lee at Fredericksburg and march another third up river to cross the Rappahannock and advance on Lee's left flank and rear from the west. The remaining third would stand in reserve, ready to reinforce either wing once fighting ensued. In addition, Hooker's 12,000-man cavalry corps under Gen. George Stoneman, mimicking Stuart's famed rides around McClellan, would maneuver behind Lee's lines to disrupt rebel communications and supply routes. Hooker called his plan perfect and predicted: "The enemy must either ingloriously fly, or come out from behind his defenses and give us battle on our own ground where certain destruction awaits him." He announced further: "May God have mercy on General Lee for I will have none."

Lee's Problems
While Hooker prepared for his sweeping advance, Lee faced a myriad of problems. His soldiers, although encouraged by the win at Fredericksburg, suffered from shortages of food, medicine, blankets, and shoes, mostly due to in-

eptitude in the commissary and quartermaster department. Lee also struggled to keep his army together as talk grew of sending a detachment of troops west to strengthen the defenses at Vicksburg. In February, Lee did divide his army, but instead of transferring troops to Mississippi, he sent James Longstreet's corps south to Suffolk, Virginia, where the Federals threatened another move up the Peninsula toward Richmond. Longstreet was also to gather food for the army from the rich farmland of southeastern Virginia. After a limited attempt to capture Suffolk, he settled into a siege, miles away from the rest of Lee's army, which remained at Fredericksburg with slightly more than 50,000 men.

In late April, Hooker began his swing around the Confederate position at Fredericksburg. All went as planned, and by the night of April 30, "Fighting Joe" had 75,000 troops across the river ready to attack. The resulting battle of Chancellorsville, May 1–5, was fought in piecemeal fashion across many miles of ground, much of it thickly wooded. Lee, taken by surprise and vastly outnumbered, would have to take risks. Accordingly, he left 11,000 troops at Fredericksburg to face Sedgwick and set out with the remaining 42,000 to meet Hooker. Once again, as at Second Bull Run, he had ignored military wisdom by dividing his smaller army in the face of superior numbers. Hooker, apparently stunned by Lee's reaction, gave up the initiative and withdrew to a defensive position.

Lee's Daring Response

When Lee next learned from his cavalry that the federal right flank was "in the air"—that is, unsecured and exposed—he gambled again. Defying all rules of conventional military strategy and tactics, he split his army a second time by ordering his trusted subordinate Stonewall Jackson to take 28,000 men and 108 guns, march 12 miles through tangled wilderness across the enemy's front, and smash Hooker's weak right flank. The absence of Stoneman's cavalry, whose raid would prove largely ineffectual, had left the Union infantry vulnerable. During the late afternoon of May 2, just as the mostly German XI Corps, which held the Union right, prepared supper, smoked pipes, and relaxed, Jackson's veterans stormed through the woods. The rout was worse than First Bull Run. One Union officer described the Union defenders "in full flight, panic-stricken beyond description." Confederate major David Gregg McIntosh recalled: "The surprise was complete. A bolt from the sky would not have startled half as much as the musket shots in the thickets . . . and then a solid wall of gray, forcing their way through the timber and bearing down on them like an irresistible avalanche."

Although darkness was fast approaching by then, the moon was full, and Jackson wanted to continue fighting. As he and his staff reconnoitered the enemy's position in wooded terrain between the lines, they became caught in the crossfire of Union and Confederate skirmishers. Hit in three places, including two bullets in his left arm, Jackson was taken to a private home to recover. Tragically, pneumonia set in after amputation of his arm, and he died on May 10. Gone was the Confederacy's first real hero of the war. Lee, upon hearing of Jackson's injury, remarked, "He has lost his left arm; but I have lost my right." Indeed, the loss of Jackson would haunt Confederates for the rest of the war, with many rebels believing that if Jackson had lived, the South's good fortune would have been assured.

Death of Jackson

The fighting raged for two more days at Chancellorsville as portions of the two armies clashed time and again. On May 3, Hooker was injured when a Confederate artillery shell struck the house where he was headquartered and a piece of debris struck him nearly unconscious. A subordinate commanded the army for the remainder of that day. Hard fighting continued, and Lee had to divide his force a third time to help beat back a Union breakthrough at Fredericksburg, 12 miles in his rear, on May 3–4. But Hooker was already a "whipped man." On the night of May 5–6, he withdrew his troops back across the Rappahannock.

Consequences of Chancellorsville

Chancellorsville gave Lee his second consecutive victory against the Army of the Potomac, but like Fredericksburg, this battle had little lasting strategic value. Often described as "Lee's masterpiece," because of the bold tactical moves that allowed him to neutralize far larger numbers, Chancellorsville was a costly victory for the Confederacy. Casualties for the Army of Northern Virginia totaled some 22 percent; those for the Army of the Potomac were 13 percent. Equally dangerous, in a surprising way, was the further boldness that it instilled in the rebel army. Despite the high losses—which included twelve brigade commanders killed or wounded—and Jackson's death, the victory added to Lee's conviction that his men could go anywhere, accomplish any task, defy any odds, against an enemy he now underestimated, as expressed by his increasingly open contempt for them. Yet, Chancellorsville would be his last significant, clear-cut victory of the war, and the overconfidence fostered along the Rappahannock would lead him to take his biggest gamble: a second invasion of the North.

Still convinced that a decisive victory could end the war and ensure independence—as he hoped it would at Antietam—Lee persuaded Richmond that another invasion was necessary. Since February 1863 he had been considering an ambitious strategy that targeted Pennsylvania, a state rich in supplies and food. Such an invasion might strengthen the growing northern peace movement and reopen the possibility of foreign recognition. He had hoped to begin his campaign in May, but Hooker's advance and the subsequent battle of Chancellorsville changed all that. Now, with Hooker defeated and enough ammunition and animals with which to go forward, Lee commenced operations.

Start of the Gettysburg Campaign

Lee was delayed once again when a Union reconnaissance mission to determine his position resulted in the largest cavalry battle of the war at Brandy Station, Virginia, on June 9. However, by June 15, Lee's advance units crossed the Potomac River into Maryland, and on June 25 his army entered Pennsylvania. All the while, Hooker was tracking rebel movements and nudging his own army cautiously toward Lee's line of advance, but having been so recently humbled at Chancellorsville, he seemed hesitant to engage the wily Gray Fox again. Hooker also bickered openly with Union general-in-chief Henry Halleck and Secretary of War Edwin Stanton over military strategy and other issues, which only added to his unpopularity in Washington. When Hooker angrily offered to resign over a disagreement with Halleck, Lincoln, who had lost confidence in "Fighting Joe" by this time, accepted his resignation and replaced him with Gen. George Gordon Meade.

Meade, who bore the nickname "Old Snapping Turtle," was a West Point graduate and Mexican War veteran who had risen steadily in the ranks from brigade to corps commander. He was intelligent, diligent, and a skilled tactician. He had an explosive temper that Grant described as "beyond his control, at times," yet Meade also steered clear of politics, and that pleased Lincoln after having dealt for so long with McClellan and Hooker. Within days of assuming his new position, Meade would face Lee in the bustling market town of Gettysburg.

George G. Meade

A battle was not supposed to be fought there, but when Confederate troops from Gen. Henry Heth's division wandered into Gettysburg on July 1 looking for provisions and signs of Union troops, they encountered Gen. John Buford's cavalry, scouting ahead of the rest of the Union army. Buford's dismounted troopers skirmished with the Confederates until federal infantry arrived. By the end of the day, the Confederates had pushed them back through the town; the Union troops then positioned themselves on Seminary Ridge, to the southwest. By the morning of July 2, both armies were concentrating on Gettysburg: 88,000 Union troops against 75,000 Confederates.

The Battle of Gettysburg

Confederate cavalry commander J. E. B. Stuart, trying to reenact his rides around McClellan and make up for the embarrassment of being surprised at Brandy Station, had embarked on a combined raid and reconnaissance mission to circle the Union army and, as a result, was entirely out of touch with his own. Lee thus found himself in these critical opening hours of the battle in a position much like Hooker's at Chancellorsville, without the "eyes and ears" of his cavalry. Consequently, on that first full day of fighting, Lee did not know what he faced, an extremely precarious situation in enemy territory.

On July 2 the Union line resembled a long fishhook that started on its right at Culp's Hill, curved southward around Cemetery Hill, ran along Cemetery Ridge, and extended toward two hills, known as Little and Big Round Top, on its left flank. Lee ordered attacks against both flanks, but it was not until late in the afternoon that fighting commenced. On the Confederate left, Gen. Richard S. Ewell, who commanded half of what had been Jackson's corps, hesitated and stumbled at Culp's Hill. On the Confederate right, Longstreet, who had rejoined Lee after the failed siege of Suffolk, struggled to organize his men for attack. The Federals, meanwhile, had troubles of their own. Gen. Daniel Sickles, acting without orders, pushed his corps forward to seek high ground in a peach orchard. The movement created an exposed *salient*, or bulge, in the Union line.

July 2 marked some of the fiercest fighting of the war. In places such as the Peach Orchard, the Wheat Field, and Little Round Top, casualties ran extremely high. The First Minnesota, charging against a rebel advance late that day, lost 215 of its 262 men. Alabamians and Texans rushed gallantly and repeatedly up the steep incline of Little Round Top before retreating, exhausted and bloodied. The Twentieth Maine Infantry, under Col. Joshua Chamberlain, finally pushed them back with a desperate bayonet charge. Col. William Oates of the Fifteenth Alabama recalled the slaughter: "My dead and wounded were then nearly as great in number as those still on duty. They lit-

The artillery duel opened up at 1 p.m. The Confederate infantry attacked at 2:30 and were beaten back with great losses.

Gregg and Custer intercept Stuart in cavalry fight 1 1/2 miles from here

Early morning attack repulsed

Chambersburg Pike
Unfinished railroad
Mummasburg Road
Carlisle Road
Harrisburg Road
Rock Creek
Hunterstown Rd.
Gettysburg and Hanover R.R.
York Pike
Gettysburg
Seminary
Hagerstown Rd.
Early
Ewell
Hanover Road
Culp's Hill
Johnson
Howard
Cemetery Hill
Slocum
Baltimore Pike
A. P. Hill
Gibbon
Cemetery Ridge
LEE
Pickett
MEADE
Willoughby Run
Longstreet
Peach Orchard
Wheat field
Sickles
McLaws
Devil's Den
Little Round Top
Round Top
Hood
Sedgwick
Rock Creek
Emmitsburg Road
Taneytown Road
Plum Run
Kilpatrick (Cavalry) Harassing action

0   1 Mile

━━━ Union forces
→   Union attack
▨▨▨ Confederate forces
⟶   Confederate attack

THE BATTLE OF GETTYSBURG raged July 1–3, 1863, and on the third day, Robert E. Lee determined to attack the Union center positioned along Cemetery Ridge. The result was the famed "Pickett's Charge," a frontal assault of some 13,500 infantrymen preceded by a massive artillery barrage. The charge failed dismally, forcing Lee to retreat on July 4.

erally covered the ground. The blood stood in puddles in some places on the rocks; the ground was soaked with the blood of as brave men as ever fell on the red field of battle."

The next day, July 3, Lee attacked again, despite the strong objections of Longstreet, who argued that the Confederates should withdraw and find a better defensive position between Meade's army and Washington. Lee originally planned to repeat his assaults on Culp's Hill and Little Round Top, but when the Federals took the initiative and attacked rebel positions below Culp's Hill that morning, Lee changed his mind. He decided to launch a frontal assault where Meade would least expect it: the center of the Union line at Cemetery Ridge. Gen. George E. Pickett's division of fresh troops, who had sat out the first two days of battle, would spearhead the attack. Portions of other infantry commands joined Pickett's Virginians, some 13,500 men in all, and an artillery barrage would precede their advance. At approximately 1 p.m., the Confederate guns opened fire.

Meade, meanwhile, was not caught unaware. Having seriously considered a withdrawal, he finally decided after a council of war with his generals on the previous night to stay and fight. Guessing that Lee would target his center, Meade reinforced the position and ordered his men to dig in.

Sometime around 3 p.m., eleven Confederate infantry brigades marched in perfectly formed columns across the gently rolling fields between Seminary Ridge and Cemetery Ridge. The temperature was exceedingly hot; the air was heavy with humidity, acrid smoke, and the foul smell of dead men and horses.

Pickett's Charge, a name coined by Richmond newspapers to highlight the role of Virginians in the advance, was a disaster. Although it later became the stuff of legend, Lee had made a terrible mistake. Only a small number of desperate Confederates pierced the Union line on Cemetery Ridge, and they soon were overwhelmed. Lee had severely miscalculated his opponent and misjudged the ability of his own men. George Meade was not Joe Hooker, George McClellan, or Ambrose Burnside. He did not lose his nerve but rather stood his ground against Lee.

Results of Gettysburg

Soon after the charge collapsed and the survivors staggered back, Lee told at least two officers that the failed effort was all his fault. In his official report, written a few weeks after the battle, he admitted: "More may have been required of them than they were able to perform." In retrospect, the attack seems little different from Burnside's futile assault against Marye's Heights. Public criticism from the Confederate press, politicians, civilians, and even a few army officers prompted Lee to ask President Davis to replace him. Davis refused, stating: "To ask me to substitute you by some one in my judgement more fit to command, or who would possess more of the confidence of the army, or of the reflecting men of the country, is to demand an impossibility."

On July 4 both armies sat and eyed each other, binding their wounds, burying their dead, and waiting for more fighting, but none came. By the evening, as rain drenched the weary troops, Lee retreated south across the Potomac River to Virginia. Meade, his own army bruised and battered, did not pursue.

Historians, poets, and novelists would look back and christen the battle of Gettysburg "the decisive turning point" of the American Civil War. In retrospect, many would argue, this was the beginning of the end for the Confederacy. Even at the time, the failure of Lee's invasion turned otherwise sober northerners giddy. At long last, the war in the East seemed to have swung in the Union's favor. "The results of this victory are priceless," enthused a New York lawyer. "Philadelphia, Baltimore, and Washington are safe. Defeat would have seriously injured all three. The rebels are hunted out of the North, their best army is routed, and the charm of Robert E. Lee's invincibility broken."

It *was* a tremendous battle, lasting three days and producing more than 50,000 casualties: the Federals lost some 23,000 men, the Confederates more than 28,000. "Pickett's Charge" became the symbolic "high-water mark" of the Confederacy and the supreme example of southern white male courage and sacrifice. For the Union, it was more of a defensive victory than a decisive one. The war lasted twenty-one more long months. Would the war have ended if Lee had won the battle? Would the Confederacy have gained its independence? A close examination of the political situation in the North and military events in the Western Theater suggest that the answer to both questions would be "No."

A Confederate victory at Gettysburg would have fueled the anger of Peace Democrats and their criticism of the Republicans, and it would have strengthened Confederate resolve, but it is doubtful that Lincoln would have been ready to give up the fight. In addition, Lee's army had been severely damaged; he would have been hard pressed to continue his bold offenses after suffering such losses in the ranks. It is highly doubtful that he could have destroyed Meade's army, which is what he needed to do to gain a decisive win. Finally, it is impossible to separate the impact of Gettysburg from what was happening out West during those first few days of July, so it is to that theater of the war that we now return.

Vicksburg Campaign

With Braxton Bragg pushed nearly out of Tennessee, Vicksburg remained the focus of federal attention in the West and so, necessarily, of the Confederates. With Vicksburg taken, the Union could claim the entire Mississippi River. The Confederates would have only Port Hudson, Louisiana, 120 miles to the south. Abraham Lincoln understood Vicksburg's importance to the western war. "Let us get Vicksburg and the country is ours," he declared. "The war can never be brought to a close until that key is in our pocket."

Navy gunboats under David Farragut had tried to capture the citadel as they had New Orleans, but the bustling river town of 5,000 inhabitants was situated more like Fort Donelson than New Orleans, high on the river's bluffs and defended by heavy guns. Farragut also ran up against one of the Confederacy's most formidable ironclads, the *Arkansas,* and low water levels in the Mississippi. The navy appeared stymied by July 1862.

This was the moment when Ulysses Grant took charge. Grant had been thinking about how best to approach the rebel bastion all that summer, long before he had any authority to implement a plan. Not until October 25, after

THE UNION'S VICKSBURG CAMPAIGN was one of the longest and most complex military operations of the war. Beginning in December 1862 with a failed attempt to advance against the Mississippi River citadel through the state of Mississippi, it did not end until July 4, 1863. This map shows the main movements of the Union army in the final drive of April–July 1863.

Bragg had begun his retreat from Kentucky, and Iuka and Corinth had been secured, did Grant receive command of the Department of the Tennessee and the freedom to act. He tried unsuccessfully during the next few months to approach Vicksburg directly from the north and the east. Confederate cavalry and guerrillas cut his long communications and supply lines, and an advance by his most trusted subordinate, William T. Sherman, down the Yazoo River and the surrounding swampy terrain, stalled at Chickasaw Bluffs, a terrace of high ground north of Vicksburg. Then, early in 1863, Grant shifted his men west of the river, to Louisiana, determined now to capture Vicksburg as he had Forts Henry and Donelson, by means of combined army and navy operations.

Grant's Army of the Tennessee spent the next three months trying unsuccessfully to attack this "Gibraltar of the Confederacy" from west of the river. Four different engineering projects, each designed to move troops along canals or across swamps and bayous into position to attack the town from either above or below, failed miserably. Some observers believed Grant never expected these "experiments," as he called them, to succeed, but only to "consume time," keep his "idle" army of 40,000 men busy during the winter months, and divert "the attention of the enemy . . . and of the public generally." All the while, he built up enormous stockpiles of food, medicine, ammunition, and other supplies for the spring campaign.

At the end of March 1863, the army began to construct a road from its main camp on Milliken's Bend southward to a point on the Mississippi 25 miles below Vicksburg. The Federals followed solid ground whenever possible, but much of the swampy route had to be laid with log roads (called corduroy roads because of their ribbed texture). The backbreaking work took four weeks to cover 70 miles, but by the end of April, Grant had 24,000 men opposite Grand Gulf. Responsibility for getting them across the river fell to Adm. David Dixon Porter, an ambitious and politically savvy fifty-year-old navy veteran who during the preceding two weeks had twice run portions of his fleet past the guns of Vicksburg to rendezvous with the weary infantry. The boats had taken a pounding, but rebel guns had sunk only one transport. The twelve transports and barges that eventually survived the run (protected by ten accompanying gunboats) could now ferry the army across the river.

Grierson's Raid   What ensued was one of the most complex and masterful joint operations of the war. The Confederates suspected that something was happening across the river, but they could not guess what it all meant. Some people thought the federal movement southward might even be a retreat, and two Union diversionary movements only added to their confusion. As most of the army prepared to cross below Vicksburg, Sherman feinted above the city with about 23,000 troops. In addition, Grant ordered a series of cavalry raids. Col. Benjamin H. Grierson, a midwestern music teacher and merchant before the war, led the most spectacular of these raids. His 1,700 men sliced their way the length of Mississippi, 600 miles from LaGrange, Tennessee, to Baton Rouge, Louisiana, between April 17 and May 2. They captured 500 rebel soldiers, 1,000 horses and mules, and 3,000 *stands of arms* (each comprising a rifle, bayonet, and cartridge belt and box). They also killed or wounded 100 Confederates, cut telegraph lines, and destroyed more than 50 miles of railroad track.

Yet, the most daring part of Grant's plan came *after* his men crossed the river. With the army poised to strike by May 1, his obvious next step would have been to capture Grand Gulf and to march against Vicksburg. The rebels, by this time having realized their peril, had made it even easier for Grant by evacuating Grand Gulf and surrendering a small nearby garrison at Port Gibson. Still, Grant did not like the looks of those daunting bluffs or relish the thought of Confederate reinforcements attacking his rear from the state capital of Jackson—only 35 miles east of Vicksburg—as he moved against the town. So, to the surprise of everyone, he marched not against Vicksburg, but toward Jackson. He did not even bother to establish a supply line from the river but cut himself adrift in the middle of enemy territory. It was a daring act that added even more drama to the campaign, but it paid off. By May 14, Grant had captured Jackson and scattered its defenders.

Pemberton's Dilemma

Gen. John C. Pemberton, defender of Vicksburg, was thoroughly confused by this time. The forty-nine-year-old West Point graduate and Mexican War veteran was a Pennsylvanian by birth, but he had married a southern woman. He knew he had a strong position along the river and miles of entrenchments and gun emplacements encircled the eastern side of the city. But Pemberton had mistaken Grant's river crossing for just another diversion, and even upon learning the truth, he refused the request of Joseph E. Johnston, who commanded the 6,000 rebel troops at Jackson, to march out of the city and combine their forces against Grant. That plan, Pemberton explained, contradicted his instructions from President Davis, which were to defend Vicksburg at all costs. The indecisive Pemberton, who was more administrator than combat officer, finally made a partial move by advancing a portion of his garrison midway between Vicksburg and Jackson on May 12.

The Siege

Grant attacked him on May 16. The resulting battle of Champion's Hill, fought 18 miles east of Vicksburg, cost Pemberton nearly 4,000 of his 25,000 men and 27 pieces of artillery. The Federals, who lost just 2,500 men, pursued but could not catch the fleeing rebels before they reentered the defenses of Vicksburg. Grant tried twice during the next week to capture the city by reckless and bloody assaults. When these failed, he laid siege to the 30,000-man rebel garrison. By mid-June, he had 77,000 troops entrenched in 12 miles of earthworks wrapping around the enemy's lines, just 600 yards away in some places. In the center of this deadly cocoon sat not only Pemberton's soldiers but also the frightened citizens of Vicksburg. More than 200 Union cannon, plus Porter's gunboats, pummeled them and their defenders for forty-six days and nights. Most people evacuated their homes to burrow into caves along the river bluffs. Black laborers did a brisk business digging these caves for $30 to $50 apiece. Although Union soldiers were able to rotate into the line during those nearly seven weeks, with half the men sleeping or resting while the other half manned the trenches, exhausted rebel soldiers, outnumbered more than two to one, stood constant vigil.

Food and water soon grew scarce in Vicksburg. Confederate soldiers received just a handful of rice and peas daily by the end of June, and civilians had even less to sustain themselves. Many people relied on rats and stray cats for sustenance. Sickness—mostly dysentery, diarrhea, and malaria—felled both soldiers and civilians. Dozens died daily. Coffin makers could not keep pace, although dead soldiers, in any event, were buried in long trenches, "a blanket for a shroud."

All the while, the artillery continued to boom. "Terror stricken, we remained crouched in the cave," recalled one woman of the conditions, "while shell after shell followed each other in quick succession. I endeavored by constant prayer to prepare myself for the sudden death I was almost certain awaited me." Many people remained defiant in the early days of the siege, but the spirits of most rebels gradually wilted under the relentless bombardment, the threat of starvation, and the uncertainty of when it would all end. They lived in hopes that Johnston would arrive to break the siege, and the general had, in fact, reassembled a force of 32,000 men at Jackson by early July. It seems doubtful, however, that he ever would have attacked Grant's rear guard, which still outnumbered his own force.

Results of Vicksburg

By July 3 it no longer mattered. As Grant pushed portions of his lines to within 100 yards of the rebels, Pemberton decided his situation was hopeless. He surrendered the next day, not knowing that at that precise moment Lee's army was retreating southward through the mud and the rain of Pennsylvania. The practical strategic value of Vicksburg to the Federals at this point in the war, like that at Gettysburg, is debatable. The capture of New Orleans and Memphis more than a year earlier had already allowed the Federals to control access to the Mississippi, although it is also true that rebel guerrillas continued to threaten navigation of the river until the end of the war. But the psychological impact of Pemberton's capitulation on Independence Day, combined with Lee's retreat, was incalculable. The twin victories, both culminating on an anniversary deemed sacred and celebrated by both North and South, seemed to symbolize God's displeasure with the Confederate cause. The rebel surrender on July 9 of Port Hudson, a strong but now completely isolated river fortress 25 miles above Baton Rouge, was anticlimactic. The Confederacy had suffered two successive blows from which it never fully recovered.

Once again, as well, the more serious blow to Confederate hopes had been struck in the West. The northern home front made more of the Gettysburg "victory" than did southerners, who, much like the soldiers who fought there, found the outcome muddled. Still, the rebels could not duck the timing of the Vicksburg surrender. "I think the 4th of July of 1863 will stand by that of 76 in the annals of [the] Country," rejoiced a northern woman upon learning of the Vicksburg triumph. A North Carolina rebel sadly agreed: "The garrison surrendered on the 4th of July. I would have waited until the 5th & not sullied our national anniversary with such an act."

Confederate Diplomacy

By July 1863, Confederate hopes for diplomatic recognition from Europe had all but died, too. Confederate diplomats and agents in England, France, and Mexico had been cajoling and pleading tirelessly for aid without success. An apparent break came in January when Emperor Napoleon III of France, hoping to exploit a political schism in Mexico, sent an army to invade that country and to establish a puppet regime. Napoleon believed that the Confederate States, which had been courting the legitimate government of Mexico under Benito Juarez, provided a convenient buffer between a resurrected French empire in North America and a United States sworn to uphold the Monroe Doctrine. That same month, the Davis government concluded negotiations with Frederick Erlanger, director of a German-based French bank who also happened to be a friend of the French emperor, for a $14.5 million loan. The Erlanger loan, using southern cotton for collateral, provided Confederate contractors with enough credit to make military and naval purchases in Europe through the remainder of the year. But England and Russia had already rejected a French proposal for a limited joint intervention in November 1862, so Napoleon thought it wise to stall the Confederates and let England make the next move.

Precisely there—with England—rested the Confederate problem. English merchants and manufacturers enjoyed a brisk business with the Confederacy. They had made enormous profits from war materials, including rifles, ammunition, **The British Situation**

VERY PROBABLE.

THIS CARTOON from the popular British magazine *Punch* represents Great Britain's important role in America's war. While it seems clear in retrospect that the chances of British intervention were slim by the end of 1863, the cartoon—which depicts Lord Palmerston, Britain's prime minister, passing Jefferson Davis in the street—suggests that some people still believed in that possibility nearly a year later.

and, most especially, the construction of swift commerce raiders like the *Alabama*. The Confederates also had two powerful ironclad "rams" under contract with an English firm, the Lairds. But despite these useful commercial ties, the Confederacy needed the backing of the English government to win legitimacy in the eyes of the world. Unfortunately for the Confederacy, recognition, let alone intervention, became entangled with other international considerations for Queen Victoria and her ministers. Britain had first to keep a wary eye on its own backyard, where Italy, Poland, and the German states seethed with political discontent. The British government even shied away from helping to break the Federal naval blockade, which at the start of the war at least would have been an easy enough assignment for the world's most powerful navy. But, looking ever to its own interests, Britain decided it would be unwise to challenge the precedent of this sometimes useful international political and military tool.

More than that, slavery still troubled the English conscience. Few British politicians or businessmen had been impressed by Lincoln's reluctant, belated, and seemingly calculated attack on slavery, but his Emancipation Proclamation had stirred much support among the working classes, which regarded the United States as a model of democratic reform. "The Emancipation Proclamation has done more for us here than all our former victories and all our diplomacy," decided Henry Adams, son and secretary to the U.S. minister to Great Britain. "Certain it is . . . that public opinion is very deeply stirred here and finds expression in meetings, addresses to President Lincoln, deputations to us, standing committees to agitate the subject and to affect opinion, and all the other symptoms of a great popular movement peculiarly unpleasant to the upper classes here because it rests altogether on the spontaneous action of the laboring classes and has a pestilent squint at sympathy with republicanism." One week later, he added, "The anti-slavery feeling of the country is coming out stronger than we ever expected, and all the English politicians have fairly been thrown over by the people."

Not that the force of "public opinion," a novel concept in nineteenth-century British politics, would ultimately dictate policy; yet, Lord Palmerston's government had grown comfortable in the belief that it could not—indeed, dared not—aggressively back the Confederacy until the rebel army had decisively demonstrated its strength of arms. What slender hope the Confederacy held for British intervention ended in July 1863 when a pro-Confederate member of Parliament, John A. Roebuck, tried to force the issue with a motion in favor of recognition. Roebuck hoped to sway Parliament by promising that the French would join any such British initiative and that he had been assured of the French position in an unofficial audience with Napoleon III. Roebuck had, indeed, met with Napoleon, who had supported just such a policy, but the always cautious emperor apparently experienced a change of heart, and when no French endorsement arrived by the time of the parliamentary vote, Roebuck's Conservative Party failed to back their own man. The episode caused a political uproar that delighted Henry Adams. "[Roebuck] has drawn public attention entirely from the question of intervention," explained Adams, "and substituted a question of veracity between himself and the Emperor, a question of dignity between Parliament and the Emperor, a question of honor between the Ministry and the Emperor, and any quantity of other side issues. . . . Mr. Roebuck has done us more good than all our friends."

Henry Hotze, the principal Confederate propagandist in England, predicted in despair before learning of Gettysburg and Vicksburg, "Diplomatic means can now no longer avail, and everybody looks to Lee to conquer recognition." News of July's twin Confederate defeats settled the matter. "I wanted to hug the army of the Potomac," exulted Henry Adams. "I wanted to get the whole of the army of Vicksburg drunk at my own expense. I wanted to fight some small man and lick him." The rebel diplomatic position then deteriorated rapidly. Judah P. Benjamin recalled John Mason in August 1863, essentially severing diplomatic ties with England. In September, responding to threats of war by Charles Francis Adams, the British government seized the nearly completed Laird rams, an action that his son Henry called a "diplomatic triumph," a "second Vicksburg." The Confederates took several sporadic diplomatic initiatives during the final year of the war, even going so far in 1865 as to promise to abolish slavery in return for British recognition, but by then it was far too late.

Developments on the Confederate home front did not bode well that spring and summer of 1863 either. It began with "bread riots" by the urban poor. Inflation, hoarding, and rank speculation had caused widespread want and hunger, and in late March, distressed citizens took to the streets of several towns in Georgia, North Carolina, and Alabama. On April 1, looters spread violence through the streets of Petersburg, Virginia, and the next day saw the Confederate capital, where working-class and middle-class women had been threatening to protest scarcities of food and outrageous prices for several weeks, erupt. By 9 a.m., a crowd had gathered in front of the home of Virginia governor John Letcher to demand bread. Gaining no satisfaction, the protesters invaded the city's commercial district. By then, the crowd had swelled to almost 1,000 women, children, and men, and real trouble soon followed. The crowd became a mob and sacked some twenty stores. When the looters ignored Mayor Joseph Mayo's threat to retaliate with armed troops, he arrested more than seventy people.

The crowd dispersed sometime after 11 a.m., more exhausted than cowed. Although composed of both poor and middle-class citizens (including a few slaveholders), the majority of the Richmond rioters seem to have been poor white women. It would be interesting to know how many of them had husbands or fathers serving in the army or how many had friends and relatives among the sixty laboring women who died in an explosion at a Richmond ordnance laboratory two weeks earlier. Whatever the circumstances, the 1863 spring riots—to be repeated on a smaller scale the following spring—demonstrated the increasingly desperate plight of many urban workers, both men and women. The sudden series of uprisings was less threatening than the Copperhead agitation Lincoln faced in the North, but it was bad enough, and it was just beginning. The confidence of the Confederate people in its government had begun to slip.

Confederate Home Front

THE RICHMOND BREAD RIOT of April 2, 1863, was the most visible of several similar protests in the spring of that year. Hundreds of citizens, mostly women, violently protested high prices and shortages of food in the Confederate capital, but their displeasure also represented growing dissatisfaction with the government's general handling of the war.

Elections of 1863

Confederate elections that summer and fall of 1863 further confirmed an alarming decline in public morale. Southerners voted nearly 40 percent of the Congress out of office, and many of their newly elected representatives had campaigned openly as "peace" candidates. A large number of the newcomers—more than two-thirds—had opposed secession at some time, and although almost all had fallen in line once the fighting started, military defeats, economic decline, and government centralization during the intervening months had led them to reevaluate the situation. Similarly, nearly every state legislature increased its antisecessionist numbers in 1863, and several governorships changed hands.

The southern elections acquired added significance in light of political events in the North. A strong reaction against the continued antiwar, antiemancipation harangues of the Democrats, which had acquired a subversive quality, could be detected in several municipal elections as early as the spring. A groundswell of patriotic fervor following Gettysburg and Vicksburg nurtured this embryonic renaissance, and the Republicans rebounded from their

1862 electoral drubbing. Patriotic political organizations, such as the Union League and Loyal Publication Society, while not officially linked to the party, boosted Republican fortunes by endorsing their legislative plans and war aims and circulating their campaign literature. Consequently, Lincoln's party made solid legislative gains in Illinois, Iowa, Minnesota, Pennsylvania, New York, Wisconsin, and Maryland. It also did better than expected in Ohio and Indiana, two states through which the rebel cavalry leader John Hunt Morgan had rampaged in a daring—and unauthorized—raid that summer, before being captured and imprisoned with most of his men.

Still, the meaning of the southern elections was not entirely clear. People wanted a change, but toward what end? Even most "peace" candidates and "unionists" rejected Confederate surrender. They were more "antigovernment" than "anti-Confederate," opposed more to the way that Jefferson Davis had managed the war than to the cause of independence. Only a few candidates desired restoration of the "Union as it was." Most favored a negotiated peace. Some candidates would only endorse reunion if slavery were protected and Union reprisals disavowed. To others, "peace" still meant some form of independence. The election results also lacked clarity because so many loyal Confederates, having fled areas of extensive enemy occupation in Arkansas, Louisiana, Mississippi, and Tennessee, had been unable to vote. Indeed, the Lincoln government, in a tentative move toward "reconstruction," had already taken advantage of refugee flight by establishing pro-Union governments in those states.

In addition was the growing personal animus against Jefferson Davis: in many respects, the elections were votes of no-confidence in his leadership. The president's six-year term of office protected him politically, but many voters clearly blamed the ills of the Confederacy on policies that they associated with his administration. The only way to loosen the oppressive yoke of conscription, impressment, taxation, restrictions on civil liberties, economic inflation, and a failed foreign policy, they believed, was to oust the politicians who served as the president's lackeys. Davis continued to suffer from an unflattering public image. Unlike the folksy, gregarious, and politically savvy Lincoln, whose gradually softening image and reputation had turned him into "Uncle Abe" and "Father Abraham," Davis could not shake his reputation—much of it deserved—for aloofness, obstinacy, and pettiness.

None of which is to suggest that Lincoln and his advisors could pause to frolic beneath sunny skies. A growing realization that Meade's victory had been less than conclusive soon offset whatever joy northerners drew from the Confederacy's internal turmoil and military setbacks. Peace remained a subject for prayers, rather than being seen as an inevitable event. Poet Emily Dickinson, observing the great pageant from her New England home, wrote in 1863:

The Northern Mood

> I many times thought Peace had come
> When Peace was far away—
> As Wrecked Men—deem they sight the Land—
> At Centre of the Sea—

Northern Conscription
The most serious new obstacle to peace, and a serious threat to Union solidarity, was conscription. When northern enlistments began to falter, Congress followed the Confederacy by passing a conscription act in March 1863, to take effect in July. At first the draft did not seem to be as heated a political or electoral issue as it was in the South. Indeed, the plight of northern slackers who found themselves "grafted into the army" became the subject of several humorous songs. Still, it was no laughing matter to able-bodied men ages twenty to forty-five, who, like their rebel counterparts, saw a class bias in the legislation. Unlike the Confederate draft laws, the North offered no occupational exemptions, but draftees could avoid service either by finding a substitute (as in the South), by proving they had dependents, or—and here was what most angered people—by paying the government a $300 commutation fee, an amount roughly equal to the annual wage of an unskilled laborer. Thousands of middle- and upper-class northerners, including William James and John D. Rockefeller, escaped military service by this means.

Northern Protests
Substitution, the equivalent of the Confederacy's "twenty Negro" clause, produced cries of a "rich man's war, poor man's fight" in the Democratic press. Violent protests soon followed, as some provost marshals, entrusted with enforcing the law, were shot, their families threatened, and their property vandalized. More than 160,000 men—a fifth of those drafted—refused to report for duty, and many thousands who did report eventually deserted. Many more thousands "dodged" the draft by fleeing their communities; perhaps as many as 30,000 wound up in Canada, beyond the arm of U.S. law. It is hard to generalize about why so many men refused to serve. It seems unlikely that so many draft dodgers were "poor." Many Democrats or men of southern heritage opposed the war on principle, just as "unionists" did in the South. Many others did not care about the war one way or another, and they certainly did not want to die in it. Not a few, too, bristled as much as any southerner at this perceived abuse of power by the national government. Only about 7 percent of northern men conscripted in 1863 and 1864 eventually entered the army. Viewed another way, draftees constituted only 4 percent of the Union army, with another 9 percent being substitutes. The equivalent numbers in the Confederate army were 10 and 11 percent.

To what extent the commutation fee favored the rich is unclear, but infuriated working-class northerners believed it did so. Immigrants who had applied for citizenship and who tended to be poor and ill-educated were among the most conspicuous grumblers. Well aware of their northern neighbors' nativist tendencies, they viewed conscription as just another form of Protestant persecution. Tens of thousands of immigrants served the Union cause—indeed, they represented as much as 25 percent of the army, more than twice the number of African Americans that enlisted. But immigrants did not, any more than other northerners, want to be told they *must* serve. Immigrants and common laborers were conspicuous in the protests and resistance against the draft that spread through northern towns and cities, including New York, Boston, Chicago, Milwaukee, and St. Paul. Protesters rioted in the streets, burned draft

ANTIWAR PROTESTS IN THE NORTH were at least as numerous and violent as mass demonstrations in the South. This scene from the New York City draft riots illustrates that African Americans were a special target of the mob, which feared that blacks would take the jobs of white conscripts.

records, looted stores, attacked affluent-looking "$300 men," and clashed with soldiers and police. Small wonder Congress repealed the commutation fee when revising the draft law in 1864.

Yet, these protests usually had hidden depths. Democratic politicians, especially Copperheads, seemingly encouraged the most violent protests. Similarly, most of the resistance came from Democratic areas of the North, especially where large numbers of immigrants and laboring poor resided. Interesting enough, many of the protests grew not from opposition to the *principle* of conscription so much as from perceived inequities of the system. It was also an ideal issue with which to challenge Republican efforts to expand the authority of the national government. Most of the violence subsided after the spring and summer of 1863. Several city governments even went so far as to pay commutation fees for poor men. Thereafter, people accepted the operation of the draft, if grudgingly.

A variety of interconnected concerns sparked the North's most famous **New York Riots** "draft riot" in New York City on July 13–15. Manual laborers and immigrants formed an important core of the protestors. After all, the nation's largest city also had the largest concentration of poor people and immigrants. More than

400,000 New Yorkers lived in crowded, unhealthy tenements. The city reported some 200,000 cases of preventable illness in 1863, and as many as 10,000 of those people died. The immigrant community was a cauldron of dissatisfaction and bitterness. But the New York riot was a complex sociological event that grew from a generation of violent protest by urban laborers and immigrants against the dislocation of the market revolution, ethnic hatred, and political impotence. The rioters targeted not just the provost marshal but all symbols of political, social, and economic power, including police, employers, pro-Republican newspapers (especially the *Tribune* of Horace Greeley, who had vigorously promoted conscription), and the homes of the wealthy.

The riot also contained a powerful component of race hatred. The working poor, immigrants as well as natives, competed with blacks for the city's skilled and unskilled jobs, yet blacks were not subject to the draft. It infuriated whites to think that they might be forced into the army while black men took their jobs. More than that, once emancipation became a war aim, immigrants believed that they would only be fighting—and possibly dying—to liberate southern slaves who would move north to depress wages and eliminate jobs. Consequently, rioters burned the Colored Orphan Asylum and rampaged through black neighborhoods. Some 300 people were injured and at least 120 killed in the New York riots. Eleven of those people killed were African Americans (six of them lynched), several of whom were brutally mutilated. It took several regiments of army troops, pulled from the lines at Gettysburg, to finally quell the riot.

The Chickamauga Campaign

And so, despite Union victories at Vicksburg and Gettysburg, the war was far from over, and the year's next dramatic military campaign had already begun. When Vicksburg was still under siege and Lee was only beginning his move toward Pennsylvania, Braxton Bragg had resumed his retreat in Tennessee. He and William Rosecrans had remained relatively inactive for several months after the bloodletting at Stones River, but as the Army of the Cumberland finally rumbled forward, Bragg fell back toward Chattanooga, one of two remaining Confederate logistical hubs in Tennessee. His problems were complicated by the fact that two federal corps under Ambrose Burnside threatened the other of those hubs, Knoxville. If Burnside captured Knoxville, an important railroad and river town in one of the most pro-Union parts of the South, he could either join forces with Rosecrans or move against Bragg's rear. In either case, Bragg would be doomed.

But Rosecrans had Bragg in his sights, with no intention of coordinating with Burnside. His army, mostly midwesterners but including several regiments of Kentucky unionists, wanted a more convincing victory than the one at Stones River. As Bragg continued to withdraw, Rosecrans guessed that the rebels might be demoralized, and when, on September 9, Bragg retreated even beyond *his* supply base at the crucial railroad depot of Chattanooga, "Old Rosey" was certain of it. He had guessed wrong: the officers who led the hard-luck Army of Tennessee—bold fighters who had always come up short of victory—were a fractious, back-biting bunch, and Bragg, no diplomat himself, had a tough time commanding their loyalty and cooperation; but their men were always ready to fight, and as Rosecrans bulled ahead, the rebels lured him into a trap.

Bragg aligned his army in a rugged patch of woods and mountains in northwest Georgia in front of Chickamauga Creek. (*Chickamauga* was an old Cherokee word that eludes precise translation, although legend says it means "River of Death.") He also had reinforcements on the way. A woefully outnumbered Simon Buckner, the lone Confederate hero from the debacle at Fort Donelson, forced to abandon Knoxville to Burnside on September 2, joined Bragg with a corps of men. Then Robert E. Lee sent James Longstreet's corps to reinforce Bragg—the only time during the war that Lee released his own troops to a western army. Bragg also knew that Rosecrans had divided his army to pass through the honeycomb of mountains that surrounded Chattanooga. All of this meant the fragmented Union force of 58,000 should have been no match for Bragg's 66,000, but the battle of Chickamauga was a confused affair from the start. Neither army actually attacked when the two-day fight began on September 19. The troops simply collided, to the surprise of both sides. With battle lines that extended across 6 miles, the two armies grappled with each other like two grizzly bears in the dense woods and tangled thickets.

The turning point came on September 20, 1863, when miscommunication and ill-timed orders removed an entire Union division from a crucial position on Rosecrans's right flank. Then luck played a hand for the rebels. Before the Federals could close the lethal gap, Longstreet—whose corps had only arrived on the battlefield the previous evening—closed on it. The Union right crumpled, and the entire army tumbled back toward Chattanooga. The retreat was an ugly sight, and only the cool action of Gen. George H. Thomas saved the Federals from annihilation. A Virginian by birth, this steady and deliberate forty-seven-year-old West Point graduate had already contributed to Union victories at Shiloh, Perryville, and Stones River. Now, by slowing the pursuit of the Union army from a defensive position on Snodgrass Hill, he bought the retreating Federals some four hours, until evening, to reach the safety of Chattanooga. About 500 Ohio infantrymen made a particularly noteworthy contribution to this delaying action. Armed mostly with the new five-shot Colt Revolving Rifle, they decimated Confederate attackers from their position on Horseshoe Ridge, on the lower right face of Snodgrass. But it was Thomas, the stubborn-looking, solidly built, 200-pound six-footer who would be remembered as the Rock of Chickamauga.

Each army suffered 28 percent casualties (16,170 Federal losses; 18,454 Confederate) in one of the bloodiest battles of the war. Bragg won a tactical victory—as he so often did—but he had missed several opportunities, both in the days preceding the battle and during the battle itself, to crush Rosecrans and significantly alter the complexion of the war. Nevertheless, he and his men now chased the Army of the Cumberland back into Tennessee. Bragg hoped that Rosecrans would evacuate Chattanooga and retreat deeper into the state. When he did not, Bragg laid siege to the town, and it looked as though Rose-

The Battle of Chickamauga

The Siege of Chattanooga

crans had blundered again. The rebels surrounded him on two sides, cut off river and railroad traffic in and out of the town, and staged a series of cavalry raids in the Union rear to disrupt communications and further diminish hopes of reinforcement. Bragg could not squeeze Rosecrans as tightly as Grant had Pemberton, but the Federals were in a bad fix. By early October, they were on half rations.

A worried Lincoln ordered reinforcements to Chattanooga, and one Union soldier who slipped through the Confederate cordon on October 23 changed everything. That soldier was Ulysses Grant, on whom Lincoln had been keeping an eye ever since the western general's successes at Henry and Donelson. Some of the president's advisors, most notably Halleck, worried about the persistent rumors of Grant's drunkenness and thought him careless and undisciplined, but Lincoln only cared that Grant won battles. Since his victory at Vicksburg, Grant had taken firm control of the Mississippi River valley by ravaging Mississippi and Alabama with a series of cavalry raids, and now Lincoln called on him to save the Army of the Cumberland. The first decision Grant made upon arriving at Chattanooga was to replace Rosecrans with Thomas as the head of the army. Then Thomas and Grant concocted a plan to acquire supplies. Their so-called "Cracker Line," laid out west of the town and out of range of Confederate artillery, used river transports, pontoon bridges, and wagon trains to funnel much-needed food into the town by November 1. Then, as reinforcements slowly arrived, Grant looked for a way to break the siege.

The Battle of Lookout Mountain

On November 24, 1863, Joseph Hooker, who had arrived with a division from the Army of the Potomac, attacked the seemingly impregnable Confederate position on Lookout Mountain. The 1,100-foot natural fortress loomed to the south of Chattanooga, and the Confederate artillery positioned there controlled all movement in the valley below, including on the Tennessee River and the railroad. But as Hooker's men rushed forward under cover of early morning darkness, fog, and mist to scale the monstrous piece of rock, they discovered that, once at the base of the mountain, they were perfectly safe. The steep elevation prohibited Confederate gunners and riflemen on top of the mountain from seeing them as they climbed through the trees and the undergrowth, and in the end, the relatively lightly defended citadel proved to be easy pickings. The mist and the height prompted soldiers to call it the Battle above the Clouds, and their victory, by forcing back the Confederate left flank, allowed Grant to focus his entire attention on the main rebel force to the east.

The Battle of Missionary Ridge

On the next day, November 25, waves of blue-clad soldiers swept across the valley east of Chattanooga toward the rebel lines on Missionary Ridge, which sloped upward to a height of 600 feet. Bragg's force had been reduced by this time, with Longstreet's corps having been ordered away to wrest Knoxville from Burnside, but he still commanded more than enough men to anchor a stout defensive position. Bragg arranged his men in three lines: one at the base of the ridge, a second midway up the slope, and the third fortifying the crest. They poured a deadly fire into Grant's men, but the Federals continued their slow, methodical advance across the mile-long plain. The

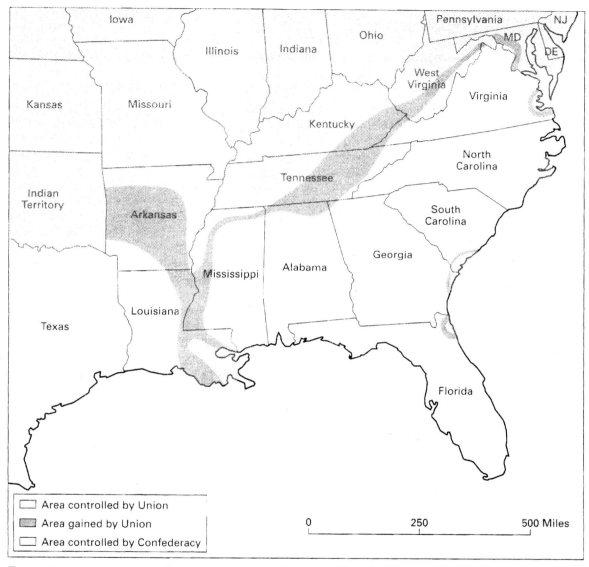

THIS MAP SHOWS the extent of Union occupation at the end of 1863. Most of the South remained free of Union troops, yet even in unoccupied areas, cavalry raids and the activities of unionist guerrillas threatened the security of the Confederacy.

bluecoats finally forced the first of Bragg's three lines back up the ridge, but as they paused, awaiting orders to resume the advance, they came under such a withering fire that, as a matter of survival, Grant's men rose up and charged the rebels of their own accord.

So began the most dramatic moment of the "Soldiers' Battle," as the fight on Missionary Ridge would be known. Many Union troops shouted "Chickamauga! Chickamauga!" as they rushed ahead, bent on avenging the September defeat. Crashing through Bragg's second line, they barely paused before scrambling to the top, where they completely overwhelmed the gray-clad defenders, who went streaming down the reverse of the ridge. It was the most complete rout of a Confederate army in the war. Bragg lost just 361 killed and 2,160 wounded (compared to 753 and 4,722 for Grant), but the Federals gobbled up 4,000 prisoners.

Results of Chattanooga

Grant's victory confirmed Lincoln's faith in the middle-aged, medium-height, average-looking general. "Well done," the president told him in a brief, understated congratulatory note written on November 25, but Lincoln had big plans for Grant. Early the next year, he would give the Ohioan command of all Union armies and tell him to win the war. Chattanooga would serve as the base from which a portion of those armies would enter Georgia in pursuit of the Army of Tennessee. Knoxville, too, had been secured by the end of the year, once Sherman had joined Burnside there. Failing to capture the city in a grand assault on November 29, Longstreet had withdrawn toward the Tennessee-Virginia border, no longer a threat. In Virginia, Lee and Meade engaged in a shoving match following the Gettysburg campaign. It ended on November 8 when Lee gave ground toward Richmond and the Army of the Potomac planted itself firmly—and permanently—below the Rappahannock River. The only bright spot for the Confederacy that autumn came in south Louisiana, where the rebels blocked a mismanaged Union effort to invade Texas.

Gettysburg Address

Lincoln had received word of the miracle at Chattanooga upon returning to Washington from a visit to Gettysburg. Several northern governors, wishing to commemorate the ultimate sacrifice made by so many Union soldiers in defense of northern soil, had joined together to create a "national" cemetery at Gettysburg. The president was invited to say a few words at its dedication on November 19. An astonishing number of people—some 15,000—arrived for the ceremonies, most of them being the wives, parents, siblings, and friends of the men to be interred. A military band, a local choral group, and the day's principal speaker, Edward Everett, preceded Lincoln on the program. Yet, as things turned out, the president's words on that occasion, his "Gettysburg Address," consummately defined the meaning of the war for the North.

As Lincoln considered whether or not to make the trip—for the president almost never left the vicinity of the capital, and then only to consult with his generals—he pondered how best to ennoble the occasion. He thought of the enormous human and material toll taken by the war. He thought of all the suffering, the political dislocation, the diplomatic danger, the entire scope of a war that had by now dragged on for thirty-one months. He decided he would use this opportunity much as he had used the "victory" at Antietam, when he had issued the Emancipation Proclamation. He would reinvigorate the Union cause, broaden the meaning of the war, and morally elevate the North's purpose in this contest. He did not want his countrymen to think of the war as a struggle between the *people* of North and South; rather, they must appreciate it

ABRAHAM LINCOLN used the dedication of the battlefield at Gettysburg. Pennsylvania. in November 1863. to redefine the purpose of the war. In this photograph of the ceremonies. the president is reputedly the figure on the horizon. left of center. in the stovepipe hat.

as a contest between competing *principles:* democracy versus tyranny, freedom versus slavery, equality versus inequality.

Everett, a former Whig congressman, governor, diplomat, secretary of state, and John Bell's vice presidential running mate in 1860, was, at nearly seventy years of age, the best-known public lecturer in the country. He droned on for two hours while the president patiently waited his turn at the rostrum, but his otherwise unmemorable oration unintentionally proved the perfect prelude to the president's "remarks." Everett, who had a reputation as a political moderate, offered an eloquent plea for national unity and the avoidance of enmity once the war ended—with a Union victory, he assumed. "There is no bitterness on the part of the masses," Everett insisted. "The bonds that unite us as one people, a substantial community of origin, language, belief, and law . . . ; common national and political interests; a common history; a common pride in a glorious ancestry . . . these bonds of union are of perennial force and energy, while the causes of alienation are imaginary, fictitious, and transient."

Polite applause followed. Then Lincoln rose to give his two-minute summation of the philosophical principles at stake in the war. He began at the beginning, with the birth of a nation that had been dedicated "to the proposition that all men are created equal." The question to be decided by the present war, Lincoln emphasized, was whether or not a nation devoted to such a principle could survive. This was not just a war to restore the Union, but one to restore a *particular type* of democratic Union, unique in the history of the world. Speaking beyond his immediate audience, he challenged the nation to equal the sacrifices of its brave soldiers, only a portion of whom rested beneath this hallowed Pennsylvania ground. "It is for us the living," Lincoln told them, "to be dedicated here to the unfinished work which they who fought here have thus far so nobly advanced." The northern public must resolve to finish "the great task," to give new life and meaning to the principle of "freedom."

Significance of Address

Northern critics lamented the fact that Lincoln had failed to mention slavery or emancipation, but the president had, in fact, proposed a far more sophisticated justification for the war than freeing southern slaves. He had *combined* the cause of emancipation with the cause of the Union. Lincoln knew that the latter—the fruit of the American Revolution nurtured by the preservation of self-government—must remain the nation's main goal. He also continued to insist that the states had been born of the nation, not the other way around. Individual states, contrary to the Confederacy's interpretation of America's revolutionary heritage, could not secede at their choosing. The United States was a single, indivisible entity. This had been Lincoln's position throughout the war. Now, however, the president implied that the *freedom* inherent in self-government was inseparable from *equality* for individuals. These two—freedom and equality—were the central doctrines of the Declaration of Independence, to which all Americans, North and South, had pledged themselves. Consequently, this war to maintain the Union was being waged to secure both ideals.

Rituals of Mourning

But the November events at Gettysburg had also been about mourning, and in that respect, they mirrored less-grand rituals witnessed daily in families and communities of North and South. The two nations seemed shrouded in black. Men wore black armbands; widows dressed in black. Black wreaths appeared on doors and in windows. Black bunting draped porches and storefronts. Relatives and friends received the bleak news of slain loved ones on stationery bordered with black and arriving in envelopes of matching pattern. The dreaded tidings, whether coming in a letter or coldly announced in the most recently posted government casualty lists, cast gloomy palls over hearts and minds. Walt Whitman wrote of one mother who received the dreaded letter:

> All swims before her eyes, flashes with black, she catches the main words only,
> Sentences broken, *gunshot wound in the breast, cavalry skirmish, taken to hospital,*
> *At present low, but will soon be better.*
> Alas poor boy, he will never be better . . . ,
> While they stand at home at the door he is dead already,
> The only son is dead.

MOURNING BECAME A WAY OF LIFE for hundreds of thousands of American families during the war. One can easily imagine the woman in this 1862 engraving by Winslow Homer as the mother in Walt Whitman's poem "Come up from the Fields, Father."

When possible, people traveled to battlefields or visited the hospitals to claim the bodies of their men. Yet, few people had those opportunities, and bodies could not always be located or recognized. Men were blown apart in battle, decapitated, disemboweled, or so disfigured as to make identification impossible. "Looking down one of the rows of corn, I saw the first corpse," reported one witness to a rather mild example of the carnage, "the hands flung stiffly back, the feet set stubbornly, the chin pointing upward, the features losing their sharpness, the skin blackening, the eyes great and white." Most of the slain were interred beneath the soil where they had fallen. Quite often, because of the large numbers involved, dozens, scores, even hundreds of bodies were unceremoniously dumped in large common graves, "in bunches, just like chickens," as one southerner put it. The bodies of officers were generally buried singly or sent home for burial in zinc-lined coffins packed with ice. "Corpse coolers," the soldiers called them irreverently.

Most often, surviving friends and relatives had only their memories and a few scattered physical reminders of the dead. This was perhaps the hardest part of the loss—never to see husbands, fathers, sons, or brothers again. The men had simply vanished. Not surprisingly, then, the Civil War was the first occasion in U.S. history where large numbers of citizens yearned for cathartic public expressions of grief, some means of sharing their emotional suffering. Never had there been such universally shared sorrow, even in past American wars. The result was an unprecedented outpouring of secular poems, songs, dramas, and literature, quite aside from all the religious sermons one might have expected. This literature assured people that their men had not died in vain, that they had sacrificed themselves "nobly," out of "duty" for "home," "family," and "country," and that they would all surely go to heaven. And that last message was vitally important. Families had to believe that however their boys may have been corrupted by the army, regardless of the fact that they had doubtless broken God's sixth commandment, that they still had died pure of heart and unsullied by war. Songs like "The Faded Coat of Blue" showcased this sentiment for northern families:

> No more the bugle calls the weary one,
> Rest noble spirit, in thy grave unknown!
> I'll find you and know you, among the good and true,
> When a robe of white is given for the faded coat of blue.

One may guess from the titles something of the lyrics sung in parlors all across America: "Just before the Battle, Mother," "Bear Gently, So Gently, the Roughly Made Bier," "O Wrap the Flag around Me, Boys," "Mother Kissed Me in My Dream," "The Vacant Chair," "Write a Letter to My Mother," "Somebody's Darling," "Tell Me, Is My Father Coming Home?" and, perhaps the most popular such song in North or South, "Weeping Sad and Lonely" (or "When This Cruel War Is Over"):

> But our country called you, darling,
> Angels cheer your way;
> While our nation's sons are fighting,
> We can only pray.
> Nobly strike for God and liberty,
> Let all nations see
> How we love the starry banner,
> Emblem of the free.
> Weeping sad and lonely,
> Hopes and fears how vain!
> When this cruel war is over,
> Praying that we meet again!

Role of Religion   Faced with such horrible loss of life, people turned to religion to buoy hopes and assuage grief. As important as religion had been to Americans in the pre-war years, it acquired even more significance as a way to sustain people in the throes of war. Formal church services, Bible reading groups, and personal devotions allowed people to accept the war as one of God's trials. "If we did not have a Bible," explained a Georgia woman, "what would we do—tis more comfort to me than anything else now." Preachers spoke of the martyrdom of men who had perished for the Union or Confederate cause. *Martyrdom* had a compelling ring to it, implying Christian sacrifice for both nation and family. For "every death now," intoned Henry Ward Beecher after Gettysburg, "a thousand lives shall be happier." Sadly, individuals would have to suffer that the nation might revive and prosper. The land, as John Brown had warned, must be purged with blood for its past sins in order to wean Americans from their unseemly pride. Both sides periodically declared national days of prayer, fasting, and humility. Lincoln, upon the suggestion of Sarah Josepha Hale, a prominent magazine editor, declared Thanksgiving a national holiday.

Some families, having been deprived of their breadwinner, required even more spiritual strength if they faced the possibility of destitution, the loss of homes, or starvation. Southerners, in particular, knew well these awful prospects by the end of 1863. Even if their men remained hale and hearty, Union—and sometimes Confederate—armies had decimated scores of southern communities. Rebel ministers sought to comfort people by embracing invasion and battlefield defeats as forms of redemption, trials by fire that would determine if Confederates were worthy of independence. All would be well in the end, they declared with moral certainty; death and defeat must be accepted in war, as part of God's plan. "We will come out of the furnace doubly purified for the good work & fight that God has given us up to," a Mississippian decided. "For to the people of the Confederacy is given the sublime mission of maintaining the supremacy of our Father in Heaven." A South Carolinian insisted, "I cannot think our Merciful Father will suffer us to sink under the weight of such a barbarous people as our foes. . . . I trust all these trials may be for our benefit and so purify us as a nation."

Beyond the churches, a wider demonstration of cultural grief afforded northerners and southerners release from their pain, bewilderment, and anger. A Virginia artist named William D. Washington produced a famous Confederate expression of cultural grief in his wartime painting *The Burial of Latané*. The allegorical scene depicted a group of women and children—those most frequently in need of these mourning rituals—laying to rest a young army officer slain in battle. The fame of the painting, which skillfully combined images of sacrifice, national loyalty, and Christian perseverance, became so widespread that it was displayed in the Confederate capital for all to admire—and as a means of soliciting financial contributions to the rebel cause. Southern poets, like South Carolinian Henry Timrod, commemorated the "ten times ten thousand" men who had given their lives. In the "Unknown Dead," Timrod touched the most exposed nerves of bereavement with a poignant depiction of the unclaimed sons and brothers who lay in unmarked graves far from home:

> I watch that gray and stony sky—
> Of nameless graves on battle-plains
> Washed by a single winter's rains,
> Where, some beneath Virginia's hills,
> And some by green Atlantic rills,
> Some by the waters of the West,
> A myriad unknown heroes rest.

THESE SOUTHERN WOMEN, seen visiting the graves of their fallen heroes in a New Orleans cemetery, were relatively lucky. As Henry Timrod's poem suggests, the remains of many thousands of soldiers rested in unmarked graves, mass graves, or places inaccessible to families and friends.

Religion also became more important to the soldiers as the war progressed. Mothers, wives, and sweethearts, when writing to their men, had always urged them to mind their souls and reject the temptations of camp life. Likewise, religious organizations and tract societies distributed Bibles and a variety of religious literature to the armies. But the clearest signs that the men were heeding this advice came through a series of religious revivals. Beginning modestly in 1862, they reached a crescendo of enthusiasm in the winter of 1863–1864. Both sides embraced the comforting reassurance of a first conversion or a recommitment to Christ, but the revival spirit took hold most strongly among the rebels. One southerner even lamented, "There is much more religion in the army now, than among the people at home." This does not mean that southerners were more religious than northerners. The enthusiastic Confederate response likely lies in the stronger evangelical underpinnings of southern society combined with the downward skid in Confederate military fortunes. Although revivals occurred at various times and places, the largest and most intense of them seem to have followed rebel defeats.

As the defeats mounted and the soldiers saw fewer and fewer of their old comrades around them, they began to recalculate their own chances for continued survival. Men feared they may have indulged too often in the evils of army life—mostly cussing, gambling, drinking, and breaking the Sabbath; it was, they decided, time to get right with the Lord. Men already strong in their religious convictions used the revivals to reaffirm their faith, but an awareness of the nearness of death inspired virtually all participants to some extent. As one soldier put it, "Life is uncertain at any time, particularly in the army where a man is exposed to so many dangers." Their officers saw additional benefits in this renewal of religion faith. Men who had made their peace with God and felt secure in their hopes for redemption were supposedly braver in battle, less fearful of death. Religion also instilled more respect for authority, improved discipline, enhanced moral behavior in camp, and underscored the importance of the cause for which they fought.

One thing religious devotion could not do was stem the tide of desertion, **Desertion** which by the end of 1863 had become a serious problem in both armies. Desertion also presents one of the knottiest problems of analysis in a very complex war. The numbers are hard to pin down, but a fairly reliable estimate is that at least 200,000 Union troops and 104,000 Confederates deserted the army. This was about 10 percent of the entire Union force and at least 12 percent of the Confederates. Desertion plagues all armies in all wars. The question—and the complicating factor—is: What causes men to desert? The explanations for both Union and Confederate soldiers are many and varied. Lost battles, retreats, and other military reverses clearly inspired desertion. So did ill health and physical discomfort when men grew too hungry, too cold, or too weary to suffer the rigors of war any longer. The year 1864 would mark the roughest time for the Union army, whereas the worst time for the rebels came in 1865, when, with defeat apparently in sight, entire companies and regiments sometimes deserted.

Conscription, as has been suggested elsewhere, also contributed to desertion. Men swept up in the draft might skedaddle at the first opportunity. So, too, the "substitutes" who took the places of drafted men. The northern conscription and enlistment systems almost encouraged desertion with their lucrative bounties. Both federal and most state governments gave cash inducements for men to enlist or reenlist. Before the summer of 1862, these inducements came in the form of monthly state supplements to a soldier's pay or a federal bounty at the time of discharge. But as enlistments slowed, bounties were often paid in a lump sum at the time of recruitment, and that caused problems. With the advent of conscription, many towns, counties, and states, concerned about inequities in the system, offered increasingly large bounties to men who would enlist rather than be drafted. Some communities, as has been noted, even raised money to hire substitutes for their residents. This began a brisk business for the so-called "bounty jumpers," who would enlist to collect the bounty in one town or state, and then desert and enlist under a different name to collect the bounty somewhere else.

Role of Communities

This exploitation of the bounty system suggests the influence that communities could have in causing desertion, but that role also became evident in other ways. The degree of support a community gave to the war, which was clearly conveyed to the men in letters from home and in local newspapers, could go a long way toward convincing soldiers either to remain loyal or to bail out. Men who believed that they would be protected rather than scorned by their neighborhood if they returned home as deserters were far more likely to abandon the war. In a state such as North Carolina, for example, where the political leaders criticized the war effort mercilessly (and which had more deserters than any other Confederate state), deserters knew that they would suffer only slight stigma and would likely face no punishment for abandoning ranks. A Union soldier believed that "copperhead ideas" most often caused desertion from his Vermont regiment in April 1863. Letters and newspapers from home could have a more profound influence on the men than battlefield fortunes, he noted unhappily. "Preach to them the justice of the rebel course," the New Englander observed, "dwell largely on their grievances, speak of the injustice and corruption of our own Government, and if soldiers will believe you, you have done more to demoralize the army than the enemy could by a thorough victory of their arms."

Role of Families

Men also left the army if they thought families or communities needed them more than did the generals and politicians. Not a few Confederates deserted to join guerrilla bands nearer home if they believed that the government had not done enough to protect their neighborhoods. Many men responded to more personal pleas when a family crisis required their presence. Both Union and Confederate soldiers were subject to this sort of pressure, but increasingly, as Union troops swept through southern neighborhoods or families suffered shortages of food, clothing, and shelter, rebel soldiers most frequently heard these pitiable pleas for help. "Before God, Edward, unless you come home we must die," a North Carolina woman wrote to her husband. "Last night I was aroused by little Eddie's crying. . . . He said "Oh mamma, I'm so hungry! And Lucy, Edward, your darling Lucy, she never complains, but she is growing thinner and thinner every day." How many fathers or husbands could resist such a lament?

Yet, to emphasize the complexity of the issue once more, not every man who "deserted" had given up on the war. Many rejoined their regiments after visiting their families and providing for them. It is worth noting, for example, that the highest desertion rates came during the winter months, when the chances for a battle were significantly reduced. Many of the war's amateur soldiers saw nothing wrong with going home during these "slow" times. A Union soldier named John Lowery did so in the winter of 1863 to support his family by working at odd jobs. When the authorities found him, he returned cheerfully to his regiment. There may not even have been an emergency; men simply missed their families—especially at Christmas—and wanted to visit. They never intended to abandon the army permanently. Not even the home folk, even those deep in crisis, expected that. "Christmas is most here again," a Virginia woman told her husband, "and things is worse and worse. . . . I don't want you to stop fightin them Yankees till you kill the last one of them, but try to get off and come home and fix us up and then you can go back and fight them."

A complicated war, indeed, and one far from over at the start of 1864. Union armies had beaten back an invasion of their soil and taken virtual control of the Mississippi River in 1863. Confederate leaders could now presume that foreign intervention on their side was unlikely. Still, the rebels remained hopeful. Northern support for the war showed serious fissures, and 1864 would be a presidential election year in the North. If the Confederates could redeem some portion of the West or trans-Mississippi, if Union armies failed to develop a more effective military strategy, if northern public opinion grew discouraged and swept the Democrats into power, time might yet be on the side of the rebels.

CHAPTER 9

A War of Exhaustion: 1864–1865

While the main Union army in the West was sweeping all before it, the Army of the Potomac hunkered down for months of relative inactivity after the triumph at Gettysburg. Unlike the cautious George Gordon Meade, commander in the East, whose undoubted popularity after Gettysburg was wearing thin, Ulysses S. Grant, hero of the Vicksburg campaign, had proven relentlessly aggressive, and admiration for him was on the rise. During the winter of 1864, Congress debated a bill that would commission Grant the first American lieutenant general since George Washington. Then, on March 3, Henry Halleck telegraphed Grant twice—to tell him the commission had been signed by the president and to order him to Washington to take over direction of the war.

Grant Comes to Washington   Short, tired, his uniform covered with a linen duster, Grant did not give the appearance of the Caesar from the West when, with his fourteen-year-old son, Fred, he quietly approached the desk of Washington's fashionable Willard's Hotel late in the afternoon of March 8. The desk clerk reckoned as how there was probably a room on the top floor, which Grant said suited him, so he signed the register "U. S. Grant and son, Galena, Ill." Seeing this signature, the clerk sprang into action, gave Grant the bridal suite and grabbed his bags to lead the hero upstairs. That was the last moment of private life for Grant in Washington. When he was recognized coming down for dinner that evening, the whole dining room rose to its feet and rhythmically shouted his name.

GEN. ULYSSES S. GRANT at City Point, Virginia, in August 1864. Six months after assuming command of the Army of the Potomac, Grant paused by his tent, perhaps to consider the bloody six weeks of battle that had led to the static and seemingly endless trench warfare at Petersburg.

Grant, who finally got up and bowed, was so embarrassed that he could not finish his meal. That evening at the White House, another cheering throng compelled Grant to stand for an hour on a crimson plush sofa so all could gawk at this plain man of whom total victory was expected.

As he took charge, Grant was evolving a grand strategy for concluding the war. He had doubtless talked through this redesign with his most trusted and brightest lieutenant, William T. Sherman, as Sherman accompanied Grant on the first leg of his train trip east. Grant intended to manage a simultaneous attack across several fronts into all regions of the Confederacy, not just to direct the Army of the Potomac.

Grand Strategy

Earlier in the conflict, following Napoleonic precedents, generals on both sides had attempted to fight and win the *climactic battle* that would annihilate the enemy army and end the conflict. That had been the intention of both armies at Bull Run, but the result, a far from complete southern victory, only led to both sides mobilizing more resources. The next year, Robert E. Lee had been angry with himself for not destroying George McClellan's army during the Peninsula campaign of 1862, and even as he approached Gettysburg, if in a somewhat muted fashion, Lee had hoped to fight the climactic battle.

Over time, however, generals on both sides came to realize that the war was too widespread geographically and too mobile, given river and coastal steamers and the railroad, to reach a simple climax in one place. Armies were relatively numerous and some of them quite big—all of which undercut the possibility of reenacting the Napoleonic dream. In effect, both sides then settled down to a war of *attrition*, where the goal was to keep punishing the enemy, wearing him down gradually, expecting not a knockout blow but the eventual destruction of enemy men, material, and finally morale.

A War of Exhaustion
Attrition in this sense had become the de facto dominant strategy until Grant took over the war. Learning from his experiences in the West, he realized, more intuitively than consciously, that a war of attrition would be insufficient to defeat the Confederacy. Beyond attrition, the Civil War now became what some military historians have termed a war of *exhaustion*. Although Grant still hoped to claim victory by overthrowing the Confederate armies, he considered exhaustion the route to victory, if it could be achieved, in his words, in "no other way." In all likelihood, the Union would have to eradicate the economic resources of the enemy until they could not sustain their armies. Of equal importance, they had to wage sustained physical and psychological warfare against the civilian population to destroy their will to resist. The men, women, and children on the home front, and not just armies, became the target of the Union army—which did not seek to slaughter noncombatants, but rather to break their material and spiritual resources, upon which the morale of their relatives, the citizen-soldiers of the Confederacy, was finally based. Explicit or not, this was the theory of war that Grant and his lieutenants implemented during the last year of the conflict.

Popular support for such a brutal war also had evolved in the Union. The long and inconclusive slaughter of earlier battles and the nastiness of a thousand bloody guerrilla attacks had hardened public opinion. No longer were Confederates errant brothers and sisters—they had become monstrous rebels whose nation ought to be destroyed by any necessary means short of genocide. With the stakes thus heightened, the greatest risk of this strategy was that its implementation would be so enormously costly to northern resources and manpower that Union morale would crumble before the Confederacy could be destroyed. Grant was aware that, particularly within the Democratic Party, an antiwar movement was growing in the North, as much of the public was sickened by the seemingly endless slaughter. Grant and his comrades knew that they would have to provide decisive-enough victories during the next eight months to convince voters to reelect the Republicans, who then would license the Union armies to finish the task.

Replacing Halleck as general-in-chief of all armies, Grant soon designed a grand strategy that flowed from the theory of exhaustion: a simultaneous Union advance on at least five fronts, penetrating as much of the Confederacy as quickly as possible. While the Army of the Potomac pushed after Lee's army, Sherman, who had replaced Grant in the West, would attack southward toward Atlanta against Joseph Johnston's forces. Benjamin Butler was to push up from North Carolina toward Petersburg along the James River, Franz Sigel was to campaign up the Shenandoah Valley, and Nathaniel P. Banks was to capture

Mobile from his New Orleans base and then march toward Sherman's army advancing from the northwest.

Sherman and Lincoln grasped Grant's point immediately. "Concurrent action is the thing," Sherman telegraphed Grant when he read Grant's strategic memorandum, while Lincoln added in his homely fashion, "those not skinning can hold a leg." Giving his agreement to the plan as a whole, Lincoln promised Grant that he would withdraw from his habit of anxious and sporadic intrusiveness that had only confused his previous commanders in the East. "The particulars of your plans I neither know nor seek to know," he assured Grant. "You are vigilant and self-reliant; and, pleased with this, I wish not to obtrude any constraints or restraints upon you." Although he still wanted to be kept well informed—and Grant found working with him pleasant enough—on the whole Lincoln kept to his word on the military front. Nonetheless, Lincoln still had plenty to say about the political meanings of Grant's unfolding campaign.

However pleased he might have been with Grant the planner, Abraham Lincoln decided to plot strategy that winter, too, although his motives and objectives ran contrary to his new commander's master plan. Lincoln had been eager to occupy a portion of Texas since the spring of 1862. By early 1864, he had decided that a joint army–navy expedition up the Red River, which ran

The Red River Campaign

NATHANIEL P. BANKS, former Republican governor of Massachusetts, was one of Abraham Lincoln's favorite political generals. Despite his having failed in three major commands previously, Lincoln placed Banks in charge of the Red River campaign in Louisiana during the spring of 1864. After another notable fiasco, Congress investigated Banks and he was discharged from the military. He returned to Republican politics in his home state.

diagonally across the northern half of Louisiana, could achieve his goal and benefit the Union economically, politically, and diplomatically. Captured cotton would enrich the government and revive a stagnant New England textile industry. A firm hold on northern Louisiana would make it easier to establish a loyal "reconstructed" government in that state, and the "relief of Texas," as a New York newspaper put it, would liberate thousands of beleaguered unionists. Finally, Union occupation of Texas would dissuade France, which had established a puppet regime in Mexico, from aligning itself with the Confederacy.

To achieve his goals for Texas, the president wanted Gen. Nathaniel P. Banks, an influential Massachusetts politician turned soldier, to coordinate a dual expedition. Banks, leading 27,000 men and a flotilla of 60 gunboats and transports (directed by Adm. David D. Porter), was to follow the Red River to Shreveport, Louisiana, near the Texas border. He would rendezvous there with a second column of 12,000 men under Gen. Frederick Steele that was marching south from Little Rock, Arkansas.

Unfortunately, 10,000 of Banks's troops would have to come from Sherman's army, meant by Grant to invade Georgia. Additionally, the expedition would spoil Grant's plan for Banks's army to join the navy in operations against the port city of Mobile, Alabama, an objective of far more strategic importance than Texas. The whole episode was a good example of the odd course Lincoln sometimes steered when demands of politics and war-making collided.

The Red River campaign lasted from mid-March to mid-May 1864. Gen. Edmund Kirby Smith, coordinating the Confederate defense, began by burning 150,000 bales of cotton worth $60 million just to keep them out of Union hands. His forces in Arkansas, commanded by Gen. Sterling Price, then fought Steele's column back before it ever reached Louisiana. Low water in the Red River slowed the advance—and nearly resulted in the destruction—of Porter's gunboats, and Gen. Richard Taylor—son of former president Zachary Taylor—defeated Banks in the battle of Mansfield, Louisiana, on April 8. The Federals got somewhat the better of it in fighting the next day at Pleasant Hill, but Banks continued his retreat.

No part of either the Union army or the navy ever reached Shreveport. The Federals lost slightly more than 8,000 men during the two months, the Confederates about 6,500. Banks was blamed—and was given the boot—for the failure, and Congress investigated not only the causes of the defeat but also rumors of cotton speculation within the army. The Confederates portrayed the Union defeat as an incredible triumph against overwhelming odds. In practical terms, too, the defeat of Steele led to a Confederate resurgence in Arkansas, as rebel soldiers and guerrillas threatened Union occupiers in the state. Nevertheless, the Union had squandered men, equipment, and time in a campaign that could not influence the course of the war.

The Union Bogs Down   Quite soon, Grant's own grand design faltered, as earlier and less ambitious plans had in the past. Butler, Banks, and Sigel, generals with more political than military qualifications, all bogged down in the face of spirited Confederate opposition, which left the two major armies of Sherman and Grant to consummate as much of this design as possible.

UNION TROOPS ADVANCING into the battle of the Wilderness, May 5–6, 1864. Both armies lost all organization in the dense woods, slaughtering each other in small-group combat. The Union lost 17,000 men and the Confederates 11,000, or 17 percent of each army. The night of May 5, hundreds of wounded men burned to death in forest fires, their screams unforgettable to the troops left to fight the second day.

In his theater, instead of remaining out of direct action in Washington as had Halleck, Grant attached his headquarters to Meade's. In theory, Meade was to execute what Grant designed, but in practice, two general headquarters at the apex of the same army proved awkward, and though Grant remained thoughtful of Meade's feelings and opinions, he soon took charge of the strategy and grand tactics of the Army of the Potomac.

In his 1884 *Memoirs*, Grant wrote that he had considered a lightning campaign to the west of Lee's army, marching southwest along the Blue Ridge Mountains, turning on Richmond after reaching Lynchburg. Such a project would have resembled his daring Vicksburg campaign of the previous year, but the risks of major failure in the election year of 1864 were greater than the more obvious, shorter, and more direct attack against which Lee was preparing. Thus, letting caution—and political considerations—govern him, the master of movement became the brutal bulldog of direct assault. On May 4, with his enormous army of perhaps 115,000 men, Grant crossed the Rapidan River to the east of Lee's army, which numbered about 85,000. Not waiting for Grant to flank him, nor to reach open ground where he might organize his forces, Lee attacked Grant on May 5 in the trackless Wilderness.

Battle of the Wilderness

Almost immediately, both armies lost their cohesion as small groups of men stumbled through dense undergrowth, firing low, the black smoke from their gunpowder further obscuring the view. However chaotic and disorganized the engagement might have been, thousands of men were cut down during numerous small-scale advances and retreats. By nightfall, the brush and trees caught fire, and those still uninjured heard the unforgettable screams of the several hundred wounded men who burned to death.

During the second day of battle, after more disorganized thrusts and counterthrusts, the Confederates held their ground, though the Union army was not routed. In the past, the retreat of the losing side followed major battles, succeeded by a combat hiatus of weeks or months. The next evening after this battle, however, refusing to concede defeat, Grant ordered his men to march southward—to continue to advance rather than retreat. Despite the bloodshed of the Wilderness—where the Union lost 17,000 men and the Confederacy 11,000 (or 17 percent of each army, which made the losses of the battle a proportional draw), Grant's men cheered their commander's aggressiveness.

The costs in human suffering of this battle had been immense, even by the standards of battle-hardened veterans. A Union infantryman wrote of the fighting on May 5, "it was a blind and bloody hunt to the death, in bewildering thickets, rather than a battle. . . . In advancing it was next to impossible to preserve a distinct line, and we were constantly broken up into small groups. The underbrush and briars scratched our faces, tore our clothing, and tripped our feet from under us, constantly." On the next day, "flames sprang up in the woods in our front. . . . With crackling roar, like an army of fire, it came down on upon the Union line. The wind drove the blinding smoke and suffocating heat into our faces. This, added to the oppressive heat of the weather, was almost unendurable." A rebel captive told one of his captors that unlike other battles, "here there ain't neither front nor rear. It's all a damn mess! And our two armies ain't nothin' but howlin' mobs." Another Confederate soldier from North Carolina vividly recalled the hellish scene in a letter to his wife: "I have neaver Saw Such a Site in no Battle as I have in this I have Saw lots of Dead bodes Burnt into a crips. . . . I Saw one man that was burnt that had the picture I suppose of his little Daughter in his pockett. . . . I neaver Saw enny thing that made me feel more Sorrow."

The Overland Campaign

As the horrified soldiers began to discern, the Wilderness was to be the opening round of a brutal six-week-long campaign. However, this Overland campaign would be different from what had come before, and arguably introduced some of the most notable combat innovations of the Civil War. The fighting, marching, and renewed fighting was almost continuous, the carnage unending Grant simply would not let go. And Lee, whose army was not strong enough to take advantage of the possibilities for counterattack, remained on the defensive, brilliantly countering Grant's ponderous thrusts. One Mississippian wrote in his journal during this period: "Fighting has become an every day business. It is no longer an occasional affair from which we can relax into peaceful camp life. Now we have become hardened to it as our normal condition."

THE FINAL YEAR OF THE WAR IN THE EAST. After six incredibly bloody weeks of campaigning, Ulysses S. Grant's relentlessly advancing army pushed Robert E. Lee's troops into trenches at Petersburg, protecting Richmond. Following eight months of siege warfare that whittled his army down to half its previous size, Lee abandoned the line and Richmond on April 2, 1865, and fled westward. Only one week later, on April 9, Grant accepted Lee's surrender at Appomattox Court House.

Spotsylvania Court House

The next major stop on the Union campaign came southeast of the Wilderness, at Spotsylvania Court House, during combat that raged from May 8 to May 20, most fiercely on May 10 and May 12. At the geographical center of this prolonged battle was the "Mule Shoe," an outward bulge in the Confederate lines a half-mile wide. The relatively open fields of Stones River and Gettysburg had become something of a relic of a past mode of warfare. As the same Mississippian who had commented about continuous battle after the Wilderness recorded in his journal: "Every time we stop we dig another hole. . . . We seldom charge 'gloriously' as we did [before]. Instead we build fortifications and try to flank the enemy. The enemy does the same."

Because of poor tactical thinking, the Confederates withdrew their artillery from their strong salient at the Mule Shoe, rendering their lines more vulnerable to assault. On the morning of May 12, the troops in Winfield Scott Hancock's corps stormed the trenches, and what ensued was hand to hand combat, with bayonets, fists, and pistols brought into use for one of the few times during the war. Although Hancock's men penetrated the Confederate trenches, they kept advancing in a straight line rather than widening the breach, and other Union troops failed to support their breakthrough. After several hours the Confederates managed to seal off the ends of the breach and then closed it by crossfire. The Union troops then withstood a powerful Confederate counterattack from the set of trenches they had dug before the battle to which they had retreated. The day ended in stalemate, twenty horrific hours after it had begun.

The next day, the "Bloody Angle," as it came to be called, was eerily quiet. Men from both sides managed to walk across the scene. "Horses and men chopped into hash by the bullets [appearing] like piles of jelly," one Union observer wrote. "Below the mass of fast-decaying corpses, the convulsive twitching of limbs and the writhing of bodies [revealed] wounded men . . . struggling to extricate themselves from their horrid entombment." The rebel trenches were filled with bodies, several dead men deep. And an oak tree, twenty-two inches thick, served as mute witness to the ferocity of the fighting: it had been cut down by the incredible intensity of musket fire at the Bloody Angle.

The Unwieldy Civil War Armies

As had been true throughout the war, poor communications and organization made the huge Union army too unwieldy to control from the command center. In fact, those engaged in both attack and counterattack responded slowly to changes in the field, falling apart at the corps and divisional levels. At the time, and later, such command disintegration was most often attributed to poor generalship on both sides below Grant and Lee. However, perhaps the larger point is that neither side had the slightest experience with battles of this level of intensity and scope. Nor was there a reliable means of communication between headquarters and units during the heat of widespread battle: the "brain" could not coordinate the distant reaches of the "body."

When their men broke in confusion, commanders on the spot were put under a pressure that many could not manage. At Spotsylvania, it was Gen. Richard Ewell's bad luck to be in the company of Robert E. Lee when Ewell's men retreated on their own. "God damn you, run, run, the Yankees will catch you; that's right; go as fast as you can," Ewell shouted furiously at the backs of his men. With his uncanny composure, Lee calmly reformed these troops on his own and then turned on Ewell. "You must restrain yourself; how can you expect to control your men when you have lost control of yourself? If you cannot repress your excitement, you had better retire yourself." A few days later, Lee removed Ewell from his command. Surely, many other such instances of commanders losing both self-control and command of their troops must have occurred out of sight of Lee or Grant.

A further reason for the slow and awkward movement of both armies during this campaign was the refusal of individuals and even whole regiments to sustain combat. Reacting to endless bloody combat, many men feigned dire illness, and countless others shot themselves in the hands or the arms or feet, and many others must have experienced combat paralysis—what later would be called shell shock. On the road to Spotsylvania, some veteran Union troops whose periods of enlistment were running out simply refused their officers' direct commands to advance. "[We] had done all that [we] were willing to do . . . and that was final," one soldier later wrote. At the height of battle on May 10, a Maine regiment balked en masse. Orders from their colonel "didn't move us a hair," one private wrote later. "We firmly refused to sign our death warrants or be driven or bullied further by him or any other drunken pimp." Later in the battle, a seasoned Massachusetts regiment watched fresh Bay Staters falling in waves as they advanced; when ordered to move up in support, they spontaneously marched to the rear instead.

Combat Refusal

Stalemated again at Spotsylvania, Grant pushed his army off to the south once more, arriving at weakly held Confederate positions at Cold Harbor on June 1. If Grant's army had been able to attack the next morning, Union prospects might have been promising, because the Confederate defenses were lightly manned, but his exhausted army simply could not be pushed to move that fast, so Grant postponed his attack until the following day. By then, far more of Lee's men had arrived, and they had the time to dig deep and well-fortified trenches. Recognizing the strengthened army they were to attack, many of the Union soldiers anticipated the slaughter that was bound to be their fate, and so, in the days before metal dog tags, many of them pinned slips of paper with their names and addresses on various parts of their bodies in hopes that enough of their carcasses would remain intact for their kin to be notified of their deaths after the battle.

The Slaughter at Cold Harbor

On the morning of June 3, the Union army advanced—and 7,000 of them were killed or wounded, most during the first thirty minutes of battle, while the Confederates lost only 1,500—the most lopsided Confederate victory since Fredericksburg. In his memoirs Grant admitted that this was the one battle he regretted ordering, but even then he did not tell the whole story. In the face of so much carnage, the refusal to give combat at Spotsylvania was repeated on this field. After a certain point, many, probably most of the men, either froze in place on the ground or refused to advance at all. Grant knew that he could not expect his men to charge into more Cold Harbors, so his tactics reached military stasis.

After the battle, the Union medical corps was unable to retrieve the wounded from the field because of Confederate sniping. Grant and Lee then entered an elaborate negotiation concerning the appropriate protocol for the exchange of white flags signaling a truce for the purpose of collecting the dead. This rather elegantly argued and completely unnecessary exchange lasted until the evening of June 7, four days after the battle, at which point almost all of the wounded, of course, had died.

On to the Siege at Petersburg

On the night of June 12, Grant pulled out of Cold Harbor and marched south once more in an attempt to flank Lee's army. By June 15, advanced units of the Union army reached Petersburg and took several lightly defended Confederate positions, piercing enemy lines temporarily the next day, but once again they failed to follow up on the opening. Although the Confederates were slow to move into trenches already prepared for them, the Union was even slower to attack, and so they lost any tactical advantage. By the afternoon of June 18, following several days of sporadic but bloody fighting, Grant called off the general assault he had intended. Once again, veteran troops had refused to advance. Indeed the sluggishness attributed to bad staff work was rife in the whole Union army by now. Grant realized that, after six weeks of battle, his men simply could not be pushed another step. Siege warfare was his only alternative, and the longer it lasted the greater the political consequences.

Grant had lost 65,000 men in those six weeks of relentless campaigning, well more than half of his army, while Lee lost perhaps 36,000. However, Lee had lost as great a proportion of his army, and the Union could replace fallen soldiers with new ones, while the Confederacy could not. Nevertheless, as news filtered back home about what had transpired, "Butcher" Grant, a name applied to him earlier by the press that now gained far wider usage, lost much of his previous stature as the Joshua from the Mississippi. At this juncture, exhaustion appeared, to the northern public at least, to be undermining Union manpower and morale more rapidly than it was affecting the South.

Defeatism in the North

As static and potentially endless siege warfare replaced bloody and inconclusive marching in Virginia, Abraham Lincoln, in common with all his most trusted advisors, believed that he was certain to lose the upcoming elections, so weary were northern voters becoming of the war. On August 23 he even prepared a secret memorandum on the transition of power to the next, Democratic administration, one that he feared, not without reason, would sue for peace on the basis of southern independence. "This morning, as for some days past, it seems exceedingly probable that this Administration will not be re-elected," the document read. "Then it will be my duty to so co-operate with the President elect, as to save the Union between the election and the inauguration; as he will have secured his election on such ground that he can not possibly save it afterwards." Lincoln had the full cabinet endorse this statement on its reverse side without reading it. In fact, Lincoln did not expect the victorious Democrats to cooperate, he later said, but wrote the document to clear his own conscience. War had become the engine driving everything in politics, and both were going badly for the Republicans.

On the other hand, the Democrats were badly muddled as a party. At a time when any opposition easily blurred into defeatism and disloyalty, all Democrats pushed for a peace conference and all opposed the Emancipation Proclamation. But when some argued for an armistice as a prelude to peace talks, other Democrats balked, as they realized that, once stopped, the war would not be restarted easily. Relatively few Democrats advocated recognition of southern independence, although a vocal minority, the Copperheads, led by Clement Vallandigham of Ohio, did. George McClellan, the Democratic presidential candidate, and a War Democrat, insisted on a full restoration of the Union, albeit with slavery intact, as a precondition for peace.

So powerful was the pressure of war on northern politics that the Republican Party also divided, many of the Radicals and some moderates being displeased with what they believed to be the less than fully engaged efforts of the Lincoln administration. For his part, Lincoln pushed successfully for renaming the Republican Party the National Union Party, in large part to attract disaffected War Democrat voters, another move that angered the Radicals. After flirting with ever ambitious Secretary of the Treasury Salmon P. Chase, the Radicals met in May 1864 and nominated John C. Frémont, the failed general who had been the first Republican presidential candidate in 1856, to oppose both Lincoln and the Democrats. A few weeks later, after the regular Republican convention renominated Lincoln, the Radical faction set a new date in late September for reconvening an alternative convention, fully anticipating another summer of inconclusive bloodletting on the field of battle. Wartime politics were in this manner divisively ferocious combat by other means, and Abraham Lincoln had good reason for his deepening gloom about his immediate political future.

Confederate Political Problems

Jefferson Davis faced intensifying political problems of his own. In the Confederacy, however, political parties had not emerged to express and channel dissent. There, members of the Confederate Congress, Vice President Alexander Stephens, and several state governors, notably Joseph E. Brown of Georgia and Zebulon Vance of North Carolina, long had attacked many Confederate policies such as conscription and the suspension of habeas corpus, often on the grounds of states' rights. As war weariness increased in 1864, southern peace advocates emerged, rather like those in the North. The best known was William W. Holden, who proposed to take North Carolina out of the war and out of the Confederacy, in effect calling for a separate surrender to the Union. Though Holden could not carry his state with him, a kind of neutralism spread through much of the Confederacy, a popular sentiment to withdraw from the war, inferentially abandoning the Confederate rebellion.

Sherman Takes Atlanta

By July 1864, paralleling Grant at Petersburg, William T. Sherman's western army was also engaged in what promised to be protracted siege warfare in front of the Confederate railroad and industrial center of Atlanta, Georgia. Sherman had gotten there, however, with far less loss of life, inflicting about 28,000 casualties on the Confederates while suffering 25,000. In the ghastly statistics of warfare, all those dead young Union men amounted to "only" 38 percent of Grant's losses.

THE ATLANTA CAMPAIGN. While Grant attacked in the East, Sherman marched on Atlanta, using flanking maneuvers to push the Confederates into Atlanta with far fewer casualties than Grant's army suffered. After a frustrating siege, several Confederate attacks, and a final movement to the rear of the Confederate forces, Sherman's army took Atlanta on September 2, 1864, rescuing both northern morale and the reelection of Abraham Lincoln.

Sherman's army had advanced this deep into Georgia during a three-month-long campaign that covered nearly 100 miles. At the onset, Sherman understood exactly what Grant expected of him. "I will not let side issues draw me off from your main plan," he wrote Grant, "in which I am to knock Joe Johnston, and . . . the resources of the enemy. I would ever bear in mind that Johnston is at all times to be kept so busy that he cannot send any part of his command" to reinforce Lee.

With one exception, Sherman used movement and indirection to push deeper into his opponent's territory, repeatedly sliding his men around to the left of Confederate positions rather than attacking them directly in the Grant mode. That exception was the June 27, 1864, assault on fortified Confederate heights at Kennesaw Mountain, which produced a smaller-scale Cold Harbor. Sherman lost 3,000 men in a couple of hours. Afterward he wrote to his wife, with a coldness that may or may not have expressed all he was actually feeling, "I begin to regard the death and mangling of a couple of thousand men as a small affair, a kind of morning dash—and it may be well that we become so hardened." Shortly after the battle, Sherman resumed his flanking movements, and Johnston abandoned Kennesaw Mountain without another fight. It was as if Sherman temporarily had forgotten what he had learned about avoiding direct attacks on entrenched enemies. In a sense he had reverted for a moment to the illusion of annihilation.

Rather than launching vainglorious assaults against his advancing enemy, Johnston used Fabian tactics to slow Sherman's advance and keep his own

AFTER FIRING THE CAUTIOUS Joseph E. Johnston as his commander in the West, Jefferson Davis replaced him with the bold and reckless John Bell Hood. Following several unsuccessful attacks on William T. Sherman's army, Hood was compelled to abandon Atlanta on September 1, 1864, thus mightily aiding the reelection of Abraham Lincoln. While Sherman marched south, Hood moved north, eventually leading his army into total destruction.

army intact by well-executed retreats. But "giving away" sacred southern soil rather than offering battle grated on Confederate public opinion and on Jefferson Davis as failing in the ideologically all-important honor department. Finally, on July 17, Davis fired Johnston and replaced him with the brave but impetuous John Bell Hood, who did Sherman the enormous favor of attacking the Union trenches three times in nine days—at Peach Tree Creek on July 20, directly before Atlanta on July 22, and at Ezra Church on July 28—squandering 13,000 of his men, while the Union lost 6,000. Rather than risking his own frontal assault in return, Sherman subsequently bombarded Atlanta for five weeks, a protracted and inconclusive posture that contributed to war weariness in the North.

But then, on the night of August 25, Sherman's men marched out of their trenches on a long flanking movement to the south of Atlanta. At first Hood thought that Sherman's empty trenches signaled a Union retreat, but after a corps of his army lost the battle of Jonesboro south of the city, thereby notifying him where Sherman's army actually had gone, Hood had to blow up his powder magazines and retreat from Atlanta, lest he be surrounded.

On September 2, after his army entered Atlanta, Sherman wired to Washington with his usual verbal flair: "Atlanta is ours, and fairly won." Suddenly electrified, northern opinion swung back behind the war. Sherman's victory in effect reelected Lincoln.

Subsequently, the smashing victories of the troops of the pugnacious Phil Sheridan over Jubal T. Early's forces in the Shenandoah Valley during September and October only added to northern euphoria. Pursuing the theory of exhaustion, Sheridan's men systematically burned out both military and civilian

THESE RUINS OF THE GEORGIA RAILROAD station greeted Sherman's troops as they marched into Atlanta on September 2, 1864. John Bell Hood's reserves of ordnance had been stored on trains that never left Atlanta. Withdrawing, the Confederates set fire to the cars to keep them out of Union hands, leading to volcanic explosions and widespread fires in the city.

targets, destroying thousands of farms and their crops. The great breadbasket of Virginia was no more, and Lee's army, as well as the citizens of Richmond and other Virginia cities, would go increasingly hungry in the months to follow.

Immediately after taking Atlanta, Sherman quite consciously heightened the war of exhaustion. He drew up plans to expel the citizens of the city and turn it into a huge Union military base. Although this project served some military purposes, Sherman knew that the main impact would be in the realm of psychological warfare. Anticipating southern reactions, he wrote on September 4 to Washington, "If the people raise a howl against my barbarity and cruelty, I will answer that war is war and not popularity seeking. If they want peace they and their relatives must stop the war."

Sherman's Psychological Warfare

Far more than casual rhetoric, Sherman's verbal assault, when combined with military aggression, amounted to a measured campaign of mass terror. Sherman intended to demoralize the civilian population of the South, who in turn would let their male kin in the army know the humiliating shapes of defeat that Sherman's army was visiting on the Confederate heartland, thereby disheartening them.

As his first act, Sherman offered John Bell Hood a ten-day truce to accept Atlanta's refugees into southern lines. Hood was, as Sherman had intended, infuriated by what he called this "unprecedented . . . studied and ingenious cruelty." In response, Sherman did everything he could to drive a jagged dagger into southern morale. In his correspondence, which he made sure to share with journalists, he stated his intent quite bluntly, that to defeat the Confederate armies, "we must prepare the way to reach them in their inmost recesses," those hidden pockets of fear that were not merely material. Sounding like the King James version of Jeremiah or Isaiah, the irreligious Sherman proclaimed: "You cannot qualify war in harsher terms than I will. War is cruelty, and you cannot refine it; and those who brought war into our country deserve all the curses and maledictions a people can pour on it. . . . You might as well appeal against the thunderstorm as against these terrible hardships of war. . . . To stop the war . . . can only be done by admitting that it began in error and is perpetuated in pride."

Following a visit from Jefferson Davis, Hood (and Davis) believed that if he headed north and destroyed Sherman's supply lines, Hood could force the Yankees to abandon Atlanta, thus also helping northern Democrats in the upcoming election. Such an action would further complement a similar move already underway in Missouri. Sterling Price had taken advantage of the Confederate resurgence in Arkansas to invade Missouri on September 19 with a hodgepodge of conventional troops, militia, and guerrillas. He hoped to stun the North by reclaiming his home state. By this means, the rebels might yet begin to salvage the war in the West. In Georgia, Sherman dispatched 40,000 soldiers to chase Hood, without success. He then recalled his troops and prepared to abandon his supply lines and march to the south on his own grand raid.

Exploring with considerable harsh insight the meanings of the abandonment and betrayal he was visiting on the enemy, Sherman planned his great raid into the heart of Dixie. With rather grim and even sadistic anticipation, he

Sherman's March to the Sea

SHERMAN'S "MARCH TO THE SEA" and up through the Carolinas. Sherman's famous raid intentionally terrorized the Confederacy, destroying enormous amounts of southern property, demoralizing civilians and almost certainly shortening the war. The war east of the Appalachians ended when Joseph E. Johnston surrendered to Sherman at Durham Station, N.C., April 26, 1865.

wrote to Gen. James H. Wilson on October 19, "I am going into the very bowels of the Confederacy, and propose to leave a trail that will be recognized fifty years hence." He added to Gen. George H. Thomas, "already the papers in Georgia begin to howl at being abandoned, and will howl still more before they are done."

John Bell Hood ignored Sherman in Atlanta and continued to march north to reclaim Kentucky. Sterling Price, following two weeks of small but sharp engagements, was already in danger of being driven from Missouri, and that, in fact, would be his fate: but Hood's army posed a far graver threat than did Price's raiders. In response, Sherman dispatched Thomas, his most dependable lieutenant, with about a third of his army, to block Hood. With no significant enemy force in sight, Sherman planned his march to the Georgia coast, not to make war against an army, but to pulverize the very notion of southern independence and rebel pride. His troops would fan out and destroy everything of material value, cutting a 60-mile-wide swath through the heart of the fertile Georgia countryside.

Grant and Lincoln, who found such disengagement from the enemy army rather too unconventional, tried to alter Sherman's planning to encourage him to go after Hood first, but Sherman almost entirely convinced them he could bring off his project. He then cut his communications with Grant and Lincoln, lest they try to change his plans at the last moment, and set off on his march to Savannah, which he gave to Lincoln as a Christmas present. The following spring, Sherman's army marched northward through the Carolinas, destroying the plantation land and buildings of the South Carolina gentry on whose patrician doorsteps he and his men laid blame for starting the war.

All along the route of their march through Georgia and the Carolinas, Sherman's army burned crops and fences and did a fair share of pillaging, enough to alarm many of Sherman's subordinate commanders. Sherman himself reveled in the freebooting of the foot soldiers, who in turn admired him all the more for allowing them such an orgy of destruction. But, unlike many armies let loose on unprotected enemy populations, this one did not destroy everything. Although Sherman's men robbed alike from rich and poor, black and white, they rarely burned down the houses of civilians who remained at home, unless the houses were owned by wealthy and leading figures. They raped or killed few white civilians. Yet, Sherman wanted to advertise that his army would do anything he willed; he knew he was considered crazy and believed his evil reputation would accelerate the level of psychological as well as material destruction. From an authentic wellspring of anger and loathing, applied with a cool intuitive intelligence, Sherman knew how to apply military means to penetrate the southern heart with fear and dread. His ferocious strategy may well have shortened the war, and thus the larger moral meanings of his great campaigns were extremely complex. With Grant both taciturn and trapped at Petersburg, the eloquently destructive Sherman became the beau ideal of a victorious Union general in northern public opinion.

As Sherman's foragers—his "bummers"—advanced, terror preceded them. The Confederates could scrape together only a ragtag cavalry under Gen. Joseph Wheeler to offer token opposition to Sherman, and although Governor Joseph E. Brown called eloquently for a *levée en masse* of Georgia men, almost none came forward. Instead, disorganized civilians awaited the Vandal hordes with a fear as dreadful psychologically as that produced by the burning, robbing, and plundering that the Union troops often enacted when they arrived. Many Union officers agreed with the opinion that Capt. O. M. Poe entered in his diary, that their soldiers stripped the local population of their dignity along with their goods, creating a human landscape "perfectly pitiable to witness," and yet, even the most civilized of Union officers would not halt the rampage, in part because it was clearly producing the demoralizing effect that Sherman had intended. Moments of humanity only accentuated the frightfulness of the Union advance. For example, one evening Mrs. Bessie Cromwell had corps commander O. O. Howard, the most avowedly Christian of Union generals, to tea while his men carried on their work. "While General Howard sat at the table and asked God's blessing," Cromwell later recounted, "the sky was red from the flames of burning houses."

Quite often, even the veneer of civility disappeared. One Monroe County, Georgia, woman recorded the damage the Yankees inflicted on her home in a rather typical visit. "The Yankees broke up and split up two of my bureau drawers," Mrs. Walton later wrote her daughter. "They took all my meat, sugar, coffee, flour, knives & forks, spoons. . . . They broke up my caster, carried off the pepper box. . . . They took all of my corn, hogs, killed the goats, took chickens. . . . They took all my home-spun dresses & one smarter one, they took all my shoes & stockings . . . scarf . . . needles, thimble, scissors & thread." They did not rape or beat her nor burn down her house. Nevertheless, in 1912, when recounting this incident yet again, she wrote, "my indignation still gets at a fever when I talk about it." The terror, of which wanton physical destruction was just the material manifestation, left scars that never healed, which helps explain the longevity and bitterness of the Lost Cause ideology and southern Yankee-hating, a deep-seated anger that has never entirely dissipated.

Hood and Thomas in Tennessee

As Sherman was marching toward Savannah, he worried, along with everyone else in the Union, about the northward march of John Bell Hood, with his 39,000 soldiers, into Tennessee. George Thomas's army of 60,000 was divided into two portions, and Hood managed to flank two corps commanded by John Schofield out of their advanced position south of Nashville, where Thomas was encamped. Schofield retreated to Franklin and dug in. At this point, on November 30, Hood's lust for combat caused him to abandon the possibilities for another flanking movement, and he decided instead to make a frontal assault on Schofield. At the disastrous battle of Franklin, Hood's army lost 6,000 men, including 12 general officers killed or wounded and captured, to Schofield's 2,000. Flanking the enemy after rather than before an utterly unnecessary battle, Hood then marched his men toward Nashville, where he entrenched his much weakened army, now down to about 23,000 men, opposite Thomas's far better supplied force of about 60,000, and awaited a Union attack.

The Battle of Nashville

At this point, concerned lest Hood slip around Nashville and march farther up into Kentucky, Grant was almost desperate for Thomas to attack. But "Slow Trot," as he was nicknamed by his peers, was not to be hurried. He had a cavalry to mount adequately, and various elements of his army needed better organization, and so forth and so on. Grant grew increasingly frustrated with Thomas, combining direct orders with almost plaintive pleas in his telegrams to him: "Attack Hood at once and wait no longer for the remnant of your cav-

AFTER THE DISASTROUS BATTLE OF FRANKLIN, on November 30, 1864, where John Bell Hood's Confederate army lost 6,000 men, including twelve generals, Hood marched north and encamped his remaining 23,000 men (seen here) outside of Nashville, where this Union army, numbering 60,000, faced him. After deliberate planning, on December 14, Union general George H. Thomas finally ordered the attack that destroyed and scattered Hood's army in one of the most decisive victories of the war.

alry. There is a great danger of delay," ran one message; a later one read, "Why not attack at once? . . . Now is one of the finest opportunities ever presented of destroying" a Confederate army. Thomas replied that he could not attack during the current ice storms. By December 14 Grant was fed up, so he sent John A. Logan, a political general but an excellent one, with orders to replace Thomas in command. Even then, Grant remained so anxious that he set off from Virginia to Washington that same night, on the first leg of a journey to take personal charge in Nashville.

Finally, on the morning of December 15, Thomas ordered his assault, and over the next two days, his men participated in the most climactic battle of the war. Hood lost another 6,000 men; the Union lost about 2,000. The remnants of Hood's army fled in disorder rather than retreating in force. Thousands deserted on the way back south. Hood's army had indeed disintegrated, and now Grant could only praise a man who so recently had driven him to distraction.

All these Union campaigns wore down the southern economy, manpower pool, and morale, as they were intended to do. Yet, with their backs to the wall, the Confederates mounted a powerful defense, and in many ways one should emphasize their pride and resistance rather than their accommodation

Confederate Morale in 1864

of themselves to the defeat that we all know was to come. Nothing was preordained. As late as August 1864, the outcome of the war remained in serious question. Yet, taken as a whole, for the Confederacy the war after Gettysburg and Vicksburg was one long trial, as the experience of the Army of Northern Virginia demonstrated.

During the entire winter of 1863–1864, a major evangelical revival, as explained in chapter 7, swept the Confederate soldiers in their winter encampments in both the East and the West. Surely noble men fighting for freedom and a Christian commonwealth far superior to that of the dishonorable and materialistic Yankee aggressors would be rewarded with final victory if only they could cleanse themselves of sin and rededicate themselves to God's purposes. This collective wave of piety amounted to a "revitalization movement," excellent for morale in the face not only of a powerful enemy but also of a shortage of food, shoes, soap, and other basic supplies. Such thinking would preclude even considering surrender until all hope was gone among those who clung tightly to the faith, in this case starting at the top, with the deeply pious duo of General Lee and President Davis.

In public, Robert E. Lee maintained his equipoise and exhorted his men to carry on the fight for independence, while privately even he sank into considerable gloom. On November 23, 1863, he wrote a trusted old friend, "God will release us from the grievous punishment with which he has thought proper to afflict us. . . . I pray it may be soon! In the meantime we must be patient & all do what we can—Our enemies are strong at every point." With such religiosity and loin girding, bolstered by an abiding faith in the justness of their cause and the power of their arms, Lee and his men prepared with steely resolve to face whatever might come.

During the terrible Union campaign of May and June 1864, Lee's men fought with considerable optimism and energy. As late as Spotsylvania, one army private insisted, "we can whip any Army the yankees can bring against us if the Lord is willing." Still, the soldiers could see what was likely to come, which made them deeply anxious. In early June, Lee wrote to A. P. Hill, a corps commander, "something more is necessary than adhering to lines and defensive positions. We ought to attack, for if the enemy is allowed to continue setting the terms of combat, we shall at last be obliged to take refuge behind the works of Richmond and stand a siege, which would be but a work of time." Many of Lee's soldiers shared this apprehension. "I see nothing but lying here in the trenches & terrible fighting in the end," wrote Georgia Capt. F. M. Croker to his wife on July 16, 1864, while J. F. Maides, a North Carolina private, wrote on September 23: "This is certainly the most cruel war that has ever been waged & instead of getting better it gets worse every day it lasts."

Lee's Army Crumbles   As the siege of Petersburg lengthened and material conditions worsened, Lee's army slowly crumbled. In partial response, even the high-minded Lee proposed legalizing and enlarging black-market trading with the Union, so scarce had supplies become. "Many officers have too many selfish views . . . to undertake the task of instructing & disciplining their commands," Lee noted in

ELABORATE ENTRENCHMENTS were dug by both sides during the prolonged siege at Petersburg, which lasted from June 15, 1864, until April 3, 1865, when the Confederates finally abandoned their positions, and Richmond, a week before surrendering at Appomattox. Shown here is a *fraise*, a defense consisting of pointed stakes projecting at a sharp angle from a rampart.

a letter to Jefferson Davis on August 13, 1864. They still went off on what he considered silly social engagements when they should have been sacrificing their all for their nation. What had become indispensable, Lee believed, was hyperdiscipline—deep habits of obedience and service—that might enable even so small an army to stand heroically in the pass against a strengthening enemy.

Exhortations from the top notwithstanding, more and more Confederate soldiers voted with their feet to desert the army. From 50,000 men present for duty in July 1864, the number was down to 38,000 by September 10. By pushing hard to recapture deserters and men absent with or without leave, and by expanding the draft age to between seventeen and fifty and closing almost all occupational exemptions to the draft, such as those for railroad, mill, and telegraph workers, the army increased to 62,000 by the end of November. This was growth in numbers but not in prime manpower, much of which lay buried at such places as Chancellorsville and Spotsylvania.

And yet, many soldiers insisted that army morale was better than that back home. "Shall we submit quietly, and go back into the union . . . or shall we fight it out," a South Carolinian asked his sister back home in December 1864. "The people must make up their mind. . . . We are a ruined people if we give up. There is a chance if we all do our duty." Grim determination struggled with despair.

Confederate Home-front Morale Plunges

This soldier demonstrated a relatively common feeling in the Army of Northern Virginia; however, many on the home front seemed to be losing heart. As well as producing severe shortages, especially when Sheridan burned the Shenandoah Valley, by now war had produced hyperinflation and other forms of severe economic dislocation over most of the South. For example, the government continued to impress crops at well below market price. During the summer of 1864, these fixed prices were increased so that, for example, flour brought $168 per bushel, up from $28. Yet, even the larger figure still lagged far behind the market price of $400 in Richmond. Such price-fixing policies created resentment against the government, active black markets, hoarding, and lying.

The Distress of Confederate Women

For many Confederate women, the war led to physical distress and depression. Mary Greenhow Lee of Winchester wrote that so much war had made her "completely unhinged." Her neighbor, Cornelia McDonald, reported: "I had lost the power of resistance and all my self command." She was also growing thin from lack of food. At the opposite end of the emotional spectrum of reactions to endless warfare, many commentators noted that conspicuous selfishness and frivolity were on the rise among civilians, especially among wealthy women. Robert E. Lee complained that even his own daughters were failing to make appropriate sacrifices for the nation. "Revelry and carousal" among the Virginia gentry, the *Richmond Enquirer* observed, amounted to "shameful displays of indifference to the national calamity." The poor deeply resented the banquets that, whether or not intentionally, appeared to mock their poverty and hunger.

Increasingly, Confederate women, fed up with the desolation of their domestic sphere, urged their men to give up the good fight and come back to the hearth, at least for a while. They often vacillated between despair and hope, frequently in the same letter, but the impact of their missives beckoned the men homeward. Thousands of letters rang with such advice as "I think you have done your share in this war," and "you have served long enough to rest awhile," and "the truth is . . . you must come." Thousands did, even though their wives may have intended them to return home and help out as a sort of intermission in combat. Given the fine point of what may have been intended as only temporary absences without leave, Jefferson Davis had to restrain their commander from shooting too many deserters, although there are no reliable statistics on just how many executions Lee authorized.

The U.S. Election of 1864

While southern morale crumbled (interrupted by periods of renewed hope, especially when any good news came in from the battlefield), northern expectations soared. Sherman's triumph in Atlanta and the other Union victories at Mobile Bay (taken by Adm. David Farragut's fleet in August) and the Shenandoah Valley rescued Lincoln from what had looked like a smashing defeat and produced his great electoral victory in November 1864. The Radical anti-Lincoln party that was backing John C. Frémont simply disbanded. The Democrats, branded as the peace at any price party, and their presidential candidate, George McClellan, fared abysmally. Lincoln won by 400,000 popular votes—winning 55 percent of the ballots—and carried all the states except Delaware, New Jersey, and Kentucky. Many soldiers had been furloughed to return home to vote, and in other states Republican administrations had sent ballot boxes to the front: Lincoln won 78 percent of the soldier vote, demonstrating the army's deep commitment to the war effort. After the election, the Republican majority in the Senate was 41 to 10, and in the House of Representatives, an astonishing 145 to 40.

In fact, George McClellan probably would have seen the war through to victory, but the well-organized antiwar arm of the party had dominated the writing of the Democrats' platform, declaring the "experiment" of war a total "failure" and demanding an immediate cease-fire, followed by a national convention to negotiate a peace treaty. In exchange for their support of McClellan, the peace

ABRAHAM LINCOLN,

ANDREW JOHNSON,

TO STRENGTHEN ITS ELECTORAL APPEAL in 1864, the Republicans called themselves the National Union Party and nominated Andrew Johnson, a Tennessee Democrat, for vice president. With the help of 78 percent of the soldier ballots, the Lincoln-Johnson ticket swept to victory with an impressive 55 percent of the popular vote, and the National Union Party won lopsided victories in both houses of Congress.

forces also named the vice-presidential candidate, the outspoken Copperhead Ohio congressman George H. Pendleton. For his part McClellan, in a letter accepting the nomination, insisted that "the union must be preserved at all hazards," and that he "could not look in the face of my gallant comrades and tell them that their . . . sacrifices . . . had been in vain." Yet, McClellan had been forced at least to accommodate antiwar Democrats by stressing future peace negotiations. If he had won, McClellan might well have been pressured into suing for peace—in part because his election would have reenergized the Confederates and demoralized the Union troops. By March 1865, when he would have been inaugurated, the Confederates would nevertheless still have been on the ropes, and McClellan could have made himself into a national hero by winning the war—that is, if the Lincoln administration had not already won it through redoubled attacks. In any event, after the fall of Atlanta, public opinion turned in favor of Lincoln and a vigorous war policy. Unfortunately for McClellan's reputation, and that of his divided party, he and the Democratic Party would be branded as pro-Confederate and traitorous long after the war ended.

Confederate Desertion Increases

For all Confederates, the unequivocal reelection of Abraham Lincoln came as a crushing blow. Four more years of war were now the best that the Confederates might anticipate, as the northern Democrats, with whom the Confederates might have negotiated peace, had been soundly defeated. After this point, Lee forced himself to recognize that many of the increasing numbers of deserters were not merely unpatriotic slackers and latecomers but brave veteran troops. By February 1865 the army was down to 50,000, and Lee issued a general clemency order to all deserters. Instead of bringing the soldiers back, this order encouraged more to leave, as they believed that in their numbers they would escape punishment. Two months later the army had dropped to 35,000 men present for duty.

If significant numbers of Union soldiers had refused orders to advance into fire during the spring campaign, this Great Skedaddle—as it well might be called—was on an even larger scale. Half the army had taken themselves home at a rate of about 10,000 each month. These men believed that all hope for southern independence was lost and that they had warred enough to retain their honor even though they had departed without permission. Many might have left with the intention to defend—now as guerrillas—increasingly exposed parts of the Confederacy near their homes. In effect, the surrender of the Army of Northern Virginia was a slow affair that began from the bottom up.

Peace Feelers: The Hampton Roads Conference

At the same time, peace advocates in the Confederacy increased pressure for a negotiated end to the war. These forces had long been concentrated in Georgia and North Carolina, but in Richmond several Confederate congressmen and Vice President Alexander H. Stephens—who was barely on speaking terms with Jefferson Davis—were among their ranks.

Well aware of both the crisis in the field and political divisions over continuing the war, Davis responded favorably to an offer carried to Richmond by Francis P. Blair Sr., a seasoned advisor to Lincoln, to convene a peace conference. Davis delegated Stephens and two other peace advocates, Senator R. M. T.

Hunter from Virginia and Assistant Secretary of War John A. Campbell, to pass through Union lines and meet with Lincoln at Hampton Roads, Virginia. At that conference, on February 3, 1865, Lincoln pledged that if the Confederates agreed to reunion, emancipation, and the disbanding of their army, he would guarantee nonpunitive postwar treatment of the rebels and promise his support for compensated emancipation. For their part the Confederates were seeking a cease-fire to precede further negotiations premised on southern independence. With no basis for further discussions, the conference collapsed in a few hours.

It is possible that, being almost certain that the negotiations would fail, Davis had sent three peace advocates to discredit them and their cause. At the same time, Davis might have thought it was just barely possible that Lincoln might prove flexible and that, in such an event, he would be more likely to respond to known peace advocates. In any case, after the negotiations collapsed, there was a resurgence of pro-war energy in the South and in the inner circles of the Davis administration. This almost evangelical faith never ended, even as the armies in the field deserted and surrendered.

Their peace option gone and their white manpower pool vaporizing, Confederate officials turned with a certain desperation to their only alternative—black soldiers. Blacks had long been used to build fortifications, and the Confederate Congress had passed a law on February 27, 1864, that allowed the army to impress slaves without the agreement of their masters, although this law was infrequently implemented. By the fall of 1864, Robert E. Lee was calling for a quasi-military black labor corps of 5,000 men, even suggesting they be paid some sort of wage, although this portion of the plan did not become law. By December 20, about 2,000 at most had ever reported, and so many deserted that perhaps 1,200 men remained of this rather ambitious project.

Confederate Experiments with Black Troops

Early in 1864, when Gen. Patrick Cleburne, an Irish immigrant, had proposed arming slaves and freeing them in the process, Jefferson Davis suppressed the document to save the support of the master class. By November 7 that year, in his annual address to the Congress, Davis hinted at arming slaves, "should the alternative ever be presented of subjugation or the employment of the slave as a soldier." Davis even argued that while legally the slave existed "merely as property," he bore "another relation with the State—that of a person." Personhood—citizenship—was precisely what slavery had forbidden, and therefore, even this late in the war, Davis's proposal aroused enormous opposition. "If slaves will make good soldiers our whole theory of slavery is wrong," Gen. Howell Cobb of Georgia insisted on January 8, 1865, and the majority of slaveholders agreed.

Nevertheless, on February 10, 1865, with Lee's private support, the Confederate Congress considered a bill to arm slaves. After a long and acrimonious debate, the bill passed on March 13, albeit not granting freedom for military service, a provision Davis added by what one historian has termed "bureaucratic fiat." Lee for one was convinced that African American men possessed suitable "physical qualifications" and had acquired "long habits of obedience and subordination" that ought to guarantee the requisite discipline to make them useful soldiers. Secure in their white supremacy, men such as Davis and Lee could support arming and even freeing blacks, whom they believed they still could continue to control. Of course Lee and Davis were also realistic enough to realize that the Union had already armed so many southern blacks that they might as well try to scoop up some of those who remained.

Even though they knew they were facing increasingly desperate odds, many masters and soldiers opposed this measure. "From today I date the history of our downfall as a nation," a Virginia artilleryman entered in his diary on March 16, while on February 18 a North Carolinian had written to his mother, "I did not volunteer my services to fight for a free negroes country but to fight for a free white mans free country."

But then, law or no law, nothing much happened. Masters kept their slaves at home. During the last week in March, about a company of black men began to drill, without arms, in the streets of Richmond. Nearly 186,000 of their brothers were under arms in the enemy army and navy by this time. Slaves, too, had voted with their feet, and then their entire bodies and hearts, to support the Union cause against their old masters.

Lee Vetoes Guerrilla Warfare

On the other hand, when it came to prolonging Confederate resistance through guerrilla warfare, Lee vetoed the idea. At the end of the war, on April 9, 1865, Edward Porter Alexander, Lee's youthful and highly capable chief of artillery, dared to advance to Lee the idea that some of the younger men in the staff had been considering: "We would scatter like rabbits and partridges in the woods," and elude the Union army, Alexander proposed. Clearly aware of the disasters guerrilla war had spread in much of the South, Lee replied to him with a word picture of the brutalities of such warfare. "The men would have no rations & would be under no discipline. They would have to plunder & rob . . . the country would be full of lawless bands." And the enemy cavalry would pursue Confederate guerrillas "with fresh rapine & destruction." Back in Richmond on April 20, eleven days after his surrender, Lee reiterated to a desperate Davis—who had polled his cabinet on the subject—that guerrilla warfare, would offer "no prospect of achieving . . . independence." Such mobocracy would be no way to end the experiment in the well-regulated Christian commonwealth that men of station had wanted to found. Better to lose the war than honor.

Lincoln's Second Inaugural Address

What, given the carnage of this struggle, did northerners believe their approaching victory had won for them in the realm of honor? On March 4, 1865, when it came time for his second inaugural address, Lincoln took as his task to frame an appropriate moral justification for the long years of bloodshed he had superintended. Though the war had begun on limited grounds—the extension or nonextension of the peculiar institution—Lincoln now argued, "All knew that [slavery] constituted the cause of the war." Yet, neither side had anticipated that the "fundamental and astounding" act of emancipation would result. Both sides prayed for moral guidance from the same God, Lincoln continued, going on, however, to insist that it "may seem strange that any man should dare to ask a just God's assistance in wringing their bread from the sweat of other men's faces." Catching himself making a sweeping moral denunciation of southerners, Lincoln then universalized the guilt of slaveholding. "This terrible war [was] the woe due to those by whom the offense came." In this formulation, the war was just punishment for *all* white Americans. Lincoln included northerners in the lists of the guilty, for through moral indifference that amounted to complicity they had allowed slavery to continue for all those generations.

If all had been guilty in the past, now all Americans were to be redeemed through blood sacrifice that would continue "until all the wealth piled by the bond-man's two hundred and fifty years of unrequited toil be sunk, and until every drop of blood drawn with the lash, shall be paid by another drawn with the sword." Almost certainly without being aware of the parallel, Lincoln had addressed the moral meaning of this war in Calvinist language that was strikingly similar to that uttered by John Brown as he mounted those scaffold stairs in 1859, when he foretold that the nation could be redeemed from the horror of slavery only with an equal remission of blood.

At the end of his sermon about collective white sin, Lincoln added his famous conclusion, "With malice toward none; with charity for all . . . let us strive to finish the work we are in; to bind up a nation's wounds [and to] achieve a just and a lasting peace." Only after enough blood had been shed could peace be made—and only God could judge the sufficiency. Yet, Lincoln did not venture to say how the newly freed African American women and men would fit into the embrace of the redeemed nation. Clearly, as he spoke he was thinking of forgiveness for white southerners when they should return to the national embrace, but when it came time to go beyond guilt about the sin of slaveholding, what would redemption for blacks and forgiveness for whites mean in actual political and social practice?

The Collapse of the Confederacy

The last campaign of the war, when it finally came, was something of a military anticlimax. Inexperienced troops, many young boys and old men, hungry and poorly clothed, manned the Confederate lines, while the Union army was augmenting in strength. In Richmond, civilian morale approached panic. During March 1865, long lines of civilians and soldiers gathered at the doors of the Confederate Treasury Department to redeem sixty (and later seventy) paper dollars for single silver-dollar coins that had not circulated since the start of the war. These coins would be hard to transport South should Richmond fall, and they also would retain purchasing power in lands controlled by Yankees when Confederate paper money no longer would. It did not take much wit to figure out the dire implications of this action.

Inflation skyrocketed as well. Even President Jefferson Davis sold his carriage horses for $12,000 in paper money. Some patriotic businessmen bought them for $240 in hard money and presented them back to Davis. People noted Davis's straits, and they also began to see the Confederate first lady's gowns and laces appearing for resale in downtown shop windows.

The endgame at Petersburg began on March 25 with a Confederate attack on Fort Stedman, one of the strongest fortifications along the Union line of trenches. Responding in considerable measure to the rapid approach of

BEFORE THEY ABANDONED RICHMOND on the night of April 2, 1865, the Confederates, or perhaps local civilians or escaped Union prisoners, set fires that destroyed a huge swath of the center of the city. Black cavalrymen were among the first Union troops to enter the formerly proud Confederate capital city the next morning.

William T. Sherman's army that had already marched well into North Carolina, Lee believed that he could not remain in place for long, and so, even knowing the weakened state of his army, he went on the offensive. Following an initial breakthrough, the Confederates fell back after taking nearly 5,000 casualties within a few hours. On March 29, Union troops including Gen. Phil Sheridan's dismounted cavalry pushed around the right of Lee's lines and, on April 1, they nearly annihilated the Confederate defenders at Five Forks, in a battle nearly as one sided and conclusive as Nashville. The following day, April 2, Grant gave the order to charge all along the line. This assault, which came at the cost of 4,000 Union casualties, drove the Confederates back into their last line of trenches.

The Fall of Richmond

That night, rather than await one final, disastrous assault, what remained of Lee's army retreated westward, evacuating Richmond after setting fire to the public buildings. On April 3, black Union cavalry were among the first troops to enter the fallen capital, followed in short order by Abraham Lincoln, who was greeted as the earthly Messiah by jubilant blacks. Most whites remained indoors and out of sight.

Surrender at Appomattox

Lee planned to move rapidly to join forces with the other remaining Confederate soldiers under the command of Joseph Johnston, who were unsuccessfully engaging William T. Sherman's advancing force in North Carolina. But as Lee's slogged westward, fast-moving Union troops cut off big chunks of the Army of Northern Virginia. Finally, on April 8, Sheridan moved around the remnants of Lee's demoralized army and blocked its retreat at the country railroad junction and county seat of Appomattox Court House. On April 9 Lee surrendered his army, now numbering less than 20,000 men. Grant offered politically uncond tional but personally generous terms, allowing the men, all of whom he paroled, to take their horses home with them and the officers to keep their side arms.

What would surrender mean? What sort of reconstruction process would the South and the nation as a whole undergo? About this central question, massive confusion abounded on all sides as the war ground to a close.

Lee embedded a political position that contained more resistance than capitulation in the general order that he issued on April 10, thanking and disbanding his army. Although he had been compelled to surrender on their behalf, Lee asserted that the Confederate national spirit had not been conquered. Pledging his men his "increasing admiration for your constancy and devotion to your country," Lee assured them that their imperishable "valor and devotion" should not have led to the "useless sacrifice" of a militarily hopeless last stand. To the contrary, Lee began his general order with a sentence that almost immediately became legend: "After four years of arduous service, marked by unsurpassed courage and fortitude, the Army of Northern Virginia has been compelled to yield to overwhelming numbers and resources." This argument assuaged southern honor while forwarding a belief that, military defeat notwithstanding, the essential righteousness of the southern cause had never perished before the monstrous Union military machine. It was as if, in this sentence, the southern goal of independence had flown free of mere physical defeat.

At this moment the Confederacy became immortal; here was born the myth of the Lost Cause. Highly idealistic, such a position fortified southerners for whatever was to come. All was not lost; the essence of southern nationalism remained. During the ensuing decades, the Lost Cause ideology would only increase in strength, serving to bolster white southerners in their often bitter resistance to Yankee power and black participation in the ruling of southern society.

The Birth of the Lost Cause

Another marker of the confusion over the meaning of the Confederate surrender came a week later, when, on April 18, Sherman negotiated the surrender of Joseph Johnston's army, the last major Confederate force. Despite the fact that he had a copy of Grant's terms with Lee in his possession, Sherman negotiated a political treaty that called, in exchange for the disbanding of all southern military forces, for "the preservation and continuance of the [Confederate] state governments . . . the preservation to the people of all political rights . . . and freedom from further prosecution or penalties." Sherman may not have noticed that he was giving his erstwhile enemies a huge political concession, so eager was he to disband Johnston's army—a goal he believed was in keeping with Lincoln's wishes. Also, he acted on his own political principles, not wanting victory to be followed by much political change, so conservative was he on issues of race and the Constitution. At least as significantly, this treaty demonstrated the degree to which southern leaders—such as Secretary of War John C. Breckinridge (former United States vice president) and Confederate Postmaster General John H. Reagan, the two men who negotiated with Sherman—began

Johnston's Surrender

to maneuver for postwar southern power, even in the act of signing one of the treaties ending the war in ostensible Confederate defeat.

Lincoln's Assassination

At this crucial juncture, on April 14, the young actor and pro-Confederate fanatic John Wilkes Booth shot Abraham Lincoln at Ford's Theater. Another assassin stabbed Secretary of State Seward, who survived his injuries. A third man assigned to kill Vice President Johnson went on a drinking binge instead. Lincoln died the next day, and the nation plunged into mourning, while Vice President Andrew Johnson of Tennessee was sworn into office.

Lincoln's death produced great anger in the North and mixed feelings in the South. Although some southerners expressed sorrow, having sensed a certain magnanimity of spirit in their leading antagonist, others celebrated. For example, in South Carolina, Emma LeConte rejoiced in her diary: "Hurrah! Old Abe Lincoln has been assassinated! It may be abstractly wrong to be so jubilant but I just can't help it—After all the heaviness and gloom of yesterday [when she had received news of Lee's surrender], this blow to our enemies comes like a gleam of light." Loula Kendall Rogers of Georgia interpreted "the tyrant Lincoln's death [as] retribution from the hand of an all powerful God," and lauded John Wilkes Booth for "the boldest deed I ever heard of in fact or fiction."

In the aftermath of the act, a military court convicted eight people of conspiracy, hanging four. Booth escaped the gallows, having been shot by Union soldiers in a burning barn in Virginia while attempting to escape. But he had fired the first shot in the terrorist response to Reconstruction that would lead southern whites back to power in their section during the next decade. And

JOHN WILKES BOOTH, a twenty-seven-year-old actor, assassinated Abraham Lincoln on April 14, 1865, plunging the nation into outrage and deep sadness. *Frank Leslie's Illustrated Newspaper* portrayed Booth in April 1865. It is impossible to surmise what Lincoln's presence might have meant for the reconstruction process.

those southern women rejoicing in his act demonstrated some of the venom behind the Lost Cause ideology, born from the Confederate experience and carried forward into the next chapters of collective white southern social and political life.

As will be shown in the next chapter, Lincoln's tentative plans for postwar reconstruction were evolving right up to the evening he was shot. As was his custom, he played these political cards close to his chest, and historians have never established the essence of his plans nor how far he had gone in the privacy of his own mind into postwar planning. Not only was Lincoln unclear, but there was also no agreement in the Republican Party, much less across the North as a whole, about what to do with the defeated South and how to give ongoing political and social meaning to black emancipation. Anger and the desire for revenge against Confederates collided with an equally passionate desire to put the evils of war to rest as quickly as possible. Lincoln's death made him a martyr, even a Christ figure, mortally wounded, eerily enough, on Good Friday, as one last blood sacrifice for the Union, the symbol of the moral war he had done so much to elucidate in his second inaugural address the previous month. Unsullied by the messy postwar politics that followed his death, the saintly Lincoln remains the leading figure of the American shrine dedicated to the very best values that Americans wish their nation might embody.

Lincoln and Reconstruction

Andrew Johnson rejected Sherman's treaty as one of the first acts of his presidency, and on April 26, Joseph Johnston signed terms similar to those Grant had dictated to Lee. On May 4, in Alabama, Gen. Richard Taylor surrendered the last Confederate troops east of the Mississippi River, while Gen. Edmund Kirby Smith followed suit for Confederate forces to the west of the river on May 26. A few guerrilla bands, particularly in Kentucky and Missouri, held out for another month or two, but Union forces tracked down and killed them, with the cooperation of the local population, many of whom formerly supported the guerrillas but now believed them to be just bandits. Some, such as the celebrated James and Younger brothers of Missouri, became just that. Stand Watie, a Cherokee chief, was the last Confederate general to admit defeat when he surrendered his battalion of Cherokee, Creek, Seminole, and Osage on June 23.

Final Confederate Surrenders

Meanwhile, in one of the strangest chapters of the war, Jefferson Davis refused to surrender along with either Lee or Johnston. After the fall of Richmond, Davis fled, first by train and then by wagon, firm in the belief that he would be able to mount a military comeback, perhaps by guerrilla means. As late as May 2, he told the remnant of the government and the military that accompanied him that times were no worse than they had been during the darkest days of the American Revolution, and that if he could scrape together 3,000 fighting men, they would be "enough for a nucleus around which the whole people will rally when the panic which now afflicts them has passed away." This fantasy was greeted with complete silence, and soon all but a few officials were gone; the soldiers in Davis's guard also disappeared, some taking to banditry. Finally, on May 10, a 150-man column of the First Wisconsin Cavalry caught up to Davis near Irwinville, Georgia, and captured him while he was attempting to reach a

THE GRAND REVIEW OF THE ARMIES. On May 23, 1865, 80,000 men from the Army of the Potomac proudly marched down Pennsylvania Avenue in Washington, to be followed the next day by 65,000 men of Sherman's western army. Then, almost all the soldiers simply went home on the next available train, one of the most rapid demobilizations in military history. These grand armies would not be available for peacetime duty enforcing Union will in the South.

nearby woods, wrapped in a rain slicker, his wife's shawl covering his head in disguise. Cartoons all over the north soon dressed Davis in woman's clothing, deriding him as a dishonorable and unmanly loser. The federal authorities imprisoned Davis in Fort Monroe, Virginia. He was charged with treason, cruelty to Union prisoners, and conspiracy to assist Lincoln's assassination, but no formal trial ever occurred. Davis was released in 1867 and lived on until 1889, spending much of his time writing bitter and self-justifying memoirs.

The new president, Andrew Johnson, talked about punishing traitors, to the approval of the more radical of his congressional partners. But beyond that shared anger, the shapes of the peace to come remained unclear. Perhaps if Lincoln had lived, he might have been able to finesse this set of problems with his tremendous political skills—after all, during the war he managed to work with the Radicals, to move in their direction while charting a more moderate course.

The Union Army Disbands   In the meantime, the Union army disbanded very quickly. After the Grand Review of Grant's army on May 24 and Sherman's the following day (parades that almost entirely excluded black troops) down Pennsylvania Avenue in Washington, the vast majority of the men soon entrained for home. Within 18 months, the army went from nearly 1 million to 65,000 men. Employing large numbers of troops as a permanent army of occupation of the South was unthinkable during demobilization, as was the whole notion of a large peacetime standing army, anathema to Americans since their nation's founding. More generally, the use of the federal government to dictate the rebuilding of the South also was remote from the thinking of the majority of power holders in Washington, although the energetic Radical faction was beginning to differ and the Freedmen's Bureau was already in place, distributing food and thinking about other forms of aid, mainly temporary, for the freedmen. The victors were puzzled and increasingly conflicted about what to do with both white and black southerners. There was no consensus about the need for a policy to promote social change and racial justice, both because such beliefs were not widespread and because there was little permanent institutional experience in using government that way. The centralization and bureaucratization improvised during war was not part of anyone's peacetime thinking. After four years of passion and slaughter, amid longing for peace and a myriad of fundamental unanswered political and social questions, the future was uncharted and full of danger.

CHAPTER **10**

Northern Politics and Southern Reconstruction: 1863–1870

he war was over, but the nation-state seemed to be in ruins. For the next several years, a great political crisis ensued while northern political leaders hotly debated how to go about reunifying the disunited states. There would be many false starts and confrontations, a variety of partial solutions, and considerable anguish and bloodshed as the executive and legislative branches of the United States government fought each other as well as the recalcitrant ex-Confederates for control of the defeated South and the redefinition of the federal union.

Mixed Responses to Peace
In the spring of 1865, belief that the war had changed everything was widespread and profound. Soon after the fighting stopped, Harvard professor George Ticknor tried to explain the vast transformation that he had experienced. It appeared, Ticknor wrote, that the war had left a "great gulf between what happened since, or what was likely to happen hereafter. It does not seem as if I were living in the country in which I was born." Ticknor was right, at least for the immediate future. American society had been altered dramatically by four years of war, and in the decade to follow, a startling amount of conflict would continue to wash over the nation. Yet, in other ways, the United States had not changed in terms of many deep social, economic, and even political assumptions and practices. In time, the promise of fundamental social reform

would be stifled, and attitudes and problems rooted deep in antebellum America would reemerge, albeit often cast in new forms.

The victorious North was eager for peace. Its industrial might and larger population had helped it win the conflict, but its people, like that of the defeated Confederacy, were weary of war. The military demobilized rapidly, reaffirming Americans' traditional aversion to a large peacetime army. Thousands of Union soldiers happily and anxiously returned home to shed their military identity and resume their prewar lives and occupations. Civilians, too, tried to return to a time when words like *Vicksburg, Fredericksburg,* or *Franklin* were little more than names of faraway and obscure towns few had wanted to visit. But these place names and a host of others where so many had died and suffered would be hard to forget. Tens of thousands of fatherless families, tens of thousands of grievously maimed veterans, would long continue to bear witness to the horrors of war.

Lincoln's shocking assassination just days after Lee's surrender made forgetting and forgiving even more difficult. "It seems *too dastardly, too cruel,*" New York diarist Cornelia Jay wrote upon hearing of Lincoln's murder. "And this," she predicted, "is the end of all our leniency." The *Washington Chronicle* similarly stated: "The indignation and horror created by this foul murder will serve, more than anything else could possibly do, to destroy the feeling of commiseration and brotherly love for the misguided people of the South, and the policy of magnanimity toward the leaders of the rebellion which had taken root in the North."

The trial of John Wilkes Booth's coconspirators demonstrated the truth of these predictions. Seven men and one woman were arrested and tried for plotting to murder the president, as well as various other charges. Those charged included Mary Surratt, who owned the Washington, D.C., boardinghouse where Booth met with some of his six accomplices. A military commission, rather than a civilian jury, convicted all of the suspects, some of them on circumstantial evidence, and sentenced four, including Surratt, to death by hanging. They met their fates on July 7, 1865. Surratt was the first woman ever executed by the federal government—photographers and illustrators captured the stark image of her limp body hanging from a rope beside the three condemned men. *Harper's Weekly* described the difficulty Surratt had in mounting the scaffold and the "ghastly expression on her face." She alone died quietly; the three men struggled in their last moments of life before hundreds of spectators. With the execution and sentencing of the conspirators, *Harper's Weekly* concluded: "Thus was completed the memorable history of that conspiracy which three months ago plunged our people into the lowest depths of grief."

Postwar Trials

Soon after the trial of Lincoln's assassins, another controversial case commenced, that of Capt. Henry Wirz, commander of Andersonville prison at the end of the war. Tales of atrocities at the Confederate prison camp had begun trickling north soon after Andersonville opened its gates in February 1864. But when survivors came home and photographs of emaciated inmates circulated, the prison's awful conditions shocked northerners. Northern prisons at places

CAPT. HENRY WIRZ, commander of the notorious Andersonville prison camp. was the only high-ranking ex-Confederate executed for war crimes. This photograph. taken the day of his hanging. shows men adjusting the rope around his neck just before his death.

like Elmira, New York, Johnson's Island, Ohio, and Camp Douglas, Illinois, were terrible, too. Slightly more than 30,000 Union soldiers (15.5 percent of those imprisoned) died in Confederate prison camps, while nearly 26,000 Confederates (12 percent) died in Union camps. Still, with the war over and the South defeated, northerners ignored stories of their own brutality, as victors are wont to do.

In May 1865, federal captain Henry E. Noyes arrested Wirz and transported him to Washington, D.C., to stand trial for "impairing the health and destroying the lives of prisoners." The Wirz trial, which lasted three months, included 160 witnesses, mostly former Union prisoners, who attested to the captain's deliberate mistreatment of prisoners. Wirz's health was so poor that he spent the entire trial prostrate on a couch, rising occasionally to protest the allegations of witnesses. It hardly mattered. On November 10, 1865, Wirz was hanged. He purportedly refused an offer of amnesty in exchange for implicating President Davis in a conspiracy to murder prisoners. "Jefferson Davis had no connection with me as to what was done at Andersonville," Wirz asserted. Just before he died, Wirz reportedly told an officer directing the hanging: "I know what orders are, Major—I am being hung for obeying them."

There were other indictments against Confederates for alleged war crimes, almost all related to prisoners, and all tinged with emotion and controversy. Navy captain John Beall died on the gallows on February 24, 1865, for his 1864 attempt to free Confederate prisoners at Johnson's Island, Ohio. Another military commission tried Maj. John Gee, commander of Salisbury Prison in North Carolina, on charges of prisoner neglect and seven counts of murder. After a five-month trial, the commission acquitted Gee and released him. Guerrilla chieftain Champ Ferguson was tried and found guilty for war crimes in the indiscriminate killing of black soldiers the morning after the battle of Saltville, Virginia, in October 1864. A detachment of U.S. Colored Troops witnessed his execution on October 25, 1865.

Federals also arrested and imprisoned Jefferson Davis, James Seddon, and Howell Cobb on charges of conspiring to assassinate Lincoln. However, as time passed and the political and legal difficulties of bringing ex-Confederates to trial became apparent, the rush to judgment somewhat waned. Seddon and Cobb were released after several months in prison; Davis, although indicted for treason and conspiracy to murder the president, was never brought to trial. He remained at Fort Monroe, Virginia, until May 1867, when he too was allowed to go home.

Overall, the federal government showed remarkable restraint, although it was also in its interest to encourage amity and not push the rebels into the prolonged

THIS POLITICAL CARTOON entitled "Uncle Sam's Menagerie" emphasizes the sensationalism of the postwar trials. This illustration represents prominent Confederates as caged wild animals in a traveling exhibition with Uncle Sam the smiling showman. President Jefferson Davis is a hyena about to die, as other condemned Confederates, "Gallow's Birds," await their fates above him.

guerrilla resistance that some Union military leaders feared. Yet, even without punishing Confederate leaders, northerners faced some difficult political questions: What was to be done with the former Confederacy? How would the federal government go about reunifying the nation, beaten and bloodied, and almost entirely torn asunder by four years of vicious fighting?

Northern Bitterness

However delicately the government might treat the leaders of the rebellion, many northern citizens were in no mood to forgive treason. They wanted visible signs of punishment and contrition. Nearly 300,000 defenders of the Union had died in the war, and many of the 277,000 wounded soldiers and sailors returned home crippled physically. Many men suffered from what would today be diagnosed as post-traumatic stress syndrome, and many others never recovered—some dying prematurely—from the physical demands of campaigning. Someone had to be held responsible for this human slaughter and slow death, said those northerners who wanted reassurance that the guilty—which included all rebels—would pay for their misdeeds.

In countless local communities that had been divided during the war, face-to-face bitterness and revenge characterized the immediate postwar experience more than did forgiveness. Particularly in the border states and upland regions of the South where guerrilla fighting had raged, many scores were settled violently, often with reprisal killings. Armed gangs from both sides frequently overrode local law-and-order forces. In Missouri, the James gang and other noted bank and railroad robbers emerged from the Confederate guerrilla population. Thousands of other veterans and civilians who had fled guerrillas during the war never returned to their home counties or states. They clung to their resentments and fears and hoped for retribution.

War in itself made reconciliation both necessary and difficult, as did conflicting northern desires both to castigate the South and to welcome it back into the Union. In his first inaugural speech, Lincoln had expressed his firm belief that not all southerners were rebels and that some would even return to the Union of their own accord. With time, however, Lincoln's ideas on reconciliation evolved and became more complex, especially with regard to slavery. When he announced the Emancipation Proclamation in 1862, the North's war aims changed radically, but the president's hopes for reunion never faded.

Lincoln's Ten Percent Plan

By the end of 1863, with large parts of the Confederacy conquered by Union armies, the timing seemed right to offer a more comprehensive proposal for occupied regions to return to the Union. Lincoln did not intend to undermine the progress made in Tennessee and Louisiana, where military governors had established some semblance of civil government; rather, he sought to accelerate the process in other rebel states. On December 8, 1863, Lincoln announced his *Proclamation of Amnesty and Reconstruction*, a pragmatic and rather flexible plan to encourage southerners to return to the Union quickly. This proclamation, also known as Lincoln's *Ten Percent Plan*, offered rebels a full pardon and restoration of their rights as citizens, except slave ownership, if they swore allegiance to the United States and pledged to accept the abolition of slavery. When the number of "loyal" southerners equaled 10 percent of the votes cast in their state election of 1860, those individuals could begin to form a new state government and draft a new state constitution. It is not clear why Lincoln was willing to use so slender a base on which to build new loyal governments, but he seemed still to have believed, as he did during the first year of war, that the number of southern unionists was large enough to restore loyal regimes in nearly every rebel state. Once recognized "as the true government of the State," the war-weary Confederates, he hoped, would gradually acknowledge the futility of continuing their rebellion and come over to the alternative Union state governments.

Of course, there were some strings attached. Lincoln excluded high-ranking Confederate political and military officials from participating in the new state governments, and he required that the new constitutions ban slavery, although he would allow for temporary measures to deal with ex-slaves as a "laboring, landless, and homeless class." His plan made no allowance for African Americans to take the loyalty oath, vote, or hold office. He affirmed the right of Congress to decide whether any members sent to Congress under his provisions would be allowed to serve. Lincoln's ideas fit his insistence that the eleven southern states never actually had left the Union but rather were in a state of rebellion, and thus should not have to undergo an elaborate or arduous process to reclaim their old positions. Perhaps most importantly under the immediate circumstances, his ideas made sound military sense by encouraging southerners to stop hostilities and seek peaceful reunion.

When Lincoln issued the Amnesty Proclamation, many northerners were pleased with it. Most Republicans praised his plan as a way to end the war and abolish slavery. New York lawyer George Templeton Strong wrote approvingly in his diary on December 11, 1863: "Uncle Abe is the most popular man in America today. The firmness, honesty and sagacity of the 'gorilla despot' may be recognized by the rebels themselves sooner than we expect, and the weight of his personal character may do a great deal toward restoration of our national unity." Southern unionists applauded it as a way to bring speedy reunion. Yet, others saw problems with the plan, especially in the provisions related to emancipation and in Lincoln's rather lenient treatment of rebels.

Democrats, in particular, criticized the president, believing that his program for reconstruction was unsound and dangerous. Northern Democrats, torn from within by the Copperhead movement, clung to their faith in states' rights and minimal federal government control. Although the party denounced secession, many northern Democrats presumed reunion without abolition of slavery was the best course to pursue—both to calm southern fears of reunion and to maintain the white man's republic in which they staunchly believed. The Democratic *New York News* called Lincoln's blueprint a "despot's edict" and a "wild, unjust, and impracticable plan for the consummation of abolition."

Confederates also blasted Lincoln's proclamation. North Carolinan Catherine Anne Edmondston, for example, wondered in her journal why Lincoln offered the South a pardon at all: "Pardon for what? Forgiveness for what? Forgive us for having himself invaded our land, ravaged and desolated our homes? Forgive us for our sin!"

Radical Ideas for Reconstruction

By the summer of 1864, Lincoln's political popularity had plunged to its lowest point, his Ten Percent Plan had not made much progress, and his reelection was very much in doubt. Radical Republicans offered an alternative and much tougher plan for rebellious states to return to the Union. The majority of Lincoln's own party believed that the president was too intent on simply *restoring* the South to the Union while paying too little attention to punishing the Confederate rebels and to rebuilding, or *reconstructing*, the southern states. To address this major flaw in Lincoln's thinking, Congress passed the *Wade-Davis Bill*, drafted by Representative Henry Winter Davis of Maryland and Senator Benjamin F. Wade of Ohio just before adjourning in July 1864. It challenged not only the loose provisions of Lincoln's plan but also the idea that reconstruction should be solely an executive initiative.

Asserting congressional authority and civilian control of the process, the bill stipulated that when the "military resistance to the United States shall have been suppressed in any state," then reconstruction could commence. At that point, a provisional governor, appointed by the president but approved by the Senate, would begin to administer the loyalty oath to all white male citizens. When this number reached 50 percent, the governor could hold elections for delegates to a constitutional convention. After taking another oath, the "Iron-clad Oath," swearing that they had never willingly supported the rebellion, these delegates would then meet and vote to ban slavery and repudiate all Confederate debts before formally drafting a new "republican form of government and ordaining a constitution" that contained these same provisions. When a majority of qualified voters ratified the constitution, the president, "after obtaining the consent of Congress," could recognize the new government's legitimacy. Only at this point could elections be held for congressional representation. The Wade-Davis Bill banned high-ranking Confederates from holding office or voting in the new state government, as had Lincoln's Ten Percent Plan, but the Wade-Davis Bill also stripped citizenship from anyone "who shall hereafter hold or exercise any office, civil or military (except officers merely ministerial and military office below the grade of colonel), in the rebel service, state or Confederate." Although authored by two Radicals, the bill had its limitations; there was most notably no provision for black suffrage.

Lincoln's Late Thoughts on Reconstruction

Unwilling either to endorse the Wade-Davis Bill or to reject it with a formal veto, Lincoln let the bill languish without his signature, thus pocket vetoing its passage. Deeming the bill unnecessarily rigid, the president explained his opposition in an unusual public proclamation. He stated that he was "unprepared by a formal approval of this bill to be inflexibly committed to any single plan of restoration." Lincoln worried that the bill would nullify the governments already established in Arkansas and Louisiana under his own plan. Lincoln added, with what seemed to be mocking sarcasm, that if any state *wanted* to accept this harsher bill, he would be "prepared to give the Executive aid and assistance to any such people."

Although most Republicans, fearful that Democrats would capitalize on any obvious splits within their party, kept quiet, Wade and Davis were angry enough to issue a formal response to Lincoln's proclamation. In the *Wade-Davis Manifesto,* the two congressmen accused Lincoln of defying the Constitution to pursue his own "personal ambition." They declared: "If he wishes our support, he must confine himself to his executive duties—to obey and execute, not make the laws—to suppress by arms armed rebellion, and leave political reorganization to Congress." Seldom have congressmen so savagely attacked a president of their own party. Congress was unable to override Lincoln's veto, but when southern representatives and senators selected under the president's Ten Percent Plan arrived in Washington, Congress refused to seat them.

An attempt at compromise between the president and Congress also failed, largely over the controversial issue of black enfranchisement. Lincoln had grown increasingly supportive of limited black suffrage, but he clung to his view that the same plan would not fit for every rebellious state. In one of his last public statements about reconstruction, on April 11, 1865, the president stated that he preferred black suffrage for "the very intelligent" and "those who served our cause as soldiers." That seemed straightforward enough, but Lincoln also recognized that "so great peculiarities pertain to each state; and such important and sudden changes occur in the same state; and withal, so new and unprecedented is the whole case, that no exclusive, and inflexible plan can safely be prescribed as to details and colatterals." "It may be my duty," he added, "to make some new announcement to the people of the South . . . when satisfied that action will be proper."

So there were numerous and complex problems about the future of the former Confederacy. The crucial question was: who would control the agenda in seeking to resolve them? In what proved to be Lincoln's final cabinet meeting, on April 14, 1865, Secretary of War Edwin Stanton suggested that military occupation of the former Confederacy might be necessary, but the president responded: "We can't undertake to run state governments in all these states. The people must do that—though I reckon that at first some of them may do it badly." That evening, an assassin's bullet mortally wounded the president, and the difficult question of how to restore the South to the Union remained unanswered. Lincoln habitually played his cards close to his vest, but he was flexible and open to congressional Radicals, often moving in their direction during the war. Had he not been lost, reconstruction policy might have been hammered out jointly by the president and Congress. Whether this would have been much more moderate than what transpired, and whether southern whites would have been more accommodating, is one of American history's great imponderables.

Vice President Andrew Johnson's unexpected ascendancy to the presidency after Lincoln's assassination initially cheered Republicans, even Radicals. A devout unionist and an antiplanter, Johnson, from Tennessee, was the only southern senator who did not vacate his seat in Congress when his state seceded. Born to illiterate tavern workers in 1808, Johnson had no formal schooling. A tailor by trade, he learned basic reading skills as an adult, acquiring the ability to write and cipher from his wife, Eliza. Johnson's ambition seemed to compensate for his humble roots. Beginning at the age of twenty-one, he won a suc-

Andrew Johnson

LINCOLN'S SUCCESSOR AS PRESIDENT, Andrew Johnson, prided himself on his humble roots and his staunch unionism.

cession of local and state offices, including the Tennessee governorship in 1853 and 1855 and election to the U.S. Senate in 1857. In 1862 Lincoln rewarded the Tennessean's loyalty to the Union by appointing him military governor of the state. In the election of 1864, Johnson replaced Hannibal Hamlin as Lincoln's running mate. Lincoln and Johnson led the coalition "Union party," which joined together Republicans and War Democrats. Republicans hoped this hybrid alignment would attract southern unionist votes and spread party allegiance into the South.

Johnson had a reputation as a bold champion of nonslaveholding whites and staunch unionism. He portrayed himself as a man of the people, "a plebian, mechanic, and not ashamed nor afraid to own it." He fostered this modest image even after becoming a large land and slave owner. At 5 feet, 8 inches tall, with impressive physical strength and dark, brooding features, Johnson seemed fearless. During the war, with his wife and children left behind enemy lines and his life threatened by assassination, Johnson determinedly administered a loyal government in Tennessee. Admirers thought him courageous and unflappable, an individual of strong principles who would not waver from his ideals, no matter the cost. But his critics—and there would be increasing numbers of them as his presidency unfolded—saw him as petty, self-absorbed, paranoid, resentful, dogmatic, and stubborn, a man who tried to mask his deep insecurities with exaggerated bravado.

Johnson's entrance onto the national scene had a rocky start. On the day of his inauguration as vice president in March 1865, ill and nervous, he self-medicated himself with too much whiskey. Clearly inebriated, he slurred his words and rambled on about his rustic roots: "I am a-going for to tell you—here today; yes, I'm a-going for to tell you all, that I'm a plebian! I glory in it; I am a plebian!" The *New York World* called the vice president a "drunken clown." Even Lincoln was embarrassed. "I have known Andrew Johnson for many years," Lincoln assured a concerned listener. "He made a bad slip the other day, but you need not be scared; Andy ain't a drunkard." Serving as vice president was, of course, different from being president, and soon both northerners and southerners discovered that his critics were right: Andrew Johnson was impossible to counsel or control. He was a man who did whatever he wanted, despite the political or personal cost, with self-righteous and impolitic rigidity, and barely concealed anger.

However, Johnson's irksome traits were not entirely apparent to Republicans when the Tennessean suddenly became president in the spring of 1865. Instead, his unexpected presidency seemed like a dream come true to Republicans, particularly Radicals who were anxious to castigate the South but had been hamstrung by Lincoln's generous policy of restoration. Johnson had repeatedly assailed the rebels, proclaiming treason a crime and affirming that "traitors must be punished." In June 1864 he had even suggested that "great plantations must be seized and divided into small farms, and sold to honest, industrious men." Radical Benjamin Wade, the coauthor of the failed Wade-Davis Bill, was delighted with the new president. "Johnson, we have faith in you," he declared excitedly. "By the Gods, there will be no trouble now in running the government."

Some northern Democrats, on the other hand, viewed the new president with mixed feelings. Alarmed by his frequent verbal attacks on Confederate leaders, they worried that their hopes to reconsolidate power with southern Democrats would flounder and that Radical Republicans would reign supreme. Still, Johnson was—or at least had been—one of their own, and some leading northern Democrats believed that his longtime devotion to states' rights and opposition to black suffrage must eventually alienate him from the Republicans. These Democrats predicted hopefully that Johnson would return to his political roots.

The new president ended up surprising everyone, moving quickly to implement his own program to restore the Union. With Congress adjourned until December, Johnson issued two executive proclamations on May 29, 1865. His Proclamation of Amnesty appeared to be less generous than had Lincoln's Ten Percent Plan, denying far more people, especially wealthy land and slave owners, easy pardons and restitution of property. Johnson's second proclamation placed control of North Carolina's provisional government in civilian rather than military hands and initially required the creation of new state constitutions

Johnson's Reconstruction Plan

before the election of any state or federal officials. In the coming weeks, Johnson issued similar directives for six more former Confederate states.

Radicals, initially pleased by Johnson's angry antiplanter tirades, grew alarmed. Despite Johnson's heated wartime rhetoric that treason was a crime and that traitors must be handled harshly, his actual plan for restoration—a term he preferred to reconstruction—punished few people and was as lenient as anything Lincoln might have concocted, almost certainly more so.

In fact, Johnson was soon offering pardons to anyone in the former Confederacy willing to swear allegiance to the United States. Even individuals exempted from his proclamation, including those who had broken prior amnesty oaths, commerce raiders, graduates of West Point and Annapolis who had served the southern cause, and those with taxable property worth more than $20,000, could personally petition the president for a pardon. Nor did Johnson require a certain percentage of citizens in rebellious states to take the loyalty oath before drafting new constitutions, not even Lincoln's extremely low 10 percent. Instead, Johnson's provisional governors were authorized to establish loyal governments based on the prewar white electorate. He did ask seceded states to repudiate the Confederate debt, renounce secession, and affirm the Thirteenth Amendment, but Johnson did not *require* that these conditions be met.

A variety of factors explains Johnson's behavior. Conservative Republican Secretary of State William Seward exerted a strong influence on the ambitious new president, convincing Johnson that offering mild terms to the former Confederacy could create a majority coalition of conservatives and moderates and isolate congressional Radicals. This coalition of northern War Democrats, moderate Republicans, border-state unionists, and antisecessionists, Johnson hoped, would join his efforts to reunify the nation, defeat extremists on both sides, and guarantee his election in 1868. In addition to Johnson's political ambitions, his personal resentments also played a role. He clearly relished the idea of slave owners coming to him, preferably with tearful wives in tow, begging for forgiveness. Churning out pardons without hesitation, Johnson issued some 13,500 of them, half of which were for individuals worth $20,000 or more. Nor did Johnson have much interest in aiding the freedmen, although at one point he urged white southerners to offer the vote to a select number of blacks as a way to disarm the Radicals politically.

Johnson had more in common with planters than perhaps he was willing to acknowledge publicly. When it came to enacting harsh measures, all the bombast about punishing his native land proved illusory. To the relief of northern Democrats, he was also an old-line Jeffersonian Democrat who was never entirely comfortable with a federal government that imposed its authority on the states. In December 1865 he boasted: "The people throughout the entire South evince a laudable desire to renew their allegiances to the Government and to repair the devastations of war by a prompt and cheerful return to peaceful pursuits, and abiding faith is entertained that their actions will conform to their professions." He predicted: "Sectional animosity is surely and rapidly merging itself into a spirit of nationality."

Johnson based his hopes for political moderation and quick reunion on the assumption that former Confederates would willingly accept his steps toward that goal. The South's rebellious spirit, however, was not so easily quelled. Many white southerners refused to repudiate the Confederate debt, secession, or slavery. Although every Confederate state except Mississippi eventually ratified the Thirteenth Amendment, they all passed *Black Codes* that were designed to ensure continued social and economic control of African Americans. Modeled after occupation codes that had been developed by the U.S. Army to regulate black laborers, these laws fit southern white fears and prejudiced assumptions about African Americans. Southern states did grant some rights to former slaves, including the right to own property, bear witness in court, sue and be sued, and marry legally, but most were more designed to restrict black rights. Defining a "negro" as anyone with one-eighth of "negro blood," the codes reaffirmed the racial caste system of the prewar South. They banned blacks from bearing firearms, consuming alcohol, and marrying whites. Alabama's 1866 state penal code stated that any white or "negro" found guilty of intermarriage or living in "adultery or fornication with each other" would "be imprisoned in the penitentiary, or sentenced to hard labor for the country, for not less than two, nor more than seven years." Vagrancy laws restricted blacks from traveling without permits and limited their ability to negotiate labor contracts. Some states passed laws that severely punished blacks who failed to present identification and passes. In Mississippi, any black older than the age of eighteen "found on the second Monday in January, 1866, or thereafter, with no lawful employment or business or found unlawfully assembling themselves together," would be "deemed vagrant" and fined $50 and "imprisoned at the discretion of the court." African Americans in the former Confederacy found their lives still ruled in draconian, often violent ways by southern whites.

White southerners were also intent on regaining political control of their states, despite military defeat. Through the summer and fall of 1865, southerners defiantly elected ex-Confederate soldiers and politicians to lead their state governments and to represent them in Congress. Termed "Confederate Brigadiers" by angry northern congressmen, this group of former rebels who arrived in Washington included ten Confederate generals, six Confederate cabinet officers, fifty-eight Confederate congressmen, and former Confederate vice president Alexander Stephens. Although this southern congressional delegation was not made up of fire-eaters or ardent secessionists, and although a few members had even advocated peace or expressed unionist sentiments during the war, every one of them had willingly supported the Confederacy in some capacity. None supported freedmen's rights. (Chapter 11 provides a more detailed discussion of conditions in the immediate postwar South.)

The election of ex-Confederates to office enraged Radical Republicans; even moderates were taken aback by the South's boldness in retaining formerly high-ranking Confederates in political power. Refusing to seat the congressmen elected under Johnson's plan, Congress considered its own plan for managing the South. It created a *Joint Committee of Fifteen on Reconstruction* to

Ex-Confederate Defiance

Congressional Reconstruction

investigate conditions in the former Confederacy and to make recommendations on how to proceed.

The Joint Committee on Reconstruction consisted of nine representatives and six senators from both the radical and the moderate Republican camps, as well as three Democrats. Maine senator William Pitt Fessenden, who chaired the committee, was a moderate Republican who disagreed with calls for punishing the South or redistributing land but agreed with the Radical view that Congress should take control of reconstruction. Republican moderates outnumbered the Radicals on the committee seven to five, but the two camps were more evenly divided in day-to-day operations. Besides Fessenden, the only other moderate to play a prominent role in the committee's work was John A. Bingham of Ohio, although Reverdy Johnson of Maryland, the most active and influential Democrat, sided with them. That still gave the three most active radicals—the irascible but driven Pennsylvanian Thaddeus Stevens, New York's Roscoe Conkling, and George S. Boutwell of Massachusetts—plenty of room to maneuver. Fessenden regarded the majority as "thorough men," but he also realized they had "resolved that ample security [for the Union] should attend any restoration of the insurgent states."

Beginning in early 1866, the committee interviewed eight African Americans, seventy-seven white northerners living in the South, and fifty-seven southerners. Among the white southerners to testify were former general Robert E. Lee, Alexander Stephens, and Virginia unionist John Minor Botts. Lee admitted that he thought the best solution for dealing with freedmen was to expel them from the country: "I think it would be better for Virginia if she could get rid of them. This is not a new opinion with me. I have always thought so." Botts stated that after Johnson began to issue indiscriminate pardons, former Confederates had

RADICAL REPUBLICAN THADDEUS STEVENS demanded that Congress champion the rights of ex-slaves or risk the condemnation of future generations of Americans.

become "bold, insolent and defiant." Committee members asked leading questions and generally found the responses they wanted to confirm their assumptions that the president's reconstruction policy was a disaster.

In June 1866 the committee issued its report rejecting the state governments established under Johnson's plan and calling for new conditions to be met before the rebellious South could have representation in Congress. The committee affirmed that the rebels "were conquered by the people of the United States, acting through all the co-ordinate branches of the government, and not by the executive department alone." Concluding that the former Confederacy had no right to representation in Congress until "adequate security for future peace and safety should be required," the committee affirmed the responsibility of Congress to ensure "civil rights and privileges of all citizens in all parts of the republic," "representation on a equitable basis," "fix[ing] a stigma upon treason," and protecting "loyal people against future claims for the expenses incurred in support of the rebellion and for manumitted slaves."

Meanwhile, Massachusetts senator Charles Sumner and Pennsylvania Representative Thaddeus Stevens, who led the Radical Republicans in Congress, introduced a vindictive note by demanding that the defeated South be treated as conquered territories. Seventy-three-year-old Stevens, clubfooted, bald, and wearing an ill-fitting red wig, seemed to delight in the image of a crazed eccentric. His contemporaries found him brusque, sarcastic, foulmouthed, foul-tempered, and entirely uncompromising in his principles. He hated both Democrats and slavery with equal passion. Just the mention of the commonly held notion that the United States was meant to be a white man's republic drove him into paroxysms. He was tactless—like Johnson and Jeff Davis, for that matter—and bitter that the rebels had destroyed his business. Though he never married, it was rumored that Stevens's longtime mistress was his devoted mulatto housekeeper, Lydia Smith. And yet Stevens was fearless and willing to look more deeply into alternatives to the American racial order than was almost any other member of Congress. He realized that unless reconstruction struck at the roots of discrimination by introducing a new regime of biracial politics, nothing would be changed for the betterment of African Americans, thus sacrificing whatever moral energy the war had unloosed.

Thaddeus Stevens and Radical Reconstruction

In a speech given soon after Congress convened in December 1865, Stevens forcefully argued that secession and war had smashed the southern states "into atoms," "severed their original compacts," and broken "all the ties that bound" North and South together. "The future condition of the conquered power," Stevens insisted, "depends on the will of the conqueror." Congress should take the helm to reconstruct the South and protect its 4 million ex-slaves. "If we leave [the freedmen] to the legislation of their late masters," Stevens contended, "we had better have left them in bondage." He added, "If we fail in this great duty now, when we have the power, we shall deserve and receive the execration of history and of all future ages." Stevens spoke for those who wanted revenge, who wanted white southerners "to learn the principles of freedom and eat the fruit of foul rebellion," and he also spoke for African American demands to participate fully and securely in public life. His aims were driven partly by humanitarian and moral impulses, but he was also a politician, determined "to secure perpetual ascendancy to the party of the Union."

Some Radicals, Stevens among them, also sought to seize planters' lands and redistribute them to former slaves. The issue of land distribution was a controversial one, even for Radical Republicans, who championed private-property owners and their continued faith in "free labor and free soil." Many Radicals were sincerely devoted to racial justice but deeply conflicted over the idea of taking land away from some Americans to give to others, no matter how determined they were to compensate former slaves for their unrequited labor and provide them with economic opportunities. Once begun, where would confiscation end? Private property was as sacred as freedom of speech and freedom from arbitrary arrest. Former slaves would discover quickly that land redistribution, something they viewed as absolutely crucial to ensuring their financial freedom and stability in the postwar South, was simply too radical even for the majority of Radical Republicans.

Congress versus the President   Moderate Republicans, uncomfortable with Radical talk about black suffrage, punishing rebels, and redistributing land to freedmen, sought some middle ground with President Johnson. Two bills presented by the prominent Illinois senator Lyman Trumbull early in the new year represented moderates' attempts to modify *Presidential Reconstruction,* check southern defiance, and nullify the discriminatory Black Codes. The first bill extended the life of the Freedmen's Bureau and gave its agents broader authority to assume jurisdiction of legal cases involving blacks. This bill also provided bureau agents with the power to discipline state officials for denying former slaves the "civil rights belonging to white persons." Provisions to redistribute seized southern lands to freedmen were soundly defeated, but in February 1866 the bill to extend the tenure of the Freedmen's Bureau passed easily in both houses, with nearly unanimous Republican support. But Johnson surprised nearly everyone by refusing to sign the bill and by rejecting the entire bureau as unconstitutional, unfair, and unrepresentative of the nation. No such economic relief had ever been offered "our own people"—meaning southern whites—and Johnson reasoned that such a law, by implying that freedmen could not make it on their own, encouraged blacks to lead a "life of indolence." Without enough votes to override the president's veto, the bill died, at least temporarily.

Trumbull's second measure, the *Civil Rights Bill,* was, as one historian has explained, "an attempt to define in legislative terms, the essence of freedom." This bill declared that anyone born in the United States, other than an Indian, was a citizen with federally protected rights, including the right to a jury trial and the right to serve on juries, the right to sue and be sued, and the right to give evidence. After a good deal of debate over the particulars of citizenship, the bill passed the Senate on February 2 and the House on March 13, 1866. An Ohio state senator wrote to Ohio U.S. Senator John Sherman: "If the President vetoes the Civil Rights bill, I believe we shall be obliged to draw our swords for a fight and throw away the scabbards."

Every member of Johnson's cabinet, except Secretary of the Navy Gideon Welles and Secretary of State William Seward, urged Johnson to sign the legislation. Instead, he vetoed it, attacking the bill as a violation of states' rights that would "resuscitate the spirit of rebellion and . . . arrest the progress of those influences which are more closely drawing around the States the bonds of union and peace." He further denounced the bill for giving preferential treatment to blacks at the expense of whites. "Can it be reasonably supposed," Johnson asked rhetorically in his veto message to the Senate, "that they [ex-slaves] possess the requisite qualifications to entitle them to all the privileges and immunities of citizens of the United States?"

Fourteen days later, when both houses of Congress overrode Johnson's veto, the *Civil Rights Act of 1866* became law. This legislation did not institute permanent federal intrusion into local affairs; only if there was an alleged violation of a citizen's rights would the federal government become involved. The measure also failed to address private acts of discrimination against citizens or to allow for black suffrage. Nonetheless, the act marked a dramatic turning point: for the first time, Congress had defined the rights of American citizenship. Its enactment also marked the first time in American history that a major piece of legislation had been passed over a presidential veto.

Later that summer, a second Freedmen's Bureau Bill made its way through both houses, and this time, when Johnson again vetoed the legislation, there were enough votes for Congress to prevail. With Republicans unified against the president, the stage was set for continued confrontations between the two branches of government.

The next major showdown between Congress and the president occurred over passage of the *Fourteenth Amendment*, the most controversial piece of legislation enacted during Reconstruction. The amendment, passed by Congress on June 13, 1866, and formally ratified on July 28, 1868, avowed that anyone born in the United States was a citizen with specific federally protected rights, and that no state could "deprive any person of life, liberty or property, without due process of law, nor deny any person within its jurisdiction the equal protection of the laws." Meant to ensure that the Civil Rights Act of 1866 would not be declared unconstitutional, the amendment echoed much of the same language of that prior law and rejected the Supreme Court's 1857 judgment in *Dred Scott v. Sanford* by endorsing African American citizenship.

The Fourteenth Amendment

The Fourteenth Amendment also gave the Republican Congress broad political power by allowing it to reduce representation for any state that restricted "the suffrage of any portion of its male inhabitants over twenty-one years of age." Responding to the South's attempt to send former Confederates to Congress, the amendment banned men from office who had previously sworn an oath to support the U.S. Constitution but then "engaged in insurrection or rebellion against the same, or [had] given aid or comfort to the enemies thereof." Finally, the amendment repudiated the Confederate debt, reaffirmed the United States' public debt, prohibited compensation to states or individual owners for the loss of slaves, and gave Congress the power to "enforce, by appropriate legislation, the provisions of this article."

Historians view the Fourteenth Amendment in a variety of ways. Some see it as watershed legislation that marked a turn toward Radical Reconstruction; others regard it as a compromise measure on the part of a Congress struggling to find unity in light of the president's stubborn and strident rejection of the relatively moderate Freedman's Bureau and civil rights bills; still others see the amendment as the Civil War's unofficial peace treaty, meting out a mild form of punishment to the rebels by denying certain elected government positions to leaders of the rebellion and renouncing the Confederate debt. It also tried to ensure that this sort of rebellion would never happen again. One scholar has argued that the Fourteenth Amendment was "a revolutionary document . . . the first amendment that operated directly upon the states rather than the federal government."

Despite its potential for radicalism, the Fourteenth Amendment, at least initially, did not dramatically alter the operations of federal or state government or even go very far in protecting the rights of American citizens, especially blacks. Through a series of landmark decisions, the Supreme Court debated and reconfigured the meaning of the amendment, interpreting it extremely narrowly and muting its guarantees of equal protection under the law. Not until the 1954 Supreme Court case *Brown v. Board of Education* did the federal government begin to restore to African Americans the civil rights that they were first promised nearly ninety years earlier. Untold numbers of blacks suffered generations of discrimination, segregation, and lynching before the rights promised by the Fourteenth Amendment, as well as the Fifteenth Amendment described below, were ensured.

President Johnson vigorously objected to the Fourteenth Amendment, as he had to all other congressional attempts to reconstruct the South. In late summer of 1866, he took his opposition to the northern people by traveling through New York, Pennsylvania, and parts of the Midwest—his *Swing Around the Circle*—giving speeches in support of conservative candidates in that year's election. Ulysses S. Grant, David Farragut, and members of Johnson's cabinet joined the president in what was supposed to be a tour to mark the dedication of a monument to Stephen Douglas, but it was soon clear that Johnson's main purpose was personal and political. He gave essentially the same speech in every city, heralding his "plebian" status, attacking his perceived enemies, and urging unity and white solidarity.

Although he never directly mentioned his opposition to the Fourteenth Amendment, Johnson did argue for state control of voting rights, and he could not restrain himself from answering hecklers. At one point, he implied that his ascendancy to the presidency, replacing the slain Lincoln, was divinely ordained. In Cleveland, Johnson proclaimed that having defeated traitors in the South, he was now "prepared to fight traitors at the north." Countering chants of "Hang Jeff Davis," Johnson shouted: "Why don't you hang Thad Stevens and Wendell Phillips?" In another speech in St. Louis, angry listeners accused

Johnson of causing bloody race riots in New Orleans. Exasperated and irritated, Johnson yelled back: "I have been traduced, I have been slandered. I have been maligned. I have been Judas Iscariot. . . . Who has been my Christ that I have played the Judas with? Was it Thad Stevens?" The tour was a fiasco. Johnson returned to Washington on September 15, his popular image sullied and his political legitimacy further tarnished.

During the 1866 campaign season, the Fourteenth Amendment dominated most other issues. Republicans ran also on platforms demanding punishment of the rebels and protection of freedmen. They railed against not only Johnson but the whole Democratic Party, inaccurately painting the entire opposition as disloyal Copperheads who were responsible for the South's postwar recalcitrance and racial violence. Indiana governor and Radical Republican Oliver Morton, for example, branded the Democratic Party as "a common sewer and loathsome receptacle into which is emptied every element of treason North and South." Such themes and images would dominate Republican rhetoric for many years to come. *"Waving the bloody shirt"*—a term originating from Ben Butler's literally waving the blood-spattered shirt allegedly worn by an Ohio carpetbagger murdered by the Ku Klux Klan—soon became a common expression to associate the Democratic Party with treason and responsibility for the war. It was a powerful way to manipulate northern public memory of the war and to use the self-sacrifice of Union soldiers for political gain.

Elections of 1866

Northern voters registered their disapproval of the president and support for Congress by giving Republicans sweeping victories in both the state and national elections of 1866. The pro-Republican *New York Times* proclaimed that the people had "decreed, not only that Congress as it now is, faithfully represents their convictions and purposes, but that the Congress which will come after shall sustain substantially the same policy." The newspaper warned that Johnson must be "content to see Congress push forward its new method of settlement, despite protestations and vetoes, or must frankly accept the verdict pronounced by the people who elected him and use his opportunities to hasten restoration on the only basis that is practicable. He has stated his own case, and the people have refused to accept it."

When Congress reconvened in December 1866, all remnants of Presidential Reconstruction vanished, and *Congressional Reconstruction* moved into high gear. Congress had already seized the initiative from Johnson by passing the Civil Rights Bill of 1866, Freedmen's Bureau legislation, and the Fourteenth Amendment. Radical Republicans, with the help of moderates alienated by Johnson's behavior and underlying ideology, assumed leadership and quickly pushed through a series of bills to check the president's power and to establish Republican political dominance in the South. Congress and the president were now set on a collision course.

Radical Reconstruction

With power firmly in its hands, Congress moved to achieve two goals: to rebuild southern society and to destroy what little remained of President Johnson's political power. It moved to achieve the first goal in a series of laws known as the *Reconstruction Acts*. These were unprecedented and bold departures from

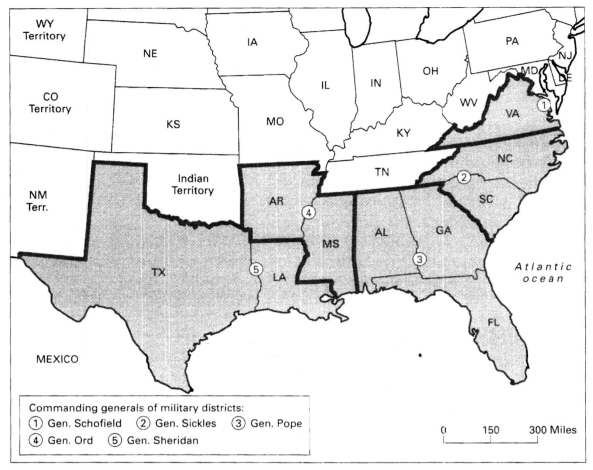

CONGRESSIONAL RECONSTRUCTION divided the former Confederate states, except Tennessee, into five separate military districts under the control of army generals.

American political practice, using all arms of the federal government, including the military, to impose fundamental political change on particular states. The first act, passed on March 2, 1867, abolished existing governments in ten of the eleven former Confederate states (except Tennessee), divided them into five military districts, instituted martial law, disenfranchised ex-Confederate leaders, and established guidelines by which these states would construct new constitutions to guarantee universal manhood suffrage and the provisions of the Fourteenth Amendment. Supplemental legislation quickly followed to authorize the army to register voters and to oversee elections. No longer would the South be able to "reconstruct" itself.

The next three Reconstruction Acts, passed between March 22, 1867, and March 11, 1868, came in response to the difficulties of protecting freedmen, ensuring black suffrage, and defeating the Democratic Party. The fourth and final act was specifically designed to outvote the Democrats and to ensure ratification of the new state constitutions. This act reduced the residency requirement to vote from one year to ten days and declared that a majority of the votes cast, rather than a majority of the eligible voters, was sufficient for ratification. By mid-1868, all but three former Confederate states—Virginia, Texas, and Mississippi—had met the requirements for rejoining the Union. These three states, with the later addition of Georgia, which returned to military rule in 1869 after its legislature expelled its black members, were not readmitted to the Union until 1870.

Johnson, never one to take challenges to his positions lightly, refused to back down. He continued to denounce Congress and to issue scores of personal pardons to ex-Confederates. Congress, irked by the president's behavior and the South's blatant defiance—all of the former Confederate states, except Tennessee and two former slave states that did not secede, Kentucky and Delaware, still adamantly refused to ratify the Fourteenth Amendment—was determined to dominate all future Reconstruction policy. Congress quickly set about weakening the president's power with the *Tenure of Office Act*, which prevented Johnson from acting without Senate approval to remove executive officials who had been appointed by and with the consent of the Senate, and the *Army Appropriation Act*, which forbade the president from giving direct commands to troops in the field. Johnson, lacking enough votes to sustain his vetoes, was unable to check this renewed legislative challenge. The Thirty-ninth Congress, after successfully passing these laws in early March 1867, quickly called the next Congress into session, disallowing Johnson any free rein while the legislative branch was in recess.

However, Republicans wanted more than just the freedom to implement **Impeachment** their own form of Reconstruction; they wanted Johnson gone. Unwilling to wait for the president's term to end, they sought to impeach him. Initially, the movement to abort Johnson's presidency was supported by only a handful of individuals, mostly Radicals. But with time and Johnson's continued provocations, more and more Republicans, including moderates, supported this radical move. Congress had proved repeatedly that it had the votes to override the president's vetoes and to establish its own agenda. The Tenure of Office Act and the Appropriations Act had stripped Johnson of his patronage and power as commander in chief of the army, yet the president's sullen and outspoken hostility enraged all Republicans. He continued to issue numerous pardons to ex-Confederates and to appoint politically moderate generals to Reconstruction districts in the South. And his official attitude encouraged southern white resistance while it undermined federal policy implementation in the South. *Impeachment*—that is, indicting Johnson in the House, holding a public trial in the Senate, and, if finding him guilty, removing him from office—seemed the only way to end his maddening presidency. The Constitution listed only a few categories for which a president could be indicted: treason, bribery, or "high crimes and misdemeanors." Thaddeus Stevens fumed: "My own impression is that we had better put it [impeachment] on the grounds of insanity or whiskey

Although this illustration shows Andrew Johnson present during his impeachment trial, Johnson's lawyers successfully convinced the quick-tempered president not to appear personally during the proceedings.

or something like that kind. I don't want to hurt the man's feelings by telling him he is a rascal. I'd rather put it mildly and say he hasn't got off that inauguration drunk yet, and just let him retire to get sobered."

But Congress needed something more concrete than insanity, drunkenness, or even being a "rascal"; they needed to show a clear violation of the Constitution. In December 1867 the House appointed a committee to draw up a bill of impeachment, but the committee failed to find any substantial charges with which to indict the president. House Republicans tried again in 1868, this time with better success after Johnson deliberately ignored the Tenure of Office Act and dismissed Edwin Stanton as secretary of war without Senate approval. Johnson first named Ulysses S. Grant as Stanton's replacement, but Grant, unwilling to be Johnson's puppet and already considering his own political future within the party, rejected the appointment. Johnson next chose Adjutant General Lorenzo Thomas to stand up to Stanton, who had been urged by Radical Republicans to defy the president. A bizarre and rather comical episode ensued in which Thomas, drunk from celebrating his new appointment, sat slumped outside Stanton's office waiting for the secretary to vacate the premises, something Stanton refused to do.

As the showdown at the secretary of war's office unfolded, the House of Representatives began to draft a bill of impeachment. On February 24, 1868, the

House, voting strictly on party lines, impeached the president, for the first time in U.S. history. In such a situation, the House of Representatives acts as prosecutor and the Senate as jury, with the trial overseen by the Supreme Court's chief justice. A seven-man committee consisting of only Republicans—mostly Radicals—drew up eleven articles of impeachment, accusing the president of "high crimes and misdemeanors," including violation of the Tenure of Office Act, hindering execution of the Reconstruction Acts, berating Congress with foul language, and denying the legitimacy of the federal legislature.

The three-month-long trial that followed was high political drama. Tickets to witness the proceedings were in great demand. Johnson's prosecutors, including Radical Republicans Stevens, who was deathly ill, and Ben Butler, gave long, impassioned speeches, insisting that they must dislodge Johnson. "If we don't do it," Stevens avowed, "we are damned to eternity. There is a moral necessity for it, for which I care something; and there is a party necessity for it, for which I care more." Stevens's words bubbled with mirth and violent imagery. He envisioned that "the ax of the executioner is uplifted" and described the necessity of "killing the Beast." Butler was his usual insensitive self, betraying his callousness when he refused to delay the trial because one of Johnson's lawyers, Henry Stansbery, fell ill.

The president's defense, led by the talented New York lawyer William M. Evarts and the respected Attorney General Stansbery from Ohio (who stepped down to defend the president), cogently disputed the legality of the Tenure of Office Act and insisted that Johnson had defied the law merely to challenge its constitutionality in court. Evarts also warned that removing Johnson would jeopardize the balance of power between the president and Congress. Nor, he stated, had the president done anything criminal. Evarts concluded: "I apprehend that no reasonable man can find it in his heart to say that evil has been proved against him here." Johnson's lawyers urged him not to appear personally at the trial, and although he very much wanted to, he deferred to their judgment. One can only imagine the theatrics if the hotheaded, loose-tongued Johnson had gone toe to toe with the likes of Stevens and Butler.

Despite the prosecution's emotion and anger, the Radicals failed to marshal enough votes in the Senate to remove Johnson from office. Republicans were split, with many admitting that despite Johnson's ineptitude and political missteps, he was hardly guilty of "high crimes and misdemeanors." Some worried about the lasting damage removing Johnson from office might inflict on the institution of the presidency itself. Others, particularly moderate Republicans, feared the ascension of Radical Ben Wade, president pro-tem of the Senate and thus Johnson's successor should the president be removed from office. Most Democrats were never convinced that Johnson had done anything warranting impeachment, let alone removal from office. In the final vote, acting with considerable courage, seven Republican senators deserted their party to vote "not guilty" and Johnson was acquitted.

Johnson finished his final year as president a broken, embattled man, but he was no less obstinate. On Christmas Day 1868, he issued a final amnesty act **Johnson's Last Days** that pardoned all former Confederates, including Jefferson Davis and Robert E. Lee. He refused to attend the inauguration of his successor, Ulysses S. Grant, instead remaining in his office until noon, signing bills and conversing with his cabinet. When he did finally vacate the White House of his own accord, he returned to his native Tennessee. Johnson gained some measure of political vindication by winning a U.S. Senate seat in 1874, but he died shortly after, in Tennessee, on July 31, 1875.

The Election of 1868

Despite Andrew Johnson's undoubted personal unpopularity, the Democrats intended to run their 1868 campaign on a white supremacist platform and as a plebiscite on Reconstruction. At their convention, they attacked the Congressional Reconstruction policy as "a flagrant usurpation of power" that they believed to be "unconstitutional, revolutionary and void." They pledged to abolish the Freedman's Bureau and all other legislation "designed to secure negro supremacy." Unable to agree on a nominee—their leading figure, Congressman George Pendleton of Ohio having been too blatant a Copperhead leader during the war to garner enough votes in the North this time—the Democrats finally settled on Horatio Seymour, the bland and frail governor of New York. Seymour's patriotism during the war had been called into question, especially when he addressed draft rioters in New York as "my friends."

But the bulk of the campaigning was turned over to Frank Blair of Missouri, who secured his vice-presidential nomination in a letter he wrote just before the Democratic convention, when he insisted that the only way to restore constitutional government was "to declare [the Reconstruction Acts] null and void, compel the army to undo its usurpations at the South, disperse the carpet-bag State Governments . . . and allow the white people to reorganize their own governments." While Seymour rested in New York, Blair took off on a national speaking tour that proved reminiscent of Andrew Johnson's catastrophic swing around the circle. The Republicans had placed the South under the brutal control of black savages who yearned to kill white men and rape white women, Blair proclaimed. Blacks in power would mongrelize the population and reverse evolution. Blair promised that White Power would be reestablished, more than implying that a Democratic administration would license as much southern white violence as necessary to bring about that result.

The Democrats handed the issue of the campaign to the Republicans, who suddenly were seen as the party of law and order. Clearly, Republicans argued, a Seymour/Blair administration would bring about a second round of civil war through implementing "government by assassination and violence, instead of government by law." And indeed, in much of the South, Democratic paramilitary units terrorized blacks, killing white and black Republicans—over 200 in Arkansas and nearly that number in Georgia, and as many as 1,000 in Louisiana. In Opelousas, St. Landry Parish, Louisiana, a white mob destroyed the Republican newspaper in town and then surged into many surrounding plantations, killing as many as 200 blacks. The Democrats carried Georgia and Louisiana, where the violence had been best organized and the fewest blacks dared to go to the polls.

And the Democratic campaign nearly worked. Grant won, but with less than 53 percent of the vote, and probably with a minority of the nation's white electorate. The United States remained bitterly divided not only by Reconstruction but, more deeply, by race relations in general. On these issues, the Republicans maintained only the thinnest and shakiest majority in the political debate.

The new president, Grant, had sought election with the campaign slogan "Let Us Have Peace," which signaled his desire to stop the squabbling over Reconstruction in the name of long-term stability and prosperity. He wanted party unity and national unity, but he was equally reluctant to fight Congress. Grant wanted to end the Civil War for good and to hasten the return of the remaining southern states into the Union. **President Ulysses S. Grant**

However, Radical Republicans in Congress had one more victory to claim before relinquishing control of Reconstruction: black suffrage. The Fifteenth Amendment, adopted by Congress in 1869 and ratified by the states in 1870, was passed to ensure the right to vote, regardless of "race, color, or previous condition of servitude." Radicals had pushed for black suffrage since the waning months of the war. They knew that with the Emancipation Proclamation and the Thirteenth Amendment, which essentially nullified the three-fifths clause of the Constitution, the potential remained for the South to have more seats than the North in Congress. Giving freedmen the vote, Radicals reasoned, would counter the possibility of the white South gaining control in Washington, help to fight northern Democrats who stridently opposed Republican Reconstruction legislation, and create a significant Republican presence in the South. Republicans assumed, with good reason, that former slaves would vote for the party of Lincoln. Radicals also saw black suffrage as a crucial component in destroying the prewar South for good. Even Grant supported the amendment, convinced that the willingness of 180,000 black men to fight for the Union had earned them the right to vote. African Americans also actively sought black suffrage. As early as 1866, Frederick Douglass had visited President Johnson to demand black suffrage as a condition of reconstruction. **The Fifteenth Amendment**

African American suffrage, however, was not an idea supported by all northerners. Postwar attempts to legalize black suffrage in northern states had failed repeatedly, and although the Fourteenth Amendment threatened to reduce representation in any state that denied the vote to all adult males, Congress declined to punish northern states that disallowed black suffrage. Republicans hesitated to make the freedmen's vote a central issue in the election of 1868 for fear of alienating northern whites and losing significant power. Racism continued to be strong throughout the nation, and many whites worried that political equality would lead to social equality and the much feared "amalgamation of the races."

To make the amendment less offensive to white northerners, and thus more likely to pass, the wording of the amendment was kept deliberately vague. Instead of declaring universal suffrage or even guaranteeing freedmen the right to vote, the amendment only prevented states from disenfranchising anyone because of race, color, or previous servitude. States could still reject voters for other reasons. The amendment also avoided the controversial issue of female suffrage. Initially, women's rights advocates argued that the right to vote should not be denied due to "sex," along with "race, color, or previous servitude." But the word was omitted, suffragists were bitterly disappointed, and the movement for female voting rights became deeply divided over race. Elizabeth Cady Stanton angrily denounced the notion that black, Asian, and immigrant men should have the right to vote over native-born white women: "Think of Patrick and Sambo and Hans and Ung Tung who do not know the difference between the Monarchy and a Republic," Stanton stated, "who never read the Declaration of Independence . . . making laws for Lydia Maria Child, Lucretia Mott, or Fanny Kemble." Women, white and black, would wait fifty more years before gaining the right to vote.

Nonetheless, even with watered-down language and avoidance of the women's suffrage issue, Radical Republicans still faced stern opposition to their amendment, especially in the far West, border South, and parts of New England, where fears of black suffrage mixed with apprehensions over immigrant voting. Only in the former Confederacy did the amendment pass easily, largely due to the strong Republican presence in the new state legislatures. Enough votes were garnered to win ratification by stipulating that the remaining southern states still under martial law—Texas, Mississippi, Virginia, and Georgia—had to ratify the Fifteenth Amendment in order to rejoin the Union.

Soon after the amendment's ratification in March 1870, white southerners set about combating it, creating all sorts of elaborate ways to stop blacks from going to the polls. African Americans faced arbitrary tests, grandfather clauses, poll taxes, and residence requirements, even violence, that dissuaded or entirely prevented them from voting. A succession of *Enforcement Acts,* passed in 1870 and 1871, sought to penalize whites who interfered with black voting, including such terrorist groups as the Ku Klux Klan. But the Supreme Court in two 1876 cases, *U.S. v. Reese et al.* and *U.S. v. Cruikshank,* deemed parts of the first Enforcement Act unconstitutional, asserting that the right to vote was a state matter, not a federal one. Not until the 1960s civil rights movement, nearly a hundred years after its ratification, would the original intention of the Fifteenth Amendment, like that of the Fourteenth Amendment, be realized.

The victorious North had sent mixed messages to the defeated South about its political plans for reunifying the nation immediately after the war. There were threats of revenge and retaliation, with some Radicals proposing dramatic and long-lasting changes to southern society. But a bitter impeachment trial and divisions within the Republican Party weakened any unified vision of how best to reconstruct the South. Americans could not imagine a permanent standing army imposing political change through an occupation. Additionally, rather than building a strong and expensive enough bureaucracy to attempt to carry though long-term social change, the American belief in limited government prevailed. It would not be until well into the twentieth century that the presence of the state in people's everyday lives, most notably during peacetime, would be tolerated. Meanwhile, the South faced its own trials of reconstruction.

CHAPTER 11

White and Black Reconstruction in the South: 1865–1872

No part of the United States, no portion of its people, ever faced a more confused and uncertain future than did the people of the South in the summer of 1865. Whites and blacks, rebels and unionists, all had cause to be anxious. All knew that their worlds had changed, but few dared to predict the extent, the cost, or the ultimate results of those changes. Some people looked hopefully to the future; others foresaw only hardship. Mostly, they were perplexed; they floated and drifted, waiting to see what would happen next. "I am at a loss what to do, in fact there is nothing left for me to do, but to wait quietly here until something turns up," conceded a Missouri ex-Confederate in May 1865. Their revolutionary new status as free people further complicated matters for former slaves. One of them recalled, "You felt jes' like you had gone strayed off a-fishing and got lost."

It took a few months just to comprehend that the war was over. Most people knew the end was near when Robert E. Lee surrendered in April, but Lee's army had been only the largest and best-known rebel force. After four years of rumors and false alarms, some suspense remained. When Joseph E. Johnston surrendered his army in North Carolina two weeks after Lee, a degree of inevitability set in, and the capture of Jefferson Davis at Irwinsville, Georgia, on May 10 seemed to seal the fate of the Confederate government. Even so, as shown in chapter 9, with scattered rebel armies only gradually admitting defeat through the early summer, the conflict did not end abruptly or dramatically; rather, it sputtered to a close. Some fervent rebels wanted to continue fighting in a guerrilla war, and the last recorded battle—a Confederate victory—was fought at Palmito Ranch, Texas, on May 13. For diehard Confederates, the reality was simply hard to bear. "It is a humiliating fact," a Tennessee woman finally lamented, "but it is so."

All parties recognized that the aftermath of war would require rebuilding and adjustments, but every group and faction developed its own agenda and its own set of assumptions about the best way to achieve those goals. White and black southerners would find particular difficulties in coping with the new political, social, and economic worlds wrought by war. Black freedom was the biggest hurdle, even for ex-slaves, who had to overcome white resistance and their own expectations in the transition from emancipation to citizenship. The relations between black wage earners and white employers produced the most friction, although a political struggle between North and South to reconstruct the old Confederacy soon overshadowed these tensions. The North, as represented by the Republican Party, won the initial battle with the help of black and white southern allies, but their triumph was short lived. By the early 1870s, ex-Confederates were reasserting southern white nationalism, and their eventual return to power meant the destruction of black political, social, and economic aspirations. After examining first the reaction of southern whites and then that of southern blacks to the end of the war, this chapter will explore some of the reasons for that reversal.

The Mood of Ex-Confederates

Judging from the ravaged physical appearance of the South, the escalating ferocity with which the war had been fought, and southern assumptions about the "meanness" of Yankees, ex-Confederates could not be optimistic in the immediate aftermath of defeat. Just as exaggerated rhetoric and fears had helped propel the nation into war, so, too, would fear-driven assumptions about how the South would be treated shape the actions of rebels and unionists alike in the last half of 1865. Indeed, uncertainty about the means and ends of northern political policy and confusion about who would direct that policy—Congress or the president—would persist for several years after the war.

Physical Condition of the South

The physical and economic condition of the South in itself depressed the spirits of most white people. Much of the capital city of Richmond lay in ruins, as did portions of Fredericksburg and Petersburg in Virginia; Atlanta and Savannah in Georgia; Charleston and Columbia in South Carolina; Selma, Alabama; Oxford, Mississippi; and dozens of smaller towns, not to mention thousands of farms and plantations. Ravaged by fire and vandals, a few of these places had been destroyed by retreating Confederate armies, but most had fallen victim to Union troops, who also ripped up hundreds of miles of railroad track, probably two-thirds of the entire southern network. They demolished factories and machinery. Livestock—especially horses, mules, cattle, and hogs—mostly had disappeared. The Union army also had confiscated property, most notably 5 million bales of cotton, which must be added to the thousands of bales destroyed by Confederates during the war to keep them from falling into enemy hands.

THESE BLACK CHILDREN sitting amidst the rubble of Charleston, South Carolina. suggest the challenges that confronted both black and white southerners after the war. With the North triumphant over the badly battered region, southerners were uncertain about what would happen next.

In all, the Union army had confiscated or destroyed tens of billions of dollars worth of property—not even counting slaves. The modern dollar value of the losses could be measured in hundreds of billions. Replacing or rebuilding all of this seemed like a life's work, nearly impossible to comprehend. The Confederate monetary system had long since become virtually worthless, and people who had invested in Confederate bonds or held Confederate insurance policies lost fortunes. Then, too, nearly 260,000 Confederate fathers, husbands, and brothers would never rejoin their family circles, and at least that many more men had been physically maimed or emotionally scarred by the war.

Exacerbating this physical collapse, terror and violence stalked the South. "We have no currency, no law, save the primitive code that might makes right," a Georgia woman observed. Gangs of deserters, jayhawkers, former guerrillas, and outlaws threatened to steal what possessions people retained and to take their lives if necessary. Many ragged, hungry veterans stole clothing and food as they straggled homeward, and horse stealing became epidemic in some communities. The war had eroded respect for human life and private property.

Soldiers had grown accustomed not only to doling out death but also to "appropriating" whatever unattended food, clothing, blankets, or other goods they desired. The crime rates in both North and South rose sharply in the postwar years as a consequence, but southerners, with no civil courts or organized governments to shield them, suffered most dramatically and most fiercely in the early months of "peace."

Race Relations   Ex-Confederates also feared the end of slavery. They could not imagine how to control black people outside of slavery, and they did not even want to consider the possibility of racial equality, so much contempt did they have for the black race. In their eyes, slave rebellions had been a constant threat before the war, and many white southerners assumed that freed blacks—to them, natural savages—now protected and encouraged by the Union army, would be emboldened to steal, assault, and murder them wholesale. Some of the tens of thousands of slaves who ran away under the protection of Union troops during the war had taunted and mocked their masters, even walking off with the family's clothes and possessions. These slaves may have regarded such thefts as compensation for years of mistreatment or unpaid labor, but masters, who saw themselves as just and humane, felt ill used and imagined even worse behavior now that all blacks had been emancipated, especially in communities where federal occupation troops were themselves African Americans.

A former South Carolina slaveholder envisioned two possible futures, but for her, one loomed far more fearfully and more likely. One of her neighbors who had fled his home at the approach of the Union army returned in June 1865 to find "his large & elegant establishment occupied by his own servants, whom he had left, & who were as humble, respectful & attentive as of old; everything kept in the neatest and cleanest style." Yet she knew that this was far from the norm, for another neighbor, a physician, had been murdered by one of his slaves, and another friend had been "chopped to pieces in his barn." In contemplating the meaning of these starkly contrasting events, given her underlying beliefs about black character, she concluded, "It is fearful to think, for an instant, the foulest demonic passions of the negro, hitherto so peaceful & happy, roused into being & fierce activity by the devilish Yankees."

Labor Shortages   Even whites who did not fear violence to this extent found their daily lives complicated by the loss of subservient black workers. If freedom did not mean bloody slaughter, it most certainly threatened a collapse of accustomed social and economic race relations. Middle- and upper-class southern women, for example, deplored the loss of their house servants. This may not seem like a serious problem to the modern world, but domestic servants were a far more common part of nineteenth-century life than they are in the twenty-first century. Upward of 7 percent of the American workforce labored as maids, cooks, and butlers in the 1860s, hired to do the exhausting, backbreaking, and in many eyes demeaning chores of the average American household. White servants were not unknown in the South, but most southern homes and hotels had always relied on black workers. When newly freed blacks, associating any type of personal service with slavery, refused to be domestics, white women who were unaccustomed to wielding their own mops, brooms, and rolling pins entered a new world. "Everybody else is doing housework," reported a white Georgian of the dismal situation. "But it does seem to me a waste of time for people who are capable of doing something better to spend their time sweeping and dusting while scores of lazy negroes that are fit for nothing else are lying around idle."

Far graver was the potential loss of hundreds of thousand of cheap and disciplined field hands, craftsworkers, and other laborers. This prospect, which could signal the collapse of the entire economy, sent panic waves through the white South. To revive economically, white southerners needed three things: land, investment capital, and labor. They possessed the land (assuming that rumors of widespread confiscation by the government had proved to be false), and they could borrow money from northern and foreign bankers (although this sometimes proved difficult). Labor was the immediate problem, and white southerners would base nearly all of their political, legal, and financial decisions about how to respond to their northern conquerors on this need.

Most people conceded that the black population provided the only practical source of sufficient labor. Some communities made furious but largely futile efforts to recruit immigrant workers from Europe and Asia. A combination of the climate, low wages, and the uncertain political and social future of the South deterred many foreigners from moving South, and many more who arrived left for a variety of other reasons. "Swedes, Germans, and Irishmen had been imported," observed a traveler in Virginia, "but the Swedes refused to eat cornbread, the Germans sloped away north-west-ward, in hopes of obtaining homesteads, and the Irishmen preferred a city career." There were plenty of native whites, but few of them seemed willing to work for wages, especially in jobs that they associated with black—and, therefore menial—labor. There seemed to be no escaping the need for black workers, and this elemental fact would help shape southern race relations for generations to come.

At the same time, ex-Confederates had to deal with threats of violence and challenges to their political and economic supremacy from white southern unionists. The home-front violence between unionists and rebels that had plagued so many wartime communities continued into the postwar years. In fact, as Confederate soldiers and civilian refugees returned to their homes, tensions often increased. "Mississippians have been shooting and cutting each other all over the state," reported a northern traveler. In such places as Arkansas, where pro-Union guerrilla bands had formed to protect their neighborhoods, men on both sides remained armed and poised to contest local sovereignty. Where unionists held the upper hand numerically or were protected by the U.S. Army, retaliation against ex-rebels became the order of the day. "Another man shot," reported a Knoxville, Tennessee, woman in August 1865. "This morning a man (southern) named Cox was in Tooles store when a Lincolnite named Foster came in shook hands with him, inquired after his health & just as Cox turned around shot him in the back." A few days later, she recorded in her diary, "There liked to have been some more shooting in town today between

**Unionist
Revenge**

Rebs and Union men." She added in early September, "We certainly live in horrible times. Scarcely a day passes some one is not killed."

Confederate Exodus

It would be misleading to suggest that such unrelenting violence, chaos, ruin, and near anarchy bedeviled the entire South. Parts of the region remained peaceful and untroubled. Yet, even people in tranquil spots never knew when their luck might run out. Therefore, many ex-Confederates fled the South, though for a variety of reasons. Some people, especially high-ranking rebel soldiers and politicians, left because they anticipated imprisonment—the fate of Jefferson Davis—or execution. Pride motivated diehards who could not tolerate the thought of living under Yankee rule or on equal terms with free blacks. A spirit of adventure invigorated many younger folk; with the war over, life at home seemed dull. Mostly, though, the emigrants doubted their ability to make a living, let alone a life, in the postwar South. "I am thoroughly impoverished like all who stood faithful to our cause," a Tennessean explained, "and like them I have no fortune—disfranchised, an object of constant suspicion, I am an exile and a stranger at my own home." A former Confederate naval officer considered, "Now that I lost my country, I must have something to occupy my ambition as well as to give me a position in life." And a Texan lamented, "This country is completely broken down; no money in it and no business done. Every thing at a stand still. . . . Every prospect is that things will get worse."

They fled by the thousands during the first year, by the tens of thousands over the next decade. They sought new homes, and they looked for them in every nook and cranny of the world. They went to England, France, Egypt, Asia, and South America. Most convenient were Canada and Mexico, and the American West, as before the war, beckoned ambitious, restless, and desperate people to prairies, silver mines, and Pacific ports. If "gold fever" had sent Americans pouring westward in the 1850s, "Texas fever," "Mexico fever," and "Brazilian fever" sent them packing in the 1860s. "Does anybody in your country have the Mexico fever?" a Georgian asked her sister in Tennessee. "Have you any authentic news from Honduras?" asked another southerner. "What of it and what have you determined on? How would California do? We are now receiving direct intelligence from our friends in Brazil all doing well and highly pleased." Mexico and some South American countries actually recruited southerners with promises of cheap land, and Mexico and Brazil drew many planters because those countries still clung to systems of forced labor, peonage in Mexico, slavery in Brazil.

Most startling of all, hundreds of former rebels moved *north* to settle—inconspicuously, they hoped—on fertile farms and in prosperous cities. These were the *Confederate carpetbaggers,* the counterparts of the better-known northern *carpetbaggers* who, pausing only long enough to dump their few belongings in a carpetbag (the nineteenth-century equivalent of a suitcase), flooded the postwar South. Ex-Confederates moved north with less fanfare than their friends and neighbors who went to Mexico and South America. The latter emigrants often embarked in widely publicized and well-organized expeditions, whereas Confederate carpetbaggers glided away as individuals or in single

THE BUSTLE, PROSPERITY, AND OPTIMISM of New York City stood in stark contrast to the condition of southern cities. This view of Broadway looking north from Spring Street was taken in 1867.

families. Northern-bound emigrants sometimes had relatives or friends already in the North to assist them. Yet, both groups had the same ambitious goal: Hopeful of improving their social and financial fortunes, they went looking for "the main chance." "New York is filled with Confederates," observed an amazed Marylander in August 1865. "They appear to have but one idea which is that the South is ruined and no longer habitable. They rush to New York as the center of wealth and they expect to obtain profitable employment at the hands of the very people who have persistently oppressed them."

Still, despite the fervor and commotion, most white southerners remained in the South, too poor, too stunned, or too stubborn to live anywhere else. Also— and crucial for understanding what happened after 1865—many people regained a sense of hope when Andrew Johnson's lenient policies suggested that the business of "reconstruction" might not be so bad after all. Indeed, Johnson seemed to be offering a sort of internal reconstruction, to be directed by southerners themselves. Encouraged by this turn of events, some whites who had fled the South now returned, especially those whose new homes had not met expectations. With a nod and a wink, former rebels took advantage of the president's

Readjustment of White Hopes

generosity to establish governments that demonstrated little of the repentance demanded by the North. This was the white South's gravest miscalculation in the first few months after the war. As shown in chapter 10 but worth reemphasizing here, northerners wanted assurances that the Union had triumphed; Republicans had to know that their party would remain in power. Ex-rebels seemed oblivious to this mood—or were just plain defiant. Yet, the Black Codes and continued dominance of Confederate leaders mocked Union victory and threatened Republican hopes of creating a strong political base in the South. Seeing the threat, Congress roared back with its Joint Committee on Reconstruction, a thumping electoral triumph in 1866, and the Reconstruction Acts of 1867. Only then did former rebels realize how gravely they had misinterpreted the situation.

As ex-Confederates scurried to readjust their political strategy, they also discovered a rising African American threat quite different from the one they had anticipated. The danger that finally emerged, far from being one of murder, rapine, and revenge, became a potent political and economic challenge to white supremacy. Aided by the Fourteenth and Fifteenth Amendments, southern blacks moved to create a new interracial social order that few whites, North or South, thought possible when the war concluded. Most white Americans, despite the Thirteenth Amendment, had continued to see the war as a struggle over the right of secession. If southern slaves had been freed as a consequence, thought northerners, that was fine, but they rarely shared the vision of complete political and social equality that African Americans struggled to create.

Black Expectations and Uncertainty Former slaves shared the uncertainty of their former masters about the political future in the first few months after the war. Most rejoiced to be free; their "day o' jubilee" had arrived at long last. Yet, most freed people remained puzzled about how to translate emancipation into freedom, how to make freedom a reality. "It came so sudden on em," recalled a former Virginia slave, "they wasn't prepared for it. Just think of whole droves of people, that had always been kept so close, and hardly ever left the plantation before, turned loose all at once, with nothing in the world, but what they had on their backs, . . . walking along the road with no where to go." A few people stayed with their old masters, sometimes out of loyalty, sometimes because they feared the unknown world beyond. Others raced away with no thought other than to test their freedom, just to see if they really would be allowed to go where they pleased. "They seemed to want to get closer to freedom," recalled a Texas freedman, "so they'd know what it was—like it was a place or a city."

Nevertheless, most ex-slaves moved with a purpose, usually to satisfy one of two immediate concerns. First, they wanted to reunite their families. This might only require that they walk to a neighboring plantation or nearby refugee camp, but it could also mean a journey of hundreds of miles. Husbands and wives, parents and children who had been separated during slavery or by the war usually had no reliable information about where to find one another. The families may have been separated for many years, and so many masters had evacuated their slaves to safe havens on the approach of the Union army that even when a freed person knew where family members were *supposed* to be, they might, in fact, be in Georgia rather than Virginia, in Texas rather than Mississippi. Freedmen's Bureau agents and northern missionaries helped to track down missing relatives by writing letters and providing transportation, but many families were never reunited. Some people, for decades after the war, continued to place newspaper advertisements and offer rewards for information about missing loved ones. One ex-slave recalled sadly, "De mostest of 'em never git togedder ag'in even after dey sot free 'cause dey don't know where one or de other is."

In addition, thousands of freed people moved either to escape or to return to old homes. This paradox well illustrates the emotional turmoil endured by ex-slaves. People who had left or been sent from their homes during the war often returned to the only place where they felt secure and safe. They were attached to the land they had tilled, and not a few of them anticipated that federal authorities would grant them ownership. There were also the familiar surroundings of old cabins and the terrain, perhaps even a cemetery where parents and children lay buried. These were emotional ties not easily broken.

On the other hand, just as many freed people had an instinctive urge to get away. They could not bear to live in their old slave quarters, amid scenes that had defined their servitude, or in close proximity to former masters. Few of them wandered far. There was no great rush to the North, as many white northern wage earners had feared, and most people eventually returned to their old neighborhoods. Yet, initially, they considered *some* degree of movement an essential means of declaring their personal freedom and independence. "The negroes don't seem to feel free unless they leave their old homes," a perceptive Florida planter noted, "just to make sure they can go when and where they choose." Even people who had been treated kindly by former masters and had no grudge to bear felt compelled to leave. As one departing slave told her mistress, "If I stay here I'll never know I am free."

This latter attitude partly explains why a large number of freed people, even those who had spent their entire lives on farms and plantations, traveled to towns and cities. Just as many Confederate carpetbaggers hoped to submerge their old identities in the anonymity of northern cities, so ex-slaves believed that "freedom was free-er" in an urban setting. "They all want to go to the cities," a white southerner proclaimed. "The fields have no attractions." Freed people who sought work could find jobs there, and everyone believed that towns afforded more protection than the countryside. Union troops—often African American troops—garrisoned many towns and cities, and the army-operated Freedmen's Bureau generally established its local headquarters in them. Freed people sensed that they could find "safe shelter" in towns, observed a white visitor to Charleston, South Carolina, "solely from the blind instinct that where there is force there must be protection."

Movement to Towns

Towns also provided security and a sense of camaraderie within visibly black communities. A curious effect of this urban migration made southern cities far more *racially segregated* than they had been before the war. Black enclaves formed where the newcomers settled in the cheapest and least-desirable housing. There, too, they established churches, schools, political clubs, benevolent societies, and other community institutions. It was a revelation to ex-slaves who had worked on farms and small plantations, and even field hands from large plantations marveled to see so many of their own race engaged openly in all the pursuits and activities of the white man's world. It reinforced their sense of independence and the reality of personal freedom. By 1870 the African American population of most southern towns and cities had at least doubled. The allure of urban life eventually faded for people who were unable to acquire good jobs or who became unhappy with living conditions in the black ghettoes. Many of these disillusioned folk returned to the countryside. Yet, a definite shift had taken place in the living patterns of many southern blacks and, consequently, for white urban residents, too.

Seeking Financial Freedom

Amid all the migration, movement, and unsettledness, the need to make a living became an urgent priority for most ex-slaves. Their immediate response to emancipation had been to stop working entirely. "We's free now, and we's not work unless we pleases," declared a Louisiana freedman. A South Carolina plantation mistress complained in March 1865, "The field negroes . . . will not work, but either roam the country, or sit in their houses." However, the full restoration of peace, joined with hard necessity, ended this brief interlude. Most ex-slaves understood that genuine freedom required financial independence, a means of supporting themselves and their families. Their chances of achieving this goal looked promising, too, with the U.S. government and sympathetic northerners ready to supply at least some of their immediate needs and help shepherd them into the future.

Northern Assistance

Even before the war ended, the Freedmen's Bureau, the Union League, and church-sponsored missionaries from the North established themselves in Union-occupied areas to distribute food and shelter, erect schools, and buoy black hopes. The Union League operated among ex-slaves as it had in the North during the war, as an arm of the Republican Party. The league reminded blacks who were keen on becoming voters and political participants that the Republican Party was the party of Abraham Lincoln and the friend of the black race. The league proved its friendship by helping to build black churches and schools and demanding that the army and the courts protect black rights. By 1868, one historian estimates, virtually every southern black voter belonged to the Union League or a similar Republican political organization.

The Freedmen's Bureau, established by Congress in March 1865 to feed and shelter both black and white refugees, gained additional responsibilities in December. Operated by the army, its *agents* promoted the doctrine of *free labor* to both former slaves and former masters. By establishing freedmen's schools and serving as mediators in legal disputes between the races, the bureau sought to educate and protect black workers. By preaching the mutual dependence of black and white in reviving the southern economy, the bureau hoped to convince employers to "give the system a fair and honest trial." "To make free labor successful," one agent explained, "it is necessary that the laborer shall be treated fairly. . . . Give to the freedmen justice, *impartial justice,* and we believe, he will work better as a

MANY FORMER SLAVES lingered in old "contraband camps" at the conclusion of the war. The people in this camp near Helena. Arkansas (pictured in 1864). may have remained in order to continue working on the adjacent government-leased plantations. which they had cultivated during the war.

freedman than he did as a slave." The bureau encouraged formal contracts between employers and laborers, so that each side might understand the nature of their new obligations and responsibilities. Bureau-directed courts tried to enforce these contracts where civil authority had not been restored.

The teachings of the Union League and activities of the Freedmen's Bureau also generated rumors that the government intended to confiscate rebel lands and redistribute them to ex-slaves. "Forty acres and a mule" became a refrain as pregnant with promise as "Manifest Destiny" and "Fifty-four forty or fight" had been for antebellum whites. "This was no slight error, no trifling idea," confirmed a bureau agent in Mississippi, "but a fixed and earnest conviction as strong as any belief a man can ever have." During the last year of the war, William T. Sherman had given substance to this rumor by turning over abandoned Confederate lands on the Atlantic coast to freedmen as a means of alleviating the refugee problem, and Congress, in early 1865, established a system by which freedmen and white unionists could have potentially leased or purchased confiscated lands. There also had been wartime efforts to establish southern blacks on confiscated or leased plantation lands in such places as the Sea Islands of Georgia and South Carolina, the Natchez District of the Mississippi River valley, and Helena, Arkansas. It seemed only reasonable to former slaves that they should be given a share of the lands that they had tilled for so many generations. "Some of them are declaring they intend to have lands, even if they shed blood to obtain them," came a more extreme report from North Carolina. "Some of them are demanding all of the crop they have raised on the former master's lands."

Black Churches   As they waited in vain for this sort of substantial economic help from the government, freed people developed thriving new institutions to solidify their still fragile sense of independence. The heart of any community, be it in town or country, became the church. Blacks quickly created other means of reinforcing their identity as free people—schools, benevolent societies, fraternal organizations, political clubs, even newspapers—but their churches, and by implication religious faith, served as the emotional glue for everything else. In fact, church buildings functioned not only as houses of worship but as schools, lecture halls, social centers, and political gathering places. Black ministers became the most influential people in developing the new communities. People depended on their preachers not only for spiritual guidance and moral leadership but also for political direction and financial counsel.

The importance of religion may be judged by the circumstances under which most freed people enjoyed regular community worship. An abandoned shed, a dilapidated shack, a person's home, or a sheltered place in the woods might well provide their "church" in rural areas. They required nothing fancy. If the building had a roof, it likely leaked; if it had windows, they probably lacked glass. Many congregations built their own structures from whatever materials they had at hand. Few congregations had a full-time minister, at least not in the early years. Even if they could afford their own preacher, there generally were not enough of them to go around. Circuit riders and itinerants, stopping to preach once or twice a month, were the norm. Local volunteers led worship the rest of the time, both on Sundays and at midweek prayer meetings.

Of course, religion had also been important in slave communities. When Babylon, as some blacks called the Confederacy, fell, newly freed slaves gave thanks by praising the Lord. "I jump up an' scream, 'Glory, glory hallelujah to Jesus! I's free!' " declared a Virginia slave. " 'Glory to God, you come down an' free us; no big man could do it.' " Another man exulted: "Golly! de kingdom hab kim dis time for sure." However, the practice of their faith—which was mostly evangelical Protestantism—had often been circumscribed during slavery. Except in a few cities, slaves had rarely worshiped in their own churches as independent congregations. A combination of white antagonism against accepting freed people as full religious partners, and black desire to control their own churches led to the segregation of the southern Protestant denominations within a very few years after the war. This separation suited white southerners, who wanted to worship Jesus in a strictly segregated setting, and it perfectly satisfied former slaves, who often described their liberation through biblical references to redemption and deliverance, most notably the flight of the Jews out of Egypt. Asked to identify the people living in an adjacent community, an Alabama black replied, "The nationality in there is Methodist," and, indeed, their churches did represent something akin to surrogate nations for black Americans.

EDUCATION WAS AN IMPORTANT THEME in the lives of former slaves. Some of the schools, like this one in the South Carolina Sea Islands, were organized by northern whites. But blacks were soon establishing and operating their own schools, which they deemed a vital part of their communities.

Black Schools

Next in importance were their schools, which might well be part of the churches. Black ministers, often being the only literate members of a community, played pivotal roles as secular teachers. So, too, did many white northerners, most of them young women, who came south after the war to take up a calling as teachers to the freedmen. Quite apart from the more politically oriented Freedmen's Bureau and Union League schools, southern blacks established as many as 500 independent schools in the spring and summer of 1865. Ex-slaves may have counted economic independence as the surest sign of freedom, but education ranked a close second. "If I nebber do anything more while I live, I shall give my children a chance to go to school, for I considers education next best ting to liberty," declared a Mississippi freedman. One Freedmen's Bureau agent estimated in the summer of 1866 that, including students in the "irregular and Sabbath schools" and those people who were "learning at home," some 150,000 ex-slaves and their children were being taught to read.

Black Disappointment

Yet, black optimism turned quickly to puzzlement when few of their expectations were realized. Most people who had left old neighborhoods soon returned, frequently even to their former masters. Many government agents proved not to be the benefactors blacks had expected, sometimes even siding with whites in legal or contractual disputes. Jobs had been hard to find. Life in crowded towns and cities had been cramped and unhealthy. Their fondest hope, land redistribution, had proved too controversial an issue for Congress to implement because it challenged the bedrock belief in private property shared by Republicans and Democrats. And cash wages remained depressed. Earning a dollar a day—the going rate for unskilled labor before the war—became a fixed idea in many black minds. "A dollar a task! A dollar a task!" they chanted. Even if seeking less, in consideration of receiving firewood, food, clothing, or shelter, former slaves expected that emancipation would give them a strong bargaining position. "I wish to tell you if you will give me twelve dollars per month I will stay with you," a Georgia freedman told his old master, "but if not, I have had good offers and I will find another place."

Labor Problems

Questions concerning wages and employment caused the most difficult problems of adjustment for black and white southerners in the first few years after the war and, as suggested earlier, it would loom like a specter over the fu-

THE FREEDMEN'S BUREAU, established by the U.S. government to protect former slaves and promote racial harmony, became a controversial player in the political and social reconstruction of the South. The motives and sympathies of individual agents were often questioned by both southern blacks and whites.

ture of the races. Neither side seemed to understand the material and emotional needs of the other. "Some folks think free labour will be cheap & that the freedmen will gladly hire out for food and clothing," a white South Carolinian observed. "But I think not, they seem so eager to throw off the yoke of bondage they will suffer somewhat, before they will return to the plantations." The freedmen's efforts to secure fair wages struck whites as just another example of black refusal to acknowledge their naturally subordinate position. Curiously, many whites expected even *more* subservience from blacks to whom they paid wages than they had from their slaves. This was especially true when ex-slaves ended up working for former masters, as did many. "Their idea of freedom," explained a Freedmen's Bureau agent of blacks in Mississippi, "is that they are under no control; can work when they please, and go where they wish." Whites routinely interpreted such demonstrations of independence as evidence of disrespect and defiance.

Changing black perceptions of labor, gender roles, and family relationships further complicated matters. If black men wanted to be treated with the respect due free laborers, black women demanded no less. As family members reunited and slave marriages became sanctioned in law, wives also demanded certain terms of labor. Many female field hands refused to return to hard agricultural labor, at least not full time. They wanted to operate their own households and raise their children, not spend all their day working for other people. Neither did they want those children to work for strangers. "The freedmen," reported a white Georgian, "have almost universally withdrawn their women and children from the fields, putting the first at housework and the latter at school." Even if consenting to work as domestic servants, as many ex-slaves wound up doing, they negotiated for limited duties and hours of labor. Housework could be even more demanding than fieldwork, and the very nature of the servant–mistress relationship meant that the latter expected the sort of loyalty and constant availability not seen in occupations outside the home.

Postwar economic realities also meant that white employers could not afford high wages, a circumstance worsened by drought and small crops in many parts of the South in 1866–1867. Both blacks and whites had trouble adjusting to the situation, although the former group had fewer options. Blacks learned that freedom could be a hard road and that they had no practical choice but to compromise and negotiate with white land owners. Planters, who still held the advantage in negotiations before 1868, adapted more slowly. They stubbornly set limits on wages and other concessions, even to the extent of blacklisting workers whom they regarded as especially stubborn or insolent. "Well I told the whole crew to go to hell, and they left," explained a Virginian who refused the wage demands of his former slaves. Here, too, the Black Codes, as explained in the preceding chapter, served to limit black bargaining power.

Republicans became convinced that white southerners would never accord blacks equal rights if left to their own devices, a conviction deepened by the violence directed against former slaves. Such violence was limited in most states during the first year after the war, but it accelerated as whites responded to assertions

Violence toward Blacks

of black freedom and equality, which they regarded as grave threats to social order and stability. Blacks were beaten and sometimes murdered for such vague offenses as "insolence" and "putting on airs." Any black suspected of violence against whites—assault or rape—would almost certainly face death, with or without formal legal proceedings. Race "riots"—almost exclusively white invasions of black neighborhoods—broke out in several southern towns in 1866, most notably Memphis and New Orleans, and by 1867 the turmoil had spread to Charleston, Norfolk, and Atlanta. Some of these outbreaks were inspired more by political than social factors, such as the New Orleans riot, in which 48 people were killed and 166 injured, but the reluctance of whites to accept blacks as citizens remained the essential element in most violence. White Union soldiers started some of the early confrontations by initiating attacks on black soldiers or civilians, but the onus always stuck to the native white population, who were by far the dominant group of attackers. This central subject of postwar racial violence, including the role of the Ku Klux Klan, is discussed more thoroughly in chapter 12.

Republican Alliance in the South

Not until the Reconstruction Acts of 1867 stripped ex-Confederates of their political power and elevated a new ruling coalition of northern carpetbaggers, white unionists (called *scalawags*), and freedmen did the situation change. After three years of false starts and frustrated plans, this sometimes uneasy alliance finally gave Republicans a working political majority in the South.

Carpetbaggers

Most of the thousands of carpetbaggers who arrived in the decade after the war were former Union soldiers or Freedmen's Bureau agents who became so taken with the financial and political opportunities open to them that they stayed in the South. They had been farmers, teachers, businessmen, lawyers, merchants, and journalists—mostly middle class and educated—before the war. Some of them were high-minded individuals who saw a chance to promote racial equality, champion free labor, and introduce what they regarded as northern "civilization" to the backward, barbaric South. Others measured success in terms of personal financial or political advancement, although some combination of ambition and idealism undoubtedly motivated many—if not the majority—of carpetbaggers. Even so, former Confederates—who apparently gave carpetbaggers their colorful name—despised these people as unprincipled and unwanted outsiders.

Scalawags

Scalawags were even more important to the new Republican coalition. The name, given to them by their political rivals, had no precise meaning, but it implied unscrupulous knaves who had turned against their own kind, "mangy dogs," "filthy sheep," "scaly pigs," "scurvy cattle," and "white negroes." In point of fact, scalawags were motivated, like carpetbaggers, by a combination of factors: Many of them believed that they acted in the best interests of a defeated South, but not a few had also calculated that the Republican Party offered the fastest ticket to personal financial recovery. Some scalawags, such as former Confederate general James Longstreet, had been unequivocal rebels, but most of them had been wartime unionists. Many, too, had been Whigs, and like many former northern Whigs, they embraced the Republicans as the natural heirs to their old party.

WHILE SECURING ECONOMIC INDEPENDENCE was the highest priority of former slaves, winning their political rights ranked a close second. When the revised southern state constitutions gave black men the right to vote and hold office, political meetings like this one became an integral part of community life.

However, southern blacks represented the largest and most crucial part of this triple alliance, though it was not the first time that they had tried to assert themselves politically. In the autumn and winter of 1865, freedmen had held mass political meetings in towns and rural communities across the old Confederacy. They drew up petitions and appeals requesting equal rights from the new postwar white governments at their own local and state conventions. The new white governments, being Confederate in sympathy, ignored their wishes. This failure naturally discouraged many blacks, as did the appearance of serious fissures in their own ranks. Political divisions and resentments, often based on social distinctions that went back decades, developed almost immediately, especially in such urban areas as New Orleans and Charleston. Free-born blacks often thought themselves superior to former slaves, and similar tensions existed between light- and dark-skinned people, the educated and the uneducated, the affluent and the poor, the skilled and the unskilled, the southern- and northern-born.

Yet, petty bickering aside, these early political conventions produced a recognized political leadership and introduced African Americans to the mechanics of the democratic process and to organized political action. With the Republican Party ready to back them, they enthusiastically embraced new political oppor-

Black Political Role

tunity. Their political ascendancy would be brief, no more than four or five years in most states, but during that short time of high hopes and progress, they enjoyed a degree of political activism not repeated for nearly another century. "You never saw a people more excited on the subject of politics than are the negroes of the south. They are perfectly wild," commented an astonished white southerner. "It is the hardest thing in the world to keep a negro away from the polls," affirmed an Alabamian, "that is the one thing he will do, to vote."

Blacks not only voted after 1867 but also ran for office, made laws, and pursued all the rights that had thus far eluded them. They revived the campaign to redistribute southern land. "Forty acres and a mule" became their cry, and this time, blacks believed they would get it. "The hunger to have the same chances as the white men they feel and comprehend. . . . That is what brings them here [to the polls]," realized a northern observer on election day in 1868. It was heady stuff, this new political clout. But it would have limits.

Limits on the Black Political Role

Although an appreciable number of carpetbaggers and scalawags wanted to do right by their African American allies, they and their northern cronies never intended that blacks should control the South. They could not, any more than southern Democrats—their main political rivals—conceive of former slaves as intelligent enough or sufficiently civilized to hold the reins of government. Someday, perhaps, but now was the white man's season, his turn to profit from power. They would use black votes, even permit a certain number of blacks to hold office, but they would call the political shots and control the economic agenda. A natural geographical division of influence evolved between carpetbaggers and scalawags. Generally speaking, carpetbaggers became most prominent in the lower South—states such as Alabama, Mississippi, Georgia, Florida, and South Carolina—that had large black populations and where many of them had purchased plantations or, as merchants, tapped into the plantation economy. Scalawags, while flourishing everywhere, gained their greatest influence in the upper South, especially Tennessee, North Carolina, Missouri, and West Virginia, all notable regions of wartime unionism.

The numbers tell the story. No southern state elected a black governor, and only three states had black lieutenant governors (a total of six men). Only South Carolina elected and maintained (for six years) a black majority in its House of Representatives, but whites controlled the state Senate. Mississippi had a black majority population but elected only forty blacks (as opposed to seventy-five whites) to its legislature. Florida, with a 45 percent black population, elected only nineteen blacks to fill seventy-six legislative seats. The South elected fourteen blacks to the U.S. House of Representatives, and in the days before the popular election of U.S. senators, two made it to the Senate. No black held a major state political office in Alabama, Georgia, North Carolina, or Texas; they were more successful at the local level, especially in Louisiana, Mississippi, and South Carolina, where many communities had black mayors, sheriffs, justices of the peace, town councilmen, and county supervisors. They also received—though not without exerting steady political pressure—patronage posts, such as postmaster and tax collector.

From one perspective, this was all rather spectacular, given the status of most of these men just a few years earlier. African Americans were making and enforcing the laws of the land; the bottom rail, as blacks were fond of saying, was now on top. It was also clear that, despite gerrymandering efforts to make legislative districts either majority white or black, at least some blacks were voting for white men. Overall, some 600 blacks served as legislators, and nearly 2,000 won election to national, state, or local office before 1877. So far as it went, and as short lived as it would be, this represented a genuine revolution in U.S. politics and society—or at least in *southern* politics and society. One favorably impressed British observer called it a "mighty revolution." Still, given the fact that blacks held the balance of electoral power in the South (carpetbaggers, for example, accounted for no more than 2 percent of the population), they expected more.

Black Leadership

One could not help but be impressed by the large number of able black leaders. A considerable number had at least some education. Nearly all of the northern-born blacks had attended school; southern blacks, both slave and free, had received a smattering of education from former masters, the Freedmen's Bureau, or missionary groups. Most of the men elected to executive positions had been free born, although the majority of legislators had been slaves.

Hiram R. Revels, a minister and educator, born free in North Carolina, had traveled widely through the upper South and the Midwest before the war, and he had helped to enlist black troops during the conflict. In 1870, having settled in Mississippi, he became the first black elected to the U.S. Senate. Jonathan Gibbs, a Philadelphia-born graduate of Dartmouth College, served as Florida's secretary of state from 1868 to 1872. His brother Mifflin became the most prominent African American in postwar Arkansas as a county attorney and municipal judge. James D. Lynch and Francis L. Cardozo served as secretaries of state in Mississippi and South Carolina, respectively. They were both free-born mulattos who had first gained prominence as ministers and teachers and, like many black officeholders, had acquired knowledge of political organization through service in the church or as educators. Other men cut their political teeth in the Union League, fraternal organizations, and volunteer fire companies.

Southern Republican Divisions

This complex mix of political interests and agendas inevitably produced divisions among southern Republicans. Although agreeing on general principles, they frequently clashed over details. Black politicians complained early on about their proportionately small share of political offices and patronage, and all joined in the heated debate about the best economic plan for their states. These and other fissures had already developed between 1867 and 1869 when the new state constitutions were being written. Special conventions—dubbed "black and tan" conventions, where blacks and mulattos reportedly held sway—had created the new governments that replaced the hastily erected, rebel-controlled concoctions. Virtually all of the new constitutions borrowed extensively from the Declaration of Independence to stress equality of the races. As it happened, women benefited, too, as they received property and legal rights rarely conceded before the war (such as the right to sue for divorce).

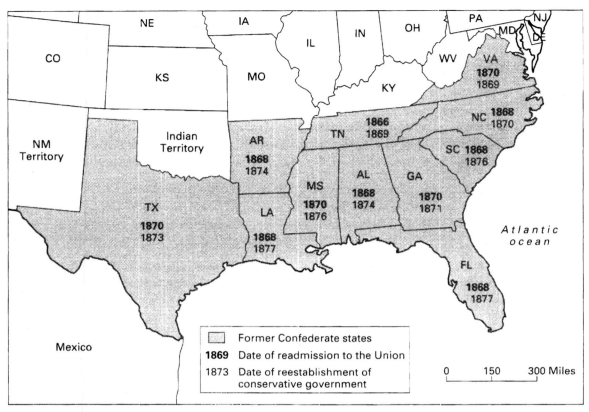

THIS MAP SHOWS the slow and disjointed process by which the southern states returned to the Union and eventual "home rule." Not until 1870—which marked a period of time longer than the war itself—had all states written new constitutions and been readmitted to the Union. On average, it took state Democratic parties another four and a half years to regain political majorities.

Still, compromise remained the rule, and trade-offs had to be made. All of the conventions praised the benefits of education, and virtually every state established a public school system. However, most schools were either explicitly or implicitly racially segregated. The conventions stressed the need for equal economic opportunity, but none provided the land distribution desired by blacks, and they placed severe restrictions on other much ballyhooed "leveling" policies, such as debtor relief and progressive tax plans.

Southern Republican Dilemma
With the new governments up and running and the new Republican coalition finally in place, controversy swirled around the treatment of defeated rebels, and on this subject, the party's southern wing betrayed its earliest vulnerability. White *Centrists* (usually, though not exclusively, identified with scalawags) were uneasy about the way the party had seized power. These moderates knew that the party had established its dominance courtesy of fed-

eral legislation, overtly rigged elections, and the presence of the army. Consequently—and likely because they were mostly southerners themselves—Centrists believed that they had to bring more southern whites into the party with conciliatory, middle-of-the-road policies. Common sense dictated that diehard ex-Confederates, although temporarily excluded from the political process by the Reconstruction Acts and the Fourteenth Amendment, must sooner or later rejoin public life. The party dare not alienate white voters on a permanent basis, warned Centrists, especially not men of influence and prestige. "It is impossible to build up and maintain a party here on the reconstruction line," explained a Georgian, "without the aid of leading Southern men who know our people and sympathize with them."

The *Radicals* (usually, though not exclusively, identified with the carpetbaggers) disagreed. They would trust to Congress, the army, and their interracial coalition to maintain an electoral majority. They believed that, come what may, they could count on the black vote; politically, black voters had nowhere else to go. Nor did the Radicals believe that scalawag allies, whatever their gripes, could seriously challenge them. Northern-born Radicals also had the ear of Congress and so controlled access to federal patronage and largesse. That was enough for them.

Depending on local circumstances and on which group—carpetbaggers, scalawags, or freedmen—held the majority, this battle played itself out differently in each southern state. The Centrists gradually won the day by making it relatively easy for former rebels in most states to reclaim the rights to vote and hold office, but their generosity angered many within the Republican Party, while securing no support from the newly reenfranchised white voters. Radicals questioned the depth of loyalty among their white southern cohorts and wondered aloud about the future of the party. A Texas Radical, typical of many hardliners in North and South, feared that the southern wing was "hopelessly broken down" by 1870. "It has recruited too many already," he declared, "and the more it takes in the worse for the cause of Republicanism."

So began the slow but steady crumbling of the South's Republican Party and the return of the region to *home rule*, meaning control by a white supremacist Democratic Party. The change came relatively soon in some states, by 1871 in Tennessee, Virginia, North Carolina, and Georgia, although it was not completed throughout the South until 1877. The removal of the occupying army provides a partial explanation for the Republican collapse. As a South Carolina newspaper predicted in 1868, "These constitutions and governments will last just as long as the bayonets which ushered them into being shall keep them in existence." That view reflects much truth, for the army played a major part in governing and maintaining order in the South during the early years of Reconstruction. However, as most of the troops—all but 20,000—were withdrawn by 1868, their role became increasingly symbolic. Consequently, more important reasons for the collapse of Republican rule lay within the nation's changing social and economic climate, especially as it related to the onset of the Gilded Age and the self-defeating policies of the Republican Party.

Southern Republican Decline

The Gilded Age   The *Gilded Age* seemed an inevitable result of Union victory in the war. Mark Twain coined the phrase in an 1873 novel of the same name, coauthored with Charles Dudley Warner. Something had gone terribly wrong with American democracy, they said. Outwardly, the United States radiated wealth, power, grandeur. It glowed like a golden icon; yet, as with all false idols, the glittering surface disguised base material, a rotten core. The nation had become fat and greedy, more so even than before the war, declared the authors. Great wealth had corrupted public behavior and public virtue to an unprecedented degree.

Because Twain and Warner wrote satire, they exaggerated the peril of the nation and the uniqueness of their depraved era. Yet, they identified precisely many of the ills that had gone unchallenged in the wake of Union military victory. They lambasted the lobbying and bribery that had grown rampant in the national capital and in nearly every state capital of the country. They exposed the politics of greed, the immorality of business, the political exploitation of southern blacks, the social rise of the nouveau riche. The tawdriness of the age became a raging disease that infected even honest folk. Their central character was just such an honest man, well meaning and generous, but even he was sucked into the world of hucksterism and promotion. "I've got the biggest scheme in the world on earth," he rejoiced naively, "and I'll take you in; I'll take in every friend I've got that's ever stood by me, for there's enough for all, and to spare." That same spirit had been one of the motivations that sent many of the Yankee and Confederate carpetbaggers scrambling to seek their fortunes. It was now inspiring and nurturing an era of scandal and *bossism* in politics, and it had begun to lay the groundwork for the rise of big business and corporate America, twin behemoths that would reach full stride in the 1880s and 1890s.

Twain and Warner were not alone in their appraisal. Reformers, writers, and social commentators of all stripes yearned for honest government, bemoaned the decline of American democracy, and deplored the new era of failure and excess. Walt Whitman blasted the "depravity of the business classes," the "hollowness of heart" betrayed by his fellow citizens, and the "canker'd, crude, superstitious, and rotten" nature of postwar government and society. Even as he rejoiced that the war had ended the "throes of Democracy," the intuitive poet sensed something still amiss:

> Democracy, the destin'd conqueror, yet treacherous lip-smiles everywhere,
> And death and infidelity at every step.

Expansion of   The political problems, especially as revealed in the process of reconstruct-
Government   ing the South, lay in the old adage that power corrupts. The triumph of the
Power   Union and the Republicans had bestowed new, unprecedented prerogatives on the national government. One could already see it coming during the war in the operation of congressional investigating committees, the restructuring of the national banking and monetary systems, and the renewed belief that government should play a more prominent role in regulating and promoting economic growth and the public welfare. With secession and states' rights in

disrepute, the federal government acted with less restraint and faced fewer challenges to the expansion of its power than ever before.

This spirit shaped the new southern state governments, too. Even though created largely by black and white southerners, the whole thrust of the Republican regime defied, in many ways, southern values, assumptions, and traditions. Determined to secure the triumph of unionism and encourage a nascent racial equality, southern Republicans necessarily adopted the guidelines of the triumphant *northern* Republican Party and a national government that, regardless of exaggerated antebellum southern rhetoric about northern domination, clearly *did* express northern values after 1868 and had the power to impose them. Therefore, as the southern wing of the party groped to reshape southern government, it was obliged to do so according to the new northern definition of public responsibility.

This way of thinking left southern Republicans politically vulnerable, and that accelerated their collapse. The story of Reconstruction in the South is really eleven different stories, one for each of the ex-Confederate states, but that was especially true after 1867 as southerners responded to the Reconstruction Acts. Because the political and economic challenges facing each state varied, each developed its own strategies and solutions to meet them. Yet, there were enough similarities, especially when considering the return to Democratic white home rule, to draw a general picture of what happened and why.

Self-Defeating Southern Republican Programs

To begin with, Republican Centrists became increasingly uneasy about the northern tinge of their southern party. They understood the need to abide by Republican principles, especially because Congress held both the power of patronage and the purse strings for southern economic development. Indeed, most Centrists heartily endorsed "the broad principles of Republican liberty and equality," as a Texas moderate declared. But it became increasingly clear to them that their Radical allies would remain the conduits by which congressional favors flowed southward, even in states with the largest and most effective Centrist wings, such as Alabama, Florida, Georgia, and Mississippi. Adding to their frustration, Centrist hopes of gaining a white southern majority by wooing ex-Confederates into the fold had been singularly unsuccessful. Thoroughly disenchanted by 1872, many of them would call the system corrupt and withdraw to join the Liberal Republican movement or the Democratic Party, to be explained in the next chapter.

Economic policies played a crucial role, too, in this southern version of Gilded Age politics. Essentially, the southern Republican governments tried to do too much too soon and at too high a financial price. In their rush to bring the backward South up to northern standards—to "modernize" it, some historians would say—they launched a slew of new state-sponsored, state-funded programs. Schools, hospitals, orphan asylums, penitentiaries, and a variety of economic schemes, especially railroads, were all wonderful ideas, and they appeared in every state—if not for the first time, then at least with vastly larger budgets to fund them. Some states experimented with free medical or legal aid for the poor. Legislation to promote racial equality in education, public transportation, and accommodations also became part of some of these programs.

But the ambitious agendas exposed two lethal weaknesses. First, not all factions—and this is what they quickly became—within the party agreed on all aspects of the plans. The division between Centrists and Radicals aside, the carpetbaggers, scalawags, and freedmen had reasons to support or criticize one or more parts of the legislation. Even so, some of the objections were surprising. For example, heated disputes erupted concerning the laws that promoted racial integration. White southerners, as one might suppose, adamantly opposed such laws, but many blacks voiced skepticism, too. Some blacks, showing their developing political savvy, feared that if the party pushed too soon for integration, its fragile coalition would splinter. They declared themselves quite content, for the moment at least, with a policy of separate but equal. Their own churches, schools, and benevolent societies had so effectively promoted and protected their well-being and were so unquestionably under their own control that racial integration outside the political realm seemed unnecessarily risky to many blacks.

Southern Economic Problems

Equally corrosive of Republican political power was the price tag of their ambitious programs. It all cost a huge amount of money, and a combination of rising taxes, public corruption, and a debilitating economic depression after 1873 divided southern Republicans at the same time that it gave Democrats an effective campaign issue against incumbents. Some Republican laws, including those affecting education and the administration of justice, won general support, but plans for economic development, most of them aimed at spreading the market revolution to southern towns and farms, rendered Republicans vulnerable. Only by wedding southern agriculture, mining, and industry to the national economy could Republicans hope to tap the financial potential of the region, generate an era of prosperity, and secure the financial and political fortunes of the new southern leadership. This would not be easy, however, for the economic interests of North and South had diverged significantly since the start of the war.

Sectional Economic Differences

A brief survey of these conflicting interests will help to explain the situation. A higher proportion of northern industry and mechanization had already differentiated the two sections in 1860, but by 1870 those and many other differences had become stark. Northern dependence on industry and the factory system grew appreciably during the war, especially in the manufacture of such war-related products as armaments, shoes, and clothing. In addition, northern business practices became streamlined and more efficient, all of which propelled the northern economy toward an era of big business and corporate organization in the last third of the nineteenth century. The war had enabled such men as Andrew Carnegie, J. P. Morgan, George Pullman, Gustavus Swift, Charles Pillsbury, Marshall Field, Philip Armour, and John D. Rockefeller to achieve significant wealth and power by the 1870s, and they would soon revolutionize the northern—and subsequently the U.S.—economic system.

Even northern farming emerged from the war more in tune with the new industrial age. Mechanization now held the key to success in the largest segment of the northern farm market: grains. Cyrus McCormick had been manufactur-

MECHANIZED FARMING helped the North win the war and made rural northern communities more prosperous than their black and white southern counterparts after the war. This scene depicts Wisconsin farmers in the 1870s.

ing harvesters, reapers, threshers, rakes, mowers, seed drills, cultivators, and binders for northern farmers for decades, but the wartime demands for grain *and* soldiers awakened northerners to the potential value of farm mechanization. An excited McCormick had told one of his Illinois salesmen at the start of the war, "Remember 20,000 militia have to leave this state . . . and these men will have to come, many or a large share of them, from the farms." Not surprisingly, the number of mowing machines manufactured in northern factories more than trebled, to 70,000, between 1861 and 1864. Even farmers who could not afford machines found their work made easier by such inventions as the chilled-iron moldboard plow, introduced in 1869 to midwestern farmers who sought to scour the tough sod and clinging loam of the prairies, and the horse-drawn "sulky" plow, which allowed farmers to ride behind their animals.

Changes in farming, industry, and business further transformed northern life by accelerating urban growth and altering concepts of labor. The mechanization of farm work meant fewer jobs on farms. The growth of industry, trade, and manufacturing meant more and larger cities. Immigration to the United States contributed to these trends when it rebounded from a slump in the late 1850s and early 1860s. Large numbers of European immigrants, who came increasingly more often from urban rather than rural areas, preferred industrial occupations to agriculture. Consequently, fewer northerners were "self-employed" either as farmers or artisans by the 1870s; more than two-thirds of the nation had become "wage earners." Also, many of these laborers were women, who, by entering the wartime workforce, had made it more acceptable for even middle-class women to seek gainful employment. Northern workers generally became more assertive, organizing more and larger labor unions to demand higher wages, shorter hours, and safer working conditions in factories, mines, and other industrial jobs. And all these changes, unsettling at best to traditional Americans, were accompanied by social stress and, quite often, outbursts of violence

Meanwhile, some southerners talked about expanding the region's industrial base or at least "modernizing" and diversifying agriculture, but they accomplished little. The traditional cash crops of cotton, tobacco, rice, and sugar were not suited to mechanization, yet they continued to dominate southern economic thinking. It would take a century beyond the Civil War before an effective tobacco harvester was invented. The cotton gin had proved indispensable since the 1790s, but the mechanical difficulties of developing an effective cotton picker would not be solved until the twentieth century. As one planter lamented, "Cotton's a ticklish plant to raise. You've got to watch it mighty close." Nor had anyone tackled the problems of cultivating or harvesting rice and sugar with machines.

Even had machines been available, southern farmers could not have afforded them. The value of the average southern farm in 1870 was $1,456, lowest of any region of the country and more than $1,000 below the national

THIS LONE FARMER at his plow cannot be identified by race, location, or date, but he perfectly represents the stagnant condition of southern agriculture—and with it the southern economy—in the aftermath of the war.

average. Moreover, with cotton prices plunging after 1868—from 43 cents per pound to only 10 cents by 1876—farmers had little liquid capital or credit. The South's postwar poverty prevented farmers from buying meaningful amounts of artificial fertilizers that would have helped them reverse the nitrogen-depleting effects of cotton and tobacco on the region's exhausted soils. A large surplus of ultimately cheap labor also dampened the incentive to purchase or develop machines. Consequently, mules and plows, hoes and rakes remained the standard tools of southern farmers.

The situation only worsened when, desperate to end the South's postwar economic stagnation and to settle the labor issue, planters and laborers turned to *sharecropping* and *tenant farming*. These two labor systems could be adapted to any type of farming, but they were most often used to produce ever greater amounts of cotton. In sharecropping, workers, who were most often black, struck a deal with planters to cultivate 20 to 40 acres of land (the average size of a family cotton farm) if the land owner provided them with a house, tools, seed, and sometimes a mule. Sharecropper and planter divided profits (though not always evenly) from the resulting crop. Tenant farming, more often involving poor whites than blacks, allowed families with a little cash, a few tools, but no land to reach similar arrangements. A land owner provided land, a house, and whatever tools or animals the tenant needed. The tenant received all the profits from the crop but used them to pay rent (usually 25 to 30 percent of the crop) and to reimburse the landowner for the initial outlay. The *crop-lien system* offered a variation on tenancy, in which farmers—black or white—borrowed enough money from the land owner (sometimes a merchant or a banker who held title to the land) to meet living and operating expenses while they planted and harvested the land owner's crop. A mortgage, or lien, was placed on the crop and any other chattel property the farmer owned to ensure repayment of the loan, plus extremely high interest.

Sharecropping and Tenant Farming

These arrangements represented the most common means by which southern planters and land owners acquired nonwage farmhands, although as one observer commented, "the details of these variations in dealings of landlord and tenant" were "practically endless." Unhappily for most tenants and sharecroppers, the system almost inevitably drove them into debt, victims of low crop yields, falling cotton prices, and high interest rates. Low cotton prices made the crop-lien system especially risky, as tenants could rarely "pay out" once they fell into debt. Hopes of saving enough money to purchase their own land rarely materialized, and they became trapped in a vicious economic cycle of more loans and deeper debt. Their drab, ramshackle cabins stood as testimony to the South's depressed economic future. Well into the twentieth century, one white southerner testified, "All of our folks before us was tenant farmers and that's all we've ever been." For blacks, it was but one step removed from slavery.

Most people agreed that the long-term solution to these woes was to expand southern economic markets, but that could only be done by rebuilding and rejuvenating the region's railroads. With a heavy reliance on river transport be-

Southern Railroads a Key Factor

fore the war, the South had constructed far fewer railroads than the North. The war widened this gap, as most southern roads fell into disrepair or were destroyed. Completion of the first transcontinental railroad in 1869 awakened everyone, including southern Democrats, to how necessary it had become for the South to catch up—and fast! Railroads would allow southerners to tap into the national economy; that meant jobs, investment opportunities, and profits for all. "A free and living Republic [will] spring up in the track of the railroad as inevitably, as surely as grass and flowers follow in the spring," a Tennessee Republican asserted. Going still further, and stressing the political benefits of railroads, a North Carolinian insisted, "The party that first completes the Internal Improvements System of the state without regard to costs will hold the reins of power here for years to come."

Unfortunately for Republicans, cost did become an issue—that and corruption. Economic development generally, not to mention all the public welfare programs, required high taxes; when the promised results were slow to materialize, existing state debts grew larger, and the days of affluence seemed farther away than ever. Construction plans were delayed or scrapped altogether. Companies went bankrupt, which caused some states to do likewise and others nearly so. Most states had sold bonds to help finance grants to private companies; when the companies folded or failed to show a profit, the states lost money and credibility.

Railroads were an especially risky business; too many things could go wrong. Most railroads far exceeded their projected construction costs. Severe labor shortages occurred when blacks opted for agricultural jobs and insufficient numbers of immigrants could be recruited. The companies and states overestimated the number of potential investors, so government and company bonds went begging or had to be sold at vastly reduced prices. Rapid construction too often resulted in shoddy work, which led to frequent breakdowns and high maintenance costs. Few railroads drew as many customers as they had expected, a problem exacerbated by the states themselves, which generally commissioned far more lines than necessary or desirable. Georgia, for example, chartered thirty-seven railroads between 1869 and 1871. Many railroads also lost business to river transport, which continued to cost less. Mississippi planters, who could ship a bale of cotton from Natchez to New Orleans for 75 cents by riverboat, had to pay $3 by rail.

Corruption, the hallmark of the Gilded Age, exacerbated all of these problems. From the passage of legislation to create a route, to the granting of a charter for a road's construction and operation, politicians and promoters all expected a piece of the action. Lobbyists bribed legislators with cash and gifts in return for charters; contractors routinely charged exorbitant prices for materials and inflated the cost of labor. "They plunder, and glory in it," declared an observer of such machinations in South Carolina, "they steal, and defy you to prove it." Politicians could also profit from what is now called *insider trading*, that is, buying stock or investing in companies before the public knows about impending charters and contracts. "I belonged to the General Assembly," a black Louisiana legislator acknowledged unabashedly, "and knew about what it could do, etc. My investments were made accordingly."

Democrats looked on gleefully—hypocritically, too, for they endorsed the goal of economic development, promoted railroad expansion, and joined with Republicans to pass the enabling legislation. However, when things turned sour, Democrats blamed the party in power and swore that they would clean up corruption, reduce taxes, and install efficient, honest government if given the chance.

Southern Democratic Resurgence

Southern Democrats had been looking for a way to win back political power. At first, a minority in the party had tried the reverse strategy of the Republican Centrists by recruiting blacks to the Democratic Party. By announcing that they had accepted the inevitable consequences of black emancipation, including suffrage and legal equality, these *New Departure*, or "soft-shell" Democrats believed that they had a far better chance of bringing blacks into the party than they did of converting longtime white political foes. More conservative Democrats, the *Bourbons*, who dominated most state parties, would have none of it. First of all, they did not believe black voters would buy the New Departure rhetoric, at least not in large enough numbers to make a difference at the polls. To them the New Departure seemed willing to sacrifice the ideological (and racial) purity of the party by compromising with the Republican regime. The great danger of the antebellum years, centralization of political power, was wildly increasing in Washington, D.C., they declared. The mission of the Democratic Party remained, as it had been before the war, to save the country from this growing evil. Even an old Whig like Alexander H. Stephens could agree: "This country must be redeemed, if ever it is redeemed, by the old line Democratic Jefferson ideas & principles."

In time, the Bourbons—who came to be known as the *Redeemers*—would gain the upper hand and claim credit for the return to home rule. They exploited Republican economic failures to swing white southerners in their direction and strengthened their appeal by pointing to a wide range of other related issues that Republicans had ignored or momentarily shuffled aside. State legislatures had ignored or diverted funds from needed river and harbor improvements, used money earmarked for education to finance failing railroad schemes, and generally forgot about land reform, at least partly because the promotion of small homesteads contradicted their vision of an industrialized New South. Tax reform became an especially important means of wooing white farmers. Southern states had received 30 to 60 percent of their revenues from the taxation of slave property before the war. Most antebellum whites had paid only a modest (25 cents to a dollar) poll tax, with virtually nothing demanded for their land. In contrast, 60 percent of Republican revenue schemes during Reconstruction relied on more progressive land and real-estate–based school taxes, which were paid by everyone on the basis of actual wealth. When a severe economic depression hit the country—the Panic of 1873—the rickety framework of the southern economy betrayed itself. A record number of farm and property foreclosures ruined small farmers and investors, thus destroying much of the tax base. Small wonder the crucial swing voters in most southern states—small and middling white farmers—entered or returned to the Democratic fold.

However, corruption, money, taxes, and railroads cannot entirely explain the Republican collapse. A powerful racial element dominated this mix, as it did nearly all southern political considerations. Then, too, political miscalculations by northern Republicans also injured the party and weakened, as a result, its ability to control its southern agenda. Liberal Republicanism, and white night-riders tied intrinsically to the triumphant Redeemers, helped finish off what remained of Reconstruction policy between 1872 and 1877.

CHAPTER 12

Destroying Reconstruction

I t would be difficult to exaggerate the profound fears that Reconstruction unleashed among the vast majority of white southerners, rich and poor alike. The very notion of change leading toward biracial democracy and toward black office holding, economic independence, and social progress threatened the core of white southern identity, even though whites dominated all Republican state governments in the South. The overwhelming majority of whites rejected black power in any form. So powerful and sustained did this opposition become that, in the face of an increasingly divided and discouraged North, southern white supremacists retook political power in every southern state by 1877. Blacks clung tenaciously to the gains they made, however, so this political change came only through the application of intense violence, coupled to Machiavellian politics. In the end, not the Reconstruction governments but those led by the Redeemers, as they called themselves, defined the South for the next eighty years—reinforcing segregation and white dominance over the decades, systematically discriminating against blacks. Their policies were nearly undisputed and unchallenged in the white South and acquiesced to when not actively supported in the nation as a whole.

Almost immediately after the Confederates lost the war, the Louisiana Democratic Party declared: "We hold this to be a government of white people, made and to be perpetuated for the exclusive benefit of the white race; and that

**The Rituals
of White
Supremacy**

people of African descent cannot be considered citizens of the United States, and that there can, in no event, nor under any circumstances, be any equality between the white and other races." Slavery might be gone, but the compelling desire to maintain a caste system remained, its founders searching for new institutions to produce total control. Alexander H. Stephens, who had been the Confederate vice president, asserted that "equality does not exist between blacks and whites. The one race is by nature inferior in many respects, physically and mentally, to the other. This should be received as a fixed invincible fact in all dealings with the subject. It is useless to war with the decrees of nature in attempting to make things equal which the Creator has made unequal; the wise, humane and philosophic statesman will deal with facts as he finds them."

As Stephens demonstrated, black power was not just an alternative political stance for southern whites to contest, but a violation of what most of them believed to be the natural order of things. They believed it necessary to stop dead any and all black efforts to move in the direction of political equality. There were no allowable gray areas in this argument: blacks would dominate whites, or whites would dominate blacks in perpetuity. As Henry W. Grady, editor of the *Atlanta Constitution* and chief publicist for an industrialized New South, would insist in 1887: "The supremacy of the white race . . . must be maintained forever, and the domination of the negro race resisted at all points and all hazards—because the white race is the superior race. This is the declaration of no new truth. It has abided forever in the marrow of our bones, and shall run forever with the blood that feeds Anglo-Saxon hearts." Such attitudes, publicly articulated by mainstream white leaders without reservation or embarrassment, were shared right down the white social scale.

ALEXANDER HAMILTON STEPHENS. As brilliant as he was tiny, Stephens had a long career in Georgia politics. A most reluctant secessionist, he nevertheless was elected vice president of the Confederacy, but he fell out with President Jefferson Davis. In 1866 he was elected to the U.S. Senate, which refused to seat him, but by 1872, following the destruction of Reconstruction in Georgia in which he participated, he was back in the House of Representatives, and in 1882 he was elected governor of Georgia, dying in March 1883.

In slavery days, so recently ended, literal ownership guaranteed nearly total white domination of blacks. After the fall of the Confederacy, blacks started from this position on the bottom, something that did not simply disappear with legal abolition. In everyday life, as in the social and economic spheres, whites still excluded blacks from the promise of equality. Whites controlled such fundamental social building blocks as naming practices. For example, when little Harry Crews called a leading black man in his Southern town "Mr. Jones," his aunt admonished, "No, son. Robert is a nigger. You don't say 'mister' when you speak of a nigger. You don't say 'Mr. Jones,' you say 'nigger Jones.' " Whites called blacks of all ages "boy," or "George," or "Jim," and black women were called "aunt" and never "Mrs." In contrast, blacks had to call white men of whatever station "mister," "boss," or "cap'n," or if they knew them well, they attached "Mr." to their first names. White women were "Miss." In the newspapers, blacks were called negro (always lowercase) and not by name, as in the famous remark in *Huckleberry Finn* that no people were killed in the steamboat disaster, only two negroes. Whites never shook the hands of blacks, nor removed their hats when in black homes, but black men had to doff their caps before whites and to yield the inner part of sidewalks when whites came their way. Blacks never entered the front door of the homes of whites, only the back. Blacks entered posh hotels, restaurants, and theaters at great peril, and they attended segregated schools. With seeming inconsistency, black women often raised young whites in great intimacy within white homes, and locales of low life— bars, racetracks, and some brothels—were not racially segregated. But those were exceptions to the rules of exclusion that would become formalized and legalized later in the century.

Although these rituals might seem minute and even trivial, most southern whites would have agreed with the North Carolinan who insisted that any and all black "assertions of independence [and] racial equality" would lead to disaster if allowed. "When the whites yield in what would be usually called 'trifles,' they may some day discover that little by little these trifles have grown into 'thunder-bolts.' " If the code of white supremacy were to crack, it might collapse: this was the logic of endemic fear and of continuous reinforcement by threat and deed. **Fear of Black Independence**

Blacks were under constant white scrutiny for any sign of "insolence" or disrespect. Offended whites would take up the matter, immediately or later, singly or with friends or mobs. Economic discrimination, beatings, forced exile, or lynching often resulted from a supposedly lewd stare at a white woman, for what was taken to be the sassing of a white man, or for other offenses to the code of black subordination as interpreted by whites. Using violence and terror to reinforce racial domination was not the last resort, but often the first.

White power defies quantification. No historian has ever been able to count the number of lynchings, the most mortal activity, as many cases were never reported, but that number was in the hundreds each year. If many of these lynchings were private acts of revenge—after which whites were never punished—many were public events where hundreds or thousands of whites **Lynching**

BEARING THE CAPTION "Verdict: 'Hang the D— Yankee and Nigger,' " this engraving appeared in *Harper's Weekly* in March 1867. No one has ever been able to calculate the number of Republicans and other African Americans who were killed in political violence during and after the period of Reconstruction. This image suggests that many influential northerners believed that such political killing was both widespread and popular among southern whites.

would gather in a picnic atmosphere to watch blacks be tortured, castrated, burned, and then hanged, with their body parts going as souvenirs, and picture postcards of the event selling briskly after the event. Such celebrations of course warned all other blacks, while reinforcing racial solidarity and superiority across class lines among whites. Some whites were lynched, particularly recent European immigrants and Republican officials. Nathan Bedford Forrest, leader of the Ku Klux Klan, for example, was more interested in killing white Republican leaders than black men. And there were lynchings in the North and West as well. But both during Reconstruction and later, the overwhelming majority of these killings was perpetrated by whites on blacks in the South.

The Softer Side of Paternalism   Lynching was most common where offending blacks were strangers. Conversely, white paternalism could afford considerable protection for blacks known to well-born whites. In court, the first question to an arrested black was likely to be "Whose nigger are you?" If the white man named were of importance in a community, the prisoner would receive a far lighter punishment than if he had no protector. In everyday exchanges, whites frequently fed appropriately respectful, hungry blacks who served them in some capacity—always, of course, at the back door. Within the southern caste system, even the best-case scenarios were intrinsically demeaning to blacks, and of course such events also convinced whites that they were kind and good to the portion of the benighted black population who were "their people."

For blacks without white protection, while beatings and lynching of those who had offended racial protocol were not uncommon, thousands more were sentenced to long prison terms for minor offenses such as petty thievery. But to avoid the costs of actual prisons, southern states leased out black convicts to private contractors who paid the state a fee, guaranteed to take care of them, and then worked them on chain gangs. Many white businessmen profited while these convicts were compelled to labor under conditions free workers would not tolerate. Much of the expanding southern railroad network was built by leased convicts, who also mined coal, drained swamps, and constructed public projects. The foremen regularly whipped prisoners, and many suffered from dysentery, gunshot wounds, sunstroke, malaria, and exhaustion. Death tolls were high, often about 15 percent annually, with Alabama reporting a death rate of 41 percent in 1870. If sharecroppers often labored for little or no profit, convicts were literal peons who were consigned to conditions frequently worse than slavery. After all, a good slave had been more valuable to his owner than a mule, while convicts always could be replaced by men captured within the legal system, one vigorously enforced when it applied to blacks.

The Convict Lease System

Collective violence was even better organized when it came to reclaiming undivided political power for white sovereignty. Many whites were convinced that they were fully justified in whatever actions they took to defend their South against what they believed was an outside tyranny seeking to impose black rule. As one upper-class North Carolinian analyzed it, outbreaks of racial violence were "the direct, natural, logical consequence of negro supremacy. White men . . . should despise our blood, our own people, if they peacefully and tamely submitted to the dominance of the African." In the best tradition of the American Revolution (and the Confederate rebellion), resistance to such a tyranny, by any means necessary, was a duty. In 1868 a Louisiana newspaper regretted that whites "should be compelled to have recourse to measures to do away with tyrants and wrong-doers in their midst," but asserted when asked who was to blame: "assuredly not we the people of the South, who have suffered wrongs beyond endurance." Rather, "radicalism and negroism" alone were to blame. "We can well pity a people forced to use such harsh means, but we have not the courage to blame them." Convinced they were victims called to defend their honor, such men did not consider the humanity of those they attacked.

Political Violence

As we have seen in the previous chapter, as early as 1866, acting on such a collective sensibility, "riots"—in fact, white mobs attacking black neighborhoods—began to break out across the South. In Memphis, between April 30 and May 2, 1866, forty-six blacks were killed, and more than eighty were injured, while no whites lost their lives. Many other explosions followed, the bloodiest of which was the Colfax, Louisiana, massacre of 1873 when 280 blacks were slaughtered, and Vicksburg, Mississippi, and the surrounding countryside, when as many as 600 were killed in 1874. The pattern was almost invariably similar. With considerable organization, whites would attack all armed blacks and well-known black leaders while burning out black-owned businesses. Then the looting and the killing would become more general and indiscriminate as the "riot" continued.

The KKK

In a more sustained way, beginning in 1866 but expanding after African Americans began to vote in considerable numbers in 1868, whites created well-organized secret militias, in effect, guerrilla armies. The best known of these was the Ku Klux Klan, which began in Tennessee and spread throughout much of the South, but other organizations such as the Knights of the White Camellia of Louisiana grew rapidly in the late 1860s. All were secret fraternities, with special handshakes and rituals, clandestine meetings, night riding, and power structures built on the local, regional, and sometimes statewide and interstate levels. But larger organizational structures were not the most important or even necessary parts of these white groups. Rather, all shared a sense of overriding political purpose: the employment of intimidation and, when need be, violence as major tools in the reestablishment of unquestioned white domination.

The caption to this photograph, "KKKlan, Ala, 1868," was written in the hand of future president Rutherford B. Hayes. On the back is the inscription "Robinson and Murphy, Photographers . . . Uniform and so-on captured by Lt. L. E. Capstein 33rd New York, on the night of October 31, 1868, in the riot at Huntsville." The photograph is still frightening, even if it was staged by Union soldiers after the riot was over.

To this end, the chief targets were Republican activists of both races and black political and social leaders more generally. Usually in the middle of the night, hooded riders would seize such men from their homes and whip them, forcing them to flee for their lives, or they would kill them right on the spot or later, sometimes after torture. As the terror spread, merely speaking up on political issues or voting for the Republican Party was sufficient cause for such a visit. At times, the Klan would attack and kill whole communities of blacks. One of the biggest such outbreaks was in Meridian, Mississippi, in 1871 when the Klan invaded a court hearing of three blacks charged with inciting other blacks to violence, shot two of the defendants and the judge, a white Republican, and then went on a rampage in the town, killing as many as thirty blacks, including almost all the local black leaders.

Because the slightest trifle might become a thunderbolt, the Klan and similar organizations attacked any African American they considered had gotten above his station, often defined as being too well dressed or too well spoken. Black prosperity and education were unacceptable for such whites. Night riders also attacked blacks for talking back to employers or even for resisting beatings at the hands of their bosses. But the Klan particularly focused on blacks accused of insulting white women, with castration the most likely outcome short of lynching. When it came to the postwar South's racial divide, the personal was political—all black assertion was the problem, and white domination defined all spheres of everyday life.

But state power was always the key, and for the white supremacist counterrevolution, after the passing of its first incarnation as the Klan, described below, similar organizations soon arose to serve as the paramilitary, terrorist arm of the Democratic Party, for example the White Line movement in Mississippi in 1875 and the Red Shirts in South Carolina in 1876. The cooperation was not always formal, although the mutual goal was clear, and often politicians and terrorists cooperated in planning major actions. Indeed, sometimes they were the same people. Particularly in the deep South states with large black populations, the White Line strategy was central, with massive uses of violence before elections coupled to an unequivocal party line of white supremacy. In Mississippi in 1875, the Democrats' election slogan was "Carry the election peaceably if we can, forcibly if we must." The worst incidents were in Yazoo County, Vicksburg, and Clinton, where white paramilitary units broke up Republican rallies and shot several white and black Republican leaders, driving others from the state. After the assault at Clinton, armed whites pursued blacks through the countryside, shooting them, as one white later said, "like birds." Additional political killings and other forms of intimidation before the election, as well as well-armed whites crowding around polling places, had the intended effect. Using the telegraph and railroads efficiently, White Liners were able to concentrate paramilitary units anywhere in the state, sometimes calling on their brethren in Alabama and Louisiana. This was necessary because in several counties blacks outnumbered whites by as much as seven to one.

The White Line

And yet, so intense was black resistance that it took a major effort to discourage African Americans from voting. The 1875 Mississippi election was perhaps the most organized and extreme campaign against political rights, but in Georgia, South Carolina, Tennessee, Louisiana, and Alabama, similar tactics ground down the Republican Party, securing victory for the Redeemers all over the South by 1876. Most white Republicans either fled or capitulated into silence or even joined the Democratic Party, and blacks became disenfranchised and politically neutered. The leaders of the Redemption movement assured the public that they decried violence and that they would look after their negroes, whom they knew and esteemed, but calm paternalism carried a rather sinister air after power had been regained through other means. The public face of white power often was bland and reassuring (in part to ward off renewed federal intervention), but in times of renewed stress, the White Line and violence remained in place to be used. In the deep South, the Redeemers threw off their robes and openly joined with legitimist Democrats who ran for office.

Bourbon Politics While employing the low road as needed, the Redeemers also presented themselves as genteel traditionalists who were, at the same time, governmental reformers. They were an alliance mainly drawn from the upper reaches of white southern society: plantation owners, merchants, and lawyers. Prior to the war, many had been Whigs who had been late but fervent converts to the Confederate cause. In places such as Virginia, this leadership cadre called themselves Conservatives to emphasize their solidarity across old party lines, but such names faded and the Democratic Party became their label, within which, as a group, they were identified as Bourbons, a name which represented their class position and their desire to restore as much of the old regime as possible, slavery excepted.

At the same time, the Bourbons rallied poor whites to their cause, staging grand parades and barbeques, much like revival meetings, where they preached white solidarity and white supremacy. In South Carolina, Wade Hampton marched triumphantly across the state, leading his armed Red Shirt units. On October 7, 1876, Hampton and his militia rode into Sumter, South Carolina, toward a speaker's platform where they beheld a human figure robed in deathly black and bound in chains. As Hampton strode to the platform, the enslaved and dehumanized figure threw off chains and robes, revealing "a radiant woman in pure white. . . . She was tall and stately, head uplifted and eyes shining like the stars," an enthralled journalist wrote. The crowd went wild, and late into the night Red Shirt horsemen raced through the black neighborhoods shouting, "Hampton or Hell!" Such ceremonies did much to bring about a reborn white Christian republic, using any means necessary, including the most violent and the most evangelical.

In reaction to what they considered the tyranny and corruption of the activist Republican Reconstruction state governments, the Redeemers slashed budgets and rolled back the employment of state power, particularly in public education. Economy, austerity, and honesty were their bywords. However, as bondholders of the railroad companies that had sprung up all over the South after the war, they insisted on full payment of the debts these roads had incurred when most of the railroads collapsed financially.

This set of policies aroused consternation among many ordinary southern whites, and by the late 1870s, political tension led to divisions and factions among the Democrats, some of whom allied themselves with Republicans, including remaining black voters. White supremacy remained the great social glue that Redeemers, and indeed all white Democratic leaders, liberally applied to counter and eventually to crush such white factionalism. A traitor to the Democratic Party, they insisted, was a traitor to the white race.

While they were able to unite the vast majority of white southerners in their powerful anti-Reconstruction crusade, the Redeemers' counterrevolution also succeeded because of ambivalence, division, and discouragement between both those northern forces who were backing Reconstruction and the outright and often angry opposition of many in the North to Republican policies. Moreover, even during the height of military Reconstruction, the national government lacked the institutional power and the will to implement systematically its policies of black enfranchisement and civil rights. **Divisions in the North**

Weary of war, unaccustomed to having anything more than the tiniest of peacetime professional forces, the government demobilized most of the huge Civil War army immediately after Appomattox. By late 1867, only 20,000 troops remained in the conquered South—a figure that shrank to 6,000 by 1876—and almost half of these Union troops in 1876 were posted to frontier duty in Texas. For traditional reasons of economy, aversion to "standing armies," and to using the federal government, much less the army, as a permanent instrument in the exercise of social policy, the notion of employing military force in any part of the nation against white civilians to protect blacks was simply unthinkable. Even the use of the federal courts to enforce social policy on the state and local level was deeply unpopular.

After four bloody years of Klan attacks and following a thorough congressional investigation, on April 20, 1871, Congress passed an anti-Klan act that President Grant and his attorney general, Amos Akerman, enforced quite vigorously. Grant sent cavalry units into the most violent counties of North Carolina, South Carolina, and Mississippi, while Akerman convened federal grand juries that indicted more than 3,000 Klansmen. Only about 600 were convicted, and they were sentenced to relatively short prison terms, but thousands more fled or stopped night riding. Although this federal action guaranteed a relatively quiet election in 1872, and shored up several state Republican regimes for two to five more years, it provided a lull rather than a fundamental change, because clandestine paramilitary units soon resumed the attack and, in fact, spread even more widely in the ensuing years. Over time, the federal government lost the energy to carry on such prosecutions. Even at the top, President Grant feared the employment of national troops in what might become an all-out race war, a sort of second round of the Civil War. Faced with the bloody White Line campaign in Mississippi in 1875, Grant's very conservative attorney general, Edwards Pierrepont, wrote to Adelbert Ames, the carpetbagger **Northern Ambivalence in Enforcing Reconstruction** governor who was pleading for troops to quash the rebellion, that the administration was growing "tired of the autumnal outbursts," and Grant remained silent. The solid South had worn down the North.

Many factors beyond the tradition of limited federal government and a small army contributed to the loss of northern will to effect a racial reformation of southern society. For one thing, the war had produced a confused and ambivalent legacy. When it began, Lincoln's own policy had been to restore the Union rather than to tamper with slavery, a position shared by almost all white northerners. This was the greatest (and the least) common denominator among the broadest reaches of white northern opinion, but even when Lincoln moved Union war aims in an antislavery direction in 1862, many white northerners bitterly resisted the change. Moreover, ending slavery was one thing, but the ideal of constructing a new order of racial justice and black equality never dominated Lincoln's thinking, nor that of any but a tiny abolitionist elite, mainly outside the Republican Party. This same lack of commitment to a biracial new order undermined Reconstruction, an ambiguity stemming in part from northern whites' ambivalence toward African Americans and their hesitation to impose social change on any fellow whites, even former Confederates.

Northern Democrats
Many white northerners remained at least as white supremacist as their southern brethren. At the height of the war, draft riots in the cities, many of which had also been negrophobic riots, demonstrated this popular sentiment. Also, after the war as well as during it, race hatred found mainstream institutional expression in the Democratic Party. This attitude was grounded in a coherent, long-term Democratic Party ideology that maintained broadly based mass appeal. The bedrock principles of the Democratic Party included the protection of natural rights for individuals; the sanctity of private property; local and state control of economic, social, and political policy; the necessity of standing vigilantly against centralizing corruption and tyranny; and the racial supremacy of white men.

Democrats believed that abolitionists and Republicans—what one of their major spokespeople called that "dark enclave of conspirators, freedom shriekers, and Bible spewkers"—had conspired to cause the war. To some extent, Democrats also blamed southern extremists, but they reserved their strongest venom for their northern political enemies. Most Democrats joined in the war effort with greater or lesser reluctance; all insisted that they were struggling for the protection of "the constitution as it is and the Union as it was." As one Democratic congressman put it in July 1861, the war was to be fought not "in any spirit of oppression . . . conquest or subjugation, or [for] interfering with the rights or established institutions" of southern states, but rather to maintain the "supremacy of the constitution, and to preserve the Union" with the rights of all states unimpaired. The code was not obscure: slavery was to be let alone.

As we have seen in chapter 7, some northern Democrats crossed the line into active support of the Confederacy during the war, and Republicans branded all Democrats as traitorous "Copperheads." This was unfair to most Democrats, both in and out of the army. What was generally true, however, was that the majority of Democrats believed that Republicans had caused the war, that it should not be turned into an antislavery struggle, and that it could and should not end on the field of battle but at the negotiating table. They tried various tactics to reach that resolution, including the suggestion of a national peace convention with Confederates included, or the sending of northern negotiators south, or inviting mediation from Britain or a consortium of European powers. Through whatever means, once this needless war ended, the South would be welcomed back to the Union with her local institutions sustained. In certain quarters this meant rescinding the Emancipation Proclamation, an alternative fully eliminated only with the ratification of the Thirteenth Amendment to the Constitution on December 18, 1865.

In part, this position had grown from their hatred of interference with local rights and private property, but it also conformed to the Democrats' belief that the United States was a white republic. As Stephen Douglas put it in his 1858 debates with Abraham Lincoln, "we here do not believe in the equality of the negro socially and politically. Our people are white people; our state is a white state, and we mean to preserve the race pure without any mixture of the negro."

With considerable consistency, northern Democrats carried their endemic white supremacism into Reconstruction. A county convention in Indiana in 1868 asserted: "we hold that this government was made for the benefit of white men and their posterity forever and that whenever the white man and the Negro comes into contact . . . the normal condition of the latter is servitude and inferiority." Another Democrat explained, in a letter to President Andrew Johnson in 1867, that suffrage for blacks was nothing but the "effort to place the African on a level with the Caucasian."

With this attitude toward African Americans coupled to an equally strong belief in local autonomy, as well as strictly limited and inexpensive central government, the Democrats stridently opposed Radical Reconstruction. Rather than offering alternative forms of reconstruction policy, they based their rejectionism on the simple proposition of immediate amnesty for ex-Confederates and the restoration of the former Confederate states to their prewar status. They opposed substantial budgets for the army, the existence of the Freedmen's Bureau, and all other civil rights legislation, including the Fourteenth and Fifteenth Amendments, as being, in the words of one New York congressman, "unconstitutional usurpations, fatal to representative government, partisan, violating the checks and balances, overriding state laws, unnatural and anti-southern." On the other hand, they either ignored the activities of the KKK, apologized for them, or denied that the Klan existed. They blamed such violence on northern and black attempts to impose a noxious tyranny on the white South. In part, of course, this support was due to the fact that the Redeemers were southern Democrats who would help northern Democrats retake Washington one day, but it also existed because most in the national party agreed with white supremacy and fully supported white southerners in their struggle to reestablish their rule.

Northern Democrats Oppose Reconstruction

The 1868 Presidential Campaign

Democratic racism reached something of an apogee during the presidential election of 1868 (recounted in chapter 10), particularly as articulated by Frank Blair of Missouri, former Union general, former Republican, and by then the Democratic vice-presidential candidate. Blair fiercely opposed the evils of miscegenation that he claimed the Republican policy had let loose in the South, where it had subjected white southerners to "a semi-barbarous race of blacks who are worshippers of fetishes and polygamists [desiring to] subject the white women to their unbridled lust." Blair proposed rolling back Reconstruction entirely and restoring white government—if need be, at the point of the army's sword. Such extremism, which almost promised a resumption of civil war, backfired in the Democrats' faces during the election, but they did not retreat from their root-and-branch opposition to Reconstruction, although no other national candidate would again be so crude and overt in his racist language.

A good sense of the milder and more widely adopted tone can be found in a letter of Redeemer support for the Democrat Party written during the 1868 campaign. Shortly after the Democratic convention, William S. Rosecrans, the former Union general, traveled to White Sulphur Springs, Virginia, where Robert E. Lee was vacationing in the company of other ex-Confederate gentlemen, several of whom were building the Conservative Party coalition that would regain political power in Virginia in 1870. Rosecrans convinced the supposedly apolitical Lee to agree to be the chief signatory, along with thirty-two others, of a public letter drafted by Alexander H. H. Stuart, a leading Virginia conservative politician, responding to Rosecrans's "patriotic [as opposed to partisan] motives" and claiming to speak "on behalf of the Southern people, and the officers and soldiers of the late Confederate Army."

Rosecrans's patriotic point was that Reconstruction, violence, and discord would end when power returned to the most conservative possible group of traditional southern leaders. Stuart, Lee, and the other southern gentlemen promised that they would exercise not violent discrimination but kindly paternalism in their governance of blacks. They explained that "the idea that the Southern people are hostile to the negroes and would oppress them, if it were in their power to do so, is entirely unfounded. They have grown up in our midst, and we have been accustomed from childhood to look upon them with kindness." Because they needed blacks as laborers, "self-interest, if there were no higher motive, would therefore prompt the whites" to protect blacks. Lee's men were as of one mind with the northern Democrats about white domination. "It is true," they wrote, "that the people of the North and West, are, for obvious reasons, inflexibly opposed to any system of laws that would place the political power in the hands of the negro race." However, and this is where they separated themselves from the sort of language Frank Blair used, their opposition to black power grew not from "enmity"—race hatred—but from a "deep seated conviction" that African Americans lacked "the intelligence necessary to make them safe depositories of political power." Because of their natural racial interiority, blacks "would inevitably become the victims of demagogues, who, for selfish purposes, would mislead them into the serious injury of the public."

These southern white leaders joined with the northern Democrats in their desire to restore the vote to all whites and to grant them "relief from oppressive misrule"—in other words, to the root-and-branch elimination of Reconstruction. Then they would take care of blacks, treating them with "kindness and humanity," but this would result from their free grant from above, not as part of any biracial power-sharing scheme.

This far politer version of Redeemer/Democratic white supremacy proved more palatable. "Inflexible opposition" did not explicitly justify violence, but neither did it condemn it. Restoration itself, after whatever measures were taken, would be warmly paternalistic, they promised. Many white northerners and, indeed, southerners preferred to think about white power that way, even if they were prepared to use violence to regain the power to extend kindness to the lowly race.

The Democratic Party maintained enormous influence, not only with the nearly half of the electorate who voted for them, but with the Republicans as well, who were compelled to come to terms with such a powerful opposition. The Democrats articulated a good part of mainstream northern discourse on race and the role of the government, and they were bound to return to power one day, as Republicans were well aware. Indeed one of the reasons Democrats did so well in the north in the 1868 election was the increasing public weariness with the aftermath of the war, the seemingly perpetual crisis atmosphere during the costly Reconstruction process. It was time for conflict to cease and the nation to return to normal channels, many believed, and the Democrats played those themes to great effect. Well before they won grand electoral victories, the Democrats would exercise great power in Congress and in many state governments, both North and South.

Even within their own ranks, Republicans disagreed about much of the thrust of Reconstruction. Many of their congressional members and voters had never been abolitionists. Indeed, their central prewar ideological position—that the federal government should open the West exclusively to free white men—was both antislavery and antiblack, and most Republicans maintained their long-term ambivalence about equal rights. Much of the language of the Fourteenth Amendment, the high-water mark of Reconstruction, was rather vague, not even hinting at ways in which the federal government could enforce equality of opportunity and due process.

Republican Faltering on Reconstruction

Moreover, after the war receded, Republicans focused most of their energies on economic development and building the power of their own party. One major reason they backed black suffrage was to support southern Republicans, and when few whites rallied to their flag, they realized that the most powerful southern forces were against them and that Republicans controlled only a permanently weak base of support in the South. With some regret, they began to conclude that they would lose their strategy to transform the electorate of the South, and that they would be able to maintain power in that region only through draconian means. Aware that eliminating white terrorism against southern blacks would be impossible without creating a large, expensive, and unpopular peacetime standing army, and fearful that such a move would erode their northern support, most Republicans refused to consider such drastic steps. Business and the electorate demanded an end to ceaseless conflict, and peace might have to be purchased at the price of help to African Americans.

Indeed, many business-oriented Republicans began to believe that Republican rule retarded their opportunities for economic penetration of the southern market and the "northernization" that would accompany it. Horace Greeley's *New York Tribune* insisted in 1872 that "had it not been for carpetbag mismanagement," the South "today would be filled with millions of Northern or foreign yeomanry carving out farms, or working . . . in iron, copper, coal, and marble."

Northern Business Expansion

Business boomed in the North after the war, while the devastated South fell further behind, a subject to be discussed later in this chapter. Railroads expanded dramatically, with larger companies spanning the continent by 1869 while smaller companies were consolidated into powerful new intrastate lines. Farmers flooded the Great Plains and the West Coast. The steel and oil industries also boomed. Industrial corporations integrated their processes, increasing dramatically in size. By 1880, John D. Rockefeller controlled 95 percent of the refining and transportation of oil, and his was but the most notable of the emerging monopolies. These large-scale companies employed thousands and thousands of new workers, often immigrants, who, along with the children of many farmers, flocked to the rapidly mushrooming urban areas. Harsh labor practices led to unionization, to socialist and anarchist movements, and to disorganized protests among the new proletariat. In 1877 a violent national railroad strike bitterly divided the North, where fear of home-grown rebellion caused far more alarm than whatever was happening to blacks in the South.

Republicans as the Business Party

As the governing party of a nation devoted to business expansion, the Republicans seemed unavoidably swept up by the tremendous promises and problems that this wildfire development produced. Although the Republicans did not propose to use the government to construct the railroads or the new factories, they were intrinsically involved in the building process; for example, they granted vast expanses of land, tax breaks, and outright construction subsidies to the railroads to finance the building of the intercontinental lines. In addition, most state governments underwrote bond issues and offered other incentives to railroad and industrial development.

As might have been expected, state and federal legislators demanded something in return. For many, the price was hefty contributions to political campaigns and to the treasuries of the political parties; other politicians demanded bribes, whether in free railroad passes and preferred freight rates or in direct kickbacks.

Scandals in the Grant Administration

With huge amounts of money greasing the legislative process, it should have come as no surprise that massive scandals broke out during the Grant administration. In 1869, Jay Gould and Jim Fisk, two entrepreneurs who specialized in unfriendly takeovers of railroads, decided to corner the gold market, and they enlisted Grant's brother-in-law to keep the government out of the market while they did their deed. Grant finally figured out what was happening and ordered the Treasury to sell gold, but this did not prevent a public uproar. In 1872 the press revealed that the promoters of the Union Pacific Railroad had set up Credit Mobilier, a dummy company, as a means of diverting profits into the pockets of selected investors. This fraudulent insider deal enriched many congressmen who had been in on the action, having bought Credit Mobilier shares at a low price at the outset of the scheme. Three scandalous years later, in 1875, Secretary of War William Belknap had to resign his post when it became known that he demanded kickbacks from merchants who traded with the Indians. Post offices, it became known, were auctioned off to the highest bidders. The secretary of the Treasury gave a friend a 50 percent commission for collecting back taxes. Also, most egregiously, whiskey manufacturers bribed Grant's private secretary and others to overlook the collecting of excise taxes due the government.

All these scandals undermined the Grant administration and thus undercut its Reconstruction policies, and they also revealed some of the myriad connections between business and the Republicans that animated the party far more than rights for blacks, an unprofitable proposition. Dealing with business, many Republican leaders turned their attention homeward, seeking to help their constituents instead of distant strangers. They felt the impulse to professionalize their activities, to bolster the party, and to sort out business tensions. In a sense, Republican politicians were part of both the problem and the solution, but in the larger sense, they were moving away from ideological politics concerning the grand issues of social change in the South. In fact, such ideological animation had been unusual historically: American politics traditionally concerned patronage and special material favors for the home states of congressmen; with the cooling of the passions aroused by the slavery controversy and the war, matters were returning to normal.

Ironically, high-minded Republicans who were revolted by the corrupt behavior of many in their own party and in the governmental bureaucracy also turned their interest from the South. By 1872 they had formed within the party a group that they called the Liberal Republicans. These reformists pushed hard for lower tariffs and civil service reform in particular, and in general for small, efficient, honest government by the better sort. E. L. Godkin, editor of the influential magazine *The Nation*, and a leading Liberal Republican, insisted that "the Government must get out of the 'protective' business and the 'subsidy' business and the 'improvement' and 'development' business. . . . It cannot touch them without breeding corruption."

The Liberal Republicans

Deeply fearing the growing and unruly proletariat and the demagogic politicians who played to them, Liberal Republican reformers began by extension to blame southern blacks and white Republican carpetbaggers and scalawags for the misrule and the corruption they observed in the South that resembled what they saw at home. If a disinterested civil service was needed to cleanse the political culture of the North by enabling well-educated and refined men to displace dirty politicians who pandered to business and the lower classes, it followed, as one of the Liberal Republican leaders wrote, that all must "recognize the fact that the South can only be governed through the part

LONG THE ECCENTRIC but powerful editor of the *New York Tribune*, a faddish prewar reformer and sometime supporter of the Republicans who turned to near pacifism during the war, Horace Greeley was the 1872 presidential nominee of the Liberal Republicans and Democrats. His campaign against Ulysses S. Grant turned him into the butt of widespread derision, and he was soundly defeated. Greeley collapsed mentally and physically, and he died less than a month after his defeat.

of the community that embodies the intelligence and capital." Another Liberal Republican observed that government left in the hands of "the more ignorant classes" could only mean that "the most active and intelligent" people would be the victims of political injustice. Therefore, the Redeemers, the natural leaders of the South, ought to be restored to power. Of course, the Redeemers were only too willing to signal their agreement with this stance. Via this route, the most socially activist cutting edge of the Republican Party turned against the Grant administration and against Reconstruction. They wanted to reform current ills, letting old questions go.

The 1872 Campaign   In 1872, happily aware of the growing schism in Republican ranks, the Democrats sought to attract the Liberal Republicans. To this end, they wrote a platform focusing on the evils of bloated government, and as their candidate for the presidency nominated their longtime enemy Horace Greeley, erstwhile Radical Republican and reformist editor of the vastly influential *New York Tribune*. Many Liberal Republicans indeed came over to their standard, although technically the Democrats endorsed the Liberals Republicans when they swallowed them. In any event Grant's great remaining prestige, large contributions to Republican coffers by interested industrialists, and the lingering sense that the Democrats had been traitors during the Civil War combined to defeat Greeley, who died shortly afterward of a broken heart. Greeley had lost not only the election but his wife, who had just died. Most Liberal Republicans then returned to their old party, which did little to diminish tensions within Republican ranks. Among other outcomes, engagement with southern blacks decreased permanently as a party priority.

Republican discord and political entropy were deepened by economic panic in 1873 and a depression that lasted for the six ensuing years. The problem stemmed from an overheated, speculative economy in general and from the watering of railroad bonds, far too many of which were issued in the postwar years in particular. Many of the roads began to default on their bonds when their revenues proved insufficient. Then, in far-off Vienna, a stock market panic pushed many Europeans to dump their American bonds, creating a chain reaction that led to the collapse of Jay Cooke's investment bank in New York. Cooke had gained enormous prestige during the war as the leading national and international salesman of Union war bonds, and his bank's collapse triggered a general stock market crash, mass unemployment for workers, and bankruptcy for many employers.

The Depression of 1873

At this juncture, during the midterm elections in 1874, the Democrats won many seats in the Senate and regained control of the House of Representatives for the first time since before the war. They used their new position to investigate many of the Grant-regime scandals, to decrease military budgets, and to detach politics from Reconstruction issues. By this point, Grant had become something of a lame duck, and his cabinet had lost almost all of what little prestige it had ever commanded. Political impetus began to swing toward the Democrats.

Shrinkage of the money supply deepened the depression. The government had long begun to reduce the circulation of greenbacks issued as a war measure, and this led to economic deflation. In the face of the worsening depression, the Treasury reissued some of these greenbacks, and the Democratic-controlled Congress passed a bill to issue yet more. Believing he was protecting the federal treasury and sound business practices, Grant vetoed this bill and instead called for a return to the gold standard, to which Congress agreed in 1875. Many ordinary people, especially farmers in the West and South, were angered by this constriction in currency, which had the effect of making the repayment of their debts all the harder, especially as commodity prices were dropping. Cotton prices plummeted by 50 percent during the depression; other southern crops also tumbled, wiping out whatever gains the painful rebuilding process in the South had begun to produce. Currency constriction led to the creation of the Greenback Party, which elected fourteen congressmen in 1878 in the South and the West, the beginning of two decades of the political expression of farmer unrest.

Massive unemployment in the cities of the North also stirred social unrest. By 1876 more than half of the railroad companies were technically bankrupt, their assets passing to receivers. When the reorganizing railroads fired many workers and slashed wages for the rest, worker fury exploded into spontaneous, disorganized, and frequently violent strikes across the nation in 1877. In this instance, unlike the response when it came to suppressing southern white night riders, the public strongly supported the use of federal troops to put down rebellious workers in several states.

As industrial capitalism expanded, it greatly altered both the rural and urban landscapes; when it now went into one of its periodic depressions, ordinary people felt caught up in new and impersonal forces beyond their comprehension. It seemed to many citizens that distant and subversive forces controlled the money supply and the economy, and many in the middle class believed that they were in danger of spiraling downward while a few rich men secretly plotted their demise. How old fashioned and distant such concerns as votes for black men began to appear. In the South, as shown in chapter 11, many voters blamed their Republican state governments for the economic ills besetting them.

The Supreme Court Undercuts Reconstruction   As the Republican will and their ability to effect social change in the South eroded, the Supreme Court announced two decisions, *the Slaughterhouse Cases* in 1873 and *U.S. v. Cruikshank* in 1876, which undercut the ability of lower federal courts to prosecute violators of black rights. Taken together, the cases argued that the Fourteenth Amendment applied only to federally guaranteed rights and that the definition of almost all the rights accorded defendants in criminal cases remained with the state and local authorities. This reassertion of states' rights meant that the national government could no longer bring cases to the federal courts when the rights of black people had been violated. As southern juries would rarely convict whites for crimes against blacks—indeed, southern authorities were unlikely to seek or secure indictments in such cases—these two decisions undermined future efforts to protect blacks, even if the Republicans still had wished to do so. Ironically, during the next twenty years, the Supreme Court would hold that the Fourteenth Amendment did apply federal constitutional protection to the rights of corporations, in this instance disallowing federal attempts at regulation.

Redeemer Tide Rising   While white northerners increasingly concerned themselves with their own problems, and while the Republicans were losing their moral authority because of the endless scandals of the Grant administration, the Redeemers were winning their battle, state by state. First retaking power in Virginia, North Carolina, Tennessee, and Georgia, in 1875 they swept back to power in Mississippi, Alabama, Texas, and Arkansas. By the end of the second Grant term, Republicans controlled only Florida, South Carolina, and Louisiana, and both national parties were sympathetic to the wave of new Redeemer regimes.

Many mainstream Republicans now agreed that the time for ideological politics and black rights was over. The *New York Times* editorialized on May 8, 1876, that "ten years ago the North was nearly united in a feeling of sympathy for the freedmen, and in a determination to defend their rights. Now," the *Times* asserted, "not a few believe that the rights of whites have been infringed upon." Former abolitionist firebrand journalist James Redpath declared even more explicitly that "Mississippi owes its present sad condition as much to sentimental abolitionists as to fiendish negro-haters. The blacks were ruined as good citizens by the chronic prattle about their rights, and they were never roused to a noble manhood by instructions as to their duties." The nation should give up sentimentality "and learn that our black ward is in very truth a barbarian and needs our best efforts to uplift him in the scale of civilization."

Catching the drift of Republican opinion, realizing that the federal government was doing less and less to aid them, African Americans increasingly believed that the Republicans were betraying them. One group of Louisiana blacks, petitioning to President Grant on May 10, 1875, for increased federal protection, accused the Republican Party of agreeing to compromises with the Democrats that gave only white politicians "more power to steal from us and to whip us and to kill us. . . . Same old whipping, murdering." Earlier that spring, the Nashville National Colored Convention was rife with backroom talk of how the Republicans had "deceived them, betrayed them, insulted them, suffered them to be massacred by the wholesale."

Despite everything, President Grant appeared to be keen to run for reelection in 1876, thus breaking the two-term tradition inaugurated by George Washington. But too much of the odor of scandal swirling around his administration clung to him, though Grant was guilty of indifference, obtuseness, and naivete in his choice of friends, rather than personal corruption. James G. Blaine of

The Election of 1876

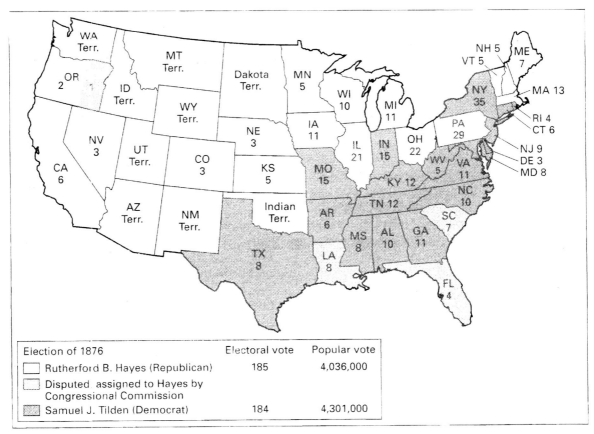

Election of 1876	Electoral vote	Popular vote
☐ Rutherford B. Hayes (Republican)	185	4,036,000
☐ Disputed assigned to Hayes by Congressional Commission		
▨ Samuel J. Tilden (Democrat)	184	4,301,000

ELECTION OF 1876. While Tilden outpolled Hayes in the popular vote, electoral votes were disputed in four states, throwing the nation into a political crisis, solved by a compromise in which Hayes was given the presidency in exchange for, in effect, the abandonment of Reconstruction.

Maine, the most attractive and charismatic Republican presidential alternative, also had skated too close to disgrace, linked as he was to some shady railroad bond dealing. Pressured by the Liberal Republicans to take a reformist stance but wanting to maintain party unity, the Republicans turned to Governor Rutherford B. Hayes of Ohio, a volunteer Union general during the war, something of a civil service reform advocate, and also a hard-money man who leaned toward a more conciliatory policy with the South. An inoffensive and solid fellow, perhaps his greatest virtue was that he was not unacceptable to any faction of his party.

For their part, the Democrats nominated Samuel J. Tilden, a rich corporation lawyer who had recently won election as a reform governor of New York. Tilden had gained fame by destroying the amazingly corrupt Tweed ring that had robbed the people of New York City blind and also by successfully prosecuting some other unsavory types in the state legislature in Albany who had bilked the taxpayers of the whole state. United behind this perfectly upright if stone-cold candidate, the Democrats campaigned against corruption while the Republicans waved the "Bloody Shirt," painting a vivid portrait of Democrats as having been traitors in the Civil War. Col. Robert Ingersoll of Indiana used such invective with the greatest creativity. "Every state that seceded from the United States was a Democratic state," he thundered in a speech during the campaign. "Every man that tried to destroy this nation was a Democrat. Every man that loved slavery better than liberty was a Democrat. The man that assassinated Lincoln was a Democrat. . . . Soldiers, every scar that you have got on your heroic bodies was given to you by a Democrat." Such rhetoric, though not ineffective, also conveyed a measure of desperation, and indeed most Republican leaders expected their party to lose.

A hung election followed. Tilden outpolled Hayes in the popular count by 4,300,590 to 4,036,298 and led in the electoral college with 184 votes to 165. However, nineteen electoral votes remained in dispute in the states of Louisiana, South Carolina, and Florida—the last three southern states still under Republican administrations—and one in Oregon. In those three deep South states, in addition to violent intimidation of potential black voters on the part of the Democrats, both sides had practiced considerable ballot-box stuffing, and after the election each party submitted its own set of returns to Congress.

The Compromise of 1877 Unfortunately, nothing in the Constitution explicitly addressed this problem, and as the Republicans controlled the Senate and the Democrats the House, deadlock ensued when the lame-duck Congress convened in December 1876. It was not clear that a resolution could be reached before the March 4 inaugural date for the next president. There even was some loose talk in the press and on the part of certain politicians about renewed warfare, but neither party had a stomach for such an outcome. All clearly believed that some sort of compromise must be reached.

After many late-night meetings, both sides agreed, on January 29, 1877, to refer the case to an electoral commission made up of five members each from the House, the Senate, and the Supreme Court. The names chosen included seven men from each party, with the final figure being Justice David Davis of Illinois, an independent Republican who had flirted both with the Liberal Republicans of 1872 and the Democrats. Many Democrats believed that Davis would be more likely to favor Democratic claims (which was apparently not the case, according to what Davis was saying privately). At just this moment, the Democrats in the legislature of Illinois, joined by members of the Greenback Party, who brought the swing votes, elected Davis to the U.S. Senate (Senate seats being filled by state legislatures until passage of the Seventeenth Amendment in 1913). With Davis out of the picture, all four remaining justices available to replace him were out-and-out Republicans, of whom the commission chose the most conservative, Joseph P. Bradley. Bradley joined with his fellow Republicans, who then voted as a bloc to give all the disputed electoral votes to Hayes. Outvoted eight to seven on the commission, congressional Democrats then threatened a filibuster, which would have prevented the inauguration.

However, while this process played out officially, leading Republicans and Democrats held clandestine meetings in smoke-filled rooms. These professional politicians finally hammered out several compromises—struck after the commission had chosen Hayes. The issue became what southern white Democrats would gain as the quid pro quo for accepting a Hayes administration. The most important of these meetings led to the *Wormley agreement*, hatched in the restaurant of the hotel owned by James Wormley, who was black. In it the Republicans allowed that if the opposition permitted Hayes to be inaugurated, the new president "would deal generously with the South." This was code for removing all remaining federal troops from active duty in the South and allowing the states of South Carolina, Florida, and Louisiana to be "redeemed." In turn, the Democrats promised that when they regained undisputed power, they would protect the rights of black men as a paternalistic grant from above, more or less along the lines laid down in the Rosencrans/Robert E. Lee letter in support of the Democrats' campaign of 1868. Other conversations led to Republican promises to support a southern transcontinental railroad and levees on the Mississippi River with federal appropriations, to place a southerner in the cabinet, and to refrain from giving federal jobs in the South to Republicans. Democrats agreed to allow the election of the Republican James Garfield as Speaker of the House (who would presumably prevent congressional investigations of yet more Republican scandals). With these secret understandings in place, the Democrats allowed the House of Representatives to accept the report of the electoral commission; Hayes went to the White House.

Once inaugurated, Hayes returned federal troops to their barracks from their positions surrounding the capitol buildings of Louisiana and South Carolina. Their Reconstruction governments, along with Florida's, collapsed, as did much of Hayes's reputation—the public remaining unaware of the secret deals that his backers had struck before he assumed office. In pursuit of a southern policy, in which he sought to entice former southern Whigs away from the Democrats, thus renewing southern Republicanism on a white base, Hayes named an ex-Confederate, David Key of Tennessee, as his postmaster

Hayes Ends Reconstruction

general, the cabinet officer with the most patronage to offer. Key then replaced Republican with Democratic postmasters in the South, thereby undercutting the southern Republican Party base. The Hayes administration also refused to support federal aid to southern railroads and other internal improvements, which killed those bills. For their part, the Democrats blocked Garfield's election to the Speakership, organized the House of Representatives for themselves, and used their control to launch yet another round of investigations into Republican corruption. They also broke their promises to protect the rights of blacks. For them, Hayes's withdrawal of federal troops from active duty in the South licensed the southern white Democratic removal of blacks from political participation, which they carried out during the next fifteen years.

Southern Democrats had achieved their supreme objective of home rule from a *Republican* president, thereby binding the opposition party to their domination in the South. This was a better outcome for them than if Tilden had won and the Republicans had continued to fight the southern Democrats' return to sectional power. With this "compromise," the Republicans essentially abandoned civil rights activities that had given concrete meaning to the Fourteenth and Fifteenth Amendments. Not for another eighty years would the federal government deploy troops in the South to protect black rights. During that period, conservative southern Democrats dug into congressional power, successfully warding off challenges to their domination at home—in part because the Republicans stuck to their 1877 bargain.

Redeemers in Power   At first, the Redeemers moved cautiously, perhaps still fearing northern intervention in the courts and the possibility of the return of federal troops should violence escalate. But move they did to exclude African Americans from voting. As early as 1877, Georgia adopted a poll tax, a device soon copied elsewhere. This worked a great hardship on blacks, most of whom were poor. Another mechanism was the use of separate boxes for each political contest during an election, labeled with the names of the offices and candidates, a system that prevented illiterate blacks from voting—black illiteracy rates remained between 40 percent and 60 percent in the southern states. The introduction of the secret ballot in the late 1880s also decreased the voting of those who were illiterate. That such measures also disenfranchised some (although far fewer) poor whites did not alarm the gentlemen in control of the voting system, whose regimes gave little support for public education or welfare measures for poor whites or for blacks.

Political control was paramount for the Redeemers and their successors in power, even at the expense of education and other engines of economic development. For a whole complex of reasons, including a more poorly educated workforce, a far slower rate of immigration and urbanization, and the fears of northern capitalists of investing in an unsettled region, the South lagged well behind the rest of the nation economically. To be sure, during the late nineteenth century, mills and other factories mushroomed in certain portions of the upper South, as did lumbering, coal, and iron-ore mining, shipbuilding, and food canning, but most of the North grew much more quickly. In 1860 the southern average income had been slightly higher than the national average, but from 1870 until 1900 the southern average remained at 51 percent of the nation as a whole. Even after the direct effects of the war diminished, structural elements kept the South relatively impoverished.

More southerners remained on the farm than was true elsewhere, and these farmers showed fewer signs of prosperity and innovation. As late as 1910, southern farms produced only 43 percent of the average for all American farms. In vast regions of the South, cotton remained the only cash crop, and production glutted the market. Increasing numbers of southern farmers lost their land. Although no other region of the nation experienced more than 39 percent tenancy rates during the period of 1880–1900, in all the upper South states the rate was above 45 percent, while in the deep South the rate was 58 percent in Alabama and Louisiana, 60 percent in Georgia, 61 percent in South

Continued Southern Poverty

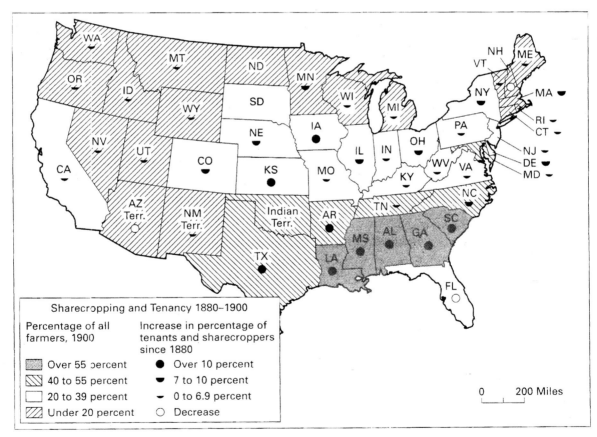

SHARECROPPING AND TENANCY, 1880–1900. During the late nineteenth century, and contrary to American notions of independence, thousands of farmers lost their land but lived on as impoverished tenants. The cotton South was hardest hit, blacks and poor whites alike being pushed to the margins of economic life.

DURING THE LATE NINETEENTH CENTURY, white southerners barred blacks from public spaces designated for whites only, first by custom and later by law. There was a great deal of racial segregation—"Jim Crow"—in the North as well. This image depicts a northern railway conductor ejecting a well-dressed black man from a passenger car, or at least from his seat, at the behest of a young woman, who wanted the seat for her and her baby.

Carolina, and 62 percent in Mississippi. Pockets of industrialization and prosperity notwithstanding, the vast majority of both whites and blacks in the South were desperately poor tenant farmers or sharecroppers.

Impoverished, suspected, and often illiterate though they might be, African Americans nevertheless continued to vote in large numbers. In the 1880 presidential election, between 50 percent and 70 percent of eligible blacks voted in the southern states. These levels of participation made the Redeemers queasy. One possible threat might be renewed Republican intervention in support of southern black voters; another was the potential for an alliance of lower-class whites and blacks, should poor whites ever place class considerations above racial animosity.

Both of these Redeemer fears nearly came to pass. In 1890, Republican Senator Henry Cabot Lodge of Massachusetts introduced a bill giving new teeth to federal control over southern elections, a measure soon termed the Force Bill, which passed the Republican-controlled House of Representatives before Democrats in the Senate defeated it. Even more threatening was the spectacular rise of the Populist Party in the late 1880s and early 1890s. Strong in the South as well the West, this angry party of the common white people, especially farmers, created tentative alliances with southern blacks against Redeemer-controlled Democratic machines. During many elections, the Democratic Party resorted to massive voter fraud in several states and to extraordinarily virulent racist campaigns to cement white solidarity.

Badly shaken by their near defeat at the hands of a home-grown, poor-people's party that contained a biracial component, fearful of renewed Republican legislation to support black voters within such an alliance in the South, the regular Democrats moved to disenfranchise blacks once and for all. State after state, starting with Mississippi in 1890, held constitutional conventions to pass literacy laws so stringent that almost no black man would be able to pass them when tested by white registration officials. Responding to white outcries that many of them, too, faced disenfranchisement if tested for literacy, later constitutional conventions, starting with Louisiana in 1897, required a literacy test only for those men who were not the sons and grandsons of voters in 1867, that is to say, for blacks only. In addition, most states passed laws that permitted only whites to vote in primary elections, and the Democrats were usually the only party that won general elections. These measures had their intended effect, which was to exclude African Americans from voting altogether, and to guarantee one-party Democratic hegemony.

Legalized Segregation

Systematic disenfranchisement in formal politics was insufficient protection against the black threat for white supremacists. All over the South, they passed laws that legalized discrimination in all public places. No longer was the traditional usage of segregation deemed sufficient; now signs went up everywhere, and blacks who tried to cross the color line were fined or imprisoned. "White Ladies" toilets were separated from those marked "Colored Women." Blacks were allowed into theaters only by separate sets of stairs leading to balconies reserved for them; whites walked in the front door and sat in the orchestra. Water fountains were segregated. On streetcars, blacks were compelled to sit at the back; white seating ran from the front backward, and blacks had to give up their seats when whites occupied more and more of the space. African Americans could not sit in first-class railroad carriages, being compelled to remain in designated smoking cars or sometimes in freight cars, the sole exception being made for black nurses caring for white babies. Schools, of course, were legally segregated, with black schools funded at a much lower level than white. Hospitals routinely refused to take blacks, and cemeteries were segregated as well. States and local communities rigorously enforced these laws, and it must be stressed that many of the same rules applied in much of the North, where school and residential and job segregation was also widespread.

Increased Lynchings

Because of continued black resistance and endemic white fears, official caste separation often needed reinforcement. After Reconstruction, lynching skyrocketed. Between 1885 and 1903, 2,585 lynchings were recorded in the South, with the number of unreported lynchings impossible to count. Many elected officials agreed with Governor James K. Vardaman of Mississippi when he pledged on the hustings in 1902 that "every Negro in the state will be lynched" to sustain white supremacy, if that would prove necessary. In particular, hysteria grew about a supposed epidemic of black rapes of white women. In 1907, on the floor of the U.S. Senate, Ben Tillman of South Carolina thundered, "I have three daughters but so help me God, I had rather find either one of them killed by a tiger or a bear and gather up her bones and bury them, conscious that she had died in the purity of her maidenhood, than to have her crawl to me and tell me the horrid story that she had been robbed of the jewel of her womanhood by a black fiend." One of Tillman's supporters back home added, "Just so long as negro men . . . outrage white women, white men will slay without mercy, judge or jury negro men." This was not because Tillman said so, but because such white vengeance was "natural" and just. Tillman gave this speech all over the South for decades.

The Antilynching Campaign of Ida B. Wells

Although whites maintained the hegemony of force in race relations, and blacks had difficulty resisting white lynch mobs that were often linked to law enforcement agents, African Americans did fight back. The most notable black spokesperson was Ida B. Wells. Born a slave in 1862 in Holly Springs, Mississippi, and trained as a teacher, by 1892 Wells was a journalist and editor of the *Free Speech*, a weekly African American newspaper in Memphis, Tennessee. After three prominent local black businessmen were lynched on March 9, 1892, for shooting back at the friends of a white business rival who was attacking them, Wells responded to the Tillman-style rationalization for such lynchings: "Nobody in this section believes the old threadbare lie that Negro men assault white women. If Southern white men are not careful, they will over-reach themselves and public sentiment will have a reaction; a conclusion will then be reached that will be very damaging to the moral reputation of their women." Wells was visiting New York when she wrote this editorial; a white mob imme-

THIS PORTRAIT of the twenty-nine-year-old Ida B. Wells, editor of the *Free Speech* newspaper in Memphis, Tennessee, appeared in I. Garland Penn's *The Afro-American Press and Its Editors*, published in 1891. The following year Wells began a courageous antilynching campaign that would result in whites threatening her and driving her out of the South. But no one stilled her voice.

diately destroyed the *Free Speech* for this affront to the moral purity of white women, and Wells never returned to Memphis.

But Wells persisted, campaigning and organizing against lynching. In the daily press, by writing several graphic pamphlets, and on lecture tours in the North and in Britain, Wells argued that lynching was not primarily a result of black men raping white women (and here she argued that white women caught in consensual relationships often charged rape), but of black actions tending toward independence. Indeed, she maintained, whites often transformed African American self-assertion into metaphorical rape—the threat that blacks might be moving to the top and whites to the bottom. To protect against this deeply feared reversal of the social order, white men then defended all white women as virtuous and condemned all black men as endlessly lustful. Conversely, Wells argued, the presence of so many thousands of mulattos in the South demonstrated that for white men, black women were below the moral pale and were assumed to be promiscuous and immoral. The charge that black males frequently and savagely raped white women and the denial that a white man was ever culpable of raping a black woman were the justifications for terrorizing and controlling black men and women, body and soul. Wells aroused enormous hatred in the white South by analyzing this potent combination of gender and race. Her views found institutional expression in the National Association of Colored Women, founded in 1896, and the biracial National Association for the Advancement of Colored People, formed in 1909. Lynching did not decline during this period, but black and a few white voices began to be raised in protest to it.

Whether vengeful and hateful or kind and paternalistic, white behavior toward blacks was systematically discriminatory. African Americans were debarred from political office, from the vote, from juries, from testifying in court against white people, from restaurants, from beaches and parks, from anything remotely resembling equal economic, social, and educational opportunities. Still, some prospered, and others began to migrate to the West and the North in numbers that would swell during and after World War I. Yet, even in the South, often with financial aid from white northern philanthropists, blacks continued to build their own institutions—schools, universities, businesses, and most notably, churches. At times, prosperous blacks and middle-class black neighborhoods became the targets of white rioters, who burned, looted, and murdered as intensely as during Reconstruction. If black poverty was a sign of black degradation in white eyes, black success was equally dangerous, for it showed that African Americans might be getting uppity, above their station.

Systematic Racial Discrimination

Far from being relaxed in their domination, whites in the segregated South continuously reinforced race lines, socializing each new generation of blacks about their appropriate caste standing. Eternal vigilance was the sign of the times: as far as whites were concerned, blacks did not rest content in their assigned place, and in this they were right. Many liberal-minded whites deplored the situation, but fearing the social ostracism and threats of violence that they rightly assumed would follow outspoken dissent, they felt powerless to contest it in public ways. Despite the prevailing ethos, acts of personal kindness continued to cross the racial divide, but private acts of subversion or softening did not change the institutional structures and general practices in any fundamental respect. Neither did the continued strength of black institutions deter white supremacists when they decided to take action—black institution building and wealth creation did not amount to independent black "agency" because whites held the whip hand and used it when they willed, undercutting and reversing hard-won black gains.

Northern Acquiescence to White Supremacists

Moreover, in support of the white South, there was an increasing convergence of white views in the North about the inferiority of blacks and the acceptability of the southern caste system. When Democrat Grover Cleveland finally ended the Republican monopoly of the White House in 1884, having been elected with great aid from the solidly Democratic South, he gave numerous posts in the diplomatic corps, in his cabinet, and on the Supreme Court to ex-Confederates. He also returned Confederate battle flags to the South. Cleveland's reintegration of southern whites in the executive and judicial branches of the federal government demonstrated the degree to which national reconciliation rested on a southern base. Indeed, the ex-Confederates also won the ideological contest over the legacy of the Civil War, in a manner discussed in the final chapter of this book.

After 1890, as waves of poor and overwhelmingly Catholic and Jewish immigrants from eastern and southern Europe entered America, older generations of white Americans, northern as well as southern, grew increasingly anxious and angry. Often employing Darwinian doctrine, scientists and social scientists began to build racial theories that they applied to the new immigrants and to blacks as well. This xenophobia matched that growing in Europe as the "white" nations conquered most of the nonwhite world in the late nineteenth and early twentieth centuries. Justification through the white man's burden was condescending when not a license for overt discrimination and, at times, slaughter. Americans joined the race for empire in 1898 when they went to war with Spain, the weakest European power, destroyed their navy and much of their army in Cuba, took Puerto Rico and the Philippines from them, and then subdued the Philippine population in a bloody colonial guerrilla war. Not coincidentally, the volunteer army of 1898 included both ex-Confederate and ex-Union officers. Many celebrated this melding of the sections through national martial glory as the best means to achieve final reunification.

The Supreme Court Accepts Segregation

Just two years earlier, in the *Plessy v. Ferguson* decision, the Supreme Court had ruled that when southern states legally enforced racial discrimination, they did not violate the Constitution. Homer Plessy, a light-skinned mulatto, was arrested for refusing to leave a whites-only, first-class railroad car in Louisiana, thus violating an 1890 law prescribing segregation. Arguing for all his brother justices save one, Justice Henry Billings Brown, a Republican from Michigan who had been raised in New England, concluded that "a statute which implies merely a legal distinction between the white and colored races— a distinction which is founded in the color of the two races, and which must always exist so long as white men are distinguished from the other race by color—has no tendency to destroy the legal equality of the two races. . . . The object of the [Fourteenth] Amendment was undoubtedly to enforce the absolute equality of the two races before the law, but in the nature of things it could not have been intended to abolish distinctions based upon color, or to enforce social, as distinguished from political equality, or a commingling of the two races upon terms unsatisfactory to either." The standard of "separate but equal" was acceptable in the eyes of the Court, although they did not use the actual phrase. Justice Brown considered it a "fallacy" for Plessy to believe "that the enforced separation of the two races stamps the colored race with a badge of inferiority." Nothing in the Louisiana law provided such a badge, one that did not exist unless "the colored race chooses to put that construction on it." With great clarity, the Supreme Court accepted the legality of the southern caste system by ruling that the Fourteenth Amendment did not apply to state laws. Following this decision, blacks had no federally protected constitutional rights.

In his dissent, Justice John Marshall Harlan, born into a distinguished Kentucky slaveholding family, ridiculed his colleagues for turning a purposefully blind eye to the motives of southern white legislators. "The thin disguise of 'equal' accommodations for passengers for railroad coaches will not mislead any one, nor atone for the wrong this day done," he wrote. Harlan could not imagine how the remainder of the Court could conclude in good conscience that such state legislation, "although conceived in hostility to, and enacted for the purpose of humiliating, citizens of the United States of a particular race, would be held to be consistent with the Constitution." Standing alone, Harlan thundered, "our Constitution is color-blind, and neither knows nor tolerates classes among citizens. In respect of civil rights, all citizens are equal before the law . . . the present decision, it may well be apprehended, will not only stimulate aggressions, more or less brutal, upon the admitted rights of colored citizens, but . . . by means of state enactments [will] defeat the beneficent purposes which the people of the United States had in view when they adopted the recent amendments to the Constitution."

Despite Harlan's solitary plea, the majority interpretation left the civil rights amendments as mere dead letters as far as the rights of blacks were concerned, in a decision that would stand until 1954. In endorsing the caste system, the Court confirmed popular opinion concerning racial segregation. Racial discrimination in educational, employment, and residential opportunities remained widespread in the North as well as the South. This 1896 decision and "the splendid little war" (as Theodore Roosevelt called it) of 1898, rather than the events of 1877, marked the end of the era of the Civil War—and the final and unequivocal acceptance of systematic, legalized, racial inequality, despite the elimination of slavery.

It has become something of a fashion for American historians to emphasize the progressive elements of Reconstruction, particularly the "legacy" of the Thirteenth, Fourteenth, and Fifteenth Amendments, which, the argument goes, remained in place for renewed use during the civil rights revolution of the

The Troubling Legacy of Reconstruction

1950s and 1960s. While it took an immense effort to destroy the tenacious struggle of blacks and their few southern white allies during Reconstruction, and while Reconstruction had been an extraordinary, if flawed, governmental experiment in racial readjustment after the war, it was the Redeemers who won the struggle, destroying Reconstruction, and their direct heirs oppressed African Americans for the ensuing eighty years, with northern acquiescence and sometimes outright support. The Redeemers enacted white supremacy—their primary goal—at a considerable cost to the white South as well as the black. To insist that the Civil War and Reconstruction had been a concerted battle for racial justice, to argue that the final collapse of the segregation system in the 1950s and 1960s proved that the Civil War had contained that promise, disappears or diminishes the lives of millions of men, women, and children who were systematically oppressed for decades by degrading and often violent means. But the Civil War, which indeed became a struggle against slavery, never had become a crusade for racial justice. Northern white ambivalence undermined Reconstruction, in tandem with determined southern white actions. The conflicting legacies of the Civil War and its aftermath give insufficient cause for American self-congratulation.

Epilogue
Remembering and Forgetting the Civil War: 1865–Present

In July 1913, veterans of Gettysburg returned to the Pennsylvania town to commemorate the battle's fiftieth anniversary. Grizzled old men in ill-fitting uniforms walked solemnly along the rolling ridges, squinting at imposing bronze monuments and posing for photographers. Their wives, children, grandchildren, and great-grandchildren accompanied them, listening as the aged soldiers recalled their distant past. Newfangled motion picture cameras captured the reunion, the grainy film exaggerating the veterans' every gesture and making them seem like actors emoting in one of the silent movies of the time.

Former Confederates and former Federals, many with long, white, wispy beards, shook hands and clapped each other's shoulder at the storied "Clump of Trees" on Cemetery Ridge, marking the high-water mark of Pickett's Charge. Spectators sought shade from the hot summer sun under tents and under trees. Hundreds of reporters and political luminaries attended, including President Woodrow Wilson, who told the crowd: "How wholesome and healing the peace has been!" The first southerner elected to executive office since before the Civil War, Wilson proclaimed: "We have found one another again as brothers and comrades in arms, enemies no longer, generous friends rather, our battles long past, the quarrel forgotten—except that we shall not forget the splendid valor, the manly devotion of the men then arrayed against one another, now grasping hands and smiling into each other's eyes."

AGING CIVIL WAR VETERANS, of the North and South, returned to Gettysburg in 1913 to remember what had happened there fifty years before.

Wilson was partially right. Americans, notably white Americans, had forgotten, at least publicly, the war's horrors. Even the actual survivors of the crisis purged from their collective memory the complicated causes and consequences of the conflict, forgetting its bitterness, chaos, and savagery, and its political ambiguities, instead recalling and recounting the war as a great morality play about honorable Americans who fought bravely for their beliefs. Forgotten, too, among the celebrations of reunion were the role of slavery in causing the crisis, the participation of black veterans, and the unfulfilled promises of racial justice and political equality.

War Becomes Myth How did the bloodiest war in American history become sanitized of its brutality and emptied of its complex meaning? Why did veterans, subsequent generations of Americans, and many historians help to create this mythology and plant it so firmly in the public's psyche? Why was slavery truncated from the history books, dismissed as unimportant and insignificant in causing sectionalism, disunion, and war?

The mythology of the American Civil War began almost as soon as the war ended. Varying interpretations of the war collided, as Americans sought to make sense of the awful conflict.

Ex-Confederates started to reconfigure an explanation and defense of their nation's short existence in a variety of published media, including newspaper articles, personal memoirs, histories of the war, poems, and novels. This *Lost Cause* ideology, which began with Robert E. Lee's farewell address to his troops in April 1865, eventually developed into several basic tenets that included the constitutionality of secession, the unity of the South, the heroism of Confederate soldiers, the loyalty of white southern women, and the faithfulness of childlike slaves. Insisting that states' rights rather than slavery caused the war was central to the Lost Cause mantra. "It was not the desire to hold others in bondage," Reverend R. C. Cave proclaimed to a Richmond audience in 1894, "but the desire to maintain their rights that actuated the Southern people throughout the conflict." Virginians were especially active in promoting this interpretation of the war, embellishing their role in the conflict over everyone else and proclaiming Virginians Robert E. Lee and "Stonewall" Jackson as the quintessential southern warriors.

The Lost Cause

Lee's image in particular was nearly Christlike, half-man, half-god, humble, honorable, inherently peaceful, but driven to war by a just and noble cause despite his personal distaste for slavery, risking everything out of loyalty to the South. If he was so noble and apolitical, the Confederate cause must have been just. Confederate defeat was due to northern numbers and might, not to any inherent weaknesses from within the southern nation. Lost Cause proponents also tended to give greater attention to events and leaders in the eastern theater, neglecting western battles and western armies. Always participating on the cultural front of the bitter politics opposing Radical Reconstruction, Lost Cause advocates also expunged the acrimonious politics of slavery from their past; yet, at the same time, they contended that the institution had been a benign one, insisting that all slaves had been well treated and happy. Self-serving, paternalistic images of docile, ignorant, grateful slaves celebrating holidays and singing spirituals permeated Lost Cause literature.

The Lost Cause interpretation of the Civil War was vital to the construction of a new form of defiant southern nationalism, replete with a heavy dose of tragedy. White southerners admitted their defeat in the war, but they used that loss to emphasize their self-sacrifice and heroic suffering. Virginian Thomas Nelson Page, one of the most prolific and influential of the Lost Cause authors, described a scene in one of his short stories where Confederate veterans slowly paraded past a reverent throng of weeping men, sobbing women, and crying children. The sight of the old soldiers profoundly moved the crowd: "they represented the spirit which when honor was in question never counted the cost." This spirit, Page avowed, was "glorious in victory . . . yet greater in defeat." Such emotional imagery helped white southerners win the peace, inspiring them to defy federal Reconstruction, block black equality, and instigate racial disfranchisement and segregation.

LOST CAUSE PROPONENTS celebrated former Confederate general Robert E. Lee as the quintessential southern hero and refined, honorable gentleman.

The Lost Cause interpretation of the war also contained clear contradictions. Although its advocates stressed the gallantry of all Confederate soldiers and the South's proud martial heritage, Lost Cause proponents also celebrated reunion and peace. They admitted Confederate defeat but refused to blame their own leaders for the loss. (The rare exception was James Longstreet, who earned the ire of his former comrades by openly criticizing Lee and becoming a Republican during Reconstruction.) For most of these aging warriors, northern might had been simply too much for the embattled Confederates, who were compelled to lay down their arms in reluctant but morally unbowed defeat.

Despite their emphasis on southern unity, some ex-Confederates bickered with each other in determining the true history of the conflict. Heated "paper wars" raged among southern veterans in the postwar years, especially in the pages of the *Southern Historical Society Papers*, *Southern Bivouac*, and the *Confederate Veteran*. Members of the pro-Lee "Virginian coalition," including Jubal Early, D. H. Maury, and William Nelson Pendleton, battled angrily with ex-Confederates in other states about the "facts" of the war. Former commanders contested different versions of specific battles and military decisions. James Longstreet fought stubbornly against repeated accusations that he failed at Gettysburg and thus had lost the battle; D. H. Hill squabbled with the pro-Lee camp about his responsibility for the "lost order" at Antietam; John Bell Hood bitterly challenged vociferous critics who said he had recklessly led the Army of the Tennessee to destruction; and Joe Johnston defended his allegedly unappreciated talents.

While some of their former commanders debated and reconstructed the South's martial history, many Confederate veterans, especially men from the ranks, were initially disinclined to remember publicly that painful past. Nevertheless, as the decades rolled by and soldiers aged and died, surviving veterans' attitudes changed. Old men *wanted* to reminisce and tried to recapture what increasingly seemed to have been the most important and exciting years of their lives. By the 1880s and 1890s, interest in Confederate organizations grew as the Lost Cause mythology evolved and spread. A coalition of state veteran groups from Louisiana, Tennessee, and Mississippi created the United Confederate Veterans in New Orleans in 1889, and UCV chapters quickly expanded throughout the South. By the early 1900s, an estimated one-third of all living Confederate veterans, some 80,000 men, belonged to the UCV.

Confederate Veterans

Ex-Confederate soldiers were not the only ones promoting the Lost Cause. The wives, sons, and daughters of veterans also helped create the mythology and shape public memory. By the 1890s, not long after the founding of the UCV, this younger generation of white southerners, especially white women, became extremely active in commemorating the war. *The United Daughters of the Confederacy* (UDC) and the *Sons of Confederate Veterans* (SCV) joined with the UCV to uphold the faith of the Lost Cause, erect monuments, build orphanages and soldier homes, celebrate Confederate Memorial Day, and petition southern legislatures and school officials to teach their version of the past, which said little about slavery's cruelties or the humiliation of defeat. Secession had not been treason but an exercise in self-government and state sovereignty. White supremacy was central to their interpretation of the war, as was their insistence on telling the "Truths of History" about the South's past. In widely disseminated pamphlets, for example, the historian general of the UDC, Mildred L. Rutherford, stated as "fact" that "Southern men were anxious for slaves to be free [and that they were] studying earnestly the problems of freedom, when Northern fanatical Abolitionists took matters into their own hands." Rutherford further insisted: "more slaveholders and sons of slaveholders fought for the Union than for the Confederacy."

The UDC and the SCV

Bitter antinorthernism was common in Lost Cause rhetoric. Yankees were crude, greedy materialists, serving themselves and Mammon in the name of the Union. While ex-Confederates pictured themselves as a beleaguered minority, they accused the North of all past and current social evils—for the sins of corrupt government, industrialization, urbanism, women's rights agitation, and racially and religiously suspect immigration. The "Old South" became an idealized utopia where the right sort of Anglo-Saxon people ruled over an inferior stock while living graciously and communally, in contrast to the divided and debased North.

Women and the Lost Cause

The leading role of women so zealously promoting such notions of social, racial, and gender hierarchy has intrigued historians. Why did white southern women play such a public and influential part in perpetuating the Lost Cause, especially in a patriarchal society, albeit a weakened and defeated one? Some have explained that southern women, particularly the well-heeled, felt a need to bolster their men's wounded masculinity; others have suggested that female Confederates were more passionate and embittered about the South's failed cause than their men and that women had more latitude to speak out emotionally than did their necessarily reserved menfolk, given contemporary gender codes. Some note that their involvement in commemoration occurred at the same time as the women's club movement, an increasingly acceptable and valued outlet for middle-class women's public persona. A recent study has explained that it was natural for women to memorialize the dead because this was a role they had played in antebellum society. Still another scholar has argued that women assumed these activities only after the federal government sought to stifle ex-Confederate soldiers' efforts to commemorate the war. It was less threatening, it seems, to have soldiers' wives, daughters, and mothers organizing public commemorative events and rituals, rather than have the veterans donning their old uniforms and marching in martial parades. Whatever the explanation, the central role of southern white women in championing the Lost Cause is undeniable.

Northern Memory

Northerners had their own version of the war to advance, but they seemed to lack the dogged persistence and determination of their former foes. They had of course saved the Union and ended slavery. For a time, there was intense debate throughout the North about how to commemorate both of these accomplishments. Eventually, however, northern whites adopted much of the southern version of the war, celebrating the courage of Confederate soldiers, the loyalty of southern women, and the irrelevance of slavery in causing the war. The troubled politics of postwar America, racial violence, and their own discriminatory policies against blacks and the waves of new immigrants, Catholics and Jews from southern and eastern Europe, made white northerners just as anxious to downplay the role of slavery in the conflict and to appreciate the notion of a hierarchical white society. Remembering the war as a contest to save the Union was simply less controversial, and in truth, it had been the principal reason many northerners had fought. As one historian noted, there was a "romance of reunion" between the victorious North and sentimentalized South.

Union Veterans

Union veterans were active participants in the process of memory-making. Their influence, like that of the Confederate veteran groups, was found in many facets of everyday life, including politics, parades, monument dedications, and making Memorial Day a national holiday. Union veterans also actively advocated their own brand of patriotism, encouraging military preparedness and demanding that public schools use certain approved history textbooks and fly the American flag. The Grand Army of the Republic, founded in Decatur, Illinois, in 1866, thirty-three years before the UCV, was the largest and most active of the various northern veteran groups. Established primarily for political purposes, the GAR lobbied successfully for veterans' interests and in support of the Republican Party until well into the late nineteenth century. They gained huge amounts of government money to provide pensions, orphanages, and homes for Civil War veterans and their families.

Generals' Wives

Wives and widows of famous commanders on both sides joined the fray, defending their husbands and helping to solidify the mythologized version of the war. Many wives of generals became "professional widows," writing books and giving lectures across the nation, celebrating a romanticized version of their husbands, the war, and their own lives. Elizabeth Bacon Custer, Helen Longstreet, and LaSalle Corbell Pickett enchanted audiences with their reminiscences of their husbands' exploits. Rarely were their memories "accurate," but few challenged them. Middle-class white women, and especially wives of famous men, were not to be confronted in public.

Monument Building

Monument building and public commemorations long remained central activities for both northerners and southerners. By the 1890s, Civil War monuments appeared across the country, forever altering the nation's landscape.

BY THE 1890s, mass-produced Civil War monuments, like the one pictured here in Greenwood, South Carolina, were placed in town squares, cemeteries, parks, and battlefields.

Before the Civil War, military shrines were uncommon in the United States. Even some of the earliest Civil War memorials were simple stone shafts, most often found in cemeteries, merely listing the names of the dead. By the turn of the century, however, monument-making became big business, with images of soldiers mass produced and replicated, North and South. There were unique ones created by the renowned sculptors Augustus Saint-Gaudens and Marius-Jean-Antonin Mercié. These granite, marble, and brass memorials, most in the neoclassic style, often evoked images of death and mourning. But as the century progressed, Civil War monuments began to idealize and romanticize the war, celebrating the heroics of individual generals, units, and nameless soldiers. Some of the most common statues depicted a single soldier, uniformed and armed, with little acknowledgment of the violence he might have inflicted or the suffering he had endured. Appearing in parks, cemeteries, and town squares, as well as on battlefields, Civil War monuments changed America's public space, as if freezing in time a legend about its past. The statues' nondescript faces and generic uniforms also helped to affirm a distinctive American whiteness devoid of ethnic or racial difference. These figures, cheap and easy to obtain, the bulk of them erected between 1890–1910, also emplaced a new nationalism in a local context. They appeared throughout the country, making an important statement about the war experience; it was not to be remembered as debilitating or dehumanizing, but as dutiful, honorable, and decidedly masculine and white.

African American Memory

African American private and public memory of the war was also conflicted and contested, and markedly different from that of whites. Some blacks openly stressed their contributions to the Union war effort and the promises of Reconstruction to justify their rights to citizenship. By recalling their strength and perseverance through decades of enslavement and their sacrifice during the war itself, blacks sought positive affirmation to counter the virulent racism of their present. Because slavery was a painful memory, for many it was best left forgotten. There was also a sense that somehow the sufferings of slavery and the trials of emancipation were all part of blacks' unique destiny, leading to an age of lasting utopian Pan-Africanism. But even these overlapping and sometimes contradictory versions of black memory were lost on whites. Black veterans found themselves excluded from veteran groups, their version of the past forgotten, their role in the war and its aftermath deliberately distorted or falsified.

It was not as though African Americans sat idly by as whites' racist commemorative activities multiplied. During those first few decades after the war, there were in fact deliberate public efforts by blacks and some northern whites to memorialize emancipation, build monuments to black soldiers, and in the process offer alternative histories to ensure that Americans remembered the war as a struggle over slavery and racial justice, with African Americans as active participants. African Americans in Charleston, for example, organized the first "Decoration Day" on May 1, 1865, to honor Union prisoners buried in the city. An estimated 10,000 people, blacks and some whites, marched in a parade, sang songs, offered prayers, listened to speeches, and decorated Union soldiers' graves with spring flowers, all in an obvious attempt to make a public statement about the meaning of the war. Southern blacks also organized Emancipation Day celebrations, often on January 1, holding ceremonies, gathering in churches, and listening to speeches. Other dates gained significance, such as April 3, the date Richmond fell to the Union, and June 19, or Juneteenth, in Texas, marking the date in 1865 when Union officials informed African Americans in Galveston that the Emancipation Proclamation had set them free. Parades often featured blacks boldly striding through urban areas normally restricted to whites. Speeches and sermons, while filled with hope and pride, echoed John Brown's original prophecy: the war was God's punishment for the sin of slavery. But they also contained warnings about the importance of memory. On Memorial Day 1878, an aging but no less fiery Frederick Douglass declared: "There was a right side and a wrong side in the late war which no sentiment ought to cause us to forget."

With time, however, African Americans' involvement in, and even record of, commemorating the Civil War would be forgotten, at least by most white Americans. By the turn of the century, black efforts at Civil War memorialization waned as they faced staggering poverty, racism, and violence.

Memorial Day

In the meantime, whites introduced their own Decoration and Memorial days in the North and South to honor their dead, which eclipsed those of blacks. In the North, Memorial Day organized by the GAR encouraged Union veterans to hold ceremonies and decorate their fallen comrades' graves. By 1890, every northern state had designated May 30 a legal holiday. In the South, a separate Confederate Memorial Day emerged, with states selecting different dates, including April 26, the date of Johnston's surrender in North Carolina, and June 3, Jefferson Davis's birthday. By 1916, ten southern states designated June 3 as the official Confederate Memorial Day, marking the occasion with martial parades, military drills, and decorating Confederate soldiers' graves.

Remembering Lincoln

Abraham Lincoln emerged as a central figure, not just in Civil War commemoration but in American memory as a whole. Lincoln became a national icon, towering over all other famed northerners, including Grant and Sherman. The martyred president entered the pantheon of America's most revered political leaders, alongside Washington and Jefferson, and it seemed that his image as the great emancipator diminished the active role of slaves in determining their own fate. Nonetheless, the massive Lincoln Memorial dedicated in 1922, and placed prominently to anchor the Mall in Washington, D.C., became a rallying point for future civil rights leaders. Martin Luther King Jr. chose the Lincoln Memorial for the backdrop of his famed "I Have a Dream" speech on the Mall in August 1963.

The Politics of Memory

Lincoln's own Republican Party became dramatically affected by the politics of memory in the decades following the war. Northern and southern leaders, quickly realizing the power that memories of the war could have on voters, often used them to telling effect. The Republican Party's tendency to "wave the bloody shirt" persuasively reminded northerners of their sacrifices and ex-Confederates of their defeat. Republicans too contrasted their image as the

THE 1898 SPANISH-AMERICAN WAR ushered in renewed nationalism and sectional reconciliation. This dramatic tableau symbolizes the reunion of northern and southern veterans to fight the Spanish and defend Cuba.

war's victors to that of the Democrats as secessionists and traitors, appealing not just to Union veterans but to new black voters.

However, by the 1890s, a new generation of Republicans wanted to distance themselves from the emancipationist legacy of Lincoln and its demand for black civil rights, choosing instead to emphasize nationalism and industrial and capitalist growth. In the election of 1896, the Republican Party tried to merge past and present by stripping from its platform demands that the federal government use military force to ensure southern black male suffrage. Republicans also continued to equate Democrats with the war, dismissing Democratic presidential hopeful William Jennings Bryan as the candidate of division. Touting former Union officer William McKinley as "the advance agent of prosperity" and national unity, the Republican Party quickened its break with its past as the party of emancipation and black civil rights.

The politics of memory extended to international affairs as well. As the end of the nineteenth century neared, Americans entered the race for empire already commenced by Europe centuries earlier. To succeed abroad, Americans needed unity at home. Thus, when the United States entered its "splendid little war" in 1898 to force Spain out of Cuba and the Philippines (where it took a protracted and brutal counterinsurgency to subdue the "natives"), Americans cheered old Confederate officers rejoining the volunteer U.S. Army—brothers again after all.

In the mid-twentieth century, the politics of Civil War memory took unexpected twists and turns. In June 1936, Democratic President Franklin Delano Roosevelt, whose New Deal would dramatically change his party to attract African American voters, told a crowd of onlookers at the unveiling of a Robert E. Lee Memorial that Lee was a "great leader of men" and a "great general." He pronounced: "But, also all over the United States I believe that we recognize him as something more important than that. We recognize Robert E. Lee as one of the greatest American Christians and one of our greatest American gentlemen." This appeal made good political sense. Much of the New Deal depended on southern Democratic segregationist voters and congressmen, and much of its programming aided blacks only incidentally.

Twelve years later, during the heated election of 1948, disaffected southern **Dixiecrats** Democrats bolted from their party convention after hearing a speech by Hubert Humphrey urging the inclusion of a civil rights plank in the party platform. Members of this new States' Rights Party, clearly conscious of the parallel events of 1860, held their own convention in Birmingham, where they nominated Strom Thurmond of South Carolina as their presidential candidate. These "Dixiecrats," as they soon became known, appropriated the Confederate flag for their cause and the slogan "Segregation Forever!" The party proved

SOUTH CAROLINA STROM THURMOND ran for president in 1948 as leader of the Dixiecrats, disaffected Democrats whose slogan was "Segregation Forever!" Here Thurmond is pictured giving a campaign speech in Austin, Texas, in October 1948.

short-lived, winning just four southern states—Louisiana, Mississippi, Alabama, and South Carolina—in the 1948 election, but their opposition to civil rights was just getting started. And they marked the weakening of the Democrats' hold on the former Confederacy. Thurmond, as did other Dixiecrats, eventually switched parties to become a devout Republican, embracing that party's turn toward conservatism. In 1999 the Republican senator addressed a Memorial Day crowd, stating that he was "irked" that anyone claimed slavery to be a cause of the Civil War. Thurmond explained that the war was fought over "the rights of the states to control their own destinies." The Party of Lincoln now included an unrepentant supporter of the Lost Cause.

Memory and Popular Culture

Changes in technology and popular culture further affected the continuing process of Civil War memorialization. Periodicals, so important during the war in spreading information to soldiers and civilians alike, remained important, and new ones were introduced with the sole purpose of commemorating the conflict. *Century Magazine*'s "Century War Series," published from November 1884 to November 1887, was so widely read—some estimate that the magazine's readership grew to nearly 2 million readers—that in 1888 the editors decided to publish all the essays in four separate volumes entitled *Battles and Leaders of the Civil War*. These volumes would have a profound effect on memory, something the editors recognized in the collection's preface. Explaining that their "main purpose" was to interest "veterans in their own memories" and instruct a new generation of Americans who had "grown up since the War for the Union," the editors asserted that the series had "exerted an influence in bringing about a better understanding between the soldiers who were opposed in that conflict." These articles, written by well-known participants, including Ulysses S. Grant, James Longstreet, Ambrose Burnside, and P. G. T. Beauregard, focused on narrow military questions of tactics, strategy, and leadership. Certainly these were points of contention among veterans, but missing was any discussion of politics, economy, culture, or race. *Battles and Leaders*, like so many commemorative expressions and events, stressed reconciliation by celebrating shared "heroic deeds" of white soldiers on both sides, muting discussion of divisive causes or troubling consequences.

The innovation of motion pictures also affected Americans' attitudes. Films such as D. W. Griffith's *Birth of a Nation* (1915) and David O. Selznik's *Gone with the Wind* (1939) conveyed histories of the war to the silver screen, seeming to relay realism by the very nature of the medium, while in fact propagating legends. Both these films, hugely successful commercially and still hailed today as classic pictures, perpetuated many of the original elements of the Lost Cause ideology. Griffith's film, based on Thomas Dixon's luridly racist 1905 novel *The Clansman*, depicts the chaos of the postwar South with scenes of hapless yet leering and threatening blacks. The final scene of the movie shows the KKK literally riding to the rescue as courageous defenders of white Christian male honor and female purity.

Gone with the Wind, based on Georgian Margaret Mitchell's novel, mixes disquiet with war, industrial capitalism, and even feminism, and one scene depicts a secretive KKK-like organization set on returning postwar political control to local whites. Blacks are caricatures: either happy and unquestionably loyal, or untrustworthy and selfish. Scarlett O'Hara's stubborn survival in the face of daunting odds was a powerful image to Americans, North and South, struggling with the vicissitudes of the Great Depression. Even future generations of Americans, troubled by the ambiguities of modern life, would be susceptible to the film's sentimentalism.

The Civil War centennial ushered in a new wave of memorialization, but it also revealed how polarized memory of the war had become. In September 1957, President Dwight D. Eisenhower signed into law the Civil War Centennial Commission to oversee commemorative activities. Ulysses S. Grant's grandson was appointed chair of the commission; ironically, his sympathies leaned more to the South than the North. States were encouraged to form their own commissions to work in conjunction with the federal government. Although the federal government sought to depict the war as a tragic but heroic and ultimately unifying experience, southern segregationists pursued a different purpose. Reinvigorating familiar messages from the Lost Cause, white southerners, increasingly under siege from civil rights activists for their discriminatory Jim Crow practices, sought to use the anniversary to celebrate their Confederate heritage and promote renewed and defiant demands for state sovereignty. From the start, the South displayed great enthusiasm for the commemoration. Mississippi alone appropriated $2 million for its efforts, and Virginia $1.4 million.

The Civil War Centennial

African Americans would also come to see the centennial as a fresh opportunity to commemorate their role in the war. Up to that time, white southerners had succeeded in propagating the Lost Cause version, even gaining widespread northern support. Civil rights leaders, initially hesitant to use the centennial as a way to advance their cause, soon realized that if segregationists were going to interpret the war's anniversary to bolster their past and present, blacks could and should do the same.

A showdown occurred at one of the first inaugural events, scheduled for April 12, 1961, the anniversary of the firing on Fort Sumter in Charleston harbor. When a Charleston hotel refused accommodation to a black female member of the New Jersey delegation, New Jersey and several other northern states threatened a boycott. The commission's chair, Ulysses S. Grant III, sided with the segregationists, arguing that the commission had "no authority or jurisdiction" to dictate to local hotel owners. President John F. Kennedy, at first hesitant to become involved, issued a statement that the commission, funded by the federal government, "should hold its meetings at places free of racial discrimination." After a compromise was reached by choosing a desegregated naval base in Charleston, most members of the state delegations who had protested agreed to attend. The secretary of the Illinois state commission, however, stated: "We're going to be commemorating Civil War events for the next four years and we might as well get this thing straight now. There can be no compromise on this."

The battle lines were clearly drawn. The incident in Charleston hurt Kennedy's public image among southern segregationists, adding to the new president's reluctance to take an active role in the fight for civil rights. Kennedy rebuffed Martin Luther King Jr.'s plea that he issue a new emancipation proclamation to coincide with planned events in Washington on September 22, 1962. But by February 1963, under increasing pressure, not just from civil rights leaders but from the international community closely watching a nation claiming to defend equality and democracy against communism, Kennedy admitted in an address to Congress that the original Emancipation Proclamation was "only a first step" in ensuring "progress for the Negro. . . . Equality before the law," Kennedy conceded, "had not always meant equal treatment and opportunity." Further, after Grant's resignation over the Charleston controversy, Kennedy appointed Alan Nevins as official historian of the centennial. Nevins, who openly backed inclusion of the African American story, also wanted to play down the military side of the war. His appointment represented a marked change in the commission's interpretation of the war and its legacy.

The latter half of the centennial was less successful in attracting popular interest. Battle reenactments drew criticism by some that the commission was trivializing and grossly commercializing the war. For white southerners, the post-1863 story of loss and defeat proved less popular to commemorate. And as a new, equally controversial war in Vietnam increasingly took center stage, Americans, black and white, had little appetite for martial celebrations of any kind.

The Confederate Flag

Still, the centennial produced a lasting impact on popular memory of the conflict. Perhaps the most obvious was the resurgence of the Confederate battle flag. During the war, this banner with an X design never was a national flag, but it seemed a better option for troops in battle than the "Stars and Bars," which looked too similar to the U.S. "Stars and Stripes." Apparently the diagonal cross emblem had been the brainchild of P. G. T. Beauregard, who sought an inspirational symbol for his army markedly different from the star-spangled banner of the United States, one easily discernable in the smoky chaos of combat. As the war raged, this design, in various forms, more often square than rectangular, and in different color combinations, flew most prominently over rebel armies. During Reconstruction, simply displaying the Confederate battle flag was illegal in parts of the South occupied by federal troops, thus lending it a certain piratical allure.

The controversial emblem enjoyed a resurgence in the midst of the Civil War centennial when white southerners returned to their past, seeking not only a historical symbol but a passionate declaration of their political stance against civil rights. For both southern blacks and whites, the flag stirred strong emotions. For white southerners, it was a proud emblem of their heritage and an assertion of states' rights; for African Americans, however, it was a painful and even threatening reminder of slavery and racism. It was no coincidence, it seemed to blacks, that the KKK as well as other hate groups had adopted the flag, and it was alarming to see white supremacists such as Georgia Governor Lester Maddox champion the Confederate flag as a symbol of segregation. Mis-

BY THE MID-TWENTIETH CENTURY, the Confederate flag became an emotional symbol for southern whites and blacks. For many whites it represented their proud heritage, but also their angry defiance of African Americans' civil rights. In this undated photograph, white male students wave the flag at a KKK rally.

sissippi had already incorporated the Confederate battle flag into its state flag in 1894; in 1956 Georgia did the same. And the red saltire in the Florida and Alabama state flags seemed to suggest the blue saltire of the Southern Cross. In the context of the civil rights movement, past and present appeared fused in these powerful and volatile symbols of southern resistance.

In recent years, the Confederate flag has continued to cause controversy as African Americans have demanded its removal from southern statehouses and state flags, stirring anger from whites determined to protect their "heritage." In Columbia, South Carolina, the Confederate battle flag flew separately over the state capitol from 1962 to 2000; although removed from the building, it is still flown elsewhere on the grounds of the capitol. In 2001, Mississippians voted by a margin of 2 to 1 to retain the Southern Cross on their state flag. That same year Georgia selected a flag that downplayed the Confederate emblem, although even today that new design remains contentious.

Nearly 150 years after the Civil War ended, defining the political meaning of the memory of the war continues to stir emotion. In the decades since the centennial, everyday Americans, mostly men but some women and even children,

**Civil War
Memory Today**

have continued to engage in reenacting combat and camp life, joining Civil War roundtables, tracing genealogy, collecting relics, books, and paintings, and touring battlefields. The Civil War has become a hobby for tens of thousands of people fascinated by this event and often drawn to it with great personal emotion. These Civil War "buffs," or enthusiasts, also read, and sometimes write, histories of the war, preferring stirring battle narratives and military biography to analytical or scholarly works. They pore over details of dress or weaponry but show less interest in complicated questions of the war's causes or consequences.

The Civil War also remains a thriving commercial venture. Opening Civil War battlefields and other historical sites to tourists has proven a profitable enterprise. Consumers gobble up books, popular magazines, and paintings, as well as T-shirts, baseball caps, mugs, chess sets, music CDs, video games, and even men's ties, all with Civil War imagery and themes. Nearly all of these products, however, depict battles and leaders, albeit sanitized of the blood and gore. If there is a political message involved in all this paraphernalia, it most frequently states: "Forget? Hell!" or "The South Shall Rise Again," affirming a determination to keep alive this rebellious Confederate heritage among considerable numbers of white southerners.

Civil War memory today remains fluid and contested, even while the Lost Cause's strong hold on the South has shown few signs of weakening. Recently, southern communities, often led by African Americans, have changed the names of streets, bridges, and schools from Nathan Bedford Forrest, or P. G. T. Beauregard to Martin Luther King and Thurgood Marshall. Even the names of school mascots and songs have changed, dropping references to "rebels" and "Dixie."

Remembering Reconstruction

If American public memory of the Civil War has largely been sanitized, depoliticized, and commemorated as a heroic "brothers' war," the memory of Reconstruction has not been so celebrated. Labeled by early twentieth-century historians as the "Tragic Era" or "Age of Hate," the decade after the war is often associated with tyranny and violence, although the victims of these abuses vary based on one's perspective. Southern whites deemed the immediate postwar era as a time of humiliation and disgrace when northern whites imposed their will and that of incompetent, licentious ex-slaves on them; African Americans like W. E. B. Du Bois, and some liberal whites like Eric Foner, have judged Reconstruction as a time of African American striving, northern betrayal, profound disappointment, and an "unfinished revolution."

Forgetting

It seems that there has been more deliberate forgetting than remembering of the real war and its painful consequences. Still rarely acknowledged are the untold numbers of impoverished widows and orphans, let alone the men who came home wounded physically and scarred emotionally; the former slaves and their struggles, impoverished, disenfranchised, and discriminated against, locally and nationally. Some of these individuals did record their painful stories for future generations: whites while seeking pensions or confiding to old comrades or family members; ex-slaves when interviewed by Works Progress Administration employees during the 1930s. These documents contain heart-wrenching stories of loss and desperation, with little discussion of honor, courage, or "the cause." Some former slaves refused to recall their grim past, or they did not see the point of trying to depict horrors that could hardly be imagined. "I could tell you 'bout it all day," one former slave explained, "but even den you couldn't guess de awfulness of it."

The "awfulness" of the war and its aftermath remains difficult for most Americans to face. It was a horrific time, leaving the nation with troubling questions unresolved by the limitations and failures of Reconstruction. It was, and continues to be, far easier to spin tales of valor and courage, self-sacrifice and patriotism than to examine the crisis honestly and critically. Better to forget the dark side of humanity exposed by the war. Like a person who endures a traumatic experience as a child, and then as an adult refuses to talk about it, most Americans appear unable to confront their civil war. The real causes, real pain, real and unsettling questions about race, power, and American society proved perhaps too difficult to articulate and to answer for the generation that survived it. Subsequent generations of Americans have been equally unwilling to face the disquieting legacy of slavery, secession, and civil war. Many have found it much more soothing and comforting to focus on fanciful stories of great men, simplistic issues, and desirable outcomes, glorious battles and heroic deaths.

The War's Lasting Legacy

Woodrow Wilson, native Virginian and ardent supporter of racial segregation, believed that the wounds of the Civil War had been completely healed by 1913. He was tragically wrong about this. These wounds *still* fester today, under thick layers of mythology, selective memory, and deliberate forgetfulness. Issues of poverty and the distribution of wealth remain considerable, as do concerns over racial justice, often linked together. Many Americans continue to interpret the Civil War and the Reconstruction period as markers of an inevitable triumph over racial injustice, a form of historical "progress." Others have used the Civil War to deny that slavery, much less institutionalized racial discrimination, was a problem at all. Only by peeling away these layers of falsely reassuring historical rhetoric can Americans start to come to terms honestly with the complex and contradictory web of victories and defeats, both immediate and long term, of that terrible war.

Documents

The Compromise of 1850

Territory gained from the Mexican War in 1848 led to stormy congressional debates about whether these new lands would be open to slavery. The result was the Compromise of 1850, a series of five separate laws. Three of them regulated the boundaries of Texas, the admission of California to the Union, and the abolition of the slave trade in Washington, D.C. The fourth, reprinted here, concerned the establishment of a territorial government in Utah, and endorsed popular sovereignty as a means for determining slavery in future western territories. The fifth and most controversial part of the compromise, the Fugitive Slave Law, also reprinted here, made many northerners believe they would be compelled to enforce slavery in their section. This part of the legislative package, feeding northern fears of a southern conspiracy to nationalize slavery, led to much northern protest and defiance.

An Act to Establish a Territorial Government for Utah.

Be it enacted by the Senate and House of Representatives of the United States of America in Congress assembled, That all that part of the territory of the United States included within the following limits, to wit: bounded on the west by the State of California, on the north by the Territory of Oregon, and on the east by the summit of the Rocky Mountains, and on the south by the thirty-seventh parallel of north latitude, be, and the same is hereby, created into a temporary government, by the name of the Territory of Utah; and, when admitted as a State, the said Territory, or any portion of the same, shall be received into the Union, with or without slavery, as their constitution may prescribe at the time of their admission. . . .

SEC. 6. *And be it further enacted,* That the legislative power of said Territory shall extend to all rightful subjects of legislation, consistent with the Constitution of the United States and the provisions of this act; but . . . all the laws passed by the legislative assembly and governor shall be submitted to the Congress of the United States and, if disapproved, shall be null and of no effect. . . .

SEC. 9. *And be it further enacted,* That the judicial power of said Territory shall be vested in a Supreme Court, District Courts, Probate Courts, and in justices of the peace. . . . Writs of error, and appeals from the final decisions of said Supreme Court, shall be allowed, and may be taken to the Supreme Court of the United States. . . .

SEC. 17. *And be it further enacted,* That the Constitution and laws of the United States are hereby extended over and declared to be in force in said Territory of Utah, so far as the same, or any provision thereof, may be applicable. . . .

An Act to amend, and supplementary to, the Act entitled "An Act respecting Fugitives from Justice, and Persons escaping from the Service of their Masters," approved February twelfth, one thousand seven hundred and ninety-three.

Be it enacted by the Senate and House of Representatives of the United States of America in Congress assembled, That the persons who have been, or may hereafter be, appointed commissioners, in virtue of any act of Congress, by the Circuit Courts of the United States, and who, in consequence of such appointment, are authorized to exercise the powers that any justice of the peace, or other magistrate of any of the United States, may exercise in respect to offenders for any crime or offense against the United States, by arresting, imprisoning, or bailing the same under and by virtue of the thirty-third section of the act of the twenty-fourth of September seventeen hundred and eighty-nine, entitled "An Act to establish the judicial courts of the United States" shall be, and are hereby, authorized and required to exercise and discharge all the powers and duties conferred by this act.

SEC. 2. *And be it further enacted,* That the Superior Court of each organized Territory of the United States shall have the same power to appoint commissioners . . . who . . . shall moreover exercise and discharge all the powers and duties conferred by this act.

SEC. 3. *And be it further enacted.* That the Circuit Courts of the United States, and the Superior Courts of each organized Territory of the United States, shall from time to time enlarge the number of commissioners, with a view to afford reasonable facilities to reclaim fugitives from labor, and to the prompt discharge of the duties imposed by this act.

SEC. 4. *And be it further enacted.* That the commissioners above named shall have concurrent jurisdiction with . . . judges . . . and shall grant certificates to such claimants, upon satisfactory proof being made, with authority to take and remove such fugitives from service or labor, under the restrictions herein contained, to the State or Territory from which such persons may have escaped or fled.

SEC. 5. *And be it further enacted.* That it shall be the duty of all marshals and deputy marshals to obey and execute all warrants and precepts issued under the provisions of this act, when to them directed; and should any marshal or deputy marshal refuse to receive such warrant, or other process, when tendered, or to use all proper means diligently to execute the same, he shall, on conviction thereof, be fined in the sum of one thousand dollars, to the use of such claimant, on the motion of such claimant, by the Circuit or District Court for the district of such marshal; and after arrest of such fugitive, by such marshal or his deputy, or whilst at any time in his custody under the provisions of this act, should such fugitive escape, whether with or without the assent of such marshal or his deputy, such marshal shall be liable, on his official bond, to be prosecuted for the benefit of such claimant, for the full value of the service or labor of said fugitive in the State, Territory, or District whence he escaped; and the better to enable the said commissioners, when thus appointed, to execute their duties faithfully and efficiently, in conformity with the requirements of the Constitution of the United States and of this act, they are hereby authorized and empowered, within their counties respectively, to appoint, in writing under their hands, any one or more suitable persons . . . to execute all such warrants and other process as may be issued by them in the lawful performance of their respective duties; with authority to such commissioners, or the persons to be appointed by them, to execute process as aforesaid, to summon and call to their aid the bystanders, or *posse comitatus* of the proper county, when necessary to ensure a faithful observance of the clause of the Constitution referred to, in conformity with the provisions of this act; and all good citizens are hereby commanded to aid and assist in the prompt and efficient execution of this law, whenever their services may be required, as aforesaid, for that purpose; and said warrants shall run, and be executed by said officers, any where in the State within which they are issued.

SEC. 6. *And be it further enacted.* That when a person held to service or labor in any State or Territory of the United States, has heretofore or shall hereafter escape into another State or Territory of the United States, the person or persons to whom such service or labor may be due, or his, her, or their agent or attorney, duly authorized, by power of attorney, in writing, acknowledged and certified under the seal of some legal officer or court of the State or Territory in which the same may be executed, may pursue and reclaim such fugitive person, either by procuring a warrant from some one of the courts, judges, or commissioners aforesaid, of the proper circuit, district, or county, for the apprehension of such fugitive from service or labor, or by seizing and arresting such fugitive, where the same can be done without process, and by taking, or causing such person to be taken, forthwith before such court, judge, or commissioner, whose duty it shall be to hear and determine the case of such claimant in a summary manner; and upon satisfactory proof being made . . . , to use such reasonable force and restraint as may be necessary, under the circumstances of the case, to take and remove such fugitive person back to the State or Territory whence he or she may have escaped as aforesaid. In no trial or hearing under this act shall the testimony of such alleged fugitive be admitted in evidence. . . .

SEC. 7. *And be it further enacted.* That any person who shall knowingly and willingly obstruct, hinder, or prevent such claimant, his agent or attorney, or any person or persons lawfully assisting him, her, or them, from arresting such a fugitive from service or labor, either with or without process as aforesaid, or shall rescue, or attempt to rescue, such fugitive from service or labor, from the custody of such claimant, his or her agent or attorney, or other person or persons lawfully assisting as aforesaid, when so arrested, pursuant to the authority herein given and declared; or shall aid, abet, or assist such person . . . to escape from such claimant, his agent or attorney, or other person or persons legally authorized as aforesaid; or shall harbor or conceal such fugitive, so as to prevent the discovery and arrest of such person, after notice or knowledge of the fact that such person was a fugitive from service or labor as aforesaid, shall, for either of said offences, be subject to a fine not exceeding one thousand dollars, and imprisonment not exceeding six months . . . ; and shall moreover forfeit and pay, by way of civil damages to the party injured by such illegal conduct, the sum of one thousand dollars, for each fugitive so lost as aforesaid, to be recovered by action of debt. . . .

SEC. 8. *And be it further enacted.* That the marshals, their deputies, and the clerks of the said District and Territorial Courts, shall be paid, for their services, the like fees as may be allowed to them for similar services in other cases; and where such services are rendered exclusively in the arrest, custody, and delivery of the fugitive to the claimant, his or her agent or attorney, or where such supposed fugitive may be discharged out of custody for the want of sufficient proof as aforesaid, then such fees are to be paid in the whole by such claimant, his agent or attorney; and in all cases where the proceedings are before a commissioner, he shall be entitled to a fee of ten dollars . . . upon the delivery of the said certificate to the claimant, his or her agent or attorney; or a fee of five dollars in cases where the proof shall not, in the opinion of such commissioner, warrant such certificate and delivery. . . . The person or persons authorized to execute the process . . . shall also be entitled to a fee of five dollars each for each person he or they may arrest, and take before any commissioner. . . .

Sec. 9. *And be it further enacted*, That, upon affidavit made by the claimant of such fugitive, his agent or attorney, after such certificate has been issued, that he has reason to apprehend that such fugitive will be rescued by force from his or their possession before he can be taken beyond the limits of the State in which the arrest is made, it shall be the duty of the officer making the arrest to retain such fugitive in his custody, and to remove him to the State whence he fled, and there to deliver him to said claimant, his agent, or attorney. And to this end, the officer aforesaid is hereby authorized and required to employ so many persons as he may deem necessary to overcome such force, and to retain them in his service so long as circumstances may require. . . .

Source: *Public Statutes at Large and Treaties of the United States from December 1845 to March 1851* (Boston, 1862), 453–58, 462–65.

Stephen A. Douglas: Speech on the Kansas-Nebraska Act

Stung by the furor his act was arousing as it was debated in the Senate, Stephen A. Douglas rose on January 30, 1854, to defend himself from the attack of several northerners who accused him of destroying historical and geographical limitations on the expansion of slavery, thus serving his political ambitions at the behest of expansionary southern slaveholders.

Mr. President, when I proposed on Tuesday last, that the Senate should proceed to the consideration of the bill to organize the Territories of Nebraska and Kansas, it was my purpose only to occupy ten or fifteen minutes in explanation of its provisions. . . .

Pertaining to the question of slavery in the Territories—it was the intention of the committee to be explicit. We took the principles established by the compromise act of 1850 as our guide, and intended to make each and every provision of the bill accord with those principles. Those measures established and rest upon the great principle of self-government—that the people should be allowed to decide the questions of their domestic institutions for themselves, subject only to such limitations and restrictions as are imposed by the Constitution of the United States, instead of having them determined by an arbitrary or geographical line.

The original bill reported by the committee, as a substitute for the bill introduced by the Senator from Iowa (Mr. Dodge) was believed to have accomplished this object. The amendment which was subsequently reported by us was only designed to render that clear and specific which seemed, in the minds of some, to admit of doubt and misconstruction. In some parts of the country the original substitute was deemed and construed to be an annulment or a repeal of what has been known as the Missouri compromise, while in other parts it was otherwise construed. As the object of the committee was to conform to the principles established by the compromise measures of 1850, and to carry those principles into effect in the Territories, we thought it was better to recite in the bill precisely what we understood to have been accomplished by those measures, viz.: That the Missouri compromise, having been superseded by the legislation of 1850, has become inoperative, and hence we propose to leave the question to the people of the States and the Territories, subject only to the limitations and provisions of the Constitution.

Sir, this is all that I intended to say, if the question had been taken up for consideration on Tuesday last; but since that time occurrences have transpired which compel me to go more fully into the discussion. It will be borne in mind that the Senator from Ohio (Mr. Chase) then objected to the consideration of the bill, and asked for its postponement until this day, on the ground that there had not been time to understand and consider its provisions; and the Senator from Massachusetts (Mr. Sumner) suggested that the postponement should be for one week, for that purpose. These suggestions seeming to be reasonable to Senators around me, I yielded to their request, and consented to the postponement of the bill until this day.

Sir, little did I suppose at the time that I granted that act of courtesy to those two Senators, that they had drafted and published to the world a document, over their own signatures, in which they arraigned me as having been guilty of a criminal betrayal of my trust, as having been guilty of an act of bad faith, and been engaged in an atrocious plot against the cause of free government. Little did I suppose that those two Senators had been guilty of such conduct when they called upon me to grant that courtesy, to give them an opportunity of investigating the substitute reported from the committee. I have since discovered that on that very morning the *National Era*, the Abolition organ in this city, contained an address, signed by certain Abolition confederates, to the people, in which the bill is grossly misrepresented, in which the action of the members of the committee is grossly falsified, in which our motives are arraigned, and our characters calumniated. And, sir, what is more, I find that there was a postscript added to the address, published that very morning, in which the principal amendment reported by the committee was set out, and then coarse epithets applied to me by name. Sir, had I known those facts at the time I granted that act of indulgence, I should have responded to the request of those Senators in such terms as their conduct deserved, so far as the rules of the Senate, and a respect for my own character, would have permitted me to do. . . .

The argument of this manifesto is predicated upon the assumption that the policy of the fathers of the Republic was to prohibit slavery in all the territory ceded by the old States to the Union and made United States territory, for the purpose of being organized into new States. I take issue upon that statement. Such was not the practice in the early history of the Government. It is true that in the territory northwest of the Ohio river slavery was prohibited by the ordinance of 1787; but it is also true that in the territory south of the Ohio river, to wit, the Territory of Tennessee, slavery was permitted and protected; and it is also true, that in the organization of the Territory of Mississippi, in 1798, the provisions of the ordinance of 1787 were applied to it, with the exception of the sixth article, which prohibited slavery. Then, sir, you find upon the statute-books under Washington and the early Presidents, provisions of law showing that in the southwestern territories the right to hold slaves was clearly implied or recognized, while in the northwest territories it was prohibited. The only conclusion that can be fairly and honestly drawn from that legislation is, that it was the policy of the fathers of the Republic to prescribe a line of demarkation between free territories and slaveholding territories by a natural or a geographical line, being sure to make that line correspond, as near as might be, to the laws of climate, of production, and probably of all those other causes that would control the institution and make it either desirable or undesirable to the people inhabiting the respective territories.

Sir, I wish you to bear in mind, too, that this geographical line established by the founders of the Republic, between free Territories and slave Territories, extended as far westward as our territory then reached, the object being to avoid all agitation upon the slavery question by settling that question forever, so far as our territory extended, which was then to the Mississippi river.

When, in 1803, we acquired from France the Territory known as Louisiana, it became necessary to legislate for the protection of the inhabitants residing therein. It will be seen by looking into the bill establishing the territorial government in 1805 for the Territory of New Orleans, embracing the same country now known as the State of Louisiana, that the ordinance of 1787 was expressly extended to that Territory, excepting the sixth section, which prohibited slavery. Then that act implied that the Territory of New Orleans was to be a slave-holding Territory by making that exception in the law. But, sir, when they came to form what was then called the Territory of Louisiana, subsequently known as the Territory of Missouri, north of the thirty-third parallel, they used different language. They did not extend the ordinance of 1787 to it at all. They first provided that it should be governed by laws made by the governor and the judges; and when, in 1812, Congress gave to that Territory, under the name of the Territory of Missouri, a territorial government, the people were allowed to do as they pleased upon the subject of slavery, subject only to the limitations of the Constitution of the United States. Now, what is the inference from that legislation? That slavery was, by implication, recognized south of the thirty-third parallel, and north of that the people were left to exercise their own judgment and do as they pleased upon the subject, without any implication for or against the existence of the institution.

This continued to be the condition of the country in the Missouri Territory up to 1820, when the celebrated act which is now called the Missouri compromise act was passed. Slavery did not exist in, nor was it excluded from, the country now known as Nebraska. There was no code of laws upon the subject of slavery either way: First, for the reason that slavery had never been introduced into Louisiana, and established by positive enactment. It had grown up there by a sort of common law, and been supported and protected. When a common law grows up, when an institution becomes established under a usage, it carries it so far as that usage actually goes, and no further. If it had been established by direct enactment, it might have carried it so far as the political jurisdiction extended; but, be that as it may, by the act of 1812, creating the Territory of Missouri, that Territory was allowed to legislate upon the subject of slavery as it saw proper . . . At the time that the Missouri act passed, namely, the 6th of March, 1820, was a provision in effect, that the people should be allowed to do as they pleased upon the subject of slavery.

The Territory of Missouri having been left in that legal condition, positive opposition was made to the bill to organize a State government, with a view to its admission into the Union; and a Senator from my State, Mr. Jesse B. Thomas, introduced an amendment, known as the eighth section of the bill, in which it was provided that slavery should be prohibited north of 36° 30′ north latitude, in all that country which we had acquired from France. What was the object of the enactment of that eighth section? Was it not to go back to the original policy of prescribing boundaries to the limitation of free institutions, and of slave institutions, by a geographical line, in order to avoid all controversy in Congress upon the subject? Hence they extended that geographical line through all the territory purchased from France, which was as far as our possessions then reached. It was not simply to settle the question on that piece of country, but it was to carry out a great principle, by extending that dividing line as far west as our territory went, and running it onward on each new acquisition of territory. True, the express enactment of the eighth section of the Missouri act, now called the Missouri compromise act, only covered the territory acquired from France; but the principles of the act, the objects of its adoption, the reasons in its support, required that it should be extended indefinitely westward, so far as our territory might go, whenever new purchases should be made.

Thus stood the question up to 1845, when the joint resolution for the annexation of Texas passed. There was inserted in that a provision, suggested in the first instance and brought before the House of Representatives by myself, extending the Missouri compromise line indefinitely westward through the territory of Texas. Why did I bring forward that proposition? Why did the Congress of the United States adopt it? Not because it was of the least practical importance, so far as the question of slavery within the limits of Texas was concerned, for no man ever dreamed that it had any practical effect there. Then why was it brought forward? It was for the purpose of preserving the principle, in order that it might be extended still further westward, even to the Pacific Ocean, whenever we should acquire the country that far. I will here read that clause in the joint resolution for the annexation of Texas. . . .

It will be seen that that contains a very remarkable provision. which is, that when States lying north of 36° 30′ apply for admission, slavery shall be prohibited in their constitutions. I presume no one pretends that Congress could have power thus to fetter a State applying for admission into this Union; but it was necessary to preserve the principle of the Missouri compromise line in order that it might afterwards be extended; and it was supposed that while Congress had no power to impose any such limitation, yet as that was a compact with the State of Texas, that State could consent for herself that, when any portion of her own territory, subject to her own jurisdiction and control, applied for a constitution, it should be in a particular form; but that provision would not be binding on the new State one day after it was admitted into the Union. The other provision was, that such States as should lie south of 36° 30′ should come into the Union, with or without slavery, as each should decide in its constitution. Then, by that act the Missouri compromise was extended indefinitely westward, so far as the State of Texas went, that is, to the Rio del Norte; for our Government at the time recognized the Rio del Norte as its boundary. We recognized in many ways, and among them by even paying Texas for it, in order that it might be included in and form a portion of, the Territory of New Mexico.

Then, sir, in 1848 we acquired from Mexico the country between the Rio del Norte and the Pacific ocean. Immediately after that acquisition, the Senate, on my own motion, voted into a bill a provision to extend the Missouri compromise indefinitely westward to the Pacific ocean, in the same sense, and with the same understanding with which it was originally adopted. That provision passed this body by a decided majority—I think by ten at least—and went to the House of Representatives, and was there defeated by northern votes.

Now, sir, let us pause and consider for a moment. The first time that the principles of the Missouri compromise were ever abandoned, the first time they were ever rejected by Congress, was by the defeat of that provision in the House of Representatives in 1848. By whom was that defeat effected? By northern votes, with Free-Soil proclivities. It was the defeat of that Missouri compromise that reopened the slavery agitation with all its fury. It was the defeat of that Missouri compromise that created the tremendous struggle of 1850. It was the defeat of that Missouri compromise that created the necessity for making a new compromise of 1850. Had we been faithful to the principles of the Missouri compromise in 1848, this question would not have arisen. Who was it that was faithless? I undertake to say it was the very men who now insist that the Missouri compromise was a solemn compact, and should never be violated or departed from. Every man who is now assailing the principle of the bill under consideration, so far as I am advised, was opposed to the Missouri compromise in 1848. The very men who now arraign me for a departure from the Missouri compromise, are the men who successfully violated it, repudiated it, and caused it to be superseded by the compromise measures of 1850. Sir, it is with rather bad grace that the men who proved false themselves, should charge upon me and others, who were ever faithful, the responsibilities and consequences of their own treachery.

Then, sir, as I before remarked, the defeat of the Missouri compromise in 1848 having created the necessity for the establishment of a new one in 1850, let us see what that compromise was.

The leading feature of the compromise of 1850 was congressional non-intervention as to slavery in the Territories; that the people of the Territories, and of all the States, were to be allowed to do as they pleased upon the subject of slavery, subject only to the provisions of the Constitution of the United States. . . .

Mr. President, I repeat, that so far as the question of slavery is concerned, there is nothing in the bill under consideration which does not carry out the principle of the compromise measures of 1850, by leaving the people to do as they please, subject only to the provisions of the Constitution of the United States. If that principle is wrong, the bill is wrong. If that principle is right, the bill is right. It is unnecessary to quibble about phraseology or words; it is not the mere words, the mere phraseology, that our constituents wish to judge by. They wish to know the legal effect of our legislation.

The legal effect of this bill, if it be passed as reported by the Committee on Territories, is neither to legislate slavery into these Territories nor out of them, but to leave the people do as they please, under the provisions and subject to the limitations of the Constitution of the United States. Why should not this principle prevail? Why should any man, North or South, object to it? I will especially address the argument to my own section of country, and ask why should any northern man object to this principle? If you will review the history of the slavery question in the United States, you will see that all the great results in behalf of free institutions which have been worked out, have been accomplished by the operation of this principle, and by it alone.

When these States were colonies of Great Britain, every one of them was a slave-holding province. When the Constitution of the United States was formed, twelve out of the thirteen were slave-holding States. Since that time six of those States have become free. How has this been effected? Was it by virtue of abolition agitation in Congress? Was it in obedience to the dictates of the Federal Government? Not at all; but they have become free States under the silent but sure and irresistible working of that great principle of self-government which teaches every people to do that which the interests of themselves and their posterity morally and pecuniarily may require.

Under the operation of this principle New Hampshire became free, while South Carolina continued to hold slaves; Connecticut abolished slavery, while Georgia held on to it; Rhode Island abandoned the institution, while Maryland preserved it; New York, New Jersey, and Pennsylvania abolished slavery, while Virginia, North Carolina, and Kentucky retained it. Did they do it at your bidding? Did they do it at the dictation of the Federal Government? Did they do it in obedience to any of your Wilmot provisoes or ordinances of '87? Not at all; they did it by virtue of their right as freemen under the Constitution of the United States, to establish and abolish such institutions as they thought their own good required. . . .

I do not like, I never did like, the system of legislation on our part, by which a geographical line, in violation of the laws of nature, and climate, and soil, and of the laws of God, should be run to establish institutions for a people; yet, out of a regard for the peace and quiet of the country, out of respect for past pledges, and out of a desire to adhere faithfully to all compromises, I sustained the Missouri compromise so long as it was in force, and advocated its extension to the Pacific. Now, when that has been abandoned, when it has been superseded, when a great principle of self-government has been substituted for it. I choose to cling to that principle, and abide in good faith, not only by the letter, but by the spirit of the last compromise. . . .

Now, I ask the friends and the opponents of this measure to look at it as it is. Is not the question involved the simple one, whether the people of the Territories shall be allowed to do as they please upon the question of slavery, subject only to the limitations of the Constitution? That is all the bill provides; and it does so in clear, explicit, and unequivocal terms. I know there are some men, Whigs and Democrats, who, not willing to repudiate the Baltimore platform of their own party, would be willing to vote for this principle, provided they could do so in such equivocal terms that they could deny that it means what it was intended to mean in certain localities. I do not wish to deal in any equivocal language. If the principle is right, let it be avowed and maintained. If it is wrong, let it be repudiated. Let all this quibbling about the Missouri compromise, about the territory acquired from France, about the act of 1820, be cast behind you; for the simple question is, will you allow the people to legislate for themselves upon the subject of slavery? Why should you not?

When you propose to give them a territorial government do you not acknowledge that they ought to be erected into a political organization; and when you give them a Legislature do you not acknowledge that they are capable of self-government? Having made that acknowledgement, why should you not allow them to exercise the rights of legislation? Oh, these Abolitionists say they are entirely willing to concede all this, with one exception. They say they are willing to trust the Territorial Legislature, under the limitations of the Constitution, to legislate upon the rights of inheritance, to legislate in regard to religion, education, and morals, to legislate in regard to the relations of husband and wife, of parent and child, of guardian and ward, upon everything pertaining to the dearest rights and interests of white men, but they are not willing to trust them to legislate in regard to a few miserable negroes. That is their single exception. They acknowledge that the people of the Territories are capable of deciding for themselves concerning white men, but not in relation to negroes. The real gist of the matter is this: Does it require any higher degree of civilization, and intelligence, and learning, and sagacity, to legislate for negroes than for white men? If it does, we ought to adopt the abolition doctrine, and go with them against this bill. If it does not—if we are willing to trust the people with the great, sacred, fundamental right of prescribing their own institutions, consistent with the Constitution of the country, we must vote for this bill as reported by the Committee on Territories. That is the only question involved in the bill. I hope I have been able to strip it of all the misrepresentation, to wipe away all of that mist and obscurity with which it has been surrounded by this Abolition address. . . .

We intend to stand by the principle of the compromise measures of 1850, . . . that great fundamental principle of Democracy and free institutions which lies at the basis of our creed, and gives every political community the right to govern itself in obedience to the Constitution of the country.

Source: Stephen A. Douglas, Speech on the Kansas-Nebraska Bill. *Congressional Globe*, 33rd Cong., 1st Sess., Part 1, January 30, 1854, 275–80.

The Kansas-Nebraska Act

This act, by extending the principle of popular sovereignty, permitted local settlers in the northern half of the old Louisiana Purchase to decide the slavery issue for themselves. It also, in effect, repealed the Missouri Compromise. Passage of this act, on May 30, 1854, drove many northern Democrats out of their party and into a new alliance with former Whigs and Know-Nothings, who together formed the Republican Party.

An Act to Organize the Territories of Nebraska and Kansas.

Be it enacted . . . , That all that part of the territory of the United States included within the following limits, except such portions thereof as are hereinafter expressly exempted from the operations of this act, to wit: beginning at a point in the Missouri River where the fortieth parallel of north latitude crosses the same; thence west on said parallel to the east boundary of the Territory of Utah, on the summit of the Rocky Mountains; thence on said summit northward to the forty-ninth parallel of north latitude; thence east on said parallel to the western boundary of the territory of Minnesota; thence southward on said boundary to the Missouri River; thence down the main channel of said river to the place of beginning, be, and the same is hereby, created into a temporary government by the name of the Territory of Nebraska; and when admitted as a State or States, the said Territory or any portion of the same, shall be received into the Union with or without slavery, as their constitution may prescribe at the time of the admission: . . .

SEC. 14. *And be it further enacted.* . . . That the Constitution, and all laws of the United States which are not locally inapplicable, shall have the same force and effect within the said Territory of Nebraska as elsewhere within the United States, except the eighth section of the act preparatory to the admission of Missouri into the Union, approved March 6, 1820, which, being inconsistent with the principle of non-intervention by Congress with slavery in the States and Territories, as recognized by the legislation of eighteen hundred and fifty, commonly called the Compromise Measures, is hereby declared inoperative and void; it being the true intent and meaning of this act not to legislate slavery into any Territory or State, nor to exclude it therefrom, but to leave the people thereof perfectly free to form and regulate their domestic institutions in their own way, subject only to the Constitution of the United States: *Provided,* That nothing herein contained shall be construed to revive or put in force any law or regulation which may have existed prior to the act of March 6, 1820, either protecting, establishing, prohibiting, or abolishing slavery. . . .

SEC. 19. *And be it further enacted,* That all that part of the Territory of the United States included within the following limits, except such portions thereof as are hereinafter expressly exempted from the operations of this act, to wit, beginning at a point on the western boundary of the State of Missouri, where the thirty-seventh parallel of north latitude crosses the same; thence west on said parallel to the eastern boundary of New Mexico; thence north on said boundary to latitude thirty-eight; thence following said boundary westward to the east boundary of the Territory of Utah, on the summit of the Rocky Mountains; thence northward on said summit to the fortieth parallel of latitude, thence east on said parallel to the western boundary of the State of Missouri; thence south with the western boundary of said State to the place of beginning, be, and the same is hereby, created into a temporary government by the name of the Territory of Kansas; and when admitted as a State or States, the said Territory, or any portion of the same, shall be received into the Union with or without slavery, as their constitution may prescribe at the time of their admission: . . .

Source: U.S. Congress. *U.S. Statutes at Large,* 1854, Vol. X. 277–90.

Dred Scott v. Stanford

In 1857, Chief Justice Roger B. Taney wrote the majority opinion refusing freedom to a slave who had been moved first to a free territory and then back to his home in the slave state of Missouri. Taney argued that slaves could never be citizens with civil rights. Furthermore, he declared the prohibition of slavery in all American territories unconstitutional. This action by the Supreme Court infuriated northern opinion, driving more voters into the emerging Republican Party.

Roger B. Taney, Chief Justice: *The question to be decided is, whether the facts stated in the plea are sufficient to show that the plaintiff is not entitled to sue as a citizen in a court of the United States.*

This is certainly a very serious question, and one that now for the first time has been brought for decision before this court. But it is brought here by those who have a right to bring it, and it is our duty to meet it and decide it.

The question is simply this: Can a negro, whose ancestors were imported into this country, and sold as slaves, become a member of the political community formed and brought into existence by the Constitution of the United States, and as such become entitled to all the rights, and privileges, and immunities, guarantied by that instrument to the citizen? One of which rights is the privilege of suing in a court of the United States in the cases specified in the Constitution.

It will be observed, that the plea applies to that class of persons only whose ancestors were negroes of the African race, and imported into this country, and sold and held as slaves. The only matter in issue before the court, therefore, is, whether the descendants of such slaves, when they shall be emancipated, or who are born of parents who had become free before their birth, are citizens of a State, in the sense in which the word citizen is used in the Constitution of the United States. And this being the only matter in dispute on the pleadings, the court must be understood as speaking in this opinion of that class only, that is, of those persons who are the descendants of Africans who were imported into this country, and sold as slaves. . . .

The words "people of the United States" and "citizens" are synonymous terms, and mean the same thing. They both describe the political body who, according to our republican institutions, form the sovereignty, and who hold the power and conduct the government through their representatives. They are what we familiarly call the "sovereign people," and every citizen is one of this people, and a constituent member of this sovereignty. The question before us is, whether the class of persons described in the plea in abatement compose a portion of this people, and are constituent members of this sovereignty? We think they are not, and that they are not included, and were not intended to be included, under the word "citizens" in the Constitution, and can, therefore, claim none of the rights and privileges which that instrument provides for and secures to citizens of the United States. On the contrary, they were at that time considered as a subordinate and inferior class of beings, who had been subjugated by the dominant race, and, whether emancipated or not, yet remained subject to their authority, and had no rights or privileges but such as those who held the power and the government might choose to grant them. . . .

In discussing this question, we must not confound the rights of citizenship which a state may confer within its own limits, and the rights of citizenship as a member of the Union. It does not by any means follow, because he has all the rights and privileges of a citizen of a State, that he must be a citizen of the United States. He may have all of the rights and privileges of the citizen of a State, and yet not be entitled to the rights and privileges of a citizen in any other State. For, previous to the adoption of the Constitution of the United States, every State had the undoubted right to confer on whomsoever it pleased the character of citizen, and to endow him with all its rights. But this character, of course, was confined to the boundaries of the State, and gave him no rights or privileges in other States beyond those secured to him by the laws of nations and the comity of States. Nor have the several States surrendered the power of conferring these rights and privileges by adopting the Constitution of the United States. Each State may still confer them upon an alien, or any one it thinks proper, or upon any class or description of persons; yet he would not be a citizen in the sense in which that word is used in the Constitution of the United States, nor entitled to sue as such in one of its courts, nor to the privileges and immunities of a citizen in the other States. The rights which he would acquire would be restricted to the State which gave them. . . .

It is very clear, therefore, that no State can, by any Act or law of its own, passed since the adoption of the Constitution, introduce a new member into the political community created by the Constitution of the United States. It cannot make him a member of this community by making him a member of its own. And for the same reason it cannot introduce any person, or description of persons, who were not intended to be embraced in this new political family, which the Constitution brought into existence, but were intended to be excluded from it.

The question then arises, whether the provisions of the Constitution, in relation to the personal rights and privileges to which the citizen of a State should be entitled, embraced the negro African race, at that time in this country, or who might afterwards be imported, who had then or should afterwards be made free in any State; and to put it in the power of a single State to make him a citizen of the United States, and endue him with the full rights of citizenship in every other State without their consent? Does the Constitution of the United States act upon him whenever he shall be made free under the laws of a State, and raised there to the rank of a citizen, and immediately clothe him with all the privileges of a citizen in every other State, and in its own courts?

The court think the affirmative of these propositions cannot be maintained. And if it cannot, the plaintiff in error could not be a citizen of the State of Missouri, within the meaning of the Constitution of the United States, and, consequently, was not entitled to sue in its courts.

It is true, every person, and every class and description of persons, who were at the time of the adoption of the Constitution recognized as citizens in the several States, became also citizens of this new political body; but none other; it was formed by them, and for them and their posterity, but for no one else. And the personal rights and privileges guarantied to citizens of this new sovereignty were intended to embrace those only who were then members of the several state communities, or who should afterwards, by birthright or otherwise, become members, according to the provisions of the Constitution and the principles on which it was founded. . . .

In the opinion of the court, the legislation and histories of the times, and the language used in the Declaration of Independence, show, that neither the class of persons who had been imported as slaves, nor their descendants, whether they had become free or not, were then acknowledged as a part of the people, nor intended to be included in the general words used in that memorable instrument.

It is difficult at this day to realize the state of public opinion in relation to that unfortunate race, which prevailed in the civilized and enlightened portions of the world at the time of the Declaration of Independence, and when the Constitution of the United States was framed and adopted. . . .

They had for more than a century before been regarded as beings of an inferior order; and altogether unfit to associate with the white race, either in social or political relations; and so far inferior that they had no rights which the white man was bound to respect; and that the negro might justly and lawfully be reduced to slavery for his benefit. . . . This opinion was at that time fixed and universal in the civilized portion of the white race. It was regarded as an axiom in morals as well as in politics, which no one thought of disputing, or supposed to be open to dispute; and men in every grade and position in society daily and habitually acted upon it in their private pursuits, as well as in matters of public concern, without doubting for a moment the correctness of this opinion. . . .

The legislation of the different Colonies furnishes positive and indisputable proof of this fact. . . .

The language of the Declaration of Independence is equally conclusive. . . .

This state of public opinion had undergone no change when the Constitution was adopted, as is equally evident from its provisions and language. . . .

Indeed, when we look to the condition of this race in the several States at the time, it is impossible to believe that these rights and privileges were intended to be extended to them. . . .

But it is said that a person may be a citizen, and entitled to that character, although he does not possess all the rights which may belong to other citizens; as, for example, the right to vote, or to hold particular offices; and that yet, when he goes into another State, he is entitled to be recognized there as a citizen, although the State may measure his rights by the rights which it allows to persons of a like character or class, resident in the State, and refuse to him the full rights of citizenship.

This argument overlooks the language of the provision in the Constitution of which we are speaking.

Undoubtedly, a person may be a citizen, that is, a member of the community who form the sovereignty, although he exercises no share of the political power, and is incapacitated from holding particular offices. . . .

So, too, a person may be entitled to vote by the law of the State, who is not a citizen even of the State itself. And in some of the States of the Union foreigners not naturalized are allowed to vote. And the State may give the right to free negroes and mulattoes, but that does not make them citizens of the State, and still less of the United States. And the provision in the Constitution giving privileges and immunities in other States, does not apply to them.

Neither does it apply to a person who, being the citizen of a State, migrates to another State. For then he becomes subject to the laws of the State in which he lives, and he is no longer a citizen of the State from which he removed. And the State in which he resides may then, unquestionably, determine his *status* or condition, and place him among the class of persons who are not recognized as citizens, but belong to an inferior and subject race; and may deny him the privileges and immunities enjoyed by its citizens. . . .

. . . But if he ranks as a citizen of the State to which he belongs, within the meaning of the Constitution of the United States, then, whenever he goes into another State, the Constitution clothes him, as to the rights of person, with all the privileges and immunities which belong to citizens of the State. And if persons of the African race are citizens of a state, and of the United States, they would be entitled to all of these privileges and immunities in every State, and the State could not restrict them; for they would hold these privileges and immunities, under the paramount authority of the Federal Government, and its courts would be bound to maintain and enforce them, the Constitution and laws of the State to the contrary notwithstanding. . . .

And upon a full and careful consideration of the subject, the court is of opinion that, upon the facts stated in the plea in abatement, Dred Scott was not a citizen of Missouri within the meaning of the Constitution of the United States, and not entitled as such to sue in its courts; and, consequently, that the Circuit Court had no jurisdiction of the case, and that the judgment on the plea in abatement is erroneous. . . .

We proceed, therefore, to inquire whether the facts relied on by the plaintiff entitled him to his freedom. . . .

In considering this part of the controversy, two questions arise: 1st. Was he, together with his family, free in Missouri by reason of the stay in the territory of the United States hereinbefore mentioned? And 2d, If they were not, is Scott himself free by reason of his removal to Rock Island, in the State of Illinois, as stated in the above admissions?

We proceed to examine the first question.

The Act of Congress, upon which the plaintiff relies, declares that slavery and involuntary servitude, except as a punishment for crime, shall be forever prohibited in all that part of the territory ceded by France, under the name of Louisiana, which lies north of thirty-six degrees thirty minutes north latitude, and not included within the limits of Missouri. And the difficulty which meets us at the threshold of this part of the inquiry is, whether Congress was authorized to pass this law under any of the powers granted to it by the Constitution; for if the authority is not given by that instrument, it is the duty of this court to declare it void and inoperative, and incapable of conferring freedom upon any one who is held as a slave under the laws of any one of the States.

The counsel for the plaintiff has laid much stress upon that article in the Constitution which confers on Congress the power "to dispose of and make all needful rules and regulations respecting the territory or other property belonging to the United States;" but, in the judgment of the court, that provision has no bearing on the present controversy, and the power there given, whatever it may be, is confined, and was intended to be confined, to the territory which at that time belonged to, or was claimed by, the United States, and was within their boundaries as settled by the treaty with Great Britain, and can have no influence upon a territory afterwards acquired from a foreign Government. It was a special provision for a known and particular territory, and to meet a present emergency, and nothing more. . . .

If this clause is construed to extend to territory acquired by the present Government from a foreign nation, outside of the limits of any charter from the British Government to a colony, it would be difficult to say, why it was deemed necessary to give the Government the power to sell any vacant lands belonging to the sovereignty which might be found within it; and if this was necessary, why the grant of this power should precede the power to legislate over it and establish a Government there; and still more difficult to say, why it was deemed necessary so specially and particularly to grant the power to make needful rules and regulations in relation to any personal or movable property it might acquire there. For the words, *other property* necessarily, by every known rule of interpretation, must mean property of a different description from territory or land. And the difficulty would perhaps be insurmountable in endeavoring to account for the last member of the sentence, which provides that "nothing in this Constitution shall be so construed as to prejudice any claims of the United States or any particular State," or to say how any particular State could have claims in or to a territory ceded by a foreign Government, or to account for associating this provision with the preceding provisions of the clause, with which it would appear to have no connection. . . .

But the power of Congress over the person or property of a citizen can never be a mere discretionary power under our Constitution and form of Government. The powers of the Government and the rights and privileges of the citizen are regulated and plainly defined by the Constitution itself. And when the Territory becomes a part of the United States, the Federal Government enters into possession in the character impressed upon it by those who created it. It enters upon it with its powers over the citizen strictly defined, and limited by the Constitution, from which it derives its own existence, and by virtue of which alone it continues to exist and act as a Government and sovereignty. It has no power of any kind beyond it; and it cannot, when it enters a Territory of the United States, put off its character, and assume discretionary or despotic powers which the Constitution has denied to it. It cannot create for itself a new character separated from the citizens of the United States, and the duties it owes them under the provisions of the Constitution. The Territory being a part of the United States, the Government and the citizen both enter it under the authority of the Constitution, with their respective rights defined and marked out; and the Federal Government can exercise no power over his person or property, beyond what that instrument confers, nor lawfully deny any right which it has reserved. . . .

The rights of private property have been guarded with equal care. Thus the rights of property are united with the rights of person, and placed on the same ground by the fifth amendment to the Constitution. . . . An Act of Congress which deprives a person of the United States of his liberty or property merely because he came himself or brought his property into a particular Territory of the United States, and who had committed no offense against the laws, could hardly be dignified with the name of due process of law. . . .

And this prohibition is not confined to the States, but the words are general, and extend to the whole territory over which the Constitution gives it power to legislate, including those portions of it remaining under territorial government, as well as that covered by States. It is a total absence of power everywhere within the dominion of the United States, and places the citizens of a territory, so far as these rights are concerned, on the same footing with citizens of the States, and guards them as firmly and plainly against any inroads which the general government might attempt, under the plea of implied or incidental powers. And if Congress itself cannot do this—if it is beyond the powers conferred on the Federal Government—it will be admitted, we presume, that it could not authorize a territorial government to exercise them. It could confer no power on any local government, established by its authority, to violate the provisions of the Constitution.

It seems, however, to be supposed, that there is a difference between property in a slave and other property, and that different rules may be applied to it in expounding the Constitution of the United States. And the laws and usages of nations, and the writings of eminent jurists upon the relation of master and slave and their mutual rights and duties, and the powers which governments may exercise over it, have been dwelt upon in the argument.

But . . . if the Constitution recognizes the right of property of the master in a slave, and makes no distinction between that description of property and other property owned by a citizen, no tribunal, acting under the authority of the United States, whether it be legislative, executive, or judicial, has a right to draw such a distinction, or deny to it the benefit of the provisions and guarantees which have been provided for the protection of private property against the encroachments of the Government.

Now . . . the right of property in a slave is distinctly and expressly affirmed in the Constitution. The right to traffic in it, like an ordinary article of merchandise and property, was guaranteed to the citizens of the United States, in every State that might desire it, for twenty years. And the Government in express terms is pledged to protect it in all future time, if the slave escapes from his owner. . . . And no word can be found in the Constitution which gives Congress a greater power over slave property, or which entitles property of that kind to less protection than property of any other description. The only power conferred is the power coupled with the duty of guarding and protecting the owner in his rights.

Upon these considerations, it is the opinion of the court that the Act of Congress which prohibited a citizen from holding and owning property of this kind in the territory of the United States north of the line therein mentioned, is not warranted by the Constitution, and is therefore void; and that neither Dred Scott himself, nor any of his family, were made free by being carried into this territory; even if they had been carried there by the owner, with the intention of becoming a permanent resident. . . .

Source: 19 Howard, 393 (1857).

Abraham Lincoln's "A House Divided" Speech

Abraham Lincoln delivered this speech when accepting his party's nomination for U.S. senator, at the conclusion of the Republican state convention in Springfield, Illinois, on June 16, 1858. This address articulated a belief widespread in Republican circles that a cabal of northern and southern Democrats was plotting to expand slavery. Republicans such as Lincoln believed that a terrible day of national reckoning could not be far away.

If we could first know where we are, and whither we are tending, we could then better judge what to do, and how to do it.

We are now far into the *fifth* year, since a policy was initiated, with the *avowed* object, and *confident* promise, of putting an end to slavery agitation.

Under the operation of that policy, that agitation has not only, *not ceased*, but has *constantly augmented*.

In *my* opinion, it *will* not cease, until a *crisis* shall have been reached, and passed.

"A house divided against itself cannot stand."

I believe this government cannot endure, permanently half *slave* and half *free*.

I do not expect the Union to be *dissolved*—I do not expect the house to *fall*—but I *do* expect it will cease to be divided. It will become *all* one thing, or *all* the other.

Either the *opponents* of slavery, will arrest the further spread of it, and place it where the public mind shall rest in the belief that it is in course of ultimate extinction; or its *advocates* will push it forward, till it shall become alike lawful in *all* the States, *old* as well as *new*—North as well as *South*.

Have we no *tendency* to the latter condition?

Let any one who doubts, carefully contemplate that now almost complete legal combination—piece of *machinery* so to speak—compounded of the Nebraska doctrine, and the Dred Scott decision. Let him consider not only *what work* the machinery is adapted to do, and *how well* adapted; but also, let him study the *history* of its construction, and trace, if he can, or rather *fail*, if he can, to trace the evidences of design, and concert of action, among its chief bosses, from the beginning.

But, so far, *Congress* only, had acted; and an *indorsement* by the people, *real* or apparent, was indispensable, to *save* the point already gained, and give chance for more.

The new year of 1854 found slavery excluded from more than half the States by State Constitutions, and from most of the national territory by Congressional prohibition.

Four days later, commenced the struggle, which ended in repealing that Congressional prohibition.

This opened all the national territory to slavery; and was the first point gained.

This necessity had not been overlooked; but had been provided for, as well as might be, in the notable argument of *"squatter sovereignty,"* otherwise called *"sacred right of self government,"* which latter phrase, though expressive of the only rightful basis of any government, was so perverted in this attempted use of it as to amount to just this: That if any *one* man, choose to enslave *another*, no *third* man shall be allowed to object.

That argument was incorporated into the Nebraska bill itself, in the language which follows: *"It being the true intent and meaning of this act not to legislate slavery into any Territory or state, not exclude it therefrom; but to leave the people thereof perfectly free to form and regulate their domestic institutions in their own way, subject only to the Constitution of the United States."*

Then opened the roar of loose declamation in favor of "Squatter Sovereignty," and "Sacred right of self government."

"But," said opposition members, "let us be more *specific*—let us *amend* the bill so as to expressly declare that the people of the territory *may* exclude slavery." "Not we," said the friends of the measure; and down they voted the amendment.

While the Nebraska bill was passing through congress, a *law case*, involving the question of a negroe's freedom, by reason of his owner having voluntarily taken him first into a free state and then a territory covered by the congressional prohibition, and held him as a slave, for a long time in each, was passing through the U.S. Circuit Court for the District of Missouri; and both Nebraska bill and law suit were brought to a decision in the same month of May, 1854. The negroe's name was "Dred Scott," which name now designates the decision finally made in the case.

Before the *then* next Presidential election, the law case came *to*, and was argued *in* the Supreme Court of the United States; but the *decision* of it was deferred until *after* the election. Still, *before* the election, Senator Trumbull, on the floor of the Senate, requests the leading advocate of the Nebraska bill to state *his opinion* whether the people of a territory can constitutionally exclude slavery from their limits; and the latter answers, "That is a question for the Supreme Court."

The election came. Mr. Buchanan was elected, and the *indorsement*, such as it was, secured. That was the *second* point gained. The indorsement, however, fell short of a clear popular majority by nearly four hundred thousand votes, and so, perhaps, was not overwhelmingly reliable and satisfactory.

The *outgoing* President, in his last annual message, as impressively as possible *echoed back* upon the people the *weight* and *authority* of the indorsement.

The Supreme Court met again; *did not* announce their decision, but ordered a re-argument.

The Presidential inauguration came, and still no decision of the court; but the *incoming* President, in his inaugural address, fervently exhorted the people to abide by the forthcoming decision, *whatever it might be*.

Then, in a few days, came the decision. . . .

At length a squabble springs up between the President and the author of the Nebraska bill, on the *mere* question of *fact*, whether the Lecompton constitution was or was not, in any just sense, made by the people of Kansas; and in that squabble the latter declares that all he wants is a fair vote for the people, and that he *cares* not whether slavery be voted *down* or voted *up*. I do not understand his declaration that he cares not whether slavery be voted down or voted up, to be intended by him other than as an *apt definition* of the *policy* he would impress upon the public mind—the *principle* for which he declares he has suffered much, and is ready to suffer to the end.

And well may he cling to that principle. If he has any parental feeling, well may he cling to it. That principle, is the only *shred* left of his original Nebraska doctrine. Under the Dred Scott decision, "squatter sovereignty" squatted out of existence, tumbled down like temporary scaffolding—like the mould at the foundry served through one blast and fell back into loose sand—helped to carry an election, and then was kicked to the winds. His late *joint* struggle with the Republicans, against the Lecompton Constitution, involves nothing of the original Nebraska doctrine. That struggle was made on a point, the right of a people to make their own constitution, upon which he and the Republicans have never differed.

The several points of the Dred Scott decision, in connection with Senator Douglas' "care not" policy, constitute the piece of machinery, in its *present* state of advancement. This was the third point gained.

The *working* points of that machinery are:

First, that no negro slave, imported as such from Africa, and no descendant of such slave, can ever be a *citizen* of any State, in the sense of that term as used in the Constitution of the United States.

This point is made in order to deprive the negro, in every possible event, of the benefit of this provision of the United States Constitution, which declares that—

"The citizens of each State shall be entitled to all privileges and immunities of citizens in the several States."

Secondly, that "subject to the Constitution of the United States," neither *Congress* nor a *Territorial Legislature* can exclude slavery from any United States territory.

This point is made in order that individual men may *fill up* the territories with slaves, without danger of losing them as property, and thus to enhance the chances of *permanency* to the institution through all the future.

Thirdly, that whether the holding a negro in actual slavery in a free State, makes him free, as against the holder, the United States courts will not decide, but will leave to be decided by the courts of any slave State the negro may be forced into by the master.

This point is made, not to be pressed *immediately;* but, if acquiesced in for a while, and apparently *indorsed* by the people at an election, *then* to sustain the logical conclusion that what Dred Scott's master might lawfully do with Dred Scott, in the free State of Illinois, every other master may lawfully do with any other *one*, or *one thousand* slaves, in Illinois, or in any other free State.

Auxiliary to all this, and working hand in hand with it, the Nebraska doctrine, or what is left of it, is to *educate* and *mould* public opinion, at least *Northern* public opinion, to not *care* whether slavery is voted *down* or voted *up*.

This shows exactly where we now *are;* and *partially* also, whither we are tending. . . .

We can not absolutely *know* that all these exact adaptations are the result of preconcert. But when we see a lot of framed timbers, different portions of which we know have been gotten out at different times and places and by different workmen—Stephen [A. Douglas], Franklin [Pierce], Roger [B. Taney], and James [Buchanan], for instance—and when we see these timbers joined together, and see they exactly make the frame of a house or a mill, all the tenons and mortices exactly fitting, and all the lengths and proportions of the different pieces exactly adapted to their respective places, and not a piece too many or too few—not omitting even scaffolding—or, if a single piece be lacking, we can see the place in the frame exactly fitted and prepared to yet bring such piece in— in *such* a case, we find it impossible to not *believe* that Stephen and Franklin and Roger and James all understood one another from the beginning, and all worked upon a common *plan* or *draft* drawn up before the first lick was struck. . . .

And this may especially be expected if the doctrine of "care not whether slavery be voted *down* or voted *up*," shall gain upon the public mind sufficiently to give promise that such a decision can be maintained when made.

Such a decision is all that slavery now lacks of being alike lawful in all the States.

Welcome or unwelcome, such decision *is* probably coming, and will soon be upon us, unless the power of the present political dynasty shall be met and overthrown.

We shall *lie down* pleasantly dreaming that the people of *Missouri* are on the verge of making their State *free*; and we shall *awake* to the *reality*, instead, that the *Supreme* Court has made *Illinois* a *slave* State.

To meet and overthrow the power of that dynasty, is the work now before all those who would prevent that consummation.

That is *what* we have to do. . . .

Does Douglas believe an effort to revive that trade is approaching? He has not said so. Does he *really* think so? But if it is, how can he resist it? For years he has labored to prove it a *sacred right* of white men to take negro slaves into the new territories. Can he possibly show that it is *less* a sacred right to *buy* them where they can be bought cheapest? And unquestionably they can be bought *cheaper in Africa* than in *Virginia*. . . .

Clearly, he is not *now* with us—he does not *pretend* to be—he does not *promise* to *ever* be.

Our cause, then, must be intrusted to, and conducted by its own undoubted friends—those whose hands are free, whose hearts are in the work—who *do care* for the result.

Two years ago the Republicans of the nation mustered over thirteen hundred thousand strong.

We did this under the single impulse of resistance to a common danger, with every external circumstance against us.

Of *strange, discordant*, and even *hostile* elements, we gathered from the four winds, and *formed* and fought the battle through, under the constant hot fire of a disciplined, proud, and pampered enemy.

Did we brave all *then*, to *falter* now?—*now*—when that same enemy is *wavering*, dissevered and belligerent?

The result is not doubtful. We shall not fail—if we stand firm, we shall not fail.

Wise councils may *accelerate* or *mistakes delay* it, but, sooner or later, the victory is *sure* to come.

Source: *Illinois State Journal*. June 18. 1858. reprinted in Roy P. Basler. ed. *The Collected Works of Abraham Lincoln* (New Brunswick. 1953). II. 461–69.

John Brown's Last Speech

On November 2, 1859, John Brown spoke before being sentenced to death at his trial for treason and conspiring with slaves to commit murder, following his raid on the arsenal at Harpers Ferry, Virginia, the previous month. Brown's eloquence inspired awe and esteem in much of the north even as he infuriated southerners, thus powerfully polarizing the nation.

I have, may it please the Court, a few words to say.

In the first place, I deny everything but what I have all along admitted,—the design on my part to free the slaves. I intended certainly to have made a clean thing of that matter, as I did last winter, when I went into Missouri and there took slaves without the snapping of a gun on either side, moved them through the country, and finally left them in Canada. I designed to have done the same thing again, on a larger scale. That was all I intended. I never did intend murder, or treason, or the destruction of property, or to excite or incite slaves to rebellion, or to make insurrection.

I have another objection; and that is, it is unjust that I should suffer such a penalty. Had I interfered in the manner which I admit, and which I admit has been fairly proved (for I admire the truthfulness and candor of the greater portion of the witnesses who have testified in this case),—had I so interfered in behalf of the rich, the powerful, the intelligent, the so-called great, or in behalf of any of their friends,—either father, mother, brother, sister, wife, or children, or any of that class,—and suffered and sacrificed what I have in this interference, it would have been all right; and every man in this court would have deemed it an act worthy of reward rather than punishment.

This court acknowledges, as I suppose, the validity of the law of God. I see a book kissed here which I suppose to be the Bible, or at least the New Testament. That teaches me that all things whatsoever I would that men should do to me, I should do even so to them. It teaches me, further, to "remember them that are in bonds, as bound with them." I endeavored to act up to that instruction. I say, I am yet too young to understand that God is any respecter of persons. I believe that to have interfered as I have done—as I have always freely admitted I have done—in behalf of His despised poor, was not wrong, but right. Now, if it is deemed necessary that I should forfeit my life for the furtherance of the ends of justice, and mingle my blood further with the blood of my children and with the blood of millions in this slave country whose rights are disregarded by wicked, cruel, and unjust enactments,—I submit; so let it be done!

Let me say one word further.

I feel entirely satisfied with the treatment I have received on my trial. Considering all the circumstances, it has been more generous than I expected. But I feel no consciousness of guilt. I have stated from the first what was my intention and what was not. I never had any design against the life of any person, nor any disposition to commit treason, or excite slaves to rebel, or make any general insurrection. I never encouraged any man to do so, but always discouraged any idea of that kind.

Let me say, also, a word in regard to the statements made by some of those connected with me. I hear it has been stated by some of them that I have induced them to join me. But the contrary is true. I do not say this to injure them, but as regretting their weakness. There is not one of them but joined me of his own accord, and the greater part of them at their own expense. A number of them I never saw, and never had a word of conversation with, till the day they came to me; and that was for the purpose I have stated.

Now I have done.

Source: John P. Lawson, ed. *American State Trials.* 17 vols. (St. Louis, 1914–36), VI, 800–802.

The Political Platforms of 1860

In 1860, the American political system had splintered into four parties. A collection of old Whigs, mainly from the Border States, called themselves the Constitutional Union Party and ran for social peace, without a real policy. The Republicans, a strictly northern antislavery party, prepared for their second presidential election by preparing a platform that was mild in tone, but clearly opposed to the expansion of the institution of slavery. The northern, or Douglas portion of the Democratic Party, argued for the acceptance of the Dred Scott decision, and sought to change the question to economic and geographic American expansionism. Finally the southern Democrats pointed toward the creation of a national slave code to protect the institution everywhere.

Constitutional Union Platform

Whereas, Experience has demonstrated that Platforms adopted by the partisan Conventions of the country have had the effect to mislead and deceive the people, and at the same time to widen the political divisions of the country, by the creation and encouragement of geographical and sectional parties; therefore

Resolved, that it is both the part of patriotism and of duty to *recognize* no political principle other than THE CONSTITUTION OF THE COUNTRY, THE UNION OF THE STATES, AND THE ENFORCEMENT OF THE LAWS, and that, as representatives of the Constitutional Union men of the country; in National Convention assembled, we hereby pledge ourselves to maintain, protect, and defend, separately and unitedly, these great principles of public liberty and national safety, against all enemies, at home and abroad; believing that thereby peace may once more be restored to the country; the rights of the People and of the States reëstablished, and the Government again placed in that position of justice, fraternity and equality, which, under the example and Constitution of our fathers, has solemnly bound every citizen of the United States to maintain a more perfect union, establish justice, insure domestic tranquility, provide for the common defense, promote the general welfare, and secure the blessings of liberty to ourselves and our posterity.

Republican Party Platform

Resolved, That we, the delegated representatives of the Republican electors of the United States, in Convention assembled, in discharge of the duty we owe to our constituents and our country, unite in the following declarations:

1. That the history of the nation, during the last four years, has fully established the propriety and necessity of the organization and perpetuation of the Republican party, and that the causes which called it into existence are permanent in their nature, and now, more than ever before, demand its peaceful and constitutional triumph.

2. That the maintenance of the principles promulgated in the Declaration of Independence and embodied in the Federal Constitution, "That all men are created equal; that they are endowed by their Creator with certain inalienable rights; that among these are life, liberty and the pursuit of happiness; that, to secure these rights, governments are instituted among men, deriving their just powers from the consent of the governed," is essential to the preservation of our Republican institutions; and that the Federal Constitution, the Rights of the States, and the Union of the States, must and shall be preserved.

3. That to the Union of the States this nation owes its unprecedented increase in population, its surprising development of material resources, its rapid augmentation of wealth, its happiness at home and its honor abroad; and we hold in abhorrence all schemes for Disunion, come from whatever source they may; And we congratulate the country that no Republican member of Congress has uttered or countenanced the threats of Disunion so often made by Democratic members, without rebuke and with applause from their political associates; and we denounce those threats of Disunion, in case of a popular overthrow of their ascendancy, as denying the vital principles of a free government, and as an avowal of contemplated treason, which it is the imperative duty of an indignant People sternly to rebuke and forever silence.

4. That the maintenance inviolate of the rights of the States, and especially the right of each State to order and control its own domestic institutions according to its own judgment exclusively, is essential to that balance of powers on which the perfection and endurance of our political fabric depends; and we denounce the lawless invasion by armed force of the soil of any State or Territory, no matter under what pretext, as among the gravest of crimes.

5. That the present Democratic Administration has far exceeded our worst apprehensions, in its measureless subserviency to the exactions of a sectional interest, as especially evinced in its desperate exertions to force the infamous Lecompton constitution upon the protesting people of Kansas; in construing the personal relation between master and

servant to involve an unqualified property in persons; in its attempted enforcement, everywhere, on land and sea, through the intervention of Congress and of the Federal Courts of the extreme pretensions of a purely local interest; and in its general and unvarying abuse of the power intrusted to it by a confiding people. . . .

7. That the new dogma that the Constitution, of its own force, carries Slavery into any or all of the Territories of the United States, is a dangerous political heresy, at variance with the explicit provisions of that instrument itself, with contemporaneous exposition, and with legislative and judicial precedent; is revolutionary in its tendency, and subversive of the peace and harmony of the country.

8. That the normal condition of all the territory of the United States is that of freedom; That as our Republican fathers, when they had abolished slavery in all our national territory, ordained that "no person should be deprived of life, liberty, or property, without due process of law," it becomes our duty, by legislation, whenever such legislation is necessary, to maintain this provision of the Constitution against all attempts to violate it; and we deny the authority of Congress, of a territorial legislature, or of any individuals, to give legal existence to Slavery in any Territory of the United States.

9. That we brand the recent re-opening of the African slave-trade, under the cover of our national flag, aided by perversions of judicial power, as a crime against humanity and a burning shame to our country and age; and we call upon Congress to take prompt and efficient measures for the total and final suppression of that execrable traffic.

10. That in the recent vetoes, by their Federal Governors, of the acts of the Legislatures of Kansas and Nebraska, prohibiting Slavery in those Territories, we find a practical illustration of the boasted Democratic principle of Non-Intervention and Popular Sovereignty embodied in the Kansas-Nebraska bill, and a demonstration of the deception and fraud involved therein.

11. That Kansas should, of right, be immediately admitted as a State under the Constitution recently formed and adopted by her people, and accepted by the House of Representatives.

12. That, while providing revenue for the support of the General Government by duties upon imports, sound policy requires such an adjustment of these imposts as to encourage the development of the industrial interests of the whole country; and we commend that policy of national exchanges which secures to the working men liberal wages, to agriculture remunerating prices, to mechanics and manufacturers an adequate reward for their skill, labor and enterprise, and to the nation commercial prosperity and independence.

13. That we protest against any sale or alienation to others of the Public Lands held by actual settlers, and against any view of the Homestead policy which regards the settlers as paupers or suppliants for public bounty; and we demand the passage by Congress of the complete and satisfactory Homestead measure which has already passed the house.

14. That the Republican Party is opposed to any change in our Naturalization Laws or any State legislation by which the rights of our citizenship hitherto accorded to immigrants from foreign lands shall be abridged or impaired; and in favor of giving a full and efficient protection to the rights of all classes of citizens, whether native or naturalized, both at home and abroad.

15. That appropriations by Congress for River and Harbor improvements of a National character, required for the accommodation and security of an existing commerce, are authorized by the Constitution, and justified by the obligations of Government to protect the lives and property of its citizens.

16. That a Railroad to the Pacific Ocean is imperatively demanded by the interests of the whole country; that the Federal Government ought to render immediate and efficient aid in its construction; and that, as preliminary thereto, a daily Overland Mail should be promptly established. . . .

The Democratic Platform of 1860

1. *Resolved,* That we, the Democracy of the Union in Convention assembled, hereby declare our affirmation of the resolutions unanimously adopted and declared as a platform of principles by the Democratic Convention at Cincinnati, in the year 1856, believing that Democratic principles are unchangeable in their nature, when applied to the same subject matters; and we recommend, as the only further resolutions, the following:

2. Inasmuch as difference of opinion exists in the Democratic party as to the nature and extent of the powers of a Territorial Legislature, and as to the powers and duties of Congress, under the Constitution of the United States, over the institution of slavery within the Territories,

Resolved, That the Democratic party will abide by the decision of the Supreme Court of the United States upon these questions of Constitutional law.

3. *Resolved,* That it is the duty of the United States to afford ample and complete protection to all its citizens, whether at home or abroad, and whether native or foreign born.

4. *Resolved,* That one of the necessities of the age, in a military, commercial, and postal point of view, is speedy communication between the Atlantic and Pacific States; and the Democratic party pledge such Constitutional Government aid as will insure the construction of a Railroad to the Pacific coast, at the earliest practicable period.

5. *Resolved,* That the Democratic party are in favor of the acquisition of the Island of Cuba on such terms as shall be honorable to ourselves and just to Spain.

6. *Resolved,* That the enactments of the State Legislatures to defeat the faithful execution of the Fugitive Slave Law, are hostile in character, subversive of the Constitution, and revolutionary in their effect.

7. *Resolved,* That it is in accordance with the interpretation of the Cincinnati platform, that during the existence of the Territorial Governments the measure of restriction, whatever it may be, imposed by the Federal Constitution on the power of the Territorial Legislature over the subject of the domestic relations, as the same has been, or shall hereafter be finally determined by the Supreme Court of the United States, should be respected by all good citizens, and enforced with promptness and fidelity by every branch of the general government.

The Democratic (Breckenridge Faction) Platform of 1860

Resolved, That the Platform adopted by the Democratic party at Cincinnati be affirmed, with the following explanatory resolutions:

1. That the Government of a Territory organized by an act of Congress is provisional and temporary, and during its existence all citizens of the United States have an equal right to settle with their property in the Territory, without their rights, either of person or property being destroyed or impaired by Congressional or Territorial legislation.

2. That it is the duty of the Federal Government, in all its departments, to protect, when necessary, the rights of persons and property in the Territories, and wherever else its constitutional authority extends.

3. That when the settlers in a Territory, having an adequate population, form a State Constitution, the right of sovereignty commences, and being consummated by admission into the Union, they stand on an equal footing with the people of other States, and the State thus organized ought to be admitted into the Federal Union, whether its Constitution prohibits or recognizes the institution of slavery.

Resolved, That the Democratic party are in favor of the acquisition of the Island of Cuba, on such terms as shall be honorable to ourselves and just to Spain, at the earliest practicable moment.

Resolved, That the enactments of State Legislatures to defeat the faithful execution of the Fugitive Slave Law are hostile in character, subversive of the Constitution, and revolutionary in their effect.

Resolved, That the Democracy of the United States recognize it as the imperative duty of this Government to protect the naturalized citizen in all his rights, whether at home or in foreign lands, to the same extent as its native-born citizens.

WHEREAS, One of the greatest necessities of the age, in a political, commercial, postal and military point of view, is a speedy communication between the Pacific and Atlantic coasts, Therefore be it

Resolved, That the National Democratic party do hereby pledge themselves to use every means in their power to secure the passage of some bills, to the extent of the constitutional authority of Congress for the construction of a Pacific Railroad from the Mississippi River to the Pacific Ocean, at the earliest practicable moment.

Source: Kirk Porter and David B. Johnson. *National Party Platforms. 1840–1956* (Urbana. Ill.. 1956). 30–33.

South Carolina's Ordinance of Secession and Declaration of Causes of Secession

Very soon after the election of Abraham Lincoln to the presidency, the legislature of South Carolina called a convention to consider leaving the Union. On December 20, 1860, the convention voted unanimously for secession. To justify their act, and to persuade other slaveholding states to join them in a new confederation, the South Carolinians issued another declaration, on December 24. They insisted that secession was the legitimate self-defense of a sovereign state against a tyrannical central government that sought, they claimed, to destroy their strictly domestic concern, the institution of slavery.

Ordinance of Secession

We, the people of the State of South Carolina, in Convention assembled, do declare and ordain, and it is hereby declared and ordained, that the ordinance adopted by us in Convention, on the 23d day of May, in the year of our Lord 1788, whereby the Constitution of the United States of America was ratified, and also all Acts and parts of Acts of the General Assembly of this State ratifying the amendments of the said Constitution, are hereby repealed, and that the union now subsisting between South Carolina and other States under the name of the United States of America is hereby dissolved.

Declaration of Causes of Secession

The people of the State of South Carolina in Convention assembled, on the 2d day of April, A.D. 1852, declared that the frequent violations of the Constitution of the United States by the Federal Government, and its encroachments upon the reserved rights of the States, fully justified this State in their withdrawal from the Federal Union; but in deference to the opinions and wishes of the other Slaveholding States, she forbore at that time to exercise this right. Since that time these encroachments have continued to increase, and further forbearance ceases to be a virtue.

And now the State of South Carolina having resumed her separate and equal place among nations, deems it due to herself, to the remaining United States of America, and to the nations of the world, that she should declare the immediate causes which have led to this act.

In 1787, Deputies were appointed by the States to revise the articles of Confederation; and on 17th September, 1787, these Deputies recommended for the adoption of the States, the Articles of Union, known as the Constitution of the United States.

. . . Thus was established by compact between the States, a Government with defined objects and powers, limited to the express words of the grant. . . . We hold that the Government thus established is subject to the two great principles asserted in the Declaration of Independence; and we hold further, that the mode of its formation subjects it to a third fundamental principle, namely, the law of compact. We maintain that in every compact between two or more parties, the obligation is mutual; that the failure of one of the contracting parties to perform a material part of the agreement, entirely releases the obligation of the other; and that, where no arbiter is provided, each party is remitted to his own judgment to determine the fact of failure, with all its consequences.

In the present case, that fact is established with certainty. We assert that fourteen of the States have deliberately refused for years past to fulfill their constitutional obligations, and we refer to their own statutes for the proof.

The Constitution of the United States, in its fourth Article, provides as follows:

"No person held to service or labor in one State under the laws thereof, escaping into another, shall, in consequence of any law or regulation therein, be discharged from such service or labor, but shall be delivered up, on claim of the party to whom such service or labor may be due."

This stipulation was so material to the compact that without it that compact would not have been made. The greater number of the contracting parties held slaves, and they had previously evinced their estimate of the value of such a stipulation by making it a condition in the Ordinance for the government of the territory ceded by Virginia, which obligations, and the laws of the General Government, have ceased to effect the objects of the Constitution. The States of Maine, New Hampshire, Vermont, Massachusetts, Connecticut, Rhode Island, New York, Pennsylvania, Illinois, Indiana, Michigan, Wisconsin, and Iowa, have enacted laws which either nullify the acts of Congress, or render useless any attempt to execute them. In many of these States the fugitive is discharged from the service of labor claimed, and in none of them has the State Government complied with the stipulation made in the Constitution. The State of New Jersey, at an early day, passed a law in conformity with her constitutional obligation; but the current of Anti-Slavery feeling has led her more recently to enact laws which render inoperative the remedies provided by her own laws and by the laws of Congress. In the State of New York even the right of transit for a slave has been denied by her tribunals; and the States of Ohio and Iowa have refused to surrender to justice fugitives charged with murder, and with inciting servile insurrection in the State of Virginia. Thus the constitutional compact has been deliberately broken and disregarded by the non-slaveholding States; and the consequence follows that South Carolina is released from her obligation. . . .

We affirm that these ends for which this Government was instituted have been defeated, and the Government itself has been destructive of them by the action of the non-slaveholding States. Those States have assumed the right of deciding upon the propriety of our domestic institutions; and have denied the rights of property established in fifteen of the States and recognized by the Constitution; they have denounced as sinful the institution of Slavery; they have permitted the open establishment among them of societies, whose avowed object is to disturb the peace of and eloin the property of the citizens of other States. They have encouraged and assisted thousands of our slaves to leave their homes; and those who remain, have been incited by emissaries, books, and pictures, to servile insurrection.

For twenty-five years this agitation has been steadily increasing, until it has now secured to its aid the power of the common Government. Observing the *forms* of the Constitution, a sectional party has found within that article establishing the Executive Department, the means of subverting the Constitution itself. A geographical line has been drawn across the Union, and all the States north of that line have united in the election of a man to the high office of President of the United States whose opinions and purposes are hostile to Slavery. He is to be intrusted with the administration of the common Government, because he has declared that that "Government cannot endure permanently half slave, half free," and that the public mind must rest in the belief that Slavery is in the course of ultimate extinction.

This sectional combination for the subversion of the Constitution has been aided, in some of the States, by elevating to citizenship persons who, by the supreme law of the land, are incapable of becoming citizens; and their votes have been used to inaugurate a new policy, hostile to the South, and destructive of its peace and safety.

On the 4th of March next this party will take possession of the Government. It has announced that the South shall be excluded from the common territory, that the Judicial tribunal shall be made sectional, and that a war must be waged against Slavery until it shall cease throughout the United States.

The guarantees of the Constitution will then no longer exist; the equal rights of the States will be lost. The Slaveholding States will no longer have the power of self-government, or self-protection, and the Federal Government will have become their enemy.

Sectional interest and animosity will deepen the irritation; and all hope of remedy is rendered vain, by the fact that public opinion at the North has invested a great political error with the sanctions of a more erroneous religious belief.

We, therefore, the people of South Carolina, by our delegates in Convention assembled, appealing to the Supreme Judge of the world for the rectitude of our intentions, have solemnly declared that the Union heretofore existing between this State and the other States of North America is dissolved, and that the State of South Carolina has resumed her position among the nations of the world, as a separate and independent state, with full power to levy war, conclude peace, contract alliances, establish commerce, and to do all other acts and things which independent States may of right do.

Source: Frank Mocre, ed. *The Rebellion Record*. 12 vols. (New York, 1861–66). Vol. I, part 2, pp. 2–4.

Abraham Lincoln's First Inaugural Address

On March 4, 1861, Abraham Lincoln used the occasion of his inaugural address to assure the South of his peaceful intentions toward them, while promising the North that he would uphold the law against the illegitimate act of secession. Lincoln still hoped for a political resolution to the crisis of disunion, but he was determined to maneuver the South into firing the first shot if a civil war were to come.

Fellow citizens of the United States:

In compliance with a custom as old as the government itself, I appear before you to address you briefly, and to take, in your presence, the oath prescribed by the Constitution of the United States, to be taken by the President "before he enters on the execution of his office."

I do not consider it necessary, at present, for me to discuss those matters of administration about which there is no special anxiety, or excitement.

Apprehension seems to exist among the people of the Southern States, that by the accession of a Republican Administration, their property, and their peace, and personal security, are to be endangered. There has never been any reasonable cause for such apprehension. Indeed, the most ample evidence to the contrary has all the while existed, and been open to their inspection. It is found in nearly all the published speeches of him who now addresses you. I do but quote from one of those speeches when I declare that "I have no purpose, directly or indirectly, to interfere with the institution of slavery in the States where it exists. I believe I have no lawful right to do so, and I have no inclination to do so." Those who nominated and elected me did so with full knowledge that I had made this, and many similar declarations, and had never recanted them. And more than this, they placed in the platform, for my acceptance, and as a law to themselves, and to me, the clear and emphatic resolution which I now read:

"*Resolved*, That the maintenance inviolate of the rights of the States, and especially the right of each State to order and control its own domestic institutions according to its own judgment exclusively, is essential to that balance of power on which the perfection and endurance of our political fabric depend; and we denounce the lawless invasion by armed force of the soil of any State or Territory, no matter under what pretext, as among the gravest of crimes."

I now reiterate these sentiments: and in doing so, I only press upon the public attention the most conclusive evidence of which the case is susceptible, that the property, peace and security of no section are to be in anywise endangered by the now incoming Administration. I add too, that all the protection which, consistently with the Constitution and the laws, can be given, will be cheerfully given to all the States when lawfully demanded, for whatever cause—as cheerfully to one section, as to another.

There is much controversy about the delivering up of fugitives from service or labor. The clause I now read is as plainly written in the Constitution as any other of its provisions:

"No person held to service or labor in one State, under the laws thereof, escaping into another, shall in consequence of any law or regulation therein, be discharged from such service or labor, but shall be delivered up on claim of the party to whom such service or labor may be due."

It is scarcely questioned that this provision was intended by those who made it, for the reclaiming of what we call fugitive slaves; and the intention of the law-giver is the law. All members of Congress swear their support to the whole Constitution—to this provision as much as to any other. To the proposition, then, that slaves whose cases come within the terms of this clause, "shall be delivered up," their oaths are unanimous. Now, if they would make the effort in good temper, could they not, with nearly equal unanimity, frame and pass a law, by means of which to keep good that unanimous oath?

There is some difference of opinion whether this clause should be enforced by national or by state authority; but surely that difference is not a very material one. If the slave is to be surrendered, it can be of but little consequence to him, or to others, by which authority it is done. And should any one, in any case, be content that his oath shall go unkept, on a merely unsubstantial controversy as to *how* it shall be kept?

Again, in any law upon this subject, ought not all the safeguards of liberty known in civilized and humane jurisprudence to be introduced, so that a free man be not, in any case, surrendered as a slave? And might it not be well, at the same time, to provide by law for the enforcement of that clause in the Constitution which guarantees that "The citizens of each State shall be entitled to all privileges and immunities of citizens in the several States?"

I take the official oath to-day, with no mental reservations, and with no purpose to construe the Constitution or laws, by any hypercritical rules. And while I do not choose now to specify particular acts of Congress as proper to be enforced, I do suggest, that it will be much safer for all, both in official and private stations, to conform to, and abide by, all those acts which stand unrepealed, than to violate any of them, trusting to find impunity in having them held to be unconstitutional.

It is seventy-two years since the first inauguration of a President under our national Constitution. During that period fifteen different and greatly distinguished citizens, have, in succession, administered the executive branch of the government. They have conducted it through many perils; and, generally, with great success. Yet, with all this scope of precedent, I now enter upon the same task for the brief constitutional term of four years, under great and peculiar difficulty. A disruption of the Federal Union heretofore only menaced, is now formidably attempted.

I hold, that in contemplation of universal law, and of the Constitution, the Union of these States is perpetual. Perpetuity is implied, if not expressed, in the fundamental law of all national governments. It is safe to assert that no government proper, ever had a provision in its organic law for its own termination. Continue to execute all the express provisions of our national Constitution, and the Union will endure forever—it being impossible to destroy it, except by some action not provided for in the instrument itself.

Again, if the United States be not a government proper, but an association of States in the nature of contract merely, can it, as a contract, be peaceably unmade, by less than all the parties who made it? One party to a contract may violate it—break it, so to speak; but does it not require all to lawfully rescind it?

Descending from these general principles, we find the proposition that, in legal contemplation, the Union is perpetual, confirmed by the history of the Union itself. The Union is much older than the Constitution. It was formed in fact, by the Articles of Association in 1774. It was matured and continued by the Declaration of Independence in 1776. It was further matured and the faith of all the then thirteen States expressly plighted and engaged that it should be perpetual, by the Articles of Confederation in 1778. And finally, in 1787, one of the declared objects for ordaining and establishing the Constitution, was *"to form a more perfect union."*

But if destruction of the Union, by one, or by a part only, of the States, be lawfully possible, the Union is *less* perfect than before the Constitution, having lost the vital element of perpetuity.

It follows from these views that no State, upon its own mere motion, can lawfully get out of the Union,—that *resolves* and *ordinances* to that effect are legally void; and that acts of violence, within any State or States, against the authority of the United States, are insurrectionary or revolutionary, according to circumstances.

I therefore consider that, in view of the Constitution and the laws, the Union is unbroken; and, to the extent of my ability, I shall take care, as the Constitution itself expressly enjoins upon me, that the laws of the Union be faithfully executed in all the States. Doing this I deem to be only a simple duty on my part; and I shall perform it, so far as practicable, unless my rightful masters, the American people, shall withhold the requisite means, or, in some authoritative manner, direct the contrary. I trust this will not be regarded as a menace, but only as the declared purpose of the Union that it *will* constitutionally defend, and maintain itself.

In doing this there needs to be no bloodshed or violence; and there shall be none, unless it be forced upon the national authority. The power confided to men will be used to hold, occupy, and possess the property, and places belonging to the government, and to collect the duties and imposts; but beyond what may be necessary for these objects, there will be no invasion—no using of force against, or among the people anywhere. Where hostility to the United States, in any interior locality, shall be so great and so universal, as to prevent competent resident citizens from holding the Federal offices, there will be no attempt to force obnoxious strangers among the people for that object. While the strict legal right may exist in the government to enforce the exercise of these offices, the attempt to do so would be so irritating, and so nearly impracticable with all, that I deem it better to forego, for the time, the uses of such offices.

The mails, unless repelled, will continue to be furnished in all parts of the Union. So far as possible, the people everywhere shall have that sense of perfect security which is most favorable to calm thought and reflection. The course here indicated will be followed, unless current events, and experience, shall show a modification, or change, to be proper; and in every case and exigency, my best discretion will be exercised, according to circumstances actually existing, and with a view and a hope of a peaceful solution of the national troubles, and the restoration of fraternal sympathies and affections.

That there are persons in one section, or another who seek to destroy the Union at all events, and are glad of any pretext to do it, I will neither affirm nor deny; but if there be such, I need address no word to them. To those, however, who really love the Union, may I not speak?

Before entering upon so grave a matter as the destruction of our national fabric, with all its benefits, its memories, and its hopes, would it not be wise to ascertain precisely why we do it? Will you hazard so desperate a step, while there is any possibility that any portion of the ills you fly from, have no real existence? Will you, while the certain ills you fly to, are greater than all the real ones you fly from? Will you risk the commission of so fearful a mistake?

All profess to be content in the Union, if all constitutional rights can be maintained. Is it true, then, that any right, plainly written in the Constitution, has been denied? I think not. Happily the human mind is so constituted, that no party can reach to the audacity of doing this. Think, if you can, of a single instance in which a plainly written provision of the Constitution has ever been denied. If by the mere force of numbers, a majority should deprive a minority of any clearly written constitutional right, it might, in a moral point of view, justify revolution—certainly would, if such right were a vital one. But such is not our case. All the vital rights of minorities, and of individuals, are so plainly assured to them, by affirmations and negations, guarranties and prohibitions, in the Constitution, that controversies never arise concerning them. But no organic law can ever be framed with a provision specifically applicable to every question which may occur in practical administration. No foresight can anticipate, nor any document of reasonable length contain express provisions for all possible questions. Shall fugitives from labor be surrendered by national or by State authority? The Constitution does not expressly say. *May* Congress prohibit slavery in the territories? The Constitution does not expressly say. *Must* Congress protect slavery in the territories? The Constitution does not expressly say.

From questions of this class spring all our constitutional controversies, and we divide upon them into majorities and minorities. If the minority will not acquiesce, the majority must, or the government must cease. There is no other alternative; for continuing the government, is acquiescence on one side or the other. If a minority, in such case, will secede rather than acquiesce, they make a precedent which, in turn, will divide and ruin them; for a minority of their own will secede from them, whenever a majority refuses to be controlled by such minority. For instance, why may not any portion of a new confederacy, a year or two hence, arbitrarily secede again, precisely as portions of the present Union now claim to secede from it. All who cherish disunion sentiments, are now being educated to the exact temper of doing this. Is there such perfect identity of interests among the States to compose a new Union, as to produce harmony only, and prevent renewed secession?

Plainly, the central idea of secession, is the essence of anarchy. A majority, held in restraint by constitutional checks, and limitations, and always changing easily, with deliberate changes of popular opinions and sentiments, is the only true sovereign of a free people. Whoever rejects it, does, of necessity, fly to anarchy or to despotism. Unanimity is impossible; the rule of a minority, as a permanent arrangement, is wholly inadmissible; so that, rejecting the majority principle, anarchy, or despotism in some form, is all that is left.

I do not forget the position assumed by some, that constitutional questions are to be decided by the Supreme Court; nor do I deny that such decisions must be binding in any case, upon the parties to a suit, as to the object of that suit, while they are also entitled to very high respect and consideration, in all paralel cases, by all other departments of the government. And while it is obviously possible that such decision may be erroneous in any given case, still the evil effect following it, being limited to that particular case, with the chance that it may be over-ruled, and never become a precedent for other cases, can better be borne than could the evils of a different practice. At the same time the candid citizen must confess that if the policy of the government, upon vital questions, affecting the whole people, is to be irrevocably fixed by decisions of the Supreme Court, the instant they are made, in ordinary litigation between parties, in personal actions, the people will have ceased, to be their own rulers, having, to that extent, practically resigned their government, into the hands of that eminent tribunal. Nor is there, in this view, any assault upon the court, or the judges. It is a duty, from which they may not shrink, to decide cases properly brought before them; and it is no fault of theirs, if others seek to turn their decisions to political purposes.

One section of our country believes slavery is *right*, and ought to be extended, while the other believes it is *wrong*, and ought not to be extended. This is the only substantial dispute. The fugitive slave clause of the Constitution, and the law for the suppression of the foreign slave trade, are each as well enforced, perhaps, as any law can ever be in a community where the moral sense of the people imperfectly supports the law itself. The great body of the people abide by the dry legal obligation in both cases, and a few break over in each. This, I think, cannot be perfectly cured; and it would be worse in both cases *after* the separation of the sections, than before. The foreign slave trade, now imperfectly suppressed, would be ultimately revived without restriction, in one section; while fugitive slaves, now only partially surrendered, would not be surrendered at all, by the other.

Physically speaking, we cannot separate. We cannot remove our respective sections from each other, nor build an impassable wall between them. A husband and wife may be divorced, and go out of the presence, and beyond the reach of each other; but the different parts of our country cannot do this. They cannot but remain face to face; and intercourse, either amicable or hostile, must continue between them. Is it possible then to make that intercourse more advantageous, or more satisfactory, *after* separation than *before*? Can aliens make treaties easier than friends can make laws? Can treaties be more faithfully enforced between aliens, than laws can among friends? Suppose you go to war, you cannot fight always; and when, after much loss on both sides, and no gain on either, you cease fighting, the identical old questions, as to terms of intercourse, are again upon you.

This country, with its institutions, belongs to the people who inhabit it. Whenever they shall grow weary of the existing government, they can exercise their *constitutional* right of amending it, or their *revolutionary* right to dismember, or overthrow it. I can not be ignorant of the fact that many worthy, and patriotic citizens are desirous of having the national constitution amended. While I make no recommendation of amendments, I fully recognize the rightful authority of the people over the whole subject, to be exercised in either of the modes prescribed in the instrument itself; and I should, under existing circumstances, favor, rather than oppose, a fair opportunity being afforded the people to act upon it.

I will venture to add that, to me, the convention mode seems preferable, in that it allows amendments to originate with the people themselves, instead of only permitting them to take, or reject, propositions, originated by others, not especially chosen for the purpose, and which might not be precisely such, as they would wish to either accept or refuse. I understand a proposed amendment to the Constitution—which amendment, however, I have not seen, has passed Congress, to the effect that the federal government, shall never interfere with the domestic institutions of the States, including that of persons held to service. To avoid misconstruction of what I have said, I depart from my purpose not to speak of particular amendments, so far as to say that, holding such a provision to now be implied constitutional law, I have no objection to its being made express, and irrevocable.

The Chief Magistrate derives all his authority from the people, and they have conferred none upon him to fix terms for the separation of the States. The people themselves can do this also if they choose; but the executive, as such, has nothing to do with it. His duty is to administer the present government, as it came to his hands, and to transmit it, unimpaired by him, to his successor.

Why should there not be a patient confidence in the ultimate justice of the people? Is there any better, or equal hope, in the world? In our present differences, is either party without faith of being in the right? If the Almighty Ruler of nations, with his eternal truth and justice, be on your side of the North, or on yours of the South, that truth, and that justice, will surely prevail, by the judgment of this great tribunal, the American people.

By the frame of the government under which we live, this same people have wisely given their public servants but little power for mischief; and have, with equal wisdom, provided for the return of that little to their own hands at very short intervals.

While the people retain their virtue, and vigilance, no administration, by any extreme of wickedness or folly, can very seriously injure the government, in the short space of four years.

My countrymen, one and all, think calmly and *well*, upon this whole subject. Nothing valuable can be lost by taking time. If there be an object to *hurry* any of you, in hot haste, to a step which you would never take *deliberately*, that object will be frustrated by taking time; but no good object can be frustrated by it. Such of you as are now dissatisfied, still have the old Constitution unimpaired, and, on the sensitive point, the laws of your own framing under it; while the new administration will have no immediate power, if it would, to change either. If it were admitted that you who are dissatisfied, hold the right side in the dispute, there still is no single good reason for precipitate action. Intelligence, patriotism, Christianity, and a firm reliance on Him, who has never yet forsaken this favored land, are still competent to adjust, in the best way, all our present difficulty.

In *your* hands, my dissatisfied fellow countrymen, and not in *mine*, is the momentous issue of civil war. The government will not assail *you*. You can have no conflict, without being yourselves the aggressors. *You* have no oath registered in Heaven to destroy the government, while *I* shall have the most solemn one to "preserve, protect and defend" it.

I am loth to close. We are not enemies, but friends. We must not be enemies. Though passion may have strained, it must not break our bonds of affection. The mystic chords of memory, stretching from every battle-field, and patriot grave, to every living heart and hearthstone, all over this broad land, will yet swell the chorus of the Union, when again touched, as surely they will be, by the better angels of our nature.

Source: Basler. IV. 262–71.

Jefferson Davis's Inaugural Address

On February 18, 1861, in Montgomery, Alabama, Jefferson Davis was inaugurated the first president of the Confederate States of America. In his address, Davis sought to demonstrate that the new nation merely wished to be left in peace to promote its own primarily agricultural interests, and to guarantee its own rights, freed from the clutches of an aggressive north.

FRIENDS AND FELLOW-CITIZENS: Called to the difficult and responsible station of Chief Executive of the Provisional Government which you have instituted, I approach the discharge of the duties assigned to me with an humble distrust of my abilities, but with a sustaining confidence in the wisdom of those who are to guide and to aid me in the administration of public affairs, and an abiding faith in the virtue and patriotism of the people. Looking forward to the speedy establishment of a permanent government to take the place of this, and which, by its greater moral and physical power, will be better able to combat with the many difficulties which arise from the conflicting interests of separate nations, I enter upon the duties of the office to which I have been chosen with a hope that the beginning of our career as a confederacy may not be obstructed by hostile opposition to our enjoyment of the separate existence and independence which we have asserted, and, with the blessing of Providence, intend to maintain. Our present condition, achieved in a manner unprecedented in the history of nations, illustrates the American idea that governments rest upon the consent of the governed, and that it is the right of the people to alter or abolish governments whenever they become destructive of the ends for which they were established. The declared purpose of the compact of the Union from which we have withdrawn was "to establish justice, insure domestic tranquillity, provide for the common defense, promote the general welfare, and secure the blessings of liberty to ourselves and our posterity;" and when, in the judgment of the sovereign States now composing this Confederacy, it had been perverted from the purposes for which it was ordained, and had ceased to answer the ends for which it was established, a peaceful appeal to the ballot box declared that, so far as they were concerned, the Government created by that compact should cease to exist. In this they merely asserted a right which the Declaration of Independence of 1776 had defined to be inalienable; of the time and occasion for its exercise they, as sovereigns, were the final judges, each for itself. The impartial and enlightened verdict of mankind will vindicate the rectitude of our conduct, and He who knows the hearts of men, will judge of the sincerity with which we labored to preserve the Government of our fathers in its spirit. The right solemnly proclaimed at the birth of the States, and which has been affirmed and reaffirmed in the bills of rights of States subsequently admitted into the Union of 1789, undeniably recognize in the people the power to resume the authority delegated for the purposes of government. Thus the sovereign States here represented proceeded to form this Confederacy, and it is by abuse of language that their act has been denominated a revolution. They formed a new alliance, but within each State its government has remained; the rights of person and property have not been disturbed. The agent through whom they communicated with foreign nations is changed, but this does not necessarily interrupt their international relations.

Sustained by the consciousness that the transition from the former Union to the present Confederacy has not proceeded from a disregard on our part of just obligations or any failure to perform every constitutional duty; moved by no interest or passion to invade the rights of others; anxious to cultivate peace and commerce with all nations, if we may not hope to avoid war, we may at least expect that posterity will acquit us of having needlessly engaged in it. Doubly justified by the absence of wrong on our part, and by wanton aggression on the part of others, there can be no cause to doubt that the courage and patriotism of the people of the Confederate States will be found equal to any measures of defense which honor and security may require.

An agricultural people, whose chief interest is the export of a commodity required in every manufacturing country, our true policy is peace, and the freest trade which our necessities will permit. It is alike our interest and that of all those to whom we would sell and from whom we would buy that there should be the fewest practicable restrictions upon the interchange of commodities. There can be but little rivalry between ours and any manufacturing or navigating community, such as the Northeastern States of the American Union. It must follow, therefore, that a mutual interest would invite good will and kind offices. If, however, passion or the lust of dominion should cloud the judgment or inflame the ambition of those States, we must prepare to meet the emergency and to maintain by the final arbitrament of the sword the position which we have assumed among the nations of the earth. We have entered upon the career of independence, and it must be inflexibly pursued. Through many years of controversy with our late associates, the Northern States, we have vainly endeavored to secure tranquillity and to obtain respect for the rights to which we were entitled. As a necessity, not a choice, we have resorted to the remedy of separation; and henceforth our energies must be directed to the conduct of our own affairs and the perpetuity of the confederacy which we have formed. If a just perception of a mutual interest shall permit us peaceably to pursue our separate political career, my most earnest desire will have been fulfilled. But, if this be denied to us, and the integrity of our territory and jurisdiction be assailed, it will but remain for us, with firm resolve, to appeal to arms and invoke the blessings of Providence on a just cause.

As a consequence of our new condition, and with a view to meet anticipated wants, it will be necessary to provide for the speedy and efficient organization of branches of the Executive Department, having special charge of foreign intercourse, finance, military affairs, and the postal service.

For purposes of defense the Confederate States may, under ordinary circumstances, rely mainly upon their militia, but it is deemed advisable in the present condition of affairs that there should be a well-instructed and disciplined army, more numerous than would usually be required on a peace establishment. I also suggest that, for the protection of our harbors and commerce on the high seas, a navy adapted to those objects will be required. These necessities have doubtless engaged the attention of Congress.

With a Constitution differing only from that of our fathers in so far as it is explanatory of their well-known intent, freed from the sectional conflicts which have interfered with the pursuit of the general welfare, it is not unreasonable to expect that States from which we have recently parted may seek to unite their fortunes with ours under the Government which we have instituted. For this your Constitution makes adequate provision; but beyond this, if I mistake not the judgment and will of the people, a reunion with the States from which we have separated is neither practicable nor desirable. To increase the power, develop the resources, and promote the happiness of a confederacy, it is requisite that there should be so much of homogeneity that the welfare of every portion shall be the aim of the whole. Where this does not exist antagonisms are engendered, which must and should result in separation.

Actuated solely by the desire to preserve our own rights and promote our own welfare, the separation of the Confederate States has been marked by no aggression upon others, and followed by no domestic convulsion. Our industrial pursuits have received no check, the cultivation of our fields has progressed as heretofore, and even should we be involved in war, there would be no considerable diminution in the production of the staples which have constituted our exports, and in which the commercial world has an interest scarcely less than our own. This common interest of the producer and consumer can only be interrupted by an exterior force which should obstruct its transmission to foreign markets—a course of conduct which would be as unjust toward us as it would be detrimental to manufacturing and commercial interests abroad. Should reason guide the action of the Government from which we have separated, a policy so detrimental to the civilized world, the Northern States included, could not be dictated by even the strongest desire to inflict injury upon us; but otherwise a terrible responsibility will rest upon it, and the suffering of millions will bear testimony to the folly and wickedness of our aggressors. In the meantime there will remain to us, besides the ordinary means before suggested, the well-known resources for retaliation upon the commerce of the enemy.

Experience in public stations of subordinate grade to this, which your kindness has conferred, has taught me that care, and toil, and disappointment are the price of official elevation. You will see many errors to forgive, many deficiencies to tolerate, but you shall not find in me either a want of zeal or fidelity to the cause that is to me highest in hope and of most enduring affection. Your generosity has bestowed upon me an undeserved distinction; one which I neither sought nor desired. Upon the continuance of that sentiment, and upon your wisdom and patriotism, I rely to direct and support me in the performance of the duty required at my hands.

We have changed the constituent parts but not the system of our Government. The Constitution formed by our fathers is that of these Confederate States, in their exposition of it; and in the judicial construction it has received we have a light which reveals its true meaning.

Thus instructed as to the just interpretation of the instrument, and ever remembering that all offices are but trusts held for the people, and that delegated powers are to be strictly construed, I will hope, by due diligence in the performance of my duties, though I may disappoint your expectations, yet to retain, when retiring, something of the good will and confidence which welcome my entrance into office.

It is joyous, in the midst of perilous times, to look around upon a people united in heart, where one purpose of high resolve animates and actuates the whole; where the sacrifices to be made are not weighed in the balance against honor, and right, and liberty, and equality. Obstacles may retard, they cannot long prevent, the progress of a movement sanctified by its justice and sustained by a virtuous people. Reverently let us invoke the God of our fathers to guide and protect us in our efforts to perpetuate the principles which, by His blessing, they were able to vindicate, establish, and transmit to their posterity, and with a continuance of His favor ever gratefully acknowledged, we may hopefully look forward to success, to peace, and to prosperity.

Source: *OR*, Series IV, vol. 1, 104–6.

Speech by Confederate Vice-President Alexander H. Stephens

On March 21, 1861, a month following his installation as Confederate vice-president, speaking in Savannah in his home state of Georgia, Alexander H. Stephens made it far clearer than had Jefferson Davis in his inaugural address that the root cause of secession was defense of white supremacy and the institution of slavery. This speech was referred to later as the "Cornerstone Speech" of the Confederacy.

Mr. Mayor and Gentlemen of the Committee, and Fellow-Citizens:

For this reception you will please accept my most profound and sincere thanks. The compliment is doubtless intended as much, or more, perhaps, in honor of the occasion, and my public position in connection with the great events now crowding upon us, than to me personally and individually. It is, however, none the less appreciated by me on that account. We are in the midst of one of the greatest epochs in our history. The last ninety days will mark one of the most memorable eras in the history of modern civilization . . . one of the greatest revolutions in the annals of the world—seven States have, within the last three months, thrown off an old Government and formed a new. This revolution has been signally marked, up to this time, by the fact of its having been accomplished without the loss of a single drop of blood. This new Constitution or form of government, constitutes the subject to which your attention will be partly invited. . . .

But not to be tedious in enumerating the numerous changes for the better, allow me to allude to one other—though last, not least: the new Constitution has put at rest *forever* all the agitating questions relating to our peculiar institutions— African slavery as it exists among us—the proper *status of* the negro in our form of civilization. *This was the immediate cause of the late rupture and present revolution.* JEFFERSON, in his forecast, had anticipated this, as the "rock upon which the old Union would split." He was right. What was conjecture with him, is now a realized fact. But whether he fully comprehended the great truth upon which that rock *stood* and *stands*, may be doubted. *The prevailing ideas entertained by him and most of the leading statesmen at the time of the formation of the old Constitution were, that the enslavement of the African was in violation of the laws of nature; that it was wrong in principle, socially, morally, and politically.* It was an evil they knew not well how to deal with; but the general opinion of the men of that day was, that, somehow or other, in the order of Providence, the institution would be evanescent and pass away. This idea, though not incorporated in the Constitution, was the prevailing idea at that time. The Constitution, it is true, secured every essential guarantee to the institution while it should last, and hence no argument can be justly urged against the constitutional guarantees thus secured, because of the common sentiment of the day. *Those ideas, however, were fundamentally wrong. They rested upon the assumption of the equality of races. This was an error.* It was a sandy foundation, and the idea of a Government built upon it—when the "storm came and the wind blew, it *fell.*"

Our new Government is founded upon exactly the opposite ideas; its foundations are laid, its cornerstone rests, upon the great truth that the negro is not equal to the white man; that slavery, subordination to the superior race, is his natural and normal condition. This, our new Government, is the first, in the history of the world, based upon this great physical, philosophical, and moral truth. This truth has been slow in the process of its development, like all other truths in the various departments of science. It is so even amongst us. Many who hear me, perhaps, can recollect well that this truth was not generally admitted, even within their day. The errors of the past generation still clung to many as late as twenty years ago. Those at the North who still cling to these errors with a zeal above knowledge, we justly denominate fanatics. All fanaticism springs from an aberration of the mind; from a defeat in reasoning. It is a species of insanity. One of the most striking characteristics of insanity, in many instances, is, forming correct conclusions from fancied or erroneous premises; so with the *anti-slavery* fanatics: their conclusions are right if their premises are. They assume that the negro is equal, and hence conclude that he is entitled to equal privileges and rights, with the white man. If their premises were correct, their conclusions would be logical and just; but their premises being wrong, their whole argument fails. I recollect once of having heard a gentleman from one of the Northern States, of great power and ability, announce in the House of Representatives, with imposing effect, that we of the South would be compelled, ultimately, to yield upon this subject of slavery; that it was as impossible to war successfully against a principle in politics, as it was in physics or mechanics. That the principle would ultimately prevail. That we, in maintaining slavery as it exists with us, were warring against a principle—a principle founded in nature, the principle of the equality of men. The reply I made to him was, that upon his own grounds we should succeed, and that he and his associates in this crusade against our institutions would ultimately fail. The truth announced, that it was as impossible to war successfully against a principle in politics as well as in physics and mechanics, I admitted, but told him it was he and those acting with him who were warring against a principle. They were attempting to make things equal which the Creator had made unequal.

Source: Henry Cleveland, *Alexander H. Stephens, in Public and Private* (Philadelphia, 1886), 717–29.

The Constitution of the Confederate States of America

On March 11, 1861, the Provisional Congress of the new Confederacy adapted the United States Constitution to reflect its own concerns. Here are some portions of that constitution that differed from the older model. In many places, slavery was explicitly mentioned and protected. Changes also included such modest innovations as single six-year terms for the president and vice-president, a presidential line-item veto on appropriations bills, and the prohibition of tariffs.

Constitution of the Confederate States of America:

We, the people of the Confederate States, each State acting in its sovereign and independent character, in order to form a permanent federal government, establish justice, insure domestic tranquillity, and secure the blessings of liberty to ourselves and our posterity—invoking the favor and guidance of Almighty God—do ordain and establish this Constitution for the Confederate States of America. . . .

Article I.

Sec. 2. 3. Representatives and direct taxes shall be apportioned among the several States, which may be included within this Confederacy, according to their respective numbers, which shall be determined by adding to the whole number of free persons, including those bound to service for a term of years, and excluding Indians not taxed, three-fifths of all slaves. The actual enumeration shall be made within three years after the first meeting of the Congress of the Confederate States, and within every subsequent term of ten years, in such manner as they shall by law direct. The number of Representatives shall not exceed one for every fifty thousand, but each State shall have at least one Representative; and until such enumeration shall be made, the State of South Carolina shall be entitled to choose six; the State of Georgia ten; the State of Alabama nine; the State of Florida two; the State of Mississippi seven; the State of Louisiana six; and the State of Texas six. . . .

SEC. 7. 2. Every bill which shall have passed both Houses, shall, before it becomes a law, be presented to the President of the Confederate States; if he approve, he shall sign it; but if not, he shall return it, with his objections, to that House in which it shall have originated, who shall enter the objections at large on their journal, and proceed to reconsider it. If, after such reconsideration, two-thirds of that House shall agree to pass the bill, it shall be sent, together with the objections, to the other House, by which it shall likewise be reconsidered, and if approved by two-thirds of that House, it shall become a law. But in all such cases, the votes of both Houses shall be determined by yeas and nays, and the names of the persons voting for and against the bill shall be entered on the journal of each House respectively. If any bill shall not be returned by the President within ten days (Sundays excepted) after it shall have been presented to him, the same shall be a law, in like manner as if he had signed it, unless the Congress, by their adjournment, prevent its return; in which case it shall not be a law. The President may approve any appropriation and disapprove any other appropriation in the same bill. In such case he shall, in signing the bill, designate the appropriations disapproved; and shall return a copy of such appropriations, with his objections, to the House in which the bill shall have originated; and the same proceedings shall then be had as in case of other bills disapproved by the President. . . .

SEC. 8. The Congress shall have power—

1. To lay and collect taxes, duties, imposts, and excises for revenue, necessary to pay the debts, provide for the common defense, and carry on the Government of the Confederate States; but no bounties shall be granted from the Treasury; nor shall any duties or taxes on importations from foreign nations be laid to promote or foster any branch of industry; and all duties, imposts, and excises shall be uniform throughout the Confederate States:

2. To borrow money on the credit of the Confederate States:

3. To regulate commerce with foreign nations, and among the several States, and with the Indian tribes; but neither this, nor any other clause contained in the Constitution, shall ever be construed to delegate the power to Congress to appropriate money for any internal improvement intended to facilitate commerce; except for the purpose of furnishing lights, beacons, and buoys, and other aids to navigation upon the coasts, and the improvement of harbors and the removing of obstructions in river navigation; in all which cases such duties shall be laid on the navigation facilitated thereby as may be necessary to pay the costs and expenses thereof:

4. To establish uniform laws of naturalization, and uniform laws on the subject of bankruptcies, throughout the Confederate States; but no law of Congress shall discharge any debt contracted before the passage of the same:

5. To coin money, regulate the value thereof and of foreign coin, and fix the standard of weights and measures:

6. To provide for the punishment of counterfeiting the securities and current coin of the Confederate States:

7. To establish post-offices and post-routes; but the expenses of the Post-Office Department, after the 1st day of March in the year of our Lord eighteen hundred and sixty-three, shall be paid out of its own revenues:

8. To promote the progress of science and useful arts, by securing for limited times to authors and inventors the exclusive right to their respective writings and discoveries:

9. To constitute tribunals inferior to the Supreme Court:

10. To define and punish piracies and felonies committed on the high seas, and offenses against the law of nations:

11. To declare war, grant letters of marque and reprisal, and make rules concerning captures on land and water:

12. To raise and support armies; but no appropriation of money to that use shall be for a longer term than two years:

13. To provide and maintain a navy:

14. To make rules for the government and regulation of the land and naval forces: . . .

SEC. 9. 1. The importation of negroes of the African race, from any foreign country other than the slave-holding States or Territories of the United States of America, is hereby forbidden; and Congress is required to pass such laws as shall effectually prevent the same.

2. Congress shall also have power to prohibit the introduction of slaves from any State not a member of, or Territory not belonging to, this Confederacy.

3. The privilege of the writ of habeas corpus shall not be suspended, unless when in cases of rebellion or invasion the public safety may require it.

4. No bill of attainder, *ex post facto* law, or law denying or impairing the right of property in negro slaves shall be passed. . . .

Article II.

SECTION 1. 1. The executive power shall be vested in a President of the Confederate States of America. He and the Vice-President shall hold their offices for the term of six years; but the President shall not be reeligible. . . .

Article IV.

SEC. 2. 1. The citizens of each State shall be entitled to all the privileges and immunities of citizens in the several States; and shall have the right of transit and sojourn in any State of this Confederacy, with their slaves and other property; and the right of property in said slaves shall not be thereby impaired.

3. No slave or other person held to service or labor in any State or Territory of the Confederate States, under the laws thereof, escaping or lawfully carried into another, shall, in consequence of any law or regulation therein, be discharged from such service or labor; but shall be delivered up on claim of the party to whom such slave belongs, or to whom such service or labor may be due. . . .

3. The Confederate States may acquire new territory; and Congress shall have power to legislate and provide governments for the inhabitants of all territory belonging to the Confederate States, lying without the limits of the several States; and may permit them, at such times, and in such manner as it may by law provide, to form States to be admitted into the Confederacy. In all such territory the institution of negro slavery, as it now exists in the Confederate States, shall be recognized and protected by Congress and by the Territorial government; and the inhabitants of the several Confederate States and Territories shall have the right to take to such Territory any slaves lawfully held by them in any of the States or Territories of the Confederate States. . . .

Adopted unanimously by the Congress of the Confederate States of South Carolina, Georgia, Florida, Alabama, Mississippi, Louisiana and Texas, sitting in convention at the capitol, in the city of Montgomery, Ala., on the eleventh day of March, in the year eighteen hundred and sixty-one.

Source: *OR*, Series IV, vol. 1, 136–47.

General Benjamin F. Butler and General John C. Frémont on Slaves

On July 30, 1861, writing from his post at Fort Monroe, Virginia, the wily Federal political general, Benjamin Franklin Butler, wrote to Secretary of War Simon Cameron, that, unless told to do otherwise, he intended to keep fugitive or captured slaves as a new species of federal property, as "contraband of war," rather than returning them to their masters. A month later, on August 30, John C. Frémont, the Republican candidate for president in 1856, then in charge of the western Union command in St. Louis, confiscated the slave property of rebels and freed them. Fearing a backlash in the Union slave states, Lincoln rescinded the order and fired Frémont. Nonetheless, the actions of these two generals demonstrated that emancipation was now imaginable.

General Butler's "Contrabands"

Head-quarters Department of Virginia, Fortress Monroe, July 30, 1861.

Hon. Simon Cameron, Secretary of War:—

SIR: . . . In the village of Hampton there were a large number of negroes, composed in a great measure of women and children of the men who had fled thither within my lines for protection, who had escaped from maurauding parties of rebels who had been gathering up able-bodied blacks to aid them in constructing their batteries on the James and York Rivers. I have employed the men in Hampton in throwing up intrenchments, and they were working zealously and efficiently at that duty, saving our soldiers from that labor under the gleam of the mid-day sun. The women were earning substantially their own subsistence in washing, marketing, and taking care of the clothes of the soldiers, and rations were being served out to the men who worked for the support of the children. But by the evacuation of Hampton, rendered necessary by the withdrawal of troops, leaving me scarcely 5,000 men outside the Fort, including the force at Newport News, all these black people were obliged to break up their homes at Hampton, fleeing across the creek within my lines for protection and support. Indeed, it was a most distressing sight to see these poor creatures, who had trusted to the protection of the arms of the United States, and who aided the troops of the United States in their enterprise, to be thus obliged to flee from their homes, and the homes of their masters who had deserted them, and become fugitives from fear of the return of the rebel soldiery, who had threatened to shoot the men who had wrought for us, and to carry off the women who had served us, to a worse than Egyptian bondage. I have, therefore, now within the Peninsula, this side of Hampton Creek, 900 negroes, 300 of whom are able-bodied men, 30 of whom are men substantially past hard labor, 175 women, 225 children under the age of 10 years, and 170 between 10 and 18 years, and many more coming in. The questions which this state of facts presents are very embarrassing.

First, What shall be done with them? and, *Second,* What is their state and condition?

Upon these questions I desire the instructions of the Department.

The first question, however, may perhaps be answered by considering the last. Are these men, women, and children, slaves? Are they free? Is their condition that of men, women, and children, or of property, or is it a mixed relation? What their *status* was under the Constitution and laws, we all know. What has been the effect of rebellion and a state of war upon that *status?* When I adopted the theory of treating the able-bodied negro fit to work in the trenches as property liable to be used in aid of rebellion, and so contraband of war, that condition of things was in so far met, as I then and still believe, on a legal and constitutional basis. But now a new series of questions arises. Passing by women, the children, certainly, cannot be treated on that basis; if property, they must be considered the incumbrance rather than the auxiliary of an army, and, of course, in no possible legal relation could be treated as contraband. Are they property? If they were so, they have been left by their masters and owners, deserted, thrown away, abandoned, like the wrecked vessel upon the ocean. Their former possessors and owners have causelessly, traitorously, rebelliously, and, to carry out the figure, practically abandoned them to be swallowed up by the winter storm of starvation. If property, do they not become the property of the salvors? but we, their salvors, do not need and will not hold such property, and will assume no such ownership: has not, therefore, all proprietary relation ceased? Have they not become, thereupon, men, women, and children? No longer under ownership of any kind, the fearful relicts of fugitive masters, have they not by their masters' acts, and the state of war, assumed the condition, which we hold to be the normal one, of those made in God's image? Is not every constitutional, legal, and moral requirement, as well to the runaway master as their relinquished slaves, thus answered? I confess that my own mind is compelled by this reasoning to look upon them as men and women. If not free born, yet free, manumitted, sent forth from the hand that held them never to be reclaimed. . . .

In a loyal State I would put down a servile insurrection. In a state of rebellion I would confiscate that which was used to oppose my arms, and take all that property, which constituted the wealth of that State, and furnished the means by which the war is prosecuted, beside being the cause of the war; and if, in so doing, it should be objected that human beings were brought to the free enjoyment of life, liberty, and the pursuit of happiness, such objection might not require much consideration.

Pardon me for addressing the Secretary of War directly upon this question, as it involves some political considerations as well as propriety of military action. I am, sir, your obedient servant,

Benjamin F. Butler.

Frémont's Proclamation on Slaves

Head-quarters Western Department.

St. Louis, Aug, 30, 1861.

CIRCUMSTANCES in my judgment are of sufficient urgency to render it necessary that the commanding General of this department should assume the administrative powers of the State. Its disorganized condition, helplessness of civil authority and the total insecurity of life, and devastation of property by bands of murderers and marauders, who infest nearly every county in the State, and avail themselves of public misfortunes, in the vicinity of a hostile force, to gratify private and neighborhood vengeance, and who find an enemy wherever they find plunder, finally demand the severest measures to repress the daily increasing crimes and outrages, which are driving off the inhabitants and ruining the State.

In this condition, the public safety and success of our arms require unity of purpose, without let or hindrance to the prompt administration of affairs. In order, therefore, to suppress disorders, maintain the public peace, and give security to the persons and property of loyal citizens, I do hereby extend and declare established martial law throughout the State of Missouri. The lines of the army occupation in this State are for the present declared to extend from Leavenworth, by way of posts of Jefferson City, Rolla, and Ironton, to Cape Girardeau on the Mississippi River. All persons who shall be taken with arms in their hands within these lines shall be tried by court-martial, and if found guilty, will be shot. Real and personal property of those who shall take up arms against the United States, or who shall be directly proven to have taken an active part with their enemies in the field, is declared confiscated to public use, and their slaves, if any they have, are hereby declared free men.

All persons who shall be proven to have destroyed, after the publication of this order, railroad tracks, bridges, or telegraph lines, shall suffer the extreme penalty of the law. All persons engaged in treasonable correspondence, in giving or procuring aid to the enemy, in fermenting turmoil, and disturbing public tranquillity, by creating or circulating false reports, or incendiary documents, are warned that they are exposing themselves.

All persons who have been led away from allegiance, are required to return to their homes forthwith. Any such absence without sufficient cause, will be held to be presumptive evidence against them. The object of this declaration is to place in the hands of military authorities power to give instantaneous effect to the existing laws, and supply such deficiencies as the conditions of the war demands; but it is not intended to suspend the ordinary tribunals of the country, where law will be administered by civil officers in the usual manner, and with their customary authority, while the same can be peaceably administered.

The commanding General will labor vigilantly for the public welfare, and, by his efforts for their safety, hopes to obtain not only acquiescence, but the active support of the people of the country.

J. C. Frémont.
Major-General Commanding.

Source: F. Moore, ed. *The Rebellion Record*, vol. 2, part 2, 33, 437–38.

Frederick Douglass: The War and How to End It

On March 25, 1862, the leading African-American abolitionist, Frederick Douglass, spoke at Corinthian Hall in Rochester, New York, urging Abraham Lincoln and the Congress to make the abolition of slavery the central war aim of the Union. This powerful oration was part of the abolitionist drumbeat that had gained a vast new audience during the first year of the war: Lincoln, the Congress and the soldiers in the field were quite aware of the swelling demand for emancipation.

I stand here to-night to advocate in my humble way, the unrestricted and complete Emancipation of every slave in the United States, whether claimed by loyal or disloyal masters. This is the lesson of the hour.

Through the certain operation of the *changeless laws of the universe,* Emancipation, which has long been a great and solemn national duty, pressing heavily on the national conscience has at last become a great and all commanding national necessity.

I choose not to insist upon these comprehensive propositions as a colored man to-night nor as one having special reasons for hating slavery, although, upon these grounds I might well base a claim to be heard, but my ground is taken as an American citizen, feeling with all others a deep and living interest in the welfare of the whole country.

In the tremendous conflict through which we are passing, all events steadily conspire, to make the cause of the slave and the cause of the country identical. He who to-day fights for Emancipation, fights for his country and free Institutions, and he who fights for slavery, fights against his country and in favor of a slaveholding oligarchy.

This was always so, though only abolitionists perceived the fact. The difference between them and others is this: They got an earlier glimpse at the black heart of slavery—than others did. They saw in times of seeming peace, for the peace we have had, was only seeming—what we can only see in times of open war. They saw that a nation like ours, containing two such opposite forces as liberty and slavery, could not enjoy permanent peace, and they said so and got mobbed for saying so. But let that pass. . . .

The first enquiry which concerned the loyal north upon the sudden outburst of this stupendous rebellion, naturally related to the strength of the rebels, and the amount of force and skill required for their speedy suppression. Even at this vital point we blundered. We misconceived the real state of the case, and misread the facts then passing before us. We were quite incredulous of the tremendous strength and vigor of the foe against whom we were called upon to battle.

We are a charitable people, and in excess of charity were disposed to put the very best construction upon the strange behavior of our southern brethren. We admitted that South Carolina might secede. It was like her to do so. She had talked extravagantly about going out of the union, and she must do something extravagant and startling to save a show of consistency. Georgia too, we thought might possibly go out, but we were quite sure that these twin rebel States, would stand alone in their infamy, and that they would soon tire of their isolation, repent of their folly, and come back to the union. Traitors fled the Cabinet, the House and the Senate, and hastened away to fan the flames of treason at home. Still we doubted that any thing very serious would come of it. We treated it as a bubble or the wave, a nine day's wonder. Calm and thoughtful men ourselves, we relied on the sober second thought of others. Even a shot at one of our ships, an insult offered to our flag, caused only a momentary feeling of indignation and resentment, such as a mother might feel toward a naughty child who had thrown away his bread and stamped defiance at her authority. It was not until Beauregard opened his slave built batteries upon the starving garrison in Charleston harbor, that the confiding North, like a sleeping lion, was roused from his lair, and shook his thundering mane in wrath. We were slow to wake, but we did awake. Still we were scarcely conscious of the skill, power and resources of the enemy. We still hoped that wiser and better counsels would ultimately prevail. We could not believe but that a powerful union sentiment still existed at the South, and that a strong reaction would yet take place there in favor of the union. To the very last we continued to believe in the border States. We could not believe that those States would plunge madly into the bloody vortex of rebellion. It required the assaults of a blood thirsty mob spilling the blood of loyal soldiers to convince us of Baltimore treason.

I need not tell you, how in all this study of passing events, we have been grossly mistaken. Every hope based upon the sanity, loyalty, and good disposition of the South has been woefully disappointed. While armies were forming, and the most formidable preparations were making, we continued to dream of peace, and even after the war was fairly begun, we thought to put down the rebellion by a show of force rather than by an exercise of force. We showed our teeth but did not wish to use them. We preferred to fight with dollars rather than daggers. The fewer battles the better was the motto, popular at Washington, and peace in sixty days trembled along the wires. We now see what we could not at first comprehend.

We are astonished at the strength and vigor of the foe. Treason had shot its poisonous roots deeper, and has spread them farther than our calculations had allowed for.. . .

Even now, you need not go far to find newspapers clinging still to the delusion that there is a strong union sentiment at the South. While the rebels are waging a barbarous war, of unparalleled ferocity, marshalling the savage Indian to the slaughter of your sons, and poisoning the wells in their retreats, we are still speaking of them as our erring brothers, to be won back to the union by fondling, rather than fighting. This has been our great error. We failed to comprehend the vital force of the rebellion. First, because we were dazzled and bewildered by the wild rapidity of the strange events, which burst upon us, and secondly because of our habitual leniency to the South and to slaveholders grimly confronting us at the outset.

I have said that the first question was how to whip the rebels. That was the bitter problem. We were sadly unprepared to fight. Treason had become the warp and woof of the army and navy. . . . The nation was at the mercy of the merciless. How to procure arms, and brave men to use them, was naturally first in order. Like the rod of Moses it swallowed all others. It even hushed the voice of abolitionists and wheeled them into line with its imperative demands.

It was the great physical question. Men of muscle understood it as well as men of mind. But now there is another and a mightier question destined to try men's souls the more severely than the first.

For not that which is spiritual is first, but that which is natural; after that, that which is spiritual. The physical part of this tremendous conflict is at last in a hopeful way. The great armies of the North are in motion. Baltimore is at the mercy of McHenry, Western Virginia clings to the union, Kentucky is no longer neutral, Missouri has gone to Arkansas. North Carolina is invaded, Florida has followed the fortunes of Bragg, and Tennessee is under Foote.

Brave hearts and strong hands, have met and disposed of the first question. I knew they would from the first. The slaveholding rebels have fought, and have fought well, and will do so again. They are proud, brave and desperate, but proud, brave and desperate as they are, I tell no secret when I say, they can run as well as they fight.

General McClellan in his recent address to his army—takes pains to compliment these traitors. He is "sad" at the thought of striking them. The traitors themselves show no such weakness. The language of their Generals is altogether of another character. There is no epithet too vile for them, by which to characterize our army. But McClellan, is careful to tell us that the Southern army is composed of foemen worthy of our steel. I do not like this. It looks bad. Instead of being foemen worthy of our steel, they are rebels and traitors worthy of our hemp.

I do not wonder that all the haters of Impartial Liberty at the North are especially devoted to this "sad" reluctant General, who instead of portraying the baseness of the traitors takes pains to compliment them. It is seriously doubted if he will ever try his steel upon them. Thus far he has entirely failed to do any thing of the sort. But, whether McClellan ever overtakes the rebels or not, the army of the Potomac has moved, and brave men sweep both the Eastern and Western border of the rebellion. So that I look upon the first question, the question as to how to break down the military power of the rebels as in good hands and the public mind is happily relieved at that point.

But now a higher and more important problem presses for consideration. It is a problem for statesmen rather than Generals. Soldiers can capture a State, but statesmen must govern a State. It is sometimes hard to pull down a house but it is always harder to build one up.

This is the question now to be decided, having broken down the rebel power in the seceded States, how shall we extend the Constitution and the Union over them? We know how to make war, we know how to conquer, but the question is do we know how to make peace? We can whip the South, but can we make the South loyal? . . . The fact is the South hates the north. It hates the Union. The feeling is genuine and all-pervading. Whence comes this hate? This is an imperative inquiry for statesmen, who would place the peace of this government on an immovable foundation. You are of the same race, the same language, the same sacred historic memories. Why do they hate you? Certainly not because you have been in any manner ungenerous or unjust to them. Why do they hate you? Is it because they are naturally worse than other men? Not at all. I hold that the slaveholder is just as good as his slave system will allow him to be. If I were a slaveholder, and was determined to remain such, I would equal the worst, both in cruelty to the slave and in hatred to the north. I should hate the declaration of Independence, hate the Constitution, hate the Golden rule, hate free schools, free speech, free press, and every other form of freedom. Because in them all, I should see an enemy to my claim of property in man. I should see that the whole North is a point blank and killing condemnation of all my pretensions. The real root of bitterness, that which has generated this intense Southern hate toward the North, is Slavery. Here is the stone of stumbling and the rock of offence. Once I felt it necessary to argue this point. The time for such argument has past. Slavery stands confessed as the grand cause of the war. It has drilled every rebel solider, loaded, primed, aimed and fired every rebel cannon since the war began. No other interest, commercial, manufacturing or political, could have wrought such a social earthquake amongst us. It has within itself that which begets a character in all around it favorable to its own continuance. It makes slaves of the negroes, vassals of the poor whites and tyrants of the masters. Pride, injustice, ingratitude, lust of dominion, cruelty, scorn, and contempt are the qualities of this rebellion, and slavery breeds them all. The tyrant wants no law above his own will, no associates but men of his own stamp of baseness. He is willing to administer the laws when he can bend them to his will, but he will break them when he can no longer bend them. Where labor is performed under the lash, justice will be administered under the bowie knife. The south is in this respect just what slavery has made her. She has been breeding thieves, rebels and traitors, and this stupendous conflict is the result. She could not do otherwise and cherish slavery in the midst of her.

Now the great question is what shall be the conditions of peace? What shall be done with slavery? We have gradually drifted to this vital question. Slavery is the pivot on which turns all the machinery of this tremendous war, and upon it will depend the character of the future of our peace or want of it.

It is really wonderful how we have been led along towards this grand issue, and how all efforts to evade, postpone, and prevent its coming, have been mocked and defied by the stupendous sweep of events.

It was oracularly given out from Washington many months ago, that whether this rebellion should succeed or fail, the status of no man in the country would be changed by the result. You know what that meant. Europe knew what that meant. It was an assurance given to the world in general, and the slaveholding states in particular, that no harm should come to slavery in the prosecution of the war for the Union. It was a last bid for a compromise with the rebels. But despite of diplomatic disclaimers, despite border State influence, despite the earlier proclamation of the President himself, the grand question of Emancipation now compels attention and the most thoughtful consideration of men in high places of the nation.

By the events of this war, Washington has become to the nation what Syracuse was to the State of New York after the rescue of Jerry, the grand centre for abolition meetings. A new Congress has assembled there.

Dr. Cheever, Ralph Waldo Emerson, Gerrit Smith, Wendell Phillips, William Goodell and William Lloyd Garrison may now utter in safety their opinions on slavery in the national capital. Meanwhile Congress has a bill before it for the abolition of slavery in the District of Columbia. Kill slavery at the heart of the nation, and it will certainly die at the extremities. Down with it there, and it is the brick knocked down at the end of the row by which the whole line is prostrate.

More and better, the infernal business of slave catching by our army in Missouri and on the Potomac, is at last peremptorily forbidden under penalty of dismissal from the service. This looks small, but is not so. It is a giant stride toward the grand result.

I thank all the powers of earth and sky, that I am permitted to be a witness to this day's events. That slavery could always live and flourish in this country I have always known to be a foul and guilty heresy. That the vile system must eventually go down I have never doubted, even in the darkest days of my life in slavery. But that I should live to see the President of the United States deliberately advocating Emancipation was more than I ever ventured to hope.

It is true that the President lays down his propositions with many qualifications some of which to my thinking, are unnecessary, unjust and wholly unwise. There are spots on the Sun. A blind man can see where the President's heart is. I read the spaces as well as the lines of that message, I see in them a brave man trying against great odds, to do right. An honest patriot endeavoring to save his country in its day of peril. It is the first utterance, and first utterances are not according to Carlyle the most articulate and perfect. Time and practice will improve the President as they improve other men. He is tall and strong but he is not done growing, he grows as the nation grows. He has managed to say one good word, and to say it so distinctly that all the world may hear. He has dared to say that the highest interest of the country will be promoted by the abolition of slavery. And this, bear in mind, is not said in the bitterness of defeat, but when every morning brought news of glorious victories over the slaveholding rebels. The message comes at the call of no desperation. The time selected for sending it to Congress and the nation must be read with the document itself in order to appreciate its true significance. . . .

But what shall be the conditions of peace? How shall the Union be reconstructed? To my mind complete Emancipation is the only basis of permanent peace. Any other basis will place us just at the point from which we started. To leave slavery standing in the rebel States, is to leave the eggs of treason in the nest from whence we shall have to meet a larger brood of traitors, and rebels at another time; it is to transmit to posterity the question that ought to be settled to-day. Leave slavery where it is, and you leave the same generator of hate towards the north which has already cost us rivers of blood and millions of treasure. Leave slavery in the south and it will be as dangerous for a Northern man to travel in the south, as for a man to enter a powder magazine with fire. Despots are suspicious, and every slaveholder is an unmitigated despot, a natural foe to every form of freedom. Leave slavery in the south, and you will fill the north with a full fledged breed of servile panderers to slavery, baser than all their predecessors.

Leave slavery where it is and you will hereafter, as heretofore, see in politics a divided, fettered, north, and an united south. You will see the statesmen of the country facing both ways, speaking two languages, assenting to the principles of freedom in the north, and bowing to the malign spirit and practices of slavery at the South. You will see all the pro-slavery elements of the country attracted to the south, giving that section ascendancy again in the counsels of the nation and making them masters of the destinies of the Republic. Restore slavery to its old status in the Union and the same elements of demoralization which have plunged this country into this tremendous war will begin again to dig the grave of free Institutions.

It is the boast of the South that her Institutions are peculiar and homogeneous, and so they are. Her statesmen have had the wit to see that contact with the free North must either make the North like herself, or that she herself must become like the North. They are right. The South must put off the yoke of slavery or the North must prepare her neck for that yoke, provided the union is restored. There is a middle path—We have pursued that middle path. It is *compromise* and by it we have reached the point of civil war with all its horrid consequences. The question is shall we start anew in the same old path?

Who wants a repetition of the same event thro' which we are passing? Who wants to see the nation taxed to keep a standing army in the South to maintain respect for the Federal Government and protect the rights of citizens of the United States? To such a man I say, leave slavery still dominant at the South and you shall have all your wants supplied.

On the other hand abolish slavery and the now disjointed nation like kindred drops would speedily mingle into one. Abolish slavery and the last hinderance to a solid nationality is abolished. Abolish slavery and you give conscience a chance to grow, and you will win the respect and admiration of mankind. Abolish slavery and you put an end to all sectional politics founded upon conflicting sectional interests, and imparting strife and bitterness to all our general elections, and to the debates on the floor of Congress. Abolish slavery and the citizens of each state will be regarded and treated as equal citizens of the United States, and may travel unchallenged and unmolested in all the states of the Union. Abolish slavery and you put an end to sectional religion and morals, and establish free speech and liberty of conscience throughout your common country. Abolish slavery and rational, law abiding Liberty will fill the whole land with peace, joy, and permanent safety now and forever.

Source: *Douglass' Monthly.* IV. (April. 1862). 624–26.

The Emancipation Proclamation

On July 22, 1862, Abraham Lincoln drafted a preliminary emancipation proclamation, but he waited until September 22, after the battle of Antietam, to issue the decree. Believing that he lacked constitutional authority to abolish slavery in Union states, Lincoln extended the decree only to slaves of those states in rebellion. Nevertheless, this promulgation heightened the meaning of the war by making abolition as well as the reunification of the nation an explicit goal of the Union effort.

By the President of the United States of America:

A Proclamation.

Whereas on the 22d day of September, A.D. 1862, a proclamation was issued by the President of the United States, containing, among other things, the following, to wit:

"That on the 1st day of January, A.D. 1863, all persons held as slaves within any State or designated part of a State the people whereof shall then be in rebellion against the United States shall be then, thenceforward, and forever free; and the executive government of the United States, including the military and naval authority thereof, will recognize and maintain the freedom of such persons and will do no act or acts to repress such persons, or any of them, in any efforts they may make for their actual freedom.

"That the executive will on the 1st day of January aforesaid, by proclamation, designate the States and parts of States, if any, in which the people thereof, respectively, shall then be in rebellion against the United States; and the fact that any State or the people thereof shall on that day be in good faith represented in the Congress of the United States by members chosen thereto at elections wherein a majority of the qualified voters of such States shall have participated shall, in the absence of strong countervailing testimony, be deemed conclusive evidence that such State and the people thereof are not then in rebellion against the United States."

Now, therefore, I, Abraham Lincoln, President of the United States, by virtue of the power in me vested as Commander-in-Chief of the Army and Navy of the United States in time of actual armed rebellion against the authority and government of the United States, and as a fit and necessary war measure for suppressing said rebellion, do, on this 1st day of January, A.D. 1863, and in accordance with my purpose so to do, publicly proclaimed for the full period of one hundred days from the first day above mentioned, order and designate as the States and parts of States wherein the people thereof, respectively, are this day in rebellion against the United States the following, to wit:

Arkansas, Texas, Louisiana (except the parishes of St. Bernard, Plaquemines, Jefferson, St. John, St. Charles, St. James, Ascension, Assumption, Terrebone, Lafourche, St. Mary, St. Martin, and Orleans, including the city of New Orleans), Mississippi, Alabama, Florida, Georgia, South Carolina, North Carolina, and Virginia (except the forty-eight counties designated as West Virginia, and also the counties of Berkeley, Accomac, Northhampton, Elizabeth City, York, Princess Anne, and Norfolk, including the cities of Norfolk and Portsmouth), and which excepted parts are for the present left precisely as if this proclamation were not issued.

And by virtue of the power and for the purpose aforesaid, I do order and declare that all persons held as slaves within said designated States and parts of States are, and henceforward shall be, free; and that the Executive Government of the United States, including the military and naval authorities thereof, will recognize and maintain the freedom of said persons.

And I hereby enjoin upon the people so declared to be free to abstain from all violence, unless in necessary self-defense; and I recommend to them that, in all cases when allowed, they labor faithfully for reasonable wages.

And I further declare and make known that such persons of suitable condition will be received into the armed service of the United States to garrison forts, positions, stations, and other places, and to man vessels of all sorts in said service.

And upon this act, sincerely believed to be an act of justice, warranted by the Constitution upon military necessity, I invoke the considerate judgment of mankind and the gracious favor of Almighty God.

Source: *U.S. Statutes at Large.* 1862. Vol. XII. 1268-69.

The Gettysburg Address

On November 19, 1863, four and one-half months after the bloody victory that had turned the Confederate invaders back from Pennsylvania, President Lincoln traveled by train to Gettysburg, to help consecrate a vast new Union cemetery. With his economical eloquence, Lincoln underlined the higher, democratic, moral principles he believed the Union war effort embodied, by effectively tying the cause of republican government to the abolition of slavery.

Four score and seven years ago our fathers brought forth on this continent, a new nation, conceived in Liberty, and dedicated to the proposition that all men are created equal.

Now we are engaged in a great civil war, testing whether that nation, or any nation so conceived and so dedicated, can long endure. We are met on a great battle-field of that war. We have come to dedicate a portion of that field, as a final resting place for those who here gave their lives that that nation might live. It is altogether fitting and proper that we should do this.

But, in a larger sense, we can not dedicate—we can not consecrate—we cannot hallow—this ground. The brave men, living and dead, who struggled here, have consecrated it, far above our poor power to add or detract. The world will little note, nor long remember what we say here, but it can never forget what they did here. It is for us the living, rather, to be dedicated here to the unfinished work which they who fought here have thus far so nobly advanced. It is rather for us to be here dedicated to the great task remaining before us—that from these honored dead we take increased devotion to that cause for which they gave the last full measure of devotion—that we here highly resolve that these dead shall not have died in vain—that this nation, under God, shall have a new birth of freedom—and that government of the people, by the people, for the people, shall not perish from the earth.

Source: Basler, VII, 23.

The Republican and Democratic Electoral Platforms of 1864, and George B. McClellan's Acceptance Letter

The 1864 Federal election was a referendum on the continuation of the Union war effort. Republicans pledged to stay the course until the unconditional surrender of the South, and offered support for a constitutional amendment abolishing slavery everywhere. In the meantime, antiwar forces, having captured control of the Democrat's platform process, declared the war a failure, and demanded an immediate cease-fire followed by a negotiated peace. In his letter accepting the Democratic presidential nomination, former general George B. McClellan showed that he did not wholly support such a unilateral antiwar position, but neither did he make it clear that he would prosecute the war until victory.

The Republican Platform

RESOLVED. That it is the highest duty of every American citizen to maintain against all their enemies the integrity of the Union, and the paramount authority of the Constitution and laws of the United States; and that, laying aside all differences of political opinion, we pledge ourselves as Union men, animated by a common sentiment and aiming at a common object, to do everything in our power to aid the government in quelling by force of arms the rebellion now raging against its authority, and in bringing to the punishment due to their crimes the rebels and traitors arrayed against it.

RESOLVED. That we approve the determination of the government of the United States not to compromise with rebels, or to offer them any terms of peace except such as may be based upon an unconditional surrender of their hostility and a return to their just allegiance to the Constitution and laws of the United States; and that we call upon the government to maintain this position, and to prosecute the war with the utmost possible vigor to the complete suppression of the rebellion, in full reliance upon the self-sacrificing patriotism, the heroic valor, and the undying devotion of the American people and its free institutions.

RESOLVED. That, as slavery was the cause and now constitutes the strength of this rebellion, and as it must be, always and everywhere, hostile to the principles of republican government, justice and the national safety demand its utter and complete extirpation from the soil of the republic; and that, while we uphold and maintain the acts and proclamations by which the government, in its own defense, had aimed a deathblow at this gigantic evil, we are in favor, furthermore, of such amendment to the Constitution, to be made by the people in conformity with its provisions, as shall terminate and forever prohibit the existence of slavery within the limits of the jurisdiction of the United States.

RESOLVED. That the thanks of the American people are due to the soldiers and sailors of the army and navy who have periled their lives in defense of the country and in vindication of the honor of its flag; that the nation owes to them some permanent recognition of their patriotism and their valor, and ample and permanent provision for those of their survivors who have received disabling and honorable wounds in the service of the country; and that the memories of those who have fallen in its defense shall be held in grateful and everlasting remembrance.

RESOLVED. That we approve and applaud the practical wisdom, and unselfish patriotism and the unswerving fidelity with which Abraham Lincoln has discharged, under circumstances of unparalleled difficulty, the great duties and responsibilities of the presidential office; that we approve and indorse [sic], as demanded by the emergency and essential to the preservation of the nation and as within the provisions of the Constitution, the measures and acts which he has adopted to defend the nation against its open and secret foes; that we approve, especially, the proclamation of emancipation and the employment as Union soldiers of men heretofore held in slavery; and that we have full confidence in his determination to carry these and all other constitutional measures essential to the salvation of the country into full and complete effect.

RESOLVED. That we deem it essential to the general welfare that harmony should prevail in the national councils, and we regard as worth of public confidence and official trust those only who cordially indorse [sic] the principles proclaimed in these resolutions, and which should characterize the administration of the government.

RESOLVED. That the government owes to all men employed in its armies, without regard to distinction of color, the full protection of the laws of war; and that any violation of these laws, or of the usage of civilized nations in time of war, by the rebels now in arms, should be made the subject of prompt and full redress.

RESOLVED. That foreign immigration, which in the past has added so much to the wealth, development of resources, and increase of power to this nation,—the asylum of the oppressed of all nations,—should be fostered and encouraged by a liberal and just policy.

RESOLVED. That we are in favor of the speedy construction of the railroad to the Pacific coast.

RESOLVED. That the national faith, pledged for the redemption of the public debt, must be kept inviolate, and that for this purpose we recommend economy and rigid responsibility in the public expenditures, and a vigorous and just system of taxation; and that it is the duty of every loyal State to sustain the credit and promote the use of the national currency.

RESOLVED. That we approve the position taken by the government, that the people of the United States can never regard with indifference the attempt of any European power to overthrow by force, or to supplant by fraud, the institutions of any republican government on the Western Continent; and that they will view with extreme jealousy, as menacing to the peace and independence of their own country, the efforts of any such power to maintain new footholds for monarchical government, sustained by foreign military force, in near proximity to the United States.

The Democratic Platform

RESOLVED. That in the future, as in the past, we will adhere with unswerving fidelity to the Union under the Constitution as the only solid foundation of our strength, security, and happiness as a people, and as a framework of government equally conducive to the prosperity of all the States, both Northern and Southern.

RESOLVED. That this convention does explicitly declare, as the sense of the American people that after four years of failure to restore the Union by the experiment of war, during which, under the pretense of a military necessity of war-power higher than the Constitution itself has been disregarded in every part, and public liberty and private right alike trodden down, and the material prosperity of the country essentially impaired, justice, humanity, liberty, and public welfare demand that immediate efforts be made for a cessation of hostilities, with a view of an ultimate convention of the States, or other peaceable means, to the end that, at the earliest practicable moment, peace may be restored on the basis of the Federal Union of the States.

RESOLVED. That the direct interference of the military authorities of the United States in the recent elections held in Kentucky, Maryland, Missouri, and Delaware was a shameful violation of the Constitution, and a repetition of such acts in the approaching election will be held as revolutionary, and resisted with all the means and power under our control.

RESOLVED. That the aim and object of the Democratic party is to preserve the Federal Union and the rights of the States unimpaired, and they hereby declare that they consider that the administrative usurpation of extraordinary and dangerous powers not granted by the Constitution—the subversion of the civil by military law in States not in insurrection; the arbitrary military arrest, imprisonment, trial, and sentence of American citizens in States where civil law exists in full force; the suppression of freedom of speech and of the press; the denial of the right of asylum; the open and avowed disregard of State rights; the employment of unusual test-oaths; and the interference with and denial of the right of the people to bear arms in their defense is calculated to prevent a restoration of the Union and the perpetuation of a Government deriving its just powers from the consent of the governed.

RESOLVED. That the shameful disregard of the Administration to its duty in respect to our fellow citizens who now are and long have been prisoners of war and in a suffering condition, deserves the severest reprobation on the score alike of public policy and common humanity.

RESOLVED. That the sympathy of the Democratic party is heartily and earnestly extended to the soldiery of our army and sailors of our navy, who are and have been in the field and on the sea under the flag of our country, and in the events of its attaining power, they will receive all the care, protection, and regard that the brave soldiers and sailors of the republic have so nobly deserved.

McClellan's Acceptance Letter
To the Democratic Nomination Committee
Orange, New Jersey Sept 8, 1864

Gentlemen:

I have the honor to acknowledge the receipt of your letter informing me of my nomination by the Democratic National Convention, recently assembled at Chicago, as their candidate, at the next election, for President of the United States.

It is unnecessary for me to say to you that this nomination comes to me unsought. [Crossed out: Since the record of my public life has been open to the world, I assume that that record was kept in view.] I am happy to know that when the nomination was made the record of my public life was kept in view. The effect of long and varied service in the Army, during war and peace, has been to strengthen and make indelible in my mind and heart the love and reverence for the Union, Constitution, Laws and Flag of our country impressed upon me in early youth.

These feelings have thus far guided the course of my life, and must continue to do so to its end.

The existence of more than one Government over the region which once owned our flag is incompatible with the peace, the power, and the happiness of the people.

The preservation of our Union was the sole avowed object of which the war was commenced.

It should have been conducted for that object only, and in accordance with those principles which I took occasion to declare when in [crossed out: command of armies, and especially in my letter to the President from Harrison's Landing.] active service. Thus conducted, the work of reconciliation would have been easy, and we might have reaped the benefits of our many victories on land and sea.

The Union was originally formed by the exercise of a spirit of conciliation and compromise.

To restore and preserve it the same spirit must prevail in our Councils, and in the hearts of the people. The reestablishment of the Union in all its integrity is, and must continue to be, the indispensable condition in any settlement [crossed out: of the questions at issue in this war]. So soon as it is clear, or even possible, that our present adversaries are ready for peace upon the basis of the Union, we should exhaust all the resources of statesmanship practiced by civilized nations, and taught by the traditions of the American people, consistent with the honor and interests of the country, to secure such peace, reestablish the Union, and guarantee for the future the Constitutional rights of every State. The Union is [crossed out: our only] the one condition of peace. We ask no more.

Let me add what I doubt not was, although unexpressed, the sentiment of the Convention, as it is of the people they represent, that when any one State is willing to return to the Union, it should be received at once, with a full guarantee of all its Constitutional rights.

But if a frank, earnest and persistent effort to achieve these objects should fail, [crossed out: it will be necessary to insist upon the preservation of the Union at all hazards, and] the responsibility for ulterior consequences will fall upon those who remain in arms against the Union. But the Union must be preserved at all hazards. I could not look in the face of my gallant comrades of the Army and Navy, who have survived so many bloody battles, and tell them that their labors, and the sacrifice of so many of our slain and wounded brethren had been in vain—that we had abandoned that Union for which we have so often perilled our lives.

A vast majority of our people, whether in the Army and Navy or at home, would, as I would, hail with unbounded joy the permanent restoration of peace, on the basis of the Union under the Constitution, without the effusion of another drop of blood. But no peace can be permanent without Union.

As to the other subjects presented in the resolutions of the Convention, I need only say that I should seek in the Constitution of the United States, and the laws framed in accordance therewith, the rule of my duty and the limitations of executive power,—endeavor to restore economy in public expenditure, reestablish the supremacy of law, [crossed out: and assert for our country and people that commanding position to which our history & our principles entitle us among the nations of the world.] & by the assertion of a more vigorous nationality reserve our commanding position among the nations of the Earth. The condition of our finances, the depreciation of the paper currency, and the burdens thus imposed on labor, [crossed out: industry] & capital show the necessity of a return to a sound financial system; while the rights of citizens and the rights of States, and the binding authority of law over President, Army and people are subjects of not less vital importance in war than in peace. Believing that the views here expressed are those of the Convention and the people you represent, I accept the nomination.

I realize the weight of the responsibility to be borne should the people ratify your choice.

Conscious of my own weakness, I can only seek fervently the guidance of the Ruler of the Universe, and, relying on His all-powerful aid, do my best to restore Union and Peace to a suffering people, and to establish and guard their liberties and rights.

Geo B McClellan.

Source: Porter and Johnson, 34–36.

William T. Sherman on the Inner Meaning of War

Following his capture of Atlanta, on September 2, 1864, the ferocious and articulate Union commander in the West, William Tecumseh Sherman, corresponded with John Bell Hood, the Confederate general opposing him, and with the mayor and city council of Atlanta. In this heated exchange, stemming from his order to banish the civilian population of Atlanta, Sherman made it clear that the war against the Confederacy extended to the entire rebel population. He intended such action and such propaganda to encourage northerners while it impoverished and demoralized southern civilians, thus leading them to discourage the citizen-soldiers and to capitulate sooner rather than later.

Hdqrs. Military Division of the Mississippi,

In the Field, Atlanta, Ga., September 7, 1864.

General Hood, Commanding Confederate Army:

General: I have deemed it to the interest of the United States that the citizens now residing in Atlanta should remove, those who prefer it to go south and the rest north. For the latter I can provide food and transportation to points of their election in Tennessee, Kentucky, or farther north. For the former I can provide transportation by cars as far as Rough and Ready, and also wagons; but that their removal may be made with as little discomfort as possible it will be necessary for you to help the families from Rough and Ready to the cars at Lovejoy's. If you consent I will undertake to remove all families in Atlanta who prefer to go South to Rough and Ready, with all their movable effects, viz, clothing, trunks, reasonable furniture, bedding, &c., with their servants, white and black, with the proviso that no force shall be used toward the blacks one way or the other. If they want to go with their masters or mistresses they may do so, otherwise they will be sent away, unless they be men, when they may be employed by our quartermaster. Atlanta is no place for families or non-combatants, and I have no desire to send them North if you will assist in conveying them South. If this proposition meets your views I will consent to a truce in the neighborhood of Rough and Ready, stipulating that any wagons, horses, or animals, or persons sent there for the purposes herein stated shall in no manner be harmed or molested, you in your turn agreeing that any cars, wagons, carriages, persons, or animals sent to the same point shall not be interfered with. Each of us might send a guard of, say, 100 men, to maintain order and limit the truce to, say, two days after a certain time appointed. I have authorized the mayor to choose two citizens to convey to you this letter and such documents as the mayor may forward in explanation, and shall await your reply.

I have the honor to be, your obedient servant,

W. T. Sherman.
Major-General. Commanding.

Hdqrs. Army of Tennessee, Office Chief of Staff,

September 9, 1864.

Maj. Gen. W. T. Sherman,
Commanding U.S. Forces in Georgia:

General: Your letter of yesterday's date [7th] borne by James M. Ball and James R. Crew, citizens of Atlanta, is received. You say therein "I deem it to be to the interest of the United States that the citizens now residing in Atlanta should remove," &c. I do not consider that I have any alternative in this matter. I therefore accept your proposition to declare a truce of two days, or such time as may be necessary to accomplish the purpose mentioned, and shall render all assistance in my power to expedite the transportation of citizens in this direction. I suggest that a staff officer be appointed by you to superintend the removal from the city to Rough and Ready, while I appoint a like officer to control their removal farther south; that a guard of 100 men be sent by either party, as you propose, to maintain order at that place, and that the removal begin on Monday next. And now, sir, permit me to say that the unprecedented measure you propose transcends, in studied and ingenious cruelty, all acts ever before brought to my attention in the dark history of war. In the name of God and humanity I protest, believing that you will find that you are expelling from their homes and firesides the wives and children of a brave people.

I am, general, very respectfully, your obedient servant,

J. B. Hood.
General.

Hdqrs. Military Division of the Mississippi,

In the Field, Atlanta, Ga., September 10, 1864.

General J. B. Hood, C.S. Army, Comdg. Army of Tennessee:

General: I have the honor to acknowledge the receipt of your letter of this date [9th], at the hands of Messrs. Ball and Crew, consenting to the arrangements I had proposed to facilitate the removal south of the people of Atlanta who prefer to go in that direction. I inclose you a copy of my orders, which will, I am satisfied, accomplish my purpose perfectly. You style the measure proposed "unprecedented," and appeal to the dark history of war for a parallel as an act of "studied and ingenious cruelty." It is not unprecedented, for General Johnston himself, very wisely and properly, removed the families all the way from Dalton down, and I see no reason why Atlanta should be excepted. Nor is it necessary to appeal to the dark history of war when recent and modern examples are so handy. You, yourself, burned dwelling-houses along your parapet, and I have seen to-day fifty houses that you have rendered uninhabitable because they stood in the way of your forts and men. You defended Atlanta on a line so close to town that every cannon shot and many musket shots from our line of investment that overshot their mark went into the habitations of women and children. General Hardee did the same at Jonesborough, and General Johnston did the same last summer at Jackson, Miss. I have not accused you of heartless cruelty, but merely instance these cases of very recent occurrence, and could go on and enumerate hundreds of others and challenge any fair man to judge which of us has the heart of pity for the families of a "brave people." I say that it is kindness to these families of Atlanta to remove them now at once from scenes that women and children should not be exposed to, and the "brave people" should scorn to commit their wives and children to the rude barbarians who thus, as you say, violate the laws of war, as illustrated in the pages of its dark history. In the name of common sense I ask you not to appeal to a just God in such a sacrilegious manner; you who, in the midst of peace and prosperity, have plunged a nation into war, dark and cruel war; who dared and badgered us to battle, insulted our flag, seized our arsenals and forts that were left in the honorable custody of peaceful ordnance sergeants; seized and made "prisoners of war" the very garrisons sent to protect your people against negroes and Indians long before any overt act was committed by the, to you, hated Lincoln Government; tried to force Kentucky and Missouri into rebellion, spite of themselves; falsified the vote of Louisiana, turned loose your privateers to plunder unarmed ships; expelled Union families by the thousands; burned their houses and declared by an act of your Congress the confiscation of all debts due Northern men for goods had and received. Talk thus to the marines, but not to me, who have seen these things, and who will this day make as much sacrifice for the peace and honor of the South as the best born Southerner among you. If we must be enemies, let us be men and fight it out, as we propose to do, and not deal in such hypocritical appeals to God and humanity. God will judge us in due time, and He will pronounce whether it be more humane to fight with a town full of women, and the families of "a brave people" at our back, or to remove them in time to places of safety among their own friends and people.

W. T. Sherman.
Major-General. Commanding.

Atlanta, Ga., September 11, 1864.

Maj. Gen. W. T. Sherman:

Sir: We, the undersigned, mayor and two of the council for the city of Atlanta, for the time being the only legal organ of the people of the said city to express their wants and wishes, ask leave most earnestly, but respectfully, to petition you to reconsider the order requiring them to leave Atlanta. At first view it struck us that the measure would involve extraordinary hardship and loss, but since we have seen the practical execution of it so far as it has progressed, and the individual condition of the people, and heard their statements as to the inconveniences, loss, and suffering attending it, we are satisfied that the amount of it will involve in the aggregate consequences appalling and heart-rending. Many poor women are in advanced state of pregnancy; others now having young children, and whose husbands, for the greater part, are either in the army, prisoners, or dead. Some say, "I have such an one sick at my house; who will wait on them when I am gone?" Others say, "what are we to do? We have no house to go to, and no means to buy, build, or rent any; no parents, relatives, or friends to go to." Another says, "I will try and take this or that article of property, but such and such things I must leave behind, though I need them much." We reply to them, "General Sherman will carry your property to Rough and Ready, and General Hood will take it thence on," and they will reply to that, "but I want to leave the railroad at such a place and cannot get conveyance from there on."

We only refer to a few facts to try to illustrate in part how this measure will operate in practice. As you advanced the people north of this fell back, and before your arrival here a large portion of the people had retired south, so that the country south of this is already crowded and without houses enough to accommodate the people, and we are informed that many are now staying in churches and other outbuildings. This being so, how is it possible for the people still here (mostly women and children) to find any shelter? And how can they live through the winter in the woods? No shelter or subsistence, in the midst of strangers who know them not, and without the power to assist them much, if they were willing to do so. This is but a feeble picture of the consequences of this measure. You know the woe, the horrors and the suffering cannot be described by words; imagination can only conceive of it, and we ask you to take these things into consideration. We know your mind and time are constantly occupied with the duties of your command, which almost deters us from asking your attention to this matter, but thought it might be that you had not considered this subject in all of its awful consequences, and that on more reflection you, we hope, would not make this people an exception to all mankind, for we know of no such instance ever having occurred; surely none such in the United States, and what has this helpless people done, that they should be driven from their homes to wander strangers and outcasts and exiles, and to subsist on charity? We do not know as yet the number of people still here; of those who are here, we are satisfied a respectable number, if allowed to remain at home, could subsist for several months without assistance, and a respectable number for a much longer time, and who might not need assistance at any time. In conclusion, we most earnestly and solemnly petition you to reconsider this order, or modify it, and suffer this unfortunate people to remain at home and enjoy what little means they have.

Respectfully submitted.

James M. Calhoun.
Mayor.
E. E. Rawson.
S. C. Wells.
Councilmen.

Hdqrs. Military Division of the Mississippi,

In the Field, Atlanta, Ga., September 12, 1864.

James M. Calhoun, *Mayor,*

E. E. Rawson, and

S. C. Wells,

Representing City Council of Atlanta:

Gentlemen: I have your letter of the 11th, in the nature of a petition to revoke my orders removing all the inhabitants from Atlanta. I have read it carefully, and give full credit to your statements of the distress that will be occasioned by it, and yet shall not revoke my orders, simply because my orders are not designed to meet the humanities of the case, but to prepare for the future struggles in which millions of good people outside of Atlanta have a deep interest. We must have peace, not only in Atlanta but in all America. To secure this we must stop the war that now desolates our once happy and favored country. To stop war we must defeat the rebel armies that are arrayed against the laws and Constitution, which all must respect and obey. To defeat these armies we must prepare the way to reach them in their recesses provided with the arms and instruments which enable us to accomplish our purpose. Now, I know the vindictive nature of our enemy, and that we may have many years of military operations from this quarter, and therefore deem it wise and prudent to prepare in time. The use of Atlanta for warlike purposes is inconsistent with its character as a home for families. There will be no manufactures, commerce, or agriculture here for the maintenance of families, and sooner or later want will compel the inhabitants to go. Why not go now, when all the arrangements are completed for the transfer, instead of waiting till the plunging shot of contending armies will renew the scenes of the past month? Of course, I do not apprehend any such thing at this moment, but you do not suppose this army will be here until the war is over. I cannot discuss this subject with you fairly, because I cannot impart to you what I propose to do, but I assert that my military plans make it necessary for the inhabitants to go away, and I can only renew my offer of services to make their exodus in any direction as easy and comfortable as possible. You cannot qualify war in harsher terms than I will. War is cruelty and you cannot refine it, and those who brought war into our country deserve all the curses and maledictions a people can pour out. I know I had no hand in making this war, and I know I will make more sacrifices to-day than any of you to secure peace. But you cannot have peace and a division of our country. If the United States submits to a division now it will not stop, but will go on until we reap the fate of Mexico, which is eternal war. The United States does and must assert its authority wherever it once had power. If it relaxes one bit to pressure it is gone, and I know that such is the national feeling. This feeling assumes various shapes, but always comes back to that of Union. Once admit the Union, once more acknowledge the authority of the National Government, and instead of devoting your houses and streets and roads to the dread uses of war I and this army become at once your protectors and supporters, shielding you from danger, let it come from what quarter it may. I know that a few individuals cannot resist a torrent of error and passion such as swept the South into rebellion, but you can part out so that we may know those who desire a government and those who insist on war and its desolation. You might as well appeal against the thunder-storm as against these terrible hardships of war. They are inevitable, and the only way the people of Atlanta can hope once more to live in peace and quiet at home is to stop the war, which can alone be done by admitting that it began in error and is perpetuated in pride.

We don't want your negroes or your horses or your houses or your lands or anything you have, but we do want, and will have, a just obedience to the laws of the United States. That we will have, and if it involves the destruction of your improvements we cannot help it. You have heretofore read public sentiment in your newspapers that live by falsehood and excitement, and the quicker you seek for truth in other quarters the better for you. I repeat then that by the original compact of government the United States had certain rights in Georgia, which have never been relinquished and never will be; that the South began war by seizing forts, arsenals, mints, custom-houses, &c. long before Mr. Lincoln was installed and before the South had one jot or tittle of provocation. I myself have seen in Missouri, Kentucky, Tennessee, and Mississippi hundreds and thousands of women and children fleeing from your armies and desperadoes, hungry and with bleeding feet. In Memphis, Vicksburg, and Mississippi we fed thousands upon thousands of families of rebel soldiers left on our hands and whom we could not see starve. Now that war comes home to you, you feel very different. You deprecate its horrors, but did not feel them when you sent car-loads of soldiers and ammunition and molded shells and shot to carry war into Kentucky and Tennessee, and desolate the homes of hundreds and thousands of good people who only asked to live in peace at their old homes and under the Government of their inheritance. But these comparisons are idle. I want peace, and believe it can now only be reached through union and war, and I will ever conduct war with a view to perfect an early success. But, my dear sirs, when that peace does come, you may call on me for anything. Then will I share with you the last cracker, and watch with you to shield your homes and families against danger from every quarter. Now you must go, and take with you the old and feeble, feed and nurse them and build for them in more quiet places proper habitations to shield them against the weather until the mad passions of men cool down and allow the Union and peace once more to settle over your old homes at Atlanta.

Yours, in haste,

W. T. Sherman.
Major-General, Commanding.

Source: OR, Series I, Vol. 29, pt. 2, 418–19.

The Farewell Messages of Jefferson Davis and Robert E. Lee

On April 4, 1865, in his surreal last message to his people, Jefferson Davis declared that, despite the fall of the national capital in Richmond two days earlier, the Confederacy still could fight on until victory. On April 10, the day after his surrender at Appomattox Court House, Robert E. Lee assured his departing troops, telling them that only overwhelming material resources had defeated them. Their moral purity remained intact, he insisted, thus beginning the southern faith in the nobility of the Lost Cause. Davis was captured on May 10, near Irwinville, Georgia, and imprisoned for two years, although he was never formally charged with war crimes.

Danville, Va. April 4, 1865.

To the People of the Confederate States of America.

The General in Chief of our Army has found it necessary to make such movements of the troops as to uncover the capital and thus involve the withdrawal of the Government from the city of Richmond.

It would be unwise, even were it possible, to conceal the great moral as well as material injury to our cause that must result from the occupation of Richmond by the enemy. It is equally unwise and unworthy of us, as patriots engaged in a most sacred cause, to allow our energies to falter, our spirits to grow faint, or our efforts to become relaxed under reverses, however calamitous. While it has been to us a source of national pride that for four years of unequaled warfare we have been able, in close proximity to the center of the enemy's power, to maintain the seat of our chosen Government free from the pollution of his presence; while the memories of the heroic dead who have freely given their lives to its defense must ever remain enshrined in our hearts; while the preservation of the capital, which is usually regarded as the evidence to mankind of separate national existence, was an object very dear to us, it is also true, and should not be forgotten, that the loss which we have suffered is not without compensation. For many months the largest and finest army of the Confederacy, under the command of a leader whose presence inspires equal confidence in the troops and the people, has been greatly trammeled by the necessity of keeping constant watch over the approaches to the capital, and has thus been forced to forego more than one opportunity for promising enterprise. The hopes and confidence of the enemy have been constantly excited by the belief that their possession of Richmond would be the signal for our submission to their rule, and relieve them from the burden of war, as their failing resources admonish them it must be abandoned if not speedily brought to a successful close. If is for us, my countrymen, to show by our bearing under reverses how wretched has been the self-deception of those who have believed us less able to endure misfortune with fortitude than to encounter danger with courage. We have now entered upon a new phase of a struggle the memory of which is to endure for all ages and to shed an increasing luster upon our country.

Relieved from the necessity of guarding cities and particular points, important but not vital to our defense, with an army free to move from point to point and strike in detail the detachments and garrisons of the enemy, operating on the interior of our own country, where supplies are more accessible, and where the foe will be far removed from his own base and cut off from all succor in case of reverse, nothing is now needed to render our triumph certain but the exhibition of our own unquenchable resolve. Let us but will it, and we are free; and who, in the light of the past, dare doubt your purpose in the future?

Animated by the confidence in your spirit and fortitude, which never yet has failed me, I announce to you, fellow-countrymen, that it is my purpose to maintain your cause with my whole heart and soul; that I will never consent to abandon to the enemy one foot of the soil of any one of the States of the Confederacy. . . . If by stress of numbers we should ever be compelled to a temporary withdrawal from her limits, or those of any other border State, again and again will we return, until the baffled and exhausted enemy shall abandon in despair his endless and impossible task of making slaves of a people resolved to be free.

Let us not, then, despond, my countrymen; but, relying on the never-failing mercies and protecting care of our God, let us meet the foe with fresh defiance, with unconquered and unconquerable hearts.

Jeff'n Davis.

Source: Richardson, ed. *Messages and Papers of the Confederacy*, vol. 1, 568 ff.

Headquarters, Army of Northern Virginia,
    April 10, 1865.
    After four years of arduous service, marked by unsurpassed courage and fortitude, the Army of Northern Virginia has been compelled to yield to overwhelming numbers and resources. I need not tell the survivors of so many hard-fought battles, who have remained steadfast to the last, that I have consented to this result from no distrust of them; but, feeling that valour and devotion could accomplish nothing that could compensate for the loss that would have attended the continuation of the contest, I have determined to avoid the useless sacrifice of those whose past services have endeared them to their countrymen. By the terms of the agreement, officers and men can return to their homes and remain there until exchanged. You may take with you the satisfaction that proceeds from the consciousness of duty faithfully performed; and I earnestly pray that a merciful God will extend to you His blessing and protection. With an increasing admiration of your constancy and devotion to your country, and a grateful remembrance of your kind and generous consideration of myself, I bid you an affectionate farewell.

R. E. Lee. General.

Source: R. E. Lee, Jr., Recollection and Letters of General Lee (New York: Doubleday & Page, 1904), 153–54.

The Wade-Davis Bill; Lincoln's Response; and the Wade-Davis Manifesto

Discontent with the generous provisions of Lincoln's interim wartime reconstruction policy, Congressman Henry W. Davis of Maryland and Senator Benjamin Franklin Wade of Ohio, introduced a tough reconstruction bill that would have disenfranchised most southern white males. Lincoln refused to sign the law, letting it lapse with a "pocket veto" after Congress adjourned for the summer in 1864. In response, Wade and Davis issued a blistering manifesto attacking not only Abraham Lincoln, but also the institution of the presidency, in the name of increased congressional control over the reconstruction policies that were sure to come. This exchange prefigured the institutional divisions that did so much to undermine the possibility of a concerted federal policy after the war ended.

An Act to guarantee to certain States whose Governments have been usurped or overthrown a Republican Form of Government.

Be it enacted, That in the states declared in rebellion against the United States, the President shall, by and with the advice and consent of the Senate, appoint for each a provisional governor, . . . who shall be charged with the civil administration of such state until a state government therein shall be recognized as hereinafter provided.

SEC. 2. That so soon as the military resistance to the United States shall have been suppressed in any such state, and the people thereof shall have sufficiently returned to their obedience to the constitution and the laws of the United States, the provisional governor shall direct the marshal of the United States, as speedily as may be, to name a sufficient number of deputies, and to enroll all white male citizens of the United States, resident in the state in their respective counties, and to request each one to take the oath to support the constitution of the United States, and in his enrolment to designate those who take and those who refuse to take that oath, which rolls shall be forthwith returned to the provisional governor; and if the persons taking that oath shall amount to a majority of the persons enrolled in the state, he shall, by proclamation, invite the loyal people of the state to elect delegates to a convention charged to declare the will of the people of the state relative to the reëstablishment of a state government subject to, and in conformity with, the constitution of the United States.

SEC. 3. That the convention shall consist of as many members as both houses of the last constitutional state legislature, apportioned by the provisional governor among the counties, parishes, or districts of the state, in proportion to the white population, returned as electors, by the marshal, in compliance with the provisions of this act. The provisional governor shall, . . . provide an adequate force to keep the peace during the election.

SEC. 4. That the delegates shall be elected by the loyal white male citizens of the United States of the age of twenty-one years, and resident at the time in the county, parish, or district in which they shall offer to vote, and enrolled as aforesaid, or absent in the military service of the United States, and who shall take and subscribe the oath of allegiance to the United States in the form contained in the act of July 2, 1862; and all such citizens of the United States who are in the military service of the United States shall vote at the headquarters of their respective commands, under such regulations as may be prescribed by the provisional governor for the taking and return of their votes; but no person who has held or exercised any office, civil or military, state or confederate, under the rebel usurpation, or who has voluntarily borne arms against the United States, shall vote, or be eligible to be elected as delegate, at such election.

SEC. 5. That the said commissioners, . . . shall hold the election in conformity with this act and, . . . shall proceed in the manner used in the state prior to the rebellion. The oath of allegiance shall be taken and subscribed on the poll-book by every voter in the form above prescribed, but every person known by, or proved to, the commissioners to have held or exercised any office, civil or military, state or confederate, under the rebel usurpation, or to have voluntarily borne arms against the United States, shall be excluded, though he offer to take the oath; and in case any person who shall have borne arms against the United States shall offer to vote he shall be deemed to have borne arms voluntarily unless he shall prove the contrary by the testimony of a qualified voter. . . .

SEC. 6. That the provisional governor shall, by proclamation, convene the delegates elected as aforesaid, at the capital of the state, on a day not more than three months after the election, giving at least thirty days' notice of such day. In case the said capital shall in his judgment be unfit, he shall in his proclamation appoint another place. He shall preside over the deliberations of the convention, and administer to each delegate, before taking his seat in the convention, the oath of allegiance to the United States in the form above prescribed.

SEC. 7. That the convention shall declare, on behalf of the people of the state, their submission to the constitution and laws of the United States, and shall adopt the following provisions, hereby prescribed by the United States in the execution of the constitutional duty to guarantee a republican form of government to every state, and incorporate them in the constitution of the state, that is to say:

First. No person who has held or exercised any office, civil or military, except offices merely ministerial, and military offices below the grade of colonel, state or confederate, under the usurping power, shall vote for or be a member of the legislature, or governor.

Second. Involuntary servitude is forever prohibited, and the freedom of all persons is guaranteed in said state.

Third. No debt, state or confederate, created by or under the sanction of the usurping power, shall be recognized or paid by the state.

SEC. 8. That when the convention shall have adopted those provisions, it shall proceed to reëstablish a republican form of government, and ordain a constitution containing those provisions, which, when adopted, the convention shall by ordinance provide for submitting to the people of the state, entitled to vote under this law, at an election to be held in the manner prescribed by the act for the election of delegates; but at a time and place named by the convention, at which election the said electors, and none others, shall vote directly for or against such constitution and form of state government, and the returns of said election shall be made to the provisional governor, who shall canvass the same in the presence of the electors, and if a majority of the votes cast shall be for the constitution and form of government, he shall certify the same, with a copy thereof, to the President of the United States, who, after obtaining the assent of congress, shall, by proclamation, recognize the government so established, and none other, as the constitutional government of the state, and from the date of such recognition, and not before, Senators and Representatives, and electors for President and Vice-President may be elected in such state, according to the laws of the state and of the United States.

SEC. 9. That if the convention shall refuse to reëstablish the state government on the conditions aforesaid, the provisional governor shall declare it dissolved; but it shall be the duty of the President, whenever he shall have reason to believe that a sufficient number of the people of the state entitled to vote under this act, in number not less than a majority of those enrolled, as aforesaid, are willing to reëstablish a state government on the conditions aforesaid, to direct the provisional governor to order another election of delegates to a convention for the purpose. . . .

SEC. 10. That, until the United States shall have recognized a republican form of state government, the provisional governor in each of said states shall see that this act, and the laws of the United States, and the laws of the state in force when the state government was overthrown by the rebellion, are faithfully executed within the state; but no law or usage whereby any person was heretofore held in involuntary servitude shall be recognized or enforced by any court or officer in such state, and the laws for the trial and punishment of white persons shall extend to all persons, and jurors shall have the qualifications of voters under this law for delegates to the convention. . . .

SEC. 11. That until the recognition of a state government as aforesaid, the provisional governor shall, under such regulations as he may prescribe, cause to be assessed, levied, and collected, for the year eighteen hundred and sixty-four, and every year thereafter, the taxes provided by the laws of such state to be levied during the fiscal year preceding the overthrow of the state government thereof, in the manner prescribed by the laws of the state, as nearly as may be; . . . The proceeds of such taxes shall be accounted for to the provisional governor, and be by him applied to the expenses of the administration of the laws in such state, subject to the direction of the President, and the surplus shall be deposited in the treasury of the United States to the credit of such state, to be paid to the state upon an appropriation therefor, to be made when a republican form of government shall be recognized therein by the United States.

SEC. 12. That all persons held to involuntary servitude or labor in the states aforesaid are hereby emancipated and discharged therefrom, and they and their posterity shall be forever free. And if any such persons or their posterity shall be restrained of liberty, under pretence of any claim to such service or labor, the courts of the United States shall, on habeas corpus, discharge them.

SEC. 13. That if any person declared free by this act, or any law of the United States, or any proclamation of the President, be restrained of liberty, with intent to be held in or reduced to involuntary servitude or labor, the person convicted before a court of competent jurisdiction of such act shall be punished by fine of not less than fifteen hundred dollars, and be imprisoned not less than five nor more than twenty years.

SEC. 14. That every person who shall hereafter hold or exercise any office, civil or military, except offices merely ministerial, and military offices below the grade of colonel, in the rebel service, state or confederate, is hereby declared not to be a citizen of the United States.

Lincoln's Proclamation on the Wade-Davis Bill

By the President of the United States:

A Proclamation.

Whereas at the late session Congress passed a bill "to guarantee to certain States whose governments have been usurped or overthrown a republican form of government," a copy of which is hereunto annexed; and

Whereas, the said bill was presented to the President of the United States for his approval less than one hour before the *sine die* adjournment of said session, and was not signed by him; and

Whereas the said bill contains, among other things, a plan for restoring the States in rebellion to their proper practical relation in the Union, which plan expresses the sense of Congress upon that subject, and which plan it is now thought fit to lay before the people for their consideration:

Now, therefore, I, Abraham Lincoln, President of the United States, do proclaim, declare, and make known that while I am (as I was in December last, when, by proclamation, I propounded a plan for restoration) unprepared by a formal approval of this bill to be inflexibly committed to any single plan of restoration, and while I am also unprepared to declare that the free State constitutions and governments already adopted and installed in Arkansas and Louisiana shall be set aside and held for naught, thereby repelling and discouraging the loyal citizens who have set up the same as to further effort, or to declare a constitutional competency in Congress to abolish slavery in States, but am at the same time sincerely hoping and expecting that a constitutional amendment abolishing slavery throughout the nation may be adopted, nevertheless I am fully satisfied with the system for restoration contained in the bill as one very proper plan for the loyal people of any State choosing to adopt it, and that I am and at all times shall be prepared to give the Executive aid and assistance to any such people so soon as the military resistance to the United States shall have been suppressed in any such State and the people thereof shall have sufficiently returned to their obedience to the Constitution and the laws of the United States, in which cases military governors will be appointed with directions to proceed according to the bill. . . .

Abraham Lincoln.

The Wade-Davis Manifesto

We have read without surprise, but not without indignation, the Proclamation of the President of the 8th of July. . . .

The President, by preventing this bill from becoming a law, holds the electoral votes of the rebel States at the dictation of his personal ambition.

If those votes turn the balance in his favor, is it to be supposed that his competitor, defeated by such means, will acquiesce?

If the rebel majority assert their supremacy in those States, and send votes which elect an enemy of the Government, will we not repel his claims?

And is not that civil war for the Presidency inaugurated by the votes of rebel States?

Seriously impressed with these dangers, Congress, *"the proper constituted authority,"* formally declared that there are no State governments in the rebel States, and provided for their erection at a proper time; and both the Senate and the House of Representatives rejected the Senators and Representatives chosen under the authority of what the President calls the free constitution and government of Arkansas.

The President's proclamation *"holds for naught"* this judgment, and discards the authority of the Supreme Court, and strides headlong toward the anarchy his proclamation of the 8th of December inaugurated.

If electors for President be allowed to be chosen in either of those States, a sinister light will be cast on the motives which induced the President to "hold for naught" the will of Congress rather than his government in Louisiana and Arkansas.

That judgment of Congress which the President defies was the exercise of an authority exclusively vested in Congress by the Constitution to determine what is the established government in a State, and in its own nature and by the highest judicial authority binding on all other departments of the Government. . . .

A more studied outrage on the legislative authority of the people has never been perpetrated.

Congress passed a bill; the President refused to approve it, and then by proclamation puts as much of it in force as he sees fit, and proposes to execute those parts by officers unknown to the laws of the United States and not subject to the confirmation of the Senate!

The bill directed the appointment of Provisional Governors by and with the advice and consent of the Senate.

The President, after defeating the law, proposes to appoint without law, and without the advice and consent of the Senate, *Military* Governors for the rebel States!

He has already exercised this dictatorial usurpation in Louisiana, and he defeated the bill to prevent its limitation. . . .

The President has greatly presumed on the forbearance which the supporters of his Administration have so long practiced, in view of the arduous conflict in which we are engaged, and the reckless ferocity of our political opponents.

But he must understand that our support is of a cause and not of a man; that the authority of Congress is paramount and must be respected; that the whole body of the Union men of Congress will not submit to be impeached by him of rash and unconstitutional legislation; and if he wishes our support, he must confine himself to his executive duties—to obey and execute, not make the laws—to suppress by arms armed rebellion, and leave political reorganization to Congress.

If the supporters of the Government fail to insist on this, they become responsible for the usurpations which they fail to rebuke, and are justly liable to the indignation of the people whose rights and security, committed to their keeping, they sacrifice.

Let them consider the remedy for these usurpations, and, having found it, fearlessly execute it.

Source: James D. Richardson, compl., *A Compilation of the Messages and Papers of the Presidents, 1789–1897,* 10 vols. (Washington, D.C., 1896–99), VI, 222–26; Edward McPherson, *The Political History of the United States of America during the Great Rebellion* (Washington, D.C., 1865), 332.

Abraham Lincoln's Second Inaugural Address

On March 4, 1865, in an address that stands beside his Gettysburg Address of 1863 for moral intensity, Lincoln articulated some of the deeper moral meanings of this terrible civil war. Although he was not conventionally religious, Lincoln appealed to a Calvinist God who had called upon all Americans to expiate the national sin of slavery with their blood.

[Fellow Countrymen:]   *March 4, 1865*

At this second appearing to take the oath of the presidential office, there is less occasion for an extended address than there was at the first. Then a statement, somewhat in detail, of a course to be pursued, seemed fitting and proper. Now, at the expiration of four years, during which public declarations have been constantly called forth on every point and phase of the great contest which still absorbs the attention, and engrosses the enerergies [sic] of the nation, little that is new could be presented. The progress of our arms, upon which all else chiefly depends, is as well known to the public as to myself, and it is, I trust, reasonably satisfactory and encouraging to all. With high hope for the future, no prediction in regard to it is ventured.

On the occasion corresponding to this four years ago, all thoughts were anxiously directed to an impending civil-war. All dreaded it—all sought to avert it. While the inaugural address was being delivered from this place, devoted altogether to *saving* the Union without war, insurgent agents were in the city seeking to *destroy* it without war—seeking to dissol[v]e the Union, and divide effects, by negotiation. Both parties deprecated war; but one of them would *make* war rather than let the nation survive; and the other would *accept* war rather than let it perish. And the war came.

One eighth of the whole population were colored slaves, not distributed generally over the Union, but localized in the Southern part of it. These slaves constituted a peculiar and powerful interest. All knew that this interest was, somehow, the cause of the war. To strengthen, perpetuate, and extend this interest was the object for which the insurgents would rend the Union, even by war; while the government claimed no right to do more than to restrict the territorial enlargement of it. Neither party expected for the war, the magnitude, or the duration, which it has already attained. Neither anticipated that the *cause* of the conflict might cease with, or even before, the conflict itself should cease. Each looked for an easier triumph, and a result less fundamental and astounding. Both read the same Bible, and pray to the same God; and each invokes His aid against the other. It may seem strange that any men should dare to ask a just God's assistance in wringing their bread from the sweat of other men's faces; but let us judge not that we be not judged. The prayers of both could not be answered; that of neither has been answered fully. The Almighty has His own purposes. "Woe unto the world because of offences! for it must needs be that offences come; but woe to that man by whom the offence cometh." If we shall suppose that American Slavery is one of those offences which, in the providence of God, must needs come, but which, having continued through His appointed time, He now wills to remove, and that He gives to both North and South, this terrible war, as the woe due to those by whom the offence came, shall we discern therein any departure from those divine attributes which the believers in a Living God always ascribe to Him? Fondly do we hope—fervently do we pray—that this mighty scourge of war may speedily pass away. Yet, if God wills that it continue, until all the wealth piled by the bond-man's two hundred and fifty years of unrequited toil shall be sunk, and until every drop of blood drawn with the lash, shall be paid by another drawn with the sword, as was said three thousand years ago, so still it must be said "the judgments of the Lord, are true and righteous altogether."

With malice toward none; with charity for all; with firmness in the right, as God gives us to see the right, let us strive on to finish the work we are in; to bind up the nation's wounds; to care for him who shall have borne the battle, and for his widow, and his orphan—to do all which may achieve and cherish a just, and a lasting peace, among ourselves, and with all nations.

A. Lincoln,
April 10, 1865.

Source: Basler, VIII, 332–33.

Andrew Johnson's Amnesty Proclamation

After Abraham Lincoln's assassination on April 12, 1865, Vice-President Andrew Johnson took the nation's highest office. A Tennessee politician of humble origins, Johnson promised to punish the southern aristocracy he personally resented and despised. However, on May 29, with Congress still on a long recess, Johnson began his own reconstruction policy with this mild proclamation of amnesty for former Confederates. By comparison, the Wade-Davis bill of 1864 had been far tougher on former enemies.

By the President of the United States of America.

A Proclamation.

Whereas the President of the United States, on the 8th day of December, A.D. 1863, and on the 26th day of March, A.D. 1864, did, with the object to suppress the existing rebellion, to induce all persons to return to their loyalty, and to restore the authority of the United States, issue proclamations offering amnesty and pardon to certain persons who had, directly or by implication, participated in the said rebellion; and

Whereas many persons who had so engaged in said rebellion have, since the issuance of said proclamations, failed or neglected to take the benefits offered thereby; and

Whereas many persons who have been justly deprived of all claim to amnesty and pardon thereunder by reason of their participation, directly or by implication, in said rebellion and continued hostility to the Government of the United States since the date of said proclamations now desire to apply for and obtain amnesty and pardon.

To the end, therefore, that the authority of the Government of the United States may be restored and that peace, order, and freedom may be established, I, Andrew Johnson, President of the United States, do proclaim and declare that I hereby grant to all persons who have, directly or indirectly, participated in the existing rebellion, except as hereinafter excepted, amnesty and pardon, with restoration of all rights of property, except as to slaves . . . but upon the condition, nevertheless, that every such person shall take and subscribe the following oath (or affirmation) and thenceforward keep and maintain said oath inviolate, and which oath shall be registered for permanent preservation and shall be of the tenor and effect following, to wit:

I, ——— ———, do solemnly swear (or affirm), in presence of Almighty God, that I will henceforth faithfully support, protect, and defend the Constitution of the United States and the Union of the States thereunder; and that I will in like manner abide by and faithfully support all laws and proclamations which have been made during the existing rebellion with reference to the emancipation of slaves. So help me God.

The following classes of persons are excepted from the benefits of this proclamation:

First. All who are or shall have been pretended civil or diplomatic officers or otherwise domestic or foreign agents of the pretended Confederate government.

Second. All who left judicial stations under the United States to aid the rebellion.

Third. All who shall have been military or naval officers of said pretended Confederate government above the rank of colonel in the army or lieutenant in the navy.

Fourth. All who left seats in the Congress of the United States to aid the rebellion.

Fifth. All who resigned or tendered resignations of their commissions in the Army or Navy of the United States to evade duty in resisting the rebellion.

Sixth. All who have engaged in any way in treating otherwise than lawfully as prisoners of war persons found in the United States service as officers, soldiers, seamen, or in other capacities.

Seventh. All persons who have been or are absentees from the United States for the purpose of aiding the rebellion.

Eighth. All military and naval officers in the rebel service who were educated by the Government in the Military Academy at West Point or the United States Naval Academy.

Ninth. All persons who held the pretended offices of governors of States in insurrection against the United States.

Tenth. All persons who left their homes within the jurisdiction and protection of the United States and passed beyond the Federal military lines into the pretended Confederate States for the purpose of aiding the rebellion.

Eleventh. All persons who have been engaged in the destruction of the commerce of the United States upon the high seas and all persons who have made raids into the United States from Canada or been engaged in destroying the commerce of the United States upon the lakes and rivers that separate the British Provinces from the United States.

Twelfth. All persons who, at the time when they seek to obtain the benefits hereof by taking the oath herein prescribed, are in military, naval, or civil confinement, or custody, or under bonds of the civil, military, or naval authorities or agents of the United States as prisoners of war, or persons detained for offenses of any kind, either before or after conviction.

Thirteenth. All persons who have voluntarily participated in said rebellion and the estimated value of whose taxable property is over $20,000.

Fourteenth. All persons who have taken the oath of amnesty as prescribed in the President's proclamation of December 8, A.D. 1863, or an oath of allegiance to the Government of the United States since the date of said proclamation and who have not thenceforward kept and maintained the same inviolate.

Provided, That special application may be made to the President for pardon by any person belonging to the excepted classes, and such clemency will be liberally extended as may be consistent with the facts of the case and the peace and dignity of the United States.

The Secretary of State will establish rules and regulations for administering and recording the said amnesty oath, so as to insure its benefit to the people and guard the Government against fraud. . . .

Source: Richardson, VI, 310–312.

Black Code of Mississippi

Once seated, the ex-Confederates who returned to southern state legislatures, passed draconian legal codes that discriminated against the freedmen. This unsubmissive and provocative legislation, which essentially turned blacks into unfree persons, if not slaves, infuriated northerners, leading Congress to push for civil rights legislation, including the Fourteenth and Fifteenth Amendments, in order to protect the legal and civil rights of African Americans.

Black Code of Mississippi

1. Civil Rights of Freedmen in Mississippi

SEC. 1. *Be it enacted,* . . . That all freedmen, free negroes, and mulattoes may sue and be sued, implead and be impleaded, in all the courts of law and equity of this State, and may acquire personal property, and choses in action, by descent or purchase, and may dispose of the same in the same manner and to the same extent that white persons may: *Provided,* That the provisions of this section shall not be so construed as to allow any freedman, free negro, or mulatto to rent or lease any lands or tenements except in incorporated cities or towns, in which places the corporate authorities shall control the same. . . .

SEC. 3. . . . All freedmen, free negroes, or mulattoes who do now and have herebefore lived and cohabited together as husband and wife shall be taken and held in law as legally married, and the issue shall be taken and held as legitimate for all purposes; that it shall not be lawful for any freedman, free negro, or mulatto to intermarry with any white person; nor for any white person to intermarry with any freedman, free negro, or mulatto; and any person who shall so intermarry, shall be deemed guilty of felony, and on conviction thereof shall be confined in the State penitentiary for life; and those shall be deemed freedmen, free negroes, and mulattoes who are of pure negro blood, and those descended from a negro to the third generation, inclusive, though one ancestor in each generation may have been a white person.

SEC. 4. . . . In addition to cases in which freedmen, free negroes, and mulattoes are now by law competent witnesses, freedmen, free negroes, or mulattoes shall be competent in civil cases, when a party or parties to the suit, either plaintiff or plaintiffs, defendant or defendants, and a white person or white persons, is or are the opposing party or parties, plaintiff or plaintiffs, defendant or defendants. They shall also be competent witnesses in all criminal prosecutions where the crime charged is alleged to have been committed by a white person upon or against the person or property of a freedman, free negro, or mulatto: *Provided,* that in all cases said witnesses shall be examined in open court, on the stand; except, however, they may be examined before the grand jury, and shall in all cases be subject to the rules and tests of the common law as to competency and credibility. . . .

SEC. 6. . . . All contracts for labor made with freedmen, free negroes, and mulattoes for a longer period than one month shall be in writing, and in duplicate, attested and read to said freedman, free negro, or mulatto by a beat, city or county officer, or two disinterested white persons of the county in which the labor is to be performed, of which each party shall have one; and said contracts shall be taken and held as entire contracts, and if the laborer shall quit the service of the employer before the expiration of his term of service, without good cause, he shall forfeit his wages for that year up to the time of quitting.

SEC. 7. . . . Every civil officer shall, and every person may, arrest and carry back to his or her legal employer any freedman, free negro, or mulatto who shall have quit the service of his or her employer before the expiration of his or her term of service without good cause; and said officer and person shall be entitled to receive for arresting and carrying back every deserting employe aforesaid the sum of five dollars, and ten cents per mile from the place of arrest to the place of delivery; and the same shall be paid by the employer, and held as a set-off for so much against the wages of said deserting employe: *Provided,* that said arrested party, after being so returned, may appeal to the justice of the peace or member of the board of police of the county, who, on notice to the alleged employer, shall try summarily whether said appellant is legally employed by the alleged employer, and has good cause to quit said employer; either party shall have the right of appeal to the county court, pending which the alleged deserter shall be remanded to the alleged employer or otherwise disposed of, as shall be right and just; and the decision of the county court shall be final. . . .

SEC. 9. . . . If any person shall persuade or attempt to persuade, entice, or cause any freedman, free negro, or mulatto to desert from the legal employment of any person before the expiration of his or her term of service, or shall knowingly employ any such deserting freedman, free negro, or mulatto, or shall knowingly give or sell to any such deserting freedman, free negro, or mulatto, any food, raiment, or other thing, he or she shall be guilty of a misdemeanor, and, upon conviction, shall be fined not less than twenty-five dollars and not more than two hundred dollars and the costs; and if said fine and costs shall not be immediately paid, the court shall sentence said convict to not exceeding two months' imprisonment in the county jail, and he or she shall moreover be liable to the party injured in damages: *Provided,* if any person shall, or shall attempt to, persuade, entice, or cause any freedman, free negro, or mulatto to desert from any legal employment of any person, with the view to employ said freedman, free negro, or mulatto without the limits of this State, such person, on conviction, shall be fined not less than fifty dollars, and not more than five hundred dollars and costs; and if said fine and costs shall not be immediately paid, the court shall sentence said convict to not exceeding six months imprisonment in the county jail. . . .

2. Mississippi Apprentice Law

(*Laws of Mississippi,* 1865, p. 86)

Sec. 1. . . . It shall be the duty of all sheriffs, justices of the peace, and other civil officers of the several counties in this State, to report to the probate courts of their respective counties semi-annually, at the January and July terms of said courts, all freedmen, free negroes, and mulattoes, under the age of eighteen, in their respective counties, beats or districts, who are orphans, or whose parent or parents have not the means or who refuse to provide for and support said minors; and thereupon it shall be the duty of said probate court to order the clerk of said court to apprentice said minors to some competent and suitable person, on such terms as the court may direct, having a particular care to the interest of said minor: *Provided,* that the former owner of said minors shall have the preference when, in the opinion of the court, he or she shall be a suitable person for that purpose.

Sec. 2. . . . The said court shall be fully satisfied that the person or persons to whom said minor shall be apprenticed shall be a suitable person to have the charge and care of said minor, and fully to protect the interest of said minor. The said court shall require the said master or mistress to execute bond and security, payable to the State of Mississippi, conditioned that he or she shall furnish said minor with sufficient food and clothing; to treat said minor humanely; furnish medical attention in case of sickness; teach, or cause to be taught, him or her to read and write, if under fifteen years old, and will conform to any law that may be hereafter passed for the regulation of the duties and relation of master and apprentice. . . .

Sec. 3. . . . In the management and control of said apprentice, said master or mistress shall have the power to inflict such moderate corporal chastisement as a father or guardian is allowed to inflict on his or her child or ward at common law: *Provided,* that in no case shall cruel or inhuman punishment be inflicted.

Sec. 4. . . . If any apprentice shall leave the employment of his or her master or mistress, without his or her consent, said master or mistress may pursue and recapture said apprentice, and bring him or her before any justice of the peace of the county, whose duty it shall be to remand said apprentice to the service of his or her master or mistress; and in the event of a refusal on the part of said apprentice so to return, then said justice shall commit said apprentice to the jail of said county, on failure to give bond, to the next term of the county court; and it shall be the duty of said court at the first term thereafter to investigate said case, and if the court shall be of opinion that said apprentice left the employment of his or her master or mistress without good cause, to order him or her to be punished, as provided for the punishment of hired freedmen, as may be from time to time provided for by law for desertion, until he or she shall agree to return to the service of his or her master or mistress: . . . if the court shall believe that said apprentice had good cause to quit his said master or mistress, the court shall discharge said apprentice from said indenture, and also enter a judgment against the master or mistress for not more than one hundred dollars, for the use and benefit of said apprentice. . . .

3. Mississippi Vagrant Law

(*Laws of Mississippi,* 1865, p. 90)

Sec. 1. *Be it enacted,* etc., . . . That all rogues and vagabonds, idle and dissipated persons, beggars, jugglers, or persons practicing unlawful games or plays, runaways, common drunkards, common night-walkers, pilferers, lewd wanton, or lascivious persons, in speech or behavior, common railers and brawlers, persons who neglect their calling or employment, misspend what they earn, or do not provide for the support of themselves or their families, or dependents, and all other idle and disorderly persons, including all who neglect all lawful business, habitually misspend their time by frequenting houses of ill-fame, gaming-houses, or tippling shops, shall be deemed and considered vagrants, under the provisions of this act, and upon conviction thereof shall be fined not exceeding one hundred dollars, with all accruing costs, and be imprisoned at the discretion of the court, not exceeding ten days.

SEC. 2. . . . All freedmen, free negroes and mulattoes in this State, over the age of eighteen years, found on the second Monday in January, 1866, or thereafter, with no lawful employment or business, or found unlawfully assembling themselves together, either in the day or night time, and all white persons so assembling themselves with freedmen, free negroes or mulattoes, or usually associating with freedmen, free negroes or mulattoes, on terms of equality, or living in adultery or fornication with a freed woman, free negro or mulatto, shall be deemed vagrants, and on conviction thereof shall be fined in a sum not exceeding, in the case of a freedman, free negro or mulatto, fifty dollars, and a white man two hundred dollars, and imprisoned at the discretion of the court, the free negro not exceeding ten days, and the white man not exceeding six months. . . .

SEC. 7. . . . If any freedman, free negro, or mulatto shall fail or refuse to pay any tax levied according to the provisions of the sixth section of this act, it shall be *prima facie* evidence of vagrancy, and it shall be the duty of the sheriff to arrest such freedman, free negro, or mulatto or such person refusing or neglecting to pay such tax, and proceed at once to hire for the shortest time such delinquent tax-payer to any one who will pay the said tax, with accruing costs, giving preference to the employer, if there be one. . . .

4. Penal Laws of Mississippi

(Laws of Mississippi, 1865, p. 165)

SEC. 1. *Be it enacted,* . . . That no freedman, free negro or mulatto, not in the military service of the United States government, and not licensed so to do by the board of police of his or her county, shall keep or carry fire-arms of any kind, or any ammunition, dirk or bowie knife, and on conviction thereof in the county court shall be punished by fine, not exceeding ten dollars, and pay the costs of such proceedings, and all such arms or ammunition shall be forfeited to the informer; and it shall be the duty of every civil and military officer to arrest any freedman, free negro, or mulatto found with any such arms or ammunition, and cause him or her to be committed to trial in default of bail.

2. . . . Any freedman, free negro, or mulatto committing riots, routs, affrays, trespasses, malicious mischief, cruel treatment to animals, seditious speeches, insulting gestures, language, or acts, or assaults on any person, disturbance of the peace, exercising the function of a minister of the Gospel without a license from some regularly organized church, vending spirituous or intoxicating liquors, or committing any other misdemeanor, the punishment of which is not specifically provided for by law, shall, upon conviction thereof in the county court, be fined not less than ten dollars, and not more than one hundred dollars, and may be imprisoned at the discretion of the court, not exceeding thirty days.

SEC. 3. . . . If any white person shall sell, lend, or give to any freedman, free negro, or mulatto any fire-arms, dirk or bowie knife, or ammunition, or any spirituous or intoxicating liquors, such person or persons so offending, upon conviction thereof in the county court of his or her county, shall be fined not exceeding fifty dollars, and may be imprisoned, at the discretion of the court, not exceeding thirty days. . . .

SEC. 5. . . . If any freedman, free negro, or mulatto, convicted of any of the misdemeanors provided against in this act, shall fail or refuse for the space of five days, after conviction, to pay the fine and costs imposed, such person shall be hired out by the sheriff or other officer, at public outcry, to any white person who will pay said fine and all costs, and take said convict for the shortest time.

Source: *Laws of the State of Mississippi passed by a Regular Session, October, November, and December, 1865* (Jackson, Miss., 1866), pp. 82ff.

The Constitution of the United States: The Reconstruction Amendments

To protect the fundamental civil, legal and political rights of blacks, Congress passed and the states adopted three amendments to the Constitution. The Thirteenth Amendment of 1865 abolished slavery once and for all. The Fourteenth Amendment of 1868 sought to define citizenship and protect black civil rights before the law, while undermining the privileges of ex-Confederates. The Fifteenth Amendment of 1870 guaranteed the right to vote to black men. After Reconstruction, white supremacists in power in the South, aided by indifference, and often hostility to blacks in the North, undermined the Fourteenth and Fifteenth Amendments, rendering them dead letters for nearly a century.

Amendment XIII [1865]

Section 1. Neither slavery nor involuntary servitude, except as a punishment for crime whereof the party shall have been duly convicted, shall exist within the United States, or any place subject to their jurisdiction.

Section 2. Congress shall have power to enforce this article by appropriate legislation.

Amendment XIV [1868]

Section 1. All persons born or naturalized in the United States, and subject to the jurisdiction thereof, are citizens of the United States and of the State wherein they reside. No State shall make or enforce any law which shall abridge the privileges or immunities of citizens of the United States; nor shall any State deprive any person of life, liberty, or property, without due process of law; nor deny to any person within its jurisdiction the equal protection of the laws.

Section 2. Representatives shall be apportioned among the several States according to their respective numbers, counting the whole number of persons in each State, excluding Indians not taxed. But when the right to vote at any election for the choice of electors for President and Vice-President of the United States, Representatives in Congress, the Executive and Judicial officers of a State, or the members of the Legislature thereof, is denied to any of the male inhabitants of such State, being twenty-one years of age, and citizens of the United States, or in any way abridged, except for participation in rebellion, or other crime, the basis of representation therein shall be reduced in the proportion which the number of such male citizens shall bear to the whole number of male citizens twenty-one years of age in such State.

Section 3. No person shall be a Senator or Representative in Congress, or elector of President and Vice-President, or hold any office, civil or military, under the United States, or under any State, who, having previously taken an oath, as a member of Congress, or as an officer of the United States, or as a member of any State legislature, or as an executive or judicial officer of any State, to support the Constitution of the United States, shall have engaged in insurrection or rebellion against the same, or given aid or comfort to the enemies thereof. But Congress may by a vote of two-thirds of each House, remove such disability.

Section 4. The validity of the public debt of the United States, authorized by law, including debts incurred for payment of pensions and bounties for services in suppressing insurrection or rebellion, shall not be questioned. But neither the United States nor any State shall assume or pay any debt or obligation incurred in aid of insurrection or rebellion against the United States, or any claim for the loss or emancipation of any slave; but all such debts, obligations, and claims shall be held illegal and void.

Section 5. The Congress shall have power to enforce, by appropriate legislation, the provisions of this article.

Amendment XV [1870]

Section 1. The right of citizens of the United States to vote shall not be denied or abridged by the United States or by any State on account of race, color, or previous condition of servitude—

Section 2. The Congress shall have the power to enforce this article by appropriate legislation.

Plessy v. Ferguson

On May 14, 1896, the Supreme Court, in a decision, written by Justice Henry Billings Brown of Michigan, accepted the principle of legal segregation—systematized white discrimination against blacks—as consistent with the basic principles of the Constitution. Justice John Marshall Harlan of Kentucky stood alone in his eloquent plea that the U.S. Constitution was color-blind on matters of justice. This decision would remain the law of the land until 1954.

Mr. Justice Henry Billings Brown, after stating the case, delivered the opinion of the court.

This case turns upon the constitutionality of an act of the General Assembly of the State of Louisiana, passed in 1890, providing for separate railway carriages for the white and colored races. Acts 1890, No. 111, p. 152.

The first section of the statute enacts "that all railway companies carrying passengers in their coaches in this State, shall provide equal but separate accommodations for the white, and colored races, by providing two or more passenger coaches for each passenger train, or by dividing the passenger coaches by a partition so as to secure separate accommodations: *Provided,* That this section shall not be construed to apply to street railroads. No person or persons, shall be admitted to occupy seats in coaches, other than, the ones, assigned, to them on account of the race they belong to."

By the second section it was enacted "that the officers of such passenger trains shall have power and are hereby required to assign each passenger to the coach or compartment used for the race to which such passenger belongs; any passenger insisting on going into a coach or compartment to which by race he does not belong, shall be liable to a fine of twenty-five dollars, or in lieu thereof to imprisonment for a period of not more than twenty days in the parish prison, and any officer of any railroad insisting on assigning a passenger to a coach or compartment other than the one set aside for the race to which said passenger belongs, shall be liable to a fine of twenty-five dollars, or in lieu thereof to imprisonment for a period of not more than twenty days in the parish prison; and should any passenger refuse to occupy the coach or compartment to which he or she is assigned by the officer of such railway, said officer shall have power to refuse to carry such passenger on his train, and for such refusal neither he nor the railway company which he represents shall be liable for damages in any of the courts of this State."

The third section provides penalties for the refusal or neglect of the officers, directors, conductors, and employés of railway companies to comply with the act, with a proviso that "nothing in this act shall be construed as applying to nurses attending children of the other race." The fourth section is immaterial.

The information filed in the criminal District Court charged in substance that Plessy, being a passenger between two stations within the State of Louisiana, was assigned by officers of the company to the coach used for the race to which he belonged, but he insisted upon going into a coach used by the race to which he did not belong. Neither in the information nor plea was his particular race or color averred.

The petition for the writ of prohibition averred that petitioner was seven eighths Caucasian and one eighth African blood; that the mixture of colored blood was not discernible in him, and that he was entitled to every right, privilege, and immunity secured to citizens of the United States of the white race; and that, upon such theory, he took possession of a vacant seat in a coach where passengers of the white race were accommodated, and was ordered by the conductor to vacate said coach and take a seat in another assigned to persons of the colored race, and having refused to comply with such demand he was forcibly ejected with the aid of a police officer, and imprisoned in the parish jail to answer a charge of having violated the above act.

The constitutionality of this act is attacked upon the ground that it conflicts both with the Thirteenth Amendment of the Constitution, abolishing slavery, and the Fourteenth Amendment, which prohibits certain restrictive legislation on the part of the States. . . .

By the Fourteenth Amendment, all persons born or naturalized in the United States, and subject to the jurisdiction thereof, are made citizens of the United States and of the State wherein they reside; and the States are forbidden from making or enforcing any law which shall abridge the privileges or immunities of citizens of the United States, or shall deprive any person of life, liberty or property without due process of law, or deny to any person within their jurisdiction the equal protection of the laws. . . .

While we think the enforced separation of the races, as applied to the internal commerce of the State, neither abridges the privileges or immunities of the colored man, deprives him of his property without due process of law, nor denies him the equal protection of the laws, within the meaning of the Fourteenth Amendment, we are not prepared to say that the conductor, in assigning passengers to the coaches according to their race, does not act at his peril, or that the provision of the second section of the act, that denies to the passenger compensation in damages for a refusal to receive him into the coach in which he properly belongs, is a valid exercise of the legislative power. Indeed, we understand it to be conceded by the State's attorney, that such part of the act as exempts from liability the railway company and its officers is unconstitutional. The power to assign to a particular coach obviously implies the power to determine to which race the passenger belongs, as well as the power to determine who, under the laws of the particular State, is to be deemed a white, and who a colored person. This question, though indicated in the brief of the plaintiff in error, does not properly arise upon the record in this case, since the only issue made is as to the unconstitutionality of the act, so far as it requires the railway to provide separate accommodations, and the conductor to assign passengers according to their race.

It is claimed by the plaintiff in error that, in any mixed community, the reputation of belonging to the dominant race, in this instance the white race, is *property*, in the same sense that a right of action, or of inheritance, is property. Conceding this to be so, for the purposes of this case, we are unable to see how this statute deprives him of, or in any way affects his right to, such property. If he be a white man and assigned to a colored coach, he may have his action for damages against the company for being deprived of his so called property. Upon the other hand, if he be a colored man and be so assigned, he has been deprived of no property, since he is not lawfully entitled to the reputation of being a white man.

In this connection, it is also suggested by the learned counsel for the plaintiff in error that the same argument that will justify the state legislature in requiring railways to provide separate accommodations for the two races will also authorize them to require separate cars to be provided for people whose hair is of a certain color, or who are aliens, or who belong to certain nationalities, or to enact laws requiring colored people to walk upon one side of the street, and white people upon the other, or requiring white men's houses to be painted white, and colored men's black, or their vehicles or business signs to be of different colors, upon the theory that one side of the street is as good as the other, or that a house or vehicle of one color is as good as one of another color. The reply to all this is that every exercise of the police power must be reasonable, and extend only to such laws as are enacted in good faith for the promotion of the public good, and not for the annoyance or oppression of a particular class. . . .

So far, then, as a conflict with the Fourteenth Amendment is concerned, the case reduces itself to the question whether the statute of Louisiana is a reasonable regulation, and with respect to this there must necessarily be a large discretion on the part of the legislature. In determining the question of reasonableness it is at liberty to act with reference to the established usages, customs and traditions of the people, and with a view to the promotion of their comfort, and the preservation of the public peace and good order. Gauged by this standard, we cannot say that a law which authorizes or even requires the separation of the two races in public conveyances is unreasonable, or more obnoxious to the Fourteenth Amendment than the acts of Congress requiring separate schools for colored children in the District of Columbia, the constitutionality of which does not seem to have been questioned, or the corresponding acts of state legislatures.

We consider the underlying fallacy of the plaintiff's argument to consist in the assumption that the enforced separation of the two races stamps the colored race with a badge of inferiority. If this be so, it is not by reason of anything found in the act, but solely because the colored race chooses to put that construction upon it. The argument necessarily assumes that if, as has been more than once the case, and is not unlikely to be so again, the colored race should become the dominant power in the state legislature, and should enact a law in precisely similar terms, it would thereby relegate the white race to an inferior position. We imagine that the white race, at least, would not acquiesce in this assumption. The argument also assumes that social prejudices may be overcome by legislation, and that equal rights cannot be secured to the negro except by an enforced commingling of the two races. We cannot accept this proposition. If the two races are to meet upon terms of social equality, it must be the result of natural affinities, a mutual appreciation of each other's merits and a voluntary consent of individuals. . . . Legislation is powerless to eradicate racial instincts or to abolish distinctions based upon physical differences, and the attempt to do so can only result in accentuating the difficulties of the present situation. If the civil and political rights of both races be equal one cannot be inferior to the other civilly or politically. If one race be inferior to the other socially, the Constitution of the United States cannot put them upon the same plane.

The judgment of the court below is, therefore,

Affirmed.

Mr. Justice John Marshall Harlan dissenting.

While there may be in Louisiana persons of different races who are not citizens of the United States, the words in the act, "white and colored races," necessarily include all citizens of the United States of both races residing in that State. So that we have before us a state enactment that compels, under penalties, the separation of the two races in railroad passenger coaches, and makes it a crime for a citizen of either race to enter a coach that has been assigned to citizens of the other race.

Thus, the State regulates the use of a public highway by citizens of the United States solely upon the basis of race. . . .

In respect of civil rights, common to all citizens, the Constitution of the United States does not, I think, permit any public authority to know the race of those entitled to be protected in the enjoyment of such rights. Every true man has pride of race, and under appropriate circumstances when the rights of others, his equals before the law, are not to be affected, it is his privilege to express such pride and to take such action based upon it as to him seems proper. But I deny that any legislative body or judicial tribunal may have regard to the race of citizens when the civil rights of those citizens are involved. Indeed, such legislation, as that here in question, is inconsistent not only with that equality of rights which pertains to citizenship, National and State, but with the personal liberty enjoyed by every one within the United States.

The Thirteenth Amendment does not permit the withholding or the deprivation of any right necessarily inhering in freedom. It not only struck down the institution of slavery as previously existing in the United States, but it prevents the imposition of any burdens or disabilities that constitute badges of slavery or servitude. It decreed universal civil freedom in this country. This court has so adjudged. But that amendment having been found inadequate to the protection of the rights of those who had been in slavery, it was followed by the Fourteenth Amendment, which added greatly to the dignity and glory of American citizenship, and to the security of personal liberty, by declaring that "all persons born or naturalized in the United States, and subject to the jurisdiction thereof, are citizens of the United States and of the State wherein they reside," and that "no State shall make or enforce any law which shall abridge the privileges or immunities of citizens of the United States; nor shall any State deprive any person of life, liberty or property without due process of law, nor deny to any person within its jurisdiction the equal protection of the laws." These two amendments, if enforced according to their true intent and meaning, will protect all the civil rights that pertain to freedom and citizenship. Finally, and to the end that no citizen should be denied, on account of his race, the privilege of participating in the political control of his country, it was declared by the Fifteenth Amendment that "the right of citizens of the United States to vote shall not be denied or abridged by the United States or by any State on account of race, color or previous condition of servitude."

These notable additions to the fundamental law were welcomed by the friends of liberty throughout the world. They removed the race line from our governmental systems. . . .

It was said in argument that the statute of Louisiana does not discriminate against either race, but prescribes a rule applicable alike to white and colored citizens. But this argument does not meet the difficulty. Every one knows that the statute in question had its origin in the purpose, not so much to exclude white persons from railroad cars occupied by blacks, as to exclude colored people from coaches occupied by or assigned to white persons. Railroad corporations of Louisiana did not make discrimination among whites in the matter of accommodation for travelers. The thing to accomplish was, under the guise of giving equal accommodation for whites and blacks, to compel the latter to keep to themselves while travelling in railroad passenger coaches. No one would be so wanting in candor as to assert the contrary. . . .

It is one thing for railroad carriers to furnish, or to be required by law to furnish, equal accommodations for all whom they are under a legal duty to carry. It is quite another thing for government to forbid citizens of the white and black races from travelling in the same public conveyance, and to punish officers of railroad companies for permitting persons of the two races to occupy the same passenger coach. If a State can prescribe, as a rule of civil conduct, that whites and blacks shall not travel as passengers in the same railroad coach, why may it not so regulate the use of the streets of its cities and towns as to compel white citizens to keep on one side of a street and black citizens to keep on the other? Why may it not, upon like grounds, punish whites and blacks who ride together in street cars or in open vehicles on a public road or street? Why may it not require sheriffs to assign whites to one side of a court-room and blacks to the other? And why may it not also prohibit the commingling of the two races in the galleries of legislative halls or in public assemblages convened for the consideration of the political questions of the day? Further, if this statute of Louisiana is consistent with the personal liberty of citizens, why may not the State require the separation in railroad coaches of native and naturalized citizens of the United States, or of Protestants and Roman Catholics? . . .

The white race deems itself to be the dominant race in this country. And so it is, in prestige, in achievements, in education, in wealth, and in power. So, I doubt not, it will continue to be for all time, if it remains true to its great heritage, and holds fast to the principles of constitutional liberty. But in view of the Constitution, in the eye of the law, there is in this country no superior, dominant, ruling class of citizens. There is no caste here. Our Constitution is color-blind, and neither knows nor tolerates classes among citizens. In respect of civil rights, all citizens are equal before the law. The humblest is the peer of the most powerful. The law regards man as man, and takes no account of his surroundings or of his color when his civil rights as guaranteed by the supreme law of the land are involved. It is, therefore, to be regretted that this high tribunal, the final expositor of the fundamental law of the land, has reached the conclusion that it is competent for a State to regulate the enjoyment by citizens of their civil rights solely upon the basis of race. . . .

The recent amendments of the Constitution, it was supposed, had eradicated these principles from our institutions. But it seems that we have yet, in some of the States, a dominant race—a superior class of citizens, which assumes to regulate the enjoyment of civil rights, common to all citizens, upon the basis of race. The present decision, it may well be apprehended, will not only stimulate aggressions, more or less brutal and irritating, upon the admitted rights of colored citizens, but will encourage the belief that it is possible, by means of state enactments, to defeat the beneficent purposes which the people of the United States had in view when they adopted the recent amendments of the Constitution, by one of which the blacks of this country were made citizens of the United States and of the States in which they respectively reside, and whose privileges and immunities, as citizens, the States are forbidden to abridge. Sixty millions of whites are in no danger from the presence here of eight millions of blacks. The destinies of the two races, in this country, are indissolubly linked together, and the interests of both require that the common government of all shall not permit the seeds of race hate to be planted under the sanction of law. What can more certainly arouse race hate, what more certainly create and perpetuate a feeling of distrust between these races, than state enactments which, in fact, proceed on the ground that colored citizens are so inferior and degraded that they cannot be allowed to sit in public coaches occupied by white citizens? That, as all will admit, is the real meaning of such legislation as was enacted in Louisiana. . . .

The arbitrary separation of citizens, on the basis of race, while they are on a public highway, is a badge of servitude wholly inconsistent with the civil freedom and the equality before the law established by the Constitution. It cannot be justified upon any legal grounds.

If evils will result from the commingling of the two races upon public highways established for the benefit of all, they will be infinitely less than those that will surely come from state legislation regulating the enjoyment of civil rights upon the basis of race. We boast of the freedom enjoyed by our people above all other peoples. But it is difficult to reconcile that boast with a state of the law which, practically, puts the brand of servitude and degradation upon a large class of our fellow-citizens, our equals before the law. The thin disguise of "equal" accommodations for passengers in railroad coaches will not mislead any one, nor atone for the wrong this day done.

I am of opinion that the state of Louisiana is inconsistent with the personal liberty of citizens, white and black, in that State, and hostile to both the spirit and letter of the Constitution of the United States. If laws of like character should be enacted in the several States of the Union, the effect would be in the highest degree mischievous. Slavery, as an institution tolerated by law would, it is true, have disappeared from our country, but there would remain a power in the States, by sinister legislation, to interfere with the full enjoyment of the blessings of freedom; to regulate civil rights, common to all citizens, upon the basis of race; and to place in a condition of legal inferiority a large body of American citizens, now constituting a part of the political community called the People of the United States, for whom, and by whom through representatives, our government is administered. Such a system is inconsistent with the guarantee given by the Constitution to each State of a republican form of government, and may be stricken down by Congressional action, or by the courts in the discharge of their solemn duty to maintain the supreme law of the land, anything in the constitution or laws of any State to the contrary notwithstanding.

Source: 167 US 537 (1896).

Selected Bibliography

Antebellum Years and Causes of War

General Works

William L. Barney, *The Road to Secession: A New Perspective on the Old South* (1972); Avery Craven, *The Coming of the Civil War* (1942); William W. Freehling, *The Road to Reunion: Secessionists at Bay, 1776–1854* (1990); William W. Freehling, *The Road to Disunion: Secessionists Triumphant, 1854–1861* (2007); Allen Nevins, *Ordeal of the Union: 1847–57*, 2 vols. (1947), *The Emergence of Lincoln: 1857–61*, 2 vols. (1950); Russel B. Nye, *Society and Culture in America, 1830–1860* (1974); David M. Potter, *The Impending Crisis, 1848–1861* (1976); Brian Holden Reid, *The Origins of the American Civil War* (1996).

Society and the Economy: The North

Jeremy Atack and Fred Bateman, *To Their Own Soil: Agriculture in the Antebellum North* (1987); Don Harrison Doyle, *The Social Order of a Frontier Community: Jacksonville, Illinois, 1825–1870* (1978); John Mack Faragher, *Sugar Creek: Life on the Illinois Prairie* (1986); Paul W. Gates, *The Farmers' Age: Agriculture 1815–1860* (1962); Patrick Rael, *Black Identity and Black Protest in the Antebellum North* (2001); Mary P. Ryan, *Cradle of the Middle Class: The Family in Oneida County, 1790–1865* (1981); George R. Taylor, *The Transportation Revolution 1815–1860* (1951); Sean Wilentz, *Chants Democratic: New York City and the Rise of the American Working Class, 1784–1850* (1984).

Society and the Economy: The South

Ira Berlin, *Slaves without Masters: The Free Negro in the Antebellum South* (1974); John B. Boles, ed., *Masters and Slaves in the House of the Lord: Race and Religion in the American South, 1784–1870* (1988); Victoria E. Bynum, *Unruly Women: The Politics of Social and Political Control in the Old South* (1992); Catherine Clinton, *The Plantation Mistress: Woman's World in the Old South* (1982); Bruce Collins, *White Society in the Antebellum South* (1985); Tom Downey, *Planting a Capitalist South: Masters, Merchants, and Manufacturers in the Southern Interior, 1790–1860* (2005); Jeff Forret, *Race Relations at the Margins: Slaves and Poor Whites in the Antebellum Southern Countryside* (2006); Elizabeth Fox-Genovese, *Within the Plantation Household: Black and White Women of the Old South* (1988); Eugene Genovese, *The Slaveholders Dilemma: Freedom and Progress in Southern Conservative Thought, 1820–1860* (1992); Lewis C. Gray, *History of Agriculture in the Southern United States to 1860*, 2 vols. (1933); Sam B. Hilliard, *Hog Meat and Hoe Cake: Food Supply in the Old South, 1840–1860* (1972); Stephanie McCurry, *Masters of Small Worlds: Yeoman Households: Gender Relations and the Political Culture of the Antebellum South Carolina Lowlands* (1995); Grady McWhiney, *Cracker Culture: Celtic Ways in the Old South* (1988); James Oakes, *The Ruling Class: A History of American Slaveholders* (1982); William K. Scarsborough, *Masters of the Big House: Elite Slaveholders of the Mid-Nineteenth-Century South* (2003); Steven M. Stowe, *Intimacy and Power in the Old South: Ritual in the Lives of the Planters* (1987); Frank Towers, *The Urban South and the Coming of the Civil War* (2004); Jonathan D. Wells, *The Origins of the Southern Middle Class, 1800–1861* (2004); Bertram Wyatt-Brown, *Southern Honor: Ethics and Behavior in the Old South* (1982).

National Politics and Political Culture

Austin Allen, *Origins of the Dred Scott Case: Jacksonian Jurisprudence and the Supreme Court, 1837–1857* (2006); William L. Barney, *The Slave Power: The Free North and Southern Domination, 1780–1869* (2000); Richard J. Carwardine, *Evangelicals and Politics in Antebellum America* (1993); C. C. Goen, *Broken Churches, Broken Nation: Denominational Schisms and the Coming of the American Civil War* (1985); Amy S. Greenberg, *Manifest Manhood and the Antebellum American Empire* (2006); David Grimsted, *American Mobbing, 1828–1861* (1998); Michael Holt, *The Political Crisis of the 1850s* (1978); Michael Holt, *The Rise and Fall of the American Whig Party: Jacksonian Politics and the Onset of the Civil War* (1999); William Lee Miller, *Arguing about Slavery: The Great Battle in the United States Congress* (1996); Roy F. Nichols, *The Disruption of American Democracy* (1948); Lewis O. Saum, *The Popular Mood of Pre–Civil War America* (1980); Joel H. Silbey, *The Partisan Imperative: The Dynamics of American Politics be-*

fore the Civil War (1985); Mark M. Smith, *Listening to Nineteenth-Century America* (2001); Kenneth M. Stampp, *America in 1857: A Nation on the Brink* (1990); Mark W. Summers, *The Plundering Generation: Corruption and the Crisis of the Union, 1849–1861* (1987); Sean Wilentz, *The Rise of American Democracy: Jefferson to Lincoln* (2006).

Northern Politics and Political Culture

Tyler G. Anbinder, *Nativism and Slavery: The Northern Know Nothings and the Politics of the 1850s* (1992); Jean Baker, *Affairs of Party: The Political Culture of Northern Democrats in the Mid-Nineteenth Century* (1983); Frederick J. Blue, *The Free Soilers: Third Party Politics, 1848–1854* (1973); Eric Foner, *Free Soil, Free Labor, Free Men: The Ideology of the Republican Party before the Civil War* (1970); George B. Forgie, *Patricide in the House Divided: A Psychological Interpretation of Lincoln and His Age* (1979); William E. Gienapp, *The Origins of the Republican Party, 1852–1856* (1987); Susan-Mary Grant, *North over South: Northern Nationalism and American Identity in the Antebellum Era* (2001); John Mayfield, *Rehearsal for Republicanism: Free Soil and the Politics of Antislavery* (1980); John R. McKivigan, *The War against Proslavery Religion: Abolitionism and the Northern Churches, 1830–1865* (1984); Michael D. Pierson, *Free Hearts and Free Homes: Gender and American Antislavery Politics* (2003); Vernon L. Volpe, *Forlorn Hope of Freedom: The Liberty Party in the Old Northwest, 1838–1848* (1990); Jean Fagin Yellin, *Abolitionist Sisterhood: Women's Political Culture in Antebellum America* (1994); Susan Zaeske, *Signatures of Citizenship: Petitioning, Antislavery, and Women's Political Identity* (2003).

Southern Politics and Political Culture

Jean Baker, *Ambivalent Americans: The Know-Nothing Party in Maryland* (1977); William J. Cooper, *The South and the Politics of Slavery, 1828–1856* (1978); Lacy K. Ford, *Origins of the Southern Radicalism: The South Carolina Upcountry, 1800–1860* (1988); Kenneth S. Greenberg, *Masters and Statesmen: The Political Culture of American Slavery* (1985); John Inscoe, *Mountain Masters: Slavery and the Sectional Crisis in Western North Carolina* (1989); John McCardell, *The Idea of a Southern Nation: Southern Nationalists and Southern Nationalism, 1830–1860* (1979); W. Darrell Overdyke, *The Know Nothing Party in the South* (1950); Elizabeth R. Varon, *We Mean to Be Counted: White Women and Politics in Antebellum Virginia* (1998); Eric H. Walther, *The Fire-Eaters* (1992).

Slavery

Ira Berlin, *Many Thousands Gone: The First Two Centuries of Slavery in North America* (1998); John Blassingame, *The Slave Community: Plantation Life in the Antebellum South* (1979); Stephanie M. H. Camp, *Closer to Freedom: Enslaved Women and Everyday Resistance in the Plantation South* (2004); Wilma A. Dunaway, *Slavery in the American Mountain South* (2003); Stanley Elkins, *Slavery: A Problem in American Institutional and Intellectual Life* (1976); Jennifer Fleishner, *Mastering Slavery: Memory, Family, and Identity in Women's Slave Narratives* (1996); Robert W. Fogel, *Without Consent or Contract: The Rise and Fall of American Slavery* (1989); George Fredrickson, *The Black Image in the White Mind: The Debate on Afro-American Character and Destiny* (1971); Eugene Genovese, *Roll, Jordan, Roll: The World the Slaves Made* (1974); Sally E. Hadden, *Slave Patrols: Law and Violence in Virginia and the Carolinas* (2001); Peter Kolchin, *American Slavery, 1619–1877* (1993); Lawrence W. Levine, *Black Culture and Black Consciousness: Afro-American Folk Thought from Slavery to Freedom* (1977); Edmund Morgan, *American Slavery, American Freedom: The Ordeal of Colonial Virginia* (1975); Leslie Owens, *This Species of Property: Slave Life and Culture in the Old South* (1976); Kenneth Stampp, *The Peculiar Institution: Slavery in the Ante-Bellum South* (1956); Brenda Stevenson, *Life in Black and White: Family and Community in the Slave South* (1996); Deborah G. White, *Ar'nt I a Woman? Female Slaves in the Plantation South* (1985).

Age of Reform

Ray Allen Billington, *The Protestant Crusade, 1800–1861* (1938); Whitney R. Cross, *The Burned Over District* (1950); David Brion Davis, ed., *Ante-Bellum Reform* (1967); Nancy Isenberg, *Sex and Citizenship in Antebellum America* (1998); Paul E. Johnson, *The Shopkeeper's Millennium: Society and Revivals in Rochester, New York, 1815–1836* (1978); Dale T. Knobel, *Paddy and the Republic: Ethnicity and Nationality in Antebellum America* (1985); Ira M. Leonard and Robert D. Parmet, *American Nativism, 1830–1860* (1971); Anne C. Loveland, *Southern Evangelicals and the Social Order, 1800–1860* (1980); Timothy L. Smith, *Revivalism and Social Reform: American Protestantism on the Eve of the Civil War* (1957); Alice Felt Tyler, *Freedom's Ferment: Phases of American Social History from the Colonial Period to the Outbreak of the Civil War* (1944); Ronald G. Walters, *American Reformers, 1815–1860* (1997); Valarie H. Zeigler, *The Advocates of Peace in Antebellum America* (2001).

Anti-Slavery, Pro-Slavery, and Abolitionist Thought

Frederick J. Blue, *No Taint of Compromise: Crusaders in Antislavery Politics* (2005); Fergus M. Bordewich, *Bound for Canaan: The Underground Railroad and the War for the Soul of America* (2005); David Brown, *Southern Outcast: Hinton Rowan Helper and the Impending Crisis of the South* (2006); John Patrick Daly, *When Slavery Was Called Freedom: Evangelicalism, Proslavery, and the*

Causes of the Civil War (2002); David Brion Davis, Inhuman Bondage: The Rise and Fall of Slavery in the New World (2006); Merton L. Dillon, Slavery Attacked: Southern Slaves and Their Allies, 1619–1865 (1989); Louis Filler, The Crusade against Slavery (1960); Elizabeth Fox-Genovese and Eugene D. Genovese, The Mind of the Master Class: History and Faith in the Southern Slaveholders' Worldview (2006); Louis Gerteis, Morality and Utility in American Antislavery Reform (1987); Julie Roy Jeffrey, The Great Silent Army of Abolitionism: Ordinary Women in the Antislavery Movement (1998); Bruce Laurie, Beyond Garrison: Antislavery and Social Reform (2006); Edward Magdol, The Antislavery Rank and File: A Social Profile of the Abolitionists' Constituency (1986); Henry Mayer, All on Fire: William Lloyd Garrison and the Abolition of Slavery (1998); William H. Pease and Jane H. Pease, They Who Would Be Free: Blacks' Search for Freedom, 1830–1861 (1974); Lewis Perry and Michael Fellman, eds., Antislavery Reconsidered: New Perspectives on the Abolitionists (1979); Mark Perry, Lift Up Thy Voice: The Grimké Family's Journey from Slaveholders to Civil Rights Leaders (2001); James B. Stewart, Holy Warriors: Abolitionism and American Slavery (1976); Ronald T. Takaki, A Pro-Slavery Crusade: The Agitation to Reopen the African Slave Trade (1971); Larry Edward Tise, Proslavery: A History of the Defense of Slavery in America, 1701–1840 (1987).

Slavery Expansion and the Crisis of the 1850s

Eugene L. Berwanger, The Frontier against Slavery: Western Anti-Negro Prejudice and the Slavery Extension Controversy (1971); Charles H. Brown, Agents of Manifest Destiny: The Lives and Times of the Filibusters (1979); Nicole Etcheson, Bleeding Kansas: Contested Liberty in the Civil War Era (2004); Don E. Fehrenbacher, The Dred Scott Case: Its Significance in American Law and Politics (1978); Thomas Goodrich War to the Knife: Bleeding Kansas, 1854–1861 (1998); Holman Hamilton, Prologue to Conflict: The Crisis and Compromise of 1850 (1964); James L. Huston, Calculating the Value of Union: Slavery, Property Rights, and the Economic Origins of the Civil War (2003); Thelma Jennings, The Nashville Convention: Southern Movement for Unity, 1848–1850 (1980); Robert W. Johannsen, The Frontier, the Union, and Stephen A. Douglas (1989); Robert E. May, Manifest Destiny's Underworld: Filibustering in Antebellum America (2002); Michael A. Morrison, Slavery and the American Civil War: The Eclipse of Manifest Destiny and the Coming of the Civil War (1997); Benjamin Quarles, Allies for Freedom: Blacks and John Brown (1974); James A. Rawley, Race and Politics: "Bleeding Kansas" and the Coming of the Civil War (1969); Edward J. Renehan, The Secret Six: The True Tale of the Men Who Conspired with John Brown (1995); David S. Reynolds, John Brown, Abolitionist: The Man Who Killed Slavery, Sparked the Civil War, and Seeded Civil Rights (2005); Jeffrey S. Rossbock, Ambivalent Conspirators: John Brown, the Secret Six, and a Theory of Slave Violence (1982); Mark Stegmaier, Texas, New Mexico, and the Compromise of 1850 (1996); Anders Stephanson, Manifest Destiny: American Expansionism and the Empire of Right (1995); Eric H. Walther, The Shattering of the Union: America in the 1850s (2004).

Secession

Jonathan M. Atkins, Parties, Politics, and the Sectional Conflict in Tennessee, 1832–1861 (1997); William L. Barney, The Secession Impulse: Alabama and Mississippi in 1860 (1974); Walter L. Buenger, Secession and Union in Texas (1984); Steven A. Channing, Crisis of Fear: Secession in South Carolina (1970); Daniel W. Crofts, Reluctant Confederates: Upper South Unionists in the Secession Crisis (1989); Richard M. Current, Lincoln and the First Shot (1963); Charles B. Dew, Apostles of Disunion: Southern Secession Commissioners and the Causes of the Civil War (2001); Michael P. Johnson, Toward a Patriarchal Republic: The Secession of Georgia (1977); Jesse L. Keene, The Peace Convention of 1861 (1961); Marc W. Kruman, Parties and Politics in North Carolina, 1836–1865 (1983); William A. Link, Roots of Secession: Slavery and Politics in Antebellum Virginia (2003); David M. Potter, Lincoln and His Party in the Secession Crisis (1962); Kenneth M. Stampp, And the War Came: The North and the Secession Crisis (1950); J. Mills Thornton, Politics and Power in a Slave State: Alabama, 1800–1861 (1978); James M. Woods, Rebellion and Realignment: Arkansas's Road to Secession (1987); Ralph Wooster, The Secession Conventions of the South (1962).

The War

Reference Works

Mark M. Boatner, Civil War Dictionary (2nd ed., 1988); Richard N. Current, ed., Encyclopedia of the Confederacy, 4 vols. (1993); George B. Davis et al., The Official Military Atlas of the Civil War (1978); Vincent J. Esposito, The West Point Atlas of American Wars (1959); Patricia L. Faust, ed., Historical Times Illustrated Encyclopedia of the Civil War (1986); David S. Heidler and Jeanne T. Heidler, eds., Encyclopedia of the American Civil War, 5 vols. (2000); Thomas L. Livermore, Numbers and Losses in the Civil War (1901); E. B. Long, The Civil War Day by Day: An Almanac (1971); Francis A. Lord, They Fought for the Union: A Complete Reference Work on the Federal Fighting Man (1960); U.S. Department of the Navy, Civil War Naval Chronology, 1861–1865 (1971); Frank J. Welcher, The Union Army, 1861–1865: Organization and Operations, 2 vols. (1989–93).

Bibliographical Guides and Literature

Daniel Aaron, *The Unwritten War: American Writers and the Civil War* (1973); David J. Eicher, *The Civil War in Books: An Analytical Bibliography* (1997); Alice Fahs, *The Imagined Civil War: Popular Literature of the North and South, 1861–1865* (2001); Sarah E. Gardner, *Blood and Irony: Southern White Women's Narratives of the Civil War, 1861–1937* (2004); James M. McPherson and William J. Cooper Jr., eds., *Writing the Civil War: The Quest to Understand* (1998); Albert J. Menendez, *Civil War Novels: An Annotated Bibliography* (1986); Eugene C. Murdock, *The Civil War in the North: A Selected Annotated Bibliography* (1987); Allan Nevins et al., eds., *Civil War Books: A Critical Bibliography*, 2 vols. (1967–69); Myron J. Smith, *American Civil War Navies: A Bibliography* (1972); Edmund Wilson, *Patriotic Gore: Studies in the Literature of the Civil War* (1966); Steven Woodworth, ed., *The American Civil War: A Handbook of Literature and Research* (1996).

Photographic Histories

William C. Davis, ed., *The Image of War*, 6 vols. (1981–84); David H. Donald, *Divided We Fought* (1952); Francis T. Miller, ed., *The Photographic History of the Civil War*, 10 vols. (1911); Carl Moneyhon and Bobby Roberts, ed., *Portraits of Conflict*, 7 vols. (1990–2001); Bob Zeller, *The Blue and Gray in Black and White: A History of Civil War Photography* (2005).

General and Interpretive Works

Richard Beringer et al., *Why the South Lost the Civil War* (1986); David J. Eicher, *The Longest Night: A Military History of the Civil War* (2001); Bruce Catton, *The Centennial History of the Civil War*, 3 vols. (1961–65); Shelby Foote, *The Civil War: A Narrative*, 3 vols. (1958–74); Stig Forster and Jorg Nagler, eds., *On the Road to Total War: The American Civil War and the German Wars of Unification, 1861–1871* (1997); William S. Freehling, *The South vs. the South: How Anti-Confederate Southerners Shaped the Course of the Civil War* (2001); Gary W. Gallagher, *The Confederate War* (1997); James M. McPherson, *Battle Cry of Freedom: The Civil War Era* (1988); Allan Nevins, *The War for the Union: 1861–65*, 4 vols. (1959–61); Phillip S. Paludan, *A People's Contest: The Union and Civil War, 1861–1865* (2nd ed., 2001); Peter J. Parish, *The American Civil War* (1974); Charles R. Roland, *An American Iliad: The Story of the Civil War* (1991); Harry S. Stout, *Upon the Altar of the Nation: A Moral History of the Civil War* (2006); Emory M. Thomas, *The Confederacy as a Revolutionary Experience* (1971), and *The Confederate Nation: 1861–1865* (1979); Russell Weigley, *A Great Civil War: A Military and Political History, 1861–1865* (2000).

Strategies and Commanders: The Armies

Carol Bleser and Lesley J. Gordon, eds., *Intimate Strategies of the Civil War: Military Commanders and Their Wives* (2001); Albert Castel, *General Sterling Price and the Civil War in the West* (1968); Ray C. Colton, *The Civil War in the Western Territories: Arizona, Colorado, New Mexico, and Utah* (1959); Thomas L. Connelly, *Army of the Heartland: The Army of Tennessee, 1861–62* (1967), and *Autumn of Glory: The Army of Tennessee, 1862–65* (1971); Thomas L. Connelly and Archer Jones, *The Politics of Command: Factions and Ideas in Confederate Strategy* (1973); Benjamin F. Cooling, *Fort Donelson's Legacy: War and Society in Kentucky and Tennessee, 1861–1863* (1997); Larry J. Daniel, *Days of Glory: The Army of the Cumberland, 1861–1865* (2004); Michael Fellman, *Citizen Sherman: A Life of William Tecumseh Sherman* (1995), and *The Making of Robert E. Lee* (2000); Donald S. Frazier, *Blood and Treasure: Confederate Empire in the Southwest* (1995); Douglas Southall Freeman, *Lee's Lieutenants: A Study in Command*, 3 vols. (1942–44); Lesley J. Gordon, *General George E. Pickett in Life and Legend* (1998); Thomas J. Goss, *The War within the Union High Command: Politics and the Generalship during the Civil War* (2003); Mark Grimsley, *The Hard Hand of War: Union Military Policy toward Southern Civilians, 1861–1865* (1995); Joseph L. Harsh, *Confederate Tide Rising: Robert E. Lee and the Making of Southern Strategy, 1861–62* (1998); Herman Hattaway and Archer Jones, *How the North Won: A Military History of the Civil War* (1983); Archer Jones, *Civil War Command and Strategy: The Process of Victory and Defeat* (1992); Robert L. Kerby, *Kirby Smith's Confederacy: The Trans-Mississippi South, 1863–1865* (1972); John F. Marszalek, *Commander of All Lincoln's Armies: A Life of General Henry W. Halleck* (2004); Geoffrey Perret, *Lincoln's War: The Untold Story of America's Greatest President as Commander in Chief* (2004); Jeffery S. Prushankin, *A Crisis in Confederate Command: Edmund Kirby Smith, Richard Taylor, and the Army of the Trans-Mississippi* (2005); Charles Royster, *The Destructive War: William Tecumseh Sherman, Stonewall Jackson, and the Americans* (1991); Brooks D. Simpson, *Ulysses S. Grant: Triumph over Adversity, 1822–1865* (2000); Emory M. Thomas, *Robert E. Lee: A Biography* (1995); Kenneth P. Williams, *Lincoln Finds a General: A Military Study of the Civil War*, 5 vols. (1949–59); Jay Winik, *April 1865: The Month That Saved America* (2001); Steven E. Woodworth, *Davis and Lee at War* (1995), and *Jefferson Davis and His Generals: The Failure of Confederate Command in the West* (1990); Steven E. Woodworth, *Nothing but Victory: The Army of the Tennessee, 1861–1865* (2005).

Strategies and Commanders: The Navies

Robert M. Browning, *Success Is All That Was Expected: The South Atlantic Blockading Squadron during the Civil War* (2002); William M. Fowler, Jr., *Under Two Flags: The American Navy in the Civil War* (1990); H. Allen Gosnell, *Guns on the Western Waters: The Story of River Gunboats in the Civil War* (1949); Chester G. Hearn, *Ellet's Brigade: The Strangest Outfit of All* (2000); Virgil C. Jones, *The Civil War at Sea*, 3 vols. (1961–62); James M. Merrill, *Battle Flags South: The Story of the Civil War Navies on Western Waters* (1970), and *The Rebel Shore: The Story of Union Sea Power in the Civil War* (1957); John D. Milligan, *Gunboats down the Mississippi* (1965); Ivan Musicant, *Divided Waters: The Naval History of the Civil War* (1995); Howard P. Nash, *A Naval History of the Civil War* (1972); Raimondo Luraghi, *A History of the Confederate Navy* (1996); Rowena Reed, *Combined Operations in the Civil War* (1978); William H. Roberts, *Now for the Contest: Coastal and Oceanic Naval Operations in the Civil War* (2004); Richard S. West, *Mr. Lincoln's Navy* (1957); Stephen R. Wise, *Lifeline of the Confederacy: Blockade Running during the Civil War* (1988).

Campaigns and Battles (chronologically)

Ethan S. Rafuse, *A Single Grand Victory: The First Campaign and Battle of Manassas* (2001); William Garrett Piston and Richard W. Hatcher III, *Wilson's Creek: The Second Battle of the Civil War and the Men Who Fought It* (2000); B. Franklin Cooling, *Forts Henry and Donelson: The Key to the Confederate Heartland* (1987); Stephen D. Engle, *Struggle for the Heartland: The Campaigns from Fort Henry to Corinth* (2001); John Taylor, *Bloody Valverde: A Civil War Battle on the Rio Grande* (1995); William L. Shea and Earl J. Hess, *Pea Ridge: Civil War Campaign in the West* (1992); Thomas S. Edrington and John Taylor, *The Battle of Glorieta Pass: A Gettysburg in the West* (1998); Larry J. Daniel, *Shiloh: The Battle That Changed the Civil War* (1997); Wiley Sword, *Shiloh: Bloody April* (1974); Chester G. Hearn, *The Capture of New Orleans, 1862* (1995); Robert G. Tanner, *Stonewall in the Valley* (1976); Stephen W. Sears, *The Gates of Richmond: The Peninsula Campaign* (1992); Gary W. Gallagher, ed., *The Richmond Campaign of 1862: The Peninsula and the Seven Days* (2000); John J. Hennessy, *Return to Bull Run: The Campaign and the Battle of Second Manassas* (1992); Stephen W. Sears, *Landscape Turned Red: The Battle of Antietam* (1983); Gary W. Gallagher, ed., *The Antietam Campaign* (1999); Joseph L. Harsh, *Taken at the Flood: Robert E. Lee and Confederate Strategy in the Maryland Campaign of 1862* (1999); James M. McPherson, *Crossroads of Freedom: Antietam* (2002); Kenneth W. Noe, *Perryville: This Grand Havoc of Battle* (2001); Earl J. Hess, *Banners to the Breeze: The Kentucky Campaign, Corinth, and Stones River* (2000); Peter Cozzins, *No Better Place to Die: The Battle of Stones River* (1990); George C. Rable, *Fredericksburg! Fredericksburg!* (2002); Daniel E. Sutherland, *Fredericksburg and Chancellorsville: The Dare Mark Campaign* (1998); Ernest B. Furgurson, *Chancellorsville 1863: The Souls of the Brave* (1992); Michael B. Ballard, *Vicksburg: The Campaign That Opened the Mississippi* (2004); William L. Shea and Terry J. Winschel, *Vicksburg Is the Key: The Struggle for the Mississippi River* (2003); Earl J. Hess, *Pickett's Charge: The Last Attack at Gettysburg* (2001); Harry W. Pfanz, *Gettysburg: The Second Day* (1987), and *Gettysburg: Culp's Hill and Cemetery Hill* (1994); Stephen W. Sears, *Gettysburg* (2003); Steven E. Woodworth, *Six Armies in Tennessee: The Chickamauga and Chattanooga Campaigns* (1998); Buck T. Foster, *Sherman's Mississippi Campaign* (2006); Ludwell H. Johnson, *Red River Campaign: Politics and Cotton in the Civil War* (1958); Gary D. Joiner, *Through the Howling Wilderness: The 1864 Red River Campaign and Union Failure in the West* (2006); Albert Castel, *Decision in the West: The Atlanta Campaign of 1864* (1992); Richard M. McMurry, *Atlanta 1864: Last Chance for the Confederacy* (2000); Mark Grimsley, *And Keep Moving On: The Virginia Campaign, May–June 1864* (2003); Noah A. Trudeau, *Bloody Roads South: The Wilderness to Cold Harbor* (1989); Jeffry D. Wert, *From Winchester to Cedar Creek: The Shenandoah Campaign of 1864* (1987); Anne J. Bailey, *The Chessboard of War: Sherman and Hood in the Autumn Campaigns of 1864* (2000); James L. McDonough, *Nashville: The Western Confederacy's Final Gamble* (2004); Richard Sommers, *Richmond Redeemed: The Siege of Petersburg* (1981).

Common Soldiers and Sailors

Michael Barton, *Goodmen: The Character of Civil War Soldiers* (1981); Michael J. Bennett, *Union Jacks: Yankee Sailors in the Civil War* (2004); Paul A. Cimbala and Randall M. Miller, eds., *Union Soldiers and the Northern Home Front: Wartime Experiences, Postwar Adjustments* (2002); Richard N. Current, *Lincoln's Loyalists: Union Soldiers from the Confederacy* (1992); Larry J. Daniel, *Soldiering in the Army of Tennessee: A Portrait of Life in a Confederate Army* (1991); Joseph Allan Frank, *With Ballots and Bayonet: The Political Socialization of American Civil War Soldiers* (1998); Joseph Allan Frank and George A. Reaves, *"Seeing the Elephant": Raw Recruits at the Battle of Shiloh* (1989); Joseph T. Glatthaar, *The March to the Sea and Beyond: Sherman's Troops in the Savannah and Carolina Campaigns* (1985); Earl J. Hess, *The Union Soldier in Battle: Enduring the Ordeal of Combat* (1997); Gerald F. Linderman, *Embattled Courage: The Experience of Combat in the American Civil War* (1987); Thomas P. Lowry, *The Story the Soldiers Wouldn't Tell: Sex in the Civil War* (1994); James M. McPherson, *For Cause and Comrades: Why Men Fought in the Civil*

War (1997); Andrew Marvel, *The Alabama and Kearsarge: The Sailor's Civil War* (1996); Reid Mitchell, *Civil War Soldiers: Their Expectations and Their Experiences* (1988), and *The Vacant Chair: The Northern Soldier Leaves Home* (1993); J. Tracy Power, *Lee's Miserables: Life in the Army of Northern Virginia from the Wilderness to Appomattox* (1998); Dennis J. Ringle, *Life in Mr. Lincoln's Navy* (1998); James I. Robertson, *Soldiers Blue and Gray* (1988); Aaron Sheehan-Dean, ed., *The View from the Ground: Experiences of Civil War Soldiers* (2006); Bell I. Wiley, *The Life of Billy Yank: The Common Soldier of the Union* (1952), and *The Life of Johnny Reb: The Common Soldier of the Confederacy* (1943).

Common Soldiers and Sailors: Minorities

DeAnne Blanton and Lauren M. Cook, *They Fought like Demons: Women Soldiers in the American Civil War* (2002); George S. Burkhardt, *Confederate Rage, Yankee Wrath: No Quarter in the Civil War* (2006); William Burton, *Melting Pot Soldiers: The Union's Ethnic Regiments* (1988); John Cimprich, *Fort Pillow, a Civil War Massacre, and Public Memory* (2005); Dudley T. Cornish, *The Sable Arm: Negro Troops in the Union Army, 1861–1865* (1966); Laura L. Gansler, *The Mysterious Private Thompson: The Double Life of Sarah Emma Edmonds, Civil War Soldier* (2005); Joseph T. Glatthaar, *Forged in Battle: The Civil War Alliance of Black Soldiers and White Officers* (1990); Robert H. Hall, *Women on the Civil War Battle Front* (2006); Laurence M. Hauptman, *Between Two Fires: American Indians in the Civil War* (1995); James G. Hollandsworth, *The Louisiana Native Guards: The Black Military Experience during the Civil War* (1995); Elizabeth D. Leonard, *All the Daring of a Soldier: Women of the Civil War Armies* (1999); Ella Lonn, *Foreigners in the Union Army and Navy* (1951); Steven J. Ramold, *Slaves, Sailors, Citizens: African Americans in the Union Navy* (2002); John David Smith, ed., *Black Soldiers in Blue: African American Troops in the Civil War Era* (2002); Noah Andre Trudeau, *Black Troops in the Civil War, 1862–1865* (1999); Gregory J. W. Urwin, ed., *Black Flag over Dixie: Racial Atrocities and Reprisals in the Civil War* (2004); Keith P. Wilson, *Campfires of Freedom: The Camp Life of Black Soldiers during the Civil War* (2000).

Desertion

Ella Lonn, *Desertion during the Civil War* (1928); Bessie Martin, *Desertion of Alabama Troops from the Confederate Army: A Study in Sectionalism* (1932); Mark A. Weitz, *A Higher Duty: Desertion among Georgia Troops during the Civil War* (2000), and *More Damning than Slaughter: Desertion in the Confederate Army* (2005).

Guerrilla Warfare

Paul C. Anderson, *Blood Image: Turner Ashby in the Civil War and the Southern Mind* (2002); Paul Ashdown and Edward Caudill, *The Mosby Myth: A Confederate Hero in Life and Legend* (2001); Anne J. Bailey and Daniel E. Sutherland, eds., *Civil War Arkansas: Beyond Battles and Leaders* (2000); Richard S. Brownlee, *Gray Ghosts of the Confederacy: Guerrilla Warfare in the West, 1861–1865* (1958); Benjamin Franklin Cooling, *Fort Donelson's Legacy: War and Society in Kentucky and Tennessee, 1862–1863* (1997); Michael Fellman, *Inside War: The Guerrilla Conflict in Missouri during the American Civil War* (1989); Noel C. Fisher, *War at Every Door: Partisan Politics and Guerrilla Violence in East Tennessee, 1860–1869* (1997); Thomas Goodrich, *Black Flag: Guerrilla Warfare on the Western Border, 1861–1865* (1995); Virgil Carrington Jones, *Gray Ghosts and Rebel Raiders: The Daring Exploits of the Confederate Guerillas* (1956); Robert R. Mackey, *The Uncivil War: Irregular Warfare in the Upper South, 1861–1865* (2004); Sean Michael O'Brien, *Mountain Partisans: Guerrilla Warfare in the Southern Appalachians, 1861–1865* (1999); David Pickering and Judy Falls, *Brush Men and Vigilantes: Civil War Dissent in Texas* (2000); Daniel E. Sutherland, ed., *Guerrillas, Unionists, and Violence on the Confederate Home Front* (1999); Jeffry D. Wert, *Mosby's Rangers* (1990).

Military Operations

Michael C. C. Adams, *Our Masters the Rebels: A Speculation on Union Military Failure in the East, 1861–1865* (1978); Robert C. Black, *The Railroads of the Confederacy* (1998); John E. Clark, *Railroads in the Civil War: The Impact of Management on Victory and Defeat* (2001); William B. Feis, *Grant's Secret Service: The Intelligence War from Belmont to Appomattox* (2002); Edwin C. Fishel, *The Secret War for the Union: The Untold Story of Military Intelligence in the Civil War* (1996); Richard D. Goff, *Confederate Supply* (1969); Paddy Griffith, *Battle Tactics of the Civil War* (1989); Edward Hagerman, *The American Civil War and the Origins of Modern Warfare* (1988); Paul A. C. Koistinen, *Beating Plowshares into Swords: The Political Economy of American Warfare, 1606–1865* (1996); Richard M. McMurry, *Two Great Rebel Armies: An Essay in Confederate Military History* (1989); Grady McWhiney and Perry D. Jamieson, *Attack and Die: Civil War Military Tactics and the Southern Heritage* (1982); George E. Turner, *Victory Rode the Rails: The Strategic Place of the Railroads in the Civil War* (1992).

Medical Care

George W. Adams, *Doctors in Blue: The Medical History of the Union Army* (1952); Stewart Brooks, *Civil War Medicine* (1966); H. H. Cunningham, *Doctors in Gray: The Confederate Medical Service* (1959); Elizabeth D. Leonard, *Yankee Women: Gender Bat-*

tles in the Civil War (1994); Lisa A. Long, Rehabiliting Bodies: Health, History, and the American Civil War (2004); Ira M. Rutkow, Bleeding Blue and Gray: Civil War Surgery and the Evolution of American Medicine (2005); Jane E. Schultz, Women at the Front: Hospital Workers in Civil War America (2004); Glenna Shroeder-Lein, Confederate Hospitals on the Move: Samuel H. Stout and the Army of Tennessee (1994); Paul E. Steiner, Disease in the Civil War (1968).

Prisoners of War

Lewis Brown, The Salisbury Prison: A Case Study of Confederate Military Prisons (1980); William O. Bryant, Cahaba Prison and the Sultana Disaster (1990); Michael P. Gray, The Business of Captivity: Elmira and Its Civil War Prison (2000); William B. Hesseltine, Civil War Prisons: A Study in War Psychology (1992); William B. Hesseltine, ed., Civil War Prisons (1962); George Levy, To Die in Chicago: Confederate Prisoners at Camp Douglas, 1861–1865 (1994); Benton McAdams, Rebels at Rock Island: The Story of a Civil War Prison (2001); F. Lee Lawrence and Robert W. Glover, Camp Ford, CSA: The Story of Union Prisoners in Texas (1964); William Marvel, Andersonville: The Last Depot (1994); Sandra R. Parker, Richmond's Civil War Prisons (1990); Charles W. Sanders, While in the Hands of the Enemy: Military Prisons of the Civil War (2005); Philip R. Shriver and Donald J. Breen, Ohio's Civil War Prisons (1964); Lonnie R. Speer, Portals to Hell: Military Prisons of the Civil War (1997).

Foreign Diplomacy

R. J. M. Blackett, Divided Hearts: Britain and the American Civil War (2001); Lynn M. Case and Warren F. Spencer, The United States and France: Civil War Diplomacy (1970); David P. Crook, The North, the South, and the Powers, 1861–1865 (1974); Norman Ferris, Desperate Diplomacy: William H. Seward's Foreign Policy, 1861 (1976); Philip S. Foner, British Labor and the American Civil War (1981); Alfred J. Hanna and Kathryn A. Hanna, Napoleon III and Mexico: American Triumph over Monarchy (1971); Charles M. Hubbard, The Burden of Confederate Diplomacy (1998); Brian Jenkins, Britain and the War for the Union, 2 vols. (1974–80); Howard M. Jones, Union in Peril: The Crisis over British Intervention in the Civil War (1992); Dean B. Mahin, One War at a Time: The International Dimensions of the American Civil War (1999); Gordon Warren, Fountain of Discontent: The Trent Affair and the Freedom of the Seas (1981).

Politics: The Union

Allan G. Bogue, The Earnest Men: Republicans of the Civil War Senate (1981), and The Congressman's Civil War (1989); Leonard P. Curry, Blueprint for Modern America: Nonmilitary Legislation of the First Civil War Congress (1968); David H. Donald, Lincoln (1995); Michael S. Green, Freedom, Union, and Power: Lincoln and His Party during the Civil War (2004); Allen C. Guelzo, Lincoln's Emancipation Proclamation: The End of Slavery in America (2004); William C. Harris, With Charity for All: Lincoln and the Restoration of the Union (1997); William B. Hesseltine, Lincoln and the War Governors (1948); David Long, The Jewel of Liberty: Abraham Lincoln's Reelection and the End of Slavery (1994); Mark E. Neely Jr., The Fate of Liberty: Abraham Lincoln and Civil Liberties (1990), and The Union Divided: Party Politics in the Civil War North (2002); Larry E. Nelson, Bullets, Ballots, and Rhetoric: Confederate Policy for the United States Presidential Contest of 1864 (1980); Phillip Shaw Paludan, The Presidency of Abraham Lincoln (1994); Heather Cox Richardson, The Greatest Nation on Earth: Republican Economic Policies during the Civil War (1997); Joel Silbey, A Respectable Minority: The Democratic Party in the Civil War Era (1977); Bruce Tap, Over Lincoln's Shoulder: The Committee on the Conduct of the War (1998); John C. Waugh, Reelecting Lincoln: The Battle for the 1864 Presidency (1997).

Politics: The Confederacy

Thomas B. Alexander and Richard E. Beringer, The Anatomy of the Confederate Congress (1972); William J. Cooper Jr., Jefferson Davis, American (2000); William C. Davis, A Government of Our Own: The Making of the Confederacy (1994); Robert F. Durden, The Gray and the Black: The Confederate Debate on Emancipation (1972); Paul D. Escott, Military Necessity: Civil-Military Relations in the Confederacy (2006); Malcolm C. MacMillan, The Disintegration of a Confederate State: Three Governors and Alabama's Homefront, 1861–1865 (1986); Mark E. Neely Jr., Southern Rights: Political Prisoners and the Myth of Confederate Constitutionalism (1999); George C. Rable, The Confederate Republic: A Revolution in Politics (1994); Wilfred B. Yearns, The Confederate Congress (1960).

Wartime Economies and Economic Change

Ralph Andreano, ed., The Economic Impact of the American Civil War (1962); Douglas B. Ball, Financial Failure and Confederate Defeat (1990); Richard F. Bensel, Yankee Leviathan: The Origins of Central Authority in America, 1859–1877 (1990); Mary A. De Credico, Patriotism for Profit: Georgia's Urban Entrepreneurs and the Confederate War Effort (1990); Paul W. Gates, Agriculture and the Civil War (1965); David T. Gilchrist and W. David Lewis, eds., Economic Change in the Civil War Era (1965); Bray Hammond, Sovereignty and an Empty Purse: Banks and Politics in the Civil War (1970); Patrick O'Brien, The Economic Effects of the

American Civil War (1988); William H. Roberts, *Civil War Ironclads: The U.S. Navy and Industrial Mobilization* (2002); David Surdam, *Northern Naval Superiority and the Economics of the American Civil War* (2001); Harold S. Wilson, *Confederate Industry: Manufacturers and Quartermasters in the Civil War* (2002); Mark R. Wilson, *The Business of Civil War: Military Mobilization and the State, 1861–1865* (2006).

Influence of Religion and Benevolence

Warren B. Armstrong, *For Courageous Fighting and Confident Dying: Union Chaplains in the Civil War* (1998); Jeannie Attie, *Patriotic Toil: Northern Women and the American Civil War* (1998); Robert H. Bremner, *The Public Good: Philanthropy and Welfare in the Civil War Era* (1980); Drew Gilpin Faust, *The Creation of Confederate Nationalism: Ideology and Identity in the Civil War South* (1988); Eugene Genovese, *A Consuming Fire: The Fall of the Confederacy in the Mind of the White Christian South* (1998); Judith Ann Giesberg, *Civil War Sisterhood: The U.S. Sanitary Commission and Women's Politics in Transition* (2000); Victor B. Howard, *Religion and the Radical Republican Movement, 1860–1870* (1990); Randall M. Miller et al., eds., *Religion and the American Civil War* (1998); James Moorhead, *American Apocalypse: Yankee Protestants and the Civil War, 1860–1869* (1978); Mark A. Noll, *The Civil War as a Theological Crisis* (2006); Gardiner Shattuck, *A Shield and Hiding Place: The Religious Life of the Civil War Armies* (1987); James W. Silver, *Confederate Morale and Church Propaganda* (1957); Steven E. Woodworth, *While God Is Marching On: The Religious World of Civil War Soldiers* (2001).

The Home Front: Union

Iver Bernstein, *The New York City Draft Riots: Their Significance for American Society and Politics in the Age of the Civil War* (1990); Joan E. Cashin, ed., *The War Was You and Me: Civilians in the American Civil War* (2002)—and for South; Paul A. Cimbala and Randall M. Miller, eds., *An Uncommon Time: The Civil War and the Northern Home Front* (2002); Adrian Cook, *The Armies of the Streets: The New York City Draft Riots of 1863* (1974); George M. Fredrickson, *The Inner Civil War: Northern Intellectuals and the Crisis of the Union* (1965); J. Matthew Gallman, *Mastering Wartime: A Social History of Philadelphia during the Civil War* (1990), and *The North Fights the Civil War: The Home Front* (1994); James W. Geary, *We Need Men: The Union Draft in the Civil War* (1991); Louis S. Gerteis, *Civil War St. Louis* (2001); Randall C. Jimerson, *The Private Civil War: Popular Thought during the Sectional Crisis* (1988)—and for South; Frank L. Klement, *Dark Lanterns: Secret Political Societies, Conspiracies, and Treason Trials in the Civil War* (1984); Melinda Lawson, *Patriot Fires: Forging a New American Nationalism in the Civil War North* (2002); James Marten, *The Children's Civil War* (1998)—and for South; Mary Elizabeth Massey: *American Women and the Civil War* (1966)—and for South; Ernest A. McKay, *The Civil War and New York City* (1990); Eugene C. Murdock, *One Million Men: The Civil War Draft in the North* (1971); Grace Palladino, *Another Civil War: Labor, Capital, and the State in the Anthracite Regions of Pennsylvania* (1990); Edmund J. Raus Jr., *Banners South: A Northern Community at War* (2006); Nina Silber, *Daughters of the Union: Northern Women Fight the Civil War* (2005); Amy Murrill Taylor, *The Divided Family in Civil War America* (2005)—and for South; Jennifer L. Weber, *Copperheads: The Rise and Fall of Lincoln's Opponents in the North* (2006).

The Home Front: Confederacy

Stephen V. Ash, *When the Yankees Came: Conflict and Chaos in the Occupied South, 1861–1865* (1995); Edward Ayers, *In the Presence of Mine Enemies: War in the Heart of America, 1859–1863* (2003)—and for North; William Blair, *Virginia's Private Civil War: Feeding Body and Soul in the Confederacy, 1861–1865* (1998); Jacqueline G. Campbell, *When Sherman Marched from the Sea: Resistance on the Confederate Home Front* (2003); Catherine Clinton and Nina Silber, eds., *Divided Houses: Gender and the Civil War* (1992), and *Battle Scars: Gender and Sexuality in the American Civil War* (2006)—and for North; Martin Crawford, *Ashe County's Civil War: Community and Society in the Appalachian South* (2002); Thomas G. Dyer, *Secret Yankees: The Union Circle in Confederate Atlanta* (1999); Drew Gilpin Faust, *The Creation of Confederate Nationalism: Ideology and Identity in the Civil War South* (1988), and *Mothers of Invention: Women of the Slaveholding South in the American Civil War* (1996); Ernest B. Furgurson, *Ashes of Glory: Richmond at War* (1996); Lesley J. Gordon and John C. Inscoe, eds., *Inside the Confederate Nation: Essays in Honor of Emory M. Thomas* (2005); A. Wilson Greene, *Civil War Petersburg: Confederate City in the Crucible of War* (2006); John C. Inscoe and Robert C. Kenzer, eds., *Enemies of the Country: New Perspectives on Unionists in the Civil War South* (2001); John C. Inscoe and Gordon B. McKinney, *The Heart of Confederate Appalachia: Western North Carolina in the Civil War* (2000); Richard B. McCaslin, *Tainted Breeze: The Great Hanging at Gainesville, Texas, 1862* (1994); Robert Tracy McKenzie, *Lincolnites and Rebels: A Divided Town in the American Civil War* (2006); Mary Elizabeth Massey, *Ersatz in the Confederacy: Shortages and Substitutes on the Southern Homefront* (1952), and *Refugee Life in the Confederacy* (1964); Kenneth W. Noe and Shannon H. Wilson, eds., *The Civil War in Appalachia: Collected Essays* (1997); Philip S. Paludan, *Victims: A True Story of the Civil War* (1981); George C. Rable, *Civil Wars: Women and the Crisis of Southern Nationalism* (1989); Sarah Anne Rubin, *A Shattered Nation: The Rise and Fall of the Confederacy, 1861–1868* (2005); Jonathan D. Sarris, *A Separate Civil War: Communities in Conflict in the*

Mountain South (2006); Margaret M. Storey, *Loyalty and Loss: Alabama's Unionists in the Civil War and Reconstruction* (2004); Daniel E. Sutherland, *Seasons of War: The Ordeal of a Confederate Community, 1861–1865* (1995); Georgia Lee Tatum, *Disloyalty in the Confederacy* (1934); Mark V. Wetherington, *Plain Folk's Fight: The Civil War and Reconstruction in Piney Woods Georgia* (2005); Lee Ann Whites, *The Civil War as a Crisis in Gender: Augusta, Georgia, 1860–1890* (1995); David Williams, *Rich Man's War: Class, Caste, and Confederate Defeat in the Lower Chattahoochee Valley* (1998); Brian Steel Wills, *The War Hits Home: The Civil War in Southeastern Virginia* (2002).

Slaves and Freedmen

Howard Belz, *A New Birth of Freedom: The Republican Party and Freedmen's Rights, 1861–1866* (1976); David W. Blight, *Frederick Douglass' Civil War* (1989); James H. Brewer, *The Confederate Negro: Virginia's Craftsmen and Military Laborers, 1861–1865* (1969); John Cimprich, *Slavery's End in Tennessee, 1861–1865* (1985); Patricia C. Click, *Time Full of Trial: The Roanoke Island Freedmen's Colony, 1861–1867* (2001); Lawanda Cox, *Lincoln and Black Freedom: A Study in Presidential Leadership* (1981); Noralee Frankel, *Freedom's Women: Black Women and Families in Civil War Era Mississippi* (1999); Louis S. Gerteis, *From Contraband to Freedman: Federal Policy toward Southern Blacks, 1861–1865* (1973); Janet Sharp Hermann, *The Pursuit of a Dream* (1981); Ervin L. Jordan Jr., *Black Confederates and Afro-Yankees in Civil War Virginia* (1995); Bruce Levine, *Confederate Emancipation: Southern Plans to Free and Arm Slaves during the Civil War* (2006); James M. McPherson, *The Negro's Civil War* (1991); Clarence L. Mohr, *On the Threshold of Freedom: Masters and Slaves in Civil War Georgia* (1986); Armstead L. Robinson, *Bitter Fruits of Bondage: The Demise of Slavery and the Collapse of the Confederacy, 1861–1865* (2005); Willie Lee Rose, *Rehearsal for Reconstruction: The Port Royal Experiment* (1964); Silvana R. Siddali, *From Property to Person: Slavery and the Confiscation Acts, 1861–1862* (2005).

Reconstruction and War's Aftermath

General Works

Eugene H. Berwanger, *The West and Reconstruction* (1981); Edward T. Blum, *Reforging the White Republic: Race, Religion, and American Nationalism, 1865–1898* (2005); E. Merton Coulter, *The South during Reconstruction, 1865–1877* (1947); Eric Foner, *Reconstruction: America's Unfinished Revolution, 1863–1877* (1988); John Hope Franklin, *Reconstruction: After the Civil War* (1961); Rembert W. Patrick, *The Reconstruction of the Nation* (1967); Michael Perman, *Emancipation and Reconstruction, 1862–1879* (1987); Kenneth M. Stampp, *The Era of Reconstruction* (1965); Daniel E. Sutherland, *The Confederate Carpetbaggers* (1988), and *The Expansion of Everyday Life, 1860–1876* (2nd ed., 2000); Hans L. Trefousse, *Historical Dictionary of Reconstruction* (2001).

Northern Reconstruction Politics

Michael Les Benedict, *A Compromise of Principle: Congressional Republicans and Reconstruction* (1974); Charles W. Calhoun, *Conceiving a New Republic: The Republican Party and the Southern Question, 1869–1900* (2006); LaWanda Cox and John H. Cox, *Politics, Principle, and Prejudice, 1865–1866* (1963); Gaines M. Foster, *Moral Reconstruction: Christian Lobbyists and the Federal Legislation of Morality, 1865–1920* (2002); Edward L. Gambill, *Conservative Ordeal: Northern Democrats and Reconstruction, 1865–1869* (1981); William Gillette, *Retreat from Reconstruction: A Political History, 1867–1878* (1979); Lawrence Grossman, *The Democratic Party and the Negro: Northern and National Politics, 1868–1892* (1976); Elizabeth D. Leonard, *Lincoln's Avengers: Justice, Revenge, and Reunion after the Civil War* (2004); Glen M. Linden, *Politics of Principle: Congressional Voting on the Civil War Amendments and Pro-Negro Measures* (1976); Eric L. McKitrick, *Andrew Johnson and Reconstruction* (1960); Earl M. Maltz, *Civil Rights, the Constitution, and the Congress, 1863–1869* (1990); John C. Mohr, ed., *Radical Republicans in the North* (1976); Keith Ian Polakoff, *The Politics of Inertia: The Election of 1876 and the End of Reconstruction* (1973); Heather Cox Richardson, *The Death of Reconstruction: Race, Labor, and Politics in the Post–Civil War North, 1865–1901* (2001); Patrick W. Riddleberger, *1866: The Critical Year Revisited* (1979); Brooks D. Simpson, *The Reconstruction Presidents* (1998); Hans L. Trefousse, *Impeachment of a President* (1975).

Southern Reconstruction Politics

Richard H. Abbott, *The Republican Party and the South, 1855–1877* (1986); James A. Baggett, *The Scalawags: Southern Dissenters in the Civil War and Reconstruction* (2003); Dan T. Carter, *When the War Was Over: The Failure of Self-Reconstruction in the South, 1865–1867* (1985); Richard N. Current, *Those Terrible Carpetbaggers: A Reinterpretation* (1988); Richard O. Curry, ed., *Radicalism, Racism, and Party Realignment: The Border States during Reconstruction* 1969); Gordon H. McKinney, *Southern*

Mountain Republicans, 1865–1900: Politics and the Appalachian Community (1978); Otto H. Olsen, ed., *Reconstruction and Redemption in the South* (1980); Michael Perman, *Reunion without Compromise: The South and Reconstruction, 1865–1868* (1975), and *The Road to Redemption: Southern Politics, 1869–1879* (1984); Howard N. Rabinowitz, *Southern Black Leaders of the Reconstruction* (1982); George C. Rable, *But There Was No Peace: The Role of Violence in the Politics of Reconstruction* (1984); Terry L. Seip, *The South Returns to Congress: Men, Economic Measures, and Intersectional Relationships, 1868–1879* (1983).

Roles of the Army and Freedmen's Bureau

Paul E. Cimbala, *Under the Guardianship of the Nation: The Freedmen's Bureau and the Reconstruction of Georgia* (1997); Paul E. Cimbala and Randall Miller, eds., *The Freedmen's Bureau and Reconstruction* (1999); Barry A. Crouch, *The Freedmen's Bureau and Black Texans* (1992); Joseph G. Dawson, *Army Generals and Reconstruction: Louisiana, 1861–1877* (1982); Randy Finley, *From Slavery to Uncertain Freedom: The Freedmen's Bureau in Arkansas, 1865–1869* (1996); Martin E. Mantell, *Johnson, Grant, and the Politics of Reconstruction* (1973); Donald G. Nieman, *To Set the Law in Motion: The Freedmen's Bureau and the Legal Rights of Blacks, 1865–1868* (1979); Claude Oubre, *Forty Acres and a Mule: The Freedmen's Bureau and Black Land Ownership* (1978); William L. Richter, *Overreached on All Sides: The Freedmen's Bureau Administrators in Texas, 1865–1868* (1991); Brooks D. Simpson, *Let Us Have Peace: Ulysses S. Grant and the Politics of War and Reconstruction, 1861–1868* (1991).

Southern State Political Studies

Randolph B. Campbell, *Grass-Roots Reconstruction in Texas, 1865–1880* (1997); Alan Conway, *The Reconstruction of Georgia* (1966); William McKee Evans, *Ballots and Fence Rails: Reconstruction on the Lower Cape Fear* (1966); William C. Harris, *Presidential Reconstruction in Mississippi* (1967), and *The Day of the Carpetbagger: Republican Reconstruction in Mississippi* (1979); Jack P. Maddex, *The Virginia Conservatives, 1867–1879* (1970); Carl H. Moneyhon, *The Impact of the Civil War and Reconstruction on Arkansas, 1850–1874* (1994), and *Texas after the Civil War: The Struggle of Reconstruction* (2004); Elizabeth Studley Nathans, *Losing the Peace: Georgia Republicans and Reconstruction* (1964); Hyman Rubin III, *South Carolina Scalawags* (2006); Jerrell Shofner, *Nor Is It Over Yet: Florida and the Era of Reconstruction* (1974); Joe Gray Taylor, *Louisiana Reconstructed, 1863–1877* (1974); Ted Tunnell, *Crucible of Reconstruction: War, Radicalism, and Race in Louisiana, 1863–1877* (1984); Sarah Woolfolk Wiggins, *The Scalawag in Alabama Politics, 1865–1881* (1977). Richard Zuczeck, *State of Rebellion: Reconstruction in South Carolina* (1996).

Society and the Economy: The South

Stephen V. Ash, *A Year in the South: Four Lives in 1865* (2002); Peter W. Bardaglio, *Reconstructing the Household: Families, Sex, and the Law in the Nineteenth-Century South* (1995); Orville Vernon Burton, *In My Father's House Are Many Mansions: Family and Community in Edgefield, South Carolina* (1985); Jane Turner Censer, *The Reconstruction of White Southern Womanhood, 1865–1895* (2003); Cyrus B. Dawsey and James M. Dawsey, eds., *The Confederados: Old South Immigrants in Brazil* (1995); Laura F. Edwards, *Gendered Strife and Confusion: The Political Culture of Reconstruction* (1997); Michael W. Fitzgerald, *The Union League Movement in the Deep South: Politics and Agricultural Change during Reconstruction* (1989); Sally G. McMillen, *To Raise Up the South: Sunday Schools in Black and White Churches, 1865–1915* (2001); Scott Richard Nelson, *Iron Confederacies: Southern Railways, Klan Violence, and Reconstruction* (1999); Ted Ownby, *Subduing Satan: Religion, Recreation, and Manhood in the Rural South, 1865–1920* (1990); Lawrence N. Powell, *New Masters: Northern Planters during the Civil War and Reconstruction* (1980); Roger L. Ransom and Richard Sutch, *One Kind of Freedom: The Economic Consequences of Emancipation* (1977); Joseph P. Reidy, *From Slavery to Agrarian Capitalism in the Slave Plantation South* (1992); James L. Roark, *Masters without Slaves: Southern Planters in the Civil War and Reconstruction* (1977); Andrew Rolle, *The Lost Cause: The Confederate Exodus to Mexico* (1965); Edward Royce, *The Origins of Southern Sharecropping* (1993); Daniel Stowell, *Rebuilding Zion: The Religious Reconstruction of the South, 1863–1977* (1998); Mark W. Summers, *Railroads, Reconstruction, and the Gospel of Prosperity: Aid under the Radical Republicans, 1865–1877* (1984); Elizabeth Lee Thompson, *The Reconstruction of Southern Debt: Bankruptcy after the Civil War* (2004); Allen W. Trelease, *White Terror: The Ku Klux Klan Conspiracy and Southern Reconstruction* (1971); Gavin Wright, *Old South, New South: Revolutions in the Southern Economy Since the Civil War* (1986).

Society and the Economy: The North

Gunther Barth, *City People: The Rise of Modern City Culture in Nineteenth-Century America* (1980); Richard Franklin Bensel, *Yankee Leviathan: The Origins of Central State Authority in America, 1859–1877* (1990); Alfred D. Chandler, *The Visible Hand: The Managerial Revolution in American Business* (1977); Gilbert C. Fite, *The Farmer's Frontier, 1865–1910* (1966); Morton Keller, *Affairs of State: Public Life in Late-Nineteenth-Century America* (1977); Walter Licht, *Industrializing America: The Nineteenth Cen-*

tury (1995); Eric H. Monkkonen, *America Becomes Urban* (1988); David Montgomery, *Beyond Equality: Labor and the Radical Republicans, 1862–1872* (1967); Walter T. K. Nugent, *The Money Question during Reconstruction* (1967); Daniel T. Rodgers, *The Work Ethic in Industrial America, 1850–1920* (1978); Fred A. Shannon, *The Farmer's Last Frontier: Agriculture, 1860–1897* (1945); Irwin Unger, *The Greenback Era: A Social and Political History of American Finance, 1865–1879* (1964); Robert H. Wiebe, *The Search for Order, 1877–1920* (1966).

African American Life

Ronald E. Butchart, *Northern Schools, Southern Blacks, and Reconstruction: Freedmen's Education, 1862–1875* (1980); William Cohen, *At Freedom's Edge: Black Mobility and the Southern White Quest for Racial Control, 1861–1915* (1991); Steven Hahn, *A Nation under Our Feet: Black Political Struggles in the Rural South from Slavery to the Great Migration* (2004); Tera W. Hunter, *To 'Joy My Freedom: Southern Black Women's Lives and Labors after the Civil War* (1997); Jacqueline Jones, *Labor of Love, Labor of Sorrow: Black Women, Work, and the Family from Slavery to Present* (1985); Leon F. Litwack, *Been in the Storm So Long: The Aftermath of Slavery* (1979); Robert C. Morris, *Reading, 'Riting,' and Reconstruction: Freedmen's Education in the South, 1865–1870* (1981); Nell Irvin Painter, *The Exodusters: Black Migration to Kansas after Reconstruction* (1976); Dylan C. Penningroth, *The Claims of Kinfolk: African American Property and Community in the Nineteenth-Century South* (2003); Howard N. Rabinowitz, *Race Relations in the Urban South, 1865–1890* (1977); Elizabeth Regosin, *Freedom's Promise: Ex-Slave Families and Citizenship in the Age of Emancipation* (2002); Joe M. Richardson, *Christian Reconstruction: The American Missionary Association and Southern Blacks, 1865–1890* (1986); Patricia A. Schechter, *Ida B. Wells-Barnett and American Reform, 1880–1930* (2001); Donald R. Shaffer, *After the Glory: The Struggles of Black Civil War Veterans* (2004); Richard M. Valelly, *The Two Reconstructions: The Struggle for Black Enfranchisement* (2004); Heather Williams, *Self-Taught: Afro-American Education in Slavery and Freedom* (2005).

Southern State Studies of African Americans

Edmund Drago, *Black Politicians and Reconstruction in Georgia: A Splendid Failure* (1982); Sharon Ann Holt, *Making Freedom Pay: North Carolina Freedpeople Working for Themselves, 1865–1900* (2000); Peter Kolchin, *First Freedom: The Responses of Alabama's Blacks to Emancipation and Reconstruction* (1972); John C. Rodrigue, *Reconstruction in the Cane Fields: From Slavery to Free Labor in Louisiana's Sugar Parishes, 1862–1880* (2001); Julie Saville, *The Work of Reconstruction: From Slave to Wage Laborer in South Carolina, 1860–1870* (1994); Leslie A. Schwalm, *A Hard Fight for We: Women's Transition from Slavery to Freedom in South Carolina* (1997); James Smallwood, *Time of Hope, Time of Despair: Black Texans during Reconstruction* (1981); Charles Vincent, *Black Legislators in Louisiana during Reconstruction* (1976); Joel Williamson, *After Slavery: The Negro in South Carolina During Reconstruction, 1861–1877* (1965).

The Supreme Court and the Constitution

Pamela Brandwein, *Reconstructing Reconstruction: The Supreme Court and the Production of Historical Truth* (1999); William Gillette, *The Right to Vote: Politics and the Passage of the Fifteenth Amendment* (1965); Harold M. Hyman, *A More Perfect Union: The Impact of the Civil War and Reconstruction on the Constitution* (1973); Robert J. Kaczorowski, *The Politics of Judicial Interpretation: The Federal Courts, Department of Justice, and Civil Rights, 1866–1876* (1985); Stanley I. Kutler, *Judicial Power and Reconstruction Politics* (1968); Keith W. Medley, *We as Freemen: Plessy v. Ferguson* (2003); William E. Nelson, *The Fourteenth Amendment: From Political Principle to Judicial Doctrine* (1988); Phillip S. Paludan, *A Covenant with Death: The Constitution, Law, and Equality in the Civil War Era* (1975); Michael Vorenberg, *Final Freedom: The Civil War, the Abolition of Slavery, and the Thirteenth Amendment* (2001); Xi Wang, *The Trial of Democracy: Black Suffrage and Northern Republicans, 1860–1910* (1997).

The Gilded Age

Ari Hoogenboom, *Outlawing the Soils: A History of the Civil Service Reform Movement, 1865–1883* (1961); William S. McFeely, *Grant: A Biography* (1981); Andrew L. Slap, *The Doom of Reconstruction: The Liberal Republicans in the Civil War Era* (2006); John G. Sproat, *The Best Men: Liberal Republicans in the Gilded Age* (1968); Mark W. Summers, *The Era of Good Stealings* (1993).

The Redeemed and New South

Edward L. Ayers, *The Promise of the New South: Life after Reconstruction* (1992); Bess Beatty, *A Revolution Gone Backward: The Black Response to National Politics, 1876–1896* (1987); Bradley G. Bond, *Political Culture in the Nineteenth Century: Mississippi, 1830–1900* (1995); W. Fitzhugh Brundage, *Lynching in the New South* (1993); James C. Cobb, *Industrialization and Southern Society, 1877–1984* (1984); Stephen Cresswell, *Rednecks, Redeemers, and Race: Mississippi after Reconstruction, 1877–1917* (2006); Paul M. Gaston, *The New South Creed: A Study in Southern Mythmaking* (1970); J. Morgan Kousser, *The Shaping of*

Southern Politics: Suffrage Restriction and Establishment of the One-Party South, 1880–1910 (1974); Leon F. Litwack, *Trouble in Mind: Black Southerners in the Age of Jim Crow* (1998); John Hammond Moore, *Carnival of Blood: Dueling, Lynching, and Murder in South Carolina, 1880–1920* (2006); Joel Williamson, *The Crucible of Race: Black-White Relations in the American South since Emancipation* (1984); C. Vann Woodward, *Origins of the New South, 1877–1915* (1951), and *The Strange Career of Jim Crow* (3rd ed., 1974).

War, Memory, and Commemoration

William Blair, *Cities of the Dead: Contesting the Memory of the Civil War in the South, 1865–1914* (2004); David W. Blight, *Race and Reunion: The Civil War in American Memory* (2001); Robert E. Bonner, *Colors of Blood: Flag Passions of the Confederate South* (2002); W. Fitzhugh Brundage, *The Southern Past: A Clash of Race and Memory* (2005); Paul H. Buck, *The Road to Reunion, 1865–1900* (1937); Thomas L. Connelly, *The Marble Man: Robert E. Lee and His Image in American Society* (1977); Thomas L. Connelly and Barbara L. Bellows, *God and General Longstreet: The Lost Cause and the Southern Mind* (1982); Kathleen Ann Clark, *Defining Moments : African American Commemoration and Political Culture in the South, 1863–1913* (2005); John Coski, *The Confederate Battle Flag: America's Most Embattled Emblem* (2005); Karen L. Cox, *Dixie's Daughters: The United Daughters of the Confederacy and the Preservation of Confederate Culture* (2003); Jim Cullen, *The Civil War in Popular Culture: A Reusable Past* (1995); Alice Fahs and Joan Waugh, eds., *The Memory of the Civil War in American Culture* (2004); Gaines M. Foster, *Ghosts of the Confederacy: Defeat, the Lost Cause, and the Emergence of the New South* (1987); Gary W. Gallagher and Alan T. Nolan, eds., *The Myth of the Lost Cause and Civil War History* (2000); David Goldfield, *Still Fighting the Civil War: The American South and Southern History* (2002); Susan-Mary Grant and Peter J. Parish, eds., *Legacy of Disunion: The Enduring Significance of the American Civil War* (2003); Stuart McConnell, *Glorious Contentment: The Grand Army of the Republic, 1865–1900* (1992); J. Michael Martinez et al., eds., *Confederate Symbols in the Contemporary South* (2001); Cynthia Mills and Pamela H. Simpson, eds., *Monuments to the Lost Cause: Women, Art, and the Landscape of Southern Memory* (2003); G. Kurt Piehler, *Remembering War and the American Way* (1995); Carol Reardon, *Pickett's Charge in History and Memory* (1997); Kirk Savage, *Standing Soldiers, Kneeling Slaves: Race, War, and Monument in Nineteenth-Century America* (1997); Nina Silber, *The Romance of Reunion: Northerners and the South, 1865–1900* (1993); John A. Simpson, *S. A. Cunningham and the Confederate Heritage* (1994); Charles Reagan Wilson, *Baptized in Blood: The Religion of the Lost Cause, 1865–1920* (1980).

Credits

Index

army, U.S.
preparedness for war, 86
in Spanish-American War, 380, 392f, 393
Army Appropriation Act (1867), 317
army soldiers. *See* soldiers
artillery, 196–197
artillery troops
Confederate, 88–90
Union, 88–90
Askew, William S., 88f
Atlanta
battle of (1864), 278
refugees from, 219, 279
Atlanta campaign (1864), 275–279, 276f, 278f
Atlanta Constitution (newspaper), 354
atrocities
at Bull Run, first battle of, 97, 98f
against prisoners of war, trials for, 299–301
attrition, strategy of
in Confederate army, 94, 266
in Union army, 266
Aunt Phillis's Cabin (Eastman), 56
aversive racism, 146–147

B
Bacon, Nathaniel, 17–18
Baker, Edward, 100
balloons, reconnaissance, 132
Ball's Bluff, battle of (1861), 100
bank(s)
managerial revolution in, 12
national, 143
in Panic of 1873, 369
Union, 143
bank notes, 143
Banks, Nathaniel P., 267f
on black officers, 163
in Grant's grand strategy, 266–267
in Red River campaign, 267f, 268
Baptist church, on slavery, 47
Barton, Clara, 225, 228
Bates, Edward, 75
battalions, artillery, 89
batteries, artillery, 89
battles. *See also specific battles*
first, 94–98
geographical scope of, 113
maps of, 129f, 131f, 271f
naming of, 89
press coverage of, 96–97, 230
Battles and Leaders of the Civil War, 394
Baylor, John R., 122
Beall, John, 300
Beauregard, Pierre Gustave Toutant
in Bull Run, first battle of, 94, 97
and Confederate flag, 396
firing of, 128
in Fort Sumter crisis, 84
in memory of war, 394
in Shiloh, battle of, 126
Bee, Bernard, 96
Beecher, Catharine, 40
Beecher, Henry Ward, 64, 259
Beecher, James C., 164–165
Beers, Ethel Lynn, 100–101
Belgium, Confederate relations with, 101–102
Belknap, William, 367
Bell, John, in 1860 presidential election, 75–78
Belmont, battle of, 118, 119

Benjamin, Judah P.
and British relations, 245
Davis' illnesses and, 212
as secretary of state, 101–102
Bible, slavery in, 40
Bingham, John A., 310
Bird, Edgeworth, 189–190
Bird, Francis W., 158
Bird, Sallie, 189
Birth of a Nation (film), 394
bitterness, postwar, 302
Black Codes
congressional opposition to, 312
passage of, 309
blacks, 155–161
in abolitionist movement, 37, 39–40
churches of, 334
on Confederate flag, 396–397
in convict lease system, 357
discrimination against (*See* racism; white supremacy)
in draft riots, 250
education of, 158, 159f, 335, 335f
fugitive slave law and, 54
on Harpers Ferry raid, 6
labor by
Confederate use of, 289
on plantations, 155–161
in Reconstruction, 326–327, 332–333, 336–337
Union use of, 155–157
land for, 158–161, 312, 333–334
Lincoln's views of, 147–148
memory of war among, 390–391, 395–397
naming practices for, 355
paternalism toward, 356–357, 364–365
political organizations of, 158–159
population of, antebellum, 26–27
in 1868 presidential election, 320
in Reconstruction (*See* Reconstruction era)
as refugees, 155–158, 156f
Republican ambivalence toward, 62–63, 146–147
in Republican Party
alliance of, 338–341
betrayal of, 370–371
as slaves (*See* slaves)
in social hierarchy, 26–27
as soldiers (*See* black soldiers)
Union abuses of, 156–157
in Union navy, 109
violence against (*See also* lynching)
political, 357–360
during Reconstruction, 337–338, 355–360
voting by (*See* suffrage)
white supremacist views of, 353–355
black soldiers
Confederate, 289–290
Union, 162–171
in combat, 166, 167–168
Congress on, 151
discrimination against, 163, 164–166
after Emancipation Proclamation, 154
execution of, 168–169
families of, 165
Lincoln's policies on, 167
number of, 163
as officers, 163

as prisoners of war, 168–171
recruitment of, 162
reenslavement of, 169–170
salary for, 165
Sherman's resistance to, 161, 166
and slavery in Union, disintegration of, 162
slaves as, 150, 162
Union views of, changes in, 150, 151
veteran, 171, 390–391
war crimes against, 301
white acceptance of, 164–165
white officers of, 163–165, 169–170
Blackwell, Elizabeth, 226
Blaine, James G., in 1876 presidential election, 371–372
Blair, Francis P., Sr., 288
Blair, Frank, in 1868 presidential election, 320, 364
Blanchard, Caleb, 190
Blanchard, Mattie, 190
Bleeding Kansas, 63–65
blood sport, 203
Bloody Angle, 272
bloody shirts, 315, 372, 391
bonds
Confederate, 141
railroad, 369
Union, 142–143
Boone, Daniel, 139
Booth, John Wilkes, 294, 294f, 299
Border Ruffians, 64
border South
Davis' hopes for, 94
remaining in Union, 85
border strategy, 114–115, 119
bossism, 344
Boston
abolitionist movement in, resistance to, 38–39
fugitive slave law in, opposition to, 54–55
Boston Female Anti-Slavery Society, 38
Botts, John Minor, 310–311
bounties, and desertion, 261–262
Bourbons, 351, 360–361. *See also* Redeemers
Boutwell, George S., 310
Boyd, Belle, 223
Bradley, Joseph P., 373
Brady, Mathew, 139
Bragg, Braxton
as army commander, 128, 139–140
in Chattanooga, battle of, 251–254
in Chickamauga, battle of, 251
in Chickamauga campaign, 250–251
in Kentucky campaign, 139–140, 178–179
in Missionary Ridge, battle of, 252–254
in Stones River, battle of, 179–181, 230–231
Brandy Station, battle of (1863), 234, 235
Brazil, ex-Confederates in, 328
bread riots (1863), 245, 246f
Breckinridge, John C.
in Johnson's surrender, 293–294
in 1860 presidential election, 74–78
in Stones River, battle of, 180
breech-loading rifles, 197
Brewster, Charles Harvey, 186
bribery. *See also* corruption
and distrust of politicians, 59
in railroad construction, 350–351